Tonic for the Woman's Soul

Tonic for the Woman's Soul

Downhome Household Almanac and Cookbook 3

Edited by Lila Mercer Young and Ron Young

Illustrated by Mel D'Souza

Editors - Lila Mercer Young and Ron Young
Illustrator - Mel D'Souza
Cover Design - Vince Marsh

Editorial Assistants:
Vince Hempsall
Janice Stuckless
Jeff Green
Sandra Dove
Maria Young

Copyright 2004 by Downhome Publishing Inc.
43 James Lane
St. John's, NL, Canada
A1E 3H3
Tel: 1-888-LUV-NFLD (588-6353)
Fax: 1-709-726-2135
Web site: www.shopdownhome.com
E-mail: mail@downhomelife.com

ISBN-13: 978-1-895109-18-4
ISBN-10: 1-895109-18-3
1st Printing April 2004
2nd Printing July 2004
3rd Printing August 2005
4th Printing June 2008

Cover photo is Co-Editor Lila Young, overlooking Cape Spear, Newfoundland, the most easterly point in North America.

If you liked this book why not look for volumes 1 & 2 in our series of almanacs.

Prologue - The Weaker Sex?

Here's a riddle that most people can't get the first time they hear it, which demonstrates how little most of us think of over 50 per cent of the world's population.

There is a doctor in St. John's who has a brother in Corner Brook, who is a lawyer, but the same lawyer in Corner Brook doesn't have a brother in St. John's, who is a doctor. Why is that?

The answer to this riddle is that the doctor in St. John's is a woman, or the weaker sex as women were often referred to in the past.

The women of the world today comprise over 50 per cent of the population, as they always have. With the way men have been running off to wars and their deadly exploits over the years, women have always held the rank of "Majority of Earth's Citizens."

Over the years circumstances made women less than equal. Old world economies provided a limited number of jobs, most of which involved hard labour capable of being undertaken only by men. Thus men became the breadwinners and dominant sex in society.

Although social attitudes have undergone major changes in the recent past, discrimination against women as the "weaker sex" still exists in most parts of the world.

But women have predominantly been the backbone of every community. That was certainly true in this province, where women worked just as hard as men, and sometimes harder. In the well-known Newfoundland song are the words, "I'se the b'y that catches the fish and brings them home to Lizer." And bring the fish home to Lizer he did. Then Lizer spread them on the flakes to dry, sometimes after splitting, gutting and salting them. At the first hint of rain she would run out and pile the salted cod into "faggots," covering them with canvas, or whatever, to keep them from going bad. Then when the sun gave her a chance of having a better grade of fish to sell, she spread them again. When the fish were dry she used a wheelbarrow to cart them off to be stored for market. All this while she was raising children, washing clothes, hoeing and weeding the vegetable garden, bringing water, chopping wood and making hay while the sun shone. On top of that she was often the person who made sure there was food for, and on, the table.

While her man was sometimes in the company of other men telling tales of jumping ice pans for seals, or in stormy seas chasing fish, she stayed at home, sewing, knitting, mending, baking and a doing host of other things.

She was the family manager and person behind the scenes who was always there to comfort him in his times of need.

She certainly wasn't the weaker sex!

Women have always been underrated. Yet there have been women in medicine, law, science and many other fields who have not been given due recognition. They have been great pilots, spies, scientists, military leaders and prominent world leaders – like Golda Meir, Indira Ghandi and Margaret Thatcher.

Today, women are considered equal to men in the developed world...yet they are different. Women are more caring, more emotional, more sensitive and more persevering. Many people still resist change in the traditional roles of women, especially in developing countries, but they are fighting a losing battle.

In this book we have endeavoured to feature the battles for equality waged by women in our province and all over the world who have made a significant difference in our lives.

We hope you will enjoy reading about these great women and be inspired by their pioneering achievements and noble deeds.

Understanding Me

*A Woman's Autobiography for Myself
and for those with whom I wish to share.
Otherwise this is Personal and Confidential.*

*For all in life, I had to face
For joys and pains this mortal took
I've earned myself eternal place
In the pages of this Woman's book*

*I am me, and I am Woman
Whether lover, mother, friend or wife
I am unique, and now I speak
Of me. This is MY life*

NOTE: This "Understanding Me" section should be entirely read before putting pen to paper. Entries need only be made on pertinent blank lines. If there is not enough space, use the blank lines in the 'biography' area at the end of the section, or extra loose leafs may be attached to these pages.

My name is _____,

and among my worldly possessions is this book, which was given to me by _____

_____ who is my (Husband, Mother, Friend, or Other) _____

on (Date) _____

When I am gone it will belong to _____

_____

Then on to others who survive, who'll keep my memory alive.

My Zodiac sign is _____

My Autobiographical Notes

I was born (Full Maiden Name) _____

on (Date of Birth) _____ **at** (Town) _____ **in the** (Prov, State, Etc.) _____

of _____, **in the country of** _____

My name was chosen because _____

My nickname was _____, **which I got because**

_____

The person responsible for bringing me into the world was (Dr, Midwife, Mrs, Mr,) _____

_____

My earliest recollections in life are _____

_____

_____

_____

I was baptized/dedicated on (Date) _____, **by** (Clergy) _____

at (Name and location of church) _____

My night-time prayer was _____

_____

_____

Which was taught to me by _____

What my childhood home was like _____

_____

_____

My Autobiographical Notes

What my bedroom was like _____

_____

_____

Outside my bedroom window I could see _____

_____

What my grandparents' houses were like _____

_____

_____

_____

Here are notes about my childhood chores and allowances _____

_____

_____

My favourite dress-up outfit as a child was _____

_____; **I would wear it on** (Occasion) _____

_____

As a child my parents expected the following responsibilities of me _____

_____

The family customs I would like to see passed on to my children and grandchildren are

_____

_____

I am thankful for the following from my childhood _____

_____

My Autobiographical Notes

My Autobiographical Notes

Over the years I have belonged to the following organizations _____

_____

_____

_____

The most meaningful advice I received was _____

_____

_____

It was given to me by _____

Some of the events from my school days were _____

_____

_____

Some of the crazy fads and fashions of my school days were _____

_____

_____

The most frightening experience I ever had was when _____

_____

The funniest thing that happened to me was when _____

_____

I remember my first trip alone. It was _____

_____

_____

I first moved away from home to _____

Here's what happened on my first job _____

_____

_____

The things I am most glad I tried were _____

_____

_____

The strangest thing I've ever seen was _____

_____

Here are some notes about my -

Parent(s): _____

_____

_____

_____

Sibling(s): _____

_____

_____

_____

Husband(s): _____

_____

_____

_____

If above you've written naught but truth, and anyone should see
Especially your present man, the truth may set you free

My Autobiographical Notes

Daughters(s):_____

_____

_____

_____

Son(s):_____

_____

_____

_____

Grandmother(s):_____

_____

_____

_____

Grandfather(s): _____

_____

_____

_____

Teacher(s): _____

_____

Friend(s): _____

_____

_____

My Autobiographical Notes

Here are some notes on my favourite -

Flower(s): _____

_____

Colour(s): _____

_____

Food(s): _____

_____

Drink(s): _____

_____

Clothes: _____

_____

_____

_____

Pet(s) and/or Animal(s): _____

_____

_____

Jewellery, perfume, etc.: _____

_____

Events during my school days: _____

_____

_____

My Autobiographical Notes

My Autobiographical Notes

Birthdays, Anniversaries or other events: _____

_____

_____

_____

Hobbies, Sports, Entertainment: _____

_____

_____

_____

_____

_____

_____

_____

Music: _____

_____

_____

_____

Book(s): _____

_____

_____

Movie(s): _____

_____

_____

TV Show(s): _____

_____

_____

Writer(s), Actor(s) or Other Achiever(s): _____

_____

_____

_____

Part(s) of the World: _____

_____

_____

_____

Place(s) to Shop: _____

_____

_____

_____

Place(s)to Eat: _____

_____

_____

Place(s) to Visit: _____

_____

_____

My Autobiographical Notes

People to Visit: _____

_____

_____

Place(s) to Relax, Meditate or Worship: _____

_____

_____

_____

Wish(es) that came true: _____

_____

_____

_____

Wish(es) that have not yet come true: _____

_____

_____

_____

My best moment(s): _____

_____

_____

My best day(s): _____

_____

_____

My Autobiographical Notes

My best holiday(s): _____

_____

_____

_____

_____

_____

My greatest achievement(s): _____

_____

_____

_____

_____

My strengths: _____

_____

_____

_____

_____

_____

_____

In general, this is how I feel about -

Women: _____

_____

_____

_____

My Autobiographical Notes

My Autobiographical Notes

Men: _____

_____

_____

_____

Children: _____

_____

_____

_____

Parenting: _____

_____

_____

_____

The society I live in: _____

_____

_____

_____

_____

Myself: _____

_____

_____

_____

What fortune teller(s) have told me: _____

_____

_____

_____

_____

_____

_____

Predictions that came true: _____

_____

_____

_____

_____

Predictions that I hope come true: _____

_____

_____

_____

My fear in life is _____

_____

_____

_____

_____

My Autobiographical Notes

My habits and quirks are _____

_____

_____

_____

_____

The most interesting thing(s) that happened to me _____

_____

_____

_____

The 'deja vu' (sights, sounds, or smells) that most take me back to my childhood are _____

_____

_____

My dream in life is _____

_____

_____

_____

_____

Before I die I want to see _____

_____

_____

_____

_____

My Autobiographical Notes

The things I love most in life are _____

_____

_____

_____

_____

Here is a short biography of my life from birth up to now: _____

_____

_____

_____

_____

_____

_____

_____

_____

_____

_____

_____

_____

_____

_____

_____

My Autobiographical Notes

My Autobiographical Notes

Life, Love
&
Laughter

Life, Love & Laughter

ABOUT THIS SECTION

The name of this section came about because we, the editors, believe that the best recipe for happiness is to "live, love and laugh." The contents of this section was conceived to please women of all cultures, social status, religions, races or ideals. Most of this section's content is acceptable family reading and is recommended reading by, and to, young children. However, some of the content is not necessarily intended for children. This includes some of the factual information, as well as the humour. Parental guidance is advised. Each item in this chapter has an easily identifiable heading to help you choose your favourites, and are listed below in alphabetical order.

Adam's Ribbing – Humourous short stories involving women.

Animal Mating – Fact and Fantasy

A factual, but satirical, whimsical and sometimes bawdy, look at the mating rituals of the "animal" species, as compared to human mating rituals. That is the **Fact** of the matter.

The Fantasy: The purpose of this chapter is a comic way to capture
The female mating rites of other creatures
This chapter will discuss, how much they are like us
As well as other unfamiliar features

Aphrodesia – Humourous shorts about a worldly woman character.

Aunt Alice says – The wit and wisdom of an older woman.

Ennellene – Our female-character poet. Turn page for more information.

Female Firsts – Women who were first throughout history.

Female Facts – Interesting facts about women.

Feminine Words & Phrases – Words and phrases with feminine connotations.

Food for Thought - Quotes for daily living.

Her Other Half - Jokes about married life.

Is That a Fact? - Misconceptions clarified.

Letters From Our Friends - Letters to *Downhomer* magazine

MABEL & MANLEY - Humourous stories about a married couple.

Out of Habit - Humourous stories from the convent.

Quillings - Poems & Thoughts.

Some Mothers Have Them - Humourous stories about a boy growing up.

Spice of Life - Humourous quotes by and about women.

The Whys of Men - Male put-downs, just for laughs.

Tickle and Bight - Humourous stories by Lucy Fitzpatrick McFarlane.

WOMEN OF THE ISLAND AND THE BIG LAND - Women of Newfoundland & Labrador.

Women Who Have Made A Difference - Contributing women in history.

PLUS — Many other stories and items of interest to women.

I am Woman, Ennellene

From the history of this land, I came
And from this heritage, got my name
I'm the beginning "enn" of Newfoundland
And the "ell'" of Labrador's big strand
I've adapted to all that I have met
Still for all, I'm woman yet
I am derived from many facets
With many sides, skills, strengths and assets
I am more than just a pretty face
While part of every creed and race
I'm Britain's lass and Eire's coleen
I'm Inuit, Innu, European
I'm from Asian, Africian, Auzzie scene
And both Americas in between
In these thoughts I write, my soul's unfurled
Befitting woman of the world
In spite of any man-made rumour
I've always had a sense of humour
For woman's human humour scene
Sometimes, robs Peter, to pay Pauline
And in a way that I hope, pleasin'
I'll add a little rhyme to reason
For in this corner of the world I'm Queen
I'm woman's woman, Ennellene

In the beginning....

 # Female Firsts

10,000 BC: (or thereabouts) The first woman on earth, according to the King James version of the Bible, was Eve. The first book of the Bible, Genesis, chapter 2, verse 22, reads, "And the rib, which the Lord God had taken from man, made a woman, and brought her unto the man." Chapter 3, verse 20 of Genesis reads, "And Adam called his wife Eve, because she was the mother of all living."

4000 BC: (or thereabouts) Anna En Hedu became the first female name recorded in technical history when she was appointed chief priestess of the moon goddess of Babylon. *See also 'Female Facts' page 427.*

3000 BC: Ka-Kum, the first brothel, was located in the city of Erech (or Urich) in Sumar.

1749 BC: (or thereabouts) Maatkare Hatshepsut became the first female head of state in world history when she declared herself Pharaoh of Egypt.

760 BC: (or shortly thereafter) Women of Greece started their own Olympic games called the Games of Hera. These were held every four years to honour the Greek goddess who ruled over women and the earth. The games were organized because women were not permitted in the original Olympics, which began in 776 BC.

600 BC: The first European brothels were located in Athens, Greece.

400 BC: (or thereabouts) Agnodice of Greece became the first woman known to dress in men's clothing to attend medical school.

400 BC: (or thereabouts) The first sculpture of a nude woman, Aphrodite, was unveiled in Greece, believed to have been sculpted by a man named Praxiteles.

♀

Women Who Have Made A Difference – *By Ron Young*

Pearl Bailey is a well-known and magnificent entertainer. But as magnificent as she is as an entertainer, Pearl Bailey's personal commitment to helping others is greater. Pearl loves people, all kinds of people, any age, any race, any nationality, any philosophy. To her, people are people. She works untiringly at problems such as AIDS, illiteracy, child abuse or family problems, and she speaks to young people throughout the nation about commitment and contribution. She is also the United States Goodwill Ambassador to the United Nations.

Halide Adivar had to flee Turkey for her life in 1909 because of her articles on women's emancipation, especially those advocating education. The Turkish nationalist later returned and became the only woman to be elected to the Ojak, the Turkish nationalist club in 1912. Halide later became Professor of English at the University of Istanbul and was a member of the Grand National Assembly from 1950 to 1954.

Marie Curie was one of the first woman scientists to win world-wide fame, and was one of the great scientists of the 20th century. She was born Maria Sklodowska in Warsaw, Poland, in 1867, and got a late start with her education, obtaining her license in physics in 1893 and the corresponding degree in mathematics in 1894. In 1903, she finally received her doctorate. Choosing radioactivity as a thesis topic, Madame Curie examined a number of substances and found that thorium and its compounds behaved the same way as uranium. Throughout her life Mme. Curie actively promoted the use of radium to alleviate suffering, and during the first world war she personally devoted herself to this remedial work with the help of her daughter, Irene. She retained her enthusiasm for science throughout her life and did much to establish a radioactivity laboratory in her native city. She won a Nobel Prize for Physics in 1903, and another for Chemistry in 1911. Ironically, it was her exposure to radium which lead to the cancer that killed her in 1934.

Jacqueline Auriol of France became the world's first woman test pilot in 1950. She had taken up flying out of curiosity in 1947 at age 30, qualified as a test pilot, and became a stunt flyer, before becoming a military pilot. In 1953 she was among the first to break the sound barrier, and she held the women's world speed record five times between 1951 and 1964. Later she was one of the first to pilot the supersonic Concorde.

Her more recent work was with the Ministère de la Coopération, using new remote sensing techniques to assist agricultural development, for example mapping crop species or locating water for irrigation. For this she was awarded the Ceres Medal of the United Nations Food and Agriculture Organization.

♀

Women's Voices

"We, the women who have come from the four corners of the earth, are here as living witnesses of thousands of women who suffer acts of violence and injustice caused by armed conflict."
– Mathilde Kayitesi, Rwanda

"Only the attainment of a just peace will allow the two people, Palestinian and Israeli, as well as all the people of the Middle East region to live and to prosper. *– Mayada Abassi, Palestine*

"I am a Kurdistani woman bringing the message of millions of women deprived of their basic human rights and status in all parts of Kurdista who resist and struggle for a better world."
– Nazand Begikhani, Kurdistan

"Anyone claiming to be a defender of justice, peace, equality and development must support around the world the woman's struggle against extremists of all stripes and religions."
– Fahima Vorgatts, Afghanistan

"We fight so that our sons and daughters do not wish for guns to play with; so that they wish for a flute, a hoe or a telescope to give free reign to their creativity and imagination; so they can dream of a free world."

– Marta Buritica, Columbia

♀

Life, Love & Laughter

WOMEN OF THE ISLAND AND THE BIG LAND

Minnie White

Original interview by June Hiscock

Photo Shane Kelly

Minnie White
The Hills of Home

Born Mary Hoskins in St. Alban's, Bay D'Espoir on April 1, 1916, Minnie attended school until she was fourteen years old. She then left school to look for work and became a housekeeper in the Codroy Valley, where she accompanied many fiddlers on piano accordion at community dances. In 1937 she married Richard Lewis White and settled down in Tompkins. She gave up performing until after her family was raised in the late 1960s. When she got back into music she did it in a big way. She began composing tunes and travelled the province, as well as on the Mainland, with her band, playing accordion and mandolin. Known as "Newfoundland's First Lady of the Accordion," Minnie performed as a regular at the Starlite Motel in Codroy Valley for 13 years. In 1993 she received the Order of Canada, in 1994 she was inducted into the Newfoundland and Labrador Arts Council Hall of Honour, and in 1995 nominated for an East Coast Music Award's Artist of the Year. During her career she released four cassette albums of her music. Minnie passed away in 2002.

*****

I first started playing the accordion when I was eight years old. I have a lot of my father's style of playing. He didn't sit down and teach me, but he gave me tips like not to shake the accordion and when he saw that I was interested, he bought me an old fashioned double-row accordion. The first tune I learned was "The Irish Washerwoman." I also fooled around with a mandolin that a sailor gave me, but I didn't get interested in the instrument until I got a real good one.

My hometown was quiet and peaceful, everyone knew each other and helped anyone who needed help. If there was a strange visitor in the Bay, everyone knew it. We all mixed together, no matter what faith or church one belonged to. Across the Bay from where I lived, there is a settlement of Micmacs called Conne River. In winter, the young men and women our age would come over to St. Alban's skating. We always had good ice to skate on; the Bay used to freeze up, and be frozen until the spring. The coastal boats could only get in five miles from St. Alban's, a place called Rody Point. There was a lighthouse there at that time and we always looked forward to the Micmac boys coming to skate with us. In the summer we would have St. Ann's Day on the 26 of July. All of us would go to Conne River to church and after, there would be a dance in their hall.

I stayed home to help my mother until I was sixteen years old. Up until I left home, I was singing in the church choir, although I am not a singer. I prefer to play music anytime. I left home and came to the Codroy Valley to work as a housekeeper and after being there a while, I got to know people who were very nice to me. I stayed one winter with an old lady who taught me how to chord with the fiddle players or violin players. There were excellent players at that time. There were three McDonald fiddlers and three McIsaac fiddlers. I learned to play the piano while I was with this lady. She taught me how to do it, and believe me, I soon caught on and got

Life, Love & Laughter

interested. I started to play piano and organ with the fiddlers. Whenever they were called to play at a dance for the church, they wanted me to play along with them and I remember playing the organ or piano with five fiddlers playing at the same time. That's what I enjoyed.

I met my husband in the Codroy Valley and we were married three years after. We had a family of six children, five girls and one boy. While I was raising my family, I had my accordion put away, but after they were grown up, I decided to get back into playing it. The accordion that I use today was given to me by a close friend. After I had it a couple of years, I knew it would do what I wanted it to do.

In the early seventies Lew Skinner of the Ducats asked me to go to St. John's to record my first album by Audat Company, so I joined them after taking a few months to fill out the contract. My first album was recorded in 1973. After my record came out, it sold so fast that I was asked to go to a local club to play on Sunday afternoons from three to six o'clock. I tried it with just a guitar to accompany me and it went over very well. That's how it started for me to be at the Starlite Lounge for thirteen seasons, playing every Sunday, unless I had a booking at the Halifax Newfie Club, or the Port au Port Peninsula, or St. John's. I finished playing at the Starlite in 1987. I enjoyed every Sunday, doing it for the hundreds of fans who used to come there. I got to meet so many people; people from Cape Breton and Nova Scotia that came to the Starlite every long weekend. I am going to miss them, but all good things come to an end; I will never forget them.

I played with a lot of different bands in those years. They were all good bands. If they were no good, I would just not have them. I have two LP records out and a forty-five. On my first album there's a jig called "Sally's Jig". Its name came from my grandmother who lived with us and she used to be humming that jig and it stuck to me. When I recorded, I put it on my album and called it after her. My second album, *Homestead Reels* has a number of my own tunes like *Saddle Mountain Jig*, *Midnight Waltz* and *Starlite Afternoon* that I first played at the Starlite Lounge.

Although I've been on a few radio shows like *The Newfie Bullet*, *Jiggs Dinner* with Neil Murray was my favourite. He was very interested in Newfoundland music and did so much in helping me get on with my music. The TV show *The Root Cellar* with The Wonderful Grand Band was a lot of fun; we all got along and had a great time working together.

In the winter months I very seldom play. I enjoy crocheting and knitting and with this break from music it gives me time to do some of the hobbies I enjoy. It's during this break from public playing I practice my music and write new material. I am not giving up music until I have to. That's what I enjoy and I believe that's what keeps me going. Music is healthy for anyone, keeps one's mind active. So, musicians keep going; it sure would be a dull life without you. The key to all musicians is to like what you are doing and like doing it for others.

From the book The Finest Kind *by Marian Frances White. Creative Publishing. Used by permission.*

♀

Female Facts

Only female mosquitoes bite humans. Male mosquitoes live on natural liquids from plants and other resources.

♀

Spice of Life

There's very little advice in men's magazines, because men don't think there's a lot they don't know. Women do. Women want to learn. Men think, "I know what I'm doing, just show me somebody naked."

♀

– Jerry Seinfeld

The Day I Lost My Tooth

By Loreen Haldenby

When I was nine years old I had never heard of a dentist. I had certainly never heard of the tooth fairy, but I knew what toothache was. I knew how it gnawed like burning coals at your jaws. How your gums throbbed and your cheeks swelled and you could think of nothing else but that hot, searing pain of the toothache.

One spring morning after such a night of toothache pain, I sat at our kitchen table waiting for Mam to give me some porridge. The porridge was cooking in the big cream-coloured pan on the old black stove. Around the edge of the pan was a dark blue border. The porridge bubbled up with big blurping sounds and as I waited, I looked out into the sunshine-lit meadow where the dandelions smiled and frolicked. To this day, the sound of porridge cooking and the sight of dandelions fill me with an inconsolable longing for my lost childhood.

"Dear child," said Mam, "there's only one thing to be done. We have to go down to the Sound and get Mr. Pittman to pull our your tooth."

I have never had a tooth pulled out, but I had heard all about Mr. Pittman down the Sound. He had a little room in his house in which he kept a wicked looking needle which he filled with something which was black like tar. Then he had an even wickeder pair of pincers which he clamped around your tooth and pulled and pulled until the tooth came right out of your head.

Not long ago, I read about Mr. Jim Pittman in the Downhomer. He was written up in an article about the settlers of Random. He was called a surrogate doctor. We didn't know any big words like that. All we knew was that he set broken bones, pulled out teeth and almost anything else he was called upon to do.

So on Monday morning, Mam takes my hand and we walk down our lilac-scented path in the warm spring sunshine. We walk over the road and out to Ted's motor boat which is moored to the government wharf.

Ted takes the mail down the sound on Mondays. Mam and I sit in boat and watch the tomcods and the connors darting back and forth around the wharf.

Ted comes out on the wharf carrying the mail bags on his back. The sun glints on his red-gold hair. He is singing.

Oh, my darling Nellie Gray

They have taken you away

And I'll never see my darling anymore - sings Ted. He is always singing. He is always happy. Everyone likes Ted.

He unties the painter from the wharf and sings out in his musical voice: "All ashore that's goin' ashore."

Then he starts the engine and we are off.

Soon we are in the deep water. The wake follows behind us. The gulls fly overhead. The sun flints and sparkles on the blue water.

We come close to Grindstone Head which is at one end of Random Island. The branches of the fir and spruce trees dip down almost on the water as we pass by. I love Random Island. I think no harm can come to us as long as Random Island juts out, in the sound, keeping guard.

We come to the wharf at Harcourt. Ted cuts the engine as we approach the wharf. Mam and I walk up through Mrs. White's garden where the honeysuckle is blooming. Mrs. White keeps the post-office in Harcourt.

We walk along the road to Mr. Pittman's house. The house sits at the bottom of a very steep hill. Mam and I have to bend over almost backward going down the hill, so that we don't fall down.

Life, Love & Laughter

Mrs. Pittman comes to the door wiping her hands on her apron. "Why, Ettie", she says, "did ye come over on the mail-boat then? Come in, come in."

"It's my little girl", Mam says, "she's got the toothache. I wonder if Jim could take out her tooth when he comes in from the lumber yard to his dinner."

"Of course he can," says Mrs. Pittman, "Dinner's almost ready. I'll just set two more places."

Before we know it, Mr. Pittman comes in from the lumber yard. He has black all-seeing eyes and a handlebar mustache.

Dinner is ready and we all sit around the table. Mr. Pittman says grace:

For what we are about to receive

Oh Lord, make us truly thankful.

We have fish cakes, pork toutons which are buns flavoured with pork and molasses, and partridgeberry jam and cream.

"This is some good, Carrie, my dear," says Mam.

"Eat up, Ettie maid," says Mrs. Pittman, "don't be shy. Make a long arm and what you don't see, ask for."

I dawdle over my food. I know as soon as we have finished dinner, my tooth will have to come out.

Mr. Pittman stands up. He says another grace. He calls this returning the thanks.

For what we have just received

Oh, Lord, make us truly thankful

He holds out his hand to me, "Come along child," he says.

Mam and I follow him into the little room off the kitchen. He motions me to sit in a chair covered with oil-cloth. Mam stands close by and holds my hand.

Out comes the wicked looking needle. Mr. Pittman fills it with the vile looking black stuff.

"Open your mouth, child," he says, and he sticks the needle in my gum.

The needle hurts. My eyes fill with tears. Mam squeezes my hand comfortingly.

"Just let 'er set a little while," says Mr. Pittman.

Next thing I know, Mr. Pittman has the pincers in my mouth and he is pulling my tooth, hard.

He screws up his face. He pulls with all his might. He takes the pliers out of my mouth and holds up my tooth.

"Idden he a beaut?" says Mr. Pittman.

Mam has fifty cents in her hand. I know it is all the money she has. I close my eyes tightly and pray silently that Mr. Pittman won't charge more than fifty cents to take out my tooth.

Mam offers him the fifty cents. Mr. Pittman waves it away.

"Put it away, Ettie, do," he says, "I don't want your money."

Mr. Pittman goes back to the lumberyard. Mam and I go back to the kitchen. Mrs. Pittman sits in the rocking chair with her knitting.

Mam and I sit on the settle. I put my tongue around the empty spot where the tooth came out. My gum feels ragged. I taste blood and it makes me sick. I snuggle close to Mam.

Mrs. Pittman and Mam settle down to gossip. "One thing, Ettie my dear," says Mrs. Pittman, knitting furiously, "we got real good children."

"That we have, Carrie," says Mam. "Every day I thank God for my children."

"Not like some of the young ones around here," says Mrs. Pittman scornfully. "Why Ettie, I've heard some terrible things about some of the young girls around here. I'd tell ye, but I couldn't get me mouth up to say it."

I wonder what some of the young girls around here have done that's so bad that Mrs. Pittman can't get up her mouth to say it.

Life, Love & Laughter

The evening wears on. It's time to go back to Harcourt to get the mailboat going back home.

Mrs. Pittman walks back to Harcourt with us. We meet people along the road. This time, they smile more broadly and are more friendly as they know that if we are friends of Mrs. Pittman, we are fine people. Very fine people indeed.

As we come to the wharf in Harcourt, we see Ted's mailboat put-putting closer and closer. It is twilight. I look at the sky and see the evening star.

Star Light, Star Bright.

First star I see tonight.

I wish I may, I wish I might,

Have the wish I wish tonight.

I wish for contentment. Contentment is a new word I have learned. Mam says it means peace of mind. I like that word, contentment.

I have to be careful not to look at that star any more for the rest of the evening. If I do, my wish won't come true.

Soon we are on the mailboat heading towards home. It is dark now. Mam shows me the Milky Way, the Big Dipper, the North Star. Phosphorous glows in the water like dark red candles.

Then we are home. The boat is tied up to the government wharf and Mam and I are walking home up the lilac-scented path and into our kitchen, dark as midnight.

Mam lights the kerosene lamp and it casts a soft glow all over the kitchen. She gets birch rind and splits and lights a few in the old black stove. She makes me some pap with bread, hot milk and sugar.

"Just sit there and eat your pap," says Mam, "I've got to go and milk Flossie. It's late and she'll be right anxious."

So I sit in the lamp-lit kitchen, and eat my pap. I stick my tongue in the hole where my tooth came out and I think what a lovely day Mam and I had down the sound.

If I get the toothache again I hope I don't get it in the wintertime. The sound is frozen over in the winter and Ted doesn't carry the mail then. If I get the toothache in the winter, Mam will have to put bricks and big rocks in the oven and heat them up. Then she'll cover them with towels and put them against my face to ease the pain.

But if I get the toothache in the summer, why then, Mam will take my hand on a Monday morning and we'll walk over the road and out along the government wharf to the mailboat. And we'll sit in the stern of the boat and watch the connors and tomcods swimming about. Then Ted will come walking along the wharf with the mail bags on his back. The sun will shine on his red-gold hair and he will be singing, and off we'll go down the sound in the mailboat.

The wake will follow behind the boat, the sun will shine on the blue water, the gulls will fly overhead, and when we get to Grindstone Head, the trees will dip almost down to the water.

When we come to Harcourt, we'll walk up past Mrs. White's house where the honeysuckle grows, and we'll walk along the road to Mr. Pittman's house. We will meet strangers along the road, and we will smile politely and say "Hello" because we must always be friendly to strangers.

And when we reach Mr. Pittman's house, we will have to bend backwards going down the steep hill so we won't fall down. We'll knock on the door and Mrs. Pittman will come wiping her hands on her apron.

"Why Ettie," she'll say, "did ye come over on the mailboat, and is anything wrong?"

"Nothing is wrong, Carrie, my dear," Mam will say, "only my little girl has the toothache and I was wondering if Jim could take her tooth out when he comes in from the lumberyard to his dinner."

♀

Life, Love & Laughter

Women Who Have Made A Difference – *By Ron Young*

Wangari Muta Maathai founded the Green Belt Movement in her native Kenya, one of the world's most successful programs to combine community development with environmental protection. The movement has built the self-reliance and self-confidence of tens of thousands living in poverty, convincing them that planting trees will make a difference in their struggle to improve their lives and those of future generations. By July 1991, the movement had planted 10 million trees, had established 1,500 nurseries and had involved 50,000 women, who plant seedlings and distribute and care for the trees. Because it is inexpensive and replicable, the Green Belt Movement has proven to be an effective method for rural development and it spread quickly to at least 12 other countries in Africa. Dr. Maathai's movement has also attracted the attention and support of people and governments throughout the developed world.

Anita Figueredo, a physician and surgeon in La Jolla, California since 1947, is the founder of Friends of the Poor, an organization devised for the purpose of receiving tax-exempted gifts for the poor in Mexico and elsewhere. The loving doctor was awarded the Papal medal Pro Ecclesia by Pope Pius XII, and in 1970, she was invested as a Lady of the Order of the Holy Sepulchre of Jerusalem, later receiving the Grand Cross of the Order. In 1973, she was made a Regional Link of the Co-Workers of Mother Teresa in America.

Elizabeth Fry spent her life trying to better the living conditions of others, particularly the poor, and prisoners and hospital patients, especially women. Her aims at Newgate prison in 1817, included the separation of the sexes, classification of criminals, female supervision for women and adequate provisions for religious and secular instruction, as well as useful employment. She visited prisons throughout Great Britain and Europe, all the time giving help and hope to those suffering the abuse of the penal system of the time. Her focus was on building self-esteem rather than on punishment.

♀

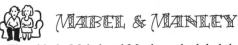

MABEL & MANLEY

The elderly Mabel and Manley scheduled their annual medical exam on the same day so they could travel together.

After Manley's examination, the doctor said, "You appear to be in good health, Manley. Do you have any medical concerns that you would like to ask me?"

"I certainly do," Manley replied. "Sometimes when I have sex with Mabel I am hot and sweaty, and then, after the next time I'm usually cold and chilly. Why is that?"

Not having an answer the doctor just shook his head and went to examine Mabel in the next room. Mabel had no questions or concerns so the doctor mentioned her husband's concerns about the way sex affected him differently at different times causing him to be hot some times and cold other times.

"Oh that crazy old fool!" Mabel replied. "That's because one time is usually in July and the next time is usually in December!"

♀

I Lost the Baby Bonus and Other Memories of Howley

By Kay Coxworthy

*"Go to sleep my dolly dear
Mama holds you never fear
Little eyelids downward creep
Dolly soon will be asleep"*

This childhood lullaby echoes down the ages – and the ghost of the little girl I was 52 years ago brings my memory back to Howley, nestled between Sandy and Grand lakes, when the railway and the telegraph were our only connection to the outside world.

It was November 1950 and I'd been chosen to sing a solo in the school Christmas concert. In those long ago days, we kids didn't know we were "poor," that a doll, a new dress and shoes were like asking for the moon. With nine small mouths to feed, on my father's leftover wages (after another visit to the local tavern on his way home from cooking in a lumber camp), my mother knew that only a miracle would allow her excited eight year old her big break.

Faith works wonders, and just a day before the big night, a new red dress, shiny black shoes and the only doll I'd ever own appeared. My mother, nine months pregnant at the time, knew she would miss the biggest night of my life. So on a frosty Sunday afternoon, she invited family and friends into our snug kitchen to "hear Kitty sing." Dressed in my new finery, I sang my heart out, crooning the lullaby as I'd heard her do countless times to her own babies. The pride in my mother's eyes is something I still cherish.

She never got to see the Christmas concert, and another child sang those lyrics; for within weeks of that kitchen performance, my young mother lay buried in our small cemetery, and I was hundreds of miles away in an orphanage.

I was born in Howley in 1942, upstairs in the rambling old railway house where my grandfather, Ken Coombs, was the Station Agent. Ken wisely left the child rearing to his wife Sarah, whose gentle spirit my own mother had inherited. My earliest memories are of that house, and the busy office where grandfather tapped out messages to other stations, receiving mysterious taps in return that he'd magically translate into telegrams.

The author circa 1945

Life, Love & Laughter

Life, Love & Laughter

And oh, the excitement in town when a train came roaring down the tracks, whistle blowing, billowing smoke into the skies, bringing the locals out to see who and what were coming or going! These trains were our lifeline to the outside world, and when a storm blocked the Gaff Topsails we were at the mercy of God and the elements.

Family names of that era remain etched in my mind – Yates, Francis, Stroud, George, Wheeler, Pelly, Samms, Gillard, Flight, Wiseman, Woolridge. One of the characters I remember well is the man we all knew as Uncle Charlie George, an old crony of my father's who shared his strong attachment to a drop of home brew. Uncle Charlie, who'd lost one arm in an industrial accident, spent many hours at our house; his family became an extension of our own. Years later, in the early 1970s, I attended a conference in Ottawa with colleagues from Newfoundland. We ended up, quite by chance, at a dance hosted by the local Newfoundland Club. Here, thousands of miles and more than two decades after they'd last seen me as an eight year old, I was reunited with Uncle Charlie's widow, son Sid and other members of the George family. What a "homecoming" that was!

I remember Doctor Parsons, who did everything from extracting teeth to delivering babies – although midwives, like the beloved Nellie Yates, brought most of Howley's babies into the world, including three sets of twins born to my mother, Margaret Dollmont, in the 1940s.

With our growing brood, I was feeding and changing infants when I wasn't much more than a toddler myself. One day when I must have had about enough of it, I asked my mother "Where do babies come from?" and learned "the doctor brings them in his bag." Then I knew where the blame lay, and I was ready for the doctor when he made his next visit. I refused to let him into the house, telling him "to take that baby in your bag and give it to someone else. We got too many here now!"

Memories from those long-ago days include frosty treats at Ginn's Ice Cream Parlour, watching my mother and her friends play broomball on frozen Station Pond, running errands to Gillard's store, visiting the beautiful farm owned by the Samms family, crossing the "Trussle" to pick berries, and visiting Aunt Lin who made the world's best date squares and chocolate cake.

Howley even had its own hotel, The Station View. Its first manager was Maxwell Simms whose son, Len, became a successful politician. Others who came through the Howley school system include businessman and recycling guru Charlie (Wes) Flight, and retired Judge Lloyd Wicks, whose father took over management of the Station Hotel from Max Simms.

I remember the meetings leading up to the referendum on Confederation, and all the talk about something called the Baby Bonus, which was going to make mothers rich! On the appointed day, I joined the long line at the Post Office. Shivering with excitement, I clasped the envelope and raced off towards home, waving the precious cheque at everyone I passed.

Unfortunately for me, there was a stiff breeze blowing off Station Pond that day, and you can guess the rest. The long-awaited Baby Bonus went flying over the rooftops of Howley! I was heartbroken, a feeling I'm sure my mother shared, but in her own quiet way she comforted me and wiped away the tears. Eventually, someone who'd found the envelope turned up at the door and all was well again in the little log cabin where we dreamed of the treats the Baby Bonus would bring and said prayers for Joey Smallwood who'd brought us such a miracle!

Today, 54 years later, many of the old landmarks of my childhood are gone. But they remain in memory and when I dream, I'm again the little girl racing home with the Baby Bonus, performing on a winter afternoon in our snug kitchen, or waiting for the train whistle to cut through the silence of early morning in the town I loved so well.

♀

WOMEN OF THE ISLAND AND THE BIG LAND

Elsie Balson Hodge

By Betty Colbourne Ranson

Courtesy - Dolly Hodge Hanrahan

In his book, *Self Matters*, Phillip C. McGraw, Ph.D., (Dr. Phil) claims that one's authentic self is determined by ten defining moments, seven critical choices, and five pivotal people.

Without a doubt, my earliest defining moment was the loss of my mother when I was only six years old. Although memory of that period of my life is dim, I believe that I made my first critical choice in 1946 when I joined the Brownies. In doing so, I placed myself under the influence of a very pivotal person, Elsie Balson Hodge, nee Wood.

Miss Wood was born in Allston, Massachusetts on Jan. 3, 1902, to Dr. Peter Henry and Alice Lillian (Heath) Wood. Both Dr. Peter and his brother, Dr. Albert John, were born in Catalina, Newfoundland. but moved to Boston at an early age. Elsie attended Boston area schools and then entered nurse's training at Emerson Hospital. There she received her degree as a registered nurse with that state's highest marks. At the age of 21, she was the youngest member of her class.

Elsie immediately began her career as a home and hospital nurse in the Boston area until a cousin, Dr. Sylvester, told her of a need for medical personnel in Newfoundland and Labrador. Dr. Sir Wilfred Grenfell had already established a hospital at St. Anthony and another was being planned for Twillingate. Having an uncle, Dr. A.J. Wood, who had returned to live and practice in Twillingate, Elsie's adventurous soul inspired her to head north. First she worked with Dr. Grenfell at St. Anthony, then accompanied him to Twillingate to help establish the Notre Dame Bay Memorial Hospital.

While in Twillingate, Dr. Grenfell was the house guest of Richard and Grace Hodge who, along with two sons, Arthur and Bertie, were proprietors of a mercantile business, Hodge Bros., Ltd. Elsie Wood and Arthur Hodge met, fell in love and were married by Dr. Grenfell in 1927.

The first meeting of the Board of Directors of the Notre Dame Bay Memorial Hospital was chaired by Arthur Hodge and, for two years, Elsie worked for no pay, first as an operating room nurse and then as head nurse.

The young couple soon started a family with a daughter, Dolly, being born in 1929, followed by Frances in 1932. Now having two daughters to raise, Elsie realized that there was very little for young people to do in Twillingate. She soon founded a chapter of the Newfoundland Rangers, then Brownie and Girl Guide troops of which she was captain and leader, respectively. She eventually became a Girl Guide commissioner and expanded Brownie and Girl Guide troops to neighbouring communities within Notre Dame Bay. She personally met Lord and Lady Baden-Powell, founders of the Girl Guide organization, and subsequently was bestowed a special award for 35 years of service.

In 1933, she, Aunt Eliza Wood and the Anglican minister's wife, established a well-baby clinic offering free nutritional advice to mothers and nursing care to babies up to two years of age. In

Life, Love & Laughter

addition, she taught a home nursing and first aid course every winter for 35 years, earning her a meritorious award.

Sundays found Elsie teaching the oldest boys in Sunday school at St. Peter's Anglican Church and, in addition to Bible verses and Catechism, she taught her boys to swim in the frigid waters of Snellin's Cove.

She was a founding member of the Twillingate Hustler's Club, a theatrical group who put on annual plays of which she was often producer and/or director. Her devotion to advancing the education of the local populace inspired her to become a founding member of the Twillingate branch of the Gosling Memorial Library of St. John's. Thus, Twillingate was brought into the larger world, not just by books, but also by American and Canadian periodicals and newspapers. Children's books were a priority with "read-aloud" sessions. This endeavour was expanded to include small lending libraries within the local schools. Teachers were taught library practices and procedures by Elsie herself.

Portuguese fishermen and other visiting foreigners were welcomed to Arthur and Elsie's gracious home. Many dinners were served without benefit of verbal communication, an open heart being a universal language.

A school friend of mine, Helen Facey White, recalls crossing frozen Twillingate harbour on snowshoes with Mrs. Hodge to trim Christmas trees at the hospital. Then summer would see her paddling across the harbour in her seal skin kayak, a gift from Dr. Grenfell. The special Inuit-made kayak has since been donated to the Newfoundland Museum.

Elsie, Aunt Eliza Wood, Maggie Ashbourne, and other friends would organize children's picnics at Minty's Farm or Purcell's Harbour Pond. Swimming, games, campfires and good food would be the order of the day. Mrs. Hodge had a fervent love of gardening and would pore over seed catalogues, planning flower and vegetable gardens. Through trial and error, she would find the right botanical mix for the short Twillingate growing season. Many a bridal bouquet or funeral arrangement came from her garden. She was, and is, the inspiration for the gardens I enjoy around my home.

Hardly a day of my life goes by without Elsie Hodge's influence playing a part in it. Whether I am setting a table with fine linens, china and silver or polishing my shoes, Mrs. Hodge has taught me how to do it. Knot-tying, semaphore, Morse code, crocheting, knitting, playing the piano, boiling a custard, wrapping a package, composing a letter or naming the stars for my grandchildren, Mrs. Hodge is guiding my hand and prodding my memory. Recognition of a piece of classical music or poetry, I owe to my mentor, Elsie Hodge. I like to think that, because I was a little motherless child, she took a special interest in me, but I'll bet if you were to ask any Twillingate girl of my generation, she will tell you that she was the special one. Such was her quiet, gentle manner and huge heart. She was diplomatic but firm, loving but demanding and her expectations were high. Her approval was more precious than gold. She introduced us to governors and premiers and, yes, we did mind our manners.

After Arthur died in 1963, Elsie travelled by train to Caribou, Maine, where she stayed with her daughter, Dolly, and family. She also worked for a period of time at the Caribou Hospital. When she finally chose to retire, she travelled by bus across America visiting landmarks, her children and grandchildren. Along the way, she continued to touch lives and make a difference to those with whom she came in contact. There were trips to Vancouver, to visit daughter Fran and family and, with Dolly, she visited Guam and spent time in the Far East. She loved it all and everyone loved her.

Elsie Balson Hodge passed away on June 12, 1994, leaving a legacy she could never have imagined in the hearts of hundreds of women. An Ecumenical memorial service was held at St. Peter's Anglican Church in Twillingate and was officiated by both Anglican and United Church ministers. Dignitaries, friends and loved ones paid tribute to her countless contributions. A reception was hosted by former Brownies and Girl Guides and her ashes are resting at Bareberry Head Cemetery in Twillingate.

On behalf of three generations of Twillingate children, I say, "Thank you, Mrs. Hodge, from the bottom of our hearts. We miss you."

♀

Food for Thought

I would venture to guess that Anon, who wrote so many poems without signing them, was often a woman.

♀   *- Virginia Woolf*

Spice of Life

When a man talks dirty to a woman it's sexual harassment, when a woman talks dirty to a man it's $3.99 a minute.

♀

Ennellene

I waited so long for my dreamboat
A man both handsome and gifted
But finally when
My ship came in
I found that his cargo had shifted

♀

Female Facts

Aelgifu, the daughter of an English nobleman, became the mistress of Cnut of Denmark around the year 1030, when he was raiding England as a young man. She remained his closest companion until his death, despite his formal marriage to Emma, the English king's sister. The eldest of their two sons, Sweyn, was made King of Norway, and Cnut appointed Aelgifu Regent there. Her rule was extremely harsh, and her reputation for tyrannical cruelty was unparalleled, eventually provoking an uprising which removed her from power in 1035.

When Cnut died she returned to England, and persuaded the nobles to recognize her other son Harold "Harefoot" as King in 1037 but no records of her from then on have been found. Incidentally, her son King Harold, was the last king of England ever conquered by a foreign nation, when William the Conqueror (of Normandy) defeated his army and killed him at Hastings in 1066.

♀

  ## MABEL & MANLEY

When Mabel and Manley got married, the groom turned to the new bride and said, "Oh Mabel my darling, to think that you will have to put up with my ugly face for the rest of your life."

Mabel looked at Manley fondly and replied, "Don't worry Darling, you'll be at work until it gets dark most days."

♀

Life, Love & Laughter

Food for Thought

The middle years of marriage are the most crucial. In the early years, spouses want each other and in late years, they need each other.   *- Rebecca Tilly*

♀

Is That a Fact?
Many things are taken as facts. Not all of them are.

Baby Boxer

It was said that Deborah Skinner, daughter of B. F. Skinner, probably the most notable psychologist since Sigmund Freud, would grow up abnormal because her father kept her in a special box as an experiment for two and a half years.

The Fact Is that Deborah grew up very normal, although her upbringing was happier than most. The box that Deborah spent the first two and a half years in was designed by her father simply to keep his daughter warm and cozy in winter without piles of blankets, as the neighbouring kids in Minnesota did. In her happy environment, which was nothing more than an air and temperature controlled crib and playpen with glass sides, Debby seldom had rashes and cried even less often. The idea was marketed but it never caught on. It seems that not many people want to raise their child in something that looks like an aquarium.

♀

Feminine Words & Phrases

Ale-wife: What the landlady of an ale-house was once called.

Amazon: Female name given to world's largest river. *See also 'Female Facts' page 351.*

Aphrodite: The Greek equivalent of the Roman goddess of love, Venus. Like many goddesses of her time in mythology, Aphrodite made love to both gods and mortals, bearing children for both. The most prominent of her half-mortal children was Aeneas, her son by an ordinary shepherd known as Anchises. According to the myth, their son became the founder of the nation of Italy, and the ancestor of the Roman people.

Berchta: A goddess of South German mythology who, after Christianity came to that part of the world, was turned into a bogy-woman. Her description, as having one large foot and a long, iron nose, was used to scare children.

Bloomers: A woman's outfit consisting of a short skirt worn over loose pants gathered at the ankles. The name (which has changed meanings over the years) is attributed to women's suffrage leader Amelia Jenks Bloomer, who was the first to wear it during a protest speech in the US in 1849. *See also 'Female Facts' page 326.*

Chaperon: A more-mature and responsible woman, who acted as protector of, and advisor to, younger, unmarried women in public places.

♀

Life, Love & Laughter

What She Sees

Author Unknown

At 3: She looks at herself and sees a Queen.

At 8: She looks at herself and sees Cinderella.

At 15: She looks at herself and sees an Ugly Sister (Mum I can't go to school looking like this!)

At 20: She looks at herself and sees "too fat/too thin, too short/too tall, too straight/too curly" -- but decides she's going out anyway.

At 30: She looks at herself and sees "too fat/too thin, too short/too tall/too straight/too curly" -- but decides she doesn't have time to fix it, so she's going out anyway.

At 40: She looks at herself and sees "clean" and goes out anyway.

At 50: She looks at herself and sees "I am" and goes wherever she wants to go.

At 60: She looks at herself and reminds herself of all the people who can't even see themselves in the mirror anymore. Goes out and conquers the world.

At 70: She looks at herself and sees wisdom, laughter and ability. Goes out and enjoys life.

At 80: Doesn't bother to look, just puts on a purple hat and goes out to have fun with the world.

♀

 # Animal Mating - Fact and Fantasy *– Ron Young*

Killer Sex

Fact:

   The female Antechinus must always raise her young without the help of her mate, because sex kills him. Once spring comes the male antechinus, a tree-dwelling marsupial (a smaller relative of the kangaroo) from Australia, has nothing but sex on his mind. He will mate for 12 hours at a time, and involve himself in marathon orgies which can include as many as 16 partners. So great is his desire to mate that he even forgets to eat, drink or sleep. Without the proper nourishment he loses weight, his hair falls out, and he will finally fall down with exhaustion. If he can gather the energy to go at it again, he will. But eventually this strenuous activity is too much for the male, and within two weeks he (and all the males around him) are dead, leaving the females to bring up the next generation on their own.

Fantasy:

The male antichinus wonder, from Auzzieland, down under
Has a sex drive that he ever must obey
He always wants to get it on, but the bugger's almost gone
I don't know if he'll live to see another day.

♀

Spice of Life

The secret of staying young is to live honestly, eat slowly, and lie about your age.

– Lucille Ball

♀

Aunt Alice says:

Women over 50 don't have babies because they would put them down and forget where they left them.

Food for Thought

The victory of success is half won when one gains the habit of work.

– Sarah A. Bolton

♀

MABEL & MANLEY

Some years after her husband, Manley, died, Mabel had a heart attack and was taken to hospital where she herself, died and went to heaven. When God saw her, he said, "There's been a mistake Mabel, you shouldn't be here. You have forty more years left on Earth yet, so I am sending you back. When Mabel regained consciousness in the hospital bed she was so thrilled to have so much of a future left that she decided she would have a complete makeover before she left the hospital. She had a complete face lift, a tummy tuck, breast implants and a nose job. On the day she was to leave the hospital she had her hair dyed and styled, and in the new clothes she had purchased she was amazed at the image that looked back at her from the bathroom mirror.

As Mabel was leaving the hospital she stepped off the curb and was hit by a bus and killed. In heaven again, she said to God, "I thought you told me I had forty more years left. What happened?"

God replied, "Sorry Mabel, I didn't recognize you."

♀

Her Other Half

My Way or the Highway

A California man whose wife got stranded in Hawaii, because she had overspent on her holiday there, was walking the beach when his toe bumped something. Picking it up he saw that it was a bottle with a cork in it. Upon popping the cork a genie appeared and thanked the man profusely for rescuing him from a thousand year entrapment within the bottle. To show his thanks the genie told the man that he would grant him one wish.

Thinking about it, the man said, "I'd like a highway from California to Hawaii."

"That's a very big wish," replied the genie. "The distance, between the two states is very far and the water is very deep. Couldn't you wish for something easier?"

The man thought about it for a minute, then said, "If you can't do that maybe you can make me understand women. I'd be satisfied with that."

"Would you like that a two-lane or a four-lane highway?" asked the genie.

♀

Life, Love & Laughter

Food for Thought

Marrying for money is often the hardest way of getting it. - *Mae West*

♀

Female Facts

In Babylon, as in many cultures, marriageable girls were, at one time, auctioned off to the highest male bidders. However in Babylon, the money collected for the prettier girls was given to the homelier ones to use as dowries to attract husbands.

♀

 The Whys of Men

Why does every woman marry the wrong man?
Because that's the only variety they come in.

♀

Spice of Life

Things are going to get a lot worse before they get worse. – *Lily Tomlin*

♀

Some Mothers Have Them

"Gosh," said three-year-old Jackson, as he saw the bottoms of the little girl next door's bathing suit fall to her knees, "I didn't know there was that much difference between Catholics and Protestants."

♀

What's The Big Deal About Beautiful Women?

Anonymous

Did you know that...

- – There are 3 billion women who don't look like supermodels and only eight who do.
- – Marilyn Monroe wore a size 14.
- – If Barbie was a real woman, she'd have to walk on all fours due to her proportions.
- – The average North American woman weighs 144 pounds and wears between a size 12 and 14.
- – If shop mannequins were real women, they'd be too thin to menstruate.
- – One out of every four college-aged women has an eating disorder.
- – The models in the magazines are airbrushed - they're not perfect!
- – A psychological study in 1995 found that three minutes spent looking at models in a fashion magazine caused 70% of women to feel depressed, guilty, and shameful.
- - Models twenty years ago weighed 8% less than the average woman; today they weigh 23% less.

♀

Life, Love & Laughter

Our Aopplgeis for the Erorrs

Aoccdrnig to a rscheearch at an Elingsh uinervtisy, it deosn't mttaer in waht oredr the ltteers in a wrod are, the olny iprmoetnt tihng is taht the frist and lsat ltteer is at the rghit pclae. The rset can be a toatel mses and you can sitll raed it wouthit a porbelm. Tihs is bcuseae we do not raed ervey lteter by it slef but the wrod as a wlohe. Tihs mkaes it hrad to fnid erorrs wchih is why tehre are Msiatkes sitll in tihs book.

♀

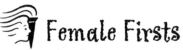 ## Adam's Ribbing

Job Action

A recently-divorced national union leader decided to try his luck with a dating service.

"Is this a union shop?" he asked the receptionist.

Upon learning that it was indeed unionized, the man asked to look at some photos of prospective dates. He was particularly attracted to the photo of one beautiful woman in her early thirties, and told the manager he would like to date her.

"You can't do that," the manager said and, showing him a photo of a 65-year-old grey-haired woman, she said, "you have to take her."

"Why should I have to take her?" bellowed the prospective client.

"Because," replied the manager, "she has seniority."

♀

Female Firsts

396 BC: A Spartan princess named Kyniska became the first woman to compete in an Olympic chariot race.

200 BC: (or thereabouts) Aglaonike, became the first woman astronomer in that after mastering the art of predicting eclipses.

1350: (or thereabouts) A Portuguese princess became Ste. Wilgefortis, making her the first female saint to have been crucified for growing a beard, according to legend.

1406: *Treatise of Fishing with an Angle*, the first known essay on sports fishing, was written by Dame Juliana Berners of Great Britain. In the book she described how to make a rod and fly hooks, and when to fish.

1492: On August 11, Vanozza dei Catanei and Giulia Farnese became the first two woman in the history of the Roman Catholic Church to witness their lover becoming a pope.

1533: Catherine de Medici, who became Queen of France, was the first woman to wear high heel shoes, which she had an artisan design for her. She wore them to impress the man who had been chosen to be her husband, as well as all the courtiers at the Royal Ball, all of whom she had recently met after travelling from her home in Medici to marry her betrothed.

1552: The term 'caddy' was first coined when Mary, Queen of Scots, started calling her assistants 'cadets.' Mary loved a game of golf, and during her reign, the famous St. Andrews Golf Course was built. *See also 'Feminine Words & Phrases' page 196 and 'Female Facts' page 386.*

♀

Life, Love & Laughter

WOMEN OF THE ISLAND AND THE BIG LAND

Cassie Brown

This story, told through interviews between Marian White and Cassie's daughter, Christine, exemplifies the truth that Cassie Brown's contribution to Newfoundland Literature is as enduring as the sea.

Courtesy – The Brown Family

Born into the Horwood merchant family at Rose Blanche, Newfoundland, on January 10, 1919, Cassie Brown identified with the sea at an early age. As a teenager, Brown was an avid reader and wrote fiction and radio plays. A five-time winner of the Provincial Arts and Letters Competition, she was also involved in amateur drama with the St. John's Players, a group that awarded her honorary membership and adapted two of her radio plays to stage.

Cassie Horwood married Donald F. Brown in 1945 and had two children, Derek and Christine. She wrote a weekly column for the Daily News from 1959-66. Between 1962 and 1965 she also wrote for, edited and published her own magazine, St. John's Woman, that later became Newfoundland Woman. After reading Joey Smallwood's Book of Newfoundland, she became interested in the 1914 sealing disaster in which seventy-eight men froze to death. A fifteen-minute story for one of her Newfoundland history radio dramatizations became the ground work for her first book, *Death on the Ice*, the success of which was phenomenal. Published by Doubleday, it sold 100,000 copies between 1972 and 1980. On September 23, 1987, Cassie Brown was inducted into the Newfoundland and Labrador Hall of Fame.

In 1976 Brown, an honorary member of the Newfoundland Writers Guild, published her second book, *A Winter's Tale: The Wreck of the Florizel*, and followed with *Standing Into Danger* in 1979. Just before her death on December 30, 1986 she completed her fourth book, and autobiography, *Who Is Amalthea*, as yet unpublished. In 1990 Flanker Press released *The Caribou Disaster and Other Short Stories*, an anthology of Cassie's stories.

*****

My mother was always writing, and as a child I thought that was a boring way to pass your days. I used to tell myself I didn't want to be like my mother in that way and she never pushed it on me. She would say, "You do what you want but I *have* to write. It's in my bones, my molecules and my atoms." She was not only an inspiration to her family, but to the public as well. She was a teacher and wrote about what she learned. Because of this she was always secure with herself since she didn't know how to be anything else but that.

I wanted to write music and my mother believed in me so much that she would continually say there would be nothing I couldn't do if I really wished it. She spent hours teaching me how to carry a tune because I couldn't sing and yet I wanted to. I don't think I really appreciated how much patience that took then, but today I look back and admire her even more for that.

My mother felt honoured to be chosen to write books about sea disasters, even though she was sometimes unwell while doing the research. If someone asked why she was writing what some considered a man's book she would say she felt she could do justice to it, and that she did not choose the book but that the book chose her. "It was as though these men who had already passed over to the other side were saying *Gotcha!* I was there. I was on the ice with those men,"

Life, Love & Laughter

she would exclaim. Sometimes I would get up and leave when she talked like this, but other times I would stay in total fascination of this woman who called herself "the sea".

It was my mother's unlimited thought that allowed her to write such books as *Death on the Ice*. Her power came from her pen; there she felt the sea - spiritually, physically and mentally. She saw the sea as a whole, as a being that she could talk to and feel it answer her. She would come back from a walk by the sea sparkling because she too had become one with it. Cassie would carry beach rocks in her car so as to have some of this sea energy with her when she drove about. Whenever questioned about it she would look surprised and say, "But you know I love the sea, and these rocks are of the sea, and so am I; these rocks have a life of their own and so do I." I would sometimes tell my mother that I thought she sustained her life by writing about the sea. She had an anemic condition and believed the sea had great healing power. After she finished writing her three most serious books, her anemic condition had balanced itself out. Strange but true. "I am too tough to surrender to the unknown," she would say. Her awareness of her task in life was so strong that she couldn't surrender "until the last word I have to write is written".

My mother seemed to have this great understanding of *why* things happen the way they do. She taught me how to contact that inner being within myself which took a great deal of patience; I was very rebellious. I was a slow learner and Mom was an amazing teacher as well as my best friend. I had no other way of learning except by listening to her and learning through her. I'm sure a lot of the disaster in her life was transmitted into her books because there is something about her disaster writing that was very healing, not only for her but for all who read her books. It was a part of her basic philosophy to turn the negative into positive and to transmit her frustrations into something creative. This was precious to me in my earlier years because I learned to write about inspirational things and I knew that if I wrote about things that were really upsetting me, I'd recognize the cause within myself. Writers, she believed, needed to accept this process and go with the flow.

My mother traveled on the sea and nearly drowned in Rose Blanche when she was about five years old. As a child she was drawn to the sea and would lie down on the wharf and look into its depths. However, she was not allowed to go near the wharf alone. One day her fascination drew her further from her home until she found herself on the dock. She started to sweep the dock to justify being there and before she knew it, swept herself right into the sea. Although none of the fishermen could swim a stroke, they formed a human chain to rescue her. What Cassie remembered of this near-drowning incident was the size of the pillars beneath the surface that kept the dock afloat!

My mother felt she had to write for Newfoundland. Cassie could see that Newfoundland women had a lot of colour and had colourful stories to tell if someone was interested enough to listen. Mom was interested. There were many heroic things that happened here, but people would just tell of them as though they were commonplace. She could see they weren't.

Cassie Brown was very non-judgmental and for that reason didn't care what other people thought. She would discuss astrology with her sister, Joan, and thoroughly enjoy their different viewpoints on the way and how of things. Cassie's destiny was to be one with her universal mind, her God-source, and in that sense she very much fulfilled herself on earth.

Mother believed she was here to touch people and she did that through her books. She was mythological in many ways, and talked of carrying around a picture in her mind of this great, great teacher that she believed was in all of us, that is in the wind, and that tests us. She would say, "I'm having a mad love affair with my greater self, that greater self who gave me life!"

From the book The Finest Kind *by Marion Frances White, Creative Publishing. Used by permission.*

♀

Adam's Ribbing
Role Reversal

A man went to bed one night, very tired from his hard day at work. He prayed he could be his wife for one day, after all, she didn't work and stayed home all day!

The next morning he woke up and realized God had granted him his wish. He got up, as his wife, got breakfast for the family, packed lunches for the day, made sure the kids had their hair combed and face washed, then drove them to school. On the way home, he/she dropped in to pick up the dry cleaning, then the grocery store to pick up a few things, went home and started the laundry, made the beds, cleaned the bathroom (especially the toilet, since men sometimes don't have good aim) and started to prepare supper. He/she then went to pick the kids up from school, took them to their soccer game, came home and finished preparing supper. The husband comes home tired from work, sits down, eats his supper, then goes for a little nap. The wife cleans up the dishes, does homework with the kids, gets them ready for bed, reads them a story and tucks them in. She then finished folding and putting away laundry from the day. She finally drops into bed at 10:30 pm. The husband wants to make love, so they do. She rolls over and prays to God to change her back to her man self, realizing his wife's day is harder than his. God replies, "Yes, my son, but you will have to wait nine months, you just got pregnant!!"

♀

Is That a Fact?
Many things are taken as facts. Not all of them are.

The Atom Bomb's Creator?

Some people are aware of the fact that the Atom Bomb was created by the Manhattan Project, led by J. Robert Oppenheimer, using information gathered by other scientists, particularly Otto Hahn, who received the Nobel Prize for discovering nuclear fission, the splitting of the atom, which makes the bomb work, in 1946.

The fact is that although Hahn got the Nobel Prize for the discovery of nuclear fission, it was actually his collaborator, Lise Meitner, who made the discovery. She couldn't stick around Germany at the time to finish the experiments because she was Jewish and Hitler was in power. She escaped to Sweden in 1938, where she continued her work, under duress. Lise was used to duress, however. Because she was female, she was not permitted to go to high school. Her father hired a tutor to prepare her for university entrance when she was 21 years old. In two years she completed 8 years' worth of school syllabus. Lise Meitner was born in Austria, but upon graduation she moved to Germany where she worked with chemist, Otto Hahn. It was there that she made the discovery that would change the world forever. Though it was Meitner who actually solved the mystery and Hahn just carried out the experiment to prove it, Hahn got all the credit and even the Nobel Prize for it. However, Meitner never complained about not getting the Nobel Prize. In 1942, when the Manhattan Project was created. she was approached by Oppenheimer to work there, but she refused. Lise didn't believe in war and would have nothing to do with working on a bomb. Indeed, the great scientist did as much as she could to distance herself from anything to do with the bomb. In 1992, several years after her death, physicists named their 109th element 'meitnerium' in honour of Lise Meitner, finally giving her official recognition.

♀

Life, Love & Laughter

Life's Funny Experiences

Where the Heart Is

My seventeen-year-old son replied to a job in the newspaper today. It was his first attempt to seek part-time work, so my husband and I were anxiously waiting around listening to him and hoping he would pick up a part-time job for the summer. The person on the other line asked him where he was calling from, to which he responded, "home," instead of "Hamilton."

Enough said, he didn't get a job interview, let alone the job.

Submitted by Nancy Rankled, Ontario, Canada

♀

One More Mile

By Loreen Haldenby

I saw you last night as I came out of the concert at Massey Hall. There was no mistaking your girl-child face, your hazel eyes, still breath-takingly beautiful in spite of the rouged cheeks, the blond spit curls. There you were in your too-short pink skirt, your black mesh stockings, your teetering high heels.

I turned my head quickly, thanking all the mercies that you didn't see me. Didn't recognize me. After all it would never do for a sixty-five-year-old matron, exuding respectability, to be seen talking to a whore on Yonge street.

How old are you now, fourteen? Yes, that seems about right. You were nine, going on ten, when you first knocked on my door. A stringy kid, shabby. You had that way of standing, first on one foot, and then on the other, and imploring, with your heart in your eyes, "is it convenient?"

Was it convenient? Did I need a grubby little girl from God knows where in my organized kitchen? I began tentatively, "would you care for a little snack?"

Would you care for a little snack? Your eyes devoured the open fridge. Yogurt, ice cream, strawberries, cereal. Large quantities found their way to your hungry little stomach. Every day you came and you left, replete and, for a short time, happy.

You became familiar as the visits went on. You played the piano, and danced to the beat of the rock and roll music on the radio. You showed me how you could do gymnastic stunts. "But, wistfully, "my mom can't afford my lessons."

And then, just a few months later, the knock on the door. The desperation. "Is it convenient? I must tell you something, but you must promise me not to call the cops.

I promised you I would not call the cops.

You twisted your hair. At last you spoke, fearfully, but yet defiantly, "My mom leaves me with my dad when she goes to work. He gets drunk and pushes me around. He hits me on the face, everywhere, and sometimes he touches me funny. Sometimes, he gets so drunk and beats me and mom up so much we have to call the cops and they come and take him away for awhile."

I didn't call the cops. I called Family Services. Whether or not they helped you, I don't know.

Lord, I believe I've gone the second mile for you, kid, but how would things have been if I'd gone the third mile, or the fourth?

♀

✍ *Letters From Our Friends*

Home is Not Just Where the Heart is

Dear Editor,

I am a Newfoundlander living in Ontario. When I recently returned from my trip home, my husband encouraged me to write this letter. While I was away Shelagh Rogers of Morningside Radio did a story on homesickness. I rarely miss the program but I did that day because of my own homesickness.

It was a Thursday night and I got a call from my Mom and oldest brother, our family home had been sold. I listened in disbelief as they celebrated the fact that "it was only on the market for one week." How could this be happening? I knew it was for sale (a fact that I had trouble dealing with) but I was counting on the slow real estate market. Surely it would be "ours" when we went home for summer vacation. Tears welled up in my eyes and before long they were spilling over as I tried to hide my heartbreak from my Mom. She was relieved and happy - something I couldn't share, but I didn't want to take that from her. Mom and Dad had raised eleven children in our home and they always had a steady stream of friends and extended family coming and going. With my father's passing six years ago, all the grandchildren getting older and more self-absorbed and our lives getting busier, the house was getting quieter and lonelier than Mom could handle. The days of sacks of flour, cases of butter and Carnation milk, and fifty pound bags of potatoes were gone. It was time to sell.

I kept myself somewhat composed until I got off the phone - and then lost it. My husband, who had recently gone through the sale of their family home with ease, was at a loss. I cried for a long time. I had to let go of the secret dream of me buying the house and telling my two children that this three-bedroom bungalow was once filled with 13 people. I had to realize that I wouldn't be taking fresh bread out of that oven as they came in from school, and on their lunch hour I wouldn't be able to challenge them to see "who can run the fastest to the Co-op for me?" I cried as I realized that the little girls I saw in my swings and in my backyard rink were me and my sisters and not my daughters.

Mostly I cried because I hadn't said good-bye. It was already the end of January and the closing date was February 23rd.

On February 1st, with baby in hand and one in my arms I walked across the runway to board my plane - a convoluted, eight-hour, three connection flight to Gander. It didn't matter that I had to rearrange several appointments, miss a few already paid-for programs, burden our meagre budget, or travel alone with two small children. What did matter was that I was bringing my children home for one last time and I was going to be able to say good-bye.

There were tears in my eyes, as always, as they announced our arrival at Gander Airport, but there was also that contentment that one can only feel from being home.

That Saturday night there was a gathering of the Dwyer clan at 23 Reid Street for one last time. This time there were no tears, just story after story about growing up in that house. We all laughed so hard as we remembered the details of memories of a small house with thirteen people. The next generation sat there in awe hanging on to every word, and added some memories of their own.

I'm back in North Bay now and life goes on. But in my heart I took 23 Reid Street with me. It will always be "where I belong to."

In my kitchen you can sometimes get a whiff of salt beef, pease pudding and - though infrequently - the sweet smell of home-made bread fills this house too. I only hope my children will feel the same love for their home as I did for mine.

A transplanted Newfoundlander, Maureen Dwyer Clout, North Bay, Ontario

♀

Life, Love & Laughter

Life, Love & Laughter

Female Facts

On January 20, 1953, US President Dwight D. Eisenhower's inauguration was televised and drew 29 million viewers. On the same night the *I Love Lucy* show, which featured Lucy giving birth to Little Ricky, was aired and drew 44 million viewers, out-hailing the new Chief by 15 million viewers.

♀

The Whys of Men

Why don't married women like going to sleazy joints? *Because they don't want to run into their husbands.*

♀

Spice of Life

A single woman is one who is foot-loose and fiancee-free.

♀

Life's Funny Experiences

Cream Scream

A few years ago, while I was visiting my sister in Newfoundland, she was painting the outside of her house. It was a hot, sunny day and she had shorts on. She got a very bad burn on the backs of her legs - so much so that she had to go to the doctor in St. John's. He gave her a prescription, and we went to the pharmacy in the mall to get it filled. After, we sat down to have a cup of coffee, I suggested that we go in the washroom so I could put the cream on her legs. In the washroom, she pulled up her dress and I got down behind her to apply the soothing cream. When I started to touch her, she cried out, "Ouch, ouch, ouch, don't do it! Mary, please. Ouch, it hurts!" Her plea was so loud that a mall employee came hurrying in and asked, "What in heaven's name is going on here?"

I looked up at her and said, "I am helping my sister get relief."

Mary Duncan - Montreal, Quebec

♀

Adam's Ribbing

The Blind Man

Just as the community-minded and charitable young housewife was about to step into the bathtub, her doorbell rang. This was not surprising because, as a volunteer, she had many people drop by to discuss projects during the day, some of whom were merely looking for charitable donations.

"Who is it?" she yelled.

"Blind man," came the answer.

In a bit of a hurry, she didn't bother to put her housecoat on as she grabbed her purse and headed for the front door, totally nude.

When she opened the door the man with the astonished look on his face took several seconds before he asked, "Where would you like these blinds put, Ma'am?"

♀

 **Aphrodesia**

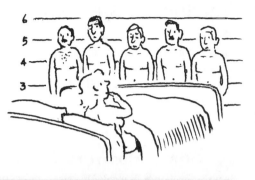

The man turned to the beautiful Aphrodesia, lying beside him in bed, and asked, "Am I the first man you've ever made love to?"

"I don't know,' replied Aphrodesia. "I have a terrible memory for faces."

♀

Is That a Fact?
Many things are taken as facts. Not all of them are.

Does sexual urge decrease with age?

When people get older they lose interest in sex, which is just as well because they wouldn't be able to perform anyway. This belief is shared by many.

The fact is that many people remain sexually active, even into their nineties. Sometimes illness, or certain medications taken for illnesses, will affect sexual drive but among healthy males and females that drive remains intact. The female goes through menopause, where hormone levels change, ovulation stops and she can no longer conceive, but this doesn't lessen her desire. Men don't experience physical menopause, but there are physiological changes. Sometimes males take longer to reach a climax as they get older, but this is not always considered to be a negative, especially by the females.

♀

10 WAYS TO KNOW IF YOU HAVE "ESTROGEN ISSUES"

Author Unknown

1. Everyone around you has an attitude problem.

2. You're adding chocolate chips to your cheese omelet.

3. The dryer has shrunk every last pair of your jeans.

4. Your husband is suddenly agreeing to everything you say.

5. You're using your cellular phone to dial up every bumper sticker

that says: "How's my driving – call 1-800 . . ."

6. Everyone's head looks like an invitation to batting-practice.

7. Everyone seems to have just landed here from "Outer Space.

8. You can't believe they don't make a tampon bigger than Super Plus.

9. You're sure that everyone is scheming to drive you crazy.

10. The Ibuprofen bottle is empty and you bought it yesterday.

♀

Life, Love & Laughter

Freedom in the Soul

The right to vote, or equal civil rights, may be good demands, but true emancipation begins neither at the polls nor in courts. It begins in woman's soul. History tells us that every oppressed class gained true liberation from its masters through its own efforts. It is necessary that woman learn that lesson, that she realize that her freedom will reach as far as her power to achieve her freedom reaches.   – *Emma Goldman, 1911*

♀

Some Mothers Have Them

Jackson was only four and, his sister three, the night their parents held their fifth wedding anniversary party in their home. Their mother was horrified when her two children, completely naked, entered the living room, where their guests were engaged in conversation. The two walked around the room, causing a moment's pause in conversation. Then everybody went back to talking again, ignoring the nude children as a way to hide their embarrassment. Meanwhile the children quietly walked around the room several times before making their exit. Silence fell again as the children left, and Jackson was overheard to say, "See Sis, I told you that was vanishing cream in the jar."

♀

Aunt Alice says:

The main trouble with old age is that you never grow out of it.

Spice of Life

They say that women talk too much. If you have worked in Congress you know that the filibuster was invented by men.
– *Clare Booth Luce*

♀

Her Other Half
Fountain of Youth

A young lady married a seventy-five year old man and, concerned about his lovemaking potential, she bought some special pills that were designed to make people feel younger. She put two in his morning coffee, three in his tea at lunch time, five in his milk at dinnertime and two in his cocoa before he went to bed.

He got into bed and immediately fell asleep.

The next morning when he got out of bed and started dressing, his new bride said in a purring voice as she patted the sheet beside her, "Why don't you come back and lay down beside me for a few minutes."

"If I do that," replied the man, "I'll be late for school."

♀

WOMEN OF THE ISLAND AND THE BIG LAND

Debbie Prim, A Life–time Winner

By Ron Young

Debbie Prim was never Prime Minister or Premier, or a dignitary of any kind by some standards, but on the day of her funeral, at age 39, the flags at all government buildings in the province of Newfoundland and Labrador flew half mast. There were as many people at her funeral at the Basilica as there were there for the funeral of the first premier of the province, Joseph R. Smallwood. Among the many dignitaries at her funeral mass was Premier Brian Tobin. The eulogy was read by the late Chief Len Power of the Royal Newfoundland Constabulary.

Courtesy – The Prim Family

A bout with polio when she was nine months old left Deborah Prim quadrapheligic, and she was confined to a wheelchair for life, but that didn't stop her from being an achiever. It only gave her a life-long cause.

Debbie's cause was to help others, especially those against whom the playing field of life is slanted. The people, like herself, who have to put much effort in doing the things most of us take for granted.

Debbie's paying job was at Royal Newfoundland Constabulary headquarters in St. John's, where she was loved and appreciated, not only by staff and citizens, but parolees, probationers, and people out on bail, who were required to report to her as part of her job. Some of them loved her so much they came to her funeral.

"You could tell who they were when they went up to her coffin," says her father, retired sea captain, Joe Prim. "They were the ones trying to hide their faces with all the police around."

There were more than 200 police officers among the throngs at the funeral, most of them part of the honour guard.

Apart from her regular job, Debbie started groups and tried to make changes to assist the disabled. She was on committees that would take more than a page to list. Among her other volunteer duties, she was President of a committee that ran HUB, which operates a printing company employing disabled persons.

"As a boss, she was supportive. She defended us to others when we got out of line and she jumped down our throats in private. Always with the best interest of the HUB at heart," said the HUB staff in a good-bye note to her.

"But Debbie was more than that. She was an inspiration. Very quickly after meeting Deb, we learned to look beyond her disability, for what was lacking in physical skills were made up in mental skills. Her memory for detail amazed all of us."

Debbie was relentless in working to help disabled persons, and would appropriate meetings with whoever was premier at the time, or any government member who could help her cause. In

Life, Love & Laughter

the last two weeks of her life she attended 22 meetings, working right up to the day before she went to the hospital for the last time.

"She would meet with the premier, or the devil himself, to help a cause for disabled people," says her father.

But Debbie Prim was also full of life and fun.

"She'd call me up and say, 'Get off the couch we're going out.' If I had a nickle for every time I took her power chair apart and put it in the trunk I could retire," said her friend and co-worker Michelle Greenham Bragg.

She liked country and western music, and on Friday nights the two would often bar hop. They also went mummering one Christmas. Debbie was the mummer dressed like Santa Claus, being pushed in a shopping cart.

Debbie loved stylish and different clothes, hats and jewellery. She had earrings to match every outfit, 100 pairs of shoes, 30 pairs of glasses and a watch for every day of the week.

But Debbie also loved giving. On one 40-minute shopping spree at the mall, she bought 130 Christmas gifts for her friends. On Christmas Day, instead of having Christmas dinner served up at her parents home by her mother, or by others who invited her, Debbie would choose to plan a dinner at the HUB for people in need.

As Chairperson of the Newfoundland and Labrador division of the Rick Hanson 'Man in Motion Tour,' she met and became friends with Hanson. In beautiful script, which her parents now have framed, he wrote, "After about thirty seconds with her you didn't notice she was in a wheelchair. She'd sweep up, stick out her hand and say, 'Hi. Debbie Prim. Polio '62. How are you?' She was, in short, a person who accepted her disability as a factor in life, not a deterrent. She hadn't beaten it (polio), but she'd wrestled it to a draw."

This was certainly attested to by Judy Gibson, who met Debbie at the RNC during an investigation, when she later wrote, "If 'dis' ability means not being able, it was obvious that Debbie was in no way disabled. She managed life from a wheelchair far better than most of us who have full use of our limbs. She was efficient, competent, organized, intelligent; all of these things, but what made her good at work was her personality. Her beautiful, unlined face, with no hint of bitterness, or self-pity, positively lit up as she answered the phone or queries at the desk, or jotted down messages for this person or that. And with a touch of the side of her hand, she controlled that wheelchair like a gymnast on the balance beam. She could navigate it around any obstruction and never bump into anything. I was so impressed. She treated me with warmth and courtesy, so besides being good at her job, she was a special human being."

Debbie was also a special human being who helped others off the job as well. And sometimes helped change their lives.

Jeannie Andrews Bowering writes, "When my son was three years old he saw Debbie in the Avalon Mall and noticed her electric wheelchair. He was very taken with it, as a young child would be. He didn't see a disabled person, he saw a really great motorized vehicle, occupied by someone else and he wanted a piece of the action."

Jeannie deterred her son, not wanting him to bother a stranger, especially one in a wheelchair and they went on with their shopping until she lost Jason.

"About 30 minutes later I was bolting through the mall hallways looking for security personel to assist me in finding my lost baby, who by now I imagined was kidnapped by a madman and taken to a secret hideaway, never to be seen again. Suddenly, I saw this huge smile and it was attached to my little boy's face as he rode happily in that wonder of a chair as she calmly searched the mall looking for the wayward mother who was sure to be frantic by now. All the while she talked to, shared with, and taught my son."

From that experience Jeannie further writes, "I learned to see beyond my own perceptions and misconceptions and try to practice that each day in my nursing career."

The Independent Living Resource Centre, which teaches disabled people how to live on their own, and which was co-founded by Debbie, is in the process of creating The Debbie Prim Memorial Garden beside the centre in her honour. The garden will be accessible to all, including those who are disabled.

Debbie was also an ideal daughter.

"She was always pleasant and never complained," says her mother Geraldine, "Even when she fell out of her wheelchair in Vancouver and came home with her leg in cast."

During her life, Debbie won a large number of medals, awards and honours for her many accomplishments, including; the 1998 YMCA-YWCA Women of Distinction Award, the 1998 Council of Canadians With Diabetes Award, as well as a medal at the National Wheelchair Games in Vancouver in 1973. But in life, Debbie was always a winner. She was a winner because she chose to be one.

"If you have a goal you should go for it," she once said.

"No matter who you are, the sky is the limit. Never let anyone stop you from reaching for the stars."

♀

Female Firsts

1539: Isobel De Soto was the first female governor in the New World when she became Governor of Cuba in the absence of her explorer husband Hernando De Soto.

1539: Francisca Hintestrosa became the first woman colonist in mainland North America.

1542: The first woman livyer in Newfoundland and Labrador was Marguerite de la Roque. She was left on an island off the coast of Labrador by her uncle, Jean Francois de la Roque, Sieur de Roberval, in 1542. *See also page 141.*

1553: Mary Tudor became the first queen to rule England in her own right. She was the daughter of Henry VIII and ruled for five years.

1561: The first European woman to use tobacco (on record) was the Queen of France, Catherine de Medici. She used it in the snuff (powdered and snorted) form as a cure for her migraine headaches. She learned about "the wonderful new drug from the New World" from Jean Nicot, her Ambassador to Portugal. Incidentally the word 'nicotine' comes from the same Jean Nicot.

1643: Goody Armitage became the first licenced tavern keeper in the American colonies. She was permitted to sell beer but not wine.

1647: Achsah Young is believed to be the first woman who was executed as a witch in Massachusetts.

1648: Margaret Jones became the first person in Boston executed for witchcraft.

1650: Anne Bradstreet became the first American woman to have her work published when her book of poetry, *The Tenth Muse Lately Sprung Up in America*, was published in England.

♀

Ennellene

When I punched out that shoe salesman
I admit that I was tipsy
When he said, "I'm looking up your thighs
I didn't know he was lipsy"

♀

Out of Habit

One day while Mother Superior was visiting a classroom she listened as one of her nun teachers asked her class to define marriage.

"Marriage is a time of torment, which some of us must experience before we go on to a better world," replied the young girl.

"No," the nun corrected. "You have just defined Purgatory, not marriage."

"Don't correct the child," said Mother Superior. "Perhaps she has been permitted to see the light."

♀

Some Mothers Have Them

Little Jackson was attending his first wedding. After the service, his friend asked him, "How many women can a man marry?" "Sixteen," Jackson responded. His friend was amazed that he had an answer so quickly. "How do you know that?" "Easy," said Jackson. "All you have to do is add it up, like the Minister said: 4 better, 4 worse, 4 richer, 4 poorer."

♀

The Perfect Dress

The wedding day was fast approaching. Everything was ready, and nothing could dampen Judy's excitement, not even her parents' nasty divorce. Her mother, Connie, finally found the perfect dress to wear and would be the best dressed mother-of-the-bride ever!

A week later, Judy was horrified to learn that her new young stepmother, Trixie, had purchased the same dress as Judy's mother had bought. She asked Trixie to exchange the dress, but Trixie refused.

"Absolutely not! I'm going to wear THIS dress; I'll look like a million in it!"

Judy told her mother, who graciously replied, "Never mind dear. I'll get another dress, after all it's YOUR special day, not hers."

Two weeks later another dress was finally found. When they stopped for lunch, Judy asked her mother, "What are you going to do with the first dress? Maybe you should return it. You don't have any place to wear it."

Connie grinned and replied, "Of course, I do, dear! I'm wearing it to the rehearsal dinner!"

Author Unknown

♀

WOMEN OF THE ISLAND AND THE BIG LAND

Helen Porter

Interviewed by Marian Frances White

Courtesy – Helen Porter

For this book is seems appropriate to take a closer, more personal look at the writer.

Helen Porter was born on the southside of St. John's on May 8, 1930, the first child of Robert W. Evelyn (Horwood) Fogwill. Following graduation from Prince of Wales College and a business course, she worked as a shorthand typist with the Dept. of Justice. She married John Porter in 1953 and lived in Corner Brook and Fortune until they moved back to St. John's in 1959 with their three children: Kathy, Anne and John. Their youngest child, Stephen, was born in 1960.

Helen began to write seriously in 1962, but it wasn't until 1973 when she resigned from her work at the Arts and Culture Centre Provincial Reference Library, that she devoted her full time to writing. She has had short stories, articles, poetry and reviews published in most major Canadian magazines and overseas, as well as plays produced on radio and stage. In 1977, she collaborated with Bernice Morgan and Geraldine Rubia to produce, *From This Pace*, anthology of Newfoundland and Labrador women writers. Her memoir-history, *Below The Bridge*, was published in 1980 and her first novel, *January, February, June or July*, released in 1988, won the Canadian Library Association's Young Adult Canadian Book Award in 1989. In 1991 Porter published *A Long and Lonely Ride*. She also enjoys writing songs; one of them, *The Southside Hills*, has been recorded by Phyllis Morrissey on her compact disc Where I Live.

Helen Porter's keen interest in politics led her to run for the New Democratic Party in Mount Pearl. Her lifelong frustration with inequality of opportunity also led her to the women's movement. Porter's husband died suddenly in 1983 and, after twenty-six years in Mount Pearl, she now lives in the centre of St John's.

*****

It's cold and white today, lots of snow around. The sun was shining earlier, when I walked down to Duckworth Street from my house on Franklyn Avenue. When the sun shines I have to get out of the house, no matter how cold it is. I've heard a lot recently about the fragility of the ozone layer, but I don't think the sun will damage me on a day like this.

Now I'm sitting in a cafe booth, having just finished a bowl of turkey soup and several cups of tea. I spend a good deal of time in restaurants these days, even do a fair number of first drafts sitting at restaurant tables. I don't mind living alone, but there's something about being alone in a house that's not conducive to writing, at least for me. I like this feeling of being in a warm place, alone but surrounded by people having quiet conversations that don't require anything from me. Also, there's the sense of rewarding myself for housework, exercise, the occasional baby-sitting I do, my journalistic writing, my writing-class work, my self-imposed obligations. There's something freeing about not having to cook supper for anyone, to come and go as I please. It's lonely sometimes but I'm not willing to give up my independence for an intimate relationship.

Life, Love & Laughter

Life, Love & Laughter

I was married for nearly thirty years to a man I'd known for seven years before that. Our marriage was, I think, as happy as it's possible for a marriage to be. Marriage can be a difficult way of life; it's not called an institution for nothing. But there were joys. My husband, John, and I had many interests in common, and a mutual attraction that never waned. We communicated well with each other most of the time; although we certainly didn't always agree, there was something solid there. When John died suddenly in 1983, I felt I had lost part of myself. I have no interest in beginning again with someone else. We had four children, two girls and two boys. They're all in their thirties now but we're still close. My grandchildren have given great pleasure but I wouldn't want to be totally responsible for them. Bringing up children is difficult and demanding work.

I began to write when I was young, as soon as I could hold a pencil, in fact. In Grade One I wrote:

I have a dog
His name is Laddie
He's a very nice dog
But he barks at Daddy.

When I look back on those four lines written when I was six, I realize that they foreshadowed the writing that was to come. Nothing was ever totally good or totally bad either. I've always been blessed - or cursed - with seeing two sides of a story; my present day writing still reflects this. Not for me, the happy endings found in Harlequins and other romances. Yet I hope that most of my stories end with the possibility of happiness even if only temporary, as all happiness is. One of the many things I admire about the work of Margaret Laurence is that, in spite of the sorrow, the unfairness, the despair contained within her stories, there is always at least a flicker of hope at the end.

At times throughout my life, however, I've identified more with Franz Kafka; everything is hopeless when I feel that way. I was fifty-one before I discovered that the awful blackness that had been descending on me periodically since I was nine was the result of clinical depression. With the help of anti-depressive medication, sympathetic doctors and nurses and the support of family and friends, I have learned to deal with those dark episodes. I'm sad that some others who suffer from depression have not been helped as I have been.

After my Aunt Jenny read my most recent book, a collection of short stories, *A Long and Lonely Ride*, she said, "I've got some advice for you: Lighten up. Your stories are too dark." I explained that the stories had been written over a period of fifteen years. The writing of most of them coincided with somber periods in my life. One story, "The Plan," grew out of the deep fear of old age and separation I experienced when I was in my forties. Often during those fifteen years I was happy, hopeful and positive; at such times I'm rarely compelled to write a short story.

I've published a number of humorous pieces in which I laugh at myself and the world around me. I can't force the mood of a place; most of my writing reflects the way I feel at any given time. I identify strongly with writers like Woody Allen, Ray Guy and the CODCO people, and I love the way my friend Gerry Rubia blends the sublime with the ridiculous. Perhaps most humourists have a dark side to their nature.

Today, at sixty-one, my life is fairly serene and busy enough to keep me out of trouble. My friends and my family mean a great deal to me. I still shiver when I contemplate the lives some people have to live, people in my own city as well as those far away. But when I compare women's lives now with women's lives in the past, I'm convinced that, with all its problems, life for women today is better than it was a hundred years ago.

I seem to be growing lazier as I grow older; perhaps that's just a natural part of aging. When I recall how much I did in a day years ago, compared with what I do now, I'm filled with admiration for the young woman I used to be, and for today's young mothers whose days are very full. My writing is important but not the be-all and end-all of my existence. I continue to enjoy Writer's Guild workshops, discussing my work with students, playing with my grandchildren, gabbing with my siblings and other family members, reading Alice Munro, the *Manchester Guardian Weekly* and *People magazine*. And lots of other things, like listening to music, singing, walking, eating alone in restaurants and watching certain television shows.

Old age doesn't frighten me nearly as much as it used to. I don't trust the pop magazine kind of stories that describe people, especially women, as being "happy at last," but I can say that at the moment I am reasonably content.

Helen is presently putting the finishing touches on her novel, *Finishing School*, which is somewhat of a sequel to *January, February, June or July*.

From the book 'The Finest Kind' by Marian Frances White. Creative Publishing. Used by permission.

♀

 The Whys of Men

Why does a woman not want to give one inch to a man ?
Because then he starts to think he's a ruler.

♀

✒ Letters From Our Friends

"...married my mother and remained in London, England..."

Dear Sir,

I was recently visiting my relatives in Griquet and St. Anthony and read letters in your July issue and I think September issues. There was a letter from an Elizabeth (Manuel) Woolfrey in Gander and Lorraine Collins (Manuel) in Windsor, Ontario. From their letters they are surely sisters. There is no way I can contact them as full addresses are not given.

I too was a Manuel. My father, Roland Allen Manuel, left Griquet and joined the Royal Navy in the first World War. He met and married my mother and remained in London, England, until he died in 1935. He had a brother Archibald who must have been from Belfast who is now dead, and that is how I came to be living in Northern Ireland.

I have visited my relatives six or seven times since 1989. I stay with Percy Roland Manuel in Griquet and Ross Manuel in St. Anthony and love being with them.

Sincerely,
Phyllis Moore, Bangor, Northern Ireland

♀

Dreams

Author unknown

The first day of school our professor introduced himself and challenged us to get to know someone we didn't already know. I stood up to look around when a gentle hand touched my shoulder. I turned around to find a wrinkled, little old lady beaming up at me with a smile that lit up her entire being. She said, "Hi handsome. My name is Rose. I'm eighty-seven years old. Can I give you a hug?" I laughed and enthusiastically responded, "Of course you may!" and she gave me a giant squeeze. "Why are you in college at such a young, innocent age?" I asked. She jokingly replied, "I'm here to meet a rich husband, get married, have a couple of kids."

"No seriously," I asked. I was curious what may have motivated her to be taking on this challenge at her age. "I always dreamed of having a college education and now I'm getting one!" she told me.

After class we walked to the student union building and shared a chocolate milkshake. We became instant friends. Every day for the next three months we would leave class together and talk nonstop. I was always mesmerized listening to this "time machine" as she shared her wisdom and experience with me. Over the course of the year, Rose became a campus icon and she easily made friends wherever she went. She loved to dress up and she reveled in the attention bestowed upon her from the other students. She was living it up.

At the end of the semester we invited Rose to speak at our football banquet. I'll never forget what she taught us. She was introduced and stepped up to the podium. As she began to deliver her prepared speech, she dropped her three by five cards on the floor. Frustrated and a little embarrassed she leaned into the microphone and simply said, "I'm sorry I'm so jittery. I gave up beer for Lent and this whiskey is killing me! I'll never get my speech back in order so let me just tell you what I know."

As we laughed she cleared her throat and began, "We do not stop playing because we are old; we grow old because we stop playing. There are only four secrets to staying young: being happy, and achieving success. You have to laugh and find humor every day. You've got to have a dream. When you lose your dreams, you die. We have so many people walking around who are dead and don't even know it! There is a huge difference between growing older and growing up. If you are nineteen years old and lie in bed for one full year and don't do one productive thing, you will turn twenty years old. If I am eighty-seven years old and stay in bed for a year and never do anything I will turn eighty-eight. Anybody can grow older. That doesn't take any talent or ability. The idea is to grow up by always finding the opportunity in change. Have no regrets. The elderly usually don't have regrets for what we did, but rather for things we did not do. The only people who fear death are those with regrets."

She concluded her speech by courageously singing "The Rose." She challenged each of us to study the lyrics and live them out in our daily lives. At the year's end Rose finished the college degree she had begun all those years ago. One week after graduation Rose died peacefully in her sleep. Over two thousand college students attended her funeral in tribute to the wonderful woman who taught by example that it's never too late to be all you can possibly be.

♀

Female Firsts

1656: America's first all-woman jury tried Judith Catchpole on a charge of murdering her child. She was acquitted. She had never been pregnant.

1658: Margaret Bourgeoys opened North America's first girls school on Montreal Island. *See also 'Female Facts' page 328.*

1660: The first woman to be hanged in America because of religious affiliation is believed to be Mary Dyer, who was hanged on Boston Common for her Quaker beliefs.

1693: *The Ladies' Mercury*, the world's first woman's magazine, was published in London, England.

1715: Ann Teresa Mathews became the first woman to have an invention patented. The patent for a process for cleaning and curing corn, was not granted to her, but to her husband.

1722: British fighter Elizabeth Wilkinson became the first woman boxer to fight in a boxing ring. Boxing gloves had not yet been introduced and Elizabeth fought with bare knuckles.

1729: On March 15th Sister St. Stanislas Hachard took her vows in New Orleans, to become the first woman to become a nun in America.

♀

The Tablecloth

The brand new pastor and his wife, newly assigned to their first ministry to reopen a church in suburban Brooklyn, arrived in early October excited about their opportunities. When they saw their church, it was very run down and needed much work. They set a goal to have everything done in time to have their first service on Christmas Eve.

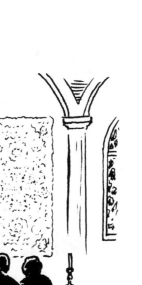

They worked hard, repairing pews, plastering walls, painting, etc. and on Dec 18 were ahead of schedule and just about finished. On Dec 19, a terrible tempest - a driving rainstorm - hit the area and lasted for two days.

On the 21st, the pastor went over to the church. His heart sank when he saw that the roof had leaked, causing a large area of plaster, about 20 feet by 8 feet, to fall off the front wall of the sanctuary just behind the pulpit, beginning about head high. The pastor cleaned up the mess on the floor, and not knowing what else to do but postpone the Christmas Eve service, headed home.

On the way he noticed that a local business was having a flea market type sale for charity so he stopped in.

Life, Love & Laughter

One of the items was a beautiful, handmade, ivory coloured, crocheted tablecloth with exquisite work, fine colours and a Cross embroidered right in the centre. It was just the right size to cover up the hole in the front wall. He bought it and headed back to the church.

By this time it had started to snow. An older woman running from the opposite direction was trying to catch the bus. She missed it. The pastor invited her to wait in the warm church for the next bus which arrived 45 minutes later. She sat in a pew and paid no attention to the pastor while he got a ladder, hangers, etc., to put up the tablecloth as a wall tapestry.

The pastor could hardly believe how beautiful it looked and it covered up the entire problem area.

Then he noticed the woman walking down the centre aisle. Her face was as white as a sheet. "Pastor," she asked, "where did you get that tablecloth?" The pastor explained. The woman asked him to check the lower right corner to see if the initials EBG were crocheted into it there. They were. These were the initials of the woman, and she had made this tablecloth 35 years before, in Austria.

The woman could hardly believe it as the pastor told how he had just gotten the tablecloth. The woman explained that before the war she and her husband were well-to-do people in Austria. When the Nazis came, she was forced to leave. Her husband was going to follow her the next week. She was captured, sent to prison, and never saw her husband or her home, again. The pastor wanted to give her the tablecloth; but she made the pastor keep it for the church. The pastor insisted on driving her home, that was the least he could do. She lived on the other side of Staten Island and was only in Brooklyn for the day for a housecleaning job.

What a wonderful service they had on Christmas Eve. The church was almost full. The music and the spirit were great. At the end of the service, the pastor and his wife greeted everyone at the door and many said they would return. One older man, whom the pastor recognized from the neighborhood, continued to sit in one of the pews and stare, and the pastor wondered why he wasn't leaving. The man asked him where he got the tablecloth on the front wall because it was identical to one that his wife had made years ago when they lived in Austria before the war and how could there be two tablecloths so much alike. He told the pastor how the Nazis came, how he forced his wife to flee for her safety and he was supposed to follow her, but he was arrested and put in a prison. He never saw his wife, or his home, again.

The pastor asked him if he would allow him to take him for a little ride. They drove to Staten Island and to the same house where the pastor had taken the woman three days earlier. He helped the man climb the three flights of stairs to the woman's apartment, knocked on the door and he saw the greatest Christmas reunion he could ever imagine.

Author Unknown

♀

 # Out of Habit

Sister Mary Catherine and Sister Constance were out for a Sunday drive in the countryside when they ran out of gas. The only container in the car was a chamber pot that was used when youngsters were taken on picnics.

The nuns went up to a nearby farmhouse and begged for enough gas to get them to the next town, a few miles away. The farmer gave them as much gas as the chamber pot could hold.

Returning to the car, the nuns started to put the gas into the tank. A farm-hand, not too far off, looked and said, "Wow, do they have faith!"

♀

🪓 WOMEN OF THE ISLAND AND THE BIG LAND 🪓

Shanawdithit – The Last of Her Race

By Ron Young

Around the year 1800 a girl baby was born in a mamateek near what is now Red Indian Lake on the Island of Newfoundland. Shanawdithit was to be the last of the Beothuks, a nomadic people who had the whole island to themselves before the white man came. Very little is known about the tribe but most of what is known was learned from Shanawdithit.

In fact, she may not have been born in a mamateek, but in a smaller dwelling known as a wigwam, depending on what time of year she was born.

In the spring of the year the Beothuks travelled from the interior of the province to the coast where they erected single family wigwams for shelter while they fished and gathered bird eggs. In the fall they went back to the mamateeks, which housed several families. There they hunted caribou, ptarmigan and other animals, until it was time again to go back to the sea.

Before the white man came, the Beothuk's only enemies were other Indians, particularly the Mi'kmaq of Eastern Canada and the Montagnais and Naskaupi of Labrador. These had no firearms before they obtained them and learned how to use them from the white man and were no serious threat to the "red-skinned" Indians. Actually, the Beothuks painted their faces with red ochre, which eventually earned, not only them, but all native North Americans, the moniker "Redskin."

Downhomer Photo

A bronz, lifesize statue of Shawnadithit stands in the woods in Boyd's Cove. Her likeness was created by Artist Gerald Squires, who claims to have seen her spirit from Exploits Island, where he was raised by his mother. See: *Women of the Island and the Big Land – Mabel Squires* - page 78

For the most part, the Beothuks never trusted the white men enough to have communication with them.

Several attempts at communications were made by the newcomers but they were too little and too late. On one occasion, long before Shanawdithit was born, there was communication and even trading between the Beothuks and British sailors on a ship captianed by John Guy. Guy promised to return the next year, but unfortunately another ship arrived instead. The ship's occupants mistook the advances toward them by the Beothuks as an attack and fired on them, killing some. This, along with other negative encounters with the Europeans, ruined the chances for communications. Fear grew between the two groups and a number of Beothuks were killed by the whites. As well, whites were also killed by Beothuks.

When Shanawdithit was a child of about 11, she witnessed another attempt by white men to communicate with her people. Led by Lieutenant David Buchan and a group of marines, they came into the little village up the Exploits River where the Beothuks were wintering, and offered gifts of knives, etc., and were given food and skins by her people. Buchan indicated that he would go back to where he had left his sleds, twelve miles downriver, to get more gifts for her people. Two of his marines remained behind and four Beothuks accompanied him and the rest of his men. Three Indians turned back before they reached the provisions, and when Buchan returned he found the two marines murdered and the mamateeks deserted. According to Shanawdithit, the Chief thought the group of marines were going for reinforcements to attack them and had the two marines killed to ensure their escape route would not be made known to Buchan and his men.

After that, things got worse and worse for the Beothuks. The tribe, which had numbered less than a thousand before the white man came in 1497, were severely depleted. In fear of the white man and his guns, which had taken a toll on them, the Beothuk were subsequently cut off from the ocean and it's important food sources and many starved. From the few contacts they had had with the newcomers, Shanawdithit's people picked up some of the white man's diseases, particularly tuberculosis. Without the antibodies to fight the new disease, many perished.

In an effort to communicate with the natives, the government of the day had offered a reward of one hundred pounds for the capture of a Beothuk. When Shanawdithit was a teenager and living on the shores of Red Indian Lake, in March of 1819, her tribe had another visit from the whites. Given the blessing of the Governor, John Peyton Jr. had organized an expedition into Indian country to try to capture an Indian and to retrieve property which the Indians had stolen from him. Among the nine men who accompanied him on this mission was his father, John Peyton Sr. who had a reputation as an Indian killer and, was hated by the Beothuks.

When the party came upon the Indian encampment the Beothuks (whose numbers were then reduced to 31) ran away, but the younger Peyton caught up to Demasduit, the wife of Shanawdithit's uncle, Nonosabasut, who had handed her infant off to her husband. Demasduit bared her breasts to Peyton to show she was a woman in hopes of obtaining mercy. Peyton had no intention of harming her, but held onto the woman. Nonosabasut, who was a giant of a man, over six feet tall (1.83 meters), came to her rescue. and in the struggle he was killed and left on the ice. This effort at communication came to naught as Demasduit also came down with tuberculosis. Her captors, who had renamed her Mary March, tried to get her back to her people but she died of tuberculosis on the way. Her body was returned to the area where she was captured and the remaining Beothuks placed her beside the body of her husband and her infant who had also died.

In 1823, which was a very severe winter, the Beothuks were starving and Shanawdithit and others went to Badger Bay on the coast in hopes of finding mussels. The three were captured while others escaped. Her father fell through the ice and drowned while trying to escape. The three were taken to St. John's but later taken back to central Newfoundland so they could rejoin their people. Her mother and sister died of tuberculosis several weeks later, without establishing any contact with the rest of the tribe. Shanawdithit was taken in by John Peyton Jr. and his family on Exploits Island where she lived as a domestic. She lived with the customs of her adopted family and grew quite fond of the Peyton children, who according to Bishop Inglis, would "leave their mother and go to her." Sometimes the Beothuk woman, who was nearly six feet tall, would openly defy Mrs. Peyton, especially when she was cross with the servants. She would laugh in her employer's face and say things like, "What de matter now Missa Peyton, what you grumble about?" Sometimes the lone Indian would wander off in the woods to communicate with the spirits of her people.

In 1828 William Cormack, who had been instrumental in starting the Beothuk Institution to try and save the remaining Beothuks, had Shanawdithit brought to St. John's. She was also suffering from tuberculosis and her health was deteriorating at that time. It was her communication with Cormack by word and drawings that gave us the little information we have about her people. When Cormack left Newfoundland to return to England, she is said to have given him a braid of her hair and two stones as a gift.

Although she was cared for by the famous Dr. William Carson, she was finally admitted to hospital where she died on June 6th, 1829.

Her skull was sent to London for further study and was destroyed by a German bomb during WWII. Her body was buried in the Church of England cemetery on the south side of St. John's harbour. In 1903, the railroad made use of the land where Shanawdithit was buried and the only marker of the existence of Shanawdithit is a plaque which reads, "Near this spot is the burying place of Nancy Shanawdithit, very probably the last of the Beothuks."

♀

Adam's Ribbing
Birthday Suit

The boss was delighted when his beautiful secretary asked him to her house for a drink on his birthday. He was even more delighted when she told him to sit on the sofa while she went to change into something more comfortable. The delighted look left his face, however, when the door opened and his young son, wife, parents and in-laws entered with a cake singing "Happy Birthday" to the man whose clothes were strewn all over the floor, while he sat on the sofa wearing nothing but the clothes he was born in.

♀

Female Firsts

1745: On July 26, the first recorded women's cricket match was played near Guildford, Surrey, England, between teams from Hambledon and Bramley.

1754: On October 11, Eleanor Power was the first woman to be hanged in Newfoundland. She was convicted along with her husband and eight other men of having murdered magistrate William Keen, and was hanged in St. John's.

1775: Mary Katherine Goddard became the first woman postmaster in the U.S.

1784: Hannah Adams became the first professional writer in the US when, after her father's business failed, she began writing to support herself. Hannah, a distant cousin of John Adams, wrote the first history that traced the United States from the Mayflower to the ratification of the federal Constitution. Many of her works were theological in nature.

1784: Marie Thible of Lyon, France, became the first female in the world to fly in a balloon. A year before a man had flown in a balloon, but Marie went higher, further and longer. Her flight lasted 45 minutes, which was 35 minutes longer than the flying trip the previous man had made. She flew in balloons many times after that, at least enough for history to refer to her as a 'balloonist.'

1785: Caroline Herschel became the first woman ever to discover a comet.

♀

Life, Love & Laughter

The Wife's Prayer

Author Unknown

Dear Lord,

I pray for the wisdom to understand my man, the love to forgive him and the patience to deal with his moods. Because, Lord, if I pray for strength, I'll beat him to death.

Amen

♀

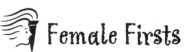 Her Other Half

The Game's in the Aim

A recently-married man was asked by his mother-in-law if she could go and watch him play golf to see what the game was all about.

He wanted to impress her and had her stand outside the green of the first hole to watch while he and his partner teed off.

"You see that woman over there," he said to his partner. "That's my mother-in-law and I want to make this first drive a good one."

"Don't be stupid," replied his partner. "You'll never hit her from here."

♀

Female Firsts

1791: Susanna Haswell became America's first best-selling novelist. Her book *Charlotte Temple*, published in 1791, went through more than 200 printings.

1796: The first cookbook to offer American recipes calling for ingredients native to that part of the world, was published by Amelia Simmons.

1798: Genevieve Labrosse became the first woman to do a parachute jump. She jumped from a balloon.

1804: Deborah Sampson, the first American woman known to have taken a male identity in order to enter the military, was offered a pension by the Massachusetts General Court for her efforts.

1804: Alice Meynell of England became the world's first woman jockey.

1805: The first ice skating race for Dutch women was held in Leeuwarden.

1805: Englishwoman Alicia Meynell, riding as Mrs. Thornton, became the first woman to defeat a leading male jockey in a horserace.

1805: On November 18th, the USA's first woman's club, 'The Female Society,' was formed by 30 women, who met at Mrs. Silas Lee's home in Wiscasset, Maine.

♀

Life, Love & Laughter

Food for Thought

Man can not degrade woman without himself falling into degradation; he can not elevate her without at the same time elevating himself.   *– Alexander Walker*

♀

Aunt Alice says:

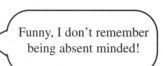

Funny, I don't remember being absent minded!

Spice of Life

There is no reciprocity. Men love women, women love children, children love hamsters.
– Alice Thomas Ellis

♀

Lucy Harris

An unparalleled example of endurance in Newfoundland history has to be the experience of nine-year-old Lucy Harris of New Melbourne, Trinity Bay.

Lucy's ordeal began on March 25, 1936, when she was lost for eleven days in the woods near her home. During that time she went without food and extra clothing, and she suffered from exposure to a variety of weather conditions including fog, rain and snow. And at night, temperatures dipped below the freezing point.

The little girl's parents discovered she was missing about 8:00 p.m. and they notified authorities in the community. Word immediately spread and the church bells tolled to attract people to come and join in a search.

The searchers spread out in all directions and covered miles of wooded area, but as each day slipped away without any trace of Lucy, hope began to diminish. By the eleventh day there was little, if any, hope of finding Lucy Harris alive.

On that day her uncle Chesley was searching in the area of Lance Cove Pond, about three miles from Lucy's home. He stopped to look under a tree and was startled by a very weak voice, which said, "Hello." When he looked at her she was sitting upright, her back against a tree, and her palms against the ground. She spoke once more, and in just above a whisper she said, "I'm the little girl who is lost in the woods."

A crowd quickly gathered, she was covered in warm blankets and was taken home. She was treated by a doctor, who then sent her on to the Old Perlican Hospital.

Before leaving, however, Lucy told her family that she had been cold and hungry all the time and ate snow to quench her thirst. She said she wasn't lonely because the birds were singing all day long and that kept her from being afraid. She added that at times she heard them crying out her name but she'd been too weak to answer.

After being treated for frostbite on her legs at the Old Perlican Hospital, Lucy was taken to the General Hospital in St. John's where both legs, unfortunately, had to be amputated, She would be remembered as a girl with remarkable endurance.

From the book, Newfoundland Fireside Stories, *by Jack Fitzgerald, published by Creative Publishing. Used by permission.*

♀

Life, Love & Laughter

Some Mothers Have Them

After the christening of his baby brother in church, little Jackson sobbed all the way home in the back seat of the car. His father asked him three times what was wrong. Finally, the boy replied, "That minister said he wanted us brought up in a Christian home and I want to stay with you guys!"

♀

Aphrodesia

Not wishing to have her lovely figure spoiled by the few extra pounds she was putting on, Aphrodesia went to see her doctor to get something that would curb her appetite, and the doctor prescribed pills for her. A few days later she was back at his office with a complaint.

"These pills have side effects. They make me even more passionate than I normally am, and sometimes I get carried away," she said. "The other night I was so passionate I even bit my lovers ear off."

"Don't worry Aphrodesia," replied the doctor. "An ear is only about 60 calories."

♀

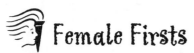

Female Firsts

1812: Lucy Brewer became the first woman marine in the U.S. armed forces.

1838: Mount Holyoke Seminary in Massachusetts became the first women's college to have a graduation.

1840: (or thereabouts) Scottish-born Fanny Wright became the first woman in the U.S. to speak out against slavery and for equality for women.

1843: Augusta Ada Byron (Lady Lovelace) developed what is considered to be the first computer program. *See also page 72.*

1845: With the publication of feminist tract, *Women In The Nineteenth Century,* and other endeavours, Margaret Fuller became the first true American feminist.

1846: Working for the New York Tribune, Margaret Fuller became America's first female foreign correspondent.

1847: Maria Mitchell became the first known female astronomer in North America when she discovered a comet.

1848: Amelia Jenks Bloomer became the first woman to own, operate and edit a newspaper.

1848: The first North American woman's rights convention was held in New York. The convention, which discussed such topics as voting, divorce and women's property rights, was organized by Lucretia Mott and Elizabeth Cady Stanton.

♀

Life, Love & Laughter

Letters From Our Friends

Stranded on 9/11

Dear Ron and Lila,

Many of the aircraft stranded in the air on 9/11 landed in Gander. We had 38 aircraft with a total of 6,656 people drop by for coffee, and they stayed for three or four days. Our population is just under 10,000, so you can imagine the logistics involved in giving each of these people a place to sleep and hot meals three times a day.

Many of us spent our time bringing people home so they could get a shower or, once the rain started on the third day, driving them to the mall or sightseeing to relieve their boredom. The diversity of the people who have been in my car and in my shower over the past few days is pretty wild.

You should have seen the look on my little girl's face when three Muslim women came home with me for a shower. With their robes, she could only see their faces, hands and feet. Their hands and feet were covered with henna paint and two of them didn't speak English. There was a king from the Middle East here, a British MP, the mayor of Frankfurt, Germany, etc., etc.

There were also immigrants from all over the world, some of whom didn't have two pennies to rub together. They all slept side by side in schools and church halls.

Except the Irish, of course! A flight from Ireland was put up at a couple of local drinking establishments! The Royal Canadian Legion and the Elks Club.

One woman here gave a driving tour to a fellow from the US. After the tour, she brought him back to his little cot in the gymnasium that he shared with many others - not exactly a world-class hotel. The two exchanged cards, she looked at his and said, "So you work with Best Western?"

He replied, "No, I own Best Western."

You should have been here, but of course, there wouldn't have been room.

What an experience!

Judy – Gander, Newfoundland

♀

Women Who Have Made A Difference - *By Ron Young*

Clare Boothe Luce, apart from being a successful journalist, playwright and legislator, was a leader in the free world's opposition to communism, an outspoken advocate of free enterprise, and a woman devoted to her family. She was the first American woman ambassador to be sent to a major country, when she was made American Ambassador to Italy in 1957.

Clare always believed in the equal opportunity of everybody, including women, but her views were sometimes disagreed with by other "feminists" of her time. Her granddaughter, Clare Luce Abbey wrote the following about her:

"One thing that often bothers me in terms of how she is remembered is the belief that she was a feminist. In the original definition of the word she was, but she did not completely identify with the feminists of the 60s and 70s. She believed in a woman's right to pursue any career and resented the attitude that women's minds were in some way inferior to that of men's. She believed in equal pay for equal work and other logical and fair notions that were the foundation of the original women's movement. She believed that femininity and chivalry were something to respect, not ridicule. The idea that a man was belittling a woman by opening a door for her was ludicrous to her. Perhaps to the feminists of today, such beliefs are contradictory. Clare didn't see anything wrong with tradition. In her mind, respectful behavior in relationships between men and

Life, Love & Laughter

women were all right, while at the same time she believed in certain aspects of equality. She possessed a razor sharp mind and a cutting wit but she was always a lady. She was not an extremist in her beliefs. She took a sensible, logical position on 'women's rights,' always wanting women to use their minds and earn the same respect (and money!) as men for their intellectual abilities."

Augusta Ada Byron (Lady Lovelace), born December 10, 1815, was one of the most picturesque characters in computer history. Ada, who was also the daughter of the illustrious poet, Lord Byron, suggested a plan in 1843 on how a new calculating engine might calculate Bernoulli numbers. This plan is now regarded as the first "computer program." A software language developed by the US Department of Defense was named "Ada" in her honour in 1979. Although only 36 when she died, Ada anticipated, by more than a century, most of what today we think is brand-new computing information.

Helen Adams Keller was stricken with an acute illness that left her deaf and blind at the age of 19 months. At the age of seven, she began her special education in reading and writing with Anne Mansfield Sullivan (later Macy) of the Perkins Institute for the Blind. She quickly learned to read by the Braille system and to write by means of a specially constructed typewriter. After only one month of study she learned how to talk in 1890 and in 1904 she graduated with honours from Radcliffe College. Throughout her life she worked and raised funds for the American Foundation for the Blind and she travelled and lectured in many countries, including England, France, Italy, Egypt, South Africa, Australia and Japan. After World War II, she visited wounded veterans in American hospitals and lectured in Europe on behalf of the physically handicapped. She wrote a number of books and her life is the subject of two movies, *The Unconquered*, in 1954, and *The Miracle Worker*, in 1962.

Odette Hallowes, although she was the mother of three young daughters in England during WWII, Odette volunteered to spy for the Allies in her native France. When she was first interviewed there were some doubts about her suitability as a clandestine SOE courier. Would she be able, as a mother of three young daughters who might be constantly on her mind, to undertake missions requiring steely nerves and an ability to concentrate on the task in question to the exclusion of all else? On the other hand, from certain points of view she seemed an ideal candidate. She was young, attractive and vivacious. She knew France and she had a winning manner. Furthermore, she had a burning desire to redeem by direct action the disgrace her country had suffered in its capitulation in 1940. Odette did her job well, but in 1943 she was captured and endured excruciating torments, including having her toenails pulled out, but still made no admissions of importance. In June 1943, Odette was condemned to death, but unlike 11 other women in her section who were executed at Ravensbrück Concentration Camp, she was still alive when the war ended. She came home emaciated, weak and gravely ill and, for a year after, she could not wear shoes and had to walk on her heels until she had several operations. Still she harboured no bitterness towards her tormentors, but instead became a beacon to others who had suffered disfigurement, pain or bereavement. She received medals of valour, including the George Cross and Legion d'Honneur and fame found her, especially through the film *Odette,* which celebrated her life. In her entry in *Who's Who*, Odette referred to herself as simply, "housewife."

♀

Life, Love & Laughter

The Ladies Home Journal – May, 1927

By Bruce Stirling

I recently got out an old (1927) *Ladies Home Journal* I had bought at a garage sale. It gave quite an insight into what women looked like and what interested them three-quarters-of-a-century ago.

The first thing I discovered is that women back then had neither breasts or behinds, or that is what the fashion plates seemed to show. Dresses show absolutely no curves, front or back. They simply go straight down from the neck, front and back. But later, as I leafed through the magazine, I understood why; a corset advertisement illustrates a contraption that would surely flatten anything.

On page 37 is an article by Florence E.S. Knapp, entitled, *A Woman Politician and Proud of It.* Her portrait shows a strong, handsome face topped by a formidable hat, while around her neck is an enormous pearl necklace. I have long held the opinion that we should let the women run the world for a change. They couldn't possibly do a worse job than we men have done.

I see that Campbell's Soup was going strong seventy-five years ago, as was Palmolive soap, Maxwell House coffee and Pepsodent tooth paste. I also noticed an advertisement by Paramount pictures, promoting, *Caberet*, starring Gilda Grey; and *Children of Divorce*, starring Clara Bow.

Page 51 contains an article by the Countess of Asquith, who advises on, "Woman's Instinct to make Herself Attractive." Unfortunately, the accompanying photo of the Countess indicates that she didn't practice what she preached.

Page 58 is taken up with an ad promoting the "Whippet" automobile. "A Real Woman's Car, Designed for safety," the ad says. "For easy parking; for lightening pick-up and quick, positive stopping. Just a little pressure with your foot - and big, sturdy, four-wheel brakes stops this car in a fraction of a second. Imagine a car," the ad continues, "that will do 55 miles an hour as easily, as smoothly, as effortlessly as a Limited Train." The Whippet, according to the ad ranged in price from $625 to $755.

The ad on page 208 warns that, "Amateur Corn Paring is a flirtation with the Gray Spectre Of Infection." In other words, Don't hack away at it. Use Blue Jay corn plasters instead.

There's no doubt that women's lives, as well as men's, have changed a lot since 1927. But many things remain constant. On page 199 a poem by Abigail Cresson is as valid today as it was way back then.

I think I never truly knew
How very much I care for you
Until I was a mother too;

Nor knew that any love could be
As deep as that you give to me.

A love that gives but does not ask;
That changes every little task
To joy; a love that stays the same,

A steady and enduring flame
This love I give to you must be
The same love that you give to me;

And gave to me through all my years;
My joy, your joy; my tears, your tears.

Mother, I never truly knew,
Until I was a mother too,
Your love for me and mine for you

♀

Some Mothers Have Them

Little Jackson became restless as the preacher's sermon dragged on and on. Finally, he leaned over to his mother and whispered, "Mommy, if we give him the money now, will he let us go?"

♀

Ennellene

I had an hourglass figure
When I was in my prime
Since then there's been a shifting
In the sands of time

♀

Female Firsts

1849: On January 23rd, Elizabeth Blackwell became the first woman to graduate from a regular medical school.

1849: The first prominent women's rights newspaper was published by Amelia Jenks Bloomer. *See also 'Female Facts' page 326.*

1850: Harriet Tubman became the first woman to run the underground railroad to help slaves escape from the U.S. to Canada.

1850: *The Wide, Wide World*, the first novel to sell one million copies in the U.S., was released by author Susan Warner.

1850: The first national American woman's rights convention was held in Worcester, Massachusetts.

1853: The first female to be ordained as a minister in the U.S. was 28-year-old Antoinette L. Brown. She became pastor of the Congregational Church in South Butler, New York. *See also page 193.*

1856: The first fitness manual for women *Physiology and Calisthenics for Schools and Families*, was published by Catherine Beecher.

1857: One hundred and nineteen British women and children were murdered in the second Cawnpore Massacre (now Kanpur) during the Indian Mutiny.

1860: The first kindergarten in New England was opened by Elizabeth Palmer Peabody in Boston.

1860: North America's first 'dime novel,' *Malaeska, the Indian Wife of the White Hunter*, was released by Ann Stevens.

♀

Adam's Ribbing

Women's Ass Size Study

A recent study was done to find out about women's anatomical feelings and, in particular, how they feel about their ass.

The study revealed that 85% of women think their ass is too big, while only 10% of women think their ass is too little.

The other 5% say that they don't care - they love him and would have married him anyway.

♀

MABEL & MANLEY

After Mabel and Manley got married, they were in their bedroom when Manley decided to assert his male dominance after an argument with his new wife. Throwing his pants in her direction he said, "Here Mable, try these on."

She did and said, "They're too big and don't fit me."

"That's right. I'm the man who wears the pants in this family and don't forget it," he smugly informed her.

She took his pants off her slender body, and removing her own panties, she threw them at Manley, saying "Put these on."

"You know I can't get into them," Manly protested.

"That's right," grinned Mabel, "And if you don't have an attitude adjustment, you never will."

♀

Quillings

Dirty Dishes

Author Unknown
Submitted by Marion Scheers,
Edmonton, Alberta

Thank God for dirty dishes,
They have a tale to tell,
While other folks go hungry,
We're eating very well.

With home and health and happiness,
We shouldn't want to fuss,
For by this stack of evidence,
God's very good to us.

Beauty of a Woman
Author Unknown

The beauty of a woman is not in
The clothes she wears
The figure she carries
Nor in the way she combs her hair
The beauty of a woman
Must be seen from her eyes,
Because that is the doorway to her heart,
The place where love resides.
The beauty of a woman
Is not in a facial mole
But true beauty in a woman
Is reflected in her soul
It is the caring that she lovingly gives,
The beauty of a woman
With passing year - only grows

♀

Life, Love & Laughter

Dear Santa,

My name is Mom and I'm middle-aged.

Thank you for the great gifts you brought in previous years, but with two small children in the house now, my needs have become drastically different.

I'll admit I haven't been that good all year but in the name of mercy, would you please bring me several items for Christmas to help ease the trauma of parenthood, especially at this age.

As a working mom, a live-in nanny is a must! All my rich friends have them and they tell me they couldn't live without them!

If I could just hint at the make up of this caregiver, I would ask that you please combine the demeanour of Mary Poppins, the singing voice of Mrs. Von Trapp (alias Julie Andrews), the entertainment ability of Barney, the patience of Job and the resourcefulness and stimulation of the world's best teacher. She (or he) must be specially trained in the area of coping with a two-year-old. You know, the potty training bit, the temper tantrums, the whining, the I'll-do-it-myself and everything-is-mine syndrome.

Santa, if you cannot fulfill my wish for a bigger house (for which I would sell my husband in a flick), please send me a top-of-the-line housekeeper! *Bad Housekeeping* magazine has been calling me for months now wanting to do a feature story. So, to avoid any further embarrassment (as all my ritzy friends have had *Good Housekeeping* approaching them), I desperately require some clean soul to scour and sanitize my humble (translation: filthy) abode. The problem is I cannot really remember what my home looked like before the kids, so this person must have prior knowledge of my decor.

One more item, Santa, and I promise to be the bestest person in the whole world: a gourmet cook (I'll settle for the decent model) would really make my season bright. I've discovered that this is one (believe me there are many more!) of the perplexing ironies of parenthood - children need good nutritional food but who has time to cook when you have kids!? Now I know why many parents look so gaunt!

A few suggestions for goodies for my Christmas stocking - a special set of ear plugs to block out the ever-cheerful (translation: irritating) voice of Barney when the children play his video tape for the millionth time (and purple used to be one of my favourite colours!); also, an innocuous concoction that will help my toddler sleep through the night so she cannot migrate to our bed and wreck havoc with my sleep; and last but not least, put in a few 'personal use' hours - finding time to myself these days is as likely as finding myself organized - not a chance in the world!

Santa, I hope you're extra nice to all the other parents out there who are also experiencing the pathos of parenting. I seek their forgiveness for all judgments rendered against them when I was childless. Boy, was I a bad little girl to have done that! Don't worry Santa, I have since mended my inconsiderate ways.

I will leave some cookies (store-bought ones) for you and your reindeer. Perhaps you can spare a reindeer or two to help the nanny entertain the kids? Nah, on second thought, reindeer, like other pets, would just complicate my life even further. Besides, my teething one-year-old might use their legs for a good chomp and then I'd be in trouble with the SPCA.

Please say "Hi" to Mrs. Claus. Tell her she must be crazy to be taking care of all those elves when she could be enjoying a nice, relaxing spa anywhere in the world. Perhaps you can suggest that she ought to hit the lecture circuit so as to enlighten the rest of us on how she manages, without hair loss, with all those wee ones? Is that smile painted on her face?

Santa, I have always believed in you (despite the other adults telling me that you're a fraud), so when you drop off the children's gifts, please, please indulge me this Christmas season. (Actually - you wouldn't know this (not having any children of your own) - indulgment is an illegal offence once parenthood is bestowed upon you, but don't let that stop you - I won't tell if you won't!)

Hugs and Merry Christmas!

Kim Ploughman

PS: Santa, I know I'm pushing it here, but if you can round up a pediatrician/advisor/counsellor all rolled into one, I'd be mighty merry. No one warned me that children came with such weird and complicated (translated: nerve-wracking) conditions and behaviour. People tell me that this might be inherited. They might be right. It would certainly explain, since becoming a parent, why I haven't been feeling myself. Those kids!

Reprinted from Downhomer *magazine.*

♀

Food for Thought

Women have always been equal to men, and now we're getting over that handicap. – *Lila Mercer Young*

♀

Quillings

A Little Mixed Up
Author Unknown

Just a line to say I'm living
That I'm not among the dead
Tho' I'm getting more forgetful
And more mixed up in my head.

For sometimes I can't remember
When I stand at the foot of the stairs
If I'm going up for something
Or if I've just come down from there.

And before the fridge so often
My poor mind is filled with doubt
Have I just put food away?
Or did I come to take it out?

And there are times when it is dark outside
With my night-cap on my head

I don't know if I'm retiring
Or just getting out of bed.

So if it's my turn to write you
There's no need of getting sore
I may think that I have written
And don't want to be a bore.

So remember, I do love you
And I wish that you were here
And now it's nearly mail time
So I must say good-bye my dear.

Then I stood beside the mailbox
With my face so very red
I forgot to mail you my letter
I opened it instead.

♀

🦆 WOMEN OF THE ISLAND AND THE BIG LAND 🦆

Mabel Squires

Courtesy Gerry Squires

Mabel Squires was born in Gander Bay into a family of thirteen on September 9, 1898. Her mother died when she was seven, after which time she lived with her uncle on Fogo Island. When she was seventeen she joined the Salvation Army and travelled extensively as a corps missionary. The following is a journal excerpt her son, Gerry Squires, and granddaughter Ester Squires, encouraged her to write before she died on October 11, 1988.

*****

I am going to try to write the story of my life, but it's a big task. I am now over eighty-eight years old and I do not find it so easy to concentrate...When I turned seventeen, I told my father I wanted to become an officer in the Army. He was determined to hold me back. When I threatened to run away from home, Father agreed to let me go but said he would not help me in any way.

St. John's Headquarters first sent me to Doting Cove, Musgrave Harbour, to teach. I walked (there) every morning...I became Cadet Payne. (Several appointments later) I decided to apply for work in China. In St. John's I used to see the Chinese people and my heart went out to them. While waiting for an answer, I was sent to Bridgeport in charge of Corps and school. I conducted my first funeral there. I never went to sleep nor touched any food from the time I was told there was a person dead until after the funeral.

In November, 1922, I got the happy news from Headquarters to come to St. John's and prepare to leave for China...we arrived in Peking Christmas Eve, 1922. On January 3, 1923, I started going to school to learn the Chinese language...In November the Army opened five food kitchens to feed the thousands of beggars who crowded the streets...(One) summer I was the only white person stationed in a village called Taku.

While working in the food kitchens, a man fell down beside me and died right there...When the police came I took hold of the dead man's arms to help (and) a louse from his head crawled on the back of my hand. I felt the bite but brushed it off...A few days later I was taken down with Typhus Fever...I became unconscious...I lost all hearing and my fever became so high the doctors said I would never survive, but I did.

When the city of Peking was captured by the Japanese in 1927, I was fortunate enough to be one of the missionaries put on a train to Tien-Sin...After two months we were taken privately aboard a cattle ship that took us to Colombo. We were to cross the Bay of Bengal, the roughest sea in the world. We were not only seasick but almost unconscious; none of us cared if we lived or died...From Colombo we were taken to Ceylon for one week, resting and enjoying the beauty of the island...fruit trees everywhere, flowers and monkeys climbing around...the saddest sight of all was the Leper Colony.

When I got to India I was told to take off my Chinese uniform and put on an Indian Sari...When I was not in the operating room, I was looking after the out-patients and saw many horrible cases; sores full of flies, ears that were sore with maggots eating the flesh...yet the time I spent at the hospital was the best time I ever lived.

In 1930, I was given my homeland ticket and sometime in March month I arrived in St. John's...The years were passing away, I was getting older and in my heart I wanted to be a mother, so I got married to a man within the Army who was two ranks below me. By marrying

Life, Love & Laughter

him, I had to go back two ranks; the rule being that the wife could not have a higher rank than her husband. This is still the case today. We were blessed with three lovely sons, but I am sorry to say my marriage was not a happy one. When World War II started, my husband was overseas against Headquarters permission and left me with three small children...Still carrying on the work in the Army, I was sent to Exploits... It was very hard with services to conduct and travelling long distances to collect for Self-Denial; it kept me away from caring for my children. They would cry when I would leave them with baby-sitters and the thought worried my mind and heart. I asked to be moved to a place where I could do my duty both to the Corps and my children. I was sent to Green's Harbour for two years and then back to Exploits. While there, my husband came back from Scotland. I was told by Headquarters that I could carry on my work as an officer but they could not accept my husband because he had wandered away from God. I considered that I had three sons to be cared for and I felt that I could not face it alone any longer, so I had to resign.

My husband went to Bonavista to visit his parents...He then went to Corner Brook to look for work and I took the children to Bonavista, intending to live there with my in-laws. Sam, my husband, wrote to tell me he would not be coming, my father-in-law became angry and laid the blame on me. I packed up again and moved to Summerside. I crossed over to Corner Brook to look for a house and I brought the children (there). My husband decided to leave home again to go to Toronto. In my heart I was glad he was going...After he was gone two years he wrote and asked me to bring the family to Toronto. I decided not to at this time but after another two years, I considered that the boys knew little of their father, so I boarded up my home and moved to Toronto in 1949.

I had to work as a nurse to help pay for our home. My husband became unsatisfied and showed his temper many times. He often drank, so life became very miserable...I told Sam he would have to move out and we were eventually divorced. After he left us, he did not support us in any way. I took in elderly ladies as boarders. The rooming house was hard to work but I was free and happy...at last.

From the book The Finest Kind *by Marian Frances White. Creative Publishing. Used by permission.*

♀

Spice of Life

I understand my teenage daughter a little, and she misunderstands me a lot.

♀

🧑‍🤝‍🧑 Adam's Ribbing
Point of Punctuation

The English professor wrote the words, "Woman without her man is nothing," on the blackboard and asked the class to punctuate it properly.

This is how the men punctuated it: "Woman, without her man, is nothing," The women in the class punctuated it thus: "Woman! Without her, man is nothing."

♀

Top Ten Things Only Women Understand

10. Cat's facial expressions.

9. The need for the same style of shoes in different colours.

8. Why bean sprouts aren't just weeds.

7. Fat clothes.

6. Taking a car trip without trying to beat your best time.

5. The difference between beige, ecru, cream, off-white and eggshell.

4. Cutting your bangs to make them grow.

3. Eyelash curlers.

2. The inaccuracy of every bathroom scale ever made.

AND, the Number One thing only women understand:

1. OTHER WOMEN

Author Unknown

♀

Female Firsts

1863: Annie Jump Cannon became the first astronomer to classify the heavens systematically. *See also page 173.*

1863: The first known charity cookbook was published by Maria J. Moss. It was dedicated to the sanitary fair held in Philadelphia that year.

1865: Mary Edwards Walker became the first and only woman to receive the Medal of Honor in the American Civil War.

1865: On July 7, Mary E. Surratt became the first woman to be hanged by the U.S. Government. She had been convicted, along with others (all male), of conspiracy in the assassination of President Abraham Lincoln. Three men were hanged for the crime as well.

1866: Sculptor Vinnie Ream became the first woman in America to win a federal commission for a statue of Lincoln.

1866: Lucy Hobbs became the first woman to graduate from a dental school when she graduated in Chicago.

1866: The first American YWCA (Young Women's Christian Association) opened in Boston.

1866: The world's first two women's amateur baseball teams were fielded by Vassar College.

1867: The first Christian Science Church was founded by Mary Baker Eddy.

1867: The first ladies golf club was founded at St. Andrew's in Scotland.

♀

Life, Love & Laughter

Quillings

Mysterious Ways
By Kim Courtney - Francois, Newfoundland

New York City dawned sunny and clear
Then airplanes like bombs brought so much despair
A homeless old man, all tattered and torn
Saw the destruction that September morn.

And, thought the old man, what horror, what loss
So many, so innocent, so much of a cost
He spent his life begging for a quarter, a penny
If God gave him a purpose, well he couldn't find any.

Gambling and drugs had cost him his wife
His only daughter, and his happy life
"That tragic event should have took me instead
Nobody would miss me if I were dead"

The doors of a church were spread open wide
Without a thought, the old man stepped inside
The sobbing young woman in the front row pew
Had the look of a heart that was broken in two

For some strange reason, the old man was drawn
To the young woman who cried there alone
He sat down beside her said "For whom do you weep?"
"My husband, Sir," she said, "Among the rubble and heap"

For some unknown reason he decided to ask
"Would you tell me about him to make the time pass?
I know I'm a stranger but I'm willing to hear
If you need to talk or to shed a few tears"

She said, "He was a good man, he was all that I had
My mom died last summer, I didn't know my dad
My mom said that he died when I was just four
I remember so little, but I love him for sure

My mom said she loved him but he lost his way
The cost was his life, that he so dearly paid
I often think about him and I love him still
I guess if God took him then that was His will

"As I sit here thinking of the husband I love
I know they are together with God up above
I married my husband and from what my mom said
I married a good man just like my dad"

"I carry a picture of my dad and me
When things were so happy and we were carefree"
When the old man saw the photo, it made his heart shudder
He was sitting beside his very own daughter.

She said, "Sir, you have done so much here tonight
Just talking to you makes me know I'm alright
For some strange reason I'd like to express
What you've given me feels like a father's kindness.

She kissed his cheek, then got up and left
He knew at that moment he was given a gift
A purpose to help, to listen, to love
His purpose, a gift from the good Lord above.

The prayers and thanksgivings, for he found the way
From a tramp on the street who saw purpose that day
From his pocket he pulled his last few cents
And to a charity box for the children it went.

He was found the next morning, dead on the steps
The shape of a smile was still on his lips
They asked what would make a man smile that day
The answer - God works in mysterious ways.

♀

Life In The 1500s

Author Unknown

The next time you are washing your hands and complain because the water temperature isn't just how you like it, think about how things used to be back in the 1500s, back when *

*Most people got married in June because they took their yearly bath in May and still smelled pretty good by June. However, they were starting to smell, so brides carried a bouquet of flowers to hide the body odour. Hence the custom today of carrying a bouquet when getting married.

*Baths consisted of a big tub filled with hot water. The man of the house had the privilege of the nice clean water, then all the other sons and men, then the women and finally the children - last of all the babies. By then the water was so dirty you could actually lose someone in it. Hence the saying, "Don't throw the baby out with the bath water."

*Houses had thatched roofs - thick straw-piled high - with no wood underneath. It was the only place for animals to get warm, so all the dogs, cats and other small animals, including mice and bugs, lived in the roof. When it rained it became slippery and sometimes the animals would slip and fall off the roof. Hence the saying "It's raining cats and dogs."

*There was nothing to stop things from falling into the house. This posed a real problem in the bedroom where bugs and other droppings could really mess up your nice clean bed. Hence, a bed with big posts and a sheet hung over the top afforded some protection. That's how canopy beds came into existence.

*The floor was dirt. Only the wealthy had something other than dirt. Hence the saying "dirt poor."

*The wealthy had slate floors that would get slippery in the winter when wet, so they spread thresh (straw) on the floor to help keep their footing. As the winter wore on, they kept adding more thresh until when you opened the door it would all start slipping outside. A piece of wood was placed in the entranceway. Hence the name "thresh hold."

*In those old days, they cooked in the kitchen with a big kettle that always hung over the fire. Every day they lit the fire and added things to the pot. They ate mostly vegetables and did not get much meat. They would eat the stew for dinner, leaving leftovers in the pot to get cold overnight and then start over the next day. Sometimes the stew had food in it that had been there for quite a while. Hence the rhyme, "Peas porridge hot, peas porridge cold, peas porridge in the pot, nine days old."

*Sometimes they could obtain pork, which made them feel quite special. When visitors came over, they would hang up their bacon to show off. It was a sign of wealth that a man "could bring home the bacon." They would cut off a little to share with guests and would all sit around and "chew the fat."

*Those with money had plates made of pewter. Food with high acid content caused some of the lead to leach into the food, causing lead poisoning and death. This happened most often with tomatoes, so for the next 400 years or so, tomatoes were considered poisonous.

Life, Love & Laughter

*Bread was divided according to status. Workers got the burnt bottom of the loaf, the family got the middle and guests got the top or "upper crust."

*Lead cups were used to drink ale or whisky. The combination would sometimes knock people out for a couple of days. Someone walking along the road would take them for dead and prepare them for burial. They were laid out on the kitchen table for a couple of days and the family would gather around and eat and drink and wait and see if they would wake up. Hence the custom of holding a "wake."

*England is old and small and the local folks started running out of places to bury people. So they would dig up coffins and would take the bones to a "bone-house" and reuse the grave. When reopening these coffins, 1 out of 25 coffins were found to have scratch marks on the inside and they realized they had been burying people alive. So they thought they would tie a string on the wrist of the corpse, lead it through the coffin and up through the ground and tie it to a bell. Someone would have to sit out in the graveyard all night (the "graveyard shift") to listen for the bell; thus, someone could be "saved by the bell" or was considered a "dead ringer."

♀

Some Mothers Have Them

Jackson's father was showing pictures of his wedding day to his son. Pointing to his mother in her wedding gown Jackson asked, "Is that the day Mommy came to work for us?"

♀

MABEL & MANLEY

Manley walked into the dentist's with his wife, Mabel. Mabel said to the dentist, "I'd like a tooth removed without novocaine or painkillers of any kind."

"Are you sure, Mabel?" asked the dentist. "Removing a tooth can be quite painful."

"Of course I'm sure," she replied. Then turning to Manley said, "Show him your bad tooth, Honey."

♀

How To Bake A Cake

Anonymous

Light the oven. Get out bowl, spoons and ingredients. Grease the pan. Crack nuts. Remove 18 blocks and 7 toy autos from the kitchen table. Measure 2 cups of flour. Remove Kelly's hands from the flour. Wash flour off. Measure one more cup of flour to replace the flour on the floor. Put the flour, baking powder and salt in a sifter. Get the dustpan and brush up pieces of bowl which Kelly knocked on the floor. Get another bowl. Answer doorbell. Return to kitchen and remove Kelly's hands from bowl. Wash Kelly. Get out egg. Answer phone. Return. Take out greased pan. Remove pinch of salt from the pan. Look for Kelly. Get another pan and grease it. Answer the phone. Return to the kitchen and find Kelly. Remove the grimy hands from the bowl. Wash off Kelly who flees, knocking bowl off the table. Wash kitchen floor, wash the table, wash the walls, and wash the dishes. CALL THE BAKERY. LIE DOWN.

♀

Life, Love & Laughter

🌳 Her Other Half

Fatherly Advice

"Always remember that there are two important ingredients in marriage," a father advised his son, who was about to become a groom, "honesty and good sense."

"What do you mean by honesty, Dad?" asked the son.

"That means that once you have given your word to your wife, you must always keep it."

"And what do you mean by good sense?"

"Never give your word," advised the father.

♀

Aunt Alice says:

> Sometimes I think I understand everything, then I regain consciousness.

Spice of Life

I refuse to think of them as chin hairs. I think of them as stray eyebrows.

– *Janette Barber*

♀

Is That a Fact?
Many things are taken as facts. Not all of them are.

Betsy Ross and the American Flag

Most Americans know of Betsy Ross, who nimbly sewed together the stars and stripes to make the original *Star Spangled Banner*, the flag of the United States of America.

The Fact Is there is no evidence to support this belief, but there is evidence to the contrary.

That Elizabeth Griscom Ross, a Philadelphia seamstress, made the first American flag, was first said by her grandson William J. Canby, at a meeting of the Historical Society of Pennsylvania. This statement was said 94 years after the flag-making supposedly took place, which was 41 years before Canby was born. He was only eleven when his grandmother died in his home.

Canby's story is that the flag bearing stars and stripes were in common use soon after the signing of the Declaration of Independence, which was in fact nearly a year before the resolution of Congress proclaimed the flag.

There were no known photographs of Betsy Ross and the picture we see of her today, which was reproduced from a painting by Charles H. Weisgerber, is actually a composite portrait made up from pictures of her granddaughters and other descendants.

Although most people who've heard of Betsy Ross believe that she created the flag, this is not the consensus of historians. It was not believed by President Woodrow Wilson, who, when he was asked his opinion of Canby's story, replied, "Would that it were true!"

♀

WOMEN OF THE ISLAND AND THE BIG LAND

Peace and Quiet for Dorothy Wyatt

By Ron Young

Courtesy City of St. John's

"Vote for Wyatt, She won't be quiet" was the winning slogan for a great lady, Dorothy Wyatt. And Dorothy was never quiet, right up to September 22, 2001, the day she passed away. That was a sad day for me, because Dorothy Wyatt was my friend.

The eight-time-elected Dottie had many friends. Two days before Dorothy passed away, Premier Danny Williams signed papers nominating Dottie for the Order of Canada, the highest recognition Canada bestows upon its citizens.

And it was with good reason that Dorothy be considered for the Order. For more than 45 years, the taxpayer's friend served her fellow citizens and her community. The love and affection that this outstanding individual had for Newfoundland and Labrador, and its people, is shown in the efforts she took to make it a better place in which to live.

Intelligent, often amusing, dedicated and determined, Dorothy used her 30 years as a member of city council to improve overall living in St. John's in particular, and in Newfoundland and Labrador in general.

Born Dorothy Fanning, to Bill and Anne (O'Brien) at 43 Patrick Street in the mid 1920s, Dorothy was later raised by her grand-uncle, the Reverend Father Patrick O'Brien, in Bay Bulls. It was in Uncle Pat's enviable library that Dottie learned about the world, about equality, justice and humanitarianism. She learned not to be racist, bigoted or unfair, in spite of the harsh blows the world had dealt her personally, even at that time. It was in Father O'Brien's library that the girl learned things that would help her later in life.

She later married and became wife to a man for whom she would work three jobs and keep four boarders to help him become a doctor. She was also a mother, a private secretary at American Overseas Airlines, an educational radio program producer and announcer, a nurse, a Director of Nursing with the Canadian Red Cross, a mayor, and had countless other roles.

It was from Uncle Pat that little Dottie learned the 11th Commandment, "You can do anything you want if you work at it."

She was the one-time nurse to the men trapped underground during the Springhill mine disaster in Nova Scotia.

But it was while with the airlines that she took to the air and saw all those places she had read about in National Geographic. She travelled to Paris, London, New York, California and Toronto. It was this worldly knowledge that helped her appreciate *Downhomer*.

Dottie was a fan of Downhomer and a friend to me, while I was one of her biggest fans and supporters. During her last municipal election campaign she ran an ad in *Downhomer*. Why? Certainly not because she needed to advertise to get re-elected. She just took the opportunity to support us.

In 1996, she came to *Downhomer's* rescue when Mayor Andy Wells couldn't make his appointment to officiate at the opening of Downhomer Shoppe and Gallery. She bravely left her

Life, Love & Laughter

wheelchair home that evening and, smilingly, hobbled into the Shoppe with the aid of her walking apparatus to speak to her gathered taxpayers.

"I'd like to see the *Downhomer* office upstairs, Ron, but I don't think this old body can make it," she chuckled.

Her remarks, when she filled in for Andy's unexpected vacancy, were kind, humourous and intelligent. She may have taken license when Andy's name came up, but her words were not unkind, and she got many a chuckle and a few hearty laughs from the crowd. She saved the thoughts she had for Mister Mayor for a time when she could meet him face-to-face in council. One remark she made in council was in reference to the many large and deep potholes congesting the streets of her fair city at the time. "When I was mayor," she said, "the taxpayers used to call them Dottie's potties, now they call them Andy's wells."

Dorothy didn't live long enough to win the Order of Canada, but she did win the love and respect of the people she served, her precious taxpayers, particularly the *Downhomer*, one of her favourite and most willing taxpayers.

Reprinted from Downhomer *magazine*

♀

Food for Thought

If you have knowledge let others light their candles at it. – *Margaret Fuller*

♀

🗝 Female Firsts

1869: Susan B. Anthony became co-founder of the first U.S. woman's suffrage organization and called the first Woman Suffrage Convention in Washington D.C.

1869: Women were first permitted to enter cycling races in Bordeaux, France.

1869: Arabella Mansfield Babb became the first American woman to be admitted to the bar.

1869: The first women's croquet championships were held in England.

1870: Esther Hobart Morris of South Pass City, Wyoming, became the first woman Justice of the Peace.

1870: Ada Kepley graduated from the Union College of Law in Chicago, making her the first woman to graduate from a U.S. accredited law school.

1870: Wellesley College, the first higher education institution for women, opened.

1871: When Frances Elizabeth Willard was made President of Evanston College in the U.S., she became the first North American woman to become a college president.

1872: Victoria Chaflin Woodhull became the first female American presidential candidate.

♀

King Arthur and the Hag

Young King Arthur was ambushed and imprisoned by the monarch of a neighbouring kingdom. The monarch could have killed him, but was moved by Arthur's youth and ideals. So the monarch offered him freedom, as long as he could answer a very difficult question. Arthur would have a year to figure out the answer; if, after a year, he still had no answer, he would be put to death.

The question: What do women really want?

Such a question would perplex even the most knowledgeable man, and, to young Arthur, it seemed an impossible query. But, since it was better than death, he accepted the monarch's proposition to have an answer by year's end.

He returned to his kingdom and began to poll everybody: the princes, the priests, the wise men, and the court jester. He spoke with everyone, but no one could give him a satisfactory answer. Many people advised him to consult the old town hag — only she would know the answer they said. The price would be high though; the old hag was famous throughout the kingdom for the exorbitant prices she charged.

The last day of the year arrived and Arthur had no alternative but to talk to the hag. She agreed to answer his question, but he'd have to accept her price first: The old hag wanted to marry Gawain, the most noble of the Knights of the Round Table and Arthur's closest friend!

Young Arthur was horrified: she was hunchbacked and hideous, had only one tooth, smelled like sewage, made obscene noises...etc. He had never encountered such a repugnant creature. He refused to force his friend to marry her and have to endure such a burden.

Gawain, upon learning of the proposal, spoke with Arthur. He told him that nothing was too big a sacrifice compared to Arthur's life and the preservation of the Round Table. Hence, their wedding was proclaimed, and the old hag answered Arthur's question thus: What a woman really wants is to be in charge of her own life.

Everyone instantly knew that the hag had uttered a great truth and that Arthur's life would be spared. And so it was. The neighbouring monarch granted Arthur total freedom.

What a wedding Gawain and the old hag had! Arthur was torn between relief and anguish. Gawain was proper as always, gentle and courteous. The old hag put her worst manners on display, and generally made everyone very uncomfortable.

The honeymoon hour approached. Gawain, steeling himself for a horrific experience, entered the bedroom. But what a sight awaited him! The most beautiful woman he'd ever seen stood before him! The astounded Gawain asked what had happened.

The beauty replied that since he had been so kind to her when she'd appeared as a hag, she would henceforth be her horrible, deformed self half the time, and the other half, she would be her beautiful maiden self.

Which would he want her to be during the day, and which during the night?

What a cruel question! Gawain pondered his predicament. During the day, a beautiful woman to show off to his friends, but at night, in the privacy of his home, an old hag? Or, would he prefer having a hideous old hag by day, but a beautiful woman by night?

The Noble Gawain replied that he would let her choose for herself. Upon hearing this, she announced that she would be beautiful all the time, because he had respected her enough to let her be in charge of her own life.

The moral of this story is: If a woman doesn't get her way, things are going to get ugly.

Author Unknown

♀

Life, Love & Laughter

👭 Adam's Ribbing
Woman's Secret

The elderly spinster was cooperative with the census-taker, but was reluctant to give her age.

"But everyone tells me their age," he coaxed her.

"Even the three "Hill" triplets, Hilda, Helen and Heather, who were in my class at school, and live down the street?" she inquired.

"Yes, they gave me their age just this morning."

"Well I'm the same age as them."

The census taker looked at her information on his clipboard and in the space for age wrote, "Old as the Hills."

♀

👩 Out of Habit

"Good morning Sister Mary Catherine, I see you got out on the wrong side of the bed this morning," said one of her fellow sisters as the good sister descended the stairs from her bedroom.

Sister Mary Catherine simply nodded a greeting and continued on. In the hall at the bottom of the stairs another nun greeted her with, "Good morning Sister Mary Catherine, I see you got out on the wrong side of the bed this morning."

Sister Mary Catherine pondered this and walked into the kitchen where Mother Superior also greeted her with, "Good morning Sister Mary Catherine, I see you got out on the wrong side of the bed this morning."

"I've never felt better in my life," replied Sister Mary Catherine. "So why is everybody saying I got out on the wrong side of the bed this morning?"

"That's probably because you have Father O'Hullihan's slippers on," smiled Mother Superior.

♀

Life's Funny Experiences
Newfoundland Nickname

My friend, who comes from Costa Rica, and I were talking about the language barrier. She could speak little English when she came to Newfoundland. She quickly learned the language however, but there were still a few local phrases used by townspeople that confused her. One day while out for a stroll she was pleased that the people had given her a nickname. She told her husband about this when he came home. A bit perplexed, he asked what nickname she had been given.

"Iddnit," she proudly told her husband.

"Why do you think they call you Iddnit?" he asked

"Because everywhere I went today people were saying, 'Nice day Iddnit,' or 'Lovely weather Iddnit.'"

She was a bit let down when her husband informed her that "Idnit" was just Newfoundlandese for "isn't it?"

Submitted by Nina Shea, Garden Cove, Newfoundland

♀

Pleasant Memories of Pleasant Street

By Lila Mercer Young

Our house at 102 Pleasant Street, St. John's, was always busy with friends and family coming and going all the time, especially at Christmas time. Mom didn't know what a stranger was, so we never knew who we would find sitting at the kitchen table when we came home. It could be somebody selling the Salvation Army *War Cry* newspaper, or anyone who just happened to be walking by – maybe even a new neighbour. But one thing that stands out in my mind is that they all kept coming back over the years.

Some Christmases we would have a child relative from "out around the bay" stay with us. Some families weren't as well off as others, but Mom made sure that the visiting children had as happy a Christmas as her own. We would each give up one of our gifts for our visiting relative.

"We don't have much, but we sure have plenty," Mom used to say.

During the Christmas season, all the stores on Water Street would be lit up, and there would be many people Christmas shopping. Mom would

L–R: Mom, Lila, Elizabeth, Madonna and Dad Mercer, Christmas 1958

take Peggy, Ada, Madonna, myself and my younger sister, Elizabeth, in turn down to Water Street to look at the sights. I couldn't wait for my turn to come. After Christmas, the toys in the stores were put away until the next year. So you can imagine a child's excitement in seeing so many toys all at once.

The bells on the horses jingled as they trotted along past us, and the windows in Ayres, Bowrings, The London, New York and Paris store, and Bon Marche were filled with toys. After we finished looking at all the wonderful sights, we would stop on Water Street and buy raffle tickets from the orphans.

Then on the way home, Mom would take me into The Cup and Saucer, a little restaurant on Queen Street, for a treat. I was so proud and happy sitting on one of the bar stools beside Mom, having a plate of chips and a glass of soft drink. While I sipped on the drink, we would talk about school and my friends.

After we finished our treat we would walk home, with Mom holding my hand. The air, although crisp and cold, had that inner warmth of Christmas, and at that moment the most important thing to me was the person holding my hand.

In the 1950s, we didn't have a lot of presents on Christmas morning, like children do now, and our gifts under the tree weren't wrapped. Sometimes I'd get a doll, or some other "girl's gift." Once the five of us girls got a hockey game between us. Mom was a very kind person, not just at Christmas time, but all through the year. She would often send parcels to needy families and friends out around the bay.

And my mom loaned money to people all the time. She kept a record of it on the calendar behind the cabinet. As each one paid, she would put an X through their names. And at the end of the year those who didn't pay got an X, too. The calendar was then torn up and placed in the fire.

Downhomer Photo

Life, Love & Laughter

Every year saw a new calendar at 102 Pleasant Street.

Christmases have come and gone since then, and I often think of Pleasant Street and my friends and siblings there. And although they no longer share the delights of Christmas with my family now, I still think of the two people who made my childhood Christmases most memorable – Mom and Dad.

Christmas will be a little different this year, but I'm sure it will be just as delightful and memorable as it was back then. Along with my husband Ron, and his daughter Lolene and my daughter Kerri, who lives in Halifax, will be with us. Hopefully I can make this Christmas as pleasant and memorable for them as my Mom made for me back then on Pleasant Street.

Reprinted from Downhomer magazine.

♀

Ennellene

Why is it that lemonade and lemon pie
Have artificial flavouring in 'em
While furniture polish and dish detergent
Are made with the real lemon?

♀

Some Mothers Have Them

"Does Jesus use our bathroom?" Jackson, at age seven, asked his mother.

"No," she answered, "Why do you ask?"

"Because some mornings I hear Dad pounding on the door and shouting, 'Christ, are you still in there?'"

♀

God's Wife

Author Unknown

A little boy about 10 years old was standing before a shoe store on the roadway, barefooted, peering through the window, and shivering with cold. A lady approached the boy and said, My Little Fellow, why are you looking so earnestly in the window?" "I was asking God to give me a pair of shoes," was the boy's reply. The lady took him by the hand and went into the store and asked the clerk to get a half dozen pairs of socks for the boy. She then asked if he could give her a basin of water and a towel. He quickly brought them to her. She took the little fellow to the back of the store and, removing her gloves, knelt down, washed his little feet, and dried them with a towel. By this time the clerk had returned with the socks. She placed a pair upon the boy's feet, and then purchased him a pair of shoes. She tied up the remaining pairs of socks and gave them to him. She patted him on the head and said, "No doubt, my little fellow, you feel more comfortable now?" As she turned to go, the astonished lad caught her by the hand, and looking up in her face, with tears in his eyes, answered the question with these words: "Are you God's Wife?"

♀

⚓ WOMEN OF THE ISLAND AND THE BIG LAND ⚓

Charlene Caines

Original interview by Marg Penney

Charlene Caines was born in St. Anthony, on Newfoundland's Northern Peninsula, in 1967. She grew up, one of four children, in a single parent family. (Her father passed away when she was young.) At age six, she became permanently blind as a result of an accident. Caines studied at the Halifax School for the Blind for five years and returned to Plum Point to complete high school. She studied English at Memorial University of Newfoundland and later took computer software courses at Key-In Technical College, as well as Electronics at the Cabot Institute. She works at the CNIB as a Technical Services Counselor doing both inventory and computer consulting. Caines is a single parent to a five year old son. She is also on the Board of Iris Kirby House, a shelter for battered women and children, and was instrumental in forming the Action Committee on Accessibility to Transition Centres.

Janette Laaning

*****

I found the school system in rural areas of this province more accommodating to a blind person. Being so far away in the boondocks, my teachers did a lot of work over and above their jobs because there were no teaching assistants like they have in St. John's. I studied subjects like biology, geology, physics and chemistry which have lots of diagrams and charts. Because I couldn't see, the teachers would have to take a pizza wheel and draw them backwards on paper so they'd be tactile. People have some bizarre feeling that blind people can't do sciences. I was the first totally blind person to enter and graduate from the school system in Newfoundland.

I came to St. John's when I was seventeen to go to University and I studied English because I was bored and didn't know what else to do. I was more interested in partying and meeting people than studying, like everybody else who comes in from a rural area. I found University much more resistant; they wouldn't let me take math or honours French. If I had 20/20 vision I would have studied the sciences, not the arts.

Right now I'm most interested in computers. I take computers apart and carry screwdrivers in my purse to change computer cards. What I do is mainly electrical, more like a computer technician. There are about fifteen people who do what I do across the country and I'm the only female as well as the first totally blind person to work in this area. We have national conferences to keep in touch. I've gone to Halifax to get recertified in Xerox Kurzweil Imaging Systems and to Toronto to do a four-week technical training course, so it's a continuous challenge which I like.

Blindness can be a perceived disability in my repair work when dealing with sighted people because they don't think I can do it. When I'm setting up cables and plugging things in, they get nervous. So that's a big problem, but it's not a big thing. As long as the system is turned off and the batteries taken out, no one is going to get fried. Once you pop the top on a computer system, there's a motherboard and accompanying boards with some outlets, the power supply, a hard drive and a few controls and cables. There was some resistance to my working with computers,

Life, Love & Laughter

Life, Love & Laughter

initially, especially since it's not something people want a woman doing anyway.

I like what I'm doing but I don't want to work with the CNIB for the rest of my life. I'd like to mainstream a bit more. I got involved with access to Transition Shelters when I realized the obstacles in the way for people with specific needs. The building in St. John's was not accessible. I kept thinking that if I were in a battered situation, accessibility should not prevent me from getting into Kirby House. Finally, we were successful in obtaining money and implementing a game plan; we had to widen doors, enlarge the bathroom and make ramps. A TDD machine (Telephone Device for the Deaf) has been donated by Taxation Canada, so communication is not as big an issue as it was before. The long-term goal is to cover all the areas of accessibility and communication, but the immediate, obvious needs were to make it wheelchair accessible. The changes necessary for a visually impaired person are mostly lighting.

There's a lot you need to do for a totally blind person. I mean, I don't have a specially designed apartment. If I'm at a friend's home, the first thing I'll do if I'm cooking supper is ask how their stove is laid out. If accessibility for blind people is part of the work to be done at Transition Shelters, they would have to adapt their kitchen by marking the buttons on the stove with something tactile.

Most of my time is taken up with work, or this "woman stuff" I'm doing now, or raising my little fella, Rick. I have my own apartment, just the two of us. My life is the same as any other single parent, I would think. The biggest problem is money, daycare and babysitters.

Attitudes about blindness can be a problem, but that can change. As I found at the Network Dinner, sponsored by the Provincial Advisory Council on the Status of women, blindness is the most feared disability by sighted people because they find it hard to walk up to you and say "Hi, how are you?" I would assume it's because the world is so visual and a blind person is perceived as having no appreciation of that "visualness," and therefore you figure they're not on the same plane as you. But that's not the reality because there's no problem about where you can't go or what you can't do. Blindness is not as confining as some other disabilities. Most people say, "You're a strange person, you're a thumb in a land of fingers and you're not supposed to be here."

Some restrictions for all people are self-imposed, but that's a personality disability and a social disability, not a physical one. If you don't have the guts to get up and do what you want, that's a whole other problem. It comes down to what you'll accept and how far you can be pushed before you say, "Look I'm not going to take it any more." People will push you to the very bottom of the pile if you let them, whether you have a disability or not. I mean, how many people live and die with nothing. Nobody's going to do it for you, that's what I've learned. I think it just comes down to how badly you want something.

From the book The Finest Kind *by Marion Frances White. Creative Publishing. Used by permission.*

♀

☺ Some Mothers Have Them

Little Jackson was telling his friend about the changes in his home life. "You see, we have this new scale in the bathroom. On the bottom, it has a dial. I keep turning it, and you can't imagine how much nicer my mother is!"

♀

 **MABEL & MANLEY**

"How dare you disobey your mother," said Manley to his son. "Do you think you're any better than I am?"

♀

 Aphrodesia

"Aphrodesia, I know we had a fling, but who told you that you could come to work when you pleased?" Aphrodesia's boss said when she came in late yet another day.

"My lawyer!" replied Aphrodesia.

♀

Female Firsts

1873: Susan Elizabeth Blow opened the first successful public kindergarten in the U.S. *See also page 185.*

1873: Ellen Swallow Richards became the first woman to enroll at MIT (Massachusetts Institute of Technology), where she earned her SB degree, then went on to become the first female chemist in the United States.

1874: The first US tennis court was set up at the Staten Island Cricket and Baseball Club by Mary Ewing Outerbridge.

1875: The first US women's college to have standards comparable to the best men's colleges, was 'Smith College' founded by Sophia Smith.

1875: On September 11, the first baseball game between two women's teams, where a fee was charged at the gate, was played with the 'Blondes' against the 'Brunettes' in Springfield, Illinois.

1876: In July, wearing 38-pound weights on each ankle, Maria Speltarini became the first woman to walk across Niagara Falls on a tightrope.

1876: Louise Blanchard Bethune became the first professional woman architect in America.

1876: The first boxing match featuring female contenders was held in the U.105. Nell Saunders defeated Rose Harland and received a silver butter dish as a prize.

1877: The first American Red Cross was founded by Clara Barton, who had been a volunteer for the International Red Cross, helping refugees of the Franco-Prussian War in Paris and other cities prior to that date. She led the American Red Cross for 23 years, and personally headed many relief expeditions to victims of forest fire, flood, hurricane and war. She did that for 23 years, until she retired at age 82 in 1904.

1877: The first woman to earn a Ph.D. in North America was Helen Magill White, who earned her degree at Boston University.

♀

Life, Love & Laughter

Food for Thought

No civilization is complete which does not include the dumb and defenseless of God's creatures within the sphere of charity and mercy.   – *Queen Victoria*

♀

Adam's Ribbing
A Change for the Worse

"Are you really going to marry Brian?" a young lady asked her friend. "He's got a reputation for being fast and loose."

"He told me he'd change if I married him," replied her friend, "but I don't know if I can live with a man who is slow and tight."

♀

The Barbie Doll Birthday Present

Author Unknown

A man was driving home the day of his daughter's birthday, when he suddenly realized he hadn't bought her a birthday present. He drove to the toy store at the mall and asked the saleslady, "How much is that new Barbie in the window?"

She replied, "Which one? We have: *Barbie goes to the nightclub* for $19.95, *Barbie goes to the beach* for $19.95, *Barbie goes shopping* for $19.95, *Barbie goes to the Ball* for $19.95, *Barbie goes to the gym* for $19.95, and we have *Divorced Barbie* for $575.00."

"Why so much for *Divorced Barbie* when all of the others are $19.95?" the man asked.

The saleslady said sweetly, "*Divorced Barbie* comes with Ken's car, Ken's house, Ken's boat, Ken's dog, Ken's cat, Ken's furniture........."

♀

WOMEN OF THE ISLAND AND THE BIG LAND
Margot Davis

During the Second World War, the voice of Margot Davis was well-known throughout Newfoundland. Davis earned her reputation as a war-time radio broadcaster from England, "Calling From Britain To Newfoundland." The popular program started under the direction of Maxwell Littlejohn, and was continued by Davis until her death.

The program originally broadcast songs, music and poetry readings performed by Newfoundland servicemen stationed in Great Britain. But after the war, Davis expanded the program and sought out Newfoundlanders living in England to speak over the radio to their families and friends at home.

Davis helped thousands of young and lonely servicemen, and she became a legend throughout this province. She was born in St. John's and moved to England in 1934. She passed away in London in 1972.

From the book Strange But True Newfoundland Stories, *by Jack Fitzgerald. Creative Publishing. Used by permission.*

♀

If I Had My Life to Live Over

By Erma Bombeck

*I would have talked less and listened more.

*I would have invited friends over to dinner even if the carpet was stained and the sofa faded.

*I would have eaten the popcorn in the *GOOD* living room and worried much less about the dirt when someone wanted to light a fire in the fireplace.

*I would have taken the time to listen to my grandfather ramble about his youth.

*I would never have insisted the car windows be rolled up on a summer day because my hair had just been teased and sprayed.

*I would have burned the pink candle sculpted like a rose before it melted in storage.

*I would have sat on the lawn with my children and not worried about the grass stains.

*I would have cried and laughed less while watching television and more while watching life.

*I would have gone to bed when I was sick instead of pretending the earth would go in a holding pattern if I weren't there for the day.

*Instead of wishing away nine months of pregnancy, I'd cherish every moment realizing that the wonderment growing inside me was the only chance in life to assist God in a miracle.

*When my kids kissed me impetuously, I would never have said, "Later, now go get washed up for dinner."

*There would have been more "I love you" and more "I'm sorry," but mostly, given another shot at life, I would seize every minute...look at it...live it...and never give it back.

*I would tell all my friends that I need and love them and that my life would be empty without them.

Newspaper columnist and humourist, Erma Bombeck died of transplanted kidney failure on April 22, 1996.

♀

✿ Her Other Half

It's About Time

A man in his 80s went to see a lawyer for a divorce from his wife of 63 years.
"Why do you want to get divorced after all this time?" the solicitor asked.
"Enough is enough," replied the husband.

♀

Aunt Alice says:

Just when I was getting used to yesterday, along came today.

Spice of Life

A male gynecologist is like an auto mechanic who never owned a car.

– Carrie Snow

♀

Some Mothers Have Them

After a church service on Sunday morning, little Jackson suddenly announced to his mother, "Mom, I've decided to become a minister when I grow up." "That's okay with us," she replied, "but what made you decide that?" "Well," said the little boy, "I have to go to church on Sunday anyway, and I figure it will be more fun to stand up and yell, than to sit and listen."

♀

Food for Thought

My share of the work of the world may be limited, but the fact that it is work makes it precious. Darwin could only work a half hour at a time; yet in many diligent half-hours he laid anew the foundations of philosophy.

Green, the historian, tells us that the world is moved not only by the mighty shove of heroes, but also by aggregate of the tiny pushes of each honest worker. – *Helen Keller*

♀

MABEL & MANLEY

As Mabel tried on the new fur coat she had just purchased, her animal-rights daughter chided her, "Don't you know that some poor, dumb animal had to suffer for you to get that coat?"

"Don't you ever talk about poor Manley like that again!" Mabel warned her.

♀

Adam's Ribbing
Dead End Relationship

"Hi darling. Is Mommy near the phone?" said Daddy as he called home from the office.

"No Daddy, she's up in the bedroom with Uncle Fred," replied the little girl.

"But you don't have an Uncle Fred," said the man after a pronounced pause.

"Well Mommy told me he was my Uncle Fred," explained the daughter, "and he's up in the bedroom now with mommy."

"Could you do Daddy a favour," he started after another pause, "and shout to Mommy and Uncle Fred that I just drove in the driveway."

"Okay, Daddy."

"I did what you said Daddy," came the panicked voice of the girl over the phone line a few minutes later, "and Mommy jumped out of bed with no clothes on and ran around the hall screaming and she tripped on the rug and fell out the window, and now she's all dead!'

"Oh my God!" exclaimed the man, "and where did Uncle Fred go?"

"He was screaming too, and he didn't have any clothes and he ran down to the back of the hall and jumped down in the swimming pool, and he must have forgot that you let all the water out last week, and he's all dead too!"

"Swimming pool?" questioned the father, "Is this 555-2822?"

♀

WOMEN OF THE ISLAND AND THE BIG LAND
Cathy Jones

Courtesy CBC

Witty and controversial with a rare ability to transform a stark stage into truer-than life scenes, Cathy Jones is an actress of impact. She's an original member of the famous CODCO troupe whose stage and national TV performances won them awards and international acclaim. Writing from everyday life experiences, Cathy is sensitive to the burden laid on women for contraception, child care and relationships. She brings these issues to light through perceptive characters who inspire rebellion. Born on April 16, 1955, in St. John's, she joined the Newfoundland Travelling Theatre Company in 1973 while still a teenager. Before that year finished she was working with CODCO in their first show "Cod On A Stick." Her strong singing voice and sharp-edged tongue enlivened such CBC TV series as *Up At Ours*, and *The Wonderful Grand Band*. Cathy has co-produced and performed in many local shows and actively participates in annual International Women's Days celebrations. In 1986, she wrote and performed her one-woman show *A Wedding in Texas*, which opened to rave reviews across the country. Cathy's film credits include *The Adventures of Faustus Bidgood* (1986) and *Secret Nation* (1992). She also played a professional wrestler in Mark Tolefson's film *Desiree's Wish*. From 1986-92, Cathy was part of the CBC series CODCO, bringing to life such memorable characters as Nervous Rex. Since 1993, she has been performing and writing for the hit show *This Hour Has 22 Minutes* with her former CODCO partner Mary Walsh. In 1995, Cathy co-hosted the Juno Awards with the rest of the cast of 22 Minutes. Later that year, she appeared at the *Just For Laughs Comedy Festival* in Montreal. In 1997, she hosted the live gala presentation of the East Coast Music Awards and co-hosted the 1998 Gemini Awards with Steve Smith (*The Red Green Show*). In addition to earning more than a dozen Gemini Awards, as well as three Canadian Comedy Awards, Cathy has also won the prestigious Earle Grey Award for outstanding contribution to Canadian TV and an honourary doctorate from Memorial University of Newfoundland.

*****

I love to entertain and laugh with people. I don't like to write funny things; I prefer the funny things to write themselves. I believe that if I tried to write *feminist* comedy it would turn out very grim and unfunny. Yet, I am a woman, writing from my experiences in this female jacket I seem to be wearing. As a place from which I write comedy, it is a decent sex.

My sex is, to me, an important tool in my learning process, and in my work. So much comedy, like so much feminism, takes itself too seriously, presuming some sort of exclusivity. Recently a "feminist" was offended that a character of mine, who was a lesbian, died, implying I suppose, that she should have been treated with kid gloves because she was a lesbian. What??? Lesbians don't die??? I have always found that the key to life is to face it head on.

And the key to comedy is reality. Reality with a twist. They say that in curing cancer, attitude is of the utmost importance. I say, why wait for cancer? In my comedy I keep a bravado attitude that makes women (and men) laugh. I act as if I've got the whole thing under control. Like I've

Life, Love & Laughter

Life, Love & Laughter

won the battle of the sexes. My character, Vave Gladney, hostess of "Fudgeos and Feminism" says: "It's great to be a woman...especially considering the alternative! Because, things are looking up for women! These days, we burn up more old calories just *making choices!* Whether to make cookies or teach up to the university."

Vave subtly hits on the inconvenience of bearing the birth control burden, and the hideous possibility of sudden unwanted pregnancy. "That old birth control is not fixed yet! I had my IUD out and I had someone else's period last month, not my own! So if anyone missed their period, don't worry...I had it." Vave says flippant, sexist things like, "My husband Bob thought that sex was like doing the dishes...if you did it badly enough you wouldn't be asked to do it again!" Vave has it all figured out, she says that "Men are like a box of chocolates...and I know what you're thinking...they're fattening and it's hard to stop at one...but you've got to learn to pick the nougats! It's no good fooling with the world of men if you're going to end up eating a load of vanilla creams! Get the guide and go for the cherries! I'm publishing a new book, *Vave's Guide to the Chocolate Box of Life*. Read it! if you've got a bordeaux, and you want something harder, like a brazil, you might have to go to the bottom layer. What of it??? The main thing is stay on top, don't get under it! Stop putting yourself down. Everybody's bum gets dimply! Don't watch the twenty minute workout, it's depressing. Don't pick up men, they're too heavy and you'll put your back out. And if some kleptomaniac wants to lift your man, take a good look at what she's getting...you might want to say "Thank you very much, Miss!" And remember the old Vave Gladney motto: "Ask not what you can do for buddy...but what buddy can do for you!!!"

And of course in my real life, off stage, I have often lived the hideous realities of my characters in their domestic fights, and I have put my back (and spirit) out picking up men. I have been the girl who drives away and never sees her mother again. I have freaked along the way with the best of them at the conditioned fear of becoming the *wife*. Yeah, yeah. But to me, life is bittersweet, and the pain intensifies the joy. I love the strength required to handle it all. It rains on the males as well as the females, though, and I feel we are heading towards a more spiritual era, when sexuality will be less relevant and marked. Yes, there is much work for women alone, but life is so much bigger than sex. If I learn to accept myself and other people, to relax and have faith, to be true to myself and you...I don't know that it will matter that in this life I was a woman.

From the book The Finest Kind *by Marion Frances White. Creative Publishing. Used by permission.*

♀

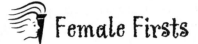 **Female Firsts**

1878: The world's first telephone operator was Emma M. Nutt of Boston.

1879: Twenty women competed in America's first National Archery Championship.

1879: Belva Ann Lockwood became the first woman to practice law before the U.S. Supreme Court.

1880: The first American beauty contest was held at Rehoboth Beach, Delaware. This later become known as the Miss America pageant.

1881: Louise Bethune became the first American woman architect.

1882: The first athletic games for women were held at the YWCA in Boston.

♀

WOMEN OF THE ISLAND AND THE BIG LAND

Emily MacDougall

Original Interview by June Hiscock

Born Emily Moore on October 31, 1911, in Jersey Harbour on Newfoundland's southwest coast, she left home at age twelve to work as a domestic in Ramea. After three years she moved to Port-aux-Basques and worked as a housekeeper until she married and settled in Wreckhouse. Emily has been diagnosed as having Alzheimer's Disease and has been living in Port-aux-Basques for the past fifteen years with her son, Leduc, who cares for her.

Courtesy Terra Transport

Wreckhouse is known for having the worst winters anywhere. The ferocious winds played havoc to the Canadian National Railway: many trains were literally swept off the rail by the hurricane force winds.

*****

I'm the woman what looked after the wind in Wreckhouse. I was born in Jersey Harbour but I lived in St. Andrews which was a good place to grow up. Everyone had big families and a lot of people lived there. My brothers and sisters and I would walk the four miles to school, carrying our dinner with us and we would all take turns bringing kindling to light the fire. I only went as far as Book Four.

When I was twelve years old, I went up the coast to Ramea and worked as a domestic for three years. Then I took the coastal boat up to Port-aux-Basques where I worked as a housekeeper for Mrs. Wilfred Gillam. I met my husband, Lauchie MacDougall, in Port-aux-Basques and after we were married we moved to Wreckhouse, the place where he was born. It was all woods up there at one time, until they cut it all out. It was a really pretty place, beautiful in the summer but no good in winter. It was lonely up there at first and I done lots of crying when I first moved up there, from being lonesome.

Now Lochie, my dear, he was some worker. He looked after the wind back then. He'd use his hand (Emily holds her arm straight up), go outdoors and come in, tell you right where the wind was. Smart my dear, he was some smart. We had the dairy farm and he'd be in the woods with her cutting wood or trapping. I tell you, he'd get his foxes and his rabbits. He was a wonderful worker and he was good as a women when it come to raising our family. We had nine boys and three girls. All my crowd was good, well, we learned 'em to be good.

I raised the twelve children while I tended the farm. It wasn't an easy life, that's for sure. The children had to walk eleven miles to get to and from the St. Andrews school. They all got good learning, though. All except for young Lauchie. He was hurted with the wind. Gale of wind took him and blowed him, broke his little back. He was only small then. But still for all, he'd keep going.

We had ten and twelve head of cattle, twelve sheep, three pigs and so many hens and ducks. You'd have to make hay and put it in the barn for winter. And I made pounds and pounds of butter. We used to sell it for sixty-five cents a pound. We sold fresh milk, too, and people would come from miles around to get it. Come right to your door and take it and go on. One time, I had fifty-five pounds of butter put away just for eating. I misses it. When I goes to Codroy Valley with my daughter Kay, I gets it from the people who got farms up there.

Life, Love & Laughter

Life, Love & Laughter

You'd have to get up at five o'clock in the morning to get water from the pond. In winter, you had to cut the ice, and then melt it on the stove to get your breakfast. I went through some there, I tell you.

Everybody loved the house at Wreckhouse. There'd be flowers up in the windows and on the table. I had a garden, you know. We had it all, my dear. And we always had a house full. Crowd from Port-aux-Basques would come up here berry picking; it was a wonderful place for berries. You'd see them coming in the morning, probably one of the men would bring a bottle of rum for Lochie and they'd stay well into the night.

The trains would run every day. You'd hear the phone ringing, "Is that you, Mrs. MacDougall, what's the wind like today?" I'd say, 'Tis good now but there's a big storm coming up." I lost two trains, blowed off the tracks. But it wasn't my fault. A big storm come on. Thank God nobody got hurt. I don't know what they got done with the trains now dear. They used to close them down when there was a gale on. There's not so much wind as there used to be, see. The wind goes down in the spring of the year. The fall is the worse.

A good many times we put people up for the night. We had to, blowing hard, see. You'd see them bringing their baskets of stuff. I must say, they were good to us. We used to hear from them afterwards. I'd get postcards and letters from people from all over. I had them all put away somewhere but I can't remember where I put them. And you know, we never used to miss a dance. I was right full of life back then. We'd go up to St. Andrews to the dances and go down to Cape Ray to parties. I loved it, dearly loved it.

It was a bard life, dear. When the poor old man was living, it wasn't so bad. God bless him, he'd dead and gone but I really misses him. And I loved it up to Wreckhouse. I'd go back today if it wasn't so lonely.

Emily passed away on February 22, 1992 at age 80.

From the book The Finest Kind *by Marion Frances White. Creative Publishing. Used by permission.*

♀

☺ Some Mothers Have Them

When Jackson went to church with his mother for the first time he watched as the ushers passed the offering plates. When they got near to the pew where they sat, he shouted out to his mother, "Don't pay for me Mommy, I'm under five."

♀

☖ Her Other Half

Flirting With Death

When their 93-year-old uncle got married to a beautiful 22-year-old woman, his family was very worried. Especially when he came back from the honeymoon bragging about having sex three times a day for the whole two weeks.

"But Uncle," they said, "don't you know that a person can die from too much activity?"

"So what?" he replied. "If she dies, she dies."

♀

Life's Funny Experiences

Cheese Please

When I worked as a demonstrator at a warehouse outlet, a customer approached me and asked if we had a cheese counter. For the life of me, I couldn't figure out why anyone would need a cheese counter. I thought, "Isn't cheese big enough so that you don't need to use a counter to count it?" I looked at the lady and asked, "Did you say a CHEESE counter?" She replied, "Yes, a cheese counter." By this time, I was searching my mind for this object and couldn't come up with anything. I again asked her if she said, "CHEESE counter." By this time, she was impatient and sighed and walked away. As soon as she left, I realized she was asking for the deli counter, which was immediately to the left of me. My face burned red with embarrassment all day. Every time I think of that day, I laugh so hard!

Dee Stead – British Columbia

♀

Ellen Dower's Ghost

By P. J. Consella

On the 10th of March, 1873, the vessel *Eleanor*, owned and commanded by John Dower of Conche, left to prosecute the seal fishery. The Dower family, father and son, had accumulated splendid returns from their annual trips to the ice; and it was with a light heart that Skipper John sailed from home once more, leaving a wife who loved him fondly, and who would count on the days until his happy return.

About a week after her husband had gone, Ellen complained of feeling unwell. She grew worse, gradually became unconscious and six hours after the seizure she was dead. The family was highly esteemed, and the deceased lady was particularly loved for her gentle qualities and charitable assistance to the needy, so the sad news spread quickly. From far and near came mourning friends. Many of them declared that the poor lady looked as if she were but sleeping, and that the hand of death had indeed dealt kindly with her.

The second night had come and gone when in the morning it was whispered that the *Eleanor* was coming up the harbour with her flag at half-mast. After viewing the approaching vessel for a little while, the watchers returned to the wake room, but had only been there but a minute when an astounding thing happened. From the body of the deceased was heard a long, weary sigh, followed by a faint motion. Then, literally back from the dead, from the very portals of eternity, from the brink of the grave, came the spirit of the dead woman. The body regained its warmth, the face, hands and limbs their colour of life, and Ellen Dower, strangely recalled, sat up, a strange and appalling figure. Consternation prevailed in the room. Some of the watchers fled, crying out in terror. Others became faint with fear. Only one or two of the older folk remained calm and gave assistance to Mrs. Dower, who had by this time almost recovered. Her first words were, "I am tired. I have been far. I have been with John."

John Dower afterwards told how his wife had come to him, her heart one with his, had caused her to cross over that great ocean of ice, though her body remained at home inanimate in the chamber of death. He had believed her dead, and half-masted his ship's flag and turned about. How sorrowfully he looked forward to that homecoming! What a joy when husband and wife met once more!

Captain Dower never went to the seal fishery again; but it was always his proud boast, that his "good wife had gone to the ice and returned in quicker time than the *Eleanor*."

♀

Food for Thought

She never quite leaves her children at home, even when she doesn't take them along.   – *Margaret Culkin Banning*

♀

Animal Mating – Fact and Fantasy – *Ron Young*

Lobster Love

Fact:

If zippers, clasps, snaps and buttons have frustrated one or more of your previous attempts at 'mating,' consider what a female Lobster has to get off before she can get it on. Crustaceans, such as lobster and crab must molt (get out of their old shell) before they can grow bigger. The female lobster must also molt before it can mate. As the time for molting and mating approaches she will go to a male's domain and, by repeatedly moving her antennules, she will poke her claws in, and see if he meets with her approval. If interested, Mister Lobster will raise up and vibrate his abdominal appendages. This may go on for several days before she decides to share his lodging and his bed. When she does, he will welcome her by tapping his claws against hers. The male appears to get more excited as the day of undressing approaches. When the day comes the female will wiggle out of her shell, a process which, depending on her size, takes a half hour or more. Without the support of her skeletal shell, and being totally exhausted by her efforts, she falls to the ground. After a half hour rest, and with the support of her temporary skeleton (created by water pressure), she is able to stand on her legs. She then approaches the male and slowly turns until her abdomen is facing him. Using the help of his two middle legs, he then helps her onto her back and mounts her in human fashion. Both sexes then rub their fanned abdominal appendages against each other, and, using the two proper appendages, the male inserts sperm into the female's seminal receptacle. The female later leaves and finds her own home to grow bigger in, regrow her shell in, and give birth to her young. This takes another nine to 12 months.

But what is her man doing in the meantime? He's just hanging around the castle for the next female wanting to remove her clothing in his presence. Then he does it all over again with a new mate.

Because of their natural habitat, under water, under rocks, and the fact that they are nocturnal, natural observation of lobsters is very difficult. That's why the information for this was taken from sources where the lobsters were observed by researchers while the lobsters were in glass aquariums. Under these conditions nature is influenced by other than natural surroundings, which may have had an affect on their normal behaviour.

Fantasy:

If your lot in all creation, is to live as a crustacean
And the only roof above your head, a stone
No matter what your spouse says, don't settle for glass houses
Lest the private life you lead, to all be known

♀

Life, Love & Laughter

Women Who Have Made A Difference *– By Ron Young*

Alice Hamilton, among the discoveries in the field of health, made a connection between improper sewage disposal and the role of flies in transmitting typhoid during the great epidemic of that disease in Chicago in 1902. She then noted that the health problems of many of the immigrant poor were due to unsafe conditions and noxious chemicals, especially lead dust, to which they were being exposed in the course of their employment. At the time there were no laws regulating safety at work and employers routinely fired sick workers and replaced them with new ones looking for jobs. Dr. Hamilton became director of the Occupational Disease Commission when it was created by the governor of Illinois in 1910. It was the first such commission in the world. She was the first woman professor at Harvard Medical School and the first woman to receive the Lasker Award in public health. Alice died in 1970 at the age of 100.

Eliza Lucas Pinckney was born on the Caribbean island of Antigua, and later moved with her family to a farming area near Charleston, South Carolina, where her mother died soon after. By age sixteen, Eliza was left to take care of her siblings and run three plantations, when her father, a British military officer, had to return to the Caribbean. In 1739, realizing that the growing textile industry was creating world markets for new dyes, she began cultivating and creating improved strains of the indigo plant from which a blue dye can be obtained. Eliza's venture was so successful that between 1746 and 1748 the volume of indigo from the Charleston area went from 5,000 pounds to 130,000 pounds. This made indigo second only to rice as a cash crop (since cotton hadn't yet become important), and made Eliza, probably, the first important agriculturalist of the United States.

Oprah Winfrey became the most famous television host of all time because she did something no other TV personality dared to do - she shared her soul with humanity. Her honesty, intelligence, and sheer charisma attracted a very wide television audience, and turned the faltering "AM Chicago," a half-hour daily television show, into a success that even outperformed the leading talk-show host, Phil Donahue, in his own market. In 1985, her show went to an hour, and was renamed *The Oprah Winfrey Show*, which became nationally syndicated. As a result, Oprah became one of the wealthiest women in entertainment, and proved herself one of the best.

In 1998, Oprah was voted the second most admired woman in America, with Hillary Rodham Clinton being the first. Oprah was followed by former First Lady Barbara Bush and former British Prime Minister Margaret Thatcher. *Vanity Fair* magazine wrote, "Oprah Winfrey arguably has more influence on the culture than any university president, politician, or religious leader, except perhaps the Pope."

But with all her greatness, her heart, which is filled with love and charity, is her biggest asset. Apart from the money she gives to others, Oprah also gives of herself to the betterment of others. She is a role model for everyone, no matter their sex, race or creed.

Her creed is, "I always feel if you do right, right will follow."

Meena, a 31-year-old Afghan woman, was no longer able to do anything about it when the fingers of blame for 9/11 started to point toward Afghanistan after the attack. She had died nearly 15 years earlier. She was killed trying to save her country from becoming something other than a battlefield, which could serve only the powerful and controlling of the world, and bring about events such as 9/11.

Meena was born in Kabul in 1956, the year Russian tanks invaded Hungary, unaware that she would someday have to face down those same invaders in her own country.

Life, Love & Laughter

As Meena grew up she saw the way the women in her country were used and abused by men, even in the university she attended, so Meena left university to devote herself to organizing and educating women. In 1977, Meena laid the foundation of RAWA, an organization meant to give voice to the deprived and silenced women of Afghanistan.

She found an enemy even worse than male Afghans at her doorstep two years later when Russia invaded. She then started a campaign against the Russian forces and their puppet regime and organized numerous processions and meetings in schools, colleges and Kabul University to mobilize public opinion.

In 1981, she launched Payam-e-Zan (Women's Message), a bilingual magazine which constantly exposed the criminal nature of fundamentalist groups within her country.

The caring Meena also established Watan Schools for refugee children, a hospital and handicraft centers for refugee women in Pakistan to support Afghan women financially.

At the end of 1981, with the Russians still causing chaos and death within Afghanistan, the French Government invited Meena, who represented the Afghan resistance movement, to the French Socialist Party Congress. When Meena boldly started waving a victory sign, bringing cheers from participants at the Congress, the Soviet delegation, headed by Boris Ponamaryev, shamefacedly left the hall. She was also invited to other European countries where she met their prominent personalities.

As Meena gained world attention with her effective advocacy against the views of the fundamentalists and the puppet regime, she provoked the wrath of her enemies. On February 4, 1987, while her country was being undermined by both the invading Russians, and the entrenched fundamentalist, she was assassinated by agents of KHAD (Afghanistan branch of KGB) and their fundamentalist accomplices in Quetta, Pakistan.

A translation of part of her poem, *I'll Never Return* follows;

I'm the woman who has awoken
I've arisen and become a tempest through the ashes of my burnt children
I've arisen from the rivulets of my brother's blood
My nation's wrath has empowered me
My ruined and burnt villages fill me with hatred against the enemy
Oh compatriot, no longer regard me weak and incapable,
My voice has mingled with thousands of arisen women
My fists are clenched with fists of thousands, compatriots
To break all these sufferings all these fetters of slavery.
I'm the woman who has awoken,
I've found my path and will never return.

Margaret Hilda Thatcher, in her younger days, earned degrees in chemistry, and from 1947 to 1951 she worked as a research chemist before later becoming a tax lawyer. She entered politics and was elected to the House of Commons in 1959. In 1979 she was elected prime minister making her the first woman to hold the office of prime minister of Great Britain. After the June 1987 elections, she became the first British prime minister in the 20th century to serve three consecutive terms. During her tenure as Prime Minister, the 'Iron Lady' sent a task force to the Falklands that defeated the Argentines. She also privatized some nationalized industries and social programs, including education, housing, and health care. Thatcher resigned as prime minister in November of 1990 and was succeeded as party leader and prime minister by her protégé, John Major.

Life, Love & Laughter

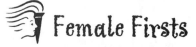 Female Firsts

1884: Women's singles tennis competition began at Wimbledon. Maud Watson won that year as well as the following year.

1885: At age 25, Phoebe Ann Moses (better known as Annie Oakley) became the world's first professional sharp-shooter. She was one of the stars of Buffalo Bill Wild West Show, and could hit a moving target while riding a galloping horse and hit a dime in mid-air. As part of her act she would also shoot a cigarette from her husband's lips.

1886: The first known women's lacrosse game was played.

1887: Susanna Madora Salter of Argonia, Kansas, became the first woman mayor of an American city.

1887: The first women's field hockey club started in Surrey, England.

1887: The first Women's French Tennis Championship was held.

1888: In August, Berta Benz became the first woman to drive on a 60-mile trip cross-country in Germany in a motorized vehicle, a 3-horse-power car with solid rubber tires.

1890: Myra Bradwell was admitted to the Illinois bar, making her the first female lawyer in the U.S. She received a licence to practice before the Supreme Court two years later.

1890: On January 25, Elizabeth Cochran Seaman, better known as Nellie Bly, became the first woman to travel around the world alone. She was a reporter for the *New York World* newspaper at the time she made the amazing trip in just 72 days.

1890: (or thereabouts) Esther Pohl Lovejoy became the first woman physician in the Klondike area of Canada's Yukon, famous for its gold rush.

1891: Women were first permitted to play golf at the Shinnecock Hills Golf Club on Long Island. The game proved to be so popular among women, that the club opened a 9-hole course for women two years later.

1891: Harriet Maxwell Converse became the first white woman to be named chief of an Indian tribe, when she became chief of the Six Nations Tribe at Tonawanda Reservation in New York. She had been adopted by the tribe seven years earlier because of her efforts on behalf of the tribe. The Seneca Indian name they gave her was Ga-is-wa-noh, which means 'the watcher.'

♀

Ennellene

The man who guesses women's ages
And always guesses right
Is a man who is smart
But not very bright

♀

Spice of Life

The graveyards are full of women whose houses were so spotless you could eat off the floor. Remember, the second wife always has a maid. – *Heloise Cruse*

♀

MABEL & MANLEY

Mabel was still upset with Manley, even while they were driving to a town nearby their home to visit a flea market one Saturday. Manley, looking for a way to break the deafening silence, pointed to a goose and a gander swimming peacefully, side by side, in a pond near the road and said, "Look at that, Mabel. Wouldn't it be great if married people could get along like these geese?"

Mabel made no reply.

On the way home later, they passed the same pond, backlit by the sinking sun, showing the silhouettes of a goose and gander, swimming peacefully in the peaceful scene.

"Look," said Manley, "the goose and gander are still happy together."

"Manley," replied Mabel, "take a closer look and you'll see that's not the same goose."

♀

Letters From Our Friends

Marriage By Mail Through *Downhomer*

Dear Readers,

My husband Dave is from Orillia, Ontario. In late 1997, he was contemplating moving to Newfoundland. His brother had brought him a *Downhomer* magazine from a business trip in Newfoundland. Thinking the move would be easier if he knew somebody here, he put his name in the "Friends Across The Miles" section. In November of 1997, I decided I'd like to have some penpals. I wrote a girl from England, a girl from Ontario, and Dave. Rarely do I write guys but something told me to write him. Mine was the only letter he received.

We found we had a lot in common and were exchanging 5-7 letters a week. Shortly after Christmas we started telephoning each other. The phone bills were extremely high and still the letters continued. Within a few months we decided it was time to meet.

Dave flew into Gander on June 22nd, 1998. We knew instantly that the love we had kindled on the phone was taking flame. Dave bought a house in Fogo and prepared to settle in. (Much to the dismay of Bell Canada and NewTel, we're sure.)

In late July, Dave took me to Ontario to meet his family. It was my first trip outside Newfoundland. We returned to Fogo on August 5th. The 7th of August Dave proposed. I said "Yes" without any hesitation.

We married here in Fogo on June 12th, 1999. We have each found our love, best friend, and soulmate, thanks to *Downhomer*. The MC at our wedding said he never knew the *Downhomer* was a mail-order bride and groom catalogue.

Mrs. Janel Mahaney, Fogo, Newfoundland

PS: Thank you very much *Downhomer* for helping us find each other.

♀

Life, Love & Laughter

WOMEN OF THE ISLAND AND THE BIG LAND

Martha Joshua

Courtesy Fran Williams

Martha tells her own story, transcribed by Fran Williams. Martha Joshua was born at Killinek, Labrador, on July 27, 1911. Her family moved to Okak when she was still a baby; however, the remainder of the family moved to Nain after the Spanish flu. This flu is said to have arrived aboard the last mail steamer in the late summer of 1918. The flu spread from areas such as Mud Lake, Rigolet and further northward to Okak. Hundreds of people died as settlement after settlement was stricken with the deadly flu.

*****

Martha was married to Titus Joshua for fifty years. Only two of seven children survived. As a young woman she did a lot of native handicrafts, such as embroidery and making boots and clothing from seal skins. She continues to contribute to the community in this fashion, but failing eyesight prevents her from making boots and other clothing. For Martha Joshua, a survivor of the Spanish flu, being outdoors, taking in the fresh air, and visiting friends is her most pleasing pastime. In 1985, Anne Budgell and Nigel Markham directed a film, *The Last Days of Okak*, based on her experience and that of the missionaries and other Spanish flu survivors.

I was around seven years old when the Spanish flu hit my family's camp. We were hunting and fishing on an island off Okak. There were five of us children there. My grandfather was chopping wood in the fall. He had his dickey on, his hood up and an armload of wood when he collapsed there and then, and died. That same night, while I was sleeping in my bed, I woke suddenly when something heavy fell on me; that was my grandmother. She also died. That left my father's sister-in-law, her daughter and Emelia Merkuratsuk's son. The old lady was making ready to row the remaining children back to Okak when she collapsed and died.

The family had made lots of *pepsi** and *nipko**, and that's what the young girl fed us for awhile. One day when the sea got calm, the young girl dressed me up and got ready to pull the rowboat to sea. I was sitting and waiting for her until she had the boat pulled out. She told me to go into the house and wait for her until the boat was pulled out because, she said, it was cold outside. I obeyed and waited inside. After a while I got tired of waiting and went out to check on her. When I looked down the river, I saw her halfway to Okak. I sat down where I was and bawled and cried.

I don't remember a lot after that except that I cried and hollered for my grandparents every night. In the shock of all this, I even forgot about the baby. One day I was so cold that I had to find more blankets. I found the baby in the bed clothes. He lived for awhile, but I guess he starved to death since I didn't really know how to feed him or what to feed him or how to care for him.

I don't remember being very hungry, thirsty or even sleepy after everyone died. The house we lived in was a small *illusuak**. The husky dogs we had for work used to fight all the time. One day they broke a sack of hard bread. I somehow managed to save a little for myself. I lived on this and a handful of snow now and again for three months or so. I remember I could only sleep

Life, Love & Laughter

Life, Love & Laughter

sitting up. That winter, many dogs came to the island. They had shiny fur and were very wild. However, there was one dog who used to guard me from the other dogs.

I later found out that the young girl had left us because she thought she might die in the middle of the ocean and leave us to drown in the boat. She managed to get to Okak and told the minister Leoni that she had left me and the baby on the island. The minister tried to row over but the fall winds prevented him from reaching the island. After a while everyone figured us dead.

One day hunters came to the island. The first people I saw where Gustave Sillit and another man whose name I forget. They were shooting all the wild dogs and also shot the dog who protected me. The men did not know I was there, but when they killed the dog who protected me from the others I started to cry for the dog. I called out *"anaanak"** because I thought this dog was my mother. The dogs had made a terrible mess of the house with flour and everything else thrown about. I, too, was covered in flour and dirt. When these men saw me, they thought they had seen a ghost. After a while they brought me back to Okak.

My hair was stuck straight up with grime and dirt. It was full of lice, but at that time it didn't bother me at all. I had no boots and was using my grandfather's longjohns. I don't remember much of returning to Okak except that I could not eat or drink for a long while. The only food I could keep down was pepsi and drinking water.

When I left the island, the only thing I took with me was my grandfather's gramophone because this was rare at the time. The minister Leoni took a thick yellow story book which belonged to my family. I was supposed to get a sum of money for that, the minister said, but I don't know what he's done with it. All I know is that I lived to tell the tale.

Martha passed away on December 2nd, 1993.

Pepsi – dried fish or dried caribou meat
Nipko – dried seal meat
Illusuak – a house made from animal skin
Anaanak – Inuit word for mother
From the book The Finest Kind *by Marion Frances White. Creative Publishing. Used by permission.*

♀

✍ Letters From Our Friends
"...adopted by an American couple..."

Dear Ron,

I just wanted you to know that I really love your magazine.

I was adopted by an American couple at the age of three months and have never been home since. Your magazine has opened my home to me. It gave me some of my history that has been closed to me since I was adopted. I can never express how much that means to me. Not many people actually know a lot about Newfoundland, and I am trying to change that.

Thank you for giving me back, through your stories and jokes and your wonderful magazine, a sense of who I am and the people who are part of my history.

Sincerely,
Sharon Niccolini - Springfield, Ohio, USA

♀

Aunt Alice says:

At my age if all is not lost, where is it?

Spice of Life

Laugh and the world laughs with you. Cry and you cry with your girlfriends.

– *Laurie Kuslansk*

♀

👩 Out of Habit

Sister Mary Catherine and Sister Constance were driving down a country road when a sudden storm came up. The sky became black and foreboding, thunder boomed deafeningly, and the lightning flashes only added an eeriness to the frightening storm. After one bright flash the two nuns saw the devil was kneeling on the hood of their car, giving them a menacing stare.

"Show him your cross, Sister Mary Catherine. Show him your cross," shouted Sister Constance.

With that Sister Mary Catherine rolled down the passenger window, stuck her head out and, staring the devil in the eyes, shouted, "Get the hell off our hood!"

♀

✒ Quillings

She Never Knew A Feminist - Tim Brown

She worked hard Lord, you know she did
For nigh on eighty years
She patched our clothes and kept us fed
And hid away her tears

On many nights I would awaken
To her muffled cry
But she never seemed to have the time
To even question, why

There were seven kids who had to eat
From thirteen years to three
When father went down to defeat
In his last battle with the sea

How strong that woman had to be
After father had to leave
I never heard her curse the sea
I never heard her grieve

She never knew a feminist
At least not by that name
In both her roles she was the best
And filled them both the same

Her sacrifices stood the test
As she raised us on her own
She never knew a feminist
But she was feminist to the bone

♀

Life, Love & Laughter

Food for Thought

Drying a widow's tears is one of the most dangerous occupations known to man. – *Dorothy Dix*

♀

Some Mothers Have Them

"Why were you wearing white when you and Daddy got married?" asked little Jackson, as he browsed through a family photo album.

"Brides wear white because they are happy. Getting married is the happiest day of a woman's life," his mother explained.

"Then how come Daddy is wearing black?" queried Jackson.

♀

Female Firsts

1892: Amy Beach was the first woman to have her work performed by the Boston Symphony.

1892: The first woman 'fellow' of the Royal Geographical Society, Isabella Lucy Bird Bishop, an English traveller, lecturer and writer, was admitted.

1892: Hessie Donahue became the first woman to ever land a knockout punch to the legendary heavyweight boxing champion John L. Sullivan. He was part of Hessie's vaudeville act at the time of the incident. The two were acting out boxing for the audience when the great John L. accidentally gave Hessie a real blow. In return she clocked him and he was out for over a minute.

1894: The first woman in the U.S. elected to a state office was Estelle Reel Meyer, when she was elected State Superintendent of Public Instruction in Wyoming.

1894: The first sisters known to compete against each other at a tennis final at Wimbledon were Maud Watson and her older sister, Lilian. Maud won.

1894: The first hockey game for College girls took place at McGill University in Montreal.

1895: Annie Smith Peck became the first woman to reach the peak of the Matterhorn. She was 68 years old at the time. When she made her last climb (Mount Madison in New Hampshire), she was 82.

1895: The first women's softball team was formed at Chicago's West Division High School.

1895: The first woman to be hanged in New Zealand was Minnie Dean, who was hanged for "baby farming." Minnie would adopt unwanted babies for a fee, then dispose of them. The three little bodies exhumed in her back yard by police were part of the evidence that convicted her.

1896: On April 4, the first women's intercollegiate basketball championship was played between Stanford and the University of California at Berkely. Seven hundred women were in attendance to see Stanford win with a score of two to one.

♀

Life, Love & Laughter

WOMEN OF THE ISLAND AND THE BIG LAND

Joan Morrissey

A special thanks to Mr. Tom Cahill, a professional and personal friend of Ms. Morrissey, and to her daughters Beverly Thistle and Debbie Stafford, for their interviews.

Courtesy – The Morrissey Family

Joan, one of ten children, was born in St. John's on January 27, 1933 to Kathleen and Charles Learning. She made her singing debut on a *CJON Variety Show* when she was nine, which led to any number of engagements, but it was not until 1959 that she took up a career as a professional country and western singer. It has been said that she took to the stage like a duck to water. In 1952, at age 17, she married Tom Morrissey. They had six children; Debbie, Beverly, Colleen, Linda, Sherry and Tommy.

Joan gained a great deal of popularity on numerous VOCM programs and by her performance in such shows as the *CBC Variety Showcase* and *All Around the Circle*. She hosted prime-time *CJON Talent Showcase* and co-hosted CBC Radio's *Jamboree*. Joan performed live at the Admiral's Keg, Hotel Newfoundland on an 18-month contract, six nights a week. She also toured the province and sang at the Newfoundland Club in Nova Scotia and Toronto. She sang with many groups including The Dipsy Doodlers. Together with Tom Cahill, she wrote such classics as *The CN Bus*, *The Mobile Goat* and *Thank God We're Surrounded By Water*.

In 1969 Joan starred in the broadway musical *Annie Get Your Gun*, with a cast of 70 and a 25-piece orchestra. Staged at the Arts and Culture Centre and produced by Tom Cahill, the show was a smash hit. Later she played the role of Gypsy Rose Lee in the musical *Gypsy*.

Joan, who was nominated for a Juno award in the late 1960s, recorded three albums.

In her early 40s she suffered from severe depression and took her own life on January 10, 1978.

"There has never been a Joan Morrissey since Joan Morrissey. In context, if she were around today she would be the grand lady of show business because she put Newfoundland on the map long before the Newf-cult revolution began." – *Tom Cahill*

This story is told by her daughter, Debbie, through interviews with Marian Frances White.

In our eyes, Mom was basically the same person at home as she was on television. Of course, the one we saw in the daytime didn't look as good as the one at night because usually when we came home from school she had rollers in her hair. I don't think she started out to make singing her career, but eventually she saw it as a way to survive and to raise her family - and it worked for her. Mom loved to do parodies of popular songs she heard on the radio with lyrics pertaining to local situations or politics. Tom Cahill often wrote songs for her to sing. We'd come home from school and there she'd be, sitting down with her guitar, scribbling out lyrics and then putting new ones in. Sometimes we'd help her, or at least listen to her while she tried them out. For the most part she was her own manager, doing her business dealings during the day while we were in school. Although when I look back, it seems she was always on the phone trying to

Life, Love & Laughter

straighten out some contract.

Mom didn't read music. She learned it all from listening and watching. For her engagements she developed her own repertoire of songs and clever monologue routines. Even during the years when her career was at its peak, she made time to sing with us. We'd get out the guitar and jam in front of the fireplace. She always made sure she was home at special times, like our birthdays; that meant a lot to us kids. Mom had job offers in other provinces but she wanted to stay here because she said she could never feel at home anywhere else. I can still see her and Helen McNiven driving off in her little Volkswagon. The two of them would pile into it, luggage, equipment and all, and go off on a tour to such places as Kelligrews, Carbonear, Ochre Pit Cove, and West Coast or the Southern Shore. We were 16 and 17 then, so we could pretty well take care of ourselves. Her hectic schedule didn't mean a row of beans to me then, but now I honestly don't know where she got her energy to do the two jobs of mothering us and singing all the time as her career.

Mom was so organized. If she worked on a show during the day there would be a gigantic note on the refrigerator when we got home explaining where she was and who should do what in the house. When we were real young we lived in a big house on a pond beside Pippy Park. The pond is still there, but the house isn't. In the summertime we'd go down to the pond and Mom would wash clothes on a board, singing while she washed. I was only seven or eight but I remember her with the big board under one arm, the laundry under the other arm and sunlight soap in her hand. We'd go swimming in the other end while she washed and watched us. We have a picture of our dog, loose while Bev is tied to a tree! The garden was so big Mom was always afraid she'd lose her... we have lots of fun memories from there, even though we didn't have conveniences like running water.

Mom was constantly striving to get recognition for herself and for other Newfoundlanders because she could see the business she was in was a tough one and she often said she hoped it would get easier for the next generation behind her. She didn't push us to follow her footsteps because she knew it was a hard road to follow. She wanted us to do what we wanted to so, just as she had, I guess. I sang with her a bit, especially at benefits; she never turned one down and was given an award as Newfoundland's Good Will Ambassador. Her work was very time consuming and pressuring; and together with the pressures of raising six kids, I think she wanted an easier life for us.

When Mom was alive I really enjoyed working with her, but afterwards I had no inclination whatsoever to continue. The tribute I did with friends of hers at the Arts and Culture Centre after she died was something I felt I had to do because she often talked about us doing a show there together. If she was alive, perhaps I would have gone on, but it was a hectic life and, on times, a rough lifestyle. She wanted to expand her career and do more musicals, so the *Annie Get Your Gun* show was a real thrill for her and for us. Three weeks before the show opened she slipped on ice and broke her ankle. The cast on her ankle wasn't removed until the day of the opening, yet few people knew that in her cowgirl boot there was a thick bandage. The show was a smash hit and ran for six nights to packed houses. Mom would talk of doing more shows at the A & C because she wanted to get out of the bars and enjoy herself more as a stage performer.

She worked very hard, needless to say, but often her hard work did not pay off as was the case when she produced an album with Marathon Music Incorporation. The album sold over 50,000 copies but she received few royalties. She spoke her mind in the media, as she was very capable of doing, and Marathon tried to sue her for libel; however, their suit was thrown out of court. The company folded so she never did receive any amount of money.

Even though Mom seemed to work constantly, every now and again she'd take time off and go to the cabin in Paddy's Pond. The best thing for her about that place was the absence of a phone.

She loved the outdoors and would walk in the woods for hours or just go fishing. When she came back she would be rejuvenated. Everyone knew her as a very outgoing personality, but she could be shy and even though she had a tremendous get up and go when it came to show time, she really liked to sit back and listen to others once she was off stage. My mother brought me up to be a good, honest, hard-working person. She always said if you worked hard enough for something you would get it. My own greatest wish, even after all these years since her death, is that people not forget her - and when they do remember her, it would be with a smile.

From the book The Finest Kind *by Marian Frances White. Creative Publishing. Used by permission.*

♀

✎ *Letters From Our Friends*

"I met my husband when he was stationed at Pepperell...

Dear Downhomer,

I have to write you and tell you how much I enjoy the magazine. My sister sent me a subscription for a year. I dearly love it. I have read it over and over again. I always find something new, and wonderful letters and photos.

There have been a lot of changes since I left there. My home is Patricks Cove, Placentia Bay. I miss Newfoundland and now I know, since I got your magazine, what is happening. It sounds so wonderful. I met my husband when he was stationed at Pepperell many years ago. He has since passed away. He would also have loved your magazine.

Keep up the great letters and stories. God bless Newfoundland and all your staff.

Sincerely,

Alice Gainey – Clinton, North Carolina, USA

PS: I hope to get your cookbook very soon.

♀

Life's Funny Experiences

Ten for a Buck

This story demonstrates how local cultural terminology can get you into trouble. In 1976 I accepted a teaching position in Georgia. Since I was new in town, I decided to attend one of the local churches and try to meet and make some new friends. This particular church was having a potluck dinner after the service. Since I was new, the church members asked that I join them - which I did. While sitting and having dinner with my new-found friends, the pastor of this church came up and inquired from me, "May I have a yankee dime?" Not knowing what he meant by this southern term, I asked him, "What is a yankee dime?" He responded, "A kiss on the cheek." I then asked this minister, "What do y'all do for a yankee dollar?" Realizing what I just said in jest, I immediately turned three shades of red.

For the next four weeks, as I would leave after the service, the minister would chuckle and say, "Here comes that yankee girl, hide your dollars."

Cynthia – Michigan, USA

♀

Life, Love & Laughter

MABEL & MANLEY

As the hymn was ending, Manley noticed that his wife Mabel was sound asleep in the church pew beside him. So when the organ's final note had almost faded into silence, he leaned over and whispered the number of the next hymn in her ear to awaken her without drawing attention. As soon as Mabel heard the number she jumped up and shouted, "Bingo!"

♀

Ennellene

Men are big on ideas
Big in the gut
Big in misunderstanding
A pain in the butt

Spice of Life

My second favourite household chore is ironing. My first being hitting my head on the top bunk bed until I faint.

– Erma Bombeck

♀

Some Mothers Have Them

When Jackson was six, his mother overheard him reciting the Lord's Prayer, "And forgive us our trash passes, as we forgive those who passed trash against us."

♀

Life's Funny Experiences

The Irate Customer

An award should go to the United Airlines gate agent in Denver for being smart and funny, and making her point, when confronted with a passenger who probably deserved to fly as cargo. A crowded United flight was cancelled. A single agent was rebooking a long line of inconvenienced travellers. Suddenly an angry passenger pushed his way to the desk. He slapped his ticket down on the counter and said, "I have to be on this flight and it has to be first class." The agent replied, "I'm sorry sir. I'll be happy to try to help you, but I've got to help these folks first, and I'm sure we'll be able to work something out." The passenger was unimpressed. He asked loudly, so that the passengers behind him could hear, "Do you have any idea who I am?"

Without hesitating, the gate agent smiled and grabbed her public address microphone. "May I have your attention please?" she began, her voice bellowing throughout the terminal. "We have a passenger here at the gate who does not know who he is. If anyone can help him find his identity, please come to the gate."

With the folks behind him in line laughing hysterically, the man glared at the United agent, gritted his teeth and swore, "F*** you!"

Without flinching, she smiled and said, "I'm sorry, sir, but you'll have to stand in line for that, too."

Submitted by Lorianne – Sheridan, Colorado, USA

♀

Life, Love & Laughter

Tickle and Bight *By Lucy Fitzpatrick–McFarlane*

The Perfect Marriage

I know Mom warned me before I took my vows there could be trouble in paradise if I married a Protestant. "You mark my words," she said, "mixed marriages never work. Couldn't you have waited a little longer until you found a good Newfoundland Catholic to settle down with?"

Well, that was 25 years ago come April and I can say with total confidence that after a quarter of a century of being together, we're still talking to each other and can argue as good as the next couple. What's the secret to our marital bliss, you might ask? Well, I'll tell you. I don't have a clue. That's the gospel truth. Note well that I have not said we have the PERFECT marriage. That only happens in the movies or in fairy tales and besides, that theory clashes with both our religious beliefs. Perfection, after all, is in the eye of the beholder. But if I have to comment on what constitutes a perfect marriage, then I'd have to say what comes immediately to mind: If a couple can get through a week without nagging each other about something or uttering the words, "when hell freezes over," then that's as close to perfection as any marriage can get.

Doesn't sound like the ideal marriage, does it. That's because I've edited the romantic trimmings and fast-forwarded to reality. We all know that the honeymoon is over when you unpack the suitcases and realize that one of you has to wash the dirty laundry and cook dinner. It's a rude awakening for newlyweds who start their lives together with great expectations of living on love the rest of their lives and clinging to the impossible dream of changing everything about each other that you don't like. I remember how it was. I had a list longer than my arm of things that needed fixing on Murray and I was convinced he'd be just perfect as soon as I made him over in my image and likeness. I even dared to hope that Mom would forgive him for not being Catholic or at the very least, that she'd stop calling him stun pole. But I was dead wrong. Trying to change that man was like trying to get blood from a turnip. And thank goodness he didn't budge, because these 25 years would've been disastrous if I had to live with someone as stubborn as I am.

It was quite a shock when we first found out that we were not compatible and the words "for better, for worse" suddenly had a new meaning. It seemed that all the BETTER things took a turn for the WORSE overnight. Trouble was, we both wanted to sleep on the same side of the bed and neither of us was willing to give it up. He had a sports injury and needed to keep his right leg on the floor while he slept and I had this thing about not being able to sleep unless I was facing the door. Finally, after a week of snarling at each other, we came up with a solution to accommodate both our needs. We moved the bed to the opposite side of the room...our very first lesson in learning how to compromise. I think that's when we realized that although we believe marriage is a union, it wasn't going to work if we both thought we were management. We couldn't agree on anything. He liked to sleep on top of the covers with the heat turned up in the winter and I liked lots of heavy blankets with the heat turned way down. It seems that every day we clashed over something. I liked to stay up all night and he liked to go to bed early. He liked sports and I hated them with a passion. My idea of romance was a candle-lit dinner with roses, while his was

Kentucky Fried Chicken from a take-out and flowers that needed to be dusted. He made decisions on the spur of the moment and I took days to deliberate. We saw a side of each other that we never knew existed and the only thing we had in common was the fact that we agreed to disagree. The time we spent trying to prove to each other that we were compatible was just not worth it, so we gave up trying and accepted the fact that we are different.

To me, marriage is like a seesaw. Sometimes you're up and sometimes you're down, but it takes two to make it work. If one or the other falls off, then you help the other climb back on again. And there's no such thing as a 50/50 arrangement. Some days one spouse gives 60% and the other 40% and then there are times when the role is reversed. The thing is, once you uncover the weakness and strengths in each other, then you have to either overlook them or accept them. Like my cooking, for instance. I was far from being a domestic goddess and I've never made a secret of that. I walked into our marriage with very little in my hope chest other than a can opener, my old diary and a dozen *Archie* comic books that I'd saved. I did my best to make the meals exciting, but there are only so many ways you can dress up beans and fried potatoes. I got really ticked off when his mother interfered and began sending him care packages every week. And when she sent me a cookbook, I was so devastated that I almost packed my grip and headed home to Newfoundland to live with Mom. Naturally I blamed Murray for complaining about my lack of culinary skills and I got very angry. "If you don't like my cooking, then you can do it yourself!" I snapped.

It took a lot of cajoling, apologizing and talking to get past that big hurdle, but we got through the arbitration stage. Once we established a few guidelines, things ran more smoothly and we decided to take turns cooking and agreed to eat whatever the other made without complaint. I promised to read the cookbook if he would tell his mother not to send food and to stop phoning collect to ask what he had for dinner. To this day, my husband does the grocery shopping and I put them away. If he wants something special to eat, he cooks it and when my turn comes, I open the cans of my choice. As for the cookbook, well I READ it, as promised, and I put it to good use - to prop up the end of the sofa that had a missing leg.

Oh, yes, you have to be flexible in a relationship and learn how to work out your differences. And believe me, you learn the hard way...through trial and error. There are no rules to follow and since it is your marriage, you can run it the way you want. And if there are things you can't change, then you may as well live with that fact. That's why I finally got my own television because I knew I'd never get custody of the remote control when Murray was watching sports. If it means having a heated argument over something occasionally, then so be it. Most happily married couples argue and if they say they don't, they're lying. Life would be pretty boring if the two of you agreed on everything all of the time. I love bickering back and forth; and what's more, I think it's healthy. Now Murray may call it an argument if we have a difference of opinion, but I call it communication. Sometimes when I can't make him see things my way, he'll agree with me just to hush me up, especially if there's a hockey game on TV. And there's nothing more infuriating to me than leaving an argument unfinished. An hour later, that man has already forgotten we ever had a discussion and by then, I've built up a grudge bigger than both of us.

He actually has to ASK why I'm mad at him. "You KNOW!" I say, fixing him with the hairy eyeball.

Now I know he doesn't have a clue why I'm so mad...sometimes I don't remember myself, but he's a husband, so a wife can always find something he's done wrong. You see, it doesn't matter which of you gives in first and says you're sorry, just as long as you can keep peace in the house. But I know that my husband hates it when I give him the silent treatment, so he eventually apologizes and promises never do it again, even though he doesn't know what he's done in the first place. Whatever works, right. Course, I've had 25 years practice to hone my skill, so I'd never recommend it to newlyweds.

I don't know...maybe we tackled things the wrong way and that's why we don't have the perfect marriage like other people seem to have. I see other couples holding hands and kissing in public and it looks so romantic, but yet I know I'd probably give Murray a black eye if he tried that mushy stuff with me in the middle of the mall. Heck, sometimes you can't even tell we're a couple. We never wear matching T-shirts, sing duets at parties, finish each other's sentences, eat off the same plate or open each other's mail. But we do respect and trust one another, enough so that we feel confident to do our own thing, to be independent and function as individuals. We're always there for each other even though we may be in separate rooms, and when we sit with our feet touching on the coffee table as he watches sports and I read my book, you can't find a more contented couple. In other words, we suit each other. We're soul mates and we've grown accustomed to our style. And that little bit I mentioned about Murray apologizing when he doesn't know what for? I'll let you in on a little secret. He knows I'm too stubborn to admit that I'm wrong or say I'm sorry to him, so he pretends it's his fault just to let me off the hook. Now what couple in their right minds would spoil a good thing like that?

Reprinted from Downhomer *magazine.*

♀

Spice of Life

Wrinkles are hereditary. Parents get them from their children. – *Doris Day*

♀

Aunt Alice says:

I've found that it's a lot easier to get older than it is to get wiser.

Food for Thought

I am an atheist, and that's it. I believe there's nothing we can know except that we should be kind to each other and do what we can for other people. – *Katharine Hepburn*

♀

♀

Her Other Half

Senior Sex

Age was taking its toll on George's virility so he decided to try Viagra. This worked so well that the couple had a better sex life than they had in the early years of their marriage. That was until his wife became ill.

After her doctor examined her at his office he said, "I don't know how to tell you this my dear, but you are pregnant."

"I can't be pregnant, Doctor, I'm 75 years old!" she exclaimed.

"Well I don't know why you are, but you are," nodded the doctor.

"My God," she said, "I'll have to call George right away. Can I use your phone?"

When George picked up on the other end she shouted, "George! I'm pregnant!"

"Who is this?" answered her husband.

♀

Spice of Life

Since we have to speak well of the dead, let's knock them while they are alive.

– Joan Sloan

♀

Is That a Fact?

Many things are taken as facts. Not all of them are.

Who was Betty Crocker?

Everybody knows Betty Crocker, the well–known writer of cookbooks.

The fact is that Betty Crocker is not a real person. The name was invented by an advertising man to use as the author of cookbooks published by General Mills. Betty was a common female name at the time and Crocker was the last name of the director of General Mills.

♀

Female Firsts

1897: Clara Brett Martin became Canada's first lawyer and the first woman to practise law in the entire British Empire.

1897: Lena Jordan became the first person to successfully execute the triple somersault on the flying trapeze. It was 12 years before a man accomplished the feat.

1898: Frances Mason became the first woman bank president when she took over the Limerick National Bank in Limerick, Maine, U.S.A.

1898: Lizzie Arlington became the first woman to sign a professional baseball contract. She was the pitcher for the Philadelphia Reserves in her first professional game.

1899: Beatrice Hinkle became the first North American woman doctor to hold a public health position when she took the job in San Francisco.

1900: The first women's ice hockey league was organized in Quebec. The league had three teams from Montreal, one from Quebec City and another from Trois-Rivieres.

1901: Annie Taylor became the first person to go over Niagara Falls in a custom-built barrel and survive.

1902: The biographical novel form was first introduced to the world by a woman writer named Gertrude Atherton.

1902: The first public school nursing system was begun by American social worker, Lillian D. Wald, who also organized the Visiting Nurse Service.

1902: The first American woman to appear on a U.S. postage was the original "First Lady," Martha Washington.

1903: A women's curling team from Quebec City became the first to defeat a men's curling team when they beat the Royal Caledonia team in Scotland.

♀

Food for Thought

I usually make up my mind about a man in ten seconds, and I very rarely change it.
– Margaret Thatcher, former Prime Minister of Britain

♀

Reading the Rights

A couple goes on vacation to a fishing resort in northern Minnesota. The husband likes to fish at the crack of dawn. The wife likes to read.

One morning the husband returns after several hours of fishing and decides to take a nap. Although not familiar with the lake, the wife decides to take the boat out. She motors out a short distance, anchors and reads her book. Along comes a law enforcement officer in his boat. He pulls up alongside the woman and says, "Good morning, Ma'am. What are you doing?"

"Reading a book," she replies.

"You're in a restricted fishing area," he informs her.

"I'm sorry officer, but I'm not fishing, I'm reading."

"Yes, but you have all the equipment. I'll have to take you in and write you up."

"If you do that, I'll have to charge you with sexual assault," says the woman.

"But I haven't even touched you," says the officer.

"That's true, but you have all the equipment."

MORAL: Never argue with a woman who reads. It's likely she can also think.

Author Unknown

♀

I Will Follow Him: A War Bride's Story

By Margaret Rowe

I was attracted to him from the minute of our meeting in the living room of an elderly friend to whose house he and his pal had been directed to spend their first leave since joining the Royal Air Force. I was on my way to hockey practice and dressed anything but conventionally in a very short guy tunic and long black stockings.

His friend, of the roaming eye, suggested a date. I agreed and volunteered my roommate Pat as a date for Ernie. We went to the Saturday night dance at the Palladium. Pat mesmerised Jack with her expertise on the dance floor and before long, I found myself discussing poetry with the tall skinny one with the incredible blue eyes. A unique approach, but it worked!

That was in October 1940. We wrote to each other when the leave was over and I was enchanted when he sent me a tiny, beautifully bound copy of the *Rubyiat of Omar Khayam* with the appropriate passage underlined. I did not need the emphasis on "a loaf of bread, a jug of wine and thou" to know that I had met the man with whom I wanted to spend the rest of my life.

We married in 1942 and had a wonderful life until his death in 1976. I have been alone for 20 years, many times longing for male companionship but reluctant to take that step that could only lead to disappointment after such happiness with my talented, loving and loveable Newfoundlander.

From the book, We Came From Over the Sea. *Published by the British War Brides Association of Newfoundland and Labrador in co-operation with ESPress. Used by permission.*

♀

Life, Love & Laughter

Spice of Life

"Lady with trailer wants to meet Gentleman with car. Object; to get hitched!"

♀

Her Other Half

Split Decision

"My wife and I don't always share the same interests," a man told his friend over a beer at a bar. "Just the other night, for example, we were going out for the evening. I wanted to see a Bruce Willis movie and she wanted to see *Phantom of the Opera*. But eventually we reached a compromise."

"And how did you enjoy *Phantom*?" asked his friend.

♀

Animal Mating - Fact and Fantasy – *Ron Young*

Porcupine Procreation

Fact:

"How do Porcupines make love? Very carefully," according to a study of a colony of porcupines kept at the Biology Department of the University of Buffalo during the 1940s.

The colony consisted of five females and three males. When the male was in the mood for love, he would get himself excited in a porcupine version of Michael Jackson on stage. He'd also sing in a whining way as he approached a female. He would then smell her all over and show off his outstanding assets. If she was not interested, she would "object vocally, strike with her front paws, as though boxing, threaten or try to bite...and run away."

When she was in the mood for mating, she would put more "vim, vigor and action" into what ever she was doing, especially when she would "ride a stick" for the same purpose and in the same manner as her male counterpart. And once she agreed to the copulation she would make the male go on until he was exhausted, and then chase after him to re-establish contact when he tried to get away. If he didn't give in to her wishes she would approach a nearby male and act out "the male role in coition with the uninvolved male." After several hours though, she would become disinterested and reject him, but throughout copulation (which is performed in the same manner as with most four-legged mammals), her sharp quills never got in the way or caused any damage. They lay limp and flat, just as his did. Isn't nature wonderful?

Fantasy:

So, if you ever should incline
To mate with a porcupine
But the prickly prospect's not that thrilling
To this, I have to say,
"Every female likes foreplay
And the prospect's pleasing when she's more than willing"

♀

Women Who Have Made A Difference – *By Ron Young*

Candace, Empress of Ethiopia, in 332 B.C. was one of the greatest generals of the ancient world and world famous as a military tactician and field commander. Legend has it that Alexander the Great would not entertain even the possibility of having his world fame and unbroken chain of victories marred by risking a defeat, at last, to a woman. So he halted his armies at the borders of Ethiopia and did not invade to meet the waiting black armies with their queen in personal command.

Agnodice of Greece in 4th century BC, dressed in men's clothing so she could attend the medical classes of the famous doctor Herophilos and practise gynecology disguised as a man. Other doctors, jealous of her fame, accused her of corrupting women. In court she was forced to reveal her sex in order to save her life. Then new charges were brought against her, of practicing a profession restricted by law to men alone. Eventually she was acquitted by the Athenian court.

Adrienne Clarkson, Governor General and Commander-in-Chief of Canada, was born in Hong Kong and came to Canada as a refugee with her family during the war in 1942. A leading figure in Canada's cultural life, Madame Clarkson has had a rich and distinguished career in broadcast, journalism, the arts and public service, including 18 years as an award-winning TV host/interviewer for such shows as CBC's, "Take Thirty," "Adrienne At Large" and "The Fifth Estate."

Joan of Arc, the French peasant girl, was only 12 when she began hearing "voices" of St. Michael, Ste. Catherine and Ste. Margaret, believing them to have been sent by God. These voices told her that it was her divine mission to free her country from the English and help the dauphin (king) gain the French throne. They told her to cut her hair, dress in a man's uniform and to pick up arms.

By 1429 the English, with the help of their Burgundian allies, occupied Paris and all of France north of the Loire. The resistance was minimal due to lack of leadership and a sense of hopelessness. Henry VI of England was claiming the French throne.

Joan convinced the captain of the dauphin's forces, and then the dauphin himself, of her calling. After passing an examination by a board of theologians, she was given troops to command and the rank of captain.

At the battle of Orleans in May 1429, Joan led the troops to a miraculous victory over the English. She continued fighting the enemy in other locations along the Loire. Fear of troops under her leadership was so formidable that when she approached Lord Talbot's army at Patay, most of the English troops and Commander Sir John Fastolfe fled the battlefield. Fastolfe was later stripped of his Order of the Garter for this act of cowardice. Although Lord Talbot stood his ground, he lost the battle, lost 1800 of his soldiers and was captured along with a 100 English noblemen.

Charles VII was crowned king of France on July 17, 1429, in Reims Cathedral. At the coronation, Joan was given a place of honor next to the king. Later, she was ennobled for her services to the country.

In 1430 she was captured by the Burgundians while defending Compiegne near Paris and was sold to the English. The English, in turn, handed her over to the ecclesiastical court at Rouen led by Pierre Cauchon, a pro-English Bishop of Beauvais, to be tried for witchcraft and heresy. Much was made of her insistence on wearing male clothing. She was told that for a woman to wear men's clothing was a crime against God. Her determination to continue wearing it (because her voices hadn't yet told her to change, as well as for protection from sexual abuse by her jailors) was seen as defiance and finally sealed her fate. Joan was convicted after a 14-month interrogation and on May 30, 1431, she was burned at the stake in the Rouen marketplace. Charles VII made no attempt to come to her rescue. She was 19 years old at the time of her execution.

♀

Life, Love & Laughter

☺ Some Mothers Have Them

The Sunday school teacher asked, "Now, Jackson, tell me frankly do you say prayers before eating?" "No Ma'am," little Jackson replied, "I don't have to. My mom is a good cook."

♀

Quillings

Lady of the Evening
Ron Young

She was a rare dark-eyed beauty
With an innocent look men admire
She was born to poor parents who loved her
They named her Shelly McGuire

She ran away to Toronto
When she was barely sixteen
And on the streets of her little home town
Shelly was nevermore seen

The streets of the city, they glistened and sang
And welcomed young Shelly McGuire
She drew men, young and old,
with her fresh innocence
And traded on their every desire

Now she sends money home to her parents
But to them, it's of no consequence
For they claim they no longer own her,
and she
No longer claims innocence

Like Cain she now walks the lean,
lonely streets
Her hopes and her dreams down the drain
She doesn't know how
she can stay one more day
Yet she never can go home again

♀

🎭 Her Other Half

Quick Change Artist

A well-known painter of nudes arrived at his loft studio one day with a splitting headache. The nude model he had hired to pose for his most recent painting was waiting for him when he arrived. As he entered she started to disrobe.

"Don't bother to do that," he said to his model. "I have a headache and I am going home as soon as I have a small brandy."

"Then at least let me get the brandy for you," offered the gorgeous lady.

"Thank you," said the artist, "and if you'd like, pour one for yourself."

The two were sitting and sipping their brandies, when the sound of familiar footsteps were heard coming up the stairs to the studio.

"It's my wife," whispered the artist. "Quick, get your clothes off."

♀

Female Firsts

1904: At the Cheyenne Frontier Days rodeo, Bertha Kapernick became the first woman to give bronco riding exhibitions.

1904: Mary McLeod Bethune became the first woman to establish a secondary school, which later became a four-year accredited college.

1904: At just 16 years of age, Amanda Clement of Iowa became the first female umpire to officiate a men's baseball game for pay.

1905: Mary Whiton Calkins became the first female president of the American Psychological Association. *See also page 179.*

1906: Madge Syers became the first female world figure skating champion. She won again the following year.

1906: The first Canadian provincial women's ice hockey tournament took place in Banff, Alberta, with a six-team league.

1907: The first organized bowling league for women took place in St. Louis, Missouri.

1907: The first pre-school for children was started in Rome by Maria Montessori.

1907: Australian swimmer Annette Kellerman became the first underwater ballerina at the New York Hippodrome.

1908: Madge Syers became the first female Olympic figure skating gold medalist at the London Games.

1909: The Canadian Criminal Code was amended to criminalize the abduction of women. Before this, the abduction of any woman over 16 was legal, except if she was an heiress. The maximum penalty for stealing a cow was much higher than for kidnapping an heiress.

1909: Sweden's Selma Lagerlof became the first woman to win the Nobel Prize for literature.

♀

Feminine Words & Phrases

Bridal: This adjective, which refers to things that are pertaining to the bride, came from "bride-ale," a drink which was specially brewed and sold to raise money for the church in which the couple were married. It was sometimes called "church-ale."

Chippie: The knee-length gown worn by a prostitute in the red light district of New Orleans, as well as the same lady of the evening who wore the apparel.

Damsel: A young woman in the era of shining knights. The name is believed to be derived from *damoisele*, the French word for the female opposite of an English squire.

Distaff side: The female side of the family tree - females, who are descendants of females.

♀

Animal Mating – Fact and Fantasy – *Ron Young*

The Small One That Got Away

Fact:

There is a tropical fish found off Okinawa that is a unique change artist. The male turncoat fish (not his real name) will mate with with one or more females until a bigger male joins the group. The smaller turncoat then, by restructuring its brain and genitalia, becomes a subservient female. When the bigger fish leaves or dies, he (or she, or whatever) will revert to its original male role.

Fantasy:

'Though I am a male at heart
My survival plays a part
To cope with bullies I do all I can
So if you move into my harem
I really don't like to share 'em
But if you need another woman, I'm your man

♀

Spice of Life

A man's got to do what a man's got to do. A woman must do what he can't.

– *Rhonda Hansome*

♀

Letters From Our Friends

"...saw a letter I had written to the *Downhomer*..."

Dear Ron and friends at *Downhomer*,

While on a recent trip to Newfoundland and other parts of Canada, I met many relatives and friends, some I hadn't seen for many years.

About 60 years ago I went to school with a girl whose family was spending two years in Burlington, on the Baie Verte Peninsula, while the father worked there. Phyllis Norman and her mother Nellie England, formerly of Harry's Harbour, now live in Sudbury, Ontario. A couple of years ago the mother saw a letter I had written to *Downhomer* and Phyllis started writing me. So it was a pleasure for me to find them again and to go to Sudbury on this trip to spend a few days with them.

I had the most magical trip in the most beautiful corner of the world, catching up with relatives, classmates I hadn't seen since school days, and many old friends.

Sincerely,
Vida Rideout – Springwood, Queensland, Australia

♀

Life, Love & Laughter

WOMEN OF THE ISLAND AND THE BIG LAND

Mary Walsh

Courtesy – CBC

Mary Walsh was born into a family of eight in St. John's on May 13, 1952. She was raised by her aunts Mary Waddleton and Josephine Walkins and her Uncle Jack Waddleton. Mary came out of high school in 1969 "bloodied but not beaten." Engaged to an American serviceman, she took a part-time job at the Arcade a Water Street department store. But in 1970 she left the Arcade and her fiancé to work with CBC Radio and CBC Television's *Here and Now*. Mary also performed and toured extensively with the Newfoundland Travelling Theatre Company where she met other members of CODCO in their first show, *Cod on a Stick*. This was the early 1970s - a time that marked an era of irreverent and award-winning work by that group, which helped establish Newfoundland's reputation as a hotbed of theatrical activity. In 1978 Mary held the lead role in the TV show, *The Root Cellar* and performed in *Up At Ours*. In 1979 she toured with Theatre Passe Muraille through England and Wales, and 1980 marked Mary's directorial work in *Terras de Bacalhua*. Since then she has directed a string of successful shows such as *A Child is Crying on the Stairs*. In 1982-83, Mary was Programme Anamateur at the L.S.P.U. Hall and in 1983 joined the Wonderful Grand Band, who toured nationally and produced a series of TV shows. In 1986, Mary starred in Newfoundland's first feature length film, *The Adventures of Fautus Bidgood*. That same year she rejoined with the CODCO group for a national TV series, which ran on CBC until 1992. During this time, Mary continued to do projects at the L.S.P.U. Hall such as *Ntesinan*, a play about the Innu of Labrador. In April 1988, her own play, *Hockey Wives*, premiered in Toronto.

Since 1993, Mary has been performing and writing on the hit CBC series *This Hour Has 22 Minutes*. She has also appeared on many TV programs such as *Major Crime* (1997), "Dooley Gardens" (1999) and *Bleacher Bums* (2002). She has also concentrated on more films, appearing in *Secret Nation* (1992), *The Boys of St. Vincent* (1993), *Extraordinary Visitor* (1998), *New Waterford Girl* (1999), *The Divine Ryans* (1999), *Violet* (2000), *Rare Birds* (2001), *Random Passage* (2001) and *Mambo Italiano* (2003). She has also just wrapped her latest film *Les Belles Soeurs*. Mary has garnered more than a dozen Gemini Awards, the Earle Grey Award for outstanding contribution to Canadian television, and honorary doctorates from Memorial University of Newfoundland, Trent University in Ontario and the University of Prince Edward Island. Mary is also a recipient of the Order of Canada.

******

Once my mother gave me a red coat.

Once when I was eleven my mother and father came out from around the bay where they moved that year and brought me, on the fleetline bus, home with them.

Once my mother sent me a Christmas card that said, in her writing, Merry Christmas, Love Mom

Once when my sister was angry with me, when I was 15 and drunk and hurling insults, my father took me outside and walked me around the yard and told me that I was his little girl.

Once when I was 18 months old, Aunt Mae and Uncle Jack and Aunt Phine took me next door

Life, Love & Laughter

to live with them because I was just out of the hospital with pneumonia and my parents' house was damp and theirs was dry...and that was it, that's where I stayed and grew up, from then on they were my parents.

And the one person who has made me, who has influenced the way I am, the way I fit into the world is Aunt Mae.

The overwhelming truth about the nature of this piece just struck me...the fact that these Almanacs are going to be hanging around in people's pocketbooks on the table next to the phone...this is not disposable stuff...this could haunt you...this could fall into your brother's hands sometime and you could receive a series of late night drunken phone calls from Alberta...see, I'm in trouble already. Well, no point worrying about the future...on with bothering the past.

If you were to ask me what the major influences on my work were...Do you want to ask me that question? Do you care even a little bit what they are? Ah, go on and ask me just for a laugh...My reply would be my family...Tho' I didn't really grow up with them, they've informed everything I've written...them and Aunt Mae.

Sometimes I actually, and I'm blushing as I write this, steal the words right out of their mouths; but mostly it's, but usually, it's an attitude I borrow from them. My oldest characters, Mrs. Budgell, Mrs. Ball, Bette Furlong, all seem to be different parts of Aunt Mae with a little of Mom thrown in and, of course, a bit of me.

In 1971, I was much more active in the women's movement than I've been ever since...at that time I was involved in a fairly destructive personal relationship...and I remember I went through a year of consciousness-raising and I never once told any of the women in the group what was happening in my life...of course I was only 19 at the time, but I just seem to have been plagued for years and years with that "Catholic I grew up in downtown St. John's and I'm not as good as everyone else" syndrome...I thought my problems to be so plebian in nature that they, of course, could be of no interest to these largely middle-class women...in truth, I have no idea what class these women were, it was just an uninformed assumption on my part. On that, thank God, I'm getting out of the habit of making.

Everyone else seems to lead a much more "Leave it to Beaver, Father Knows Best" kind of life...with a white-collar dad, a car, a house in around the back of town, and sisters who were head of the student council...we lived on Carter's Hill, right in the centre of town. One year I waited at the bus stop in front of the Basilica...I went to Mercy School...pretending to be getting the bus to my well-appointed home "in around the back of town" 'til everyone else had gotten on their busses and I could trip down over the hill to my well-appointed home on Carter's Hill.

What is she getting at now, you ask. Are ya askin that? Are ya? Go ahead ask me just for amusement sake...well, aside from family, matters of class distinction between the haves and the have-nots, between the upper class and the under class, would seem to be the other theme that informs my work.

Well, that's it. Except to say that I find getting older is better, a lot better. You just get so sick and tired of the upkeep and maintenance costs of the castle of hurts that you've been building brick by miserable brick since the first real or imagined rejection in your life...you just get so weary of it. You're forced to start a demolition process...now of course, you're not a fool, you don't bring the huge wrecking ball...It'd be too frightening...God where could I live if not in the castle? Anyway, you start dismantling the huge, costly west wing bit by bit and maybe you rip it all down; or maybe you're left with a small manageable cottage of hurts by the end.

From the book The Finest Kind *by Marian Frances White. Creative Publishing. Used by permission.*

♀

Women Who Have Made A Difference – *By Ron Young*

Cleopatra VII was the most popular of seven queens with the same name. She came to power at the tender age of 17 and was instrumental in making Kemet (Egypt) into the world's number one super power at that time.

Eka Esu-Williams founded the Society of *Women Against AIDS in Africa* (SWAA) in Nigeria in 1988. Traditionally, African girls and women were taught to be submissive to their husbands and accepting of the practice of polygamy and wife inheritance. At the time she founded SWAA, 80% of all women with AIDS were living in Africa. SWAA held workshops for the purpose of educating girls and women about this disease and instructing them in safe sex practices. In the SWAA workshops women also learn about self-esteem and how to gain control of their own lives.

Williamina Paton Stevens Fleming obtained work as a maid in the home of Professor Edward Pickering, then director of the Harvard Observatory. After she was abandoned by her husband, while pregnant with their child. Pickering was unhappy with the work performed by his male employees and declared that his maid could do a better job than they did, so he hired her in 1881 to do clerical work and some mathematical calculations at the Observatory. Fleming proved not only to be a good clerk, but also a good scientist. She devised a system of classifying stars, which was later named after her. She was also the first person to discover stars called "white dwarfs," a discovery of astronomic proportions in itself.

Balkis Makeda, Queen of Sheba, was ruler of Ethiopia a thousand years before Christ was born, when that nation was second only to Egypt in power and fame in the world. She was so impressed by the exciting story of King Solomon, brought back to her from Israel by her servant Tamrin, that the great queen decided to visit the king herself. This visit was extraordinary, even by ancient standards. The beautiful, black African woman and her vast array of resplendent attendants travelled over the Sahara desert into Israel with gold, spices of very great store, precious stones, carried by more than 797 camels, plus donkeys and mules too numerous to count. The value of the gold alone, which she gave to King Solomon, would be $3,690,000 today and was of much greater worth in antiquity. Makeda was very impressed with King Solomon and his young nation.

"Your wisdom and goodness," she told him, "are beyond all measure. They are excellence itself. Under your influence I am placing new values on life."

Solomon was also much impressed with Makeda; he wished to have a son from her regal African lineage. On the night before Makeda returned to Ethiopia, Solomon coerced the queen into having sex with him.

The following day as the queen and her entourage prepared to leave Israel, the king placed a ring on her hand and stated, "If you have a son, give this to him and send him to me."

The queen did have a son who visited his father when he became an adult. While her son was in Israel, she sent a message to Solomon to anoint their son as king of Ethiopia and to mandate that thenceforth only the males descended from their son should rule the land of Sheba, changing the history of her country, which up to then had seen a line of "virgin" queens.

Menelik, as he was renamed by his father, returned to rule the Land of Sheba and his famous line has continued down to the 20th century. Even now, the ruler of Ethiopia is the "conquering lion of Judah," descended directly from King Solomon and the Queen of Sheba.

♀

Life, Love & Laughter

Life, Love & Laughter

The Whys of Men

Why don't women blink during foreplay?
Because they don't have enough time.

♀

MABEL & MANLEY

"What do the cards say about me, Mabel?" asked Manley as he sat across the table from his wife, who was reading his fortune in the cards.

"They say you're handsome, witty and a great sex partner," she told him as she scrutinized the cards facing her.

"Really?" said Manley.

"Yes, Manley," she smirked, "and they got your age and weight wrong, too."

♀

Spice of Life

Liquor is a substance that makes a married man see double and feel single.

♀

Female Firsts

1910: On March 8, Baroness Raymonde de Laroche became the first woman in the world to be issued a pilot's license.

1910: Québec legislation reduced the working hours for women in the textile industry from 60 to 58 hours per week, the first of other legislative amendments to reduce women's work week.

1910: The first general-education school for girls in Cairo was organized and begun by Huda Sha'arawi.

1910: Ms C. J. Walker became the first self-made female millionaire in America.

1910: Mrs. John B. Dodd started the tradition of Father's Day.

1911: The first women's flying school was founded in France, run by qualified pilot Jane Herveux.

1911: The famous United Artists motion picture production company was begun by Mary Pickford to give her control over her own movies. The associates she chose as partners were Douglas Fairbanks, D.W. Griffith and Charlie Chaplain.

1911: Helene Britton became the first woman to own a major league baseball team, the St. Louis Cardinals.

1912: On April 16, Harriet Quimby became the first woman to fly over the English Channel.

1912: The Girl Scouts of America was founded by Juliette Low, who became its first president.

1913: Georgia "Tiny" Broadwick became the first woman to make a parachute jump from an airplane. At the height of 2,000 feet she released herself from the trap seat of a biplane piloted by Glenn L. Martin, after taking off from Griffith Park, California. Also during that year, she became the first person to begin a parachute flight from a seat in front of an airplane on a level with the propeller.

♀

The *Florizel* Disaster

By Cassie Brown

Mrs. Mike McDonald doesn't think too much about it these days because the memory of the wreck of the *Florizel* has not been a pleasant one. She does recall it as a terrible experience and it ended her hopes of ever seeing a bit of the world before she settled down.

Kitty Cantwell was going to visit her sister in New York that winter and was eager to see some of the United States before her marriage to Mike McDonald, and it was a happy young girl who boarded the *Florizel* that Saturday, February 23, 1918.

Kitty's travelling companion was her good friend, Miss Annie Dalton of Western Bay, who was also going to New York to take up a position in a clothing factory.

It was a nasty night when the *Florizel* left the port of St. John's. When she was an hour out of port, a southeast gale and snowstorm came on that continued until midnight when the wind chopped around to the east-northeast, and blew with violence.

Kitty's good friend Annie got sick, but Kitty didn't mind the rolling of the ship at all. She actually enjoyed the rough motion of the *Florizel* as she pitched through the rough seas, and still greatly excited about the whole trip, she was unable to sleep.

She was wide awake when the *Florizel* was impaled on Horn Head Point off Cappahayden on the Southern Shore at dawn.

In the roar and confusion that followed, Kitty got her friend up and dressed; then as they left their stateroom, the lights went out.

Clinging together, they were swept along by the seas rushing in through the broken ship. It was Kitty who encouraged her friend along, for Annie was still weak and shaken from her bout of seasickness.

Pushed and battered by the heavy seas, the two girls were carried along, Kitty clinging to whatever her hands found and Annie clinging to her.

The afterpart of the ship was submerged beneath the heavy seas and she was fast disintegrating. People were being swept overboard, disappearing in the huge waves sweeping the ship. Kitty was grimly concerned with survival as she and Annie worked their way to the fore of the ship still above sea level.

A young stalwart appeared beside them and Kitty appealed to him for help for Annie, but he said he couldn't help and soon disappeared from their view in the combers sweeping the ship. Kitty didn't know if he survived or not.

They were nearing safety and the Marconi room was up ahead of them when a huge wave caught Annie Dalton off-balance and swept her overboard.

Kitty found herself alone, crawling on her hands and knees across the deck to the door of the Marconi room. She pounded on it and called out, demanding to be let in.

At first a voice called back that it was all filled, but another voice cried, "It's a woman, let her in!"

After a while, as she huddled resignedly outside, the door opened and someone pulled her in to safety.

There were 22 other survivors in the tiny room, a precarious shelter, spared only because the huge smoke stack of the ship took the brunt of the huge, savage seas.

Altogether, 42 people survived the disaster, including one other woman besides Kitty. Her name was Minnie Denief.

Kitty never did get to New York. She married Mike McDonald a few months later, cured of her desire to travel. From that day on, relatives in the United States could not get her to travel to visit them.

From the book, The Caribou Disaster And Other Short Stories. *Published By Flanker Press. Used by permission.*

♀

Ennellene

Us women, we have many faults
Men have only two
Everything they say
And everything they do

♀

Just a Mum

I was applying for a credit card and the bank teller was filling out my details. "And what is your occupation?" asked the career-oriented woman behind the desk, in an almost demanding voice of superiority.

"Mother," I replied.

"Maybe 'housewife' would cover it? 'Mother' isn't on the list," she abruptly answered.

In a flash, I uttered, "I'm really working in Childhood Development and Human Relations." Looking up at me as though she wasn't hearing correctly, I repeated for her my declaration. The space on the questionnaire was completed.

"May I ask what exactly your chosen career entails?" asked the woman.

"Oh, I have a continuing programme of research (what mother doesn't)," came my answer. "I'm working for my masters (all the family), and I have two credits already (a son and a daughter). Of course, my job is most demanding (any mother disagree?), and I often work 16 hours a day (24 is more like it). It is a very challenging job, but the rewards are in the satisfaction I receive, rather than money."

After completing the form, she walked me to the door. As I entered my home I was greeted by my lab assistant, aged three; and in the workroom, our new experiment of three months could be heard testing new vocal patterns for the child development programme.

I felt buoyed with my preferred career; what was more, I was victorious. I had beaten bureaucracy. I was now on official records as someone more essential to mankind than just another homemaker...I have an admirable career. What mother doesn't?

By Leonie Mitchell – Lennox Head, Australia

♀

Life, Love & Laughter

WOMEN OF THE ISLAND AND THE BIG LAND
From Italy to Newfoundland: A War Bride Story
By Daphne Collins

I was born in Blackheath, London, England, even though my family's residence was Naples, Italy.

My grandfather originated from Northumberland but in the late 1800s, decided to emigrate to Italy in order to start a business of his own. Eventually, my father, having finished his studies in England and Scotland, joined the firm to settle permanently in Italy where he, too, married and started a family.

However, when I was due to be born, the doubts that this offspring may not be granted British nationality if born in a foreign country brought the family back to Great Britain.

I was three months old when we returned to Naples, and it was there that I grew up and attended school.

In 1940, never believing that Mussolini would join forces with Hitler, we were still in Italy. When he did, we became "the enemy" and were taken from our home, jailed, separated and sent to various camps and interviewed.

It would be too long to narrate all the events that took place at this time. Suffice it to say that we were eventually reunited as a family in a small village, Pescasseroli, in the province of L'Aguila in the centre of Italy, from where we were going to be exchanged with some Italian prisoners of war and repatriated. This was possible as my father was over 65 and not eligible for war duty and my mother, sister and I were all women.

We left Italy on January 7, 1943, to be taken by train, under escort, through France, Spain and Portugal and from there we flew over to Bristol on January 23. From Bristol we were taken up North to Leeds, where we were billeted in the Quarry Hill Flats. Jobs were also found for my father, sister and I.

My sister's godfather, Mr. H. Rae, who was a family friend and who originally had also been part of the British Colony in Naples, came to visit us. This visit resulted in my leaving the job I had with the Admiralty in Leeds and I headed South to reside on the Raes' estate. I worked there as a Land-Arm girl producing vegetables for sale, thus contributing to the war effort.

It was on this estate Foxbush, Hildenborough, Kent - that the headquarters of the 59th Newfoundland Heavy Regiment R.A. was billeted. Mr. Rae wasted no time in telling me, "If you ever go out with any of these Newfoundlanders I will send you straight back to your father!"

I met Wick for the first time in May. In June, for my 21st birthday, he invited me to go up to London with him for dinner and a show. It was to be a whirlwind romance. We were engaged in September and married on the 1st of December in a little church in Tonbridge. Father Lawrence Farrell, the regimental padre, officiated.

Jacob Lee was the best man and my sister, the bridesmaid. The reception, a gift from the officers at headquarters, was held at the Hilden Manor in Hildenborough. The brief honeymoon was spent at the Moor House Hotel, Hindhead, Surrey.

War separated us for many months. Wick fought in France on the Western Front from the

Life, Love & Laughter

beaches of Normandy, through Caen, Falaise, Brussels, Antwerp, Arnhem across the rivers Maas and Waal, the Oder and the Seine, to the Baltic under Field Marshal B.L. Montgomery, Commander in Chief of the 21st Army group.

In April 1946, after the birth in England of our first child, we sailed from Tilburn on the SS *Corner Brook* for Newfoundland. It is here in St. John's that we lived, toiled and raised our family of three children. Our marriage lasted 43 years - up to September 13, 1987, the day Wick died.

From the book We Came From Over the Sea. *Published by British War Brides Association of Newfoundland and Labrador in co-operation with ESPress. Used by permission.*

♀

Spice of Life

A divorcee is a woman who gets richer by decrees.

♀

Ennellene

My husband is understanding
In life he has really been through it
And he knows the best time
To dust, sweep or clean grime
Is right after I tell him to do it

♀

Mary's Mark

There is a stone marker halfway between Ladle Cove and Aspen Cove in the Province of Newfoundlandand Labrador, Canada, that bears the inscription "The Mark of Mary Cap." The significance of the marker is all but forgotten except by a handful of old-timers in the area.

During the mid-1800s, the husband and son of Mary Cap died of starvation at Ladle Cove. It was mid-winter, and Mary decided to walk to Aspen Cove to stay with friends.

A storm came up and she became lost. Weeks later, friends found her body. Mary had frozen to death. She was buried at the site where her body had been found and friends carved into a nearby stone the words: "The Mark of Mary Cap."

From the book, Newfoundland Fireside Stories, *by Jack Fitzgerald. Published by Creative Publishing. Used by permission.*

♀

Is That a Fact?
Many things are taken as facts. Not all of them are.

Proper Foods and Cancer

When Adelle Davis the famous nutritionist who had advocated longer life through healthier eating in hospitals, schools and health clinics, and later through her best selling books, including, *Lets Eat Right to Keep Fit*, got cancer and later died, it was said that her teachings had no value. She unfairly blamed herself and the junk food she had eaten before shifting to a diet emphasizing healthier foods in the 1950s.

The Fact Is that even though she did blame herself and her earlier diet on her disease, there was never any evidence to show that the bone cancer that took her life at age 70 had anything to do with her diet.

♀

Food for Thought

Success has made failures of many men. – *Cindy Adams*

♀

Some Mothers Have Them

Jackson had heard how long the preacher at their church had preached and was a bit concerned about that when the man of God visited his family for supper. However the preacher made the grace short and to the point. As everyone started in, Jackson looked at the preacher and said, "You don't pray as long when you're hungry, do you?"

♀

Life's Funny Experiences

Stocking Statement

Hi, I want to tell you this story about my sister. There are six of us sisters and she is a bit larger than the other five. One day she was in a bedding store with her seven-year-old son. When they were looking at some mattresses, she came to one that was a queen size. Her son looked at her and said in a very loud voice, "Look Mom, this bed is the same size as your panty hose!"

Chrissy – Newfoundland, Canada

♀

Second Honeymoon

On July 20, 1969, as commander of the Apollo 11 Lunar Module, Neil Armstrong was the first person to set foot on the moon. His first words after stepping on the moon, "That's one small step for man, one giant leap for mankind", were televised to Earth and heard by millions. But just before he reentered the lander, he made the enigmatic remark: "Good luck, Mr. Gorsky."

Many people at NASA thought it was a casual remark concerning some rival Soviet Cosmonaut. However, upon checking, there was no Gorsky in either the Russian or American space programs.

Over the years many people questioned Armstrong as to what the "Good luck, Mr. Gorsky" statement meant, but Armstrong always just smiled when asked the question.

On July 5, 1995, in Tampa Bay, Florida, while answering questions following a speech, a reporter brought up the 26 year old question to Armstrong. This time he finally responded. Mr. Gorsky had died and so Neil Armstrong felt he could answer the question.

In 1938 when he was a kid in a small midwest town, he was playing baseball with a friend in the backyard. His friend hit a fly ball, which landed in his neighbour's yard by the bedroom windows. His neighbours were Mr. and Mrs. Gorsky. As he leaned down to pick up the ball, young Armstrong heard Mrs. Gorsky shouting at Mr. Gorsky. "Sex! You want sex?! You'll get sex when the kid next door walks on the moon!"

– *Anonymous*

♀

Life, Love & Laughter

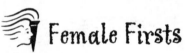 Her Other Half

Winning by a Nose

The honeymoon was over for two years and the man sat in the living room watching the horse races on television while the wife made dinner, cleaned up, and tried to keep an ear on her son who was crying and sniffling in the playpen in the living room.

"Baby's nose is running again," the man shouted in the direction of the kitchen.

At this point the wife lost her temper and shouted back, "Don't you ever think of anything but horses?"

♀

Food for Thought

Far away there in the sunshine are my highest aspirations. I may not reach them, but I can look up and see their beauty, believe in them, and try to follow where they lead.
— *Louisa May Alcott*

♀

Aunt Alice says:

Now that I have the maturity to get my head together – my body is falling apart.

Female Firsts

1914: The term 'birth control' was coined by Margaret Higgins Sanger.

1914: On June 21, Miss Georgia "Tiny" Broadwick became the first person to make an intentional free-fall parachute jump from an airplane.

1916: Jeannette Rankin of Montana became the first woman representative elected to the U.S. House, making her the first woman in the world elected to a parliamentary body. This was four years before women throughout the U.S. had the right to vote.

1916: Suffrage activist and rabble-rouser Emily Murphy became Canada's first female judge.

1916: On September 12, two sisters, Adeline and Augusta Van Buren, arrived in San Francisco on their motorcycles, thereby becoming the first women to ride motorcycles across the U.S. They had started the trek in Brooklyn on July 5.

1917: Jeannette Rankin became the first woman in U.S. Congress.

1918: Nina Bang became the first female member of the Landsting (the Upper House) in Denmark's first Social Democratic government. In 1924 she became Minister of Education and in 1926 was promoted to Minister of Commerce.

1918: Anne Martin of Nevada became the first woman to run for U.S. Senate.

♀

Life, Love & Laughter

Life's Funny Experiences

Poor Labour Relations

My water broke and I told my husband to get dressed, it was time to go. He helped me into the van and we started to go to the Grace Hospital in St. John's. I told him to back up, as I didn't have my bag. After he went to get the bag it got cold, so I got out of the van and went into his sister Rita's house next door to get warm. "Where are you going this time of night?" she asked me. I told her Ed was getting my bag and that it was time to go to the Grace. The very next moment, I noticed the van was pulling out of the driveway.

My husband said he had gone about a mile, talking to me all the way, before he realized I wasn't in the van. Rita and I were laughing so hard I could barely get in the van when he came back. I was still laughing when we got to the hospital. The nurses laughed when I told them. Poor Ed, he was so embarrassed.

Jean Brown – Topsail, Newfoundland, Canada

♀

Three Aisles Over

Feeling the call to return to my roots, I packed the Ontario family up to spend the entire summer in the land of my ancestors - the Rock. Maybe it was the peaceful calm that permeated the outport, or my spirited 95-year-old nan, or maybe it was actually hearing the church bells ring or simply the distant ghosts of past ancestors that seemed to draw so near. I don't know. But, whatever it was, I found more than just my roots on this trip.

At first, I looked in all the wrong places: the university, the archives, the genealogical society. Old records and family trees told me many interesting facts and situations past. Graveyards were filled with once hearty people who were outlived by the houses and churches they built. Weathered diaries whispered secret anecdotes and old timers shared sacred stories passed on to them by their parents.

I should have known. It was there all the time in the grocery store only three isles over. There always seems to be that elusive grocery item that cannot be found anywhere. You spend priceless time searching every aisle only to conclude the item does not exist until, finally, in sheer frustration, you break down in humiliation and ask for help.

"Yes, me dear," a friendly voice responded to my desperate plea for assistance. She looked me right in the eyes.

"It's t'ree aisles over. Here, let me show you, now." The kind lady proceeded to take me right to the coveted grocery piece. "There you be," she said as she handed me the missing package of food and the angel of mercy then disappeared.

I stood there stunned for a moment. It had been years since someone actually showed me where something was in a store. Most often, my Ontario merchant friends would continue their busy job and rattle off a list of directions without even bothering to make eye contact with me. I would then proceed to toddle off in a fuzzy and uncertain search of my mecca.

It struck me that this attitude of helpfulness, connection with people, and sense of community were in fact much more important than the name of my great-grandfather and more meaningful that the country from which he came or the name of his father. Newfoundlanders were survivors; survivors in the sometimes inhospitable land. And, why? They were survivors because of their willingness to take the time to show - not tell - the path to greatness. I found what I was looking for last summer. The questions about my ancestry were resting inside me all the time - only three aisles over.

- Heather Down – Cookstown Ontario

♀

Life, Love & Laughter

Food for Thought

I'm a Roman Catholic and I take a dim view of 2,500 celibates shuffling back and forth to Rome to discuss birth control and not one woman to raise a voice.

– Laura Sabia, Chairperson Ontario Advisory Council on the Status of Women
Quoted in The Toronto Star, 22 Aug 1975

♀

Saving Faith

The broad smiles she received when entering a senator's office were not so much due to her grey matter, she knew, as to the above-the-knee skirts she favoured. Sometimes it was as simple as dangling a shoe. She was talking about children dying, families living in sewers in far-off lands, and these men were fixated on toe cleavage. God, testosterone was a man's greatest weakness and a woman's most powerful advantage. At least it helped to level a playing field that had always been tilted in favour of the males.

– David Baldacci, from the novel, Saving Faith *published by Time Warner Books.*

♀

5 Secrets to a Perfect Relationship

1. It is important that a man helps you around the house and has a job.

2. It is important that a man makes you laugh.

3. It is important to find a man you can count on and doesn't lie to you.

4. It is important that a man is good in bed and loves making love to you.

5. It is really important that these four men don't know each other.

♀

The Mermaid

A strange story from our past is the one recorded by Sir Richard Whitbourne. He described coming face-to-face with a creature in St. John's Harbour that strongly resembled a mermaid.

The creature described by Whitbourne appeared again a few miles from St. John's Narrows during 1912. The two fishermen who witnessed the appearance described it as a mermaid. The men said they saw the creature come up from the ocean and try to climb aboard a dory near them. The dory belonged to two fishermen from Little Bay West.

The creature looked around, then came over to the boat and tried to climb into it. The fishermen fought it off and it disappeared into the ocean. The description of the creature of 1912 was similar to the one given by Whitbourne more than 150 years before. He wrote in his diary, "The creature came to within the length of a long pike from me and was about 15 feet long. I was standing by the riverside in the Harbour at St. John's when it very swiftly came swimming toward me looking carefully at my face, like a woman. The face seemed to be beautiful and well proportioned. It had about the head many blue streaks resembling hair but it certainly was not hair."

From the book, Strange But True Newfoundland Stories, *by Jack Fitzgerald, published by Creative Publishing. Used by permission.*

♀

Women Who Have Made A Difference *– By Ron Young*

Catherine Booth, an avowed feminist and wife of English Methodist minister William Booth, started preaching in 1860, even though her husband was opposed to it. Catherine's sermon was so impressive that William changed his mind about female preachers. In 1864 the couple began the Christian Mission in London's East End, which later developed into the Salvation Army. The Church of England was at first extremely hostile to the Salvation Army. One of the main complaints was Booth's "elevation of women to man's status." In the Salvation Army a woman officer enjoyed equal rank with a man. William later wrote, "The best men in my Army are the women."

Bette Davis was the first woman to receive the American Film Institute's Life Achievement Award and a special César for her life's work in films from the French motion-picture industry. During her lifetime, she received ten Academy Award nominations and appeared in more than 80 films.

   One of her least-known awards was the Distinguished Civilian Service Medal, the U.S. Defense Department's highest civilian award for her efforts as president of the Hollywood Canteen Foundation, which donated money for various services for the soldiers of WWII. She received the award 40 years after the war ended.

Princess Diana was born Diana Frances Spencer in Sandringham, Norfolk, England. She worked as a kindergarten teacher in London until her engagement to Prince Charles, the heir to the British throne. By the time of her divorce from the Prince, Diana had already adopted charity work as her royal duty. She withdrew from public activities for a period of about four months in 1993, in an effort to avoid the negative publicity focused on her separation from Prince Charles. After that, however, Diana continued to give active support to many charities related to homeless and deprived children, drug abuse, and victims of acquired immune deficiency syndrome (AIDS). Diana shocked many people in 1987, when she shook the hand of an AIDS patient. She was the vice president of the British Red Cross and served as a member of the International Red Cross advisory board after 1994. She continued to serve her country and the world until a tragic auto accident in France took her life on August 31, 1997.

Florence Nightingale, born in Florence, Italy, on May 12, 1820, but raised mostly in Derbyshire, England, is famous as being "The Lady With the Lamp" during the Crimean War, but achieved much more than that in her lifetime. Before her time, female doctors were mostly unheard of, and the females who assisted doctors and did other nursing duties were largely untrained personnel whose job was considered nothing but a menial chore.

   Under Nightingale's supervision, efficient nursing departments were established in the Crimea, during a war that saw many injured and sick soldiers. Through her tireless efforts, the mortality rate among the sick and the wounded was greatly reduced.

   At the close of the war in 1860, with a fund raised in tribute to her services, Nightingale founded the Nightingale School and Home for Nurses at Saint Thomas's Hospital in London. The opening of this school marked the beginning of professional education in nursing. Florence Nightingale's contributions to the evolution of nursing as a profession were invaluable and led to the great profession that nursing is today.

♀

WOMEN OF THE ISLAND AND THE BIG LAND

Patti Au

Interview by Marian Frances White

Linda Boddie

Patti Au was born Chiu Shuet Lin on November 26, 1944 in Canton, China. At a young age, she and her sister studied dance there and today her sister is a well-known Chinese dance teacher. At 16 Patti moved to Hong Kong, where she trained for three years as a teacher and taught grades two to five. In 1970, at the age of 26, Patti took her first flight - from Hong Kong to Tokyo to Vancouver, then to Toronto, and finally to St. John's. Immigration laws at that time stated you had to marry right away or you would not be able to stay, so within one month of her arrival she married her husband, Wing, at Gower Street United Church. She and her husband have five children: four girls and one boy. When she first came to Newfoundland, Patti worked at a restaurant in the Goulds where her working hours were 9:00 am until 2:00 am; then for many years, she worked at the E & W Restaurant on Water Street in St. John's, which she and her husband owned. Her life is indicative of hundreds of Chinese who immigrated to Canada, though she is quick to point out that those who come here with a knowledge of the English language have better opportunities to work in their chosen field. Patti has a strong identity with her culture, and keeps it alive through her activities in the local Chinese community and her contact with her family in China.

*****

When I first came to Newfoundland I wanted to go back to Hong Kong right away. My family lived there and 17 years ago there were not many Chinese people here. The buildings downtown made no view; I saw no colour and the houses really looked all the same. It was not the height of the buildings that made me sad, but the look.

The markets in China and Hong Kong are open six o'clock in the morning to ten o'clock in the night, so people can buy fresh Chinese vegetables any time. I remember here you could only get cabbage, tomato, celery and vegetables like that. My husband and his uncle and his family always tried to find Chinese food for me; they thought this would make me want to stay here. Today I still miss my food. Even in the restaurant, Chinese do not cook Chinese food; they cook Canadian Chinese food like chicken fried rice. Everyone love the french fry here - even my children want to eat the french fry more than rice and vegetables - but still I never eat french fries. I cook the Chinese way.

In Hong Kong I learned English in school, but just a little, so first when I come over here I didn't understand not one word. My husband teach me a little and his uncle show me the cash in his restaurant, but until I learned enough to work the cash, I just wash and work in the kitchen.

I think it would make it easier for other women who come here if they had people to talk to.

Not far from this restaurant there is a woman who just came from China and works in the kitchen. She never went to English school in China; I'm lucky that I knew a little. The first time I met her I understood what she was going through because I was like that when I first came over. I talked to her to tell her that one day she would understand well; I tell her to listen to the radio and watch the news. I understand 80% of what is said now. I love to learn and understand what people say.

It seems Chinese people mainly work in restaurants and in laundries because there is not much more unless they learn English. I know when my children grow up they do not want to work in a restaurant; that makes me happy. I work like this for 17 years with not much time off. I work seven days a week, and when I had young children I took care of them between the time I worked in this restaurant. Sometimes that's okay, but sometimes that's awful because the baby wants milk and you hear the baby cry but you cannot leave the customers. I don't think it's good to work seven days a week, 16 hours a day. Now sometimes other Chinese families come here after hours and we open the restaurant for them. That makes for a social time.

In China life was very different. Even in Hong Kong everyone spoke the same language so people did more things together. My children understand me when I speak to them in Chinese; my oldest daughter, Michelle, answers me sometimes in Chinese, but my youngest son Richard, only answers me in English. I see no future for the Chinese like this. They can read and write and talk well in English but if they do not have their Chinese tongue I think they lose our culture. They learn a little in school but that is like when I learned English in Hong Kong; I did not learn much because I did not speak English outside the school.

Right now in St. John's there is a Chinese community, but for many years there was no place except where we work to be together. I used to stay at the restaurant because I had no friends. There were not many women my age, but when more and more people came here I found lots of friends. It was hard to try to make friends with Newfoundland people. Once they did not like the Chinese people because we were very different. It is so difficult when you do not speak the language. Newfoundland people really like to go out and drink and dance, and often the men and the women do that together; but the Chinese don't like that so much. I like to dance but my husband don't like it, so we cannot enjoy that together.

My kids really like to listen to me talk of when I was young in China and in Hong Kong, but if I do not tell them, and if not much happens here like in China, they lose their culture. In 1983 I took Richard and Michelle to my home in Canton where I was born. Richard did not like it so much, but Michelle spoke Chinese and she enjoyed the stores and my family. I think it's too late when they are older to learn the Chinese way of life. A few years ago I taught my two daughters and a friend's two daughters a Chinese dance for the Chinese New Year celebrations. I made the dress for the dance just like in China because I know the dress they use for each dance, but when the Chinese New Year was over everything went back to the way it was. That's not so good.

Today I wish I could teach like I did in China. I really enjoyed the work in the Hong Kong schools, and I really enjoy the dance. The government tells you lots of reasons why you should come over, but I wish now I thought about it more before I come. I think some day I got to move to Toronto because there the Chinese culture is strong. They got a Chinese school and Chinese books and they learn when they are very young the Chinese culture. I hope the government will do more for the Chinese people. I know every year they give some money to help celebrate the New Year but they could help us more, especially with the new people who come in and do not speak English and must work right away.

From the book The Finest Kind *by Marion Frances White. Creative Publishing. Used by permission.*

♀

Life, Love & Laughter

Food for Thought

List to that bird! His song - what poet pens it?
Brigand of birds, he's stolen every note!
Prince though of thieves - hark! how the rascal spends it!
Pours the whole forest from one tiny throat!
                    "The Mockingbird" – Edith Proctor (Clarke) Hayes

♀

Her Other Half

Par for the Hearse

As a funeral procession slowly made its way past a golf course, George, an avid golfer, paused before teeing off. Then he took his golfer's hat off, in a respectful manner, and attentively watched as a funeral train of cars slowly went by. His golfing partner, surprised to see anything but golf get any attention from his friend, said, "I never knew you cared about anything but golf, George."

"It's the least I could do," sighed George. "Tomorrow would have been our 40th anniversary."

♀

Female Firsts

1919: Nancy Witcher Langhorne Astor became the first woman to be a member of Parliament in Britain when she was elected by a substantial majority.

1920: (or thereabouts) Englishwoman Dorothy Annie Elizabeth Garrod became the first woman to do research in Paleolithic archeology and to study early humans.

1920: Margaret Hill M'Carter of Kansas became the first woman delegate to address a Republican national gathering.

1920: Florence E. Allen became the first woman judge in the U.S.

1920: The first women's Olympic springboard diving competition was won by 14-year-old Aileen Riggin.

1920: Mary Anderson, a Swedish immigrant, became the first woman to rise to a government position through union activities when she was made first Director of the Women's Bureau of the Department of Labor in the U.S.

1921: Margaret Gorman became the first Miss America.

1921: In May, Monaco's first all-woman *Olymiades Feminines* games were held.

1921: In June, aviator Bessie Coleman became the first African American pilot, as well as the first woman to be licensed as an international pilot.

♀

Life, Love & Laughter

😊 Some Mothers Have Them

Jackson's mother's rich, oldest sister was about to visit, and his mother told him he must be on his best behaviour and speak only when spoken to while his aunt was there. Jackson behaved very well and didn't speak, but he did stare at his aunt throughout the entire meal. Finally the aunt could take it no longer and asked Jackson why he was staring at her.

"I was waiting for you to do your trick," answered Jackson.

"And what trick is that?" asked his aunt.

"Well, Daddy says you drink like a fish, and I've never seen that," Jackson responded.

♀

Newfoundland and Labrador's First Woman Settler

On June 18, 1542, Marguerite de la Roque became the first woman to set foot in Newfoundland and Labrador. For three years after, she went through a living hell.

Before coming to Newfoundland, Marguerite was the darling of French society; bright, witty and beautiful. When she learned that her uncle had been appointed by family friend King Francis I to the position of first Viceroy to Canada, she begged him to take her along.

Marguerite felt it would be adventurous and romantic to live in the frontiers of the New World. The uncle agreed to her request and Marguerite was accompanied by her nurse, an old Norman peasant woman named Damiene. During the voyage to the New World, she flirted and fell in love with a common soldier. The affair angered her uncle who held strong Calvanistic beliefs. It also damaged his French pride.

When Marguerite refused to break off the romance, the uncle decided to teach her a lesson. He arranged for her marriage to protect the family name and then set her ashore on a cold, drab desolate island off the coast of Labrador known as Harrington Island. Marguerite's experience there provided the new name for the island and it became known as the Isle of Demons.

Following the marriage the uncle gave Marguerite some provisions, three guns and some ammunition. He ordered the old nurse to go with her. Her husband was to be put in chains, but he managed to grab some guns and ammunition and jumped into the water and swam ashore. The three struggled to survive in their wild environment. When Marguerite's child was born it died shortly after. Her husband went mad during the first winter and threw himself off a cliff. The following winter Damiene died, leaving Marguerite to try and survive on her own.

Surprisingly, Marguerite showed great determination and courage. She built a tiny hut and hunted small game, while all the time watching the horizon for a ship. After a while she began hearing voices and turned to reading the New Testament to avoid becoming insane.

Three years passed and just when Marguerite was ready to give up, a ship passed close to the island, saw the smoke from her campfire and rescued her. She was still beautiful, wore an animal skin dress as her only form of clothing, and was of sound mind when taken aboard the rescue vessel.

Having lost the desire for further adventure, Marguerite de la Roque returned to France and became a school mistress.

From Jack Fitzgerald's Notebook, *by Jack Fitzgerald, published by Creative Publishing. Used by permission.*

♀

Life, Love & Laughter

Ennellene

For every man made to look the fool
By a woman, as part of her plan
Without ridicule, there's been many a fool
By a woman, made into a man

♀

Her Other Half

A Year For Languages

When the couple decided to adopt, they learned that there was a lovely Japanese infant boy available for adoption.

"I don't mind having a Japanese boy as a son, but won't it cost a lot for us to take lessons to learn Japanese?" the man asked his wife.

"Why would we need to learn Japanese?" she replied.

"Because when he starts to talk, I think it's important that we know what he's saying."

♀

Quillings

Somebody's Mother

The woman was old, and ragged, and grey
And bent with the chill of the winter's day
The street was wet, with a recent snow
And the woman's feet were aged and slow,
She stood at the crossing and waited long
Alone, uncared for, amid the throng
Of human beings who passed her by
Nor heeded the glance of her anxious eye.
Down the street, with laughter and shout,
Glad in the freedom of "school let out,"
Came the boys, like a flock of sheep,
Hailing the snow piled white and deep.
Hastened the children on their way,
Past the woman so old and gray
Nor offered a helping hand to her.
So meek, so timid, afraid to stir.
Lest the carriage wheels or the horses' feet
Should crowd her down in the slippery street,
At last came one of the merry troop,

The gayest laddie of all this group;
He paused beside her, and whispered low,
"I'll help you cross, if you wish to go."
Her aged hand on his strong young arm
She placed, and so, without hurt or harm,
He guided the trembling feet along,
Proud that his own were firm and strong.
Then back again to his friends he went,
His young heart happy and well content.
"She's somebody's mother, boys, you know,
For all she's aged, and poor, and slow;
And I hope some fellow will lend a hand
To help my mother, you understand,
If ever she's poor, and old, and grey,
When her own dear boy is far away."
And "somebody's mother" bowed low her head
In her home that night, and the prayer she said
Was "God be kind to the noble boy
Who is somebody's son and pride and joy!"

Anonymous

♀

Life's Funny Experiences

Patient's Patience

I am a nurse and I was in the process of adapting myself to a new department in our little rural hospital. Of course, for the staff members who had been on the unit for some time, it was no problem for them to know every patient and their families exceptionally well. For me, it was a struggle trying to familiarize myself with the floor plan, let alone all the faces, names and special desires and routines of 32 patients.

One early evening stands out in my memory as a "watershed" moment. A young lady walked up to me and asked, "Nurse, can Dad have something to eat?"

Well, my mind raced - Who is Dad? So, in an effort to clarify who Dad was, and where he was, I carefully chose my words and asked, "And your father is...?"

The little face looked up at me strangely as she said softly, "Hungry."

Bonnie Jarvis–Lowe, R.N. – Shoal Harbour, Newfoundland, Canada

♀

Animal Mating - Fact and Fantasy – *Ron Young*

Double the Pleasure

Fact:

Scientists at Oregon State University have recently discovered that the snake is right-handed, even if it doesn't actually have even one hand. But it betters its human counterpart in another way. The snake has not one penis, but two, known as a hemipene (plural for hemipenis). The snake has a preference the same as humans have in their hands. Scientists have discovered that not only is the right hemipenis of the snake predominately bigger than the left, but it is the most favoured hemipenis when he has sex on his mind, and two procreative objects from which to chose.

The findings were a result of the bodies of some 500 garter snakes that suffocated while trying to keep warm under a Manitoba woodpile. The findings seem to have no value to humans as yet, the researchers say, but, "it could lead to future studies regarding humans' hand preferences."

Fantasy:

Go flaunt your sexual prowess
And think that I'm the lowest
But don't forget I sport a working pair.
While one may get deflated
My mate remains elated
Because I have another one to spare

♀

Women Who Have Made A Difference — *By Ron Young*

Esther Ocloo is a model to women and men in Africa and worldwide, producing creative solutions to the problems of poverty, hunger and the distribution of wealth. In 1942, with ten shillings given to her by her aunt, she bought oranges and made 12 jars of marmalade. Today, her business packages foods using Ghanaian produce ranging from fruit juice to soups. Among her many accomplishments and firsts, at a workshop in Mexico City preceding the International Women's Year conference in 1975, she put forth the idea of an international bank directed specifically to women. The result was Women's World Banking, which gives women access to credit so that they may start their own enterprises.

Trieu Thi Trinh aka Trieu Au, was born in AD222 when her homeland, Vietnam, was a territory of China. She was treated more like a slave than a relative by her sister-in-law, who was possibly Chinese, and with whom she lived after she was orphaned as a young girl. To shed herself from bondage, Trieu killed her sister-in-law and escaped to the hills where she raised an army of at least a thousand men and women. When her brother tried to discourage her military aspirations, she is reputed to have said to him, "I will not resign myself to the lot of women, who bow their heads and become concubines. I wish to ride the tempest, tame the waves, kill the sharks. I have no desire to take abuse." Leading her army, Trieu fought and won more than 30 major battles against the Chinese before she was 21 years old. The Chinese defeated her army in AD248 and rather than surrender, she jumped into a river and died at the age of 26.

Golda Meir was born in Kyyiv, Russia (now Ukraine) in 1898, and immigrated to the US in 1906 with her family. She later became a school teacher, but while still in her teens she became a Zionist, dedicated to building a homeland for Jews. In 1921 she and her husband immigrated to Palestine (now Israel), where she remained active in Zionist affairs and in the labour movement. Meir served throughout the 1930s and 1940s in various Zionist organizations in Palestine, Europe and the United States. She was one of the signers of the proclamation of the independence of the state of Israel in 1948 and served as her country's first minister to the USSR in 1948 and 1949. In 1956 she became Israel's minister of foreign affairs and held that post until 1966. She was prime minister of Israel from 1969 to 1974. Meir died in Jerusalem on December 8, 1978.

Rigoberta Menchu (born in 1959) and her family, like all the Quiche Indians in Guatemala, were very poor. The small plot of land that the family owned did not produce enough to feed everyone. And like their neighbours, who were in the same predicament, they travelled to the coast to work as labourers on large coffee or cotton plantations, working up to 15 hours a day for eight months a year. Rigoberta started working on a plantation at the age of eight and did not have an opportunity to attend school. Two of her brothers died on the plantation; one from pesticide poisoning, the other from malnutrition.

   Then the military-led government and the wealthy plantation owners started taking Indian-occupied lands by force. Her father was arrested and imprisoned many times for leading the peasant movement opposing this action. In 1979, Rigoberta's 16-year-old brother was kidnapped by soldiers, tortured and burned alive while his family watched. In 1980, her father, along with 38 other Indian leaders, died in a fire at the Spanish embassy while protesting violations of Indian human rights abuses. Rigoberta's mother, also a leader in her community and a healer, was kidnapped, raped, tortured and killed the following year.

Wanted by the Guatemalan government herself, Rigoberta fled to Mexico. The book she published there in 1984 about the plight of her fellow Indians, and the campaign she led for social justice, brought international attention to the problems of her people.

Awarded the Nobel Peace Prize in 1992, Rigoberta used the $1.2 million cash prize to set up a foundation in her father's name to continue the fight for the human rights of her people.

Princess Noor Inayat Khan was a Muslim woman who was born in Russia and was living in England as Nora Baker at the outbreak of WWII. To help the cause she enlisted in the Women's Auxiliary Air Force (WAAF), and was deemed suitable for spy operations in occupied France. Given the code name "Madeline," she arrived in France only to find that many of her fellow agents were being captured by the enemy and her support network had been severely compromised. London offered her a chance to return, but she refused and stayed to keep the vital radio links to London open. Incredibly enough, the Princess eluded the dreaded Gestapo for many months; cycling, with transmitter in tow, from one safe house to another. It was even reported that she solicited the help of an enemy officer to string up a clothesline, which in fact was her radio antenna. Eventually she became her French Resistance unit's only link to home base. She was later betrayed, captured and paid the price of spies - execution.

Clara Hale was a rare individual who had left her loving imprint on the lives of thousands in the U.S. In 1940 she became a foster mother and over the next 25 years became "Mommy" Hale to more than 40 children of all ethnic and religious backgrounds. Later, when drug abuse reached astronomic proportions in the Harlem community, the black woman turned her five-room apartment into a home for 22 babies of heroin-addicted women. She then helped establish a home for infants addicted before birth. Hale House was the first and only known program in the U.S. designed to deal with infants born addicted to illegal drugs. Over 500 children found a nurturing, loving, comforting woman who genuinely cared about the future of these otherwise friendless children.

♀

Nail in the Fence

There once was a little girl who had a bad temper. Her mother gave her a bag of nails and told her that every time she lost her temper, she must hammer a nail into the back of the fence. The first day the girl had driven 37 nails into the fence. Over the next few weeks, as she learned to control her anger, the number of nails hammered daily gradually dwindled down. She discovered it was easier to hold her temper than to drive those nails into the fence.

Finally the day came when the girl didn't lose her temper at all. She told her mother about it and the mother suggested that the girl now pull out one nail for each day that she was able to hold her temper. The days passed and the young girl was finally able to tell her mother that all the nails were gone. The mother took her daughter by the hand and led her to the fence. She said, "You have done well, my daughter, but look at the holes in the fence. The fence will never be the same. When you say things in anger, they leave a scar just like this one." You can put a knife in a person and draw it out. It won't matter how many times you say I'm sorry, the wound is still there.

A verbal wound is as bad as a physical one. Friends are very rare jewels, indeed. They make you smile and encourage you to succeed. They lend an ear, they share words of praise and they always want to open their hearts to us.

– Author Unknown

♀

Life, Love & Laughter

Ennellene

In past years there was bliss, in remembered first kiss
And that memory, for many years carried
But the woman of late, can't remember first date
Or even the first man she married

♀

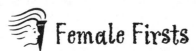 Adam's Ribbing

Dead Engine

A young man-on-the move was driving down a moonlit country road with his glamourous date when the engine coughed and sputtered, and the car came to a halt.

Shaking his head the man said, "I wonder what that knocking was?"

"Well, I don't know what it was," she icily replied, "but it sure wasn't opportunity."

♀

Female Firsts

1922: Lila Acheson, along with husband DeWitt Wallace, launched Reader's Digest.

1922: Lilian Gatlin became the first woman pilot to fly across the continental U.S.

1922: The first women's Australasian Tennis Championship was held.

1923: Margaret Grace Bondfield became the first woman to attain cabinet rank in Great Britain. Prior to her election she had been a British trade union leader.

1924: Englishwoman Alexandra David-Neel became the first European woman to travel to the forbidden city of Tibet.

1924: On November 4, Miriam Ferguson of Texas was elected as the first female to become a state governor in the U.S.

1924: Ruth Law became the first woman to be granted an international hydroplane licence.

1925: Nellie Tayloe Ross became the second woman governor of the U.S. and the first woman governor of Wyoming, when she was elected to serve out the term of her deceased husband. *See also Female Firsts page 164.*

1925: The Canadian federal divorce law was changed to allow a woman to divorce her husband on the same grounds that a man could divorce his wife - simple adultery. Before this, she had to prove adultery in conjunction with other acts, such as sodomy or bestiality.

1925: Massachusetts Republican, Edith Nourse Rogers was the first woman to serve in the U.S. House of Representatives.

♀

WOMEN OF THE ISLAND AND THE BIG LAND
Dorothy Clarke
Interview by Marian Frances White

Linda Boddie

Dorothy Clarke was born into the Antle family in St. John's on July 11, 1937. She lived at the Battery with her sister and brother, and attended St. Joseph's School. Most of her summers were spent in Paradise where the air was considered drier for her mother who had tuberculosis. Dorothy's mother died when she was six. Her family moved to Paradise when she was 14; however, they commuted daily to school in St. John's with their father who worked there.

For seven years, Dorothy worked as a chef at Chateau Park in Mount Pearl. In 1978 she became a foster parent and since then has given care to 32 children, besides raising her own family of five. On November 11, 1987, Dorothy and four other foster parents got together to reinstate the Avalon Newfoundland Foster Parent Association that had died out five years previously. She has served as the president of this association, which lobbies and directs questions at government to help improve the present conditions for both foster parents and the children they have in care. Dorothy continues to live in Paradise and still hears from all her charges, who refer to her and her husband as Nan and Pop.

*****

The way I see it, children are children no matter where they have come from. The only difference is the needs of foster children are greater. I found that if you sat down and talked to them and made them feel that they were just as special as your own, then they thought of you as their family. In that way, they don't feel left out or that they are just boarding.

When I first became a foster parent I received just over a hundred dollars a month. It has increased a bit since then, but there is never enough money to give the kids what you want to give them. I mean, you can't put your own children in school dressed in Levi jeans and Nike sneakers and have a foster child getting on the bus with a pair of jeans too short or too long. They stand out like a sore thumb and people spot them as foster children. Over the past 10 years I have seen a lot of needless hardship for foster children.

After a decade of fostering over 30 children, I seldom look forward to the day when the children go back with their natural parents because I've seen so few of those cases work out. I feel Child Welfare should have someone investigate those children that are sent back home up to six months or even longer. I don't mean appointed visits, because then everything is prepared; I mean drop in on them from time to time. I've had children with me that did not want to go home, who went home for two or three years and are now teenage pregnancies. They can't be put back in foster homes, so they are in homes for unwed mothers or living with their boyfriends for as long as that will last. Probably a year or so down the road that child will end up in care; so the trend is repeated. More money needs to be spent on hiring social workers to have a follow-up on these children.

Because only a week's notice is given before a child is returned home, some foster parents feel they have to stand off a bit from their foster child. The child leaves, but you're the one left

Life, Love & Laughter

behind. Regardless of how long you've had a child, you do become attached. Their problems become your problems.

Every child that comes into foster care is a special needs child because that child has been taken from his or her family. Foster parents need to be trained so they will know how to cope with a child's problems. The foster parent needs help to learn how to survive from day to day with children who have often learned that how to get attention is by throwing a tantrum. We now meet every last Tuesday of the month at the Social Services building in Mount Pearl. There we can discuss our concerns and borrow books on fostering. Our association is also trying to obtain an emergency phone for foster children who are being abused and are afraid to call from their home. It's such an important tool to have, yet we are one of the few provinces in Canada who do not have this service.

Child Welfare is an over-burdened system, which means the social workers have case loads up to a hundred. Obviously, we need more child welfare workers who are trained to deal with foster children. When you're talking of fostering, you are talking of meeting children with all kinds of problems, from families who have separated or a parent died, or the child has been abused or the adoption has broken down. I have known more than one child from an adoption breakdown. You take it, those children are rejected by their birth parents, probably they have been in foster care, they are rejected by them, then they go into adoption that breaks down, so they are put back in another foster home. What help is there for that little child? And these children are our future, yet through no fault of their own they will probably end up on the street one day.

The law says that at the age of 16 a foster child can leave fostering. That is too young. You wouldn't say to your own child, you're 16 today, you can leave now. Anyway, you would take them back if it didn't work out, but not so with fostering. If they come back it is as a boarder; whereas, if they stay with you, all education is paid, even through university. I think they should stay in care until they are at least 19.

If foster parents have a child in care for a few years and they grow to love that child, then they should be given first priority to adopt. We are lobbying to make a subsidized allowance available for adoption because presently once you adopt you are on your own financially. If you are average working class person with a few children of your own, it is next to impossible to put them through university with the child you've adopted. Some of that financial concern should remain with the Department of Social Services.

I think that in place of many of the group homes there should be more foster homes because group homes are more like an institution or an orphanage and it is very impersonal. It's run by staff and it doesn't have a family atmosphere. Payment for one child in a group home for one month is more than a foster parent receives in six months, but I know that some foster children do need special care above the love he or she will receive in a family setting. It is sad when you realize that foster children are given no special allowances for Christmas time or special occasions like birthdays.

Many of you could be foster parents. If you are the type of person who has time, love and comfort to give a child who has some problems, call me at 1-709-782-1547. Let's face it, fostering is for the children. The only benefit we get is knowing that we did something to help a child in need. We need a lot more foster parents. A lot, lot more.

From the book The Finest Kind *by Marion Frances White. Creative Publishing. Used by permission.*

♀

Survived Because of Love

By Cassie Brown

In times of great disaster, when death seems inevitable, there are many things that give man the will to stick it out just a little while longer.

On March 31, 1914, when over 150 men of the SS *Newfoundland* were caught in a raging blizzard on the icefields off the northeast coast of Newfoundland during the annual seal hunt, 78 men would die and the survivors would have been exposed to the vicious elements in zero weather.

Cecil Mouland of Doting Cove, Bonavista Bay, a cheerful man with a sunny disposition, was not 20 years old when he went to the icefields that year on the *Newfoundland*, and he survived because he was in love. Said Cecil, "I was courting a girl at that time, and I wondered who was going to have her if I died out on the ice. I made up my mind nobody else was going to get her."

It was a simple as that.

Today, October 27, 1964, he still has that girl, and they are celebrating their 49th wedding anniversary.

Going back to the *Newfoundland* disaster, Cecil Mouland recalls that they left the *Newfoundland* around 7 a.m. and made it to the SS *Stephano* around noon. It was snowing a little and they got aboard and had a mug-up, but some of them hadn't finished their mug-up before they were ordered over the side.

"We left everything up to the second hand, George Tuff," said Cecil. "But when Captain Kean told us we had to walk back to our own ship in such weather, we began to murmur like the children of Israel in the wilderness; we went for George like they went for Moses.

"That night we were waist-deep in snow, it was a real blizzard, and we began to get uneasy although it was snowing first, then raining and not too bad, but halfway through the night the wind chopped around and it began to freeze. It was a bad night after that."

In Cecil's crew, six men died that night. Two of the men fell in the water but were pulled out. However, the wet sealers lay on the ice and that is where they died.

They selected Jesse Collins as their boss, and he decided they should go through the motions of fishing in order to keep warm. First they went jigging, and he'd say, "There's not much on the jigger today, b'ys."

They all agreed and Mr. Collins would say, "We'll go with hook and line." They would bait their imaginary line, pulling in and in until they got warm.

When that was finished, Jesse Collins would say, "Alright b'ys, we'll go on parade now," and they would line up single file and march around and around, hitting one another on the shoulder. Then they would stop and huddle together, and everyone would try to get in the middle, boring in through the crowd. "Next thing, you'd be on the outside," said Cecil Mouland.

Cecil never stopped or sat down. He watched all the fellows as they gave up. All would say, "I'm awful tired and sleepy. I think I'll sit down for five minutes and take a little rest."

They sat down and never got up.

Cecil saw his own cousin, Ralph Mouland, lay down to die, and he said to him, "You going to die, Ralph?"

Ralph replied, "Yes, I can't stick it any longer."

Said Cecil, "Well, I wouldn't die if I were you. I wouldn't give it to them to say back home, that you died on this old ice." He then got Ralph to his feet, punched him and pushed him around, rousing him thoroughly. "He came through," said Cecil, "and died only a few years ago."

After the sealing disaster, Cecil Mouland moved to Brooklyn, N.Y., where he eventually became an American citizen. At the outbreak of World War II, the U.S. government asked for carpenters to volunteer to go around the world to build army, navy and airforce bases. Naturally, Cecil volunteered for Newfoundland!

But he was working one day at Fort Pepperell when he was stricken with pneumonia, from which he suffered a relapse. After he had recuperated from that he was run over by a car on Prince of Wales Street, right opposite Buckmaster's Field gate, was dragged about a hundred feet, and suffered over a dozen broken ribs, each broken in three places; a broken collar bone; and cuts and bruises. He was in hospital on a fracture board for six weeks.

Cecil returned to the United States after the war, but when he retired at the age of 65, Cecil and his wife, Jessie, came back to Newfoundland to live, and bought a home in Hare Bay, Bonavista Bay. He has been here for six years, and has applied to become a Canadian citizen.

This year, the 50th anniversary of the *Newfoundland* sealing disaster, Cecil Mouland was trying to get together all the 13 survivors for a reunion, but the men were too scattered.

Cecil attained his 71st birthday, Sept. 27, and still retains his sunny disposition. Said Mrs. Mouland, "I don't think there's anyone else like him. He's a very nice man, I don't know what I'd do without him."

Mr. Mouland is a Salvation Army man, and at one period was an usher for Billy Graham for four months.

From The Caribou Disaster and Other Short Stories. *Published by Flanker Press. Used by permission.*

♀

 ## MABEL & MANLEY

"You haven't agreed with a thing I've said in 15 years, Mabel, " said Manley to his wife.

"It's been 17 years," replied Mabel.

♀

Aunt Alice says:

A friend of mine confused her valium with her birth control pills. She had 14 kids, but she doesn't really care.

Spice of Life

The phrase "working mother" is redundant.

– Jane Sellman

♀

Women Who Have Made A Difference – *By Ron Young*

Colleen McCrory discovered that Canada is losing one acre of forest every 12 seconds, so she decided to do something about it. For nearly two decades she has been crusading to protect the world's largest remaining temperate rainforest in British Columbia, which is being threatened by the over-cutting by loggers. More recently, she has been advocating for the protection of endangered northern boreal forests throughout Canada and the world. She has formed a number of societies to preserve nature. Among other things, these societies were responsible for the establishment of the 49,600 hectare Valhalla Provincial Park and later (in 1987), the South Moresby National Park Reserve in the Queen Charlotte Islands.

Candy Lightner founded MADD (Mothers Against Drunk Driving) in the U.S. when her 12-year-old daughter, Cari, was killed by a drunk driver. Today MADD has chapters throughout the U.S., Canada and with many international affiliates. Candy's outreach is felt through her lectures, speeches, writings and personal appearances. She speaks about survivors of alcohol-related crashes, victim's rights, legislative advocacy, grass roots organizations, and the need to recognize the contributions of women and children. After MADD came on the scene in the 80s, there was a noticeable drop in drivers being caught impaired at police road checks. The movie, *Mothers Against Drunk Drivers: The Candy Lightner Story*, starred Mariette Hartley.

Eleni Gatzoyiannis, a woman from a small village in Greece, was given the tribute to motherhood award, which is presented by Women's International Center and is now called the Eleni Award in her honour. When her village and her very home were taken over, "liberated" as the soldiers called it, she did not disobey. She made do with what food and other items she could find for her family, food that was not already taken by the soldiers. She worked at hard labour every day, and even let an older daughter join the soldiers to fight, all in the name of a cause she didn't understand. But when they told her she must give up her children so that they could be raised as Communists in another country, she went against all her cultural and familial teachings. She defied authority and arranged for her children to escape from Greece and go to their father in America. She was charged with treason, tortured and condemned to death by firing squad. As Eleni stood before them, ready to die, she raised her arms and shouted her last words, "My Children!"

Eleanor Roosevelt, a niece of President Theodore Roosevelt, was born in New York to a prominent family of Dutch ancestry and learned how to deal with disappointments at an early age. Her mother died when she was eight, and her father when she was 10. Eleanor later did social work in New York before marrying her distant cousin, Franklin Roosevelt, in 1905. She faced another disappointment in 1918, when she learned her husband was having an affair with her social secretary, Lucy Page Mercer. Although she resolved to have a career of her own, that didn't stop her from becoming active in Democratic party politics as a means of keeping alive the political career of her husband, who had become handicapped by poliomyelitis.

   She not only assisted him in his bid for the presidency, which he won in 1932, but continued to assist him; and although she held no office, she soon became an influential figure in his administration. To help offset the devastation of the Great Depression during the 1930s, Eleanor sponsored an experiment at Arthurdale, West Virginia, designed to bring small-scale manufacturing to impoverished coal miners in a self-sustaining community.

Life, Love & Laughter

Eleanor was even more liberal than her Democrat husband and worked to promote racial equality. In a famous incident, the president's wife resigned from the Daughters of the American Revolution when black singer Marian Anderson was denied the use of their facilities.

During World War II, during which her husband died, she visited American soldiers around the world, all the time championing desegregation of the armed forces. After the death of her husband she became a delegate of the newly-founded United Nations where she chaired the commission that drafted the Universal Declaration of Human Rights. Eleanor Roosevelt, whose creed was, "No one can make you feel inferior without your permission," died in New York City on November 7, 1962.

Bridget "Biddy" Mason was born a black slave in Mississippi, but moved with her masters to Utah and then to California, herself herding the cattle westward as she also prepared meals, acted as a midwife and took care of her own children.

Obviously unknown to her master, California had been admitted to the Union in 1850 as a "free state," and slavery was forbidden there. Biddy petitioned the court and in 1856 won freedom for herself and for her daughters. She then moved to Los Angeles and found employment as a nurse and midwife. With the money she saved from her hard work and her nursing skills she bought a site on Spring Street for $250. In 1884, she sold a parcel of the land for $1500 and built a commercial building with spaces for rental on the remaining land. Using her great business skills, Biddy became very rich. Her grandson would later become the richest African-American in Los Angeles.

But Biddy was not only smart and rich, she was also caring and giving. She gave generously to various charities and provided food and shelter for the poor of all races. In 1872 she and her son-in-law, Charles Owens, founded and financed L.A.'s first black church.

♀

👥 Her Other Half
Troublesome Twosome

Two men playing golf were annoyed by the two lady golfers playing on the course ahead of them. The two took a lot of time in making their shots and were holding up the men's game. One man said to the other, I think I'll talk to those women to see if they'll let us play through them and get on with our game. When he got near the spot where the women were about to tee off, he suddenly turned around and ran back to his playing partner.

"I can't talk to those two women," he said, "One of them is my wife and the other is a woman I am having an affair with. You go talk to them."

But the second man turned around before he even got as far as the first, and when he came running back said, "Small world, isn't it?"

♀

Life, Love & Laughter

🧠 Her Other Half
Premature Put–Down

In the middle of a furious row with her husband, the wife yelled, "I should have listened to my mother. She told me years ago that you and I were incompatible."

"And all these years, how I've wronged that poor woman," the man sighed.

♀

 # Aphrodesia

"I have a good surprise for your husband, Aphrodesia," her doctor told her.

"I don't have a husband," said Aphrodesia.

"Then your boyfriend is in for one hell of a surprise," the doctor returned.

"I've never had a boyfriend in my life," insisted Aphrodesia.

The doctor walked over to the window and looked up at the night sky, while shaking his head.

"What are you looking for?" asked Aphrodesia.

"Well, I never believed in miracles, but right now I'm looking for a star rising in the east."

♀

💇 Female Firsts

1926: On April 21, Elizabeth Windsor was born in a London townhouse, making her the first British monarch to be born at a private address.

1926: At age 19, Gertrude Ederle became the first woman to swim the English Channel. On that swim she set a new time record for the distance; one hour and 52 minutes faster than the previous male record.

1926: Helena Frecker became the first person to complete the university program at Memorial University College of Newfoundland.

1927: Elsie Eaves became the first woman admitted to full membership to the American Society of Civil Engineers (ASCE).

1928: Anna Dexter became queen of the airwaves as Canada's first woman radio broadcaster.

1928: (or thereabouts) Englishwoman Kathleen Mary Kenyon became the first female president of the Oxford Archeological Society. She was later responsible for the excavations at Jericho, one of the earliest continuous settlements in the world.

1928: Canada's Olympic Team included women for the first time.

1928: Alice Catherine Evans became the first female president of the Society of American Bacteriologists (now the American Society for Microbiology). *See also page 168.*

1928: American Betty Robinson became the first woman to win a gold medal in track and field at the Olympics for the 100-metre race.

♀

Life's Funny Experiences

Laundry Deterrent

This story proves how much some Newfie wives spoil their husbands. My husband and I had been married about a year and a half. I was having some trouble with my clothes dryer. Gord is a jack-of-all-trades, so I asked him to go downstairs and take a look at the dryer to see if he could fix it. He marled off down into the basement, and soon I heard the rattle of tools being put in to place. About five minutes later the call came, "Babe!!" I went to see what he needed, and he asked, "Which one is the dryer?" True story. He still couldn't wash a load of clothes if he had to.

Tina – Grande Prairie, Alberta, Canada

♀

 **Out of Habit**

Margaret had been a model nun all her life, but then she was called to her reward. As she approached the pearly gates, Saint Peter said, "Hold on, Sister Margaret...not so fast!"

"But I have been good all my life and dedicated to the work of the Lord. From the time I was taken in as an infant by the sisters at the convent to my dying breath...I have lived for this moment!" Sister Margaret exclaimed in disbelief.

"That is just the problem," replied St. Peter. "You never learned right from wrong and to get into heaven, you must know the difference between right and wrong."

"Well, what can I do? I will do anything to get into heaven!" Sister Margaret pleaded.

"I am going to have to send you back down to Earth. When you get there, I want you to smoke a cigarette and call me when you are finished...we will discuss your situation then," ordered St. Peter.

Sister Margaret returned to Earth, smoked a Camel and then immediately called St. Peter, coughing and hacking.

"Saint Peter," she gasped, "I can hardly breathe, my mouth tastes terrible, my breath stinks, I feel dizzy, and I think I am going to throw up."

"Good!" replied the old saint. "Now you are finally getting a feel for right and wrong. Now go out tonight and drink some hard liquor and call me back when you are ready."

Sister Margaret phoned St. Peter immediately after taking several belts of Jack Daniels.

"Saint Peter...I feel woozy...that vile liquid burned my throat and nauseated me...it is all I can do to keep it down."

"Good...good! Now you are starting to see the difference between right and wrong," said St. Peter with delight.

"Tomorrow I want you to seek out a man and know him in the biblical sense, then call me."

A week passed before Sister Margaret called St. Peter and left a message: "Yo, Pete...it's Peggy. It's gonna be a while!"

♀

Life, Love & Laughter

Animal Mating – Fact and Fantasy – *Ron Young*

Love is in the Air

Fact:

   Bats are the only mammals to have been given the gift of flight. Apart from the fact that they give birth to their young live, instead of laying eggs like birds and insects, they also mate in a different way - the male bat rides on the back of the female and they mate while they are flying.

   In 1947, a bat biologist was flyfishing when he thought he saw a bat fall out of the sky. What he was actually seeing were two bats: a female bat, with her male mating-partner still hanging on for dear life. Actually he (the bat) wasn't hanging on for dear life, but had gotten so caught up in the act, that his copulative-clinging had restricted his female mate's flying ability, and both had crash-landed.

Fantasy:

Sometimes I find myself complyin'
With your advances while we're flyin'
And I have to say it makes me quite excited
Making babies in the sky
Is the only way to fly
And I love it when you say, "Let's fly united"

♀

Female Facts

Cassie the Con Artist

   Cassie Chadwick was born in Eastwood, Ontario, Canada in 1857. She became a forger, and at the age of 22 was arrested in Woodstock, Ontario. She was able to convince the court that she was insane and was not convicted of the crime. Dr. Wallace S. Springsteen of Cleveland, Ohio, met, and fell for the charms of Ms. Chadwick, not knowing of her background. In 1882 he married her, but 11 days later, found out about her past and threw her out. In 1886 and 1887 Cassie became a fortune teller using the names Lydia Scott and Madame Lydia DeVere. In 1889 she was again charged with forgery, this time in Toledo, Ohio. She was convicted and sentenced to 9 1/2 years, but she was lucky enough to be paroled, by then-governor William McKinley, after only four years.

   In 1897, while she was living in Cleveland as Mrs. Hoover, she met and married Dr. Leroy Chadwick, who knew nothing of her criminal activities. One day, while Mrs. Chadwick was visiting New York she met a banker friend from Cleveland and had him drive her to the home of Andrew Carnegie, once dubbed the richest man in the world. Mrs. Chadwick had the banker wait in the car while she went into Carnegie's house. At the door, the con artist merely asked for directions, but she was such a good actress that she was able to convince the banker that she was Carnegie's illegitimate daughter who would inherit everything when her father died. Thinking he could make money, the banker offered to loan her money at high rates of interest until she got her inheritance. Other Cleveland bankers got into the act and over a nine-year-period loaned her more than $5 million, causing several Ohio banks to collapse. In 1904 she was exposed and sentenced to 14 years. She died in Ohio State Prison in 1905.

♀

🐑 Her Other Half

Disguised As Married

As the happy couple neared the hotel where they would spend their honeymoon, the bride became embarrassed. "Oh," she sighed, "I don't want the people in the hotel to know that we're newlyweds. Couldn't we do something to make them think we've been married for a long time?"

"That's easy," said the taxi driver. "When you get out of the cab, carry all the suitcases yourself."

♀

Life's Funny Experiences

O Newfoundland

A few years ago while we were driving through the States, at every rest room, hotel or beach, we were asked where we were from. Our answer was, "Newfoundland." The automatic response to this was, "Where is Newfoundland?" We explained where the province was located, and that it is in Canada. After two weeks, while we were heading back home, we stopped for gas and along came the usual question from the gas attendant: "Where are you from?" This time we answered, "Canada." His reply was, "Is that in Newfoundland?" (He had noticed our Newfoundland licence plates.)

Betty – Newfoundland, Canada

♀

 Female Firsts

1929: Lowe Barnes became the first woman stunt pilot in motion pictures.

1929: Katherine Bement became the first person to conduct a national U.S. survey of sexual attitudes.

1929: Amy Johnson became the first British-trained female ground engineer,

1930: For the first time in Canada, federal divorce laws changed to allow a woman deserted by her husband to sue for divorce after two years of being abandoned from the town her husband lived in before separation. Before that, a woman's legal residence was wherever her husband lived, even if she didn't know where he lived.

1930: Britain's Amy Johnson became the first female to fly solo from England to Australia, a distance of 11,000 miles.

1930: On May 15, Ellen Church, a registered nurse, became the world's first airline stewardess.

1930: Anne Morrow Lindbergh became the first woman granted a glider pilot's license.

1930: Jennie Kelleher of Wisconsin became the first woman to bowl a perfect 300 game.

1931: Jane Addams, of the U.S., became the first woman to receive the Nobel Peace Prize.

1931: Jackie Mitchell became the first woman in organized baseball when she signed on as a pitcher for the Chattanooga Baseball Club.

♀

Life, Love & Laughter

Spice of Life

Cynicism is an unpleasant way of saying the truth. – *Lillian Hellman*

♀

Is That a Fact?

Many things are taken as facts. Not all of them are.

Gone With The Wind

Not everybody knows that *Gone With The Wind* was the only novel that Margaret Mitchell wrote.

The Fact Is that although it was the only novel the writer penned, it wasn't originally called that. Her title was *Tomorrow is Another Day,* which is the saying Scarlet O'Hara is famous for in the book and the movie. Her publisher, however, felt that at the time there were too many novels with the word "tomorrow" in them so it was changed. The heroine was to have the floral name of "Pansy," but the author changed her mind about that as well.

♀

Letters From Our Friends

"...spent six years in Newfoundland..."

Dear *Downhomer,*

Courtesy – The Baldwin Family

Since we have been receiving *Downhomer* here in Georgia (about two years), we have found some interesting, sincere, and comical items in your magazine.

I spent six years in Newfoundland while based at Fort Pepperrell with the US Air Force in the 50s and 60s. I was fortunate enough to find me a Newfie girlfriend the first year I was there. We got married in March 1953, in "the worst snow blizzard in 20 years," according to our taxi driver at the time.

My wife is from Charlottetown, Bonavista Bay. She was working at the London, New York and Paris store on old Water Street when I met her. She has three brothers and one sister still living in Newfoundland. Her sister and husband come to Clearwater, Florida, each year and we drive down from Georgia to visit with them.

I used to take leave each summer and we would spend one month visiting with her aunts and uncles in Charlottetown, Newfoundland; cod fishing and jigging was at its peak in the 50s. We still remember old Water Street, Bannerman Park, Bowring Park and also the old theatres: Cornwall, Nickel, Star, Paramount and Capital. Those were the best days of our lives.

We have been married 47 years now and have five grown children. They were born here in the U.S. My wife is now a U.S. citizen. However, we truly cherish the years we spent at Fort Pepperrell.

Attached is a photo of us taken in 1953. Some of the old folks may recognize us.
Respectfully,
James (and Madge) Baldwin – Cedartown, Georgia

♀

Life, Love & Laughter

WOMEN OF THE ISLAND AND THE BIG LAND

Gerry Rogers

Interview by Marian Frances White

Photo Peggy Norman

Gerry Rogers was born on August 17, 1956 in Corner Brook. Before she was a year old, her family moved to Montreal where her father was stationed in the army. Besides Montreal, throughout her school years, she lived in Toronto, Germany and Winnipeg where she completed her high school education. Gerry then entered the convent in Edmonton. In 1977 she left the convent and returned to Winnipeg where she worked in a juvenile group home for girls. In 1978 she returned to Newfoundland with her family and shared co-ordination of the Women's Centre in St. John's with Barbara Doran. In 1984 Gerry moved to Montreal to work with the National film Board of Canada. Since then, she has produced 17 films, most notably *To A Safer Place* and directed the film *After The Montreal Massacre*.

Gerry moved back to Newfoundland in 1998. In 1999 she was diagnosed with breast cancer. In 2000 she released a stunning, award-winning biographical film, *My Left Breast*, that details her journey to recovery.

*****

My experience of Newfoundland has always been with me because wherever my family lived, we identified as Newfoundlanders. Our family wasn't a closed system. We were like tumble weeds, transplanting our Newfoundland culture in the communities where we lived. I think this is why I can be at home wherever I am because I have a sense of bringing my home with me.

I'm a survivor of the Catholic school system and I'm a recovering Catholic, but when I look back on my life, some of the strongest role models I had were nuns that were my teachers. I was a sponge growing up, absorbing whatever was around me. I knew I wanted to learn things and travel and work with people, and I didn't want to be owned. Because of my parent's influence and encouragement, I learned I had a right to be happy and to fully participate in the world as I wanted to.

I entered the convent thinking I was taking a step toward freedom, but I certainly didn't find what I was looking for there. I was not a religious person, but I was spiritual. I loved communal prayer and meditation, and on those occasions I was able to go places spiritually that I couldn't on my own. There I was able to get in touch with the deep respect for life that I always felt and my intense curiosity that pushed me beyond borders.

However, my eyes were like layers of onion skins being peeled away to reveal the inherent sexism in the Church. The religious life I experienced within the Church was not so much a process of discernment and spiritual reflection as one of the value of obedience to the point where you cannot interpret your own feelings and your own spiritual movements. I was being taught to be suspicious of what my mind was saying, and I saw that this was distancing me from my own experience. At that point I began to tell myself this is not spirituality and liberation, and

Life, Love & Laughter

tonic for the Woman's Soul

this is not where I want to be. This is a box and this is destructive. When I left, I felt like I had been wearing a pair of super tight shoes and I had taken my shoes off and wiggled my toes. My decision fit into the hypothalamus of my soul and for the first time I felt I had truly done something that was life-giving for myself.

I went back to Winnipeg with the three hundred dollars they gave me after three and a half years and I got work in a juvenile home for girls. Everything was so different. I had come from a place where my environment was so controlled; the convent not only defines who you are, but what you're wearing, and it also defined how others react to you. So all of a sudden I didn't have that anymore and I felt like I had entered a new world of music and sound.

If anyone had told me then that I would eventually leave the Church, I would not have believed them. There were pockets of the Church that I really liked, the social activism and the community action, so I imagined I would continue to be involved. As I looked closer I had no choice but reject it as one of the most serious patriarchal, misogynist institutions on the face of the Earth. This was the mid-1970s, long before the Mount Cashel revelations, but then I was always aware that there was violence within the Church. My father quit school in grade nine because he couldn't stand the violence of the Christian Brothers in the classroom.

Indirectly, because of the fundamental formative message of the Church, which was that pain and sin and evil are brought into this world through a woman, I became a feminist. To not become a feminist you would have to actively decide to close your eyes, deny reality and experience.

One of the last times I was in a Church was at midnight Mass with my parents. Here was this old man, supposedly celibate, saying that the epitome of womanhood was to be like Virgin Mary, a woman who could give birth and still be a virgin, and all I could see in front of me was this sea of tired women who could never be virginal mothers, but who had given and given of themselves all their lives. I had to leave because I saw this as the ultimate abuse.

When I returned to Newfoundland, I felt I was where I belonged and stayed for five years, but I had to reconnect with the Rock in a physical way and that was exciting for me. To reconnect with the ocean, the rocks, the forest and the woods, happened with my family and also with women like Sandy Pottle, who is a strong feminist activist. To go out to the ocean at night and watch the breakers and feel the wind and taste the salt on my lips is something that will never leave me, and it's something that I'll have to constantly return to.

My involvement in the women's community coincided with this return to my roots. I finished my social work degree at Memorial and became involved with the Women's Centre, which was one of the best things that ever happened to me and marked the beginning of my formalized initiation into the women's movement. I remember having to do an impact evaluation of unified family court and I'd sit in on court proceedings and watch the many battered women that passed through the court system. I observed how women were treated in court and I watched the fear on the faces of these women as they were not protected from the men who were hurting them. My life was radically transformed by these observations as I began to see women's reality through their eyes. Women like Barbara Doran and Bonnie Jarvis helped push me into things that I never thought I would be able to do. I ended up representing NAC (National Action Committee on the Status of Women) and being a spokesperson in Regina and Ottawa for women in the Province of Newfoundland and Labrador. I never felt more alive in all my life!

I grew up not wanting to be like regular girls, and began to see that my most profound connections were with women. It's funny because I also went through a period in my life where I didn't like women a whole lot; I didn't like who we were supposed to be in this society. I always envied lesbians and felt they were so lucky to have found each other. Although there is no closet big enough to contain me, it took awhile for me to find my identity; but when I did, that was a

Life, Love & Laughter

Life, Love & Laughter

true celebration of self discovery. It was another life-giving decision I made for myself.

My work with film gives me a deep connection with the grassroots struggles I had experienced with women in Newfoundland. I remember saying to Kathleen Shannon, who had been to Newfoundland to launch *Not a Love Story*, that the strength and power of women's voices are not being heard. We needed films about the experience of being a Newfoundland woman, not films that someone from the outside will make about us; we need to speak to ourselves, our experiences and our dreams. So I went to Montreal in 1982 for six weeks to try and express some of these ideas.

As Newfoundlanders coming from that God-forsaken Rock, we always feel marginal and as an anglophone in Quebec and as a lesbian and a radical feminist activist, I could be quite marginalized, but I feel like I'm in the centre of where I want to be. I think that political activism and community building and identity is all about creating your own space in the world. Although I speak French more now and I understand the struggle of the Quebecois, I feel very much like a guest in Quebec; not a formal guest, but a cousin hanging out with the family. "Alors, je suis chez ma cousine." A few years ago I almost left here because my French wasn't so great. It was during the Chantal Daigle case and I wanted to express my activism on the pro-choice issue. We worked entirely in French and I felt that I finally had found a feminist activist community that I had a commonality with.

Working on *To A Safer Place* with Shirley Turcott changed my life. I had wanted to do a film about incest that would reach out to women and say you're not crazy or alone, and I wanted to work on a film that would be healing, but I could never have dreamed that it would have the impact that it's had. Filmatically it's won awards all over the world, but more importantly is how it has touched so many lives.

Producing the international women's film festival in Nairobi was such an empowering experience because it taught me so much about racism and imperialism. One of the biggest payoffs in filmmaking is seeing your film with an audience because I am not a separate, objective expert. I am often accused of being subjective and I ask since when has this come to be an accusation, when to be subjective means to do work about something that you are passionate about and know about. I believe this journalistic standard of objectivity is a myth that will keep us separate from each other. Filmmaking is a communication of many voices so that we can speak to one another and break silences and empower one another.

Woman-talk excites me because women are such wonderful storytellers. I want to produce a film that will look closer at women and body image; not just as a critique of the media and the "male stream" portrayal of women, but I want to look at how we take our space and our power, and I want to use music and poetry and dance, and I want this work to be an explosion of the celebration of our lives, despite all the restraints and contemporary efforts to make women smaller and smaller until we barely exist. Somehow, we're breaking through and I want to show these survival mechanisms and give each other permission to explode and to take our place in celebrating our survival.

I've learned that it's so important to be in touch with your gut and to trust your gut feeling and follow those rhythms even though sometimes you don't know where that is going to lead. When I look at the existing structures and systems that exist today, they're not working so well, so to me, to fit into those systems and structures is not a sign of success. Things can be really tough financially, but that should not get in our way of daring to dream. To dare to dream is not being naive or stupid. I think it's one of the most courageous things we can get in touch with.

I have a sense of myself and Newfoundland as rocks that float; not fighting or being tossed around in the wind. I go home and I hear music and we dance and pick blueberries and sit by the ocean, that's home. And yet I feel it is within me wherever I go, so I have a sense of living in a transmutable home. The uncertainty of my life is not frightening. I feel I am like a kid in a candy store in terms of how much there is to learn, but I do not have the same sense of urgency because I know all the changes are not going to happen today; but I have the time and energy to help them happen for our continued struggle.

From the book The Finest Kind *by Marian Frances White. Creative Publishing. Used by permission.*

♀

Aunt Alice says:

When I'm finally holding all the cards, why does everybody want to play chess?

Spice of Life

A woman starts lying about her age when her face starts telling the truth about it.

♀

 MABEL & MANLEY

Manley excused his wife and himself as they squeezed past the elderly man on the outside of the church pew and Mabel sat next to him.

Mabel became increasingly aware that it was hot inside the church and thought that the air conditioner must not be working. Suddenly the old man who had been sweating so opulently beside her, lurched forward.

"Put your head between your knees," said Mabel as she knelt beside the bent-over old man, holding his head down with her hand. "You'll feel better if the blood can get to your head."

"For God's sake, Mabel," said Manley, "will you let him up. The man is trying to pick up his hat that you kicked up under the front pew."

♀

Life's Funny Experiences
Stealing is Unethical

When I was in college, I happened to take an ethics course (Philosophy Dept.). One day when I went to lunch in the college cafeteria, I put my books down, as usual, on the shelves at the entrance. My ethics textbooks were among them. When I finished lunch, my books were nowhere to be seen! I put up signs all over the campus: "To whoever took my ethics books: please keep them. You obviously need them more than I do!" The next day, all my books mysteriously reappeared on the shelf where I had left them.

Debbie – New York, USA

♀

Life, Love & Laughter

Women Who Have Made A Difference — *By Ron Young*

Marilyn Bell, a Toronto schoolgirl, became the first person to swim across Lake Ontario when she emerged from the waters on the Canadian side shortly after 8:00 p.m. on September 9, 1954. When the 16-year-old stepped into the water at Youngstown, New York at 11:00 p.m. the previous evening she had more challenges facing her than she realized. Forced to swim much further than the 51.5-kilometre (32-mile) route straight across the lake due to poor conditions, she also had to contend with choking oil slicks, lamprey eels and overwhelming fatigue. Two other swimmers were attempting the crossing at the time. One was well-known American marathon swimmer Florence Chadwick; the other, Toronto swimming star Winnie Roach Leuszler. While both were competing for the $10,000 prize offered by the Canadian National Exhibition, Marilyn decided to attempt the swim herself even though she had not been invited or offered any money to do so. She was the only one to make it, so the Exhibition gave her the prize money anyway. She was also showered with gifts from Canadians everywhere and became an immediate celebrity. Marilyn later became the youngest person to swim the English Channel, as well as the youngest to swim the Strait of Juan de Fuca.

Queen Victoria became Monarch of Great Britain and Ireland at age 18. The prime minister, Lord Melbourne, served as her educator in political decision-making. Before long, however, Victoria's iron will caused her to dispense with the prime minister's advice and ruled by her own power. She was married to Prince Albert of Saxe-Coburg-Gotha for 21 years, raising nine children together. When Albert died in 1861, the Queen went into a prolonged state of mourning and depression. Eventually, Victoria became one of Great Britain's most popular and prominent monarchs. Before she died in 1901, her long reign saw progress in her own country as well as expansion of the British Empire.

Dian Fossey, an American zoologist, spent 22 years studying the ecology and behavior of mountain gorillas. Her field studies of wild gorillas in the Virunga Mountains of Rwanda and Zaire served to dispel many myths about the violent and aggressive nature of gorillas. She was found murdered at her campsite in 1985 and although the murder was never solved, some authorities believe she was killed in retaliation for her efforts to stop the poaching of gorillas and other animals in Africa. Mountain gorillas are now protected by the government of Rwanda and by the international conservation and scientific communities, due mostly to the efforts of Dian Fossey.

Huda Shaarawi, who was born in Egypt in 1879, grew up envying her brother and all the advantages he had, because he was a male. Among the other disadvantages of women in Egypt, they were confined to the house or harem, and when in public, women were expected to show modesty by covering their hair and faces with veils. Young girls were also forced to marry at an early age. Against her wishes, at age 13, she herself was betrothed to her much older cousin as a second wife. Huda later started organizing lectures for women on topics of interest to them, bringing many women out of their homes and into public places for the first time. Huda convinced the royal princesses to help her establish a women's welfare society to raise money for poor women of their country, and in 1910 she opened a school for girls where she focused on teaching academic subjects, rather than practical skills such as midwifery. In 1919, after WWI, Huda helped organize a large women's demonstration against the British rule. In defiance of

British orders to disperse, the women remained still for three hours in the hot sun. After her husband's death in 1922, Huda returned from a conference in Europe and when she stepped off the train she removed her veil. This, at first, shocked the women who came to greet her. Then they broke into applause, some of them taking off their veils as well. This was the first public defiance of the restrictive tradition. In 1923 Huda was elected president of the Egyptian Feminist Union, which she helped to found, and for the rest of her life in that position, she campaigned for various reforms to improve women's lives. Among her accomplishments was the raising of the minimum age of marriage for girls to 16, increasing women's educational opportunities and improving health care.

She was instrumental in the founding of Egypt's first secondary school for girls in 1927. Huda also led Egyptian women's delegations to international conferences and organized meetings with other Arab feminists, and in 1944 she founded the All-Arab Federation of Women.

Helen Sawyer Hogg, an astronomer who was considered a world expert on the night sky, developed a technique for measuring the distance of galaxies beyond the Milky Way. She was the first woman president of the physical sciences section of the Royal Society of Canada in 1960. She was also the first female president of the Royal Canadian Institute (1964-1965) and founding president of the Canadian Astronomical Society (1971-1972). Hogg received honorary degrees from six Canadian and U.S. universities. Both the Canadian National Museum of Science and Technology's observatory in Ottawa, and the University of Toronto's southern observatory in Chile were named for her. When Helen Sawyer Hogg died of a heart attack in 1993, she had been a leading authority in astronomy for more than 60 years.

Princess Yasmin Aga Khan is the daughter of Rita Hayworth. After her mother died with Alzheimer's Disease, the princess chose to use her name and position to help fight this most misunderstood and fatal disease. Yasmin has since established a world-wide network to coordinate Alzheimer's Disease research, and has brought together this global connection by her many published interviews and by making scores of public appearances. Through public awareness about Alzheimer's disease, Yasmin Aga Khan has reached scientific and monetary sources which might otherwise have been left untouched. She also serves on many boards and committees because she believes that someday a cure for Alzheimer's Disease will become a reality.

♀

Life's Funny Experiences
Microbrain

We often fondly refer to my daughter Amanda as "Bubbles" (having nothing but bubbles between her ears). One night, Amanda was supposed to go help her brother with one of his jobs. He was pacing and ready to go, but Amanda had to finish her supper first. He then came to me and said that she had her supper back in the microwave. Amanda replied that she was cooling it off. I told her that you cook in the microwave. Very indignantly she said, "I know that. I have it on defrost."

Brenda McPherson– Ontario, Canada

♀

Life, Love & Laughter

Ennellene

I've taunted fate and survived to date
And side-stepped life's little crinkles
And time has healed most of my wounds
But it's been hard as hell on my wrinkles

♀

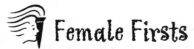 Her Other Half

The Lion's Share

"I'm the head of my house," said a recently married man to his friend, as they sipped a beer at the pub. "After all, I should be. I'm the one who earns the most money."

"I have a different arrangement with my wife," replied the second man. "I decide on the major problems and she decides on the minor ones."

"How does that work out for you?" queried the first husband.

"Great!" replied his friend. "In 10 years we've never had a major problem."

♀

Female Firsts

1932: Amelia Earhart Putnam became the first woman pilot to fly solo across the Atlantic.

1932: Dr. Elizabeth Bagshaw became director of Canada's first family planning clinic, when such clinics were illegal.

1932: American Helene Madison became the first woman to swim the 100-yard freestyle in a minute at the Los Angeles Olympics.

1933: Nellie Tayloe Ross became the first woman director of the U.S. Mint, a position she held until 1955. *See also Female Firsts page 146.*

1933: The first chocolate chip cookie was created by Ruth Wakefield.

1934: Anne Morrow Lindburgh became the first woman to win the National Geographic Society's Hubbard Gold Medal for distinction in exploration, research and discovery.

1934: Mary Hirsch became the first woman to be a licensed trainer of thoroughbred horses.

1934: Evangeline Cory Booth, at age 69, became the fourth elected commander and the first woman general of the Salvation Army. She was the seventh child of Salvation Army founder, William Booth.

1934: Phyllis Dewar of Moose Jaw, Saskatchewan, became the first Canadian woman to win four gold medals for swimming at the 1934 British Empire Games. That record lasted until 1966.

♀

🔥 WOMEN OF THE ISLAND AND THE BIG LAND 🔥

Marilyn John

Interview by Marian Frances White

White Photographic

Marilyn John has taken on the mammoth task of claiming aboriginal rights for the Newfoundland Micmac Indians. She was born on the Conne River Reserve, Bay d'Espoir, on September 20, 1951. By 1973 she had been elected secretary/treasurer of the Native Association of Newfoundland and Labrador. The first group attempted to organize all aboriginal people in the province; it included the Nascapi, Montagnais, Micmac and Inuit. Over the next five years, as vice-president and president of the Micmac Band, she encouraged them to go back to their tribal systems. To determine the status of people living in Conne River, Marilyn worked with the Department of Indian Affairs doing genealogy research. The 580 Micmac Indians were finally given Indians Status in 1984 under the Indian Act of Canada. As international spokesperson for the Band, Marilyn has lobbied in Geneva to have the United Nations establish a statement of principles for indigenous people of the world. She negotiates for reserve lands, for Indian control of education, and for more say in the Indian social and welfare system.

*****

As a child I was taught English as my first language. Later on in life, I began to realize there was a part of my culture missing and I wanted to know what that was. I never learnt the Micmac language fluently because the old people around me were discouraged from using it. The Micmacs were even discouraged from saying their Catholic prayers in their own language. I would like to see the school systems changed to take into account the Indian culture.

Culture is a big part of the development of an individual; that is, knowing who you are and what you are. Because this has not been taught in the schools, kids today are caught between two worlds. To change this, we have finally introduced the Micmac language as an extra-curricular activity in the schools. Up until our booklet on the culture history of the Micmacs was printed, everything that was written about us was written by non-Micmacs. We are finally beginning to express ourselves as we see ourselves.

As aboriginal people, we see the right to land as one of our basic rights. The attitude that the Micmacs are not aboriginal to this island is ludicrous. The Micmac Indians have been in Newfoundland since time immemorial and once occupied a land mass of what is today known as Eastern Canada. They were a nomadic people and travelled back and forth between here and Nova Scotia. This is where the old mythology that the Micmacs were brought over here to kill off the Beothucks is slowly losing ground. In the research done on genealogy, we have been able to document that both Beothuks and Micmacs lived in the same community but have not been able to document any major clashes or wars between them. It seems apparent that many of the people here today are a mixture of Beothuk and Micmac. Every summer an archaeologist comes here to do excavating and talks to the old people. He has documented so many similarities between them that he believes what other archaeologists have labelled as Beothuck could very well be Micmac. Today the government is saying that the Beothuks are the aboriginal people. I

Life, Love & Laughter

venture to say that if there were Beothuk people around today to claim aboriginal rights, the attitude would be the opposite. I have come to recognize that people's attitudes are born out of ignorance. You have to teach people your history and make credible arguments for them to realize that what they have always believed is not necessarily truth.

In June 1984, the Micmacs were finally recognized as Status Indians under Canada's Indian Act. Since then the Band's social conditions have improved greatly. However, when it comes down to reserve lands, the provincial government tries to make things very sticky for us by attaching so many conditions to granting land for a reservation. We don't feel they have land to grant us because the land was ours to start with. We have aboriginal rights as the first people here. We are not a minority group but indigenous people, and the problems generated from other people who left their own country and came to ours...we have problems because they came to ours. We feel we have the right to fish, hunt and to make our own laws and to develop ourselves in a manner that we feel is fit for our people.

Before April 17, 1985, if an Indian woman married a non-Indian man, legislatively she was cast out of the tribe and was not allowed to live on reservation land; neither was she entitled to any programs or services of the Band. We negotiated Clause 12 1 B so that this would not apply to our women. Clause 12 1 B now states that even if you have intermarried we do not cast you out. However, we also realize that a time may come when too much intermarriage will seriously threaten our culture.

Employment is very scarce in Newfoundland and, to say the least, desperate for Indian women. It is especially scarce for non-professional women with no education and also women who are young, unwed mothers. Because of this problem I have been working on a training program to bring women back into the workforce. We are using skills that are in the community like basket weaving, leather work, bead work, and reviving the old art of doing embroidery with caribou hair. Employment and Immigration partially sponsors these programs. Under *Micmac Crafts* we sell our work all over Canada in trade shows. This project works well because some of the older people here offered to teach their skills to the younger generation.

As a counsellor for the Band, I see the problems of child welfare and medical services as serious ones. The immune system of the Indians here does not seem to be strong, whether that is genetic or not I don't know, but it certainly seems to have a lot to do with diet and the kinds of food we eat. In my genetic research, I have found that the people today are not as healthy as those who lived off wildlife. Now that we are federally funded, we have more money to put into these programs.

I think as women, especially aboriginal women, we have a role to play in developing our culture and providing for our own people. We should strive to ensure that the life we want to provide for them is the best one possible. I am dedicated to improving the life and lifestyles of all Indian people, and making the culture thrive and flourish where it would otherwise die. I think the answer lies in taking parts of our culture and using it in modern day situations. I don't think my work stops or starts regionally or internationally; you have to recognize the work on both ends to find the meeting point. Indian women have to start making this awareness grow so that somewhere in the middle we will all reach a happy medium.

These days I am keeping very busy running my restaurant, Dashwood. It's located between Bay D'Espoir and Harbour Breton; a perfect place to stop when you are travelling along the Trans Canada Highway and need a cup of coffee or tea.

From the book The Finest Kind *by Marion Frances White. Creative Publishing. Used by permission.*

♀

Women Who Have Made A Difference *– By Ron Young*

Emily Carr is one of Canada's most noted artists, but was also a good writer, receiving a Governor General's Award for her book, *Klee Wyck,* in 1941.

Sally James Farnham was convalescing in a New York City hospital when, in 1901, the urban housewife was given some modelling clay to play with. The figures she made while lying in bed were the beginning of a hobby that led to a profession, which brought her international fame. The Soldiers and Sailors Monument in Library Park, Ogdensburg, New York, was one of Mrs. Farnham's early works. Although she had no formal artistic training, in 1917 she was chosen over a long list of many famous sculptors to do a statue of Simon Boliver, the South American liberator. This project took four years to complete and when finished, stood 15 feet high and rested on a 16-foot pedestal. She sculpted busts of President Harding, Herbert Hoover and Theodore Roosevelt and many famous international subjects, as well as many larger statues at home and abroad.

Louisa May Alcott (1832-1888), the U.S. author best known for her creation of the classic work *Little Women*, was born into and grew up in poverty. The family was rich with friends, but didn't become financially secure until Louisa's book was published. This book has been immortalized in the movies as well. Jo, one of the characters in *Little Women*, was played by Katherine Hepburn. The author spent her life working for the right of women to vote and for the temperance (anti-alcohol) movement.

Anne Frank, along with her Jewish family, had escaped Nazi Germany into Holland in 1933. While hiding from the Nazis in the sealed-off back rooms of an Amsterdam office, she kept a diary describing with humour and tenderness her two arduous years in seclusion. They went into hiding in 1942 in order to avoid arrest by German occupation forces. The family's hiding place was revealed in August, 1944, and they were taken into custody. Anne, still in her teens, died in a German concentration camp at Belsen less than one year later. The diary was found in the hiding place and published in 1947 as *Het Achterhuis* (*The House Behind*). In 1952 it appeared in the U.S. as *Anne Frank: The Diary of a Young Girl*. It was dramatized for the stage under the title, *The Diary of Anne Frank* in 1956 and filmed in 1959.

Charlotte Friend discovered the link between viruses and cancer when she showed that leukemia could be induced experimentally by a virus. The oncologist and microbiologist also founded the Hampstead Child Therapy Course and Clinic in London in 1947 and served as its director after 1952. The author of numerous scientific books and papers, she also helped found the annual periodical *Psychoanalytic Study of the Child*, in 1945.

Marian Anderson was born the daughter of a black seller of ice and coal in Philadelphia in 1897. Her talent for music was noted when she was still in elementary school. After high school she applied to an all-white music school in Philadelphia, but her application was rejected because of her colour. She continued private studies and in 1925 won first prize at the New York Philharmonic voice competition. In the early 1930s she went on a concert tour of Europe, where her reputation was established. She performed at Town Hall and Carnegie Hall in New York. In the late 1930s she sang for the Roosevelts at the White House.

In 1939, Howard University sought to bring her to perform at Constitution Hall. The request was denied by the Daughters of the American Revolution (DAR), who owned the Hall, because she was black. Eleanor Roosevelt, who sat on the board of DAR, resigned her membership in protest over this decision and other prominent women followed suit. Mrs. Roosevelt then arranged a concert for Anderson at the Lincoln Memorial which was attended by 75,000 people. Millions more listened to the radio broadcast of this event. Four years later DAR invited Anderson to take part in a concert for China Relief at Constitution Hall, which she accepted.

In 1955, she became the first black person to join the Metropolitan Opera in New York. She also sang at the inaugurals of U.S. Presidents Eisenhower and Kennedy.

Alice Catherine Evans became the first female scientist to have a permanent appointment in the U.S. Dairy Division of the Bureau of Animal Industry; and in 1928, she became the first woman president of the Society of American Bacteriologists (now the American Society for Microbiology). The second "first" for Alice was partly because in 1917 she demonstrated that raw milk could transmit a bacterium, Bacillus abortus, which caused disease in cattle and in humans. Evans contracted this disease, brucellosis (undulant fever), herself and suffered from it for seven years. She advocated pasteurization of milk to effectively kill this disease-causing bacterium. Her findings and recommendations were not taken seriously by other scientists, partly because she was a woman and she had no Ph.D. She encountered a great deal of difficulty convincing physicians, public health officials, veterinarians and farmers that pasteurization was needed to halt the spread of this disease. Eventually she succeeded and in the 1930s, pasteurization of milk became mandatory in the U.S. dairy industry.

Jodie Foster made her debut as "The Coppertone Girl," then went on to cross the formidable boundary from child actor to adult star, director and producer, and according to *Cosmopolitan* magazine, "the most powerful woman in Hollywood." Foster had regular roles in a number of TV series, including "Mayberry, RFD," "The Courtship of Eddie's Father," "My Three Sons," and "Paper Moon," before her first feature part in Disney's *Napoleon and Samanta* in 1972. She received her first Academy Award nomination for her performance as a teenage prostitute in *Taxi Driver*. Her first Academy Award was for her role in *The Accused* in 1988. She produced her first movie, *Little Man Tate*, in which she also starred in 1991. That same year she won her second Oscar for playing an FBI agent in *Silence of the Lambs*. She was executive producer and star of *Nell* in 1994. Foster has created her own company, Egg Pictures, which gives her the opportunity to "develop something totally protected from the outside environment," said the single parent of two boys, "until it's ready."

♀

Aunt Alice says:

I think if God had really wanted me to touch my toes he would have put them on my knees.

Spice of Life

Every time I close the door on reality it comes in through the windows.
— *Jennifer Unlimited*

♀

Life, Love & Laughter

A Real Love Story

By Bette Murphy

Courtesy – The Ramos Family

This is a true love story, one that has lasted 33 years and has overcome all kinds of obstacles. It is the story of Ruby Amminson, an all-star softball player who was born and raised on Signal Hill in St. John's, and Brasilino Ramos, a marine engineer who was born and raised in Gafanha da Nazare, Portugal. It is a story of dedication to each other and a combined determination to allow nothing to stand in the path of their marriage. When they met at Walsh's Juke Joint on Shea Heights in 1968, Ruby was working at a food processing plant and Brasilino was an engine room worker on the Portuguese vessel, *Pedro de Barcelos*. As Ruby tells it, "I knew he was the one for me from the first time I saw him. I've always been stubborn, so I suppose I would have married him even if I knew all the problems we would have before we settled down in St. John's. Our life together has really been worth all the problems."

And there were plenty of problems. When they wed May 14, 1970, Ruby could speak a few Portuguese words and Brasilino could speak a few English words. They exchanged vows at St. Joseph's Church in the East End of St. John's, followed by a reception at a friend's home. Within two days, Brasilino was back on the Grand Banks providing power for his ship.

"From the time we met to two years after we were married I saw Brasilino about 40 days," Ruby remembers, "and 15 of those days came in one spurt while his ship was being repaired in St. John's. It would have been nice if we could have spent more time together, but that was just the way it was."

While Ruby is an outgoing individual, overflowing with energy and ready to talk to anyone, anywhere, Brasilino is a laid-back, relaxed person and a great listener. He was the first, and maybe only, Portuguese fisherman to watch entire female softball games at Wyatt Park in St. John's. Ruby played for Newfoundland and Labrador at the first Canada Summer Games in Halifax in 1969, and in the Canadian senior female championships in Fort Erie the same year. It appeared to be a simple case of "opposites attract."

The major trouble started in July 1970, when Brasilino was back in Portugal and the couple had decided that he would become a Canadian citizen. Despite the fact that he was legally married to a Canadian, the Portuguese government was very reluctant to issue passports to young citizens with specific training to leave its country. Though it would take time, Canada would eventually provide citizenship. But getting Portugal to provide immigration papers would be the problem.

"I sold some of my wedding gifts and scraped enough money together to fly to Portugal," Ruby recalls. "I guess I was nervous, but I really wasn't scared since I was going to be with Brasilino. His family was very kind to me, and I started to pick up more Portuguese words. The food was all right, but because it was all cooked in olive oil, I had a little trouble getting to like it. Overall, the stay with his parents and only brother was a good experience. I came to love and respect them just as I think they came to love and respect me. Our big dream was to get both of us back to St. John's."

The return to Newfoundland for Ruby started one night when, she says, "I knew something was happening. Brasilino packed a suitcase and left. I found out later that, for a fee, he had been smuggled across the border into Spain without a passport or any other papers. He became a real

Life, Love & Laughter

refugee. The next day I took a train, along with a lady who (I would find out) was seven months pregnant, and legally crossed into Spain. Brasilino and the lady's husband met us at a train station. We were crowded into the train like sardines, but overnight got across the next border into France, where Brasilino had an uncle."

Ruby describes her arrival in France as "really frightening. Since the lady and I had our passports we had no trouble, but Brasilino and her husband were separated from us and went to the refugee line. We sat on our suitcases at the train station for two or three hours waiting for our husbands. I went to a small store to get something to drink for us and suddenly saw what looked to me like a Nazi concentration camp, like in the movies. Brasilino was there behind barbed wire. I was really frightened and started to cry as I ran over a small hill and talked to him through the wire."

Fortunately, Brasilino was granted refugee status. His uncle took Brasilino and Ruby into his home and, again for a fee, they obtained work in a French manufacturing plant that turned out automobile parts in the French city of St. Claude. While they stayed with Brasilino's uncle for a short time, Ruby says that she and Brasilino soon moved into "our own two-room place." It wasn't a mansion but it wasn't too bad. "I was the first Canadian to work in the plant and made the total number of different nationalities reach 10. The money wasn't great, about $40 Canadian a week, but the 13 months we spent in Leone was a good time. We were together, and we were working on getting a Canadian passport for Brasilino. It was a strange situation...Brasilino could speak a few words of English, I could speak a few words of Portuguese and we could both speak very little French."

Very few homes or apartments in Leone had a telephone. "I would go to the post office every week and call the Canadian Embassy in Paris. It was one of the highlights of the week, but it was very (often) disappointing. I wrote plenty of letters, but the biggest problem was the change in Embassy people who handled Brasilino's case. It seemed like there was a different person every week, and this went on for 13 months. I remember I cried a lot about that because it seemed like the Embassy was dragging its feet. There was never any encouragement from the Embassy and, as a refugee, Brasilino had to check with the French police station every week."

Finally, Ruby had probably the happiest phone conversation of her life. Canada had agreed to accept Brasilino into the country and the papers were at the Embassy to be picked up. However, Ruby continues, "I was also told that while Brasilino could get into Canada, there was no guarantee France would let him leave since he was still officially a refugee." Regardless, they headed to Paris to pick up the papers and bought two tickets to Newfoundland, scheduled departure in four days. Ruby says, "After picking up the Canadian papers, it was a hard three days waiting for our flight."

In what Ruby describes as "the roughest day of my life," the couple arrived at Orly Airport near Paris, "about five hours before our flight was to leave. We reached the French immigration room and sat down. When I went to the official at the gate I was told to return to my seat and he would let us know if Brasilino had been approved to fly out of France. I went back to the man every 20 or 30 minutes and always got the same answer. I could see he was getting upset with me but I just wasn't able to help myself. We were so near to getting home, I guess I got emotional."

About 45 minutes before the plane was due to leave, there was a call for passengers to move to the departure area, and that's when Ruby completely broke down. "There were buckets of tears streaming from my eyes when I went back to the French guy. In fact, I still cry my heart out when I talk about it now. But I heard the nicest French word in the world when the official snarled *allez*. I grabbed Brasilino's hand and we nearly ran through the gate. We were so quick I didn't even get my Canadian passport stamped.

"We were finally on our way home."

They experienced another delay when their flight was grounded at Gander because fog in Torbay prevented their landing at St. John's airport. But at least they were in Newfoundland. "We hired a Gander taxi to drive us to St. John's and a big party at my parents' home," says Ruby. "We had about $300 left from our year's work in France but that was plenty."

Five years later, on October 28, 1976, Brasilino Ramos became a Canadian citizen. The couple have lived in Newfoundland ever since, except for two years in Toronto "to get work." They lived in Harbour Grace for six years while Brasilino was on a ship that fished out of that town.

Now, they sail together. "Brasilino is engineer on the *Ocean Concorde*, and I'm the first cook," explains Ruby. "It's a clam boat. I signed on about nine years ago as a factory worker and I've worked my way up to cook. I had to go to Gerry Crewe at the College of the North Atlantic and I earned my red seal certificate. We are out to sea for six or seven weeks together, and then we're back in St. John's for the same length of time. It's a pretty good setup but I'm thinking about giving it up next year or so."

The couple have two children: daughter Susie who has "a couple of degrees" and is a teacher, and son Lino who is involved in child care and the arts and culture. "They live with us and that's great because neither of them are any trouble; but I figure it's time for them to settle down and make Brasilino and me grandparents. That would be nice."

While their courtship, marriage and return to Canada could have been easier, both have no regrets about the whole situation. "It has been worth every bit of the effort," Ruby smiles. "We've had 31 great years of marriage, have two fine children and Brasilino has been a wonderful husband. It's been a good life and really I don't think I'd change any of it even if I could. I figure we've both been very lucky."

Reprinted from Downhomer *magazine.*

♀

Female Facts

In prehistoric times, women had 50 menstrual cycles or less; in Colonial America women were having approximately 150 cycles per lifetime; and currently in America, women average 450 - 480 menstrual cycles per lifetime. [Segal, 2001]

♀

Ennellene

Of the men that we married, the many and varied
The prizes of varied seductions
Have you ever asked why, your particular guy
Didn't come with pre-packaged instructions?

♀

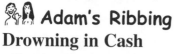 **Adam's Ribbing**
Drowning in Cash

"I can't believe that your husband, even though he couldn't read or write, left $5 million to you when he drowned," exclaimed a hairdresser to the lady whose hair she was giving a perm.

"And he couldn't swim either," commented her customer.

♀

Life, Love & Laughter

MABEL & MANLEY

Manley was wondering if his wife Mabel was having a hearing problem in her advancing years, so one night he stood behind her while she was sitting in her lounge chair. He spoke softly to her, "Mabel, honey, can you hear me?" There was no response, so Manley moved a little closer and said again, "Honey, can you hear me?" Still, there was no response. Finally he moved right behind her and said, "Honey, can you hear me?"

"For the third time, Manley! Yes! I can hear you," replied Mabel.

♀

Her Other Half

Private Detective

"Did you follow my wife last night?' the man asked the private detective he had hired.

"Yes, Sir, I did," he replied. "I followed her to a bar, a singles dance, and then finally to someone's apartment."

"Then I've got her!" the man exclaimed. "Is there any question about what she was doing?"

"No, there isn't," the detective replied. "She was following you."

♀

Female Firsts

1934: Jacqueline Cochran became the first woman to fly in the Bendix Trophy Transcontinental Race. *See also page 227.*

1935: Amelia Earhart Putnam became the first person to fly solo from Hawaii to California.

1936: For the first time, women's gymnastics was made part of the Olympic program at the Berlin Games.

1936: Sally Sterns became the first woman coxswain of a male rowing team at Rollins College.

1936: American Kit Klein became the first woman World Champion of Speedskating.

1937: Jacqueline Cochran became the first woman to make a blind landing in an airplane when she landed in Pittsburgh, Pennsylvania. *See also page 227.*

1937: Anne O'Hare McCormick, who worked for the *New York Times*, became the first woman to win a Pulitzer Prize in foreign correspondence.

1938: Jacqueline Cochran became the first woman to win the Bendix Trophy Transcontinental Race. *See also page 227.*

1938: Helen Stephens became the first woman to create, own and manage a semiprofessional basketball team.

♀

Life, Love & Laughter

Women Who Have Made A Difference – *By Ron Young*

Annie Jump Cannon, born in Dover, Delaware, USA, in 1863, was the first astronomer to classify the heavens systematically. Her "Henry Draper Catalog," which contains information on about 225,000 stars, is still accepted as an international standard.

Edith Louisa Cavell, a British nurse, was matron of a large training centre for nurses in Brussels, Belgium, when the First World War broke out. This school became a Red Cross hospital, and she attended many wounded German and Allied soldiers there. On August 5, 1915, during the German occupation of Brussels, she was arrested by the Germans for having sheltered 200 British, French and Belgian soldiers in her house, and for having helped them to escape from Belgium. In spite of protests by American and Spanish ministers to Germany, she was shot by a firing squad on October 12, 1915.

Sylvia Tyson made the big time in music as Ian and Sylvia with Ian Tyson, her husband at the time. The two recorded 13 albums for U.S. labels Vanguard Records, MGM, Ampex, and Columbia, which put them at the forefront of the 60s North American folk movement. The duo parted ways in music and marriage in the mid-70s, and Sylvia built an impressive solo career hosting television shows and releasing seven of her own albums. Some of the great songs written by Sylvia include "You Were on my Mind," and "River Road," which was also recorded by Crystal Gayle in 1980. In 1994, along with three of Canada's top female singer/songwriters, Sylvia formed the country/folk act Quartette, which has since released four albums.

Mother Teresa (of Calcutta) was born Agnes Gonxha Bojaxhiu in Skopje, now the capital of Macedonia. She entered the Sisters of Our Lady of Loreto and trained in Dublin, Ireland, at the age of 18. Taking her religious vows in 1937, she later served as principal of a Roman Catholic high school in Calcutta. She was moved by the presence of the sick and dying on the city's streets, and in 1948 was granted permission to leave her post at the convent and begin a ministry among the sick. Mother Teresa and her associates were approved within the archdiocese of Calcutta as the Missionaries of Charity in 1950, an order which was later recognized as a pontifical congregation under the jurisdiction of Rome. A fourth vow, pledging service to the poor, was added to the three basic vows of poverty, chastity, and obedience of nuns, in Mother Teresa's order. The work of Mother Teresa eventually  made its way to five continents and in 1979 she was awarded the Nobel Peace Prize. Mother Teresa died in 1997 at 87.

Alice Zukor is an internationally acclaimed floral designer who is known as "the flower lady with heart." Alice has owned and operated Broadway Florist, in the heart of the homeless area in downtown San Diego, California, for more than 40 years. The plight of those in need around her does not go unnoticed by Alice. Apart from her funding of charities, she also volunteers with the San Diego Rescue Mission, the Salvation Army and the YMCA.

The charity of the big-hearted volunteer begins, but does not end, in downtown San Diego. She also is world-renowned for her humanitarian efforts and has received the Key to the City from Leon, Mexico, as well as awards from such cities as Lisbon, Portugal; and Madrid, Spain.

Life, Love & Laughter

For the part she played in furthering goodwill between nations, the San Diego Business and Professional Women's Clubs gave her the "Outstanding International Achievements" award. As well, she received the Living Legacy Award.

Alice gives to charities in another way. If you don't see her at a charity or civic fund-raising function in San Diego, there is a good chance that flowers arranged in her world-famous floral designs will be there to give the place a cheery atmosphere. Donated, of course.

When Alice had triple by-pass heart surgery in 1992, those around her didn't expect her to ever work again, but within two weeks she was back up and working to help others. When someone told her she should slow down and take it easy, her reply was, "We can't relax now. There is so much to do. So many in need. The fight to help must go on."

Greer Garson is one of the most beloved actresses of our time, whose honours and awards are too numerous to enumerate in this space, but include "most loved" and "best actress" tributes from 11 countries. Her charitable and civic causes have earned her many Honorary Doctorates from various universities. Among the many acting roles she played was that of another famous woman, Marie Curie.

Nanette Fabray is the only woman to have received the Public Service Award from the American Academy of Otolaryncology (apart from Helen Keller). Besides her acting and performing abilities on stage and TV, which have won her a Tony and three Emmy Awards, Nanette has worked to bring sign language and captioning to television.

Handicapped for most of her adult life until four operations restored her hearing, Nanette has been in the forefront of the rights of all disabled people. Her many official, private and governmental memberships and appointments, including being a Trustee of the House Ear Institute, note Miss Fabray as an international leader for the handicapped. She has also received the Women's International Center's Living Legacy Award.

Laura Secord, was living in the Queenston area of Ontario, Canada when the Americans invaded. Her husband, James Secord, was not among the Canadian men over 18 who were marched off as prisoners of war in May of 1813, but was allowed to remain in his home due to the wounds which he was still recovering from after the Queenston battle of October 13, 1812. Some months later, Laura Secord overheard the three American officers, lodged in their home with James and herself, planning a surprise attack on the Canadian forces under FitzGibbons at Beaverdams.

She told the American sentry she was going to St. David's to visit her sick brother and she did briefly stop there, but continued on into Black Swamp, in spite of the midday heat and the rattlesnakes and wolves known to frequent the area. The 38-year-old woman then climbed the Niagara Escarpment, an 18-hour ordeal. Exhausted and lost, she was stumbling through the woods into a clearing when she was surrounded by Mohawk and Caughnawaga Indians, who were loyal Six Nations allies. With trepidation Laura pursuaded the warriors to take her to FitzGibbon to warn him of the attack. When the Americans attacked, 50 soldiers and 200 warriors stood ready. All but six of the American soldiers were captured and their attempt to control the Niagara Peninsula ended.

♀

Female Facts

Of all Canadian women 15-45, 28% reported that they had an unintended pregnancy (1998 Canadian Contraception Study).

♀

Quillings

Remember – By Christina Georgina Rossetti

Remember me when I am gone away,
Gone far into the silent land!
When you can no more hold me by the hand
Nor I half turn to go, yet turning stay.
Remember me when no more, day by day,
You tell me of our future that you planned:
Only remember me; you understand
It will be late to counsel then or pray.

Yet if you should forget me for a while
And afterwards remember, do not grieve
For if the darkness and corruption leave
A vestige of the thoughts that once I had,
Better by far you should forget and smile
Than that you should remember and be sad.

♀

Animal Mating – Fact and Fantasy – Ron Young

Dancing With the Devil

Fact:

There is not much love involved in the mating of Scorpions, but they do dance before the act. The scorpion, whose sting can be fatal, generally leads a solitary life and will eat other scorpions on sight if he or she can do it. When the male gets in the mood for mating he will start noisily vibrating to signal his intentions to a prospective female. Since the female scorpion is larger than the male he must approach her cautiously, for he knows she may be more in the mood for a meal than for mating. He will sometimes give her a non-fatal sting as a warning as he approaches her. There, linking their claws together, he leads her in a strange waltz as they keep each other at "arm's" length to avoid being eaten by the other. He then deposits his sperm on the ground (a flat rock or flat surface if possible) and manoeuvres his dance partner over it. If he can do it properly the sperm is sucked up into a genital pore on her underside. He will then get as far away from her as possible and not just because she's so ugly.

Fantasy:

Don't Save The Last Dance For Me
When lookin' for romancin'
Many males must take up dancin'
In human cultures, that's the way it goes
For Scorpion to do it rightly
He must learn to two-step lightly
His dancing partner really keeps him on his toes

♀

Female Firsts

1940: Belle Martel became the first woman boxing referee when she officiated eight bouts in San Bernardino, California.

1940: Québec women first obtained the provincial vote.

1940: On August 14, the first Rebakah Lodge (the female version of the Odd Fellows) was set up in Newfoundland.

1941: Jacqueline Cochran became the first woman to pilot a bomber across the Atlantic Ocean. *See also page 227.*

1941: Québec allowed women to practise law.

1941: The first Canadian bank strike was organized by Eileen Tallman.

1941: Linda Darnell became the first woman to sell securities on the New York Stock Exchange.

1942: Margaret Bourke-White, a photographer, became the first accredited female war correspondent.

1942: Julia Flikke of the Nurse Corps becomes the first woman colonel in the U.S. Army.

♀

Her Other Half

Six Again

A man asked his wife what she'd like for her birthday. "I'd love to be, uhm, six again," she replied.

On the morning of her birthday, he got her up bright and early, and off they went to a local theme park. What a day! He put her on every ride in the park: the Death Slide, the Screaming Loop, the Wall of Fear, everything there was! Wow! Five hours later she staggered out of the theme park, her head reeling and her stomach upside down.

Right to a McDonald's they went, where her husband ordered her a Big Mac along with extra fries and a refreshing chocolate shake. Then it was off to a movie, the latest epic, and hot dogs, popcorn, pop, a chocolate bar and candy.

What a fabulous adventure! Finally she wobbled home with her husband and collapsed into bed.

He leaned over and lovingly asked, "Well, dear, what was it like being six again?"

One eye opened. "You idiot! I meant my dress size."

The moral of this story: Even when a man is listening, he's still gonna get it wrong.

– *Author Unknown*

♀

WOMEN OF THE ISLAND AND THE BIG LAND
Constance Chretien
Original interview by Marie-Annick Desplanques.

Marie-Annick Desplanques

Constance Chretien was born in Cape St. George on June 14, 1913, the only girl among nine children. Her parents, Joseph Lainey and Marguerite Cornect, were francophone - one from Acadia and the other from France. Like her brothers, she did not have a chance to go to school and although she does not know how to read or write, she knows all the joys and pains of life outdoors. She and her husband, Henri, had 16 children, two of whom died when they were young. While raising her children she also took care of the farm and the two cows while her husband was off to sea. In her leisure time, she sings and plays the accordion. She has been a widow for a number of years but is alive and well. At age 90, Constance lives with her daughter, Margaret Alexander, in Kippens, Newfoundland.

*****

I grew up in a French community, Cape St. George, and never heard English spoken in my younger years. Most women around me worked on the farms while men were out fishing, but I fished *and* farmed. I went fishing in the morning and milked cows in the evening. I did everything men did and when I would come back home, I had to do the housework while my brothers relaxed. In those days, women's life was much harder than the men's life.

With all this work, there was not much time left for leisure, but women would get together and spin. That was the time for stories, too! Some of us would play cards, some would spin and some would knit. There were no "me," only "us," only women. When we were finished we would drink homebrew and joke around and I would play my accordion. I learned to play that myself.

From the book The Finest Kind *by Marion Frances White. Creative Publishing. Used by permission.*

♀

Female Facts
Women blink twice as often as men.

♀

Food for Thought
Love is more easily illustrated than defined.

♀

Ennellene

If you're feeling downcast by that face in the glass
That's not fit to be anyone's pin-up
Give yourself the gift of a brand new face-lift
It's one sure way to help keep your chin up

♀

Life, Love & Laughter

Women Who Have Made A Difference – *By Ron Young*

Margaret Cochran Corbin fought alongside her husband in the American Revolutionary War and was the first woman to receive a pension from the United States government as a disabled soldier. She had been wounded by grapeshot, which tore her shoulder, mangled her chest and lacerated her jaw as she manned a cannon during an attack on Fort Washington. She never recovered fully from her wounds and was left without the use of her left arm for the rest of her life.

Elizabeth Arden was born Florence Nightingale Graham in Ontario and was the youngest of five children of a Scottish grocer. She received little education and worked at several jobs before setting off for New York. There she became an assistant in a cosmetics shop, then partner in a beauty salon before changing her name and going into business on her own on Fifth Avenue in 1909. Elizabeth eventually owned more than 100 exclusive salons in America and Europe, and manufactured over 300 cosmetics products.

Sirimavo Ratwatte Dias Bandaranaike was elected Prime Minister of Sri Lanka in 1959, making her the world's first female Prime Minister. Her husband had became Prime Minister in 1956 but was assassinated by a Buddhist fanatic in 1959. To the public's surprise, Mrs. Bandaranaike emerged from her retirement to tour the country, campaigning as his successor in highly emotional speeches on behalf of the Sri Lanka Freedom Party.

Jean Augustine, who was born in Grenada, became the first African Canadian woman elected to the Parliament of Canada in 1993. From 1994 to 1996 she was the Parliamentary Secretary to the Prime Minister of Canada. On May 26, 2002, Ms. Augustine became Secretary of State. She served in many capacities, including Chair of the Sub-committee on Violence in Toronto's black community.

Anna L. Fisher is a NASA astronaut who has received many awards, including a National Science Foundation Undergraduate Research Fellowship in 1970 and 1971. She graduated from UCLA cum laude and with honours in chemistry She is the recipient of the NASA Space Flight Medal, the Lloyd's of London Silver Medal for Meritorious Salvage Operations, the Mother of the Year Award in 1984, the UCLA Professional Achievement Award, and the UCLA Medical Professional Achievement Award. Dr. Fisher also received the NASA Exceptional Service Medal in 1999.

Vigdis Finnbogadottir was elected President of Iceland in 1980 and re-elected in 1984 and 1988. Since 1976 she had been a member of the Advisory Committee on Cultural Affairs of the Nordic Council, serving as its chairman since 1978. The dynamic and popular leader of the people of Iceland also taught French drama at the University of Iceland and has been employed by Iceland State Television, giving French lessons and introducing theatre in a popular cultural series. Vigdis also served as director of the Reykjavik Theatre Company from 1972 to 1980. On January 26, 1990, Women's International Center presented the International Leadership Living Legacy Award to President Finnbogadottir.

Lettie Pate Whitehead Evans took over her husband's part of his business when he died. He and a friend had started selling Coca Cola in bottles seven years prior to his death. Lettie served as Chairman of the Board and President of the firms that were the major assets of the family

Life, Love & Laughter

fortune. She became one of the first female directors of a major American corporation when she was appointed to the board of The Coca-Cola Company in 1934, a position she held for almost 20 years. In her lifetime, she contributed to more than 130 charities and when she died she left much of her estate to the Lettie Pate Evans Foundation to support charity, education and religion.

During World War II, Mrs. Evans was awarded the Order of the Purple Heart and Wings of Britain for her personal donations to the Queen's Fund for air raid victims.

Eleanor of Aquitaine was one of the most powerful and fascinating personalities of feudal Europe. At age 15 she married Louis VII, King of France, bringing into the union her vast possessions from the River Loire to the Pyrenees. Only a few years later, at age 19, she knelt in the cathedral of Vézelay before the celebrated Abbé Bernard of Clairvaux offering him thousands of her vassals for the Second Crusade. It was said that Queen Eleanor appeared at Vézelay dressed like an Amazon, galloping through the crowds on a white horse and urging them to join the crusades.

In 1152 her marriage to King Louis was annulled and her vast estates reverted to Eleanor's control. Within a year, at age 30, she married 20-year-old Henry who, two years later, became King Henry II of England.

Dora Bakoyiannis was born in Athens, the daughter of the Greek Prime Minister. With the overthrow of the government in 1968, Dora and her family were forced out of Greece. Six years later, the military regime was ousted and the family returned. She grew up to marry Pavlos Bakoyannis, another member of Parliament. When Dora's husband was assassinated by terrorists in 1989, her political involvement turned from passive to active. She turned this devastating loss into a tribute to her husband by being overwhelmingly elected to take over her husband's position in Parliament. She carried on what he had begun, and did so with the strength and spirit displayed in only the greatest of leaders.

Mary Whiton Calkins, a female pioneer in psychology, was responsible for the creation of a method of memorization called the "right associates" method. She also founded the psychology department at Wellesley College, and was the first female president of both the American Psychological Association (APA) in 1905 and the American Philosophical Association in 1918. She developed and advocated a self-based psychology, even as behavioural psychology began to dominate the field.

♀

Spice of Life

Whatever women must do, they must do twice as well as men to be thought half as good. Luckily, this is not difficult.   *– Charlotte Whitton, former Mayor of Ottawa*

♀

Aunt Alice says:

Any man who laughs at women's clothes has never paid the bill for them.

Female Facts

When public opinion turned against her, former Philippine first lady, Imelda Marcos, reportedly wore a bullet-proof bra.

♀

Her Other Half

One Good Turn

A man has six children and is very proud of his achievement. He is so proud of himself that he starts calling his wife, "Mother of Six" in spite of her objections. One night, they go to a party. The man decides that it's time to go home and wants to find out if his wife is ready to leave as well. He shouts at the top of his voice, "Shall we go home mother of six?"

His wife, irritated by her husband's lack of discretion shouts right back, "Anytime you're ready, Father of Four."

♀

Quillings

Heroes and Villains

Author Unknown. Submitted by Fay Herridge, Fortune Bay, Newfoundland

There are heroes and villains in all walks of life,
There's laughter and teardrops, there's pleasure and strife;
There's joy and there's sorrow, there's sunshine and rain,
But heroes and villains will both cause you pain.

Now heroes will bury their feelings too deep,
While villains make promises they never keep;
Just when you need them they both will be gone,
For heroes and villains will both lead you on.

There's heroes and villains in cities and towns,
There's success and failure, there's ups and there's downs;
There's right and there's wrong and there's good and there's bad,
And heroes and villains will both make you sad.

Now you will find heroes so gentle and kind,
They'll tug at your heart strings and mess with your mind;
And you will find villains who will treat you so good,
That they'll make you think they are misunderstood.

There's heroes and villains wherever you go,
There's love and rejection, there's highs and there's lows
There's dreams and there's nightmares, there's smiles and there's frowns,
But heroes and villains will both let you down.

♀

What This Woman Has Learned

I've learned that I like my teacher because she cries when we sing "Silent Night." - Age 6

I've learned that our dog doesn't want to eat my broccoli, either. - Age 7

I've learned that when I wave to people in the country, they stop what they are doing and wave back. - Age 9

Life, Love & Laughter

I've learned that just when I get my room the way I like it, Mom makes me clean it up again. - Age 12

I've learned that if you want to cheer yourself up, you should try cheering someone else up. - Age 14

I've learned that although it's hard to admit it, I'm secretly glad my parents are strict with me. - Age 15

I've learned that silent company is often more healing than words of advice. - Age 24

I've learned that brushing my child's hair is one of life's great pleasures. - Age 26

I've learned that wherever I go, the world's worst drivers have followed me there. - Age 29

I've learned that if someone says something unkind about me, I must live so that no one will believe it. - Age 39

I've learned that there are people who love you dearly but just don't know how to show it. - Age 42

I've learned that you can make someone's day by simply sending them a little note. - Age 44

I've learned that the greater a person's sense of guilt, the greater his or her need to cast blame on others. - Age 46

I've learned that children and grandparents are natural allies. - Age 47

I've learned that no matter what happens, or how bad it seems today, life does go on, and it will be better tomorrow. - Age 48

I've learned that singing "Amazing Grace" can lift my spirits for hours. - Age 49

I've learned that motel mattresses are better on the side away from the phone. - Age 50

I've learned that you can tell a lot about a man by the way he handles these three things: a rainy day, lost luggage and tangled Christmas tree lights. - Age 52

I've learned that keeping a vegetable garden is worth a medicine cabinet full of pills. - Age 52

I've learned that regardless of your relationship with your parents, you miss them terribly after they die. - Age 53

I've learned that making a living is not the same thing as making a life. - Age 58

I've learned that if you want to do something positive for your children, work to improve your marriage. - Age 61

I've learned that life sometimes gives you a second chance. - Age 62

I've learned that you shouldn't go through life with a catcher's mitt on both hands. You need to be able to throw something back. - Age 64

I've learned that if you pursue happiness, it will elude you. But if you focus on your family, the needs of others, your work, meeting new people, and doing the very best you can, happiness will find you. - Age 65

I've learned that whenever I decide something with kindness, I usually make the right decision. - Age 66

I've learned that everyone can use a prayer. - Age 72

I've learned that it pays to believe in miracles. And to tell the truth, I've seen several. - Age 75

I've learned that even when I have pains, I don't have to be one. - Age 82

I've learned that every day you should reach out and touch someone. People love that human touch - holding hands, a warm hug, or just a friendly pat on the back. - Age 85

I've learned that I still have a lot to learn. - Age 92

Author Unknown

Life, Love & Laughter

Female Facts

First North-American Feminists

The first people to practise true feminism in North America were probably the Iroquois of Canada. For each Iroquois clan there was a clan mother who chose the male chief. Once chosen, this man was chief for life, unless he made a serious mistake, in which case the clan mother had the authority to remove him from office and replace him.

♀

 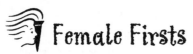 **MABEL & MANLEY**

Mabel and Manley had been married for some years, and Mabel started to find that wedded bliss was not what it used to be, so she visited her minister to see if he could give her some advice.

"Manley doesn't do anything with me anymore," Mabel told the man of the cloth. "He won't take me anywhere, and he won't go anywhere with me. He won't even come to church with me."

"Does he believe in life after death?" asked the minister.

"Reverend," she retorted, "Manley doesn't even believe in life after supper!"

♀

Female Firsts

1943: Actress Betty Grable became the first woman to insure her legs for $1 million. *See also 'Female Facts' page 448.*

1944: Nurse Elizabeth Lawrie Smellie became the first woman promoted to Colonel in the Canadian Army.

1944: Dorothy McElroy Vredenburgh of Alabama became the first woman appointed secretary of a national political party, the Democratic National Committee.

1945: Jacqueline Cochran became the first woman to receive the Distinguished Service Medal. *See also page 227.*

1946: On July 7, Francesca Xavier Cabrini became the first American citizen to be declared a saint. Four years later she was named the Patron Saint of Immigrants.

1947: Mary Eugenia Charles became the first female lawyer of Dominica. She was also Prime Minister of that country from 1980 to 1995.

1947: For the first time, Canadian women no longer lost their citizenship automatically if they married non-Canadians.

1947: Ann Shaw Carter became the first licensed helicopter pilot.

1947: Agatha Barbara became Malta's first female Member of Parliament. *See also 'Female facts' page 331.*

1947: Barbara Washburn became the first woman ever to climb Mount McKinley.

♀

Life, Love & Laughter

Feminine Words & Phrases

Grass widow: A woman who is divorced or separated from her significant other. It formerly meant an unmarried woman who had a child. There are several theories as to the origin of this phrase. It may have been as simple as "putting her out to grass" after she became pregnant or, as one source suggests, that "grass" means "straw" which infers "bed." Another source suggests that it may come from making love in the grassy fields. In Newfoundland and Labrador we used to call that "grassing."

Lady: Gentlewoman (as in the female counterpart of gentleman). The name comes from the old English hlaf (loaf, as in bread) and dige (to knead), hlafdige (breadkneader) originally meant, "female head of the family." Pronounced "lad gee," hlafdige eventually became "lady."

Old Maid: An elderly, unmarried spinster. Also, a card game where the person stuck with the Old Maid card in the end loses the game.

Spinster: A woman who never marries. Some of the men, who were our forefathers, thought that no woman was capable of being a wife unless she could spin a complete set of table, bed and body linen. Many women who subscribed to that philosophy did a great job of spinning but never found a man. They became known as "spinsters."

♀

The Woman and the Cow

   From 1696 onwards, Bay Bulls, Newfoundland, was captured five times by the French. A dozen or more ships were sunk in Bay Bulls Harbour, the most famous being the British Man o' War *Sapphire*, which was excavated during the 1970s.

   On one occasion at least, the French did not act as conquerors. On January 26, 1705, about 400 French soldiers landed at Bay Bulls to mass for an attack on St. John's.

   Instead of attacking the settlers there, the French pleaded with them for shelter and were allowed to stay there for several nights in the homes and barns of the people.

   In 1762 the Justice of the Peace there led volunteers from Bay Bulls over land to Petty Harbour, where they joined the schooners of Lord Colville in his successful effort to drive the French from St. John's.

   During the see-saw battles between French and English, it wasn't always the men who showed courage. Following the French attack on Bay Bulls in September 1796, a lady resident stood up and defied the French.

   The French attack came after they had been driven from St. John's. They took out their frustrations on the people of Bay Bulls. The people there fled into the woods for safety.

   Upon returning to the smouldering ruins of cottages and barns, one old woman was so outraged at the French who had stolen her only cow, that she rowed alone out to the French commander's ship. She shouted at the French Admiral that she wanted her cow back. She made such a fuss, and the Admiral was so impressed by her courage, that he ordered his soldiers to load the cow on a raft and return it to her.

   From the book, Strange But True Newfoundland Stories, *by Jack Fitzgerald, published by Creative Publishing. Used by permission.*

♀

Animal Mating – Fact and Fantasy – *Ron Young*

The Ecology and Mating

Fact:

Zebrafish used to reproduce like most other fish, but pollution is causing that to change, according to a study by Dr. John Trant and his team at the University of Maryland Biotechnology Institute. The overall effect of personal hygiene products and other man-made products being dumped into the water where the fish lives, is causing the male Zebrafish to show less male traits than normal. "This is significant because a male who fails to display all of the appropriate male behaviours is not likely to attract a female," says Dr. Trant. But the human waste products also cause the female to behave like a male, which does nothing for the heterosexual male zebrafish. The only way to solve the problem is to stop the polluting.

Fantasy:

We should look for a solution to results of our pollution
Which for many of our species is a pain
So when you brush, or wash a dish, think of little zebrafish
Whose sex life may be going down the drain

♀

Letters From Our Friends

"...adopted from Newfoundland to New York..."

Dear *Downhomer*,

I am a Newfoundlander adopted by an American family. I was adopted from Newfoundland to New York at the age of five months. I was fortunate enough to find my birth family in 1998 and was welcomed. Through my search I was amazed to find many other adoptees from Newfoundland who were adopted to the States, especially in the late 1960s and early 1970s.

I have also been fortunate enough to return to Newfoundland twice. Once in the summer of 97 before I found my birth family, when I camped around the island, and again in the summer of 99 I came to visit members of my birth family. I can't wait to return, but with six-month-old twins it seems a bit of an undertaking!

Even though I have grown up in New York and have made my home here, whenever someone asks where I am from, my answer is Newfoundland. Ever since I can remember I have always wondered about Newfoundland and tried to seek out any information I could find, which wasn't always easy, especially before the Internet became available and my discovery of *Downhomer*. It seemed weird to miss a place I didn't really know. So thanks to *Downhomer* for bringing me a little piece of my history and heritage every month.

Donna Dugan – Staten Island, New York, USA

♀

Women Who Have Made A Difference – *By Ron Young*

Charlotte Auerbach, a Scottish geneticist of German birth, was the first to discover the deadly weapon of chemical warfare, mustard gas. She considered her most important work, however, to be the in-depth study of mutagenesis as a biological process. She used the fruit-fly Drosophila and the fungus Neurospora to analyze the selective action of certain mutagens on certain genes. In 1947 the University of Edinburgh awarded her a DSc and in 1967, a personal Chair. She also received several honorary degrees and awards, including medals from the Royal Society of Edinburgh and the Royal Society of London.

Clara Brown was born a slave in Virginia, USA, in 1803. Clara was 55 years old when her third owner died in Kentucky. She was now able to buy her freedom but, according to Kentucky law, she had to leave the state immediately or she would lose it. She joined a caravan going to Denver, Colorado, and paid for the trip by bartering her services as a cook, laundress and nurse. She invested in mining claims and made about $10,000 by the mid-1860s. With her wealth, Clara Brown helped many other African-Americans go west in search of a better life by paying for their trips on a number of wagon trains.

Renée Bordereau watched as her father was killed by revolutionary forces during the French Revolution. Afterwards she disguised herself as a man and joined Bonchamps' cavalry to avenge his death. She led the troups into more than 200 battles, on foot and on horseback, and proved herself an adept soldier. In one battle alone she personally killed 21 enemy soldiers. She liberated 50 priests at one time, and on another occasion saved 800 people from the guillotine. Renée saw 42 of her relatives killed before her attempt to restore the monarchy was put down by Napoleon. To keep Renée from starting another uprising, Napoleon put a price of 40,000 francs on her head. She was captured and imprisoned for five years, until Napoleon met his Waterloo on June 8, 1815. Two years later Renée was received by King Louis XVIII with honours.

Shirley Jane Temple Black was the biggest box-office attraction in Hollywood at the height of her popularity from 1935 to 1938. The large gross revenues from her films helped to make 20th Century Fox a major film studio. Propelled by an ambitious mother, Shirley Temple had, in 1931, made her film debut at the age of three, then went on to become one of Hollywood's biggest film stars before retiring from acting in 1949.

Temple became a member of the U.S. delegation to the United Nations (1969-1970), was U.S. ambassador to Ghana (1974-1976) and became the first woman in U.S. history to serve as chief of protocol (1976-1977), during the administration of President Gerald R. Ford. In 1989 President George Bush appointed her ambassador to Czechoslovakia.

Susan Elizabeth Blow opened the United States' first successful public kindergarten at St. Louis' Des Peres School in 1873 to offer more education to poor children who were forced to leave school at age 10 to work. By 1883 every St. Louis public school had a kindergarten, making the city a model for the nation and was instrumental in establishing kindergartens throughout North America.

Pocahontas, as a little girl saved Captain John Smith from apparent death as he lay "on two large, flat stones and Indians stood over him with clubs as though ready to beat him to death if

Life, Love & Laughter

Life, Love & Laughter

ordered."

Smith was leading an expedition near Jamestown, Virginia, when, in 1607, he was captured by Indians. Several days after that he was brought to the official residence of Powhatan. At first he was welcomed by the great chief, before finding himself being menaced on the flat stones. It was then that the Indian girl rushed in and taking Smith's "head in her arms and laid her owne upon his to save him from death," she pulled him to his feet and her father, Chief Powhatan, adopted Smith as his son.

Later when relations between the whites and the Powhatans worsened, and believing that John Smith was dead, Pocahontas was kidnapped by the English. The ransom for Pocohontas that the English demanded of Powhatan was the English prisoners Powhatan held, the arms and tolls that the Indians had stolen and also some corn.

The full ransom was not met by her father and Pocahontas was taken to Henrico, a new settlement, where she began her education in the Christian Faith and where she met a successful tobacco planter named John Rolfe, whom she married on April 5, 1614.

A general peace and a spirit of goodwill between the English and the Indians resulted from this marriage. Then, in the spring of 1616, the leader in Henrico, Sir Thomas Dale, asked Pocahontas, her husband and their young son, as well as other Algonquian Indians, to accompany him to England, where he wished to find finances for his venture. The Indians were to bring more attention to his efforts. Pocahontas was presented to King James I, the Royal Family and the rest of the best of London society.

In London, she again met her old friend, Captain John Smith, whom she had not seen in eight years and believed dead. According to Smith she was at first too overcome with emotion to speak. After composing herself, Pocahontas talked of old times. At one point she addressed him as "father" and when he objected, she defiantly replied: "Were you not afraid to come into my father's Countrie and caused feare in him and all of his people and feare you here I should call you father: I tell you I will, and you shall call mee childe, and so I will be for ever and ever your Countrieman."

She never saw Smith again and during the trip back to Virginia it became apparent that Pocahontas was deathly ill from pneumonia or possibly tuberculosis and would not survive the voyage home. She was taken ashore and when she died at the young age of 22, was buried in a churchyard in Gravesend, England.

Ginetta Sagan was tortured, starved and suffered unspeakable inhumanities after she was captured by the Nazis at age 20. Her parents were tortured and killed but Ginetta was lucky enough to survive. While a captive she learned well the suffering of prisoners and how long, even an hour in captivity can be. Since then, Genetta spent 45 years liberating others by facing the captors and demanding release of prisoners. She was personally responsible for the release of political prisoners in Poland, Czechoslovakia, Latin America and South Africa. Due to Ginetta's unrelenting campaigns, 6,000 prisoners in Vietnam have been set free. Ginetta died September 1, 2000.

Mary Kay Ash, founded Mary Kay Inc. in 1963. Since then the company has grown from nine original sales staff to an independent sales force numbering over 950,000. Mary Kay does business in 33 markets on five continents and nearly $1.6 billion in wholesale sales worldwide. Mary Kay also consistently ranks among the best-selling brands of facial skin care and colour cosmetics in the United States.

Still one of the few female Horatio Alger Award recipients who hails from the business world, Mary Kay Ash left an indelible mark on American business and on opportunities open to women.

WOMEN OF THE ISLAND AND THE BIG LAND

Mary McDonald

Interview (through letters) by Marian Frances White

Laura Jackson

Self-taught fisherwomen from the age of 15, Mary McDonald continued to be outstanding in her chosen career. Born in West St. Modeste on May 14, 1940, into a family of eight sisters, she often took on roles that were considered only for men. Her father, reluctant to let his daughter follow his footsteps in the boats, soon gave up trying to persuade her otherwise when he recognized her capabilities. For the following 25 years Mary and her sister, Josephine, fished for a living. She acquired her own gear for salmon fishing and continued to fish for salmon and cod until her licence was cut. Mary now works in the fishplant on the stages as a "layer" and "salter" during the fishing season. She lives close to her environment, cutting wood and planting potatoes, cabbage and other vegetables that last throughout the winter. In 1978 the CBC-TV programme "Land and Sea" produced a show on her while she fished. Although her specialty in fishing is salmon, she catches a variety of fish and ice fishes in winter.

*****

I suppose I was 13 when I started fishing. That was just for fun back then. I would go out in the boats with my father jiggin' fish. It was very exciting. It wasn't long before I realized I could make a living by fishing so I started to take it more seriously. There were no boys in a family of nine girls so we often found ourselves doing things that normally only men did. My father didn't want me to go fishing all the time, but I wanted to do it, so I did.

I had very little education, just up to grade seven, so I had to think of a way to make a living. Fishing seemed fine to me. The men then didn't seem to mind me in the boats even though it was unusual. It was only when I got me own gear that they started making something of it. I guess they thought I had no business doing what they thought was men's work. As the years rolled on their attitude got better. I fished in the boats for 25 years. I've caught a lot of salmon and cod in that time. One year I sold fish to a buyer with 19 different grades of cod. That's quite a variety for anyone to have. I had West Indian (the kind that is sun burnt). I had tom cods, choice and many more. It's all in the way you cut it up and put it up and lay it out to dry. It's cut for different grades. I think a women can do anything a man can do, and even sometimes do it better.

Most often I'm treated fairly with the federal government but sometimes the inspectors give me a hard time. Once I wasn't quite so lucky. I had 25 barrels of herring that usually sell for $28 a barrel. The herring inspector turned them down, said they weren't good. What he said was he couldn't tell if they were bad, so he figured they were no good. He tore them abroad and heaved them away. I had to dump them because the inspector couldn't tell if they were good or bad.

In the time I've been fishing I haven't seen many women in the boats. I think that's changing a bit nowadays. Some think you got to be different to do this work, but I think it's all a matter of putting your mind to one thing and doing it because you want to. My sister, Josephine. fishes with me. She can use a compass as good as any man. One winter me and Josephine, hauled 112

Life, Love & Laughter

Life, Love & Laughter

loads of wood out on the Ski-doo. That kept us busy right up until Christmas. When we aren't fishing or hauling wood in the summer and fall, we're picking berries. The bakeapples around here are right plentiful. A few years ago I bought an old-fashioned wood stove for $450 out of bakeapple money alone. Whatever I do, I enjoys it. I wouldn't rather be anywhere but here in West St. Modeste.

In 1982 a few things changed around here concerning me and fishing. I left me boat and started working as a layer and salter in the fishplant here. There were lots of salmon and I caught lots, but there were no buyers, so I couldn't get enough money for me work. If you don't work during the salmon season, June and July, you don't get stamps to tie you over with unemployment insurance during the winter.

The problem was, after I took a job in the fish plant, my salmon licence was cut from 200 permitted to catch to 100 I could catch. They called me a part-time fisherman, which I don't understand since I only work in the plant for about ten weeks. I don't know why the federal people got to make it so hard. If I want a full-time licence again I have to fish two years to qualify. I don't like that (their rules) too much. If they don't expect me to fish salmon and cod, I don't know what they think I can do with me gear I've bought over the years, the nets and rope and anchor. I'd get about $200 for it, but what I really want is to be able to fish when the season comes around. I'm the only woman who fished in the boats around here for a living, but that seems to make it more difficult rather than easier. There's poor communication in Ottawa and I know a lot of the problem is because I'm a fisherwoman.

The first year I applied for unemployment as a woman fishing for a living, I had me unemployment insurance cut off in March. I thought this strange since none of the men around me had theirs cut off, so I inquired as to why. The taxation people told me directly that they figured I'd used me father's stamps. Somehow I managed to convince them I did the fishing and I got me money rolling in again; got all the back pay, too. It wasn't that long ago that the wife of fishermen couldn't get UIC.

In most ways I learned what I know from being out on the water here in Labrador. One winter, though, an inspector come up here from the College of Fisheries in St. John's and taught a four-week course on mending gear and the like. I enjoyed that. I always mended me own gear. I was the only woman in the class. Me and Josephine have done a lot of fishing, so has me mother when she had the chance. There's equal pay for both men and women in the fishing industry now, but before the 80s that wasn't the case. The way I sees it, fish is fish, no matter who catches them!

Mary passed away on May 30, 2000.

From the book The Finest Kind *by Marian Frances White. Creative Publishing. Used by permission.*

♀

🌳 Her Other Half

Employee Propaganda

At the office Christmas party the office manager was intercepted by his wife on his way back from the bar. "That's the tenth time you've been to the bar this evening," she warned. "What are your employees going to think of you?"

"Don't worry," he replied. "I tell them they're for you."

♀

Aunt Alice says:

Some days I feel like a dog and other days I feel like a hydrant.

Spice of Life

Thirty-five is when you finally get your head together and your body starts falling apart.

– *Caryn Leschen*

♀

Ennellene

Come home my love and you won't starve
There'll be food as well as libations
I'm making my favourite thing tonight
Restaurant reservations

♀

 Female Firsts

1948: Barbra Ann Scott became the first Canadian woman to win the Olympic, World and European figures skating titles.

1948: Patty Berg became the first president of the Ladies' Professional Golf Association, which she founded that year.

1948: Frieda Hennock became the first female commissioner of the FCC (Federal Communications Commission of the U.S.).

1948: Marie Maynard Daly became the first black woman to earn a Ph.D. in Chemistry.

1948: Margaret Chase Smith became the first female U.S. senator. Even though she didn't have the support of the Republican Party she won by a large majority, collecting 70 per cent of the votes of the people of Maine where she was elected.

1949: Vietta M. Bates became the first enlisted woman sworn into the U.S. Army after legislation was passed making the Women's Auxiliary Army Corps part of the regular Army.

1949: Conchita V. Cintron became the first U.S. woman bullfighter in Spain.

1949: Bobbie Rosenfeld became the first Canadian Woman Athlete of the Half Century, excelling in many sports, including ice hockey and softball, as well as winning a gold medal in Olympic track and field in 1928.

1950: Florence Chadwick, of San Diego, California, became the first woman to swim the English Channel both ways.

♀

Life, Love & Laughter

Spice of Life

Even a stopped clock is right twice every day. After some years, it can boast of a series of successes. – *Marie von Ebner-Eschenbach*

 MABEL & MANLEY

"The insurance company paid me $50,000 for the injuries I got when me and Manley had that car accident, and they only gave Manley $10,000," Mabel told her friend over tea.

"I guess Manley was lucky that he wasn't hurt as much as you," implied her friend.

"He wasn't even hurt," said Mabel, "but before he got out of the car I had enough sense to kick him in the head."

Aunt Alice says:

Amazing! You hang something in your closet for awhile and it shrinks two sizes!

Spice of Life

Oh for a man to take me out
And feed me fowl or sauerkraut
Without first asking where to dine
If such there be, would he be mine!
　　　– *Margaret Fishback*

Life's Funny Experiences

Sleep Easy

My husband and I reluctantly agreed to go on a camping trip to the Rockies, despite my anxiety about grizzly bears. We lived in Calgary, so we didn't have far to go.

As night fell, I grew increasingly nervous about the idea of sleeping outdoors. In order to be assured there were no bears terrorizing the campground, I insisted that we go to the ranger station.

"We haven't seen grizzlies here all season," the ranger said, "or black bears, either."

I asked what the difference was between the two. "If you climb a tree and it climbs up after you, it's a black bear," the ranger explained. "If it stays on the ground and shakes the tree until you fall out, it's a grizzly."

We spent the night in a motel.

Martina MacDonald - Dartmouth, Nova Scotia

Under the "B"

By Jennifer Howlett

These days I am about as popular as an outgoing premier. I am simultaneously loved and hated by large numbers of people on a daily basis. By day, I am a mild-mannered, stay-at-home mom, but by night my alter ego emerges. You see, I am a dum-da-da-dum - bingo caller.

Yes folks, you heard me correctly. I call bingo, in a hall, in front of people. As most of you know, Newfoundlanders take their bingo seriously. Just look at the differences in bingo here and on the Mainland. My husband came back from a business trip recently and said, "You should see what they call bingo halls up along. They look like little houses!"

Cute. But here we all know that bingo is serious business.

It is so serious that some nights I feel like I should have a police escort to my vehicle. Is it any wonder that I live in a different city from the hall I work in? Some of these people can be down right scary, and I, like so many other callers, have been threatened on more than one occasion.

I would like to take a moment to address my personal lynch mob; but anyone who has stalked or threatened a bingo caller would do well to heed the following message. I do not secretly watch your cards and then not call your numbers. I do not cast any spells on the bingo machine so that "O 74" does not come up once on any given night. If I have taken a 10-minute break it is because I have been told to do so, not to make you bored. I call by a computer-set timer and yet I can call both too fast and too slow at exactly the same time. Now that's talent!

I could tell you bingo stories that would make any soap opera seem dull. I could tell you, that as a bingo caller, I have gotten quite good at reading lips - and don't like the names that you people are calling me!

But I am still better liked than the people who call satellite bingo. At least there is only one hall full of players criticizing me at any given time. For the satellite caller, once the link is set up, they have over 20 halls of people to please.

"I can't believe he's calling again. Sure he says 'sex' instead of six! That shouldn't be allowed."

Perhaps I should explain the satellite game to you. At nine o'clock, so many halls throughout the province join together via satellite and play one common game of bingo for a $50,000 grand prize. There is a guaranteed payout of $2000 and every hall pays out $100 when the $2000 is gone. And heaven forbid that the same hall should win two consolation prizes close together. Then you should hear the mumbles.

"Fixed. They win every night. Maybe I should drive to Tilton to play bingo, they're always

Life, Love & Laughter

lucky out there."

I have seen women play close to 60 cards for the jackpot game. It is really something to watch. They have about 15 seconds to dab the numbers and their set of cards take up an entire table. These women are quite proficient at dabbing, smoking, drinking and eating, while also giving a running commentary on the quality of my work.

"My Gawd, girl, could you call a little faster?"

Sometimes I wonder, if I called any faster than I do, would smoke come out of their dabbers?

It often amazes me how much money is spent in a hall on any given night. You can actually see some of the money circulate throughout the hall and it never leaves. It is given as change for the card purchase, spent on tickets or extra cards, paid out as prize money, spent again, and finally put in the float for the next night's business. Some of these bills get so decrepit that I send them to the bank just to put them out of their misery.

Bingo also has a complex social net. Mrs. O'Leary, for example, can't sit next to Mrs. Brown because four years ago they had an argument over which side of the table to sit at. Marg can only sit at one particular table every single night. I have actually seen people ask others to move because they are sitting in "their" spot. You know that you spend too much time in a place when...

It also baffles me why people with no blood in their bodies have to sit by the doors. They are always cold! We had a glorious summer this year (ha-ha Environment Canada, you were wrong) and without air-conditioning, any room with 200 people will get a little sticky. Of course, the first logical thing to do is to open the doors and windows. I can guarantee that someone will want the doors closed within five minutes; they are sitting by the door wearing a cardigan and jacket done up to the neck. The only reason that don't wear mittens is because they would interfere with the dabbing process. Then, as soon as you close the door (you don't want them to catch pneumonia; after all, it's only 20 degrees out), 35 people start complaining. Then, the icing on that cake is the 400-pound woman who is threatening to strip if the doors aren't re-opened immediately. You quickly move the cardigan lady to another table and open all of the doors.

People sometimes arrive an hour-and-a-half before the first game begins. They buy their cards, fill out their "Pick-Your-Own" cards, glue them together, lay them out just so, have something to eat and watch other people arrive. Others bring along craft projects to work on, novels to read and cards. I often exchange book reviews with some, while admonishing others (card players) for having the nerve to gamble in the bingo hall.

But don't get me wrong, some bingo patrons are also my fiercest protectors. People have argued over my merits (and lack thereof) to the point of almost coming to blows. There are some players who go seven nights a week and to them it is not about gambling - it's about a night out. For some, it's the only contact they will have with other people during any given day. More than once I've been thanked for taking a minute out of my night to chat and see how things are going, just interacting with a lonely person. And besides, if you've never heard old ladies telling jokes dirty enough to make a sailor blush, you've never truly experienced bingo to its fullest extent.

And that's why I keep going back (dirty jokes aside). I like talking to these people and if I can make their night doing so, great. If I can call them the $1000 jackpot game as well, so much the better.

Reprinted from Downhomer *magazine.*

♀

Women Who Have Made A Difference – *By Ron Young*

Antoinette Louisa Brown became the first American woman ordained as minister on September 15, 1853, when she became minister of the First Congregational Church in South Butler, New York. Oberlin College in Ohio objected to a woman studying theology but the school charter decreed that no student could be excluded on the basis of sex, so Brown prevailed and finished the theological course in 1850. The Oberlin College faculty, however, refused to award her a college degree and she did not receive a license to preach. The degree was eventually awarded to her 28 years later.

Barbara Bodichon gave evidence to the British House of Commons committee looking into the legal position of married women that made a change in history. The Matrimonial Causes Act that followed allowed divorce through the courts, instead of the slow and expensive business of a Private Act of Parliament. This new act also protected the property rights of divorced women. In 1866 Bodichon formed the first ever Women's Suffrage Committee.

Elizabeth Boit was one of the first women to break into management in the male-dominated British textile industry and was the first woman in the country to serve as a bank director. She set a lasting example for other textile industry executives by improving the working conditions of her employees, giving them health care and an innovative bonus plan which shared the company's profits.

Nora Astorga's bedroom was where the notorious General Perez Vegas of the Nicaraguan National Guard was lured and then murdered by the Sandinistas on March 8, 1978 (International Women's Day). The CIA later managed to block her appointment as ambassador to Washington, but in 1986 she became the Nicaraguan ambassador to the United Nations in New York, where she was known both for her fierce, logical argument and her highly feminine style, sending red roses with her diplomatic notes. She died in 1988 at the age of 38, after a gruelling battle against cancer.

Aung San Suu Kyi was awarded the Nobel Prize for Peace in 1991, by which time she had been under house arrest in her native Burma for two out of what was to become six years. She first came to prominence in 1988 when she left England, where she received her university education, to return to Burma, a country whose human rights record has been rated one of the worst in the world after Algeria. She became the leader of a burgeoning pro-democracy movement in the aftermath of the brutal repression of a pro-democratic uprising earlier that summer.

The movement quickly grew into a political party that went on to win an overwhelming majority of 82 per cent in national elections in 1990. The military regime, however, refused to relinquish power and stepped up intensified repression of her party, the National League for Democracy.

No longer under house arrest but still restricted in her movements, Aung San Suu Kyi, has come to be seen internationally as a symbol of heroic and peaceful resistance in the face of oppression.

Dorothy von Beroldingen became a judge in 1982, but before that she had a number of "Firsts" to her credit. She was the first female sales promotion manager at Clarion Radio in Chicago from 1937 to 1939. She passed her bar exam at age 39 in 1955 and in 1956 served as the first woman reader for the California Bar Examinations. Between 1956 and 1959 von Beroldingen served as

Life, Love & Laughter

the first female lecturer for the Carson-Sack Bar Review Course. She was the first woman to serve as professor of federal taxation and legal accounting at Lincoln University School of Law. She was the first woman to serve on the panel of the Civil Service Commission and was the first woman selected to chair the board's Finance and Budget Committee, regarded under San Francisco's laws of official succession as the third highest ranking elected position in the city. In the early 1970s she became the city's first elected official to envision and actively champion a concept for using underdeveloped land in San Francisco's South of Market area.

Von Beroldingen was the first woman appointed to the Golden Gate Bridge, Highway and Transportation District in 1976. And she was the only woman and San Francisco's only representative to serve on the Governor's statewide Commission on the Law of Pre-Emption between 1966 and 1967.

She served as presiding judge from 1982 to 1983 and was assigned primarily to the court's criminal division until early in 1997, when she was appointed the city's Senior Municipal Court Judge.

Maria Gaetana Agnesi of Italy was by far the most important and extraordinary figure (male or female) in mathematics during the 18th century. When her work was published in 1748, it caused a sensation in the academic world. It was one of the first and most complete works on finite and infinitesimal analysis. The oldest of 21 children, she retired from public life when her mother died. Maria then had to take care of her 20 siblings and her lonely father. Later she devoted the rest of her life to poor, homeless and sick people, especially women.

Hélène Ahrweiler, although born in Athens, Greece, was elected president of the famous Sorbonne university in France in 1976, the first woman in such a position in its 700-year history. She became Chancellor of the Universities of Paris in 1982 and became Vice President of the Council of National Education in 1983. She also worked with UNESCO.

♀

Female Firsts

1950: Jacqueline Auriol of France became the world's first female test pilot. *See also page 30.*

1950: Kathyrn Johnson became the first female to play Little League Baseball when she joined the King's Dairy team in Corning, New York, at age 12.

1951: Pat McCormick became the first springboard diver to ever win all five national U.S. championships.

1952: Manitoba women were first permitted to serve on juries.

1953: On August 12, when Ann Davidson sailed into Miami, she became the first woman to have sailed solo across the Atlantic Ocean.

1953: On September 7, at the age of 16, Maureen Connolly, became the first woman to score a Grand Slam in tennis. After winning at Wimbledon, at the French and Australian Opens, she won the U.S. singles title at Forest Hills.

♀

Spice of Life

He was so narrow-minded he could see through a keyhole with two eyes.

– Esther Forbes

♀

Is That a Fact?

Many things are taken as facts. Not all of them are.

Humphrey Bogart and Gerber Baby

For years many people thought that the baby on the label of Gerber's baby food jars was Humphrey Bogart.

The Fact Is however, that is not the case. The portrait was painted by Bogart's mother, Maude, which is probably the reason for the misconception.

♀

Animal Mating – Fact and Fantasy – *Ron Young*

Odd Couples

Fact:

Although there are similarities between the **Black Widow Spider** and the **Eider Duck**, there are many differences besides their size. Contrary to popular belief, the spider is not an insect but is part of the arachnid (has four pairs of walking legs) family. This family includes spiders, scorpions, ticks, mites and others, as well as the ocean-dwelling, horseshoe crabs. Both the eider and black widow are carnivores, and both species lay eggs to reproduce (widows up to 900, and eiders up to five at a time). The black widow eats insects, but never birds, while the eider will eat fish, shellfish, mollusks and arachnids, in the form of the young aforesaid horseshoe crabs.

While the female eider duck may keep the same man for up to 20 years, the female black widow has a more fatal attraction to her mate. The drake (male) eider will not eat while courting, nor the female while she is incubating her eggs. The black widow female, on the other hand, is famished during mating and will sometimes eat her mate after the act is consummated. He serves her no further purpose after mating, as she mates only one time in her life, whereas eiders mate many times. If she doesn't eat him at this point, the male spider will have a leisurely life from then on, living off the insects captured by the female in her web.

With its powerful bill, an eider could easily crush a black widow, but any duck would be foolish to try it. The widow's venom is 15 times as toxic as the venom of the prairie rattlesnake, and her bite is capable of killing ducks, as well as humans. She will especially do this after mating, to protect her unborn children.

Fantasy:

Eider drake (after drinking much cider)
Offered sex and a meal to a spider
Said Black Widow, "Too late
I just ate my mate
So now I don't really want eider"

♀

Life, Love & Laughter

✒ Quillings

Sixty-five and Counting
Author Unknown

In nineteen hundred and ninety-two
My working days shall all be through
I'll be the happiest person alive
For then I shall be sixty-five.

Each month I watch those old folks grin
Each month those pension cheques roll in
Each month they get that bit of gold
All simply just for being old.

Who ever thought they'd see the day
When getting old meant getting pay
And if you're paying too much rent
You just apply for supplement.

And if that isn't quite enough
You get all kinds of other stuff
Like discounts off on bus or planes
And then you also get the gains.

And ten percent off all your clothes
Plus senior rates on first row shows
And travel tours are all the rage
But only when you come of age.

Now, if I'd known when I was twenty
The real true meaning of land of plenty
I would have moved both heaven and earth
To falsify my date of birth.

So politicians please take note
You'll wish you'd lost by just one vote
When I wake up in ninety-three
If there's no pension left for me.

And even worse if on that morn
Old Gabriel should blow his horn
He'd better plan to keep on blowing
Without my pension, I'm not going.

♀

Feminine Words & Phrases

Casket Letters: Reputedly found in a small chest (casket) the letters, eight in all, probably were the biggest downfall of Mary, Queen of Scots. In fear of her life at the hands of her husband Henry Stuart, Earl of Darnley, because she had seen him murder her secretary, Mary had estranged herself from him. He was later murdered while she had an adulteress affair going on with James Hepburn, the fourth Earl of Bothwell. Because of the interpretations of her letters to her lover, he was imprisoned until he died and she was held in custody on the tiny island of Loch Leven. She escaped and sought help from her cousin, Queen Elizabeth of England, only to have translated copies of the casket letters again used against her, never the originals. She was held in one prison or another for 18 years. A plot to free Mary and assassinate Elizabeth was discovered in 1786 and the Queen ordered Mary's execution. In 1787, at the age of 44, Mary was executed. *See also pages 46 and 386.*

Children of the Casket: Respectable middle-class were girls sent by the Mississippi Company to New Orleans to hopefully become brides of the Acadian-French settlers there. The casket was really a hope-chest of suitable clothing, which each young lady was given. Woman arriving with these caskets could be distinguished from female released prisoners being sent there in large numbers from the Salpetriere Prison between 1728 and 1751. "La filles a la cassette" (girls of the casket) were much preferred by the men of New Orleans. The descendants of these couplings have been treated with old-family respect ever since.

♀

FROM HALL'S BAY TO BADGER

My story dates back to 1923, when I was the first woman to travel the Hall's Bay Line with my two small children, Norma, two years and Charles, five months.

This was a trip I want to forget. My husband had secured a contract in the lumber woods and I persuaded him to let me go along. So after he had gone to Badger and built our cabin he came back for me at Pilleys Isl'and, Notre Dame Bay. There, with other men who were walking to Badger to get work in the lumber woods, I got aboard a small motor boat which took us 18 miles to South Brook. My husband had come from Badger by horse and carriage. On our arrival at South Brook, the carriage was there but the horse was gone. So my husband tried persuading me to go back by the same boat, but that didn't work. I had come from Chicago just three years previous and Pilley's Island was a lonely spot for me when my husband was not there. While he was coaxing me to go back, I looked around and the six or seven men who had come with us were not to be seen. I asked for them and my husband said they were walking to Badger and already were on their way. I convinced my husband I was walking also. I remember that I had two coats and my five-month-old baby in my arms. And my husband had a lunch box with food for two days and two blankets, and our two-year-old daughter in his arms. We started our walk, which was up grade, and the mosquitoes were out in thousands. We met them in cloud formation and we did not have our hands free to brush them away. The timber was very tall in places, and the smoldering heat and a burst of sun here and there made it very convenient for the mosquitoes. It was almost unbearable.

We walked six miles, all upgrade. Then we were on a high level and with just enough wind to keep us from smothering with flies. At that distance I could not hold up my baby. My arms had lost their strength. So I suggested a rest and a lunch at a little camp not far from the road. It was made of bough, and had been used by the men who put the road through, namely the Halls Bay Line.

As we laid our children down, they were bitten by flies and badly sunburnt. My husband was disgusted with me for talking him into letting me walk. I kept telling him someone may be coming through from Badger and would give us a lift, and sure enough, before I could open our lunch box we heard in the distance the sound of a horse trotting. We weren't long getting out of the thicket to the road. This was a good friend, Con Simms. He had seen the horse my husband had taken to the Bay to bring us to Badger and knowing same, had caught it. Thinking he might catch the boat we were coming on, he decided that he might get a trip back to Pilley's Island to see his girlfriend. So Con and my husband went back six miles to get the carriage and our clothing and luggage. They told me to prepare lunch while they were gone. But the creaking of the trees made me fear the creatures of the forest, especially bears. So I stood in the centre of the road with a child on each arm and waited for them to return, and my arms did not give out. After lunch, we started by carriage. We rode until dusk, when we found an old camp with the ground for a floor. The men who had walked ahead of us were there, trying to smoke out the mosquitoes by burning sods.

On my arrival with the children they extinguished the burning sod. Then came the rain. The men had made a bed of boughs, and in their humble hospitality, gave me their bed. The children slept for a while until the rain soaked through and made our ground floor very wet.

The next morning, after a dry breakfast, we started in misty rain. We rode as far as Gull Pond where there was another camp. This one had a stove, so we dried our wet clothing and had lunch, then continued to Badger. We arrived about 6:30 p.m., just as the people were finishing their supper.

We went to the home of Mr. and Mrs. Pinkston at Badger where we had spent our honeymoon. They were astonished to see us and we enjoyed a wonderful meal. Now our winter camp was about seven or eight miles from Badger so the next day we went to the woods. There was a very large camp nearby and two other small ones. The large one was operated by a Mr. Jones and they had their own private little camp, also. Our camp was not quite finished, such as doors and walls, etc. I covered the walls or logs with sheeting paper and put up a heavy blanket for a door. It was August and very warm. We used a young bull to pull the logs in place in the timber yard. Then the men cut wood until winter frost came. However, during the warm weather I spent many lonely nights and was frightened of bears. My husband's army rifle was the only consolation I had. I would sit up and think and plan night after night.

My husband would be in Badgertown on business, mixed with a little bit of pleasure. He would laugh at me when I would tell him of my fear. But it was not until we got a door to our camp that they told me how the men in other camps had set traps and caught many bears.

When winter set in, the children did not get as many colds as I expected. But they both got a severe dose of "white mouth," and the baby had to go to Badger because his circumcision was causing problems.

On our way back to camp from Badger I drove the horse myself. On arrival, my brother-in-law took the horse, fed it and watered it. A short while later, it dropped dead with jawlock colic.

I wanted my husband to buy another horse as the A.N.D. Co. had several old ones for sale. But no, he was fed up. He went to Badger to borrow 15 dogs. We packed up, got a komatic or large sleigh, put a small feather bed on it, lunch box, coats and my two babies. Then in the month of February, we started the journey back again to Pilley's Island, 52 miles; 32 by land, 20 by frozen bay.

The ice was very thin but we made the trip in two days and one night. We passed thousands of rabbits hung up on high scaffolds waiting for the roads to get broken to take them north for packing. We broke the road through mountains of snow in places. About one hour before we arrived at Pilley's Island a snow and wind storm came on and we could not see one yard ahead of us. The only thing we could do was leave it to the instinct of the dogs. And although the dogs had never been that way before, as they were from Badger, they took us to the right landing place. It was very slippery and the dogs were tired and hungry. The sleigh upset, spilling us in a snow drift about five minutes from our home. But a neighbour, Mrs. Tom Campbell, who lived by the side of the hill, came out and helped us in her house. She wasn't long getting a cup of tea.

My husband went back to Badger to get our luggage and to his dismay, our camp had been broken into and our possessions were gone. Among the loot were his rifle and my skates and many little things we treasured—all gone. On the trip I had left a coat with my camera, new shoes for the children and several little things in the pocket, at one of the camps on the road.

Since then I have had 11 more children. My husband was killed in the mines at Bell Island in 1939 when my baby was three months old and the children were all small. Now most of them are married and I am a grandmother 31 times over.

Author Unknown

Life's Funny Experiences
A Prickly Situation

We live in Guelph, Ontario, but my husband is originally from Miles Cove, Green Bay, Newfoundland. One night he came home from work at 12:30 a.m. and ran frantically into the house to wake me up so that I could help him catch the cat. He had seen the cat sitting in the yard when he came in and figured she must have somehow gotten out. Before I could stop him and tell him that the cat was in bed beside me he ran outside. From outside I could hear, "Here kitty, kitty!" The cat looked up at me as if to say, "Is he calling me?" I ran outside and there was my husband chasing a porcupine around the house and still repeating, "Here kitty, kitty!"

Submitted by Julie–Dee Hewlett – Guelph, Ontario

♀

Animal Mating - Fact and Fantasy – *Ron Young*

The Parrot's Language of Love
Fact:

Although parrots have the ability to mimic human words, they do not communicate with other parrots this way, even their mates. Parrots (male and female), who come in beautiful colour combinations, use other languages of love to bond with their mates. Although they use no English words (nor the words of any language they may have picked up) to show affection to their mates, they do sometimes appear to whisper sweet nothings into their mate's ear. This is when they trim the feathers of the other, especially in the head and neck area, with their beaks (this is called preening). They will lovingly nibble each others bills and feed each other and not only at times when mating is an issue.

When mating becomes an issue, it is actually the female parrot who initiates copulation of the pair. With her body lowered, her tail raised higher, her head up and neck withdrawn from the body, while her wings are lifted and quivering, she will emit a low, wordless, cackling sound as she sidles up close to her man on the perch.

Her mate will sidle closer to her way and placing his foot on her lower back, he will swing his tail under hers so that their cloacae touch. (The cloacae are the sex organs of both male and female parrots.) During mating, the two organs, which resemble human lips as much as anything else, join in a highly exuberant "cloacal kiss." The mating of parrots can last as long as eight minutes, but usually lasts for only about three. During successful copulation the male squeezes sperm from his cloacae into hers and with any luck there will soon be baby parrots joining the parents in the nest.

Fantasy:

When two parrots become a pair
They always show how much they care
In other words, they're just a couple of
Our feathered friends, the birds
Who don't communicate in words
But in the universal language known as love

♀

Feminine Words & Phrases

Blue-gown: A one-time name for a prostitute. This was once the dress of public disgrace for a prostitute who had been in jail.

Blue-stocking: A woman of learning who tends to care little for feminine graces or their accessories. The name probably came from "The Blue Stocking Society" founded by a Mrs. Montagu about 1750. One member of the society, a Miss Monckton, later became Countess of Cork. When she died in 1840, the Countess was the last remaining member of the society.

Bobby-sox: White cotton socks worn by teenage girls in North America in the 1940s and '50s.

Bobby-soxers: Teenage girls who raved at live performances of bands of the 1940s and '50s.

Maid of all work: As the name suggests, a female servant who does a variety of chores.

Locksmith's daughter: Term once used to refer to a key.

♀

Female Firsts

1953: Jacqueline Cochran became the first female airplane pilot to break the sound barrier. *See also page 227.*

1953: Oveta Culp Hobby became the first Secretary of the U.S. Department of Health, Education and Welfare.

1954: New Brunswick women were first permitted to serve on juries.

1954: Toronto schoolgirl Marilyn Bell became the first person to swim across Lake Ontario. *See also page 162.*

1955: Louise Arner Boyd became the first woman to fly over the North Pole. *See also 'Female Facts' page 380.*

1955: For the first time in Canada, restrictions on married women in the federal public service were removed. In the past, women public service employees were fired upon marriage.

1956: Lucille Wheeler of Montreal won Canada's first Olympic medal for skiing, a bronze in Austria.

1956: Australian swimmer Dawn Fraser became the first woman to win four Olympic gold medals.

1956: Prince Edward Island women were first permitted to serve on juries.

♀

✍ Letters From Our Friends

"...sailed all the way from Houston, Texas."

Dear Ron,

Greetings from Lewisporte. My name is Irene King-Benoit and I am enclosing a copy of a letter from an American couple who visited Newfoundland during the summer of 1998. I met Mark and Bunny Thompson at the Lewisporte Marina one lovely August evening. Sometimes I stroll down there just to see some of the sailboats and yachts from away.

My ten-year-old daughter Nancy and myself met the "crew of two," Mark and Bunny, and were invited aboard the sailboat, *The Wild Goose*. They had sailed all the way from Houston, Texas. During the brief visit, they gave us a tour of their boat and we shared some stories. They were a very nice couple. She is an author back in Texas and I believe both were engineers, and were just taking a couple of years off for themselves. They mentioned that they were expecting a family member to fly into Gander from

Wild Goose

Texas the next day and then they were off to Twillingate. And from there, they were leaving to return home to the United States.

Later that same evening, I returned to the *The Wild Goose* with a loaf of homemade sweet bread and a couple of books. One was Cassie Brown's *Death on the Ice*. The couple were nowhere to be found, so I left the bag of goodies hanging on the cabin door with a note attached. Never to be in contact again, I thought. *To my surprise, a couple of months later I received a very nice letter of appreciation from them.

After reading the "Letters to the Editor" in the January 2001 issue of *Downhomer*, the letter from Judy (Sparkes) de Mare of Townsend, Massachusetts, regarding the book and movie, *The Shipping News*, prompted me to write this letter. I thought that Americans Mark and Bunny Thompson's bird's eye view of Newfoundland would show what Newfoundlanders are truly made of to the whole world.

Regards,
Irene Benoit – Lewisporte, Newfoundland
PS: Here is the note I received from Mark and Bunny.

Dear Irene and Nancy,

Thank you for the book by Cassie Brown, *Death on the Ice*. I read it as we were sailing from Lewisporte to St. John's. It really made me thankful for the warm summer in Newfoundland. It also reinforced my admiration for Newfoundlanders. Once we were back in the States, I found another of Cassie's books, 'Standing into Danger', also a great read. Once more, as an American, I thanked God for the help provided by Newfoundlanders that day, some 50 years ago.

Thanks also for the sweet bread you left aboard *Wild Goose*. You're right, it was great toasted; but unlike the book, it was finished before we reached Twillingate.

Long may your big jib draw.
Mark and Bunny, Houston, Texas, USA

♀

Life, Love & Laughter

Tickle and Bight　*By Lucy Fitzpatrick-McFarlane*

Having a Bad Hair Day, Huh?

I don't know about you but I get all out of sorts if my hair is not neat and tidy all the time. I could never wear those hairdos that stand up like a birch broom in the fits, because it would drive me crazy. Every time I see someone with a piece of hair out of place or tufts of hair going awry, I have this uncomfortable urge to spit on my finger and smooth it back in place. I believe this thing I have about untidy hair goes back to when I was a youngster, for hair was a big issue with Mom. Four of us girls had long hair and Mom always fussed over us, making sure that every hair was brushed and in place before she let us out the door. My father did most of the barbering around the Cove back then, so his clippers were always in use on my brothers and their friends.

Lord, how I hated my long, mop of curls. Not only was it thick, but it was RED, the colour of blasty boughs and along with it, came freckles . . . big, fat ones. I'd fly into a snit if someone said anything about my hair colour and I got called names like Spitfire and Carrot Top. No matter how much I begged, my parents wouldn't let me get it cut. The worst thing about having long hair was getting the tangles out. Every Saturday night Mom washed our hair, curled it into ringlets and tied up the ends in either rags or brown paper to keep it in place for Sunday mass. Once she caught you between her knees in that deathgrip, escape was impossible. Trust me, she knew how to keep us from complaining or squirming. She'd simply ask that dreaded question that none of us dared answer. "Do you want to feel this brush on your backside?"

With each passing year as my hair got longer I hated it more. I was 12 before I finally got it cut. When summer holidays started that year, I wanted so badly to be able to wear my hair shoulder-length in a flip like the older girls. That one night, when my parents went out, I talked my sister, Helena, into cutting my hair. I sat in front of the looking glass for an hour explaining exactly the style I wanted, and Helena assured me she could do it. I was so excited as I rattled on about what I'd look like, that I didn't notice Helena was picking up hair all over and snipping. It wasn't until I heard those awful words that I reacted.

"Whoops ... Oh, my gosh!" I heard her say.

My eyes flew open just in time to catch her trying to kick my curls under the stove, and in a panic, I ran to the looking glass. Talk about a mess! She had lopped off one side of my hair up over the ear and the rest was all different lengths. I screeched and bawled as she tried to even it up, but it just kept getting shorter and shorter. When Daddy walked in on us after, there was hair flying everywhere ... and it wasn't just mine either. What a Ree-raw that was! I can't remember ever seeing my father so angry. Suffice it to say, Helena spent the rest of the night in her bedroom while Daddy tried to salvage what was left of my hair. It was shock enough seeing myself for the first time, but getting a shingle-bob was something I hadn't counted on. For the rest of the summer, I went around with a bandana tied around my head. I kept the knot so tight under my chin that I got a rash and eventually had to take it off.

It took several years before I got used to short hair and once I experimented with rollers, I became quite good at styling my hair. I even got used to sleeping on those brush rollers because

Life, Love & Laughter

we didn't have the luxury of hair dryers then and if I was in a hurry to get my hair dried, I'd stick my head in the oven of the wood stove. My friends even let me work on their hair and I did very well...except for the first time I gave someone a cold wave and some of the hair came off on the rods. I thought the directions said to leave the solution on overnight. Besides, she was always complaining that her hair was too thick anyway and you could hardly notice those thin patches under the little squiggly curls. It was an honest mistake and I tried my best to correct the situation. I conditioned her hair with a good dose of vaseline to fix the burnt ends and granted, it took several days to get that sticky muck out, but mom's home-made lye soap did the trick.

As I got older, my interest in hair grew and because I worked mostly on women, I wanted to try my skills on men. I used to watch my father cutting hair with his scissors and hand clippers, so it looked easy enough. Problem was, none of the boys would let me near their hair. When my father invested in a pair of electric clippers, I was itching to try them and I got my chance one afternoon when I was home alone and a teenager (I'll call him Bob because he doesn't know this story yet) came for his monthly haircut. It took a lot of coaxing but I finally bribed him with a piece of bakeapple pie and one of his favourite comic books...*Archie*. I didn't want anybody to catch me, so I took him in the store beside the house where Daddy had just connected the electricity. I didn't realize there was a problem with the outlet, so I plugged in the cord and not knowing how to use the new clippers, I laid it flat against the back of Bob's head. I guess something must have shorted out because when I turned on the button, sparks flew from the plug and my hand started to vibrate, leaving a zig-zag trail up the back of Bob's hair. It went right smack to the scalp, but Bob was so engrossed in his comic book, that he didn't even notice. To make a long story short, when my father got home and saw the predicament I was in, he took over. Thankfully he never uttered a word about the mess to Bob's head. So I scravelled back into the house.

The next time I saw Bob through the window, the only place he had hair was on the top of his head, because the rest was skinned from one ear to the other, not unlike the Mohawk haircut from a few years ago. I was terrified when I saw him return a few minutes later with his two buddies, for I thought he was seeking revenge for that ugly looking haircut. Who would have figured that he actually liked it and was bringing his friends back to get Daddy to cut theirs? Later my father told me that he had asked Bob if he wanted to be the first in the Cove to get a new "flat top" haircut, and he readily agreed. And to this day, Bob still doesn't know how that new hair style originated.

Daddy always kept a close eye on me whenever I did somebody's hair after that. I guess he knew I was a natural because it was he who suggested that I go to college "to find out how to cut hair properly before you gets yourself into more trouble."

Perhaps it was because I actually did become a hairdresser that I pay so much attention to hair. Oh, sure, I still have trouble with my own sometimes, but who doesn't? Just recently, when I was going out with my friends, my hair just wouldn't go right somehow. In desperation, I stuck my head under the bathroom faucet and washed it again. This time it dried beautifully and had a brilliant shine. "That new green shampoo you bought did wonders on my hair," I told my husband. "What is it?"

"You used the GREEN stuff?" he asked with an amused look on his face. "That's the flea shampoo I got for the cats."

Oh, well, what did I care? I got more compliments on my bouncy hair that night than I've had in years. Who knows...maybe I've stumbled on the solution to my problem. Having a bad hair day? Try Hagen's Flea and Tick Shampoo. It works for me.

Reprinted from Downhomer *magazine.*

♀

Spice of Life

I wish I had married a plumber. At least he'd be home by five o'clock.

– Betty Ford

♀

Food for Thought

If you always do what interests you, at least one person is pleased.

– Katharine Hepburn

♀

Ennellene

Oh, the shrewdness of our shrewdness when we're shrewd
And the rudeness of our rudeness when we're rude
But the shrewdness of our shrewdness
And the rudeness of our rudeness
Ain't nothing to our goodness when we're good

♀

Life's Funny Experiences
He's Not Kidding

When we were living on an apple orchard west of Sydney, Australia, we offered to care for our neighbour's goat for a few months. This made more work for my husband, since he had to chase the goat out of places it shouldn't have been, such as the orchard or garden.

One morning my dearest came in late for breakfast looking as though he had been working for hours. I suggested he take the day off to "stop and smell the roses."

Glumly, he replied, "Can't. The goat ate them."

Leonie Mitchell – Lennox Head, Australia

♀

Female Facts
Mother of Suspension

The bra was invented in 1913, when Mary Phelps, a Manhattan debutante, became frustrated because her corset kept showing above the low necklines if her dresses. Using two handkerchiefs and ribbons she and her maid designed an undergarment which enabled her to "move more freely," and gave her a "delicious, nearly-naked feeling, and in a glass I saw that I was flat and proper."

She gave many of her "backless brassieres" to friends but when the demand became great she patented her product. Mary had no marketing skills and she eventually gave up on the idea.

Some years later she met an old boyfriend who was in the corset business. When he showed her invention to his employees, Warner Brothers Corset Company, they gave her $1,500 for patent rights and made a fortune from her idea.

♀

Life, Love & Laughter

Women Who Have Made A Difference *– By Ron Young*

Josepha Abiertas was born in the Philippines in 1894, and although orphaned at an early age, she became the first woman to graduate from law school. She then devoted her life to the welfare of her people. After her death from tuberculosis in 1929, a welfare home, the Josepha Abiertas House of Friendship, was named after her.

Linda Richards was the first person to enroll in, and the first one to graduate from a nurse-training program at the New England Hospital for Women and Children. The program was offered by Miss Susan Dimock, the resident physician at the hospital. As the first trained nurse in the U.S., Linda became the night supervisor at Bellevue Hospital in New York City where she met Sister Helen, a nun of the All Saints Order, who had trained in the Nightingale System in London. While at Bellevue, Nurse Richards created a system for charting and maintaining individual medical records for each patient. This was the first written reporting system for nurses which even the famous Nightingale System later adopted.

Aretha Franklin, the daughter of a Baptist minister and singer, was greatly influenced by the gospel singers who visited her father's church. The lady with the great vocal capabilities began her recording career in 1960, and in 1967 her album, *I Never Loved a Man,* as well as five single records each sold more than 1 million copies. Among her many honours and awards are a Grammy Legends Award in 1991, a Kennedy Center Honours Award for Lifetime Achievement in the performing arts in 1994 and a Grammy Lifetime Achievement Award, the same year.

Pauline Frederick Robbins, who was the "Voice of the United Nations" as correspondent for NBC News for 21 years, has many firsts to her credit. She became the first woman to moderate a Presidential debate, the first woman to be awarded the Paul White Award for her contributions to broadcast journalism and the first woman to receive the Peabody and the DuPont Awards for news broadcasting. She was the first woman to be elected President of the UN Correspondents Association. She has also been honoured as one of the "Ten Most Admired Women" and has received honorary doctorates from 23 colleges and universities.

Judy Garland was born Frances Gumm and into a show business family. After her name change she went on to become one of classic Hollywood's most popular musical entertainers and actresses. Although mostly remembered as Dorothy in *The Wizard of Oz*, which helped her win an Oscar in 1939, she went on to gain greater recognition for her acting abilities and was nominated for Oscars in "A Star is Born" in 1954 and "Judgement at Nurenberg" in 1961.

Lakshmi Bai was the wife of Gangadhar Rao, Maharajah of Jhansi in northern India. When her husband died, the British refused to accept her adopted son as Maharajah, so Lakshmi assembled a volunteer army of 14,000 rebels and ordered that defenses of the city itself be strengthened. Jhansi was attacked by the British in March 1858. Shelling of Jhansi was fierce and the British were determined not to allow any rebels to escape, while the Ranee (wife of the Maharajah) was determined not to surrender. The British noted that the Indian soldiers fighting them showed more vigor than they ever had while following British orders. Women were also seen working the batteries and carrying ammunition, food and water to the soldiers. The Ranee herself was seen constantly active in the defense of the city. Jhansi, however, fell to the British forces after a two-week siege.

Lakshmi escaped on horseback and was later influential in convincing other rebel Indian rulers

Life, Love & Laughter

to go on the offensive and seize the fortress of Gwalior. The British attacked the fort and after a long siege captured it. Among the dead in the fort was Rani Lakshmi Bai.

Sir Hugh Rose, the commander of the British force, wrote later, "The Ranee was remarkable for her bravery, cleverness and perseverance; her generosity to her subordinates was unbounded. These qualities, combined with her rank, rendered her the most dangerous of all the rebel leaders."

Dr. Justina Ford, despite the fact that she had two strikes against her (she was black and a female and was therefore denied hospital privileges for a number of years), still persisted in her commitment to bring medical service to the disadvantaged and underprivileged of Denver. Specializing in gynecology, obstetrics and pediatrics, the "Lady Doctor," as she became familiarly and lovingly known, delivered more than 7,000 babies of varied ethnic backgrounds and from all walks of life. Dr. Justina Ford was the first African American woman doctor in the State of Colorado and a true Humanitarian. Today, the lovely Victorian house which served as both home and office for Ford, stands as a beacon of light to the community, and as a lasting tribute to a magnificent woman and is known as the Dr. Justina Ford House.

Chris Evert, became the first professional tennis player to win 1,000 singles matches in 1984. Evert turned professional at the age of 17 in 1972, after winning the Virginia Slims Championship tournament and the United States Clay-Court Championship earlier the same year. In 1974, she won singles titles at Wimbledon and the French and Italian opens. In 1975, she again won the French title, in addition to winning her first U.S. Open women's singles competition by defeating Evonne Goolagong at Forest Hills. She beat Goolagong again in 1976 at Wimbledon. Evert went on to win a total of six U.S. opens, seven French opens, three Wimbledon titles and two Australian opens. She retired from competitive tennis in 1989 and became a colour commentator for network-television broadcasts of major tennis tournaments. Evert earned a rare unanimous selection to the International Tennis Hall of Fame in 1995.

Qiu Jin, who was born in 1875 into a moderately wealthy family in China, felt that a better future for women lay under a Western-type government instead of the corrupt Manchu government that was in power at the time. Along with her male cousin Hsu Hsi-lin, she worked to unite many secret revolutionary societies to work together for the overthrow of the Manchu government. On July 12, 1907, she was arrested by government troops and although she refused to admit her involvement in the plot, incriminating documents were found and she was beheaded.

♀

Aunt Alice says:

The only time the world beats a path to my door is when I'm in the bathroom.

Spice of Life

I try to take one day at a time, but sometimes several days attack me at once.

– Jennifer Unlimited

♀

MABEL & MANLEY

When Manley turned 65, he and his wife Mabel got dressed in their best and off they went to the government building to register for his old-age pension. When they got to see the clerk, she asked for some identification. Upon discovering that Manley had forgotten his wallet, the clerk asked him to open his shirt to show that his body was full of gray hair. Sure enough, when he took off his shirt his body was covered with gray hair. The clerk approved his application. On the way out off the office Mabel smacked him up the side of the head and said, "Manley, you should have dropped your underwear and applied for a disability pension too."

♀

Female Facts

Collaborating with the Enemy

In 1994, Miss Lebanon, Ghada Turk, was participating in the Miss World competition in South Africa when she inadvertently fell into disfavour with her country. During a photographing session, Ghada was standing beside Miss Italy. When Miss Italy stepped away for a minute a photographer snapped a picture which appeared in the papers the next day. The photograph showed a smiling Miss Lebanon standing beside a smiling Miss Israel. Since Lebanon and Israel were at war, Ghada's act was considered "collaboration with the enemy." In fear, Ghada hid out in London for four months before returning home. Upon her return she was interrogated for two and a half hours and charged with violating Lebanon's boycott of Israel. Luckily the judge let her off with a warning.

♀

Female Firsts

1956: After overcoming polio as a child, Tenley Albright became the first female in America to win a Olympic gold medal in figure skating.

1956: Pat McCormick became the first female to win back-to-back springboard and platform diving events at the Olympics.

1958: Maria-Teresa de Filippis of Italy became the first female to compete in a European Grand Prix auto race.

1959: Lorraine Hansberry became the first African-American woman to write a Broadway play.

1959: Jacqueline Cochran became the first female to serve as president of the Fédération Aéronautique Internationale.

1960: Sirimavo Ratwatte Dias Bandaranaike of Ceylon became the world's first female prime minister. *See also page 178.*

1961: J.G. Travell became the first female personal physician to the President of the U.S.

♀

Life, Love & Laughter

The Whys of Men

Why were men given larger brains than dogs?
So they won't hump women's legs at cocktail parties.

♀

Life's Funny Experiences
Out Of Her Habitat

My dad, Ron, and my mom, Lottie, are both from Norman's Cove. Dad has a real sense of humour and you never know what he's going to say. They came to visit during our anniversary party and Dad started telling everybody about seal oil capsules. Dad said, "Lot (he calls mom, Lot) is taking the seal oil capsules but I got one problem with that."

"What is that?" someone asked.

"Every morning when I get up," replied Dad, "Lot is looking out the window waiting for the ice to come in!"

Margaret McCarthy – Bellevue, Newfoundland

♀

Letters From Our Friends
Christmas Surprise

Dear Editor,

In 1991, I had a very special Christmas. My dad, along with my two sisters and two brothers, decided to give my mother a big, wonderful surprise. You see, my mother hadn't spent Christmas with her mother in more than 30 years! Us kids had never spent a Christmas with Grandma Pittman, because she lived 2,500 miles away in St. John's, Newfoundland, and had little money for travelling.

So, we all saved up and bought two airline tickets - one for Grandma and one for my aunt Sandra, who lived with Grandma. They arrived a day before our Christmas gathering and stayed secretly at my house. My brothers, sisters and their families all arrived early on the big day, and excitement was in the air! We couldn't wait for Mom and Dad to arrive. Our hearts were pounding with anticipation!

Just as Mom and Dad pulled into the driveway, we hid Grandma and Aunt Sandra upstairs in a bedroom. They came in the door and Mom just couldn't figure out why we were all acting so suspiciously. We then blindfolded Mom and told her that her Christmas present was soooo special she just had to open it right away. Mother still couldn't imagine why we were all so excited! We removed the blindfold and standing in front of her was her mother and baby sister. They screamed and they cried and they laughed like hyenas! It was joyously overwhelming. I was so full of happiness just to be a part of that wonderful surprise. It was the best Christmas I ever had.

Grandmother has since gone on to heaven. That was the only Christmas we ever spent with her. I'm so thankful that we were able to put together our big surprise. Our family is very close to our Newfoundland relatives and one of our family traditions at Christmas is to read *The Night Before Christmas In Newfoundland*.

Debra S. Carlisle Smith – North Muskegon, Michigan, USA (Born in St. John's, Newfoundland)

♀

Life, Love & Laughter

Tickle and Bight *By Lucy Fitzpatrick–McFarlane*

'Til Birth Do Us Part

A friend of mine recently became a
grandmother for the first time and naturally I
went to see her new grandson. As I was
admiring the baby, the new mother asked me a
question that made me bivver all over. "Would
you like to see the video of the baby being
born, Lucy?" she asked enthusiastically? "My
boyfriend got everything on tape...me
screaming my head off, the crowning...
everything. It's awesome!"

I could feel the corner of my mouth twitch
and the hives popping on my thighs. She said
the words so easily that you'd think she was
asking me to watch an episode of *The Young
and the Restless*. The thought of watching something so intimate on a big screen over cake and
coffee made me blush and I politely declined, telling her I had to rush home to water my plants.
Let's face it, I know where babies come from. I've had two myself and even the thought of
having my husband in the delivery room with me was a strain on my nerves 23 years ago. After
all, in my mother's day, babies were born at home with the help of a midwife, but the men were
never present at the actual birth. Oh, they participated alright because they had the important task
of boiling water for the midwife. Mind you, Mrs. May Isaacs, the midwife who delivered all of
my mother's children, once told me she never really needed all the gallons of water the men
provided. It was more to keep them busy so they wouldn't get in her way and they wouldn't dare
poke their noses in the bedroom door because that was a private matter...a 'woman thing', if you
will.

However, things change, so when my husband expressed a wish to go into the delivery room
with me, I reluctantly agreed. In all fairness, he was there for the conception, so I figured he was
entitled to be there for the birth as well. As it turned out, he didn't quite witness his son's birth
and perhaps it was just as well because we might never have made it to our 23rd anniversary. If
Murray had attempted to stick a video camera in my...er...face, in my heightened state of misery,
I might have resorted to violence like Lorena Bobbit did. My chances of having a second son
would've been very slim had I been able to get my hands on a scalpel, and since I was not in any
condition to help police search for Murray's missing appendage, divorce would've been
inevitable.

As I watched the new mother getting ready to go see the movie *Independence Day* with her
boyfriend, I marveled at her recovery from childbirth after only three days. Was it just me, I
wondered, or is this new generation of women physically and mentally stronger than mine? In
my mother's day, after childbirth the woman stayed in for 10 days or more, so I thought that was
normal. But I later found out from the midwife that it wasn't because the women were so
delicate, but it was more for their mental well-being. "If it was a woman with a large family, I
always told the husbands that their wives had to have complete bed rest," she said. "After all,
that was probably the only chance the poor dears would get to get off their feet and God knows
they needed that time for themselves."

Oh, yes, I liked her way of thinking. Fact is, I needed the time to let my body shrink back to normal. I had enough stretch marks to reach from Ontario to Newfoundland and permanent ring-around-the-buttocks from having to sit on a rubber doughnut ring. I hung on to the bed springs for three weeks before I was evicted and even then, I didn't go willingly. And I'm not ashamed to admit that I took full advantage of all the pampering I got from Murray when I got home. He did everything...the cooking, cleaning, groceries, washing diapers and getting up for the baby's night feeding. But I figured that I had done enough in the delivery room, so now it was his turn. After all, I gave him a son and a snap to put in his wallet to replace the old one of Marilyn Monroe, didn't I? And he did, after all, miss the actual birth. You see, I was in labour for almost 40 hours before our son made his grand entrance. That's why we always celebrate his birthday for two days. Naturally my husband was beside me every second and after the first 30 hours, I was exhausted from pain and the more he tried to help, the more frustrated I became. I didn't handle giving birth graciously, but Murray remained in complete control, holding my hand, giving me directions on how to breathe and telling me not to push whenever I tried to speed things up. I'll be frank with you, even in normal times I get my dander up when someone tells me what to do, so you can imagine my reaction under stress. My dark side emerged and I was like a raving lunatic. Between the panting and heavy breathing, I focused all my attention on the center of my pain...HIM. I don't even recall the words I spit at him or the rotten names that flew like knives off my tongue, but the woman in the next room later told me that she knew every time I got a pain because I screamed at my husband, "I feel a cramp coming on and it's got your name on it, so get out of my face!"

When I threatened to rip out his mustache one hair at a time, a wise nurse who had given birth three times herself, sent him to have a coffee. And wouldn't you know it, before he got back, our son was born. I felt terrible about all the verbal abuse I showered on him then, but he was so wrapped up in our new son that he didn't even remember that just an hour earlier I was threatening immediate divorce upon delivery. Instead, he brought me roses, chocolates and all kinds of lovely gifts. I could tell by the proud look on his face when he held the baby that all was forgiven, but I worried that the trauma of childbirth had taken its toll on him. Perhaps it was my weakened state that made me feel the way I did, but I thought he was acting really queer the way he'd stand outside my room stopping passers-by and dragging them off to see the baby. He took up permanent residence outside the nursery window, making goo-goo sounds and reciting nursery rhymes in baby talk. It was pitiful to watch a grown man with his face plastered against the nursery window showing sports equipment to a newborn who had barely had a diaper change yet. Thank God our son couldn't see the crazed look in his father's eyes when he held up the hockey stick and skates as he blubbered on about the Boston Bruins, or he might have been traumatized for the rest of his life.

It wasn't until three years later that our second child was born and Murray saw my ugly side emerge again during labour. But this time he was prepared for any adverse reaction on my part. Since the first delivery was so long, we assumed that the second might be the same, so when Murray went to take our three-year-old to a friend's house, it happened. After only 24 hours of labour, I was whisked into the delivery room and by the time Murray returned half an hour later, I was sitting up in bed holding our second son. He was very disappointed and apologetic for not being there and just to make it up to me, he actually hired someone to come to our house for a week so I could rest up in bed. Naturally I accepted his gift because I knew I wouldn't get the opportunity of being pampered for a long time now that I had two children to attend to. I was ecstatic the first morning when he brought her to my bedroom. After he left I just lay there relaxing while the pleasant young lady went to meet my toddler. Finally, I decided to start my day with a hot bath..."You know what would be great to start the morning," I said to her as she looked in the door,"...a long, hot bubble bath."

Her response was immediate. "I'll run the bath right away," she said and before I could blink an eye, she was headed for the bathroom.

Now I knew Murray said she was supposed to do light housework, but drawing my bath water? I thought I'd died and gone to Heaven! I called Murray at work and thanked him for finding this wonderful gem. "She's going to work out great," I told him excitedly. "You won't believe this, but she's running a bubble bath for me as I speak. I feel like a queen!"

My excitement was short-lived, however, when I made my way to the bathroom and heard my "hired help" splashing and singing in HER bubble bath. I could've used a video camera then. Somehow this young college graduate was under the impression that she was supposed to be on the receiving end of the "pampering", because I ended up doing all the work while SHE rested. I knew I should've set her straight on the first day, but I thought I'd give her another chance to redeem herself and besides, I didn't want Murray to know. But the poor angishore didn't have a clue about anything. Instead of two babies, I now had three to look after. She talked on the telephone while I made lunch and did laundry, lay on the sofa reading her Harlequin Romance novel while my toddler watched cartoons, and took longer afternoon naps than he did. Every time I crawled back in bed, she'd yell up the stairs to tell me the baby was crying or come into the bedroom to ask if she should pick him up. When she woke me up to tell me we were out of chips and dip on the second day, I lost my cool and broke the news to her that the health spa was closed for the season and sent her home in a taxi so I could get a rest.

But that's all in the past now and I've chalked it up to inexperience. Had I known then what I know now about love, marriage and babies, I might have re-written our vows. The words uttered so willingly at the altar might have set a new trend for women had I altered one little word before he slipped that wedding band on my finger. "Till birth do us part..."

My, it has such a nice ring to it, doesn't it?

♀

How Mrs. Peddle Caught a Tuna Fish in 1939

The unusual and plucky performance of Mrs. Thomas Peddle by Dan Benson of Rantem, Trinity Bay.

Mrs. Peddle belongs to Chance Cove, but was spending some time at Rantem Harbour. The mouth of Rantem Harbour is about two hundred yards wide. One day a school of what our Newfoundland fishermen call horse mackerel – their proper name is tuna fish – came in on one side of the harbour and went out again on the other side, where the water is quite shoal.

Mrs. Peddle was watching the big fish and noticed that one of them was coming along quite near to the shore. She ran and caught a piece of rope, made a half-hitch in it, and ran out in the water to her arm-pits, from which position she threw the rope over the tuna fish's tail, jerked it tight, and then hurried back to the shore and wound the rope around a heavy tree growing near the edge of the water. This brought the big fish up standing and of course in a moment the fish was in a rage of splashing and plunging.

Mrs. Peddle held on grimly to the rope and as he weakened she gradually shortened the rope until she had him landed. The tuna fish was eleven feet long, seven feet on the round, and filled four barrels when cut up.

From the book The Best Of The Barrelman *(1938-1940), edited by William Connors, published by Creative Publishing. Used by permission.*

♀

Life, Love & Laughter

Life, Love & Laughter

Spice of Life

The successes of today belong to bold mediocrity. — *Esther Forbes*

♀

MABEL & MANLEY

"I remember when you used to hold my hand at every opportunity," Mabel told her husband Manley as they sat together on the sofa.

Feeling obligated, Manley reached across and gently held Mabel's hand.

"I also remember," said Mable wistfully, "when you used to nibble on my neck and send chills down my spine."

At that, Manley got up and headed out of the room.

"Was it something I said Manley?" asked Mabel. "Where are you going?"

"I'm going to the other room to get my teeth," replied Manley.

♀

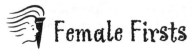

Female Firsts

1963: On June 16, Soviet cosmonaut Valentia Tereshkova, became the first woman in space.

1964: Australian swimmer Dawn Fraser became the first swimmer (of any sex) to win an event in three straight Olympiads, having won in 1956 as well as 1960.

1964: Jerrie Mock became the first woman to complete a solo airplane flight around the world. She was flying a 1953 Cessna 180 single-engine monoplane, called the Spirit of Columbus.

1964: Australian author Kath Walker became the first Aborigine to have writings published, when her best-selling book *We are Going* was published.

1965: Donna De Varona became the first woman sports broadcaster on U.S. national TV when she started as broadcaster for ABC.

1965: Vivian Malone became the first black person to graduate from the University of Alabama.

1966: On March 24th, Cheng Yen, who was born Mien-Yuan in Taiwan, began the first Buddhist organization which sought out the needy, poor and aged, and rendered whatever assistance was necessary.

1966: Indira Gandhi became the first woman president of India. *See also page 295.*

1967: On December 28, Muriel Siebert became the first woman to own a seat on the New York Stock Exchange.

1967: Nancy Green of Canada became the first woman's season champion in the World Cup of ski racing.

♀

The First War Bride

By Isabella Allen - Rimbey, Alberta

I was the first war bride to come over from Scotland to the shores of Newfoundland during WWII. My husband, Milven Allen, was in the British Navy; I met him shortly after he came overseas in 1940. We fell in love almost immediately and were married May 24, 1941.

My husband's ship was torpedoed, so he spent some time in hospital in England. The navy people wanted him to go back to his homeland to recuperate, and I was to follow him after the war. But Milven wouldn't have any of that – if I couldn't go, he wouldn't go either. Plus my family wouldn't allow me to travel by myself. So with the help of our minister, and my doctor and family, we were allowed to travel together.

On July 7, 1942, we boarded a ship which was part of a huge convoy. It was quite a frightening thing – being escorted up the *Clyde* from Glasgow to the Atlantic by destroyers, which turned back when we reached open water.

It was a long journey in tough seas. They were dropping off depth charges for days and a couple of ships in the convoy were lost; we were lucky. During the 19-day crossing, my husband had to do duty – eight hours on, four hours off – until we reached the coast of the United States of America.

We sailed past the Statue of Liberty and into New Jersey harbour. From there we boarded a bus that took us to New York City, where we were put up in a hotel on the 25th floor. I thought I was in another world, with all the lights and large buildings. I said to my husband, "There's no war over here." We were there for a week, which was good as I needed to regain my "land legs."

We took a train from New York to the Canadian border. There we encountered some trouble. The customs official boarded the train to check peoples' tickets and passes, and when he got to us, I didn't have the pink slip to admit me into Canada. I thought, 19 days on the ocean avoiding torpedoes and I might be sent back! Well, all the servicemen in our car told the official not to even try putting us off the train, after all we'd gone through to get to that point.

The conductor of the train said he'd get in touch with the American consul; he did and they said it was okay to let us go, and we were on our way to North Sydney, Nova Scotia. We stayed there another few days awaiting the *Baccalieu*, which took us to my husband's home in St. Jacques, on the shores of Fortune Bay.

When I got there I thought I'd gone to the end of the world. But I will say this: the people in Newfoundland are the best I have ever known. They helped me by being my friends.

Life, Love & Laughter

My husband and I moved from St. Jacques to St. John's in January 1943, and we immigrated to Montreal in January 1949. Then in March 1949 came Confederation, which in my book was a godsend for Newfoundland.

Milven passed away on May 22, 2000, just two days before our 60th wedding anniversary. Life has certainly changed without him. I still love to visit his family and I was there in Newfoundland this past summer. Believe me, I didn't recognize the city of St. John's – it's grown and flourished so much since I lived there.

Here I'll end my story. I hope other war brides will read it and remember.

♀

Quillings   *From Your Aged Mother*

When I spill some food on my nice clean dress
Or maybe forget to tie my shoe
Please be patient and perhaps reminisce
About the hours I spent with you

When I taught you how to eat with care
Plus tying shoe laces and your numbers too
Dressing yourself and combing your hair
Those were precious hours spent with you

So when I forget what I was about to say
Just give me a minute - or maybe two

It probably wasn't important anyway
And I would much rather listen to you

If I tell a story one more time
And you know the ending through and through
Please remember your first nursery rhyme
When I rehearsed it a hundred times with you

When my legs are tired and it's hard to stand
Or walk the steady pace I would like to do
Please take me carefully by my hand
And guide me now as I did for you.
Author Unknown

♀

Feminine Words & Phrases

Cicisbeo: A married woman's escort or lover. To the married men of Italy at one time, the cicisbeo was his wife's gallant escort, since it was unfashionable in Italy at the time for a husband to be seen in public with his wife, his cavaliere servante took his place.

Cuckhold: The husband of a cheating wife. Ironically there are many places in Newfoundland and Labrador such as *Cuckhold's Cove, Cuckhold's Point, Cuckhold's Rocks,* that begin with that definer. The place names were originated by sailors. Who else?

Good Jack makes a good Jill: A good husband creates a good wife. The inference being, a good husband is one who has sense enough to know that, a happy wife is a happy life.

Jill: A generic name for female, woman, girl and sweetheart.

Love in a cottage: A term referring to a married couple who do not bring in enough money to sustain their social status.

♀

Women Who Have Made A Difference – *By Ron Young*

Jan Davis became an astronaut in June 1987. Now a veteran of three space flights, Dr. Davis has logged more than 673 hours in space. She flew as a mission specialist on STS-47 in 1992 and STS-60 in 1994 and was the payload commander on STS-85 in 1997.

Margaret Eleanor "Peggy" Atwood, prolific novelist, poet and critic, is one of Canada's major authors. A number of her writings have won awards, including her novel, *The Handmaiden's Tale*, which won her the Los Angeles Times Prize, the Governor General's Award, "runner-up" Booker Prize and Ritz-Paris-Hemmingway Award.

Melchora Aquino of the Philippines began her political career at the age of 83 when she was involved in the successful revolutionary attempt made in 1896 which gained her country freedom from Spain in 1898. The Spanish authorities caught her and she was imprisoned in a Bilibid prison and then exiled to the Marianas Island. She was set free when the Americans arrived in the Philippines. She lived to be 107 years old.

♀

The Ghost of Alice

The diary of Aaron Thomas, preserved at the Provincial Archives of Newfoundland and Labrador, describes the area between Springdale Street and Flower Hill in St. John's (during the 19th century) as being the most beautiful, natural flower garden in the world. That area was later used as a race track and the local gentry spent many an enjoyable evening there. It was also the site haunted for a decade by the spirit of Alice Janes, who was among the city's most ardent racing enthusiasts. With her Irish-knit shawl and jug of brew, Alice was a fixture at the race track.

During one of the many races there, Alice suffered a sudden heart attack and died instantly. The whole town turned out for the funeral and she was given a respectable send off at the old cemetery adjoining the Anglican Cathedral.

A year passed. On the anniversary of Alice's death, a young woman was being escorted through Flower Hill field by a male companion. Darkness was just beginning to set in and the girl complained of a strange, cold feeling. She asked her friend to take her home. As they neared the edge of the field they came upon a sight that sent them screaming from the area. They later described the apparition that had frightened them. At first it seemed like an old woman sitting on a rock holding a jug in her hand. When the couple neared the figure, it slowly stood up and stared straight at them. Her eyes were burning red and her white hair stood out like whisks of a broom.

The couple recognized the figure as the spirit of Alice Janes. When word of the apparition spread throughout town, several friends of the late Alice Janes visited the race track and then the gravesite to pray. While at the graveside they noticed that the tombstone which had marked the grave had disappeared. They searched the graveyard, but were unable to find it.

The apparition was reportedly seen on the anniversary of Alice's death for about a decade. Then one day the caretaker at the cemetery, while clearing an area of the graveyard, found the missing tombstone. He placed it back on the gravesite. The apparitions ceased and Alice's spirit was never heard from again.

From the book, Strange But True Newfoundland Stories, *by Jack Fitzgerald. Creative Publishing. Used by permission.*

♀

Life, Love & Laughter

Spice of Life

It takes all the fun out of a bracelet if you have to buy it yourself. – *Peggy Joyce*

♀

MABEL & MANLEY

Mabel said to her husband, "Manley, tomorrow will be our 25th wedding anniversary. Why don't you kill the two hens we have in the barn for dinner?"

"You don't mean to tell me that you're blaming what happened 25 years ago on them two hens," queried Manley.

♀

Ennellene

I am a bold lass, I'm brazen as brass
I'm personified women's genetics
I'm of feminine race, and won't hide my face
In spite of my female cosmetics

♀

Quillings   Fatal Flowers *- By Tim Brown*

I sent her flowers this morning
Roses of red
And begged her forgiveness
For the cruel things I said
I sent her flowers this morning
'Cause I felt so bad
I hope that tomorrow
She won't make me mad
I sent her flowers this morning
'Cause I beat her last night
I sent her flowers this morning
'Tho she caused the fight
I sent her flowers this morning
Carnations I think
Beautiful flowers
Purple and pink
I sent her flowers this morning
The best I could get
I know she still loves me
She'll forgive and forget
I sent flowers this morning
To the hospital door
She won't press charges

She loves me I'm sure
I cried when I told her
How sorry I feel
I kissed all her scars
And the bruises will heal

She'll get flowers this morning
From friends everywhere
She'll be buried this morning
And I can't be there
'Tho I begged and pleaded
They won't set me free
But she can't go away
Without flowers from me
I never meant
To hurt her that bad
But it seems she was always
Making me mad
I'll send her flowers this morning
Or first chance I get
She'll know I still love her
Even in death

♀

Her Other Half

Fair Deal

"I got a new television with a built-in DVD player for my wife's mother," a man told his friend.

"Good trade," his friend replied.

♀

Ennellene

Man's way is guided by his will
Yet we, as women, guide him down aisles
And he may have his will, but still
We women have our wiles

♀

Aphrodesia

Aphrodesia tried on a new dress for her husband, which appeared to be plastic and was completely transparent.

"But Aphrodesia," her husband gasped, "people will see right through it!"

"No, they won't silly," she countered, "I'll be inside it."

♀

Feminine Words & Phrases

Capon: Now means a castrated rooster but once meant love letter. This probably came from the French word poulet which not only means chicken, but fancy writing paper.

Lady Day: March 25, the first day of the year on the old Gregorian calendar, which was in existence before 1752. It originally commemorated the annunciation of the Virgin Mary and has also been known as Saint Mary's Day.

Hot stuff: Refers to a woman of perceived amorous inclinations.

Maid Marian: A female character in old English May Day games. In the Robin Hood tales that came later, Maid Marian was the sweetheart of Robin Hood. Plays featuring Robin Hood became popular at the May Day festivities. In these plays, Maid Marion was often played by a man in female costume.

Mistletoe kissing: The custom of kissing under the mistletoe is English and dates back to the early 1600s. Back then the correct procedure was for a man to pluck one of the berries from the mistletoe when he kisses the girl under it. When the last berry is gone the kissing is no longer permitted.

♀

WOMEN OF THE ISLAND AND THE BIG LAND

Top Golfer's Brave Fight Against Cancer

By Dee Murphy

Dee Murphy

Before breast cancer finally took her in 2002, at age 48, those who knew Marg Davis well were not surprised by the manner in which she dealt with the disease when it first came calling. That was back in 1997.

In fact, they'd be surprised if she had reacted to the dreaded disease in any other manner than she did.

"The first impact of knowing I had breast cancer was startling. It was something I never thought of having and the initial knowledge was frightening," Davis said in 2000.

"I was lucky that I had a strong family and a close group of friends to offer support, but still it was not a pleasant thing to happen."

"I was very, very concerned, as was to be expected and I had big worries about my future," the native of Fox Harbour, Placentia Bay offered.

"I have been extremely active all my life and just how the cancer would affect my activities was one of my big concerns. Having strong parents who held strong beliefs was a plus for me."

"I don't think I thought long or a great deal about dying from the cancer, but I was more than concerned about its immediate and long range effect on my lifestyle."

For ten months, physical education teacher Davis was off work and received chemotherapy treatment. It was successful and she went back to work at Holy Family School in Paradise for three years.

"You don't really appreciate your family and friends as much as you should until something like that happens," she stressed. "Money and other material things can be nice, but they are certainly not nearly as important as family and friends, particular at a time like that."

Regarded by most observers as the best female athlete the province has ever produced, Davis was an established "winner" prior to her cancer, and she's demonstrated well that she continues to be an established "winner" after her cancer.

For three straight years after her cancer, Marg Davis earned a spot on the team representing Newfoundland and Labrador in the Canadian senior female golf championships, played at the Admiral's Green Course in St. John's.

Golf is the sixth sport in which she has represented her native province at national championships.

Prior to her cancer, she was an outstanding softball, soccer, field hockey, ball hockey and ice hockey performer, and had a short but successful curling career. She was also inducted into the Canadian Softball Hall of Fame and the Newfoundland and Labrador Sports Hall of Fame, among others.

She was deeply involved in squash when her cancer was detected and returned to dominate that sport at the provincial and Atlantic levels following treatment and recovery.

"My breast cancer was certainly a major event in my life and I'm certainly happy that its treatment was successful, but I'm not the type to dwell on it all the time," Davis said.

"It was something that happened within my life but, as with other things, I've moved on from it."

Life, Love & Laughter

She is quick, and very emphatic however in urging "the need for medical checkups on a very regular basis. "Naturally, I extend that checkup need to breast and other cancer, especially breast cancer."

"I really urge women to have regular breast cancer checks. It's a very necessary step to take."

"I realize I was lucky. My breast cancer responded well to treatment and I'm able to go on with my life. I guess the good Lord was watching out for me."

A 'private' person, despite all her athletic achievements, Davis is a great example of what a determined and confident individual, backed by family and friends, can do.

♀

Aunt Alice says:

I started out in life with nothing - and I still have most of it.

Spice of Life

I'm not offended by all the dumb blonde jokes because I know I'm not dumb...and I'm also not blonde.   – *Dolly Parton*

♀

 Female Firsts

1967: Brigadier General Adams-Ender of the U.S, became the first woman in the Army to receive the Expert Field Medical Badge.

1967: Women student protesters succeeded at integrating women into the University of Toronto's Hart House, for which women students paid fees but were restricted from entering

1968: Sandra Post of Oakville, Ontario became Canada's first female professional golfer when she won the Ladies Professional Golf Association Championship at Sutton, Massachusetts.

1968: The first gender tests in international sports were conducted at the Winter Games in Grenoble, France.

1968: The Presbyterian Church first ordained women in Canada.

1969: On July 26, Sharon Sites Adams became the first woman to sail across the Pacific, solo.

1969: Diane Crump became the first woman jockey to ride in a parimutuel horse race in North America.

1970: On May 2nd, Diana Crump became the first woman to ride in the Kentucky Derby.

♀

Life, Love & Laughter

Life, Love & Laughter

Spice of Life

I'm not going to vacuum 'til Sears makes one
you can ride on.   — *Roseanne*

♀

Ennellene

When people tell me I look young
'Though older I am growing
The inspiration of their tongue
Tells me my age is showing

♀

Food for Thought

Money alone can't bring you
happiness, but money alone
has not brought me
unhappiness. I won't say my
previous husbands thought
only of my money, but it had a
certain fascination for them.
          — *Barbara Hutton*

♀

Life's Funny Experiences

'Tis Not Downhome

My husband, a Newfoundlander, and I, a Mainlander (and a new bride to boot) were sent to
pastor a church in Grand Bank, Newfoundland. My next door neighbour kept continually talking
about going Upalong. After many months of wondering where in Newfoundland Upalong was, I
finally asked the question to which he replied, "That's where you are from my child."
Rev. Grace Vaters – Perth, Ontario

♀

Animal Mating - Fact and Fantasy – *Ron Young*

Sock it to Me

Fact:

The female rabbit likes her sex "rough and often." Unlike her human counterpart who ovulates
once a month, the female rabbit can ovulate on demand. While the human female practises the
"rhythm method" to get pregnant (or avoid pregnancy), the female rabbit can conceive at any
time. She's always ready and willing to produce more rabbits. Moreover, she loves to be treated
roughly while mating - not out of promiscuity, but in order to enhance her fertility. Roughness
during sex ruptures a follicle in her ovary and releases an egg that grows into another Easter
bunny.

Fantasy

If you are with your Honey
Don't treat her like a bunny
Or else, for you she will not care.
But it's okay with a rabbit
'Cause rough sex is just a habit
But only if her partner is a hare

♀

Life's Funny Experiences
Kiss of Death

In October 1996, my husband's late brother was being laid to rest and all the family were in the viewing room of the funeral home saying our last good-byes. When the time came to close the coffin we all took turns giving Douglas his last goodbye kiss.

When it was my turn I leaned over the casket and bent down to kiss Douglas. At that point, I accidentally pushed the casket backward. The back edge of the casket came up against the wall, which in turn pushed the lid forward and down. Before I knew what was happening, the cover had come down and struck me on the head. I saw two arms coming to my rescue. I was so embarrassed that I walked straight out of the room with my head down staring at the floor.

I thank God it wasn't a steel casket.

Bulah Morgan – Conception Bay South, Newfoundland, Canada

♀

Letters From Our Friends
"...rather than spend the few cents it cost to heat the porridge..."

Dear Ron,

A "Did You Know" on page 102 of the February *Downhomer* reads, "Did you know that Henrietta Howland Green, born in 1835, was so thrifty that she lived almost entirely off cold porridge for most of her life, rather than spend the few cents it cost to heat the porridge? She died in 1916 leaving a fortune of $95 million."

I was given Henrietta's engagement ring which in turn I gave to the Vermont State Museum, (Montplier, Vermont) USA.

My late husband's great-aunt Helen Guild was given this ring from Sylvia Green Astor Wilkes, Henrietta's daughter.

I have a sugar spoon which also belonged to Sylvia. I also acquired Henrietta's diary, amongst other items. I burnt the diary many years ago, as it was so sad what Hettie (Henrietta) did to her daughter Sylvia and her son Ned. He lost a leg after being hit by a cart in New York. Hettie took him to a charity hospital, rather than a reputable institution, to have him treated and was recognized as a lady of great wealth. Her son was therefore refused treatment. Because of her miserliness, her son lost his leg. Ned grew up to be a playboy, buying railroads and having many affairs, but with only one leg, when, if his mother hadn't been so stingy, could have kept his leg.

Henrietta's daughter, Sylvia, married Astor Wilkes when she was 38 years old. He was much older than her. They had no children together. She lived at times in Bellows Falls, Vermont, USA and became friendly with my Aunt Helen, who was a music teacher in that town.

I think they were both sad people, but they were friends. They are all buried in the Emmanuel Church Yard Cemetery. Helen is in the Guild plot, while Sylvia, Ned, Hettie and Mr. Green are under the one stone. I have never regretted burning the diary.

When Hettie (Henrietta) died she was the world's richest woman and her fortune was more than the $95 million mentioned in *Downhomer*. Aunt Helen and Mrs. Bolling were privy to the interest of some of the money for their lifetimes. Mrs. Bolling used hers, but Aunt Helen never did. My husband used to bring Aunt Helen food and other items at the end of her life.

Lorraine Hynes Louunis – Reading, Massachusetts, USA.

♀

Tragedy at St. Jacques Island

By Cassie Brown

The Christmas of 1963 was a Christmas of tragedy as a three-day storm battered the Atlantic Provinces and took the lives of 28 men. In the ocean surrounding Newfoundland, six of the seven-man crew of the 124-ton Newfoundland coastal freighter, *Mary Pauline*, were lost when the vessel sank in mountainous seas off St. Pierre and Miquelon; 12 crew members of the French freighter, *Douala*, were lost a little farther up the coast off Burgeo, and two other Newfoundlanders were swept into the sea from the Island of St. Jacques.

The two men swept into the sea were Eric Fiander and Hughie Myles, lighthouse keepers on St. Jacques Island. They disappeared at the beginning of the three-day storm and left a young woman to keep a lonely vigil with her three small babies, for three bitter, frightful days.

Katherine Fiander had been married for five years. Her 26-year-old husband, Eric, and their three small babies, Alton 3, John 2, and Karen 1, were happy and cosy in the residence of the lighthouse at St. Jacques Island, a small rocky island less than a mile from the mainland on the south coast of Newfoundland.

Eric was the assistant lighthouse keeper, and was in charge, since the head keeper, Hubert Myles, was ashore on leave. Meanwhile, Hubert's nephew, 17-year-old Hughie Myles, was also on the island to help Eric.

The island itself is less than a mile in length and is roughly shaped like a horseshoe; the cliff bridging the middle is less than 175 yards in width.

The residence was approximately 200 yards from the lighthouse and the whistle, on the outer tip of the island facing the Atlantic. In a small building by itself, apart from the residence, was the diesel generator which supplied electricity to the residence, lighthouse and whistle. During this particular period the generator had to be started by hand with a crank because of weakening batteries. New batteries had not yet arrived.

Contact with the mainland was maintained by water, and a shed housing the Department of Transport's boat's engine and other equipment was on the strip of beach on the other side of the island. Contact was also made twice daily with the D.O.T. station at Burin, through radio-telephone, at 10:30 a.m. and 8:30 p.m.

The residence itself was heated by a hard-coal furnace, with additional heat coming from the kitchen oil-range. The oil drum connected to the stove was on the back of the house, but the main supply of oil was near the whistle house, 200 yards away. As a precautionary measure in stormy weather, a lifeline spanned the distance between the residence and lighthouse.

The storm struck on Thursday night, December 19, and by Friday was raging in all its fury with winds gusting up to 100 m.p.h. when contact was made with the DOT station in Burin, at 10:30 that morning by Eric Fiander.

The men then made their rounds, checking the lighthouse, whistle and the shed on the beach. They returned to the house dinnertime with the news that the shed was being blown over, and decided that as soon as they had finished dinner they would return to the beach with a rope to secure it.

They had left immediately after dinner and Katherine had her hands full with the children and the housework until 3 o'clock when she heard Eric call, "Katherine!"

Above the whine of the wind his voice sounded as if it came from the basement, and as she was fully occupied with the small children at that moment, she didn't answer.

He called again, louder this time, "Katherine!"

She called back, "What?"

He did not reply and she kept doing what she had been doing for a few moments, then was suddenly alert and frightened. Had she heard Eric calling—or was it the wind?

She listened uneasily for a moment to the howling wind, then gave herself a mental shake. Of course it was Eric, she told herself. She had heard him call her name twice.

She gave the basement a hurried check but found no sign of her husband or his young helper, and a nagging fear took possession of her; she decided firmly that it had been the wind and not his voice after all....even if she knew she had heard him call her.

She worked about the house, keeping her hands busy and her eyes glued to the windows facing the island, watching for a glimpse of the men. Her ears were alerted for other sounds than that of the wind and sea, but the afternoon passed and still the men hadn't returned.

Now, fear was growing, but she would not give in to it. She made many excuses for their continued absence. Perhaps the cliff was too icy for them to climb; perhaps they were staying in the shed until the worst of the storm was over; perhaps.

When the men did not return for supper, Katherine Fiander changed her thinking and forced herself to admit that something must have gone wrong. Perhaps, she reasoned, Eric has been hurt and had decided to remain in the shed.

She would think no further than that.

Now a problem presented itself to Katherine. With daylight going she had no light in the house, and the lighthouse had no light unless she could go out to the generator and get it started, but one look at the lifeline changed her mind. Ice, six inches thick, coated the lifeline, and ocean spray had also coated the ground with slick, treacherous ice. To try to cross that stretch to the shed in the half-light would be suicide in that hurricane.

Black night descended, bringing no relief from the fury of the storm, serving only to heighten its intensity. There was no friendly light shinning from the residence window, and no warning light emanating from the lighthouse. All was in darkness. With no generator there could be no contact with the DOT stations, either.

Katherine had put the two smaller children to bed, but let 3-year-old Alton stay up to keep her company, and the two sat in the kitchen, lit only by the flickering light of the oil stove. Alton's endless chatter was, for the first time, a Godsend.

Later, after little Alton finally went off to bed and to sleep, Katherine found the house growing cold. A hurried check showed her the kitchen stove was out; a further check revealed that the furnace too, was completely out. In her anxiety about the men she had forgotten to keep the furnace stoked. The oil tank for the kitchen stove must have emptied too, and she was now without heat, as well as light.

Katherine Fiander kept a long, lonely vigil that night, her mind full of fears for her man and for Hughie Myles as she paced endlessly. The storm hadn't slacked at all when daybreak came.

She tried to light the furnace, but could not get the hard coal to ignite. The men had always started the furnace by throwing stove oil on the hard coal but there was not a drop of oil in the

Life, Love & Laughter

house. It was all in the tank 200 yards away, and the system used by the men to transfer it to the tank attached to the kitchen stove, involved a pump and hose and was too cumbersome and complicated for Katherine who had never bothered with those things.

Later, as the last vestige of heat left the house, Katherine dressed, and grasping the ice-coated lifeline ,made it somehow to the shed where she began to work on the generator, as she had seen the men work on it. If she could get the generator working she could get heat from the hotplates, the iron and the electric kettle, and she would have warm food for the children.

Snow had seeped into the shed and covered the batteries which were quite cold and weak. When Katherine tried to start the generator with the hand crank, it gave not a gig. She didn't know it, but there were compression levers to pull as well, before the engine would start.

A strength greater than hers was needed to get the generator going, and at last, her arms aching with the strain, she gave up and fought her way back to the residence.

By now she had the children dressed in every bit of heavy clothing they had, and she worked about the house, feeding the children cold meals, keeping her hands busy; answering the numberless questions little Alton put to her because it kept her mind off the future.

One certainty she still resisted. "Eric would be alright," she told herself.

The second day was passing with no let-up in the storm, and thrown upon her own resources, she searched the house for something, anything, that might give them light for the long black night ahead. She found an old kerosene lamp with a broken flue and enough oil to give a tiny light during the night.

Katherine passed the second night without food or rest. She hadn't eaten a morsel since the men had left the residence after dinner on Friday, nor had she rested or slept. She felt neither hungry nor tired as the second night passed, but alert and confident and full of hope that somehow Eric and Hughie were still alive.

Just before dawn on Sunday the wind stopped and the silence was frightening. She waited in silence, listening for the fall of a footstep—for anything to indicate that there was life on the island outside the residence.

Then it was dawn, and dawn showed a brilliantly-beautiful day it was as if the fury and havoc of the three preceding nights had never happened. Katherine went outside, her eyes searching the island, and now another fear took possession of her. Supposing she went to the shed to look for the men and they weren't there?

This fine, calm Sunday was not so pleasant now, and while her eyes scoured the cliffs where Eric and Hughie might appear, she was a woman afraid to the core of her being. She was afraid to go to the shed because Eric might not be there. As long as she did not know for sure, she could hope, and hope was the only thing that kept her from going to pieces.

Later she saw two men coming along the cliff toward the house and for a fleeting moment thought it was Eric and Hughie, but in the same moment recognized two friends, Tom Osbourne and Roland Stoodly from Coombs Cove, and in that split-second she accepted the inevitable, that Eric was gone forever and she had known it all along—from the moment she had heard him call her name.

As the two men came up to the residence, the self-control she had exercised for three days, deserted her. She ran to them, screaming at the top of her lungs, "Eric and Hughie are gone!"

On the beach, high water marks showed that the seas had gone right up the cliffs behind the shed, and it was evident that the seas had swept both men away while they were trying to secure the small building.

As she left the island that same day, Katherine's eyes swept the beach, searching the base of the cliff, hoping she might see Eric or Hughie; they might have been too weak or cold to reach home, but they might be still alive, she thought, in one last, vain outburst of hope. Her eyes were still riveted to the island as her friends took her into Coombs Cove.

Hughie's body was recovered on the beach on Monday, but Eric Fiander's body was never found. The sea claimed him and never gave him back.

Tragedy followed Katherine Fiander, who returned to her own family in Rose Blanche that summer of 1964, then settled in nearby Harbour Le Cou. It was discovered after her ordeal, that another baby was on the way. On September 13, another son was born to Katherine, and she named him Eric Bruce. On October 22, baby Eric died in his sleep.

From the book The Caribou Disaster And Other Short Stories, *by Cassie Brown. Flanker Press. Used by permission.*

♀

 Out of Habit

Sister Mary Catherine went into a liquor store and asked for two bottles of wine. The clerk, surprised to see the holy woman buying alcohol, questioned selling it to her.

"I am buying it for Mother Superior's constipation," she told him.

An hour or so later when the clerk was on his way home, he saw Sister Mary Catherine staggering down Main Street. He approached her and said, "You lied to me Sister, you told me that wine was for Mother Superior's constipation."

"She won't be constipated any more after she sees me like this," slurred the Sister.

♀

Female Firsts

1971: Canadian Debbie Brill became the first woman to high jump six feet.

1971: Mina Rees became the first woman president of the American Association for the Advancement of Science.

1971: Quebec finally allowed women jurors after eight Québec women were jailed earlier in the year for protesting the all-male jury law.

1971: On June 30, riding California Lassie, jockey Mary Bacon became the first woman to ride to 100 wins in horseracing.

1972: Anne L. Armstrong became the first U.S. woman to hold a Cabinet-level post of counselor to the President (first to Nixon then to Ford).

1972: International Surfing champion, Laura Blears Ching, became the first woman to go up against men in a surfing meet in Hawaii.

1972: At the age of 20, Asma Jahangir became the first person to challenge the Bhutto government of Pakistan when she launched her legal battle there to free her father whom she believed had been arrested illegally. Ten years later, after she had become a lawyer, she won her case.

1972: The first female FBI agents, Susan Lynn Roley and Joanne E. Pierce were sworn in.

♀

Life, Love & Laughter

Is That a Fact?
Many things are taken as facts. Not all of them are.

Mona Lisa's First Name
Many have heard of the Mona Lisa, Leonardo Da Vinci's most famous painting.

The Fact Is the painting is named La Gioconda after the lady in the painting, the wife of merchant, Francesco del Gioconda. The custom of women shaving their eyebrows was considered a sign of beauty in Mrs. Gioconda's time, that is why "the lady with the mystic smile" has no eyebrows. Over time the painting was called Madonna Lisa by someone, and a short while later this was shortened to Mona Lisa.

♀

Letters From Our Friends

Just a Tree

Hello Everybody,

Merry Christmas to all my family and friends in Newfoundland. I am 55 years old, and ever since I can remember, Christmas has always had a special place in my heart. When I was a child, my parents, like a lot of families living on the outskirts of Newfoundland, didn't have access to a lot of money, and things were very slow for the lack of an industry in my community of Traytown.

My father worked all his life in the woods cutting logs or as a cook in the cookhouse. The people that he worked for usually gave him credit for household supplies, groceries, and things that we didn't grow. I always wondered what Christmas was all about and why we didn't have a Christmas tree. I used to go to my friend Jean LeDrew's house and look at their tree.

Once, when I came home from viewing my friend's tree, I spoke to my father who was down in the barn feeding the horse he used for hauling the logs and wood. I asked him why we couldn't have a tree like the one that the LeDrews had, "Aren't we just as good as they are?"

When my father was excited or worried about something he would always draw in this big sigh and scratch the left side of his head on top. "Golly, Pats," he said. (Only my family called me Pats). "I guess we could get a tree and hang it in the corner."

The next day, Christmas Eve, it was snowing so bad you couldn't see a hand before your face. In those days it snowed a lot more than today. Dad got dressed and went outside and was gone for a long time. When he came home later that day, he had a tree that was the most beautiful tree in the world. My mother looked at it and said, "Boy, you're foolish, what are we going to put on it?" I can't remember who was there at that time, but my older sister Pearl and my two brothers helped colour paper strings and things to decorate the tree. We didn't have any electricity or coloured bulbs, but it was just as nice.

I know this is a very long letter explaining my most memorable Christmas, but when you are young and poor like we were, any little thing would make Christmas a very special place in your heart. I always said I would have a tree for Christmas every year for the rest of my life, no matter where I was or who I was with. That day meant everything in the world to me.

Patricia Davis – Seabeck, Washington, USA

♀

Food for Thought

What we usually pray to God is not that His will be done, but that He approve ours.
– Helga Bergold Gross

♀

Female Facts

Among single young women who had sexual intercourse during a six-month period, only 60% of 15-17 year-olds and 69% of 18-24 year-olds always used a method of contraception (1998 Canadian Contraception Study)

♀

Ennellene

That "all men are created equal"
Is too much to presume
And disavowed by any
Who've been in a men's locker room

♀

Spice of Life

When women are depressed they either eat or go shopping. Men invade another country.
– Elayne Boosler

♀

Women Who Have Made A Difference - *By Ron Young*

Dr. Ellen S. Baker became an astronaut for NASA in June 1985. Since then, she has worked a variety of jobs at NASA in support of the Space Shuttle program and Space Station development. A veteran of three space flights, Dr. Baker has logged more than 686 hours in space. She was a mission specialist on STS-34 in 1989, STS-50 in 1992, and STS-71 in 1995.

Joan Baez, a traditional folk artist, became closely associated with the song "We Shall Overcome," which she sang at the great civil rights marches and rallies of the early 1960s. Joan Baez has been a member of the advisory council of Amnesty International since 1974, and visited Hanoi in 1975. She was co-founder of Humanitas, the International Human Rights Commission, in 1979, and in the same year conducted a fact-finding mission in refugee camps in South East Asia. She also sang to Solidarnósc strikers in Poland and worked with the Mothers of the Disappeared in Argentina.

Jacqueline Cochran, although raised as an orphan, was the first woman to fly in the Bendix Trophy Transcontinental Race in 1934, the first woman to win it in 1938, the first woman to pilot a bomber across the Atlantic Ocean in 1941, and, as head of Women's Airforce Service Pilots of World War II, she was also the first woman to receive the Distinguished Service Medal in 1945. She was the first woman to break the sound barrier in 1953, and in 1959 she was the first woman to serve as president of the Fédération Aéronautique Internationale. She was the first woman to take off from and land on an aircraft carrier in 1960, and the first woman to attain a flying speed of 1355 km/hr (842 mph) in 1961.

♀

MABEL & MANLEY

"My doctor told me that I have the body of a woman only half my age," bragged Mabel after a visit to her physician.

"What about your 65-year-old ass?" inquired her husband.

"He never once mentioned you," replied Mabel.

♀

Quillings

Lila – By Ron Young

Of all the things that touched my life
No similes can I compile
To show the glow that lifts my soul
Each time I see you smile

Behind your eyes the secret lies
Of love and life and then some
Humility, mirth and character
Naivety, and wisdom

Your smiles inspire all you meet
They share with each a part
Of sincerity and caring
From within your giving heart

Something in the smile you gave me
Touched a part of me
Made my earth-bound spirit rise
And gave it melody

You found the door into the essence
Of what I was about
You gave my life new meaning
And deleted any doubt

I've had the knocks of knock-abouts
And in many ways was wise
But the things that matter most to me
Are found behind your eyes

The beauty in horizons
Metaphorical and real
The uniqueness in each sunset
And the magic moon's appeal

When we kissed beside a waterfall
Or cuddled near a stream
Nightbird's song, a melody
To sleep by, and to dream

When sun sank red behind the hills
Or purple in the ocean
We viewed from special settings that
We only found by notion

The flowers you know well by name
Our game of show and tell
Are flowers that, before in life
I never stopped to smell

You found hidden parts of me
In corners of my soul
Pieced them all together
And made the portions whole

What roll of dice? What happenstance?
What timing by the fates?
What infinity in a glance?
What allurement of soulmates?

What was the attraction?
What ever did you see
When you looked into my eyes?
When you looked at me?

And when I ask these questions
She reflectively replies,
"When I looked at you I saw
The sadness hidden in your eyes."

♀

The Whys of Men

Why does it take 1 million sperm to fertilize one egg?
Because they don't stop to ask directions.

♀

WOMEN OF THE ISLAND AND THE BIG LAND

The Female Seal Hunter

A valiant attempt by a young Newfoundland girl to get food for her starving family almost cost the loss of two lives.

Adelaide Barker was a teenage girl from Elliston, Trinity Bay, who walked out onto the ice of that bay during an overcast March day in search of a seal to feed her family.

Ordinarily, her father would have been the one to have gone out but he was in failing health, and since the family was running low on food supplies, young Adelaide felt they could certainly use a supply of seal meat, and the few dollars a seal skin would fetch.

As she approached a patch of seals, the wind suddenly changed and began to blow offshore. Very quickly the ice began to move, carrying the helpless teenager further and further away from land. Fortunately, some people on shore saw what was happening and rushed to tell her father.

William Baker, realizing the extreme danger his daughter was facing, ignored his own sickness and went out on the ice-floes to rescue her. He was an experienced seaman and seal hunter and knew only too well the terrible death that awaited his child if she was not rescued. Witnesses recalled that the ailing man seemed to gain a superhuman strength as he arrived on the shore, just as the last pan of ice was moving off. He managed to leap to it and then, by jumping from pan to pan, he finally reached his frightened and helpless daughter. Now they were both in danger because they were far from shore and the ice pans were spreading even further. When the wind increased and moved then out of sight of land, it seemed that only a lifeboat could save them.

Baker thought it would take a miracle. Both father and daughter huddled together for comfort and warmth and prayed for that miracle. Just as darkness was setting in and temperatures were dipping to below freezing, the Bakers got their miracle. The winds suddenly abated, temperatures rose and they managed to survive their first night on the tossing pan of ice.

Meanwhile, family and friends at Elliston had given them up for lost.

Baker, however, didn't give up hope, and seemingly out of nowhere, came the sealing vessel *Dart,* under the command of Captain Coleman. He took the Bakers onboard and three days after their disappearance they were delivered safely to their home at Elliston.

That night at Elliston, there were celebrations and prayers of thanksgiving to the Lord for answered prayers.

From the book, Newfoundland Fireside Stories, *by Jack Fitzgerald. Creative Publishing. Used by permission.*

♀

Life's Funny Experiences

Catastrophe

My brother Jim and his wife were visiting her family in Newfoundland one year. His brother-in-law, (also Jim) suggested the two of them go down to the shop. As they left, the family cat scampered out the door as well.

On the way back the cat ran in front of their car and was killed.

They got out to investigate and the brother-in-law's heart sank as he looked at the cat. "Oh my! Oh my! I've killed the wife's cat," he exclaimed!

They went back to the shop where they got a shovel and buried the cat in a field.

When they returned home, they said not a word about the incident. Some time later, while sitting with the family in the kitchen, they heard a scratching against the door.

The wife opened the door and in walks the cat, all nine lives intact. The two Jims looked at each other and could hardly contain themselves.

My brother has told the story many times, but the other Jim has been very quiet about it for a very good reason.

In a field in a town in Newfoundland, in an unmarked grave, lies the wrong cat.

Phyllis Barrett – Brampton, Ontario

♀

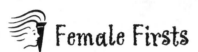 # Female Firsts

1972: In June, Sally Jan Priesand was ordained a rabbi, making her the first woman Rabbi in the U.S.

1973: Khatijah Ahmad of Kuala Lumpur, Malaysia started KAF Group, Malaysia (int'l edition), which would make her the first businesswoman of her country to become a multi-millionaire.

1973: Pauline Jewett became the first woman President of a co-educational university, Simon Fraser in Burnaby, BC.

1973: On September 20, at a match in Houston, Texas, Billie Jean King became the first woman to beat male tennis star Bobby Riggs.

1973: The first rape crisis centres in Canada opened - in Vancouver and Toronto.

1974: On July 29, the first 11 women priests in the Episcopal Church were ordained.

1974: The RCMP hired its first woman member.

1974: When Lanny Moss was hired by the minor league Portland Mavericks, she became the first woman to manage a professional men's baseball team.

1974: The first issue of *Women's Sports* magazine was published.

1975: Karen Stead was the first female to win the All-American Soap Box Derby at age 11.

1975: Marion Bermudez was the first U.S. woman to compete in the formerly all-male Golden Gloves boxing tournament in Mexico City. She beat the first man she fought.

♀

Female Facts

Avon products were named for "Stratford-on-Avon," the birthplace of William Shakespeare.

♀

Her Other Half

A Promise Made is a Debt Unpaid

There was a man who had worked all of his life and had saved all of his money. He loved money more than just about anything, and just before he died, he said to his wife, "Now listen, when I die, I want you to take all my money and place it in the casket with me. I wanna take my money to the afterlife."

So, he got his wife to promise him with all her heart that when he died she would put all the money in the casket with him.

The man eventually died and during the funeral ceremony his wife sat beside his casket. Next to his wife sat her best friend. Just before the undertaker got ready to close the casket, the wife said, "Wait just a minute!"

She had a shoe box with her which she placed in the casket. Then the undertakers locked the casket down and rolled it away.

Her friend said, "I hope you weren't crazy enough to put all that money in the casket."

She said, "Yes, I promised. I'm a good Christian, I can't lie. I promised him that I was going to put that money in that casket with him."

"You mean to tell me that you put every cent of his money in the casket with him?"

"I sure did," said the wife. "I got it all together, put it into my bank account and I wrote him a cheque."

♀

Women Who Have Made A Difference – *By Ron Young*

Dianne Feinstein became the 35th Mayor of San Francisco after the assassination of Mayor George Moscone in 1978, making her the first woman to ever hold the office. She was later elected to two full terms as mayor, the second time with a 81 per cent majority. Among her many accomplishments as Mayor was a decrease of 30 per cent in the serious crime rate over a six-year period. She also served as first woman president of the Board of Supervisors, and received the Living Legacy Award from the Women's International Center. She was also elected as U.S. Senator from California.

Hannah Senesh was born in Hungary in 1921. Hungary had been a relatively decent place for Jews before WWI, but the aftermath of that war's destruction had caused anti-Jew sentiment among her friends and neighbours. As Hannah grew up, anti-Semitism became stronger in Hungary, starting out as minor injustices that rapidly became government-sponsored anti-Semitic policies. When Hungary, the country her forefathers had chosen to call home, announced that it would take the Nazi German side in a European war, Hannah came to the conclusion that a return to the Jewish homeland was the only long-term solution for the Jews. Knowing that agricultural knowledge would be far more useful in Palestine than poetry, she gave up her dream of being a university-educated writer, and went to agricultural school in Nahalal. However in

1943, as the invasion of Palestine seemed more and more possible, Senesh volunteered for the underground Jewish self-defense army. On one of the missions in which she was later involved, Senesh parachuted into Yugoslavia, near the Hungarian border where she met with other underground partisans. Soon after however, she was captured with a radio transmitter and imprisoned. A long and brutal imprisonment did not gain her tormentors any useful military information, and Hannah Senesh, whose dream was to one day grow crops in Palestine, was executed by a firing squad on November 7, 1944, at the age of 23.

Irmgard Flugge-Lotz made contributions to to the aircraft industry that have spanned a lifetime during which she demonstrated, in a field dominated by men, the value and quality of a woman's intuitive approach in searching for and discovering solutions to complex engineering problems. During the 1960s she was one of Stanford University's most distinguished professors and has received such honours as the Achievement Award by the Society of Women Engineers in 1970, an honorary Doctor of Science degree by the University of Maryland in 1973, and a selection by the American Institute of Aeronautics and Astronautics (AIAA) to give the prestigious annual von Karman Lecture in 1971.

Maggie Lena Walker, the daughter of former slaves, later became the first woman in the United States to become a president of a local bank. This required dedication and hard work, which Maggie continued throughout her life, despite her many personal tragedies. These tragedies included her father being murdered by a robber, when she was just a girl, and in 1907, she fell on the front steps of her home and injured her knees. The damaged nerves and tendons continued to trouble her for the rest of her life. Then her husband died in 1915 when her son, Russell Ecles Talmage, mistook his father for a prowler on the porch and shot him. Maggie also suffered from diabetes and was confined to a wheelchair after 1928. She died of "diabetes gangrene" in 1934. The house her family occupied is now the Maggie L. Walker National Historic Site and is located at 110 1/2 East Leigh Street in Richmond, Virginia.

Estée Lauder, aka Josephine Esther Mentzer, the daughter of immigrants, started an enterprise by selling skin creams concocted by her uncle, a chemist, in beauty shops, beach clubs and resorts. It is said that her only employee would change her voice on the phone to become receptionist, shipping, or billing department, as needed. Josephine was a great saleslady, who had a good product and who, outworked everyone else in the cosmetics' industry. She followed the bosses of New York City department stores around until she got some counter space at Saks Fifth Avenue in 1948. And once in that space, she utilized a personal selling approach that was every bit as good as the promise of her beautiful-skin enhancers and perfumes. Estée Lauder, the little business Josephine started, went on to control 45% of the cosmetics market in U.S. department stores. The company now sells in 118 countries and the family shares are worth more than $6 billion.

♀

☺ Some Mothers Have Them

Jackson said to his mother, "Mom, you know that $10 you promised me for getting a good report card? I just saved you the expense."

♀

Tickle and Bight *By Lucy Fitzpatrick-McFarlane*

Treasures in the Attic

Everybody should have an attic. It was one of the nicest things I remember about our old house when I was growing up in Lord's Cove. The attic was always my favourite place to play and even though my childhood home no longer exists, I still miss it.

I remember how excited my sisters and I would be when the time came to re-open the attic after a long winter. Every year when the warm May sunshine coaxed the steam from the freshly thawed earth, Mom would throw open the windows and doors to let in the fresh breeze. Before our old rooster could muster up a throaty cock-a-doodle-do, Mom would come upstairs and start whipping the feather mattresses and blankets off the beds, sometimes with us in them.

"What are ye all doing in bed on a beautiful morning like this?" she'd holler. "We've got to open up the attic and put all the winter stuff away, so get out of bed everybody!"

That was one chore my sisters and I never complained about, for we couldn't wait to get back in the attic again.

Not many people knew it was there. Our two-storey house had a peaked roof, so the attic ran the whole length of the house, with a small window under the eaves at both ends. There was ample space to play in at the highest point, but it gradually sloped, so you had to coopy down to look out the windows. The opening to the attic was in a large closet that was built in a semi-circle around a brick chimney and you had to climb a ladder to get up there.

Our attic had a personality all its own. At one time, our house belonged to a merchant who had a shop in the back of the house and he used the attic for storage. There was nothing of value left there, but to us it was a special place where we could rummage through the nooks and crannies to see what treasures we could find. As I recall, there was a gramophone, a spinning wheel, old albums, slates that my oldest sister and brothers used in school, Christmas decorations, a rocking chair and an old suitcase full of knick-knacks.

It was full of cobwebs, dust and spiders, but that just added to the atmosphere. I can still smell the musty scent of clothes that hung on hooks, and bolts of old wallpaper that were piled in the corners.

However, it wasn't the things in the attic that intrigued me, but rather the way I felt when I was there. Over the years, it became my refuge – a place where I could have time to myself.

As a child, I loved playing dollhouse and hide-and-go-seek, and I would lie on the floor listening to the rain on the roof just inches above my head. The pungent scent of the felt after the sun dried up the rain always made me feel so contented that often I'd curl up in front of the window and watch the cobwebs glimmer in the sun.

Once when I fell asleep, I awoke to find a big spider walking across my face. I couldn't see my sisters, so I started screeching as I scravelled on hands and knees to get to the ladder. Before I knew what I was doing, I found myself down in the chimney room looking up at the hatch where my sisters were laughing their heads off.

"I'm telling Mom on ye and you're gonna get your ticky-tumps when I tells her!" I snivelled.

Later, when I realized that I had finally mastered the ladder without the help of my sisters, there was no stopping me from going up there alone.

When my sisters got too old to play in the attic, my friends Lorraine and Eileen would hang out with me. There we read comic books, played cards, played Snakes and Ladders and did a little play-acting. My father often let me borrow his battery-operated radio, so we listened to the music and learned the words of every song we heard. Sometimes we dressed up in the old clothes from the boxes and waltzed to the music, pretending that the mop or broom was a bewitching stranger.

Oh, yes, romance flourished in our attic – at least in our imaginations. We used to read romance novels whenever we could get our hands on them. We called them nurse novels, for usually they were stories about nurses and doctors falling in love.

We knew better than to let our mothers know about them, for they thought they were "dirty books." That's why we hid them behind the chimney, just like we did with Mom's old medicine book. I suspect she anticipated that my sisters and I would be snooping, because we noticed that a few pages were conspicuously missing.

Years later, when I asked Mom about it, she confessed that she had torn out the anatomy pictures and the ones of a woman giving birth.

"I figured what you didn't know wouldn't hurt you and that's all I have to say about it," she said indignantly.

Still, the nurse novels made up for that. We'd sit with our backs against the chimney and read passages out loud, especially the endings where the doctor finally kisses the nurse. Then we'd swoon and giggle, for that was pretty risqué reading for us back then. It's no wonder that we all wanted to be nurses when we grew up.

The poor boys around home had no clue that up there in our attic, we were setting high expectations for them in the romance department. But it didn't matter, for they had their own suave style that could turn a girl's head.

As a teenager, I saw many changes, but the attic always stayed the same. In a way, that attic represents a coming of age for me, for even though I knew every item in it, I saw them differently as I grew older. The suitcases that once held knick-knacks are reminders of sad goodbyes when my brothers and sisters began to leave home one by one. I missed them terribly.

The rocking chair was not just a piece of discarded furniture anymore, but rather a source of comfort. It was there I penned my first poem, wrote stories in my scribbler and cranked the old gramophone as it eked out a song on the only record we owned. The spinning wheel and the old slates from school spoke of days gone by and made me wonder what the future had in store for me. But it wasn't until I discovered my sister's journal on a shelf in the attic that I finally understood the importance of family. Marceline, the eldest child in our family, was 16 when I was born and she had gone away by the time I was six years old. Before I read her daily journal, I knew very little about her. I was the youngest of the family and never had the opportunity of knowing any of my four grandparents, but my sister's observations about them made me feel close to them. She recorded birth dates, the names of people who had lived and died in our community, and the hardships that our own parents had to face in raising nine children.

Her last entry before she left home was about me. She made notes on when I took my first steps for her, how she'd rock me to sleep and take care of me as if I was her own child. By the time I'd finished reading it, I felt like I'd known her all my life. Now, whenever I picture her sitting in the attic in the same rocking chair where I sat years ago, it makes me smile. I wonder if she knew that with each word she wrote, she was leaving threads of the past – treasures in the attic for me to discover.

♀

Feminine Words & Phrases

Clipper: A sleek, stylish and beautiful woman. Perhaps named after the sailing "clipper" ships of yesteryear.

Clippie: A female conductor on an English bus, who for many years had to clip the tickets of bus users.

Doll: A Newfoundland and Labrador colloquialism for a pretty or nice lady.

Dolly: An American colloquialism for female.

Iris: The coloured membrane surrounding the pupil of the eye, also, a family of plants with bright-coloured flowers. Both got their name from Iris, the goddess of the rainbow in classical mythology.

♀

Letters From Our Friends

Good Samaritans at St. John's Airport

Dear *Downhomer*,

This year was my first trip to Newfoundland. Travelling with me were five members of my family (my husband, my son, my daughter and two cousins). When we arrived in Toronto, we were informed that the original plane had some problems so Air Canada sent a much smaller plane. There weren't enough seats on the smaller flight for all of the passengers, so some people had to stay back in Toronto and wait for the next plane. Our names were called, but since there were only four seats and six of us travelling together, two from our party had to stay back.

My husband and cousin stayed back and sent me off with the three children. Realizing that the only two who had ever been to Newfoundland were still in Toronto, I started to panic, thinking that I would either have to find someone who was willing to help us lost Americans in St. John's, or stay at the airport and wait until my husband and cousin arrived. And I didn't know when they would arrive, if at all that same day.

Well, off the plane we came, trying to gather all of the luggage, when guardian angels appeared in the form of two sweet people. They knew who we were because my son looks exactly like my husband, and they remembered my husband from years ago when he used to 'go home' (to St. Lawrence) with his grandparents. It was amazing. From Toronto, my cousin called Uncle Don and Aunt Suzanne in Newfoundland to tell them what had happened with the flight, and so these two wonderful people took the time out of their busy day to come rescue us at the airport. They also found the Hertz rental phone (which happens to be hidden behind a desk), called the company (which was supposed to be there when we arrived), got the luggage into the courtesy van, took the children to the car rental office and lead us to Hotel Newfoundland. It was one of the longest days of my life, but that was the start of a wonderful 'true Newfoundland' experience. Thanks Aunt Suzanne and Uncle Don!! We are looking forward to our trip next summer, only this time if we get separated we will all know that Aunt Suzanne and Uncle Don will be there to save us once again!

Sincerely,
Regina – Wexford, Pennsylvania, USA

♀

Life, Love & Laughter

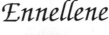 **Adam's Ribbing**

Long Winded

The company president had to make a speech and asked his secretary if she would draft it for him. The following day he stormed into his office and confronting his secretary said, "I asked for a 20-minute speech, but the one you wrote lasted for an hour. Not only that, it was so boring that some people fell asleep."

"I did write you a 20-minute speech," replied the secretary, "and I also supplied you with two carbon copies."

♀

Ennellene

As we sat in the terminal building
After missing our plane on the run
He said, "If you weren't so long getting ready
We would have been on that plane, Hon"
I answered, "Indeedy! If you weren't so speedy
We wouldn't be waiting so long for next one"

♀

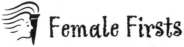 **Female Firsts**

1975: On May 16, Junko Tabei of Japan became the first woman in the world to reach the top of Mount Everest. She was leading an all-female Japanese expedition at the time.

1976: Competing against mostly men, Margaret Murdock became the first markswoman in history to win an Olympic medal.

1976: Anne L. Armstrong became the first woman to serve as U.S. ambassador to Great Britain.

1976: Barbara Walters became the first woman to anchor a network evening newscast, when she joined Harry Reasoner at the anchor desk of *ABC Evening News*.

1976: Pauline Frederick, the United Nations correspondent for NBC, became the first woman to moderate a televised presidential election debate.

1976: Brigadier General Adams-Ender became the first nurse and first woman to be awarded the degree Master of Military Art and Science at the U.S. Army Command and Staff College. In 1991 she was made commanding general at Fort Belvoir, Virginia.

1976: On March 28, Krystyna Choynowski-Liskiewicz of Poland became the first woman to sail around the world solo.

1976: Hélène Ahrweiler, although born in Athens, Greece, became the first woman president of the famous Sorbonne university in France. This made her the first woman in such a position in the Sorbonne's 700-year history. *See also page 194.*

1976: On January 22, the first Lioness' club in Newfoundland was set up in Bay Roberts. The first president was Anne Lake.

♀

Life, Love & Laughter

Food for Thought

No one can argue any longer about the rights of women. It's like arguing about earthquakes
– Lillian Hellman

♀

MABEL & MANLEY

Manly was lying in bed, very weak, and expecting to die any moment, when he caught the smell of his favourite sweet - chocolate chip cookies - being baked by Mabel downstairs. In spite of his weakened condition, Manley managed to drag his decrepit body out of bed and onto the floor. On hands and knees he slowly made it to the top of the stairs, where he bump, bump, bumped his backside to the bottom. He crawled down the long hall to the kitchen and strained his body so his hand could reach the plate of steaming cookies on the counter. He just about got one when Mabel slapped his hand and scolded, "Leave them cookies alone Manley, they're for the wake."

♀

WOMEN OF THE ISLAND AND THE BIG LAND

The French Empress Eugenie's Newfoundland Connection

William Johnston, one of the founders of the prominent Newfoundland firm Baine-Johnston, was a cousin of the wife of Napoleon III, the Emperess Eugenie of France, and even made a strong effort to visit her in Paris. Aides to Napoleon blocked Johnson's attempt because they suspected he was a conspirator against the Emperor.

The incident began while Johnston, was researching his family tree, discovered a connection with the family of the Empress and another famous figure in history — EL Cid Campeador of Spain. Johnston's search established a relationship between his family and the Earl of Fingal, who held the position of British Ambassador to the Spanish court at Madrid, one of the highest honours given by the Crown at that time.

The Earl's daughter married a Spanish Don who was a descendent of El Cid Campeador. This daughter was an ancestress of Empress Eugenie. While the branch of the family bearing the Earl's name had died out, the family fortune remained unclaimed in London. Johnston gathered his evidence and set out for Paris to meet with the Empress, to establish the link that would assure both of them a claim to the fortune. Johnston had no difficulty with his business connections, of introduction to the French Court. For a week he was treated well and entertained by members of the French Court, who were impressed by his claim to be a relative of the Empress. But Johnston spoke very little French; and by the end of the week French officials became suspicious — during this period Napoleon had to contend with powerful enemies in his own country.

One newspaper editor so strongly believed Johnston was a conspirator that he refused to help him in any way. Based on these suspicions, Napoleon's aides refused to allow him to see the Empress. Johnston returned to Newfoundland in disgust; but after recovering from his disappointment, he delighted in telling his friends what an insurmountable difficulty it is, at certain times, to have a friendly chat even with one's cousin.

From the book, Strange But True Newfoundland Stories, *by Jack Fitzgerald. Creative Publishing. Used by permission.*

♀

Life, Love & Laughter

Life, Love & Laughter

Life's Funny Experiences

Hospital Humour

Last week, I was having dizzy spells and my husband took me to the emergency room at the hospital. As I was describing my symptoms to the doctor and he was checking me out, he asked my husband, "Has she been acting goofy?"

"Compared to what?" replied Phillip, ever so sweetly.

Submitted by Carolyn Steele, Nova Scotia, Canada

♀

Food for Thought

It is said in love we idolize the object, and, placing him apart and selecting him from his fellows, look on him as superior to all others. We do so; but even as we idolize the object of our affections, do we idolize ourselves: if we separate him from our fellow-mortals, so do we separate ourselves, and glorying in belonging to him alone feel lifted above all other sensations, all other joys and griefs, to one hallowed circle from which all but his idea is banished: we walk as if a mist, or some more potent charm, divided us from all but him, a sanctified victim, which none but the priest set apart for that office could touch and not pollute, enshrined in a cloud of glory, made glories through beauties not our own.

— *Mary Wollstonecraft Shelley*

♀

Animal Mating – Fact and Fantasy – *Ron Young*

Built Like a Seahorse

Fact:

The Seahorse makes an ideal husband. He not only keeps his mate until death do them part, but also gives birth to the baby seahorses. The male has a pouch similar to that of the female kangaroo, and during mating the female seahorse inserts her ovipositor (egg tube) into the male's pouch, depositing up to 200 eggs. There the eggs are fertilized and a system of support veins grow around the eggs to provide nutrition. When the eggs are fully developed, which takes from two to six weeks, the male assists the young in leaving his pouch by muscle contractions which squeeze the pouch, pushing the newly born seahorses into the ocean. The birthing process, which can take up to two days, leaves the male too fatigued to fight, so to hide itself from its enemies among the ocean vegetation, it camouflages itself by changing colours from white, to ebony, greens, and bright oranges and reds.

Fantasy:

"My Seahorse is The King
(Though he does a woman's thing)
Good men, like him, are very seldom found
And to keep himself alive
He'll change colours to survive
But as a father, doesn't horse around

♀

Life's Funny Experiences
That Does Not Compute

On meeting my grade students for the first time in September, one eager young boy excitedly showed me his new "Student Organizer" which included a calculator. I looked at my enthusiastic student wide-eyed as he explained the instrument's capacity "to do adding, take-aways, multiplying and even dividing sums."

"Wow," I exclaimed, "that sounds wonderful!"

"Ask me a really hard dividing sum," he suggested.

"Okay, here's a really hard one," I queried, "what is twelve divided by three?"

My eager beaver looked carefully at his calculator and then in a very dejected voice explained, "That's a bit too hard - the numbers only go up to nine!"

Ms. Bronac Gallagher – Lakecrest School, St. John's

♀

WOMEN OF THE ISLAND AND THE BIG LAND
The Irish Princess Who Married a Newfoundlander

Sir Hugh O'Connor of county Connacht, Ireland was the claimant to the Irish throne. The on-going struggle between Irish and English patriots was causing a rift among the inhabitants of Sir Hugh's county. The struggle resulted in a split in the Irish royal family which caused Sir Hugh to become concerned for the safety of his daughter, Princess Sheila. Sir Hugh made arrangements for the Princess to be sent to a convent in France where her aunt was the Abbess.

While en route to France, Dutch pirates captured the Irish ship, looted it and took Princess Sheila captive. However, before the pirates could get their prize to port they were intercepted and captured by Captain Peter Easton, who later became one of Newfoundland's most infamous pirates. At that time Easton was the Commander of a fleet of British warships. Princess Sheila was taken on board Easton's ship, which was heading for Newfoundland. Easton was being sent to this country by the British King to protect the English fishing fleet.

During the trip the Princess met and fell in love with Easton's Lieutenant, Gilbert Pike. Captain Easton arranged for his ship's chaplain to marry the two. Upon arriving at Harbour Grace, Pike and his Irish Princess decided to settle down at Mosquito, a community now known as Bristol's Hope. They had two children and the Pikes played a major part in developing that community. Princess Sheila, who had managed to conceal her identity as an Irish princess, was recognized by Irish immigrants who added the Gaelic name Nageira to her title. Nageira is the Gaelic word for beauty and Princess Sheila was described by many as a natural leader and a most beautiful lady. The one day tragedy struck Bristol's Hope. The community was attacked by pirates. Princess Sheila gathered the women and children and hid them in the nearby hills. Her husband, Gilbert Pike, was taken by the pirates and never heard from again. Princess Sheila moved with her children to Carbonear where she died on August 14, 1753 at the age of 105. Newfoundland's Irish Princess is buried in the garden of Hubert Soper of Carbonear.

From the book, Strange But True Newfoundland Stories, *by Jack Fitzgerald. Creative Publishing. Used by permission.*

♀

Life, Love & Laughter

Food for Thought

Let not the atom bomb
Be the final sequel
In which all men
Are cremated equal
— *Kaye Phelps*
♀

Spice of Life

Why does a woman work ten years to change a man's habits then complain that he's not the same man she married.
— *Barbra Streisand*
♀

Quillings

The Molly D — *By Ron Young*

Foaming white waves wash over docks
Strain anchor chains, smash on the rocks
With booming noise like thunder.
Receding, flinging boats like toys
Sucking dead seabirds, marker buoys
And debris completely under.

With her overcoat on
She waits at dawn
In her arms she holds her daughter.

As the lighthouse blinks at Fleur de Lys
She waits for his boat, the *Molly D*
Searching every square inch of the water.

Daylight grows dim
Still waiting for him
She watches wave after wave repetitious.
One last look at form
She walks slowly home
And puts away yesterday's dishes.
♀

Is That a Fact?
Many things are taken as facts. Not all of them are.

Who Was Mother Goose?

Mother Goose was actually a real woman named Elizabeth Goose, who lived in Boston, and her grave there in the Old Granary Burying Ground is a tourist attraction.

The Fact Is the grave is there and the graveyard is a tourist attraction, however, there has never been any evidence to show that the *Mother Goose Rhymes* written in 1719, were penned by the grave's occupant. *Mother Goose Rhymes* was the phrase used by Charles Perrault in a collection of eight fairy tales which included "The Sleeping Beauty," "Little Red Riding Hood," "Cinderella," "Bluebeard," and others published in 1697.

The term has been traced to Loret's 1650 La Muse Historique in which appeared the line, Comme un conte de la Mere Oye ("Like a Mother Goose story"). Two French Queen Berthas have also been conjectured as a "Mother Goose" but there is no traceable evidence that either was the reference in Loret's remarks. Mother Goose is first known to have appeared in America somewhere between 1760 and 1766, printed by a company owned by John Newbery. Mother Goose's Melody: or Sonnets for the Cradle was a little volume, believed to have been edited by Oliver Goldsmith.

But despite the facts, nursery rhyme pilgrims continue to visit the gravesite to pay homage. Except Elizabeth Goose's grave has no marker. There is however a marker there for a "Mary Goose."
♀

Female Facts

The Gun that Won the West and Haunted a Widow

The famous Winchester rifle made a fortune for the Winchester family, especially during the American Civil War. The gun's creator, Oliver Winchester, left the fortune to his son, William, who married Sarah Pardee in 1858. The couple had a daughter, Annie, who died causing Sarah to be so traumatized that she became very ill. Sarah attributed her daughter's death to a curse on the Winchester rifle which had taken so many lives. When her husband became stricken with tuberculosis and died in March of 1881, she became convinced that a curse was upon her and went to see a medium.

Legend has it that the medium confirmed her fears and instructed her that she must, sell her home in New Haven and "follow the setting sun to the west." Sarah was told that she would find a house which she must purchase and then she should buy it and continually build upon it.

"If you continue building you will live," the medium is said to have told her. "Stop and you will die."

The house she bought was on 162 acres of land in San Jose, California. From the day she bought it in 1884 until she died 38 years later, she had carpenters working on it 24 hours a day. The house went from 17 rooms to 160 rooms, with some 2,000 doors, 10,000 windows, six kitchens, two ballrooms, and 40 staircases, some of which went nowhere. The house was so vast and complex that servants needed a map to get around. Sarah slept in a different bedroom every night to confuse the spirits that haunted her. Meanwhile, the carpenters kept working until Sarah died in her sleep in 1922 at the age of 82.

On Friday the 13th of May, 1974, the Winchester Mystery House was designated California Historic Landmark number 868, and sees many visitors, especially around halloween.

♀

Feminine Words & Phrases

Cancan: A fast dance with multi-positions, some rather risque, first performed in the casinos of Paris.

Call Girl: A prostitute who makes use of the telephone as a way to arrange business.

Come out: In past years, said of a girl who has become a woman and finally 'come out' in society among her peers.

Confetti: A recent substitute for corn (and later rice) which were symbols of fertility, to assure that the couple would go forth and multiply. In modern churches all fertility symbols, even confetti, are almost obsolete. It is too much of a strain on the budgets of many churches to pay for the cleaning bill.

Cradle Crown: The fine (instead of penance) a mediaeval English priest paid for keeping a mistress and fathering a child.

Curtain Lecture: What is said by a woman to a man after they are in bed for the night.

♀

Ennellene

His memory for dates has never been that great
And in passing, time leaves him, much more at a loss
He forgets to give me praise, as well as my birthdays
And he sometimes forgets who's really boss

♀

Aunt Alice says:

One of life's mysteries
is how a two-pound box of
candy can make a woman
gain five pounds.

Spice of Life

People are more violently
opposed to fur than leather
because it's safer to harass rich
women than motorcycle gangs.
– Unknown

♀

Female Firsts

1977: Bette Davis became the first woman to receive the American Film Institute's Life Achievement Award.

1977: On May 29, Janet Guthrie, a 39-year-old physicist, became the first woman to participate in the Indianaoplis 500 auto race.

1977: Marie Ledbetter became the first woman to win the World Accuracy Title at the 12th annual Parachuting Championship in Rome.

1978: Sally Aw Sian of Hong Kong began beaming the pages of her *Sing Tao* newspaper via satellite to Chinese communities around the world, making it the first truly international Chinese newspaper.

1978: The law changed so that Canadian women could no longer be fired for pregnancy in federally-regulated industries.

1978: Nancy Lopez became the first female golfer to win Rookie of the Year and Player of the Year in the same year.

1978: Lynn Rippelmeyer became the first female to go from flight attendant to pilot. She had become a TWA flight attendant in 1972.

1978: July 26, in England, Louise Joy Brown became the world's first test-tube baby.

1978: The first U.S. coin to honour a woman, the Susan B. Anthony dollar, was minted.

♀

Life, Love & Laughter

Twenty-one Memos to My Mom

1. Don't spoil me. I know quite well that I ought not to have all I ask for. I'm only testing you.

2. Don't be afraid to be firm with me. I prefer it, it makes me feel more secure.

3. Don't let me form bad habits. I have to rely on you to detect them in the early stages.

4. Don't make me feel smaller than I am. It only makes me behave stupidly "big."

5. Don't correct me in front of people if you can help it. It'll take much more notice if you quietly talk to me in private.

6. Don't make me feel my mistakes are sins. It upsets my sense of values.

7. Don't protect me from consequences. I need to learn the painful way, sometimes.

8. Don't be too upset when I say "I hate you." It isn't you I hate, but your power to thwart me.

9. Don't take too much notice of my small ailments. Sometimes they get me the attention I need.

10. Don't nag. If you do, I shall have to protect myself by appearing deaf.

11. Don't forget that I cannot explain myself as well as I should like. This is why I'm not always very accurate.

12. Don't make rash promises. Remember that I feel badly let down when promises are broken.

13. Don't tax my honesty too much. I am easily frightened into telling lies.

14. Don't be incoherent. That completely confuses me and makes me lose faith in you.

15. Don't tell me my fears are silly. They are terribly real and you can do much to reassure me if you try to understand.

16. Don't put me off when I ask questions. If you do, you will find that I stop asking and seek my information elsewhere.

17. Don't ever suggest that your are perfect or infallible. It gives me too great a shock when I discover that you are neither.

18. Don't ever think it is beneath your dignity to apologize to me. An honest apology makes me feel surprisingly warm toward you.

19. Don't forget how quickly I am growing up. It must be very difficult to keep pace with me, but please do try.

20. Don't forget I love experimenting. I couldn't get on without it, so please put up with it.

21. Don't forget that I can't thrive without lots of understanding and love, but I don't need to tell you, do I?

Author Unknown

♀

Life, Love & Laughter

Life, Love & Laughter

Spice of Life

I can never understand why women want to be equal.
Why would they willingly accept a demotion?
— *Allan Fotheringham, Maclean's 4 Sept 1978*

♀

Food for Thought

You don't seem to realize that a poor person who is unhappy is in a better position than the rich person who is unhappy, because the poor person has hope. He thinks money would help.
— *Jean Kerr*

♀

Ennellene

Subtracting age, is now all the rage
And to show it, we dress to the nines
And cosmetics help some
To keep others from
Reading between the lines

♀

Her Other Half

She's a Good Sport

"You love hockey more than you love me," said the housewife to her couch potato husband.
"Yes," he replied, "but I love you more than lacrosse."

♀

Quillings

Laughtertown
By Katherine D. Blake

Would ye learn the road to Laughtertown,
Oh ye who have lost the way?
Would ye have young heart though your hair be gray?
Go learn from a little child each day.
Go serve his wants and play his play,
And catch the lilt of his laughter gay,
And follow his dancing feet as they stray;
For he knows the road to Laughtertown
O ye who have lost the way?

♀

Spice of Life

Clare Luce Booth attended a fashionable dinner party one evening and found herself seated next to a man whose name she could not remember. He was actually David Burpee, chairman of Burpee's Seed Company.

Burpee, realizing her predicament, and in an effort to put her at ease, leaned over and whispered in her ear, "I'm Burpee."

"That's all right," replied a puzzled looking Clare, "I get that way sometimes myself."

♀

Spice of Life

Don't be humble. You're not that great. – *Golda Meir*

♀

Women Who Have Made A Difference *– By Ron Young*

Jane Russell began a organization called WAIF during the 1950s which has resulted in the adoptive placement of at least 38,000 children. Russell was also the champion of the passage of the Federal Orphan Adoption Amendment of 1953, which allowed, for the first time, children of American servicemen born overseas to be placed for adoption in the United States. For more than 30 years, Russell turned the extraordinary publicity of her acting career to focus on the plight of waifs, the homeless children whom she believes have the right to a permanent and loving family.

Dame Millicent Garrett Fawcett became active in the woman suffrage movement shortly after her marriage to Henry Fawcett, at age 20. She subsequently served as president of the British National Union of Woman's Suffrage Societies. During the Boer War, she was appointed to inquire into conditions in internment camps for Boer women and children. After the triumph of the suffrage movement in 1918, her organization became the National Union for Equal Citizenship. In 1925 she received the Grand Cross and Order of the British Empire. She also has four novels to her credit.

Jennifer Openshaw was raised in a family with little financial means. Her parents were divorced and her mother worked two full–time jobs as a waitress while Openshaw took care of her younger brothers. When Jennifer tried to enter the world of business, which was dominated by men, her experiences would ultimately lead her to create a unique company tailored to women's specific needs. The original Women's Financial Network, an Internet company designed specifically for women who are looking for a way to make dealing with money matters easier. Ms. Openshaw has since become a nationally recognized financial expert, TV commentator, and motivational speaker.

Rosalyn Sussman Yalow desperately wanted to go to medical school after graduating with honours in physics and chemistry from Hunter College in New York, but being Jewish and a woman, she realized she had no chance of being admitted, so she instead applied to study physics at Purdue University. The answer from Purdue was, "She is from New York. She is Jewish. She is a woman. If you can guarantee her a job afterward, we'll give her an assistanceship." Since no one would give her such guarantee, she went to secretarial school. Then when men of the United States were being called to fight in WWII, the universities found themselves with a shortage of students, so women were admitted to keep them from having to close their doors. Rosalyn took advantage of that situation and in 1945 she graduated from the prestigious University of Illinois, with a PhD in nuclear physics.

Dr. Yalow went on, not only to teach, but was part of an important discovery in the development of radioimmunoassays of peptide hormones which won her the 1977 Nobel Laureate in Medicine, along with her many other esteemed positions, honours, awards and medals.

♀

Life, Love & Laughter

Wild Bob's Gift

By Marie Foley (nee Duffenais) – Miramichi, New Brunswick

Bitter winds pounded my back as I stood in the emptiness of Stephenville, searching for a cab to take me to Winterhouses, my isolated home some 40 miles away on the rugged edge of the Gulf of St. Lawrence. It was Christmas Eve in Newfoundland, 1953.

My parents were expecting me to arrive with gifts, but a blizzard had whipped up and my chances of getting home were bleak.

"We wouldn't even try to venture out there in this. The road won't be plowed for days," a taxi driver said regretfully.

"But I have to get home, I'm Santa Claus!"

"Sorry, miss. I have a family, too."

I kept an eye on my two cardboard boxes, sheltered in an alcove of Kearney's Clothing Store. I think I knew then how Mary and Joseph must have felt when they couldn't find any help on that first Christmas Eve in Bethlehem. I hailed a second taxi. The cabby smiled politely and refused. "I'm the last cab tonight. You better get to a warm place."

Though the chill pierced my skinny frame, I wasn't about to give up. As I stooped to check the cartons, I felt the weight of a hand on my shoulder. I was startled. I turned to face a stranger in black oilskins. A sou'wester covered his eyes and a long black beard masked his face.

"I have an old ton truck." He pointed to a badly rusted heap, half-covered in snow. "I'll fill 'er up with gas, put the chains on 'er, and throw some weight in the back." He paused, "But it will cost you twenty or thirty dollars."

He was asking for all the money I had.

"Who are you, anyway?" I asked.

"I was watching ye from the windows of the Brown Derby Tavern. Ye haven't had much luck, eh? They call me Wild Bob — but don't let the name scare ye."

His breath reeked of beer, but he was my only hope of getting home. As we headed out, I whispered a prayer: "Please, God. Let me get home safely tonight."

The storm seethed around us. Ice clung to the wipers. "Storm is wild near the ocean. The telephone lines been down all day, b'y."

Conscious of being alone with a stranger, I edged my body closer to the door. "I've got to get home. I'll walk if I have to."

Suddenly, the tires began to whine. We were stuck in a snow bank. Tears trickled down my cheeks. Without speaking, Bob left the cab and grabbed a shovel. I offered to help but he yelled, "Stay where yer to, girl...yer not dressed for this!" He was shoveling furiously. The headlights shone on his face, sweat glistening on his forehead, ice and snow crusting his beard. In spite of my fears, I smiled to myself when I thought how much he resembled a young Santa Claus.

After what seemed like a year in solitary confinement, we were again on our way. But we'd only travel another mile before we'd be stuck again! I glanced at the dash. It was 3:00 a.m.

I began to sob, blurting out family details too intimate to share with strangers. "Do you know we are poor?" (My father lost his trawls and traps in a fall gale). "No money except the baby bonus. I was so happy to be able to help over Christmas." (My tongue seemed to have a mind of its own). "I have 11 brothers and sisters. I'm the oldest and I'm only 17! Can't you see? I just have to get home with these gifts!"

"Yes, b'y," he answered, staring straight ahead.

The rusty blue Ford turned the corner toward home. Only five more miles! My heart raced. We were so near the end of this nightmare. It was four o'clock now and the blizzard had eased.

Finally, I could see my house. Huge snowdrifts had covered our gate. That meant we'd have to go through the schoolyard next door. As we climbed out of the Ford and sank into waist deep snow, the sky was alive; Northern Lights dancing in celebration all around us! And a kerosene lamp was burning in the parlour window of our home.

In no time, Mom and Dad came trudging through the snow to greet us. The soft light of their lantern was a warm welcome. "Thank God you're okay. We tried all day to reach you but the lines were down."

They thanked Bob over and over again for bringing me safely home. Dad said, "You're some brave, my son."

"Come in and have some hot rabbit pie," offered my mom.

Before long we were all watching as my wide-eyed siblings raced to their swollen wool stockings and sat together on the canvas floor in the warmth of the white wood range. The look of gratitude and love on my parents' faces will always stay with me.

Wild Bob said nothing. He just stared, tears flowing freely down his flushed cheeks. Then, I saw him glance at the old clock on the wall. "Jeez, 10 o'clock. Gotta go, b'y. I 'ave a sister somewheres in St. George's...might go to see her."

I followed him out to the porch and held out my hand to give him the payment he'd asked for...all the money I had to my name. He gently pushed my hand away. Looking at his rubber boots he said, "Keep yer money. Can't remember a Christmas that I wasn't loaded drunk. Don't expect I'll ever ferget this one." As he walked away, he added — more to himself than to me — "Yer one crazy woman, b'y."

I was choking on the lump in my throat. Tears again welled in my eyes. I wanted to tell him, "I'll never forget this," but in that moment I was speechless. Silently I watched as wild Bob slowly climbed into his truck and drove away that quiet Christmas morning in 1953.

Reprinted from Downhomer *magazine.*

♀

Female Facts

The world's most expensive bra is sold by Victoria's Secret and has 1,300 gems, including diamonds and rubies, inset in the garment. It comes with matching panties and sells for $15 million.

♀

Aphrodesia

Aphrodesia was lying nude on the bed one night when her husband came home early. He started to undress when he saw a cigar in the ashtray on the night table.

"I'll kill you unless you tell me where that cigar came from," he shouted.

From under the bed came a quivering voice, "Havana."

♀

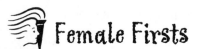
MABEL & MANLEY

When friends and family came to visit Manley in his coffin they noticed the smile on his face and mentioned it to his wife Mabel.

"Yes," she replied, "Manley's smiling because he died in his sleep and he don't know he's dead yet. He's dreaming he's still alive so when he wakes up and finds he's dead the shock will kill him."

♀

Female Firsts

1978: The first "Take Back the Night" march was held in Vancouver.

1978: Female flight attendants in Canada won the right to continue working after marriage and past the age of 32.

1978: Shirley Muldowney became the first woman to win the National Hot Rod Association points title.

1978: Mary Clarke became the first female to be named major general in the U.S. Army.

1958: The first Kinnette's Club in Newfoundland was chartered in St. John's with Isabelle Goodridge as president.

1978: On December 8, the first game of the Women's Professional Basketball League was played between the Chicago Hustle and Milwaukee Does.

1978: On December 30, the first all female crew on any U.S. scheduled airline were Pilot Emily Jones and co-pilot Lynn Rippelmeyer, when they flew a DHC-6 for Air Illinois.

1979: Maria Pintasilgo became the first female Prime Minister of Portugal.

1979: Dr. Sylvia Earle became the first person in the world to dive to a depth of 1,250 feet.

1980: Shirley Muldowney became the first driver to win two National Hot Rod Association points titles.

♀

Aunt Alice says:

My mind not only wanders, it sometimes leaves completely.

Spice of Life

Behind every successful man is a surprised woman.
— *Maryon Pearson*

♀

Is That a Fact?
Many things are taken as facts. Not all of them are.

How To Spell Mrs.
The title, Mrs, is sometimes spelled and often pronounced "Missus" in Newfoundland and Labrador, which is not the proper spelling.

The Fact Is the title is not an abbreviation at all, but in itself the title of respect given to married women. It was originally the short form for Mistress, but since that word has taken on a whole new meaning, Mrs has to stand on it's own. Except of course, in Newfoundland and Labrador where a man often misses his missus, and she often misses him.

♀

Letters From Our Friends
"...like a kid again herself."

Dear *Downhomer*,

As my mother, Effie Mae High, nears her 80th birthday, reflections of her childhood are ever present. She tells many stories of growing up in St. John's, Newfoundland and her trips to New Chelsey to visit her grandmother.

Last summer she returned to Newfoundland and by good fortune, her four children, their spouses and one grandson and his spouse were able to make the trip with her. She returned to her old neigbourhood by Bishop Field College in St. John's and visited with friends there.

When we went to Trinity Bay to visit with family there, it was simply magical. In Heart's Content, her Aunt Clarice Avery celebrated her 102nd birthday. Aunt Clarice was given a party at her home and even had a dance with her son Albert. (Aunt Clarice passed away in October)

In Winterton, her Aunt Emily Green gave us use of her family home and we met many, many relatives and made some new friends. Our cousin Marie Evans made a jiggs dinner for the whole crowd when we got there. Folks who heard about our visit, stopped by the house to say hello and introduce themselves as a cousin or friend of the family.

How about that, going home and visiting your Aunts the year before you turn eighty. She felt just like a kid again herself.

What a wonderful, magical place Newfoundland is, made possible by the friendly, down to earth people.

Diana Leonard, Harrowsmith, Ontario

♀

Life, Love & Laughter

Life, Love & Laughter

Feminine Words & Phrases

In the family way: Pregnant.

Gentle sex: Women in past times.

Daughter of Joy: In French, fille de joie, or prostitute.

Camilla: Queen of the Volscians, according to Roman legend.

Daughter of Eve: A term used as a reference to female curiosity.

Brandy Nan: A nickname given to Queen Anne, who is reputed to have loved her brandy. On her statute, which faced away from St. Paul's Church in London, England, toward a tavern that once existed there, someone once inscribed the following rhyming graffiti: "Brandy Nan, left in the lurch - Her face to the gin-shop, her back to the church."

Breach of Promise: This was part of English law until it was abolished in 1971. It gave women, who became engaged, the right to some settlement should her intended husband break the engagement. The plaintiff was allowed to claim any monies she had lost in marriage preparation, as well as other damages she might claim. Men had the same rights, but very few took advantage of it.

♀

WOMEN OF THE ISLAND AND THE BIG LAND

Mary Travers

During Newfoundland's first election in September 1832, the tavern and boarding house of Mrs. Mary Travers, located on the corner of King's Road and Duckworth Street, had been used by authorities for voting and other purposes connected with the election.

On December 26, 1832, Traver's Tavern became the seat of the Newfoundland Government with the Legislature holding all it sessions there. One of the first items to be discussed by the first legislative session was an appropriation for rent of Mrs. Travers. Although rent was approved, many months passed without rent being paid.

At first the landlady petitioned the House for her rent and when this failed she initiated legal action. She had the Court issue a restraint order and seized the speaker's chair, the cocked hat and sword of the Sergeant-at-Arms and the books and papers belonging to the Legislature. She also took possession of the mace.

The Legislature then moved to new quarters at the old Court House. Meanwhile, Mrs. Travers placed an ad in the newspapers announcing she was going to auction the objects taken from the Government. The Legislature demanded she return the items. But the strong-willed Mrs. Travers refused and threatened to go ahead with the auction.

The Government finally gave in and paid her the $350 she was owed.

From the book, Newfoundland Fireside Stories, *by Jack Fitzgerald, published by Creative Publishing. Used by permission.*

♀

Spice of Life

Life is easier to take than you'd think; all that is necessary is to accept the impossible, do without the indispensable, and bear the intolerable. – *Kathleen Norris*

♀

Quillings

Life

By Anna Letitia Barbauld

Life! We've been long together
Through pleasant and through cloudy weather
'Tis hard to part when friends are dear -
Perhaps 'twill cost a sigh, a tear;
Then steal away, give little warning,
Chose thine own time;
Say not good night - but in some brighter clime
Bid me Good Morning

Adoption

Author Unknown

A special kind of love
Not flesh of my flesh
Nor bone of my bone
But still miraculously my own
Never forget for a single minute
You didn't grow under my heart
But in it

♀

Is That a Fact?
Many things are taken as facts. Not all of them are.

Who Was Tokyo Rose?

During WWII everyone knew of Tokyo Rose, who was actually Iva Toguri d'Aquino, a Japanese-American woman, who was convicted of treason for broadcasting propaganda from Japan to Allied troups in the South Pacific.

The Fact Is that d'Aquino was found guilty of one of the eight charges of treason against her, but was later given a full pardon.

Although an American citizen, Iva was visiting a sick relative in Japan in 1942 when war was declared between Japan and America. Pressured by Japanese military police to renounce her American citizenship, Iva refused, and instead, learned Japanese and took two jobs to support herself while she sought a way to return home. One of the jobs she took was as a typist for Radio Tokyo. While there, she met American and Australian prisoners of war who were being forced to broadcast radio propaganda. Iva scavenged black-market food, medicine, and supplies for these POWs. When Radio Tokyo wanted a female voice for their propaganda shows, the POWs selected Iva. She was one of many female, English-speaking voices on Radio Tokyo, and she took the radio name of "Orphan Ann." Her POW friends wrote her scripts and tried to sneak in pro-American messages whenever possible.

After the war Iva was offered money, which she and her new husband desperately needed, to be interviewed by reporters. In the statement she signed, she admitted to being the voice of Tokyo Rose, and in 1948 she was tried for treason in the US and sentenced to 10 years in jail. After being released for good behaviour in 1956, Iva told her version of the story on the TV news show "60 Minutes" in 1976, which led to a full pardon in 1977.

♀

Life, Love & Laughter

Quillings   King of the Castle - By Ron Young

You've seen him in bars
He's a regular bloke
He's the fellow who's laughing
Whatever the joke

He's a good family man
(He would have you believe)
But he's first to arrive
And the last one to leave

And she waits at home
Her life unfulfilled
She hopes he's all right
And she hopes he'll get killed

Yet he pleases others
(As much as he's able)
And orders a round
For the boys at the table

He is always around
He's funny and loud
But he's still "Whats-his-name"
To most of the crowd

And when the nights over
And there's no one around
He makes his way home
And puts his wife down

He's King of his castle
He rules around here
His subjects pay homage
Through shame and through fear

He beats her and beats her
She never knows why
If it weren't for the kids
She's give up and die

He can't feel her pain
But her pleas and her screams

Give vent to his failures
And frustrated dreams

When his frenzy abates
And his anger is through
He tells her, "Now look at
What you made me do!"

She doesn't know what she's done
To her lover and mate
To make him this monster
Now so full of hate

He hates her because
The kids like her better
He knows she'd leave with them
But he'd never let her

But she'll never leave
She prefers not to change
The devil she knows
For one that is strange

And he hates her because of
The life she goes through
And because of the things
That she lets him do

He hates her because of
The way she shows fear
And because she's his wife
And because she is here

He hates her because
He owns her, she's his
And because she lets him see
The person he is

But as much as he hates her
He hates her much less
Than the devil inside him
That makes him do this

Life, Love & Laughter

Female Facts

In 75 per cent of households, women manage the money and pay the bills.

♀

Spice of Life

Acting is the most minor of gifts. After all, Shirley Temple could do it when she was four.   – *Katharine Hepburn*

♀

Women Who Have Made A Difference – *By Ron Young*

Dorothy Annie Elizabeth Garrod who was born in 1892, was the first woman to do research in Paleolithic archeology and to study the early man. As part of her life work she was able to conclude that the more "advanced" type of Neanderthal Man found in Tabun, Palestine existed at the same time as the more "primitive" type found in Europe. Her findings created an upset in current theories about simple linear evolution of man. When Garrod was elected Disney Professor of Archeology at Cambridge in 1939, she became the first woman to become a professor in any field at either Oxford or Cambridge.

Janice Glasgow is the president of the Canadian Society for Computational Studies of Intelligence, one of the oldest national AI societies in the world. She is also a principal investigator in the Intelligent Robotics and Intelligent Systems Federal Centre of Excellence, and the principal researcher on an AI project for the Canadian Space Agency.

Kate Gleason was the first woman to be president of a national U.S. bank, First National Bank of Rochester, New York. She was also the first woman member of the American Society of Mechanical Engineers. Henry Ford credited Kate with the invention of a machine that produced beveled gears quickly and cheaply, saying it was "the most remarkable machine work ever done by a woman." In 1913, she branched out on her own and restored a machine-tool company to financial solvency. As a result of her business leadership, Gleason Works became a leading U.S. producer of gear-cutting machinery. While at the bank, she promoted large-scale development of low-cost housing, and in 1921, she started selling low-cost concrete box houses in East Rochester, New York, after developing a method of pouring concrete. These became a model for many future suburban developments. She later became the first woman member of the American Concrete Institute.

Elizabeth Cabot Agassiz, a U.S. naturalist and educator, saw a need for a college for women to be taught by the Harvard University faculty. In 1979, she helped open the Harvard Annex, which became Radcliffe College. She served as president there until her retirement in 1903, when a scholarship and a student hall were endowed in her honour.

Mary Anderson of Alabama took a trip to New York City in 1903. Touring the city on a streetcar she was captivated by the shivering motorman who continually had to get out to wipe off the snow and ice that collected on the windshield. From this Mary got an idea which she sketched in her notebook and patented a year later. The device allowed the motorman to manipulate a lever from the inside that "activated a swinging arm that mechanically swept off the ice and snow." While she never sold her invention, her "windshield wipers" did catch on, and by 1913 they were standard equipment on American cars, saving lives and making it easier to drive through storms.

♀

Life, Love & Laughter

🍎Her Other Half
Orders From Above

Saint Peter arrived at the pearly gates one morning to find a large number of men lined up in front of the sign that read, 'Henpecked Husbands Line Up Here,' and only one small man in front of the 'non-henpecked husbands' sign.

"Why are you standing here?" the heavenly gatekeeper asked him.

"I'm not sure," replied the little man, "this is where my wife told me to stand."

♀

🗣 Female Firsts

1980: Liz Claiborne was named the fashion industry's first Entrepreneurial Woman of the Year. *See 'Female Facts' also page 435.*

1980: Carolyn Farrell became mayor of Dubuque, Iowa, making her the first Roman Catholic nun to become mayor of a major U.S. city. Before being elected to city council in the late '70s, she had been Sister Mary Consolatrice, a Sister of Charity of the Blessed Virgin Mary. She was made mayor by her peers in 1980.

1981: Taiwan's Diane Ying Yun-peng launched *CommonWealth* magazine, the first business magazine published by a Taiwanese woman. The magazine later became the top business and financial magazine and a major force in Taiwan.

1981: On July 31, Arnette Hubbard became the first woman president of the U.S. National Bar Association.

1981: Sandra Day O'Connor became the first woman on the U.S. Supreme Court.

1981: Betty Ellis became the first woman to officiate at a professional soccer match.

1982: Shirley Muldowney became the first driver, male or female, to win three National Hot Rod Association points titles.

1982: On March 4, Bertha Wilson was appointed to the Supreme Court of Canada, making her the first woman to sit on the country's highest court.

1982: Runner Mary Decker became the first woman to win the Jesse Owens Award, which is presented annually to the best U.S. track and field athlete.

1983: For the first time, it became a criminal offence in Canada for a man to rape his wife.

♀

WOMEN OF THE ISLAND AND THE BIG LAND

The Angel of Hope

By Ron Young

Jack Barrett

Charity is not just giving
In gifts and in deeds
But in understanding
What the needy one needs

I wrote this little rhyme for Enid Barrett of Bishop's Cove, and others like her who give with understanding. Enid has been a giving person all her life. Among other things, she has collected for the blind and the Canadian Red Cross, and she has been a monumental help to the Newfoundland Cancer Treatment and Research Foundation (NCTRF).

Lila and I met Enid at a friend's house where she sold us a cookbook, one of many she was selling to raise money for the Cancer Foundation. We later met with her and her husband Jack at their home, where we had a great chat and a tasty meal.

Over dinner, Enid told us of her own personal challenges that have kept her motivated on fund-raising for cancer research. Over the years she has had three bouts with cancer herself. In 1982 she had breast cancer. Then in 1989, the disease visited her again, causing the removal of her second breast. In 1997, when she thought she was in the clear, she found out she had cervical cancer. Now Enid, at 75, is thankful for every day she is alive and uses her time to do what she can for others, especially those with whom she can identify.

Cancer is not only a physical disease, but a mental one as well. It brings on depression and a loss of hope. When one is in this state, it is the caring of others that brings back the hope and the will to live on. Enid knows what cancer patients in hospital feel like, so she visits them around the province, especially at the Dr. H. Bliss Murphy Cancer Centre in St. John's, which is run by the NCTRF. By visiting these people in need, the "angel of hope" from Bishop's Cove brings sunshine and kindness – and a little something extra, handmade with love.

Enid presents every patient she sees with a special reminder of her visit. You see, in addition to being a kind person with a warm and bubbly personality, Enid is an excellent crafts person. Some of her crafts she sells, but one very special creation is made to give to others. The little guardian angels, which she calls Angels of Hope, are a simple but beautiful design. They are much enjoyed by the patients, as is Enid's company. Really, she's giving the most precious gift of all – time.

Aside from craft making, Enid is also good at raising money. To date she has reached her personal goal and sold more than $25,000 worth of cookbooks, put out by the NCTRF. At $12 apiece, that's a lot of work and a great help to the project. It was for efforts such as these that she was given a certificate of recognition by the NCTRF in 1995, and was made the province's Volunteer of the Year for 2001.

In nominating Enid for that honour, Dr. Lear, of the Dr. H. Bliss Murphy Cancer Centre, wrote:

Life, Love & Laughter

Life, Love & Laughter

"Enid has worked just as hard caring and doing for her church as for the Cancer Foundation. She has an intense love for children and will use any opportunity to present them gifts at Easter, birthdays, Christmas and special events. Her gifts are usually personal and hand-made, and God is never far from the picture."

Enid has been a volunteer at the Anglican Church for decades. After 32 years as the organist, she finally retired from that voluntary job, but a replacement couldn't be found. So guess who is still the organist for the Anglican Parish of Upper Island Cove?

Enid also reads stories to children at church, and every Easter she knits little hens that hold an egg for each of the 42 kids. In December, she gives each child a Christmas tree ornament, fashioned from jigsaw puzzle pieces gathered in the shape of a wreath.

But it's Enid's work the rest of the year that earned the praise of Bertha Paulse, CEO of the NCTRF. "When she comes here to the centre it's like old-home week. She's one of our favourite people. She has been a tremendous supporter of our organization," she says.

In return, Enid had kind words for the people at the centre: "The people at the cancer clinic at Health Sciences are great. They all treat you so good. Dianne (Abbott) is the angel at the desk. If you go in, you wouldn't believe the smile on her face."

The Dr. H. Bliss Murphy Cancer Centre is sponsored by the government, but it still requires a certain amount of fund-raising, "for all the little extra bits and pieces for patients who can't afford to travel from Labrador into St. John's," Bertha says.

"And if patients are having some financial hardships, we will provide them with some support," Bertha continues. "We have a recreational and leisure program that we fund for people who have to come to us for six weeks. And you can imagine, if you're from some little place in Tickle Harbour and you come to St. John's, you may not know a lot of people."

One of the biggest needs was for information, so centre employees created a Patient and Family Library on the premises. To raise money for this project, they put together a cookbook, which, of course, Enid sold.

"She'll go to, maybe, the Tax Centre or the bank or the phone company, or some other place, and she'll say, 'Have you got a Garden of Hope cookbook?' and they'll say, 'Never heard of it,' and she'll say, 'What, you never heard of the cookbook' She'll then turn to her husband and say, 'Jackie, go out in the car and get a cookbook.' Before she leaves there she's probably sold 10," Bertha says.

Enid will even raise funds at her personal celebrations. On her 50th wedding anniversary, she had a party and asked people not to bring a gift but to make a donation to the cancer foundation. This venture raised more than $1,200 for the centre.

"If everybody associated with our organization made a personal goal like that, we would be truly well-endowed in terms of additional resources for our patients," Bertha said.

For 20 years now, Enid has been an angel of hope for cancer patients. She has been a giving person much longer than that, but it was having cancer herself that gave her the focus.

If you are in need of an angel of hope, call Enid at 709-589-2933. If you are not, call her anyway and say hello. And while you're at it, buy a cookbook from her. It makes a great gift, because you'll be giving twice.

Merry Christmas everyone.

♀

Spice of Life

For most folks, no news is good news; for the press, good news is not news.

- Gloria Borger

♀

Female Facts
The Song Most Sing

The biggest-selling recorded song to date is "Candle in the Wind" by Elton John, followed by "White Christmas" and "Rudolph the Red-Nosed Reindeer." The music for the most-sung song in history however, was written by Mildred and Patty Smith Hill, two sisters from Louisville, Kentucky, who composed the music and lyrics for a song called "Good Morning To All". The song was published in a kindergarten song book and sung by children to greet each other each morning. In 1924, the publishing company published the music with new lyrics, entitled "Happy Birthday to You." This was done without the Hill sisters' knowledge or permission. The song became popular and in 1933 it was used in a Broadway play. At that point, Jessica Hill, a third sister, sued for copyright infringement and won. Many singers stopped using the song rather than pay the royalty fee. Some people would use the words but not the music. Actress Helen Hayes did this in a play called "Happy Birthday." To this day, anyone who uses the song in any commercial way must pay royalties to the Hill sisters. This is why we see bigger chains such as Swiss Chalet come up with their own birthday songs to sing to customers.

♀

Letters From Our Friends
"...I'd love to go north and visit New England and Canada..."

Hi,

I just read two *Downhomers* for the first time. I had never seen one before and found how very downhome interesting and informative they are. I had a friend up there some years ago who told me a little about Newfoundland and sent me a tape about the resettlement, but the magazines told me lots more about the country itself, the people and so much else. The letters from all over were great. I live way down south, about 300 miles from the Gulf of Mexico, and I'd love to go north and visit New England and Canada one of these days.

Juanita Bodiford – Monticello, Arizona, USA

♀

Life's Funny Experiences
She Was Taking No Bull

The first encounter my mother had with a bull was when she let the door open and the bull walked right inside the house. Mom went after Mr. Bull with her broom and broke the handle on his horns as he backed out the door.

The next encounter Mom had with a male bovine was when she was 78 years of age. Mom was on her way to Mass and took a short cut off the main road. A big bull spotted her and started chasing her. As the bull closed in on her she started backing up until she fell on her back on a pile of rocks with the bull staring down at her.

She was alone and the only help she could get would have to be from God.

"Jesus, Mary and Joseph help me!" she said as she made her hand into a fist.

With that she raised her fist over her head and let the bull have it between the eyes. The startled bull took off and Mom got up, brushed herself off, and made her way to Mass.

M. T. Duncan – LaSalle, Quebec

♀

Life, Love & Laughter

Ennellene

He told me my looks, are what drew him to me
By that I was flattered, and greatly
But that earlier look, should not be mistook
With the looks I've been giving him lately

♀

Aunt Alice says:

It's not hard to meet expenses - they're everywhere.

Spice of Life

Some men break your heart in two,
Some men fawn and flatter,
Some men never look at you
And that clears up the matter

– *Dorothy Parker*

♀

Quillings

Be Your Best - *Author Unknown*

If you can't be a pine on the top of the hill
Be a scrub in the valley - but be
The best little scrub by the side of the hill
Be a bush if you can't be a tree

If you can't be a bush, be a bit of the grass
And some highway happier make
If you can't be a muskie then just be a bass
But the liveliest bass in the lake

We can't all be captains, there's got to be crew
And the task we must do is the near
There's big work to do and there's lesser too
As a crew we will surely get there

If you can't be a highway, then just be a trail
If you can't be the sun, be a star
It isn't by size that you win or you fail
Be the best of whatever you are!

♀

Letters From Our Friends
Good Samaritans in Alberta

It was in February 2000 in Brooks, Alberta, that my son and I were walking across a very busy street. As soon as I stepped onto the sidewalk, I slipped and hurt myself. Out of all the people around, the only people who stopped to see if I needed help were two Newfoundland gentlemen. As soon as they spoke, I knew they were from home.

I said to them, "You guys are Newfoundlanders, right?" They said yes and asked how I knew. I said it was because they were the only ones that stopped to help.

I just want to thank them for stopping and caring about someone other than themselves, unlike most people here.

Ada Ford (Walsh) – Brooks, Alberta (formerly of Baie Verte, Newfoundland)

♀

Food for Thought

If you have a great career why should you want a
man trailing around after you.   *– Mary Garden*

♀

Is That a Fact?
Many things are taken as facts. Not all of them are.

Immaculate Conception

Everybody, especially those who are Roman Catholic, knows of the Immaculate Conception,
when the Virgin Mary gave birth to baby Jesus.

The fact is Immaculate Conception actually refers to the birth of the Virgin Mary herself,
who was considered to have been conceived free of all original sin, and therefore holy
enough to give birth to the son of God. According to Biblical scholars, Mary was just 15 or
16 years of age when she became the mother of Jesus.

♀

Animal Mating – Fact and Fantasy – *Ron Young*

Ain't Had No Lovin' in a Long, Long Time

Fact:

In spite of the fact that it lives its entire life in the ocean, the blue whale is not a fish, but like
humankind, a mammal. The word "mammal" comes from the same base word as "mammary
glands" which means "female breasts." Mammals, unlike other classes of animals, suckle their
young with warm breast milk. The other distinction of mammals is that the young are born live
and not hatched or given life in any other way.

Mister Blue is a showoff like most men, especially when seeking the sexual attention of Mrs.
Blue. His way of getting her attention is by doing fancy dives.

The blue (both female and male) makes a low-frequency moan, which is not necessarily a
mating call, but on the other hand, the ultrasonic whistles and chirps it makes is a definite sign
that it is feeding. Although this description of whale communication doesn't sound like much on
the written page, the sound (the low-frequency one) a whale makes is louder than that of any
other living creature. It is louder than a jet plane, and a whale's sounds can be heard for hundreds
of miles.

Whales can live about as long as humans (up to 70 years), but are not as sexually active. They
mate only once every three years, but when they do mate, they do the human, belly-to-belly,
nose-to-nose, way.

Fantasy:

Though I only get to mate
Every three years (on some date)
You may wonder at my smile from ear-to-ear
Yes, it has been a while
And the reason for my smile
Is that finally it's time, this year's the year

♀

Ennellene

He used to say, "This is my 'little' woman"
Which was something I just couldn't take
And he wouldn't relent, so wherever we went
I'd call him, "My 'big' mistake"

♀

 ## MABEL & MANLEY

A neighbour paying her last respects to Manley as he lay in his coffin said to his wife, "Mabel, I touched Manley and he is still warm."

"Warm or cold," replied Mabel, "he's going to the cemetery tomorrow."

♀

 ## Female Firsts

1983: The Canadian Human Rights Act prohibited sexual harassment in workplaces under federal jurisdiction. Before this, women in these workplaces had no legal recourse if their employers demanded sexual favours.

1983: Dr. Sally Ride became the first American woman in space, aboard the space shuttle, Challenger.

1984: Jean-Mathilde Sauve became the first female Governor General of Canada.

1984: Geraldine Anne Ferraro, became the first female vice-presidential nominee of a major U.S. party when she was chosen by Walter F. Mondale of the Democratic Party.

1984: On July 18, Lynn Rippelmeyer and Bev Burns became the first women in the world to captain a Boeing 747. The two asked to fly their first trips on the same day so they could share the honour. Lynn flew TransAtlantic, Newark to Gatwick in London, England, and Bev flew TransContinental, Newark to Los Angeles.

1984: On August 5, Joan Bennett, of Augusta, Maine, won the first ever women's Olympic Marathon.

1984: Soviet cosmonaut Svetlana Savitskaya became the first woman to walk in space.

1984: Chris Evert became the first professional tennis player to win 1000 singles matches. *See also page 206.*

1984: Geraldine Ferraro became the first major party U.S. vice-presidential candidate.

1984: Joan Benoit Samuelson became the first woman to win an Olympic marathon at the Summer Games in Los Angeles.

♀

Life, Love & Laughter

Life's Funny Experiences

Rear View Mirror

My sister and I went out looking for bridesmaids dresses for my wedding. When we got to the bridal shop, I noticed that there were floor-length mirrors everywhere. After we had been there for a while, my sister turned around and said, "Look over there at that woman, her butt is huge." When I looked to where she was pointing, I started to laugh. She asked me what was wrong. I asked her if she noticed what the woman in the mirror was wearing. When she took a closer look she started to blush because the woman was her.

Liz Thomas – Newfoundland

♀

Quillings

Touching Shoulders

There's a comforting thought at the close of the day,
When I'm weary and lonely and sad,
That sort of grips hold of my crusty old heart,
And bids it be merry and glad.
It gets in my soul and it drives out the blues,
And finally thrills through and through.
It is just a sweet memory that chants the refrain:
"I'm happy I touched shoulders with you".

Did you know you were brave? Did you know you were strong?
Did you know there was one leaning hard?
Did you know that I waited and listened and prayed,
And was cheered by your simplest word?
Did you know that I longed for that smile on your face,
For the sound of your voice ringing true?
Did you know I grew stronger and better, because
I had merely touched shoulders with you?

I am glad that I live, that I battle and strive
For the place that I know I must fill;
I am thankful for sorrows - I'll meet with a grin
What fortune may send - good or ill.
I may not have wealth, I may not be great,
But I know I shall always be true,
For I have in my life that courage you gave
When once I rubbed shoulders with you.

Author Unknown

♀

Life, Love & Laughter

Food for Thought

I don't look down on men, but I certainly don't look up to them either. I never found a man I could love, or trust, the way I loved myself. – *Mae West*

♀

Is That a Fact?
Many things are taken as facts. Not all of them are.

Went to the Dogs

When Ms. Eleanor Ritchley, the unmarried grand-daughter of Quaker State Oil founder Philip Bayer died, people said all her fortune went to 150 stray dogs the spinster had adopted as pets.

The fact is that, except for 1,200 boxes of stationary and 1,700 pairs of shoes, which she left to the Salvation Army, her entire fortune, worth $12 million, went to her best friends, her adopted dogs. Her will stipulated a trust that saw her strays living in the lap of luxury for the rest of their lives. Money left after that was to go to Auburn University. In 1968, Musketeer, the last of Eleanor's friends, and the richest dog in America died, and Auburn got what was left.

♀

Feminine Words & Phrases

Iron Lady: The title given to Margaret Thatcher, Prime Minister of Britain from 1979 to 1990. She was given the name on January 24, 1976, by the *Red Star*, a newspaper operated by the Soviet Defense Ministry, after a speech she made warning of Russia's impending threat to the West. That was before Russia gave up being an iron-curtain nation. *See also page 104.*

Jump over the broomstick: Living together as a couple without the formality of a church or civil wedding ceremony. The source of this information is not known, but there as been an allusion by some writers that "jumping over the broomstick" was sometimes the only ceremony allowed to slaves in America, who may not be together forever. This was especially true if one of them should be sold to someone who lived far away.

Lily: Flower which, in tradition, sprang from repentant tears that fell from the eyes of Eve in the Garden of Eden.

♀

Ennellene

After we both said "I do," and started out anew
And before we had the marriage day all mastered
Me and my new spouse were like a brand new house
I was all painted up, and he was plastered

♀

Tickle and Bight *By Lucy Fitzpatrick–McFarlane*

The Height of Style

I can still see a bunch of us teenage girls pouring through the pages of the Eaton's catalogue and marveling over the beautiful clothes that we could only dream about owning. "Oh, luuuhhhh... I wish I could buy that green dress for the garden party next month! I loves that stand-up collar... it looks right stylish, don't it?"

"Yis, my dear, and that colour would look some good with your red hair. And luuuhhh... see that frilly blouse there? My, I wish I could get that for myself. We'd be right in the height of style, wouldn't we?"

"I wish... I wish..."

Seemed like we were always wishing for something we couldn't have back in Newfoundland in my younger days, but you know what, we were none the worse for it. No, siree...wishing and hoping didn't stunt our psychological growth at all. It did, however, give us hours of entertainment and enjoyment, as well as teaching us to appreciate the value of things. Even though we had little connection with the outside world, we were still conscious of wearing clothes that were the latest fashion. Granted, styles came and went, and often, by the time we had seen it with our own eyes in the catalogue, that something new had gone out of style again, but it didn't really matter. We wore it anyway, for we knew we had seen it with our own eyes in the catalogue, albeit several years ago. With the nine of us in our family, we didn't exactly have a choice but to wear whatever the oldest kids had outgrown. And with second-hand clothes, they came in three sizes only... big, small, or one-size-fits-all. With most of the families, it was the same thing, so it was difficult at times to tell if children were under-nourished or overweight. If you had to squeeze into something that was too small, your clothes puckered at the seams and rode up over the wrists and ankles. "My, what are you feeding that child," someone might ask. "Sure he's getting so big, he's popping out of his clothes."

On the other hand, if you were tall, skinny and gawky looking like I was, you looked like a streel with the clothes hanging off you. I supposed that was why kindly old ladies looked at me with pity in their eyes.

"My dear girl, you're so skinny, a puff of wind would knock you down. Eat more and put some fat on your bones."

When I'd grumble and throw a fit because I didn't want to wear a pair of hand-me-down slacks that didn't reach to the top of my ankles, mom would try to reason with me. "My dear, you're lucky you can wear slacks because you got nice long legs," she'd say. "Just pull your socks up a bit more and you'll be right in style."

Many years have passed since then, but now when I look around at the younger generation, I realize they're wearing exactly the same fashions as we did back then. The only difference is that we didn't actually KNOW we were in style. We couldn't afford to buy new clothes all the time, but for special occasions, like Easter or St. Patrick's Day, mom made dresses or outfits for the girls. Sometimes, when we weren't around, she'd look through the catalogue and duplicate a dress style at her sewing machine, but she'd never let on to us that she did it. Then she'd act surprised if someone pointed out the similarities in the wish book. "Well, look at that," she'd say. "That's almost like the dress I made for you, Lucy, except yours is a nicer colour. It looks right stylish on you, too."

Course I'd be prouder than a peacock, to say the least. But she always made us feel that whatever we wore was the height of fashion and I supposed we believed her. And like all mothers, she couldn't keep her tongue still if she saw us wearing something that she thought wasn't appropriate. She hated the mini skirts when they were in style and when that changed over to the maxi lengths, she complained that they were too long. But my favourite was the hot pants. You remember them, don't you ladies? It was an outfit with a short dress worn over a pair of matching shorts. Mom disapproved of them vehemently and claimed they were unladylike because it looked like the dress was too short to cover the unmentionables. Oh, my...those were the days. I still have a snap of myself and my girlfriend posing in our beautiful floral hot-pant fitout and wearing paten-leather boots that came to the knee. I just wish I kept that outfit, because one never knows when they may come back on the fashion scene again. And they just might, you know, for a lot of things from the past have been resurrected in the fashion industry. There really is some truth to that old saying "what goes around, comes around," you know. Just this winter when I saw the young teenagers wearing plaid, pleated skirts, I rushed home and dug out my old reversible, pleated skirt and the mohair, boat-neck sweater I had in high school. I was in my glory as I dusted off my wedge-heeled shoes and I mentally patted myself on the back for having the foresight to keep them all those years. Not that I thought they'd ever make a come-back, mind you, because it really was for sentimental reasons that I kept it all. Still, it made me feel good. Then, when I saw the bell-bottom jeans and trousers in the stores last year, I kicked myself for throwing mine away. Course the now-generation don't call them bell-bottoms anymore...now they're FLARES, but the idea is the same. And along with that, the girls are wearing the polyester, floral blouses with the big collars and the chunky shoes with the thick heels that we referred to as wedgies. Fact is, that word too, has several different connotations these days. I understand, one of which is along the line of having your underwear creep up on you and wedge itself in a certain uncomfortable place that makes sitting a bit difficult. Worse still, I'm told, is having a prankster yank your undies up from behind in what they call a "wedgie," for I hear it can be very painful.

I think what pleases me most is that the younger generation are wearing their clothes with pride because they're not in the least concerned with what other people think, or whether clothes actually fit properly or not. They don't give a hen's tooth if it is too small or too big or that the loud colours may clash with their latest hairshade. All that really matters is that it is fashionable and by golly, I admire their tenacity, because their self-image will never be damaged by feeling insecure about their choice in clothes.

Truth is, I'm happy about the way the styles have made a come-back, because I'm tired of having to buy new clothes just so I can blend in with everybody else. And no more buying spandex that can stretch from a size 10 to 16, just so I can tell everybody that I can still fit into a size 10. Now that the trend is more liberal, I can go from wearing something three times too big to something that fits like a latex glove and nobody will blink an eye. And the best thing about it all is that I won't have to buy any more new clothes. I can just rummage through the boxes I've kept over the years and bring out the clothes I wore twenty years ago. If I feel like going to work with my hair standing on end or wearing bobby socks with my pumps or perhaps even piercing my navel, then I'll do it. From now on for me, it's out with the new and in with the old no matter what happens, I'll wear everything I have with confidence because I know that I'll be right smack in the height of style.

♀

Spice of Life

A woman never really makes a fool of a man - she just directs the performance.

♀

Female Facts

Eighty-five per cent of all women wear the wrong bra size.

♀

Ennellene

In my widow's cardigan, I mourned for my man
Whose recent cheating caused me pain and sorrow
When someone passing by asked "When did he die?"
I answered back, "When he comes home tomorrow."

♀

Animal Mating - Fact and Fantasy – *Ron Young*

Feeding the Cat

Fact:

The Lynx, which is found in many parts of the world, is seldom seen in Newfoundland and Labrador (or anywhere they reside for that matter). They are around however, but are such a quiet and private animal that they are seldom heard or seen. During mating season however, both the male and female become more vocal, making shrieking sounds. Although most of us couldn't find a male lynx for love nor money, the female knows how to find him for lovemaking. To gain his affection she will enter his territory and make meowing sounds until she gets a reaction. If you've ever owned a domestic cat while she was in heat, you may have some idea of how "catty" a feminine feline can be, especially a wild, wanton one, wanting to be a mother.

The male lynx however, prefers catting around, as well as eating, to parenthood. He leaves his lover after three or four days in search of food and other possible sex partners. But if he is not out of her territory by the time the babies are born, she will chase him out. That's because the male lynx has been known to kill and eat his children, especially when there is a shortage of rabbits or hares to eat.

Fantasy:

From mother lynx, a warning
If you're still around, just yearning
To make a meal of daughter or of son
Beware my instinct as a mother
Take that for granted, Brother
And before I claw out your eyes, you'd better run

♀

Adam's Ribbing

Doing His Part

At the end of the trial, when the family court judge said, "Young woman, this court is going to see that you receive $1,500 a month as alimony, her estranged other-half spoke up and said, "Thanks, your Honour, and I'll even throw in a few bucks myself."

♀

Aunt Alice says:

The older you get, the tougher it is to lose weight because by then, your body and your fat are really good friends.

Spice of Life

In politics, if you want anything said, ask a man, if you want anything done, ask a woman.
– *Margaret Thatcher*

♀

Female Firsts

1984: Billie Jean King became the commissioner of World Team Tennis, making her the first woman head of a professional athletic league.

1984: On October 8, Anne Murray became the first woman to win the Country Music Association's Album of the Year Award, with her album, *A Little Good News*.

1985: On March 20, Libby Riddles was five hours ahead of her nearest competitor when she won the Iditarod dogsled race to become the first woman to win the event.

1985: Penny Harrington became North America's first woman police chief of a major city when she took over as the head of the Portland, Oregon police force.

1986: Mountaineer and guide, Sharon Adele Wood of Halifax, Nova Scotia, became the first woman from the Western World to stand atop Mount Everest.

1986: Ann E. Bancroft became the first woman to reach the North Pole on a dogsled. She was a vital member of the 1986 Steger International Polar Expedition, giving emergency medical aid to men and dogs. She was also the expedition photographer and cinematographer for National Geographic.

1986: When Nancy Lieberman-Cline joined the USBL's Springfield Fame, she became the first woman to play in a men's professional basketball league.

1986: On January 28, Christa McAuliffe became the first woman citizen passenger on a space mission. Unfortunately Christa, and all the occupants aboard *Challenger,* were killed when the ship exploded on re-entry.

1987: Wilma Mankiller became the first elected Chief of the Cherokee Nation.

♀

WOMEN OF THE ISLAND AND THE BIG LAND

Setting the Seeds of Humanity

By Ron Young

Marian Frances White sets the seeds of humanity, the safety of the environment and equal rights for all, wherever she goes. The garden that she, and her husband, Beni, "the circus clown" Malone, planted in such a wild and terraced fashion is now our garden, so I know what I'm talking about. We bought their house and that's when I learned some of her qualities, including honesty. The seeds of the environment that she and Beni sowed are certainly apparent all the way from our back yard down to the falls on the Waterford River.

Marian White

Lila and I thank Marian and Beni for wanting a larger property where they can grow foods that are healthy, and thereby made this home available to us at an opportune time. Since then we have become friends and have gotten to know other sides of Marian even better.

Marian loves to write poetry. When we spoke she was putting the finishing touches on her second book of poetry, *Mind Your Eyes*. She has also written in genres other than poetry. She wrote a number of Almanacs for women of Newfoundland and Labrador for six years before broadening the scope of her stories to include all the Atlantic Provinces. This is part of the "equal rights for all" part of Marian that inspired her to write and produce *The Untold Story* about the women's suffrage movement in this province. The documentary won her a major award at the San Luis Obispo International Film Festival in California. Considering that famous producers such as Steven Speilberg took part in the festival, it was quite an accomplishment. Marian was also named Artist of the Year by Newfoundland and Labrador Art's Council in 2000, for her many other efforts in promoting art and artists of the province. Not bad for a little girl from Carbonear, who was one of 12 children.

The award Marian received for her work is well deserved. *The Untold Story* is entertaining, informative and well produced. It brings to life an era in this province when there were no liquor laws, when men and boys were often paid in rum rather than wages. Meanwhile, at home, mothers watched their children go hungry, and do without life's necessities. Worse than that, there was nothing women could do about it, the deck was stacked against them. They didn't even have the right to vote to change the system.

Marian tells me, "When I set out to do the *The Untold Story*, I thought I would write a book, but when I saw all the words and stories of these wonderful women, I wanted to bring back the voices of those who were silenced by the oppressive government of the time." The prolific writer didn't just want the words about these women to be on the written page.

"I wanted to not only hear them, but see them and feel their anguish over unjust laws. It was an opportunity for me to do a re-enactment and bring them back to life."

With the success of *The Untold Story*, television broadcasters such as Vision TV and NTV gave

Life, Love & Laughter

Life, Love & Laughter

her a licence to do another film of her choice.

"I wanted to do something that was lighthearted," Marian says, "something that I had knowledge about, so having a partner who owned a small circus, and a daughter who was about to run away and join an international circus in Switzerland, I thought I could do a good job on this topic. *Fool Proof* has been released and was featured at the Atlantic Film Festival in Halifax." In *Fool Proof* you can see Anahareo, her and Benni's daughter, do several spectacular aerial manoeuvers.

Lila and I watched the show on NTV on New Year's Day several years ago. It was humourous, and heartwarming. It took us to circuses around the world, and around Newfoundland and Labrador, to the happy eyes of children who just got to meet a clown face to face.

Even back when she was growning up, Marian realized that although the world was good in many aspects, there was room for improvement. Her loving mother, Florence, raised 12 children under very adverse conditions and no doubt had a lot to do with Marian's inspiration. For one thing, Marian decided that she would have only one child, to give her more time to attend to her needs. Anahareo grew up with her sights set even higher than Marian's, at least in the physical sense. She now performs her aerial artistry high above the crowds for people all over Europe - as a circus aerialist. She is a lovely person, and a child any mother would be proud of. Marian certainly is.

Marian's father, Terrence, was also an inspiration to her.

"I grew up with a father who performed recitations and poetry. I think I was born lucky. My father always said, 'Better to be born lucky, than rich.' I have had a lot of opportunity that has allowed me to become part of a global community of people and I really love that."

Marian was asked to showcase her work across Canada, in parts of the U.S, as well as at the prestigious Cannes Film Market in France. Marian likes being part of the global community because that's where big changes can be made. Preserving the environment requires a world-wide effort, and Marian is especially concerned with keeping Newfoundland's environment intact.

"It seems that change is the only constant we can really count on. But some of the changes are not really for the better. I try in my life to find harmony; harmony in my work, as well as harmony with nature. The outside is as important as the inside; I mean that both elementally as well as physically in our bodies. One reason I love living in Newfoundland is that I can go to a pond and swim if I like. I can eat the fruit that I pick, like blueberries and strawberries, and wild herbs and mushrooms. It is quite amazing the feast Newfoundland has to offer. I'm glad my eyes have been opened to the magic that is life in Newfoundland and Labrador."

A number of excerpts from Marian's Almanac, *The Finest Kind,* appear on these pages.

♀

Ennellene

I knew I was right, and after having a fight
He said, "I'm sorry if I seemed unkind
In spite of the fight, I now think you were right"
I said, "It's too late now, I've since changed my mind"

♀

Food for Thought

Nobody speaks the truth when there's something they must have.
                                    - Elizabeth Bowen

♀

Public Hanging in Newfoundland

The first woman to be publicly hanged in Newfoundland (and believed to be the first in British North America) was Eleanor Power of Freshwater Bay, near St. John's. She was convicted, along with her husband and eight other men, of having murdered Magistrate William Keen.

The last woman to be publicly hanged in Newfoundland was Catherine Snow. She had been charged, along with Tobias Mandeville and Arthur Spring, of having murdered her husband, John Snow. She was hanged on July 22, 1834.

♀

Life's Funny Experiences

Don't Go Near the Water

I remember when my Aunt first came to Ontario from Newfoundland and we all used to giggle at the way she talked. Some of the things she said were funny to us as we weren't used to hearing these expressions.

Well, this one day we were going to the beach and my Aunt was left in charge of us while our parents were setting up camp. When we were all running towards the beach we could hear her in the background saying: "If any of ye drowns I'm gonna have to kill ya". Needless to say we all rolled around laughing and my poor Aunt never lived it down.

Submitted by F. O'Brien – Ontario, Canada

♀

Is That a Fact?
Many things are taken as facts. Not all of them are.

I'll Take You Home Again Kathleen

Many people remember the old Irish ballad, "I'll Take You Home Again Kathleen." We can visualize an Irish lass pining away in New York, far away from her beloved "Aulde Sod." We can see her, pale of face, crying as her husband, who well knows how she misses Ireland, sings .... "to where your heart has ever been, since first you were my bonny bride. The roses all have left your cheeks. I watched them fade away and die."

The fact is that the song is not an Irish ballad at all. It was written in Indiana, USA, by Thomas Paine Westondorf, who originally came from Virginia.

Several things apparently inspired the song. One of these was the fact that Westondorf's new wife, for whom he was lonesome because he had to live in Plainfield, Indiana, where he had a teaching job, while she was visiting her parents in Ogdensburg, New York. Another influence was actually another song, "Barney, Take Me Home Again" by Arthur W. French and George W. Parsley. Incidentally, the name of Westondor's wife was Jenny, not Kathleen. The author obviously found the name Kathleen more romantic than Jenny.

♀

Food for Thought

I've got a woman's ability to stick to a job and get on with it when everyone else walks off and leaves it. – *Margaret Thatcher*

♀

👩 Out of Habit

At the Saint Patrick School for Girls, one of the teachers, Sister Constance, was asking the girls what they wanted to be when they became women. The chorus of proposed careers ranged from nurse, through mother to even a few nuns, but when one of her girls shouted out that she wanted to be a prostitute, Sister Constance fainted away to the floor.

She regained consciousness to the anxious faces of her students ringed around her.

"I'm sorry," said the young lady who had taken the nun's breath away, "my sister used to be a teacher, but she makes more money as a prostitute, and you don't even have to go to university for that, so I decided to be a prostitute when I'm older."

"Praise Jesus," said the good sister as she sat up. "I thought you said *Protestant*."

♀

Female Firsts

1987: Aretha Franklin became the first woman to be inducted into the Rock and Roll Hall of Fame.

1987: The first Women's World Hockey Tournament was held at the Centennial Arena in North York, Ontario.

1987: Aside from the swimsuit edition, Jackie Joyner-Kersee became the first woman athlete to be featured on the cover of *Sports Illustrated*.

1987: Lynne Cox became the first person to swim the Bering Strait from Alaska to the former Soviet Union.

1988: In June, Kay Cottee of Australia became the first woman to sail single-handed and non-stop around the world.

1988: Jockey Julie Krone became the first woman to compete in the prestigious Breeders' Cup.

1988: Barbara C. Harris of Massachusetts was elected the first woman Episcopal bishop.

1989: Phyllis Holmes of Greenville College in Illinois became the first woman president of the National Association of Intercollegiate Athletics in the U.S.

1989: Takako Doi, Chair of the Japan Social Democratic Party from 1986 to 1991, became the first real female voice in Japanese politics when she lead the Socialists to a stunning victory over the ruling party in the Upper House elections. This inspired hundreds of politically inexperienced housewives and mothers to run for political office, many of whom were elected.

1989: Audrey McLaughlin became the first female leader of a federal political party with sitting members after being elected to the House of Commons as MP for the Yukon in 1985.

♀

Life, Love & Laughter

Spice of Life

Money is what you'd get along beautifully without if only other people weren't so crazy about it. – *Margaret Case Harriman*

♀

Life's Funny Experiences
Here's Looking at Ya...

A few years ago while attending a music festival on the Port au Port Peninsula, my friend Bernice and I had brought along a tent to sleep in during our weekend stay. After partying all day, and half the night, we headed back to our tent in the now crowded field. Once there I discovered we had forgotten to bring pillows, so out to the car I went to find something to rest my head on. I finally decided on my gym bag and then called to my friend Bernice to see if she wanted hers as well. The conversation went like this: "Bernice do you want a bag for your head?" No answer. Again I asked: "Bernice do you want a bag for your head?" Suddenly, from a few tents over a man called out, "How ******* ugly is she??"

Sheila – Ontario, Canada

♀

Animal Mating – Fact and Fantasy – *Ron Young*
Not Crabby

Fact:

Unlike the female capelin, which is chased ashore by males for mating, and the female lobster, which molts before it mates, the female Horseshoe Crab (which is an arachnid, not really a crab) carries her mate ashore and doesn't have to molt to mate.

The largest population of the American horseshoe crab, which are found along the western shores of the Atlantic Ocean from Maine to the Yucatan Peninsula, mate in spring at times when the tide is getting high. Thousands of males, which are one third smaller than the females, wait in groups at the shoreline for their prospective mates to arrive. When a couple "hit it off," he will hang on to her back with the glove-like claws on his first pair of legs, while she drags him up the beach to the high tide line. Every few feet along the way she will pause to dig a nest-hole, into which she deposits up to a total of 20,000 eggs. She then drags the male over the nest while he fertilizes the eggs. The incoming waves then cover the eggs to protect them.

Fantasy:

Though my presumed mating notion, as I waited in the ocean
And your arrival found you, ready, able, willing
Instead of blushing bride, I got taken for a ride
And the outcome of the act was unfulfilling
And though I couldn't wait for more, as you dragged me up the shore
(And hanging on to you was sometimes scary)
When you brought me within reach, of baby-making on the beach
'Twas more like planting wheat seeds on the prairie

♀

Life, Love & Laughter

Life, Love & Laughter

The Whys of Men

How many men does it take to put a toilet seat down?
It's not known. It hasn't happened yet.

♀

Aphrodesia

"For months I didn't know where my husband was spending his evenings," Aphrodesia told her friend.
"Did you find out?" asked her friend.
"Yes, I went home early one evening and that's where he was."

♀

Some Mothers Have Them

"I don't know what your father will say when he finds out you were fighting with your friends?" scolded Jackson's mother one day.
"He threw a rock at me," answered Jackson. "So I threw one back at him."
"Why didn't you come to me before you threw the rock?"
"What good would that have done? My aim is better than yours," answered Jackson.

♀

Ennellene

As I older grow, and my aging starts to show
I look at myself in looking glass, and I sigh
For my darling little figure is less curvier, and bigger
And my face is changing into corduroy

♀

Life's Funny Experiences
Keeping up With the Mess

I worked at the central supply room at the Grace General Hospital in St. John's in the mid-70s. One day a co-worker accidentally dropped a bottle of solution on the marble floor causing quite a mess. Mrs. Ryan, the supervisor, asked the worker to call housekeeping to send someone to clean up the mess. The phone rang a while later and my co-worker answered. A man said, "This is housekeeping. Is Mrs. Ryan there?" Handing the phone to her supervisor, she said. "It's for you. It's Mr. Keeping."

Beulah Morgan – Conception Bay South, Newfoundland

♀

Tickle and Bight *By Lucy Fitzpatrick–McFarlane*

Garage Sale Anyone?

Up until a few years ago, I've always found the idea of garage sales distasteful, for I couldn't imagine why anybody would want to buy other people's junk. Lord knows we had enough at our own house, because my husband is a hoarder and he hates to part with anything. As far as I'm concerned, if something can't be used, then it should go in the garbage...but not Murray. Oh, no, he just keeps everything "...just in case I need it."

Then, one sunny day in May, when I was doing my yearly house cleaning, I had a sudden change of heart brought on by the frightful sight of junk crammed into every nook and corner of the house. I made the decision that it was all going to the dump, no matter what Murray said and when he saw that I meant business, he suddenly announced that he was going to have a garage sale. At first I balked at the idea because I didn't want our neighbours to think that we were desperate for money. But then I decided to keep my mouth shut, for I was willing to sacrifice anything that would give me the freedom to walk through the house without getting my shins bruised. I actually got excited about the whole thing as I watched Murray gather up all the things I wanted desperately to get rid of. For almost four hours, he carted 20 years of junk from the house to the back yard and when he was finished, we both stood back and surveyed the enormous pile. My excitement was overwhelming and all I could do was prattle on about my plans for all the extra space in the house. When he didn't answer me, I turned and saw the expression on his face. He looked like he had a heavenly vision, for his face was all aglow and his eyes were glazed over. When he finally spoke, my enthusiasm shrunk to the size of a pea. "I had no idea I had so much stuff...and it's all mine," he whispered as he beheld the shrine before him.

I should have known better than to believe a man who still has boxer shorts he wore 25 years ago. He was never going to part with any of his loot. It was a losing battle to begin with, so I decided to gather up another pile of things for the garage sale. You'll have to trust me when I say our two sons are cut from the same cloth as their father, for they suddenly become very possessive of their "STUFF" and don't want to part with it. Most of the things have been condemned, broken or outgrown anyway, but as soon as I touched them, everything suddenly looked better than it did before and they insisted on keeping all of it. After hours of indecision, they finally parted with a decapitated Cabbage Patch doll, a broken baseball bat and a frayed jock strap that they used as a slingshot. Naturally, that went in the garbage, but I managed to weasel a few things from Murray's pile when he wasn't looking. I spent days cleaning and polishing items, for I had no intention of letting the neighbours think I was selling dirty junk. When I set up the tables in the garage, Murray began repairing everything that was broken. And the rest is history. Once he fixed everything, he refused to part with them and started carting

Life, Love & Laughter

them back into the house. "Guess what?" he'd say, "I fixed that old purple lamp Aunt Olive gave us for a wedding present. It's just as good as new...do you want it in our bedroom or the living room?"

By the time my dear hubby finished, there was nothing left to go out in the garage sale. Except two broken door knobs, a few hinges, an old pair of his football cleats and a box of popsicle sticks. I was at my wits end because he had been running a newspaper ad for a whole week advertising a GIANT THREE-DAY GARAGE SALE. The contents of the one remaining table looked pitiful, but still Murray insisted on going ahead with the sale. I resorted to sneaking things out of his pile while he slept and the next time I'd look, they'd be gone. The day before the sale, I was so distraught that I started putting out my good dishes from the kitchen cupboards. That was when I realized that I'd have to do something that I vowed I would never do. So, hiding behind sunglasses and a big hat, I hopped in my car and went to my very first garage sale, praying that I wouldn't meet anyone I knew. I cleaned out the first three sales I came upon, loaded up the car and heading home with my loot. Murray was like a kid in a toy shop when he saw what I'd bought and he actually wanted to keep all of that stuff too, but I was adamant. "After this sale is over," I sputtered, "don't you ever mention a garage sale to me again. From now on, anything that's not being used is going in the garbage and God help the person who brings it back inside this house!"

So, we ended up having a garage sale to sell other people's junk. I was determined to at least get back the money I had spent on that heap of trash. It was more like a nightmare. People were ringing our doorbell before we were even out of bed and when we opened the garage door, they practically ran over us. You'd think K-Mart was having a blue-light special the way they grabbed things from each other. I was amazed that they would negotiate and hassle over items priced for a quarter and after one hour of this, my temper was starting to rise. I just wanted to end the whole fiasco with my dignity still intact, so I started throwing things in boxes and put a FREE sign on them. Throngs of people who had been browsing converged on the boxes and we nearly got trampled in the stampede. It was terrifying to watch grown people arguing over who got what first as they pushed and shoved each other. And just when I had almost lost faith in the whole human race, an elderly man pushed his way through the mob and handed me a loonie. I gestured to the Free sign, but he just smiled and said "I couldn't possibly take anything for free."

"God bless you sir," I sniveled, thankful that I had made one sale without having to make change for a quarter.

When everything was over, we didn't even make enough money to pay for the newspaper ad, let alone what I had spent buying the other stuff. And still there was all that junk of our own that Murray refused to part with to be put back in the house. Nothing had changed, except my frame of mind. Depressing is the only way to describe it. And that's what it's been like every summer at our house since that first garage sale. It's a vicious circle. I gather up the junk from the house, clean it up and Murray takes it all back. Then I have to start going to garage sales again to get enough stuff for the one that I know Murray will insist on having next year. I keep praying that he'll get over his urge to hoard up things, but I'm not holding much hope. You see, now Murray has started going to garage sales and judging by the size of the storage shed he's building to put all his newly acquired junk in, I'd say my chances are...well slim, to say the least, wouldn't you agree?

♀

Food for Thought

Giving advice is like cooking - you should try it before you feed it to others.

♀

Spice of Life

If high heels were so wonderful, men would still be wearing them. *– Sue Grafton*

♀

Letters From Our Friends

A Friend out of Reach

Dear Friends,

A couple of years ago I sent in a poem to your magazine entitled "Flanders Fields."

I made several pen pals through this poem and I have kept in touch with several of your readers. One of my pen pals was from Virginia and the other, a lady from Toronto.

We three have been pen pals ever since I wrote this poem, but now my friend from Toronto is very sick. She is such a nice person and she has a real good sense of humour. She has told me all about her travels and sent post cards.

The last letter I had from her she was so full of fun and she described her view from her window. I forgot to say that she has been confined to her wheelchair and walker for a year or more.

As she described her view I made up a poem to send back to her and told her, whatever she saw and told me about, I would make it into a poem and send it to her. I didn't know then that I would never be able to write to her again because now she has since lost her memory and doesn't even recognize her own sister. She is also too sick to leave the hospital so they have put her in a home because her sister is unable to care for her due to sickness and her age.

"I am going to enclose the poem I wrote for her. It's entitled "Scenes From Mablel's Window." This lady became a very dear friend and I already miss her letters and her talks.

Sincerely,

Mrs. Edith Burrage, New Perlican, Newfoundland

Scenes From Mabel's Window

As I sit here by my window
Watching all the scenes below
Now my mind is apt to wander
To the scenes so long ago

Today the sun is brightly shining
And the grass a lovely green
There are times for which I'm pining
Things that now can never be

I can see the park below me
And the people there at work
Women there are very busy
Making flower beds in the park

There are people out there walking
Leisurely across the street
Walking puppies, yapping, yapping
At the people that they meet

All the scenes they pass before me
As I watch them come and go
Watching, watching, ever thinking
Of a time so long ago

Memories are precious keepsakes
And I'm storing them away
As I look out from my window
Sitting here from day to day

Dedicated to a dear friend Mabel Black, Toronto, who has been taken seriously ill. May God hold her in the palm of his hand. Edith

Life, Love & Laughter

Life, Love & Laughter

Spice of Life

Have you noticed how no man ever tells a woman she's talking too much when she's telling him how wonderful she is. – *Goldie Hawn*

♀

Ennellene

When you say that marriage left me in this contract fifty-fifty
I can tell you without laughing, "you can shove it"
No matter your intent, the rules for me were bent
And you never understood the halving of it

♀

 ## MABEL & MANLEY

When Mabel's husband Manley, died, his insurance company was very prompt on settling his life insurance and showed up at her door with a $250,000 cheque, less than 24 hours after he died.

"He was such a good husband," sobbed Mabel as she accepted the check, "that I'd give half of this money just to have him back right now."

♀

Animal Mating – Fact and Fantasy – *Ron Young*

Avoiding Labour Pains

Fact:

   Scientist, Karen Strier, has discovered that the female Muriqui (woolly spider monkey) of Brazil consumes a plant, known as monkey's ear (because of the shape of its leaf) as a means of birth control. The plant contains stirmasterol, a chemical that has similar properties as the pregnancy hormone progesterone. Scientists believe that these primates may have been practising birth control long before humans.

Fantasy:

   The dilemma of each nation
   Is a booming population
   Much unlike the Muriqui, who have no fear
   Their numbers have been stagnant
   And seldom they get pregnant
   Because they always chew on monkey ear

♀

Tickle and Bight   *By Lucy Fitzpatrick–McFarlane*

Shopper Smart

I love a good bargain, don't you? Just the sight of a flashing blue light or a big SALE sign in a store makes my heart do flip-flops. In the past year though, I just don't get out shopping much unless I absolutely have to get something, because I'm too darned busy all the time, but I call it being thrifty. Even as a youngster I was like that and it's not surprising, for we certainly didn't have spare money to spend on anything. If someone gave me a dime back then, I thought carefully before I ever parted with it. Course we didn't have the opportunity to do comparison shopping back in the Cove then, for there were just two shops. It was either Rob Lambe's or Jim Harnett's store, although later on when I was a teenager, a Co-op store opened. Most of the time I'd go to Rob Lambe's, put my dime on the counter and ask

if I could have ten coppers. It always looked like so much more in the palm of my hand and then I could go from one shop to another and spend a penny here and there, at my own discretion. Now I don't want to brag, but I pride myself on being what I call 'Shopper Smart,' because I like to get my money's worth. I don't purposely go looking for a sale, but if I'm buying something for myself or for the house, then I have no qualms about purchasing a sale item. However, I do have my standards when it comes to buying a gift for somebody else, for I always pay the regular price. Besides, I wouldn't want to risk getting my name besmirched if they had to return the item and find out I bought it on sale. Heaven forbid that should happen.

Now, if I buy something for myself at regular price in the clothing line, and discover, as often happens, that the same item is on sale a week later, I'll take it back to the store and exchange it. It makes sense to me to get the money back so it can be put to better use, but trying to make my husband understand that I'm actually saving him money is another story. He maintains that I buy things just because they're on sale and it's usually something that we have no use for. Naturally I don't agree with that, and besides, I've only done that a few times that I remember. Just after Christmas this year, for instance, I went to the mall to get wallpaper. As usual, I went to look around Wal-Mart and spent almost two hours rummaging through the sale bins. When I got home, Murray stuck his head out around the kitchen door. "Well, how did you make out?" he asked.

"Oh, I got some great bargains," I said, putting the four bags on the table, "Wait 'til you see all the stuff I got!"

"Can you show me later because I want to get started on the wallpaper," he said as he opened one of the bags. "Where is it?"

Good night...I totally forgot the wallpaper! I knew I had a purpose for going to the mall, but I got so caught up in the sales, that I never even reached the wallpaper store. Feeling very annoyed at myself, I tried to stall and pulled out a little plastic do-jigger. "Look what I got for you to put

Life, Love & Laughter

in the vegetable patch," I said. "See, the little flaps move when the wind blows and it scares the birds away. What a buy that was...only $1.25, eh?"

"We don't have a vegetable patch," he said dryly, "and the back yard is snowed in. Which bag did you put the wallpaper in?"

"...Uhh...ummmm, well, there's no rush to get the paper done tonight..." I began.

Murray looked at me scow-ways. "Let me guess...you forgot to get the paper and you spent the money on all this stuff we'll never use...right?"

Well, what can I say? The very next morning I went back to Colour Your World and as luck should have it, I found exactly what I was looking for...and 50% off too, so in the long run, I got twice as much for my money. Course my dear husband maintains that I make a profit everytime he buys me a gift because often I return things, as I've said...but only if I can save money. He has his own theory on the way I operate, but I'll let him tell you his version further down the page. But just so you'll give me the benefit of a doubt, let me explain what happened. I've admitted that I love to get a good bargain, but I don't go searching for a sale. Oh, no. You know how some women go to a health spa or a salon to get all dickied up when they feel down in the dumps? Well, for me, a little shopping spree cheers me up. It's the thought of doing it that counts, for often I'll hop in the car, go to a mall and spend hours just window shopping or trying on clothes that I have no intention of buying. Most of the time I'll come home empty-handed or I'll just buy something small, like a pair of knee-highs or a box of Q-tips. "You mean after being out shopping all day this is all you bought?" Murray will ask.

I think men just don't understand how we women can just go shopping for the sake of shopping. Now, if Murray needs something, he concentrates on that one item, marches into the store, goes straight to the item, buys it and is back home before I can blow my nose. What fun is there in that, I ask you? And he never seems to understand why I take things back to exchange at the store, but I did promise him I'd let him have his say in his own words, so the following is his version of what happened with the gift he bought for me this Christmas:

"Lucy is unique. She makes money from every gift I buy for her. Although I can do reasonably well choosing clothes for her, I know it doesn't really matter if she likes it or not because she WILL return it. And the more they cost originally, the better. You see, Lucy is such a great shopper that she not only returns items, getting more in quantity in return, but she usually pockets a great deal of the money. This year, I bought her a two-piece suit that cost $199. Two days later she saw the same suit at a different store for $129, so she returned the original suit bought at the other store, and instead of giving me back my money, she put the $70 plus tax back into her own wallet. The day after, she saw a suit at a different mall that she liked better which was listed at $190.00 and which happened to be on sale for $49. Back went the $129 suit and she bought the $49 special and added a matching blouse and two sweaters on sale for $35. So, into her pocket goes another $45 or $50. As you can see, I put out the $199 originally, Lucy ends up with a great suit, two sweaters, a blouse and about $120 cash.

But, I did get my payback though, because she got caught returning one item that I gave her. I received a free gift (an alarm clock), for opening up an account in a store, so I wrapped it up and put it under the tree for Lucy. When she asked where I bought the clock, I told her, but I had no idea she would return it as I had no sales bill for it. On one of her 20 trips to the mall looking for sales, she took the clock and tried to get the money back, but was informed that it was a free gift. She actually called me a cheapskate and once her pride let her bring the subject up again, I was informed that from now on if I am to buy her a present, that she'd like me to pay cash for everything, or at least give her the money and let her buy for herself. To this day, my wife will never admit that she makes money on everything I buy for her and I daresay I'll never live long enough to hear her admit to that. I can't wait to see how much profit she'll get when I choose her gift for Valentine's day this year. I wonder...will she be able to return a box of chocolates?"

Humph...have I got news for him!

He's already bought my Valentine's gift, but he doesn't know it yet. You see, I was browsing through the mall the other day and I saw this great sale I just couldn't resist. You'd be surprised how many thing I can get in a 70% off sale, and not even Murray will complain about the amount of money I spent when he sees all the stuff I got tucked away in the closet. I can't wait to see the look on his face.

♀

Food for Thought

The first idea that the child must acquire, in order to be actively disciplined, is that of the difference between good and evil; and the task of the educator lies in seeing that the child does not confound good with immobility and evil with activity.   – *Maria Montessori*

♀

Life's Funny Experiences
More Than Just Hair

When my oldest son was eight, he decided he was going to have a bath all by himself one Saturday night, so I told him to go ahead. I was busy getting ready for Sunday, so he was just about ready to get out of the tub when I finally checked on him. I noticed that the bottle of Head and Shoulders shampoo, which had been full earlier, was now empty. I was upset that he had used the whole bottle and told him so. As a matter of fact, I grumbled for several minutes about the fact that there were three more children who had to get a bath, and that he shouldn't be so wasteful. When there was finally a lull in my muttering, and he could get a word in, he said, "But Mom, by the time I got my shoulders done there was nothing left!"

Carol Hancock – Roddickton, Newfoundland.

♀

Her Other Half
Not Late for the Wedding

An 81-year-old man from Newfoundland applied to participate in the track event in the upcoming Newfoundland and Labrador Summer Games.

"Don't you think you're too old for this kind of activity?" asked the surprised official.

"Not at all," replied the Octogenarian, "My father is 102, and he was going to sign up too, but my grandfather is getting married and Dad is best man at his wedding today."

"Well how old is your grandfather?"

"He's123."

"I can't imagine that a man of that age would want to get married."

"Want to get married?" Grandfather didn't want to get married, he had to get married."

♀

Ennellene

I think that when God made man to live upon this land
The plan for man was really not that sound
And when God did create, for womankind a mate
I think She was only in the mood for foolin' 'round

♀

Her Other Half

Little Gift

"I'd like a small bottle of Chanel No. 5," the man told the salesclerk at the perfume counter. "It's for my wife's birthday.
  "A little surprise?" inquired the clerk
  "Yes, a little surprise," responded the man, "She's expecting a cruise."

♀

Female Firsts

1989: Chan Heng Chee became Singapore's first female ambassador, when she was appointed permanent representative to the United Nations.

1989: Chris Evert became the first tennis player, male or female, to reach 1,000 wins.

1990: On March 9th, Antonia Novello became the first woman and the first Hispanic to be appointed Surgeon General of the U.S.

1990: In June, when Bernadette Locke joined the University of Kentucky as an assistant coach to Rick Pitino, she became the first female Division I coach of a men's basketball team in the U.S.

1990: The first International Ice Hockey Federation Women's World Championship were held in Ottawa, Ontario. Team Canada beat the U.S. team 5-2.

1990: Martina Navratilova became the first woman in history to win Wimbledon nine times.

1991: Khaleda Zia became the first female Prime Minister of Bangladesh.

1991: Gertrude Elion became the first woman inducted into the U.S. National Inventors Hall of Fame.

1991: Hassiba Boulmerka, who was born in Algeria, became the first woman from an Arabic or African nation to win a world track championship when she won a gold medal in the 1,500 meters at the world track and field championships in Tokyo.

1992: Skeet shooter Zhang Shan of China became the first woman to earn a gold medal in a mixed shooting event.

♀

Life, Love & Laughter

Spice of Life

Oh, to be only half as wonderful as my child thought I was when he was small, and only half as stupid as my teenager now thinks I am.   *– Rebecca Richards*

♀

WOMEN OF THE ISLAND AND THE BIG LAND

Patricia Murphy

During the 1970s, Patricia (Murphy) Kiernan would often pilot her own private aircraft from New York to Florida, spend a few days resting at her 48-acre luxury estate, and then return to New York to operate her multi-million dollar restaurant-chain business.

Mrs. Kiernan was a successful New York businesslady who had received the rare Papal Honour of Lady of the Equestrian Order of the Holy Sepulchre of Jerusalem. Her story is of interest to Newfoundlanders because Mrs. Kiernan was the former Patricia Murphy of Placentia Bay.

She first arrived in New York during the fall of 1929 with a scholarship to study music. She had been born during the early 1900s, the daughter of Frank Murphy, a general-store operator at Placentia. Shortly after arriving in New York, while living with her uncle, she decided to drop her music studies and strike out on her own. She rented a furnished room in Manhatten for $4 a week, and got several part-time jobs. These included playing the piano during lunch hours at a restaurant near Columbia University, working in a cafeteria, and hand-colouring postcards at $3 a hundred.

One day in 1929, at the start of the depression, she dropped in for her usual 45-cent lunch at the Step-In Restaurant in Manhatten. But the restaurant had gone out of business. She decided to operate the business herself, and made arrangements to rent the place for $25 per week. She changed the name to the Candlelight and introduced her own speciality, called popovers. In 1938, she purchased a second restaurant in Manhatten and later another on Long Island. Eventually, she had a chain of ten luxurious Candlelight restaurants, with her main restaurant catering to one million customers a year. She also owned several gift shops in Florida.

At one of her restaurants she had an 800-car parking-lot, with a special limousine shuttling-service to take customers to the main entrance. It included a pond, a bridge, and a dazzling assortment of flowers and plants.

She married a New York stock broker in 1930 but that marriage was annulled. In 1948, she met Navy Captain James E. Kiernan at a New Year's Eve party. They were married shortly afterwards, but Kiernan died in 1954.

Patricia owned a spectacular estate in Florida, which included greenhouses, a swimming pool, a marble cabana, and 48 acres of floral beauty, illuminated at night by thousands of lights.

She had a special interest in horticulture, specializing in orchids. She extracted perfume from them and marketed the perfume under the names of Green Orchid, Gold Orchid and Regina Rose.

Patricia Murphy won recognition in this field, and for her outstanding flowers, won numerous awards, including a commendation from Queen Wilhelmina of the Netherlands.

From the book, Strange But True Newfoundland Stories, *by Jack Fitzgerald, published by Creative Publishing. Used by permission.*

♀

Life, Love & Laughter

The Lady and The Pirates

I'm indebted to Mrs. Doctor V.P. Burke for this amazingly interesting pirate story of old-time Newfoundland. It concerns a Newfoundland woman named Lucretia Parker, and whether Lucretia Parker has any descendants living in this country today, or whether any descendants of the same family are living here now, I'm afraid I can't say. This story occurred in the year 1825, so it could be that Lucretia was the great-grandmother of some of the present-day generation of Parkers.

*****

It seems that one of her brothers, Thomas Parker, had purchased a plantation and was making his home in Antigua, one of the more southerly of the West Indian Islands. He wrote to his sister Lucretia in St. John's, where she was living, and where in all probability, he had previously been living himself, asking her to take passage to Antigua to live with him and his wife. And accordingly, on February 28, 1825, Miss Parker took passage aboard the sloop *Eliza Ann*, whose captain was a man named Charles Smith.

They had a favourable wind from the time they left Newfoundland, and it looked as though the trip was going to prove quite a humdrum and uneventful one. Little did Captain Smith and his men dream that they were on their last voyage – that never again would they set eyes on Newfoundland – that within a fortnight they would all be dead.

On the 14th day out from St. John's they sighted a small schooner standing toward them, with her deck swarming with men. They knew at once that it was a pirate ship. The pirate ship ran up alongside them, and in an instant the deck of the sloop was crowded with blood-thirsty cut-throats armed with pistols, cutlasses and knives. Without ceremony the pirates fell on the sloop's small crew, and the scene was a bedlam of curses and blows.

Lucretia Parker fell on her knees and began to pray. From the one pirate who seemed to be master of the others she begged for mercy – begged to have her life spared. The pirate captain heeded her pleas, and led her to the companionway and ordered her below into the cabin, and locked the door of the companionway behind her. From her position in the cabin she could hear the shouts and curses on deck, and concluded that the crew of the *Eliza Ann* were being butchered by the buccaneers.

After she had been there for more than an hour the noise died down, and then the door of the companionway opened and down came eight or 10 of the pirates, led by their captain, pouring into the cabin. But they were only looking for the money they supposed the captain of the sloop had hidden there–they made no move whatever to molest their female captive. Then the pirates returned to the deck and, leaving so many aboard to sail the sloop, went back to their own schooner.

Lucretia Parker had no idea of what was happening, or whether the two vessels were bound, till at length they arrived at a small island which proved to be the pirates' rendezvous. Then she learned that the captain and crew of the *Eliza Ann* had not been murdered, for when the sloop's hatches were removed, the men came up on deck in response to the pirate captain's order. They had been in the hold of the sloop all the time. But it was not in the pirates' minds to spare them –

Life, Love & Laughter

far from it. As soon as they had all landed on the island, the brutal buccaneers began to torture the men. Captain Smith was killed instantly with a knife thrust. Others were killed with blows from clubs. Lucretia Parker was forced to look on while the entire crew of the sloop was butchered. Then she was taken into a shack and locked in.

On the following morning the pirate captain appeared in the cabin. He was nearly six feet in height, of a swarthy complexion, with black and penetrating eyes – she never learned of his nationality, but it was plain to see that all the pirates – there were forty of them – stood in considerable awe of him. At sight of him she fell on her knees and began to pray again, and after gazing intently at her he left the shack again. She spent a terribly uneasy day and night, and on the following morning the pirate chief again visited her. But he had no sooner entered the shack than there was the sound of a bugle-call. It was the signal from the pirate stationed on the look-out that there was a sail in sight, and instantly the captain turned about and left again. Mustering up her courage, Lucretia Parker stood up on a box to peer through the window, and a glad sight it was that greeted her eyes. A short distance from the island she spied a vessel which appeared to be lying to, and a few miles to windward of her another, which appeared to be bearing down toward her under press of sail. She hoped it might mean rescue – and the pirates who knew what the two ships were, began a feverish activity. All but four of them jumped into their small boats and rushed to get to their own schooner with a view to making their escape before the British warship could cut them off.

By the time, however, they had reached the schooner and begun to get her underway, the two warships had opened fire on them. Some of them jumped into the water to swim ashore, but every man of them was captured and taken aboard the two British ships. But to her anguished disappointment they turned about and departed without coming on the island, and here she was left alone in the charge of the four pirates who still remained on the island.

Perhaps it was the fright they'd got from the appearance of the British warships, and the capture of their buddies, but in any event, the four remaining pirates changed their attitude toward the Newfoundland girl, and they announced their intention of getting away from the island as quickly as they could, and to get her to some place of safety.

One of the four pirates was an Englishman, and he told her his story, claiming that he had been forced into piracy. He told her that the pirate band had captured and plundered dozens of vessels. The plunder they'd sent to somebody on one of the populated islands of the West Indies to sell for them. Once their decision to leave the island was taken, the four men set about demolishing the remaining shacks, and then dug up a hole in the earth from which they took several bags of money, which they put aboard their boat. They took her with them and set sail. About midnight they landed her on the shore of another island, which they told her was Cuba, gave her some water and hard biscuit, and directions as to what direction to take when she landed.

That was the last she ever saw or heard of them, and to make a long story short, she followed their instructions and came to an isolated house, whose occupants she guessed, were friends of the pirates, and the man of this house took her to the Cuban town of Mantansies, where she found many Americans and Europeans. She struck passage on a vessel bound to Jamaica, and in Jamaica, where she was treated with the greatest possible kindness and consideration by the Governor and officials, she had the last installment of her thrilling and gruesome adventure. She discovered that the thirty-six pirates captured by the two British warships had been brought here, and were then lying in jail awaiting trial! She was asked to accompany the officials to the prison to see if she could identify them. She recognized the pirate captain and most of the others, and through her evidence they were all sentenced – seven of them to execution by hanging, the others to various other forms of punishment. Lucretia Parker was invited by the Governor to stay and witness the execution of the seven condemned men – they had queer ideas about hanging in those old days – but she'd had enough horror to last her a lifetime, and she firmly declined.

After spending nine days in Jamaica she was lucky enough to obtain a passage with a Captain Ellsmore direct to St. John's, where she arrived back safe and sound after one of the most thrilling and adventurous experiences it has even been the fate of a woman to undergo, in Newfoundland or any other country. Lucretia Paker afterwards wrote the story of her adventures while a captive of the pirate gang, and published it as a pamphlet, and all the facts given have been compiled from that publication.

From the book, Strange But True Newfoundland Stories, *by Jack Fitzgerald. Creative Publishing. Used by permission.*

♀

Ennellene

"If you can't telegraph, telephone - tell a woman"
And other past put-downs as such
Have been given the can, 'cause you can tell a man
But you really can't tell him that much

♀

Female Firsts

1992: For the first time ever, girls won all three divisions in the All-American Soap Box Derby.

1992: In October, Ann E. Bancroft led the first all-women's expedition across Antarctica to the South Pole. She and her four female companions, Kellie Erwin-Rhoades, Sue Giller, Luch Smith and Anne Dal Vera, covered the 1,700 miles of ice cap using skis and sleds pulled by huge parasails. The trip took four months.

1992: Carol Moseley-Braun became the first black woman ever to be elected to the United States Senate.

1993: Queen Elizabeth II became the first British monarch to pay income tax.

1993: Tansu Ciller became Turkey's first female prime minister.

1993: Kim Campbell became the first woman leader of Canada's Progressive Conservative Party.

1993: Anson Chan became the first woman and the first Chinese to hold the post of Deputy Governor of Hong Kong.

1993: Canada's refugee guidelines were changed to include women facing gender-related persecution.

1993: Julie Krone became the first woman jockey to win a Triple Crown race, riding Colonial Affair in the Belmont Stakes.

♀

Is That a Fact?
Many things are taken as facts. Not all of them are.

Women Have More Money
In America, men are still the biggest money makers and as such are richer than women.

The Fact Is that between 70 and 80 per cent of the wealth of the U.S. is owned by women. This is mostly due to the fact that husbands die earlier than their wives, leaving all their worldly goods to their widows.

♀

Aunt Alice says:

I gave up jogging for my health when my thighs kept rubbing together and setting my pantyhose on fire.

Spice of Life
I have yet to hear a man ask for advice on how to combine marriage and a career.
– *Gloria Steinem*

♀

Quillings

The Mighty Rock
By Barbara (Reynolds) Somers, Fort McMurray, Alberta, formerly of Western Bay, Newfoundland

To say farewell to "The Mighty Rock"
was all that I could do,
as I packed my bags
and headed home feeling rather blue

My morning strolls along the beach
as I watched the seagulls soar,
with the taste of salt upon my lips
and forever wanting more

Binoculars glued to my piercing eyes
I viewed the ocean wide
and watched the many humpback whales
swimming side-by-side

The treasured visits with my friends,
as I dropped in for a tea,
they always have the kettle on,
expecting company

It was a special year for celebrations
from every port and shore,
reunions, picnics, folk festivals,
who could ask for more

It was an exceptional time this summer
for the people of Newfoundland
where once stood our forefathers,
now, indeed we stand

It was a sad time for our classmates though,
as we said our last goodbye,
a final chapter now is closed,
but will never die

Fond memories of Newfoundland,
savor every moment in your heart,
Never let them fade with the passing years,
never let your soul depart.

♀

Life, Love & Laughter

Spice of Life

Oh! The good old days when I was so unhappy. - *Sophie Arnould*

♀

☺ Some Mothers Have Them

"You're home from school early today," Jackson's mother said as he walked in the door, "Did everyone get off early?"

"No just me, Mom, I got the right answer to the question."

"What question was that, Jackson?"

"Who put the glue on Miss Wilkinson's chair?"

♀

Animal Mating - Fact and Fantasy – *Ron Young*

What a Shot

Fact:

The Eastern Spotted Skunk does not have the sexual "staying-power" of some other mammals. Its coital coupling with his mate lasts only a minute, but his "ready-again" power is better than many. He can hang around for up to 20 repeat performances. The mating season for this species of skunk peaks in April, but can go on throughout July if the female is capable of having a second litter. Throughout this time the male's testosterone levels are higher and his testes bigger than normal. When wishing to mate, the male will chase the female and grabbing by the back of her neck, guide her into a lying position on her side, beside him, where they mate. During mating season, male skunks develop a condition known to scientists as "mating madness." Skunks showing signs of this condition will spray any large animal they encounter.

The eastern spotted skunk is the only skunk capable of climbing trees, and is noted for its handstand method of spraying other creatures with its noxious-smelling odour. It will stand on its front paws and lifting its back legs and anal area in the air, turn its head back to aim its "weapon" directly at the face of its intended victim. Lucky for humans this skunk is nocturnal, making walking in the woods during the day fairly safe from the vileness of this animal, especially males that may be suffering from "mating madness."

Fantasy:

If your intended thesis
Is on the spotted species
Of the Eastern as it procreates its race
And you find a male handstanding
Aiming at the place you're standing
Just remember that his weapon's much like mace
And he never aims to please
When he aims to cut the cheese
So for heaven's sake remember, "Hide your face!"

♀

Food for Thought

You better live your best and act your best and think your best today; for today is the sure preparation for tomorrow and all the other tomorrows that follow.
– Harriet Martineau

♀

Is That a Fact?
Many things are taken as facts. Not all of them are.

Women Are Better At Math
It is traditionally believed that in math especially, men are better than women.

The Fact Is a 1990 study that tested more than 4 million students, showed that female students scored higher than male students in math.

♀

Aunt Alice says:

I wish the buck stopped here - I sure could use a few.

Spice of Life

A woman is like a teabag, you never know how strong she is until she gets in hot water.
– Eleanor Roosevelt

♀

Life's Funny Experiences
Hush Little Baby

I was a mother who breast-fed my babies—some were over a year old before they quit. They ate solid food, but still needed the comfort of being cuddled and nursed.

So one day my daughter and I took my 11-month-old son to visit my mom in St. John's. When we got the bus for home to Foxtrap there weren't many people on-board, but two very well dressed ladies were sitting ahead of us. The baby started getting snuggly around me. It was getting dark and everyone on the bus was chatting so I thought it was a good time to nurse him, as I really needed to get rid of it myself. Well, he was nursing away until we went over a bump in the road, and he pushed my breast away so quick that it spurted some milk on the side of one of the nice lady's faces in the seat ahead of us. She screamed and of course the baby stood up on my lap and my blouse dropped down. The driver stopped, turned on the lights and said, "What's wrong lady?"

"Someone peed on me!" she screamed "The baby did it!"

I said, "Lady, he's got pampers on and little jeans with the straps in place."

She glared at a few men on the bus and said, "Someone peed on me."

Everyone was laughing all the way home. I felt bad for the poor woman, everyone thought she was dreaming — she kept wiping her face all the way to Kelligrews.

Myra Pearline Porter – Foxtrap, Newfoundland

♀

Life, Love & Laughter

Women Who Have Made A Difference – *By Ron Young*

Aduke Alakija, who was born in 1921, was a member of the Nigerian delegation to the United Nations (1961-1965), and a trustee of the Federal Nigeria Society for the Blind and of the International Women's Society. She was also Adviser to the International Academy of Trial Lawyers, the first black African woman Director of Mobil Oil, and President of the International Federation of Women Lawyers (FIDA).

Mary Anderson, who was born in Linköping, Sweden in 1872, at the age of 16 emigrated to the U.S., where her first job was washing dishes at a boarding house for lumberjacks in Michigan. She later found a job at an Illinois shoe factory, where she became a union executive. In 1920, she was made first Director of the Women's Bureau of the Department of Labor, the first working woman to rise through union activities to a government position.

Corazon Cojuangco Aquino took over as President of the Republic of the Philippines, one of the world's most volatile nations, two and one half years after her husband's assassination on August 21, 1983. At the time she was a politically inexperienced homemaker and mother of four daughters and one son. What is even more impressive, she maintained her power and fortitude despite several attempts to take away her leadership. President Aquino's awards and distinctions are numerous, some include: Woman of the Year, *Time* magazine; the Eleanor Roosevelt Human Rights Award, the United Nations Silver Medal, as well as the Canadian International Prize for Freedom.

♀

🖋 Quillings

The Song of the Shirt   *By Thomas Hood*

With fingers weary and worn,
With eyelids heavy and red,
A woman sat, in unwomanly rags,
Plying her needle and thread,
Stitch! stitch! stitch!
In poverty, hunger and dirt
And in a voice of dolorous pitch
She sang the "Song of the Shirt"

"Work - work - work
'Til the brain begins to swim!
Work - work - work
'Til the eyes are heavy and dim!
Seam and gusset, and band
Band, and gusset, and seam
'Til over the buttons I fall asleep
And sew them in a dream

"O men, with sisters dear!
O men, with mothers and wives!
It is not linen you're wearing out,
But human creatures' lives
Stitch - stitch - stitch
In poverty, hunger, and dirt,
Sewing at once, with a double thread,
A shroud as well as a shirt!

"But why do I talk of death -
That phantom of grisly bone?
I hardly fear his terrible shape,
It seems so like my own
It seems so like my own
Because of the fasts I keep:
O God that bread should be so dear,
And flesh and blood so cheap!"

♀

Life, Love & Laughter

Food for Thought

However dull a woman may be, she will understand all there is in love; however intelligent a man may be, he will never know but half of it. – *Madame Fee*

♀

Ennellene

Get rid of your man
If he's nothing but trouble
But before you remarry, remember
Present trouble, could double

♀

Spice of Life

I am a marvelous housekeeper. Every time I leave a man I keep his house.

– *Zsa Zsa Gabor*

♀

Feminine Words & Phrases

Madonna: Meaning 'my lady' in Italian, this title is usually applied to the Virgin Mary.

Maiden: A type of guillotine used in the 16th and 17th centuries for beheading criminals.

Marriage made in heaven: Implying that people getting married were preordained to be together.

Mary of Arnhem: Real name Helen Sensburg. She broadcasted Nazi propaganda to the British troops in northwest Europe between 1944 and 1945.

Mother-sick: Pining for one's mother.

Mother-wit: Quick-wittedness, which one is said to have gotten from mother.

♀

Animal Mating - Fact and Fantasy – *Ron Young*

The Love Song of the Eastern Whipbird

Fact:

"If I could sing like Bing, I could do my thing," is probably the theme song of the Eastern Whipbird of Australia. After about 100 hours of taped recordings of singing by five pairs of eastern whipbirds in captivity, zookeeper Tristen Bird of Adelaide Zoo, and his colleague, Dr. Greg Johnson, have electronically analysed the recordings and discovered that the better the singing of the male, the more receptive his mate was to sex. The more bass it was, the more the female liked the singing. She was not as turned on by the higher notes.

Fantasy:

If you wish to copulate with your lovely whipbird mate
Don't take your music lessons from a tenor
But if musically you know, just how low to go
With your music-loving mate you'll be a winner

♀

Life, Love & Laughter

Spice of Life

Conversation must have been difficult between Adam and Eve at times because they had nobody to talk about. – *Agnes Reppler*

♀

Life's Funny Experiences
Hair-don't

Many years ago, my dad and his brother were walking down the street in Sept-Iles, Quebec, where they were working. A woman walked passed them sporting a new and very popular hair-do. "Now, that's what I would called teased!" my dad exclaimed, as she walked past them. "Go on b'y," said my uncle, "I wouldn't call that teased, I'd call that tormented!"

Ivy Bromley – Quebec

♀

Animal Mating - Fact and Fantasy – *Ron Young*
Gender Choice

Fact:

Can the female Howler Monkey decide the sex of the baby she conceives? Dr. Ken Glander of Duke University believes she can. Over two decades Glander watched female howler monkeys eat certain plants, before and after copulation, that they don't usually eat. During the long study, he found out that some females gave birth to only boy howlers, while others gave birth to only girls, an outcome unlikely to be a coincidence.

Fantasy:

A female Howler received the following written marriage proposal from a male she had been dating.

"I'm tired of being a prowler
So I propose, Ms. Howler
That we should wed and live our life as one
Except I thought that maybe
We could have a baby
And since you have a choice, I'd like a son

Here is the written answer he received...
Now that you have made a reference
To the baby of your preference
Before our coupling life even begins
The question makes me queasy
'Cause raisin' babies, sure ain't easy
But I'll marry you if you don't ask for twins

♀

Spice of Life

A self-made man is one who believes in luck and sends his sons to Oxford.

– Christina Stead

♀

Her Other Half
Money-Back Guarantee

"I listened to your sermon about it being a great sin to profit from the mistakes of others," one of the male parishioners told the priest after mass, "and I wondered if I could get a refund of the fee you charged me for marrying me to the wife?"

♀

Life's Funny Experiences
Got to Get Me Moose!

I was living in Newfoundland and had waited a year to apply for a set of moose tags. After not receiving any notification in the mail, I decided to phone the Department of Wildlife in St. John's. The receptionist answered and said: "Department of Wildlife, how may I hurt you? Oh my God, I mean, help you."

Jacinta Cormier, Edmonton, Alberta

♀

Female Firsts

1993: Jean Augustine, who was born in Grenada, became the first African Canadian woman elected to the Parliament of Canada. *See also page 178.*

1994: Chandrika Kumaratunga, of Sri Lanka, became the first president of a country whose parents had both been presidents of the country.

1994: Cassie Clark and Stephanie Brody became the first two women on a men's national junior weightlifting squad.

1995: On February 2, Eileen Collins became the first American woman to pilot a spacecraft.

1995: When Kerri McTiernan was hired to coach men's basketball at Kingsboro Community College in Brooklyn, she became the first female ever to coach a men's team at such a high level.

1995: Barbara J. Easterling became the first woman in history to serve as secretary-treasurer of the AFL-CIO, the 13-million member federation of labor unions.

1996: Germany's Uta Pippig became the first female to win the Boston Marathon for a third consecutive year.

1996: Christina Sanchez became Europe's first qualified woman bullfighter at age 24.

♀

Life, Love & Laughter

Spice of Life

He who laughs, lasts.
    – *Mary Pettibone Poole*
    ♀

Female Facts

Female-run businesses are more likely to remain in business than the average U.S. firm.   ♀

Life, Love & Laughter

WOMEN OF THE ISLAND AND THE BIG LAND

Innu – A Way of Life

Sheilagh Harvey of Wabush, Labrador, is the artist behind a series of paintings depicting the Innu Culture. The project was inspired by old photographs taken in the 1920's and 1930's by Monsignor Edward O'Brien.

It was an undertaking that soon required help. There was a lot to learn and even from the onset of the first painting, the Innu were there to provide much needed information.

"Bart Jack, David Huke and George Gregoire, whom I met by chance (or so it seemed at the time), came to my home; they began naming the people in the photos and explaining some of what was happening in them. That made everything so much more real," says Harvey.

Courtesy Sheilagh Harvey

With their continued encouragement she went on to complete 10 of the 20 watercolours. At which time she felt it necessary to bring the paintings to Sheshatshit where she met with some of the elders and Chief Greg Andrew, as well as Greg Penashue.

"I was happy with the trust they extended my way and since then whenever I became stuck or needed direction, someone from the Innu Community was there."

Judy Hill researched and wrote stories in both Innu and English to accompany each painting. Mary Anne Michel told Harvey stories of the old ways; Simon Michel explained about the "drum" and Mary Jane Nui, along with Madeline Michelin, helped her experience some of their culture by teaching Harvey to make a pair of moccasins for her grandson.

Three years passed all too quickly. Now armed with 20 watercolours and a lithograph, she was part of the exhibition "Labrador on the Edge," held at the CBC building in Toronto in November 1996.

Harvey says the encouragement from the Innu Community coupled with the support from family, friends, businesses, towns and other sponsorships was overwhelming.

"There was so much to be done and without that kind of help it could not have been accomplished."

Harvey will be giving ownership of the paintings to the Innu Nation to promote and preserve the Innu culture.

♀

Female Facts

In 1977, less than 9% of U.S. doctors were women.

♀

Ennellene

With a woman, a man
Could command centre stage
By remembering her birthday
And forgetting her age

♀

Spice of Life

The hardest years in life are those between 10 and 70.

– Helen Hayes (at 73)

♀

Feminine Words & Phrases

Bun: The bun a woman creates when she puts her long hair up at the back, did not get its name from baked buns, but from the way it resembled the tail of the bunny.

Bun in the oven: A reference to a pregnant woman.

Bunny girl: A woman who appears at functions in bathing-suit-like apparel, to serve food and/or drinks to groups where men are present. Some even wear false bunny ears and bunny tails.

Gardy loo: Edenburgh housewives and servants yelled this out before they dumped the contents of their slop bucket out from their windows into the street below. It probably comes from the French gare de l'eau (watch out for the water).

Land-girl: A female who was recruited for farm work during WWI and WWII. In WWII they were organized as the Woman's Land Army.

Mermaid: A creature which is half woman half fish. The belief in mermaids may have come from sailors watching a dugong, a member of the whale family. Like all whales, dolphins and porpoises, the dugong suckles its young like humans do, but unlike other whales the dugong has a head somewhat similar to human features.

Petticoat Merchant: A female fish merchant in Newfoundland.

Morganatic Marriage: A marriage where a woman of lower class marries a man of royal rank, or a rank higher than her own. In a Morganatic Marriage, the wife does not acquire the husband's rank. She is not entitled to inherit any of his possessions, nor is any of their children.

Widow's peak: The V-shaped of the peak of the cap once worn by widows gave its name to the V-shaped disappearance of men's hair from the forehead back.

Sweater girl: Term used for a woman who was well enough endowed with breasts to demonstrate the stretchy qualities of wool.

♀

Life, Love & Laughter

Life, Love & Laughter

Spice of Life

A man of courage never needs weapons, but he may need bail. – *Ethel Watts Mumford*

♀

The Whys of Men

Why did God make men before women?
Because a rough draft was needed before the final copy could be made.

♀

Ennellene

For courtin' we'd be more keen, if treated more like Queen
If men who, like the Queen's Prince Charming, got it right
He offered her his honour, and she honoured his offer
Which he offered often, on, into the night

♀

Animal Mating – Fact and Fantasy – *Ron Young*

Just Being Crabby

Fact:

Like the lobster, the female Crab of some species must remove her outer shell before mating. Before she manages to "get her clothes off" however, the male will grab her and take her off to some place where there will be no competitors around when her chastity belt is gone. Before long however, the couple are joined by another couple, and another couple, and more and more, until the two or three feet high mound of mating crabs can be a thousand or more.

But do they change partners during this orgy of copulation? A reliable source says, "Moulting crabs are protected in the centre of the heap and males are always on standby for the receptive females." The same source gives some idea of how long this orgy lasts, "The mounds can stay in one place for months over the summer."

Fantasy:

If you're waiting for your mate
Who lately stays out late
And your own hungry heart could use some grub
Don't sit around and moan
In your domicile alone
Get yourself a life and join the club

♀

Women Who Have Made A Difference – *By Ron Young*

Rhonda Fleming Mann is not only a famed film, television and stage actress, with more than 50 appearances to her credit, she is also a wife, mother, humanitarian and philanthropist. Dealing with a sister, who had cancer, taught Rhonda the compassion needed to find an effective means to take care of the emotional, spiritual and psychosocial aspects of people with the disease. To provide the comprehensive care that Rhonda had otherwise found missing, she, along with her husband, Ted Mann, established the Rhonda Fleming Mann Clinic for Comprehensive Care at the UCLA Medical Center, as well as the Rhonda Fleming Mann Research Fellowship at the City of Hope, to advance research and treatment associated with women's cancer.

Emily Dunning Barringer earned a medical degree in 1901 from the Cornell University Medical School in New York City, graduating second in her class. She later applied for a position at the Gouverneur Hospital in New York. The position was denied her because she was a woman. Later, Dr. Dunning re-applied to the hospital and, this time, she was accepted, although the (male) medical interns in the city had petitioned against this appointment. From 1903 to 1905 she worked as an ambulance surgeon. In June 1903, when she went on her first emergency call in an ambulance, some doctors at the hospital cheered her on but many were hostile toward her. In 1905, she joined the hospital staff as a surgeon and was the first woman in a New York City hospital to occupy this position.

Indira Gandhi, before becoming India's third President, joined the National Congress party and became active in India's independence movement. Ghandi, along with her husband, Feroze Gandhi, were arrested by the British on charges of subversion and spent 13 months in prison. When India gained independence in 1947, her father, Jawaharlal Nehru, became the country's first president and, Indira, whose mother had died in 1936, became her father's official hostess and confidante on national problems, accompanying him on foreign trips.

In 1955, she was elected to the executive body of the Congress party, becoming a national political figure in her own right; in 1959 she became president of the party for one year. In 1962, during the Chinese-Indian border war, she coordinated civil defense activities. When her father died in 1964, Indira became minister of information and broadcasting in the government of his successor, Lal Bahadur Shastri. Upon Shastri's death, she became prime minister, and in 1971 led her party to a landslide victory. Her party was defeated in 1977 and Indira lost her own seat, but in 1980 she made a spectacular comeback and was able to form a new majority government.

On October 31, 1984, after she had moved vigorously to suppress Sikh insurgents, she was shot to death by Sikh members of her own security guard.

♀

Spice of Life

With today's prenuptial agreements, it would be virtually impossible for a marriage to be made in heaven.

♀

Spice of Life

When women's lib started, I was the first to burn my bra and it took three days to put out the fire.

– *Dolly Parton*

♀

Ennellene

We've come a long way to get to this day
And its status, which further enhances
The working woman's chance, to survive and advance
While rejecting male colleagues' advances

♀

# Aphrodesia

At a dinner party the ladies present were discussing Aphrodesia, a woman known to all for her free spirit and liberal attitude toward sex.

"She actually confessed her past to her new boyfriend," said one.

"All those affairs," another commented. "What courage she has."

"And what a memory," sighed another.

♀

Some Mothers Have Them

When Jackson joined the military he took his date on a tour of the base where he was stationed. As they passed the firing range the sudden sound of rifle fire caused her to fling herself into Jackson's arms, and holding him tightly close said, "I'm sorry I didn't mean to get that frightened."

"Oh, that's all right," said Jackson with a grin. "Now we'll go and watch the heavy artillery."

♀

Her Other Half

In Absentia

A typical macho man married a typical good-looking lady and after the wedding, he laid down the following rules: "I'll be home when I want, if I want, and at what time I want-and I don't expect any hassle from you. I expect a great dinner to be on the table unless I tell you that I won't be home for dinner. I'll go hunting, fishing, boozing and card-playing when I want with my old buddies and don't you give me a hard time about it. Those are my rules. Any comments?"

His new bride said, "No, that's fine with me. Just understand that there will be sex here at seven o'clock every night whether you're here or not."

♀

Life, Love & Laughter

 **Quillings**   *The Dream-Bearer* - *By Mary Carolyn Davies*

Where weary folk toil, black with smoke   *I went to bitter lanes and dark*
And hear but whistles scream   *Who once had known the sky*
I went, all fresh from dawn and dew   *To carry them a dream - and found*
To carry them a dream   *They had more dreams than I*

♀

Life's Funny Experiences
Cyber Spaced

My husband and I have been signing on to a Newfoundland chat line for several months during which time we have gotten friendly with two couples from St. John's, Newfoundland. After chatting with them every night for a period of about three months, we got to know them pretty well. The male partner in one of the couples we spoke to went by the nickname of 'Chuck,' while 'Fluff' was a nickname used by the other couple. Chuck came on the chat line one night asking anyone if they had a cure for hemorrhoids. At first we were serious with him trying to help him, until someone piped up with a very strange cure and the seriousness turned into a big joke.

We got to know these people so well that we agreed to meet them at St. John's airport, on our way back from our visit to Newfoundland in August of this year.

Two weeks later when we arrived at the airport, I called Chuck and he said he would come to meet us within the hour. He described himself so that we would recognize him. After I described myself, I told him to meet us at the airport bar. My husband and I sat and waited. There was no sign of them for about an hour. Then a couple came in, looking around. I went over and spoke to them and they told me that they were indeed looking for someone and that I fitted the description. They introduced themselves by their proper names and not their nicknames. We all shook hands, planted kisses on cheeks and exchanged little hugs!

I leaned over and whispered into Chuck's ear, "How are your hemorrhoids?"

He smiled, but his only reply was "Huh?"

We talked on for a while, then something seemed off, so I asked, "Where is Fluff?" The answer was "Who's fluff?"

I looked at my husband and he looked at me. We were talking to the wrong people!

We wanted a hole to sink in so bad!

The man said, "Well, it sure was nice meeting you guys!"

We went back to our seats and laughed our heads off - after the embarrassment wore off, of course!

Anyway, when Chuck and his wife, and Fluff and her husband finally did come, we sure had a lot to tell them. That was a night at St. John's airport we will never forget, or live down.

E. Meade, Brampton, Ontario

PS: Everytime I'm on the chat line now I'm always asked the same old question - "Kiss any strangers today?"

♀

Animal Mating - Fact and Fantasy – *Ron Young*
You Light Up My Life

Fact:

Anyone watching the flashing of a Firefly in the warm spring night air and the same blinking light coming from a Glow-worm on the ground, are watching synchronous love messages being exchanged between two lovers that could end in a night of sex between the two. The firefly is a male glow-worm after it has spread its wings of adulthood (the female has no wings and is flightless). In his search for a lover, the male sends out precisely timed flashes to any interested female on the ground. If a female is turned on by his glow, she will respond with her own "Morse code" of flashes. The chemical reaction that lights up the firefly's sex light, also serves another purpose. The nitric oxide which lights his lantern also serves as "Spanish fly" for the male, by regulating blood vessel restriction in penile erection. The nitric oxide in Viagra serves the same purpose in human males.

Fantasy:

So, if your sexual drive is lagging (and other things are sagging)
You can't be blaming problems on your age
There is no alibi, since they brand-named Spanish fly
"Viagra" for the aged's now's the rage

♀

Women Who Have Made A Difference *By Ron Young*

Jane Goodall went to Tanzania in 1960 and began the longest continuous field study of animals in their natural habitat. Although it was unheard of for a woman to venture into the wilds of Africa, her methodology and profound scientific discoveries revolutionized the field of primatology. One of the discoveries she chronicled was that of chimpanzees making and using tools, a skill once believed exclusive to humans. Later in 1977, Dr. Goodall founded The Jane Goodall Institute to provide ongoing support for chimpanzee research.

Jessie Catherine Gray, was not only a surgeon, lecturer and researcher, and one of four leading cancer surgeons in North America, she was Canada's "first lady of surgery." She was also the first female member of the Central Surgical Society of North America. Dr. Gray was Surgeon in Chief at the Women's College Hospital in Toronto from 1945 until she retired in 1965.

Lisa Thorson was confined to a wheelchair, but that didn't stop her from making an impact in the world of jazz, it only gave her a better understanding of just how far we have to go to make the world accessible to the handicapped. An injury in 1979 left the jazz singer, songwriter and actress to spend the rest of her life in a wheelchair. In 1982 Lisa created Spokesong, a musical production designed to educate the public about disability issues in the form of a delightful performance. Lisa incorporated a very skillful presentation by American Sign Language Interpreter to not only, make it possible for the hearing impaired to enjoy the performance, but this, along with her other endeavours, helped demonstrate by example what can be done.

♀

Life, Love & Laughter

Tickle and Bight   *By Lucy Fitzpatrick–McFarlane*

They Came Bearing Gifts

I've always believed that gift-giving is a very special part of Christmas and I'd like to think that everything I give or receive is from the heart, no matter how little or how big it may be. Over the years, though, it seems that the whole idea of Christmas has become too commercialized and for a lot of people, a financial burden. Let's face it, gone are the days when you can get anything half-decent for $10, and as much as we'd like to do something nice for everybody, it just isn't possible anymore. Take my situation, for instance. We have such a big crowd in the Fitzpatrick family and what with the

dozens of nieces, nephews and their families, I'd be down to my last copper if I bought gifts for everybody. The rest of the family felt the same way, and that's why, a few years ago, we did something about it. After a lot of discussion, we decided that there would be no gifts exchanged during the festive season... just good wishes and a phone call would be sufficient. That way, everybody could relax, enjoy the festivities and not feel guilty or left out in any way. I was afraid that Murray's family might think that the Fitzpatrick's were cheapskates when Murray mentioned our agreement, but his sister thought it was a great idea and so the McFarlane family decided to do the same thing. Matter of fact, a few of our best friends thought we should extend that deal to the other couples we hang around with and it was all settled. As far as everybody was concerned, it was the perfect plan for Christmas. Well ... at least it started out that way.

I should've left well-enough alone, but when the time came to buy greeting cards, I made the decision to but, back in that area too. Usually I send at least 120 Christmas cards every year and I'd noticed that many of the people I send to no longer return that gesture. My husband usually does half the cards and he was indignant when I told him my plan to eliminate the people who never send us cards. "You do what you want, but I'm sending the same as usual," he said. "Besides, maybe the ones who didn't send cards to us last year will send this year and then you'll be sorry."

My, but it galls me to no end when that man is right! Sure enough, for the first time in years, the cards rolled in from the very ones I took off my list, and the people I sent to didn't bother to send cards at all. I was caught red-faced and rushing like crazy to get cards in the mail the day before Christmas Eve. After that fiasco, I got to thinking about the agreement we all made. What if somebody failed to keep their promise and sent presents anyway? Worse still, what if everybody was thinking the same thing and decided to buy gifts at the last moment and forgot to tell me? I couldn't sleep thinking about going empti-handed to his mother's house where all the McFarlane family were gathering for Christmas dinner, so I went out and bought presents for everybody. I knew Murray would be upset, so I never told him until after I loaded up the trunk of the car. And boy, did he get saucy about the whole thing! "You did WHAT?" he bellowed. "What are you trying to do, spoil Christmas for my family? A deal's a deal, so you should've stuck to it!"

I chose to ignore him and as usual, he was right again, for I was the only one who showed up with gifts. I felt like the Grinch who stole Christmas, and judging by the cold shoulder I got from everyone, I got the impression they didn't appreciate my good intentions at all.

But that wasn't the end of it, either. I was determined not to make the same mistake twice in one Christmas, so I made sure I stuck to the 'no gift' decision with our friends who came to our house on Boxing Day. And wouldn't you know it, they showed up bearing gifts for us. Feeling very guilty because I had nothing for them, I decided to take a bottle of wine from the many that were given to my husband from different companies he'd worked. While they were busy talking, I grabbed one, wrapped it and stuck it under the tree. Feeling very proud of myself, I casually asked Murray to give them their present. "Present? What present?" he repeated, gaping at me with that stunned look a deer gets when caught in the headlights of a car.

I fixed him with the hairy eyeball immediately. "You know, the present under the tree right beside the box of chocolates your mother gave us for Christmas," I said sweetly.

I could tell nothing was registering, so before he said another word, I snatched the box from under the tree and gave it to my friend. She seemed extremely pleased as she passed it to her husband and it was at that moment, I saw Murray's mouth drop open. "Thank you so much, you guys," she said. "You didn't have to buy us such an expensive wine... you really shouldn't have, you know!"

"They didn't buy it dear," her husband said with a twinkle in his eye. "Somebody else gave it to them. Look, there's another tab under the label of the bottle. It says, 'Merry Christmas, Murray and Lucy from McNamara Construction Company.'"

That few seconds of embarrassed silence seemed to last an hour, until our friends confessed they had done the same thing. Apparently at the last minute, they re-wrapped a vase someone had given them just in case we reneged on our deal. And that's what kept happening for the past two years. Even though the no-gift agreement still stands, there's always someone on both sides of the family who buys something at the last minute. Last year, when I went to my sister Leona's house, I brought presents because she had welshed out on our deal the year before and I had kept my end of the bargain. So you see, it was a vicious circle.

I'm beginning to realize now, that maybe this system will never work, for none of us seem to be able to break the tradition of gift-giving. Perhaps that's because we still want to follow in the footsteps of the Wise Men who brought gifts of gold, frankincense and myrrh to the newborn Saviour in Bethlehem so many years ago. Perhaps it is something within ourselves that makes us want to show our appreciation and gratitude to those we lose, or maybe it is as simple as people needing to reach out to others with open hearts. But whatever the reason, I know the feeling of giving takes on new meaning at Christmas, and it has nothing to do with the price of things we purchase. At least that's the way I remember it when I was a child in Newfoundland. Nobody could afford to go out and buy gifts, so things were hand made to give to neighbours and friends. Once the children were looked after then there wasn't much left over to give to someone else. Baked goods, breads, buns and pies were the usual presents exchanged and it was all greatly appreciated, for it was the spirit in which it was given that mattered. Things got passed around from one house to another, be it personal belongings, keepsakes or family recipes passed from one generation to the next.

I can recall an incident years ago when someone in the Cove brought me a present wrapped in a bit of tissue paper. Mom had nothing prepared to offer in return and reluctantly, she decided to give away part of her sugar and creamer set, the only one she had that matched. She wrapped up the sugar bowl in the same piece of tissue paper and gave it to the woman, who was overjoyed with her treasure. The very next year, the lady returned again with a present and when mom opened it, she discovered the sugar bowl from her set. Knowing that the kindly widow was forgetful, Mom pretended she'd never seen it before and thanked her for the kind gesture. "Gettin' my bowl back that I treasured so much was the best Christmas present I ever got," she said.

And now, here it is Christmas again and I've given my word to both families that I will not renege on our agreement this year. "Don't worry," I told them, "I'm not buying anything for anybody...I promise."

I must admit that I rather enjoyed the hustle and bustle of looking for gifts to suit everybody and now that we don't have to do it, I miss it. Funny, isn't it? Perhaps though, just to get myself in the Christmas spirit, I'll pick up a few things here and there...just in case. Maybe I'll choose things so that, if need be, I can wrap it up if someone shows up bearing gifts when they're not supposed to. I mean, I won't be breaking a promise if I just buy things that I like for myself, now will I? Besides, Christmas just won't be Christmas without presents, so if I can't give them to anyone, at least I can use them around the house. But, if any of the family reads this, I just want you to know that I won't be bringing gifts this year. As of now, that's my story and I'm sticking to it, so as agreed. I'm extending only my good wishes this year.

Merry Christmas everybody!

♀

Spice of Life

A straight line is the shortest distance between a baby and anything breakable.

♀

Ennellene

Down through the ages, in well-written pages
Our story's been told, without fibbin'
Now woman's word, is at last being heard
Since we finally got 'round to add "libbin'"

♀

Feminine Words & Phrases

Scarlet Letter: The scarlet letter was the letter 'A' for Adulteress. It was worn on the dress of Puritan New Englander women who were found guilty of the crime. Adulterers were not required to wear the 'A' symbol of sin.

Scarlet Woman: The woman seen in a vision by St. John who described her in the bible as, "The mother of harlots (whores) and abominations of the earth," and, "Mystery, Babylon the Great."

Shotgun Wedding: A wedding in which the couple are forced to marry to conform with the expectations of their parents, particularly the father of the bride. He was sometimes known to use a firearm to induce the dissenting groom into a marriage against his will, particularly if his daughter was pregnant.

Sob Sister: A term applied to women, who in newspapers, answered personal questions from readers, particularly women readers.

Pig-wife: A woman who sold pottery. A pig was a small mug, cup or bowl. A piggin was a larger piece of crockery, such as a milk pail.

♀

Feminine Words & Phrases

Penny weddings: Weddings for poor people in Scotland and Wales. Each guest at the ceremony brought a small sum, not more than a shilling. Any money left over was given to the newlyweds.

Perfume: Originally used as a means of dealing with the nasty smell of burning flesh at religious sacrifices, the name originates from the Latin, per fumum which means, 'from smoke.'

Piece of skirt: Male slang term for a woman.

Platonic: The word for non-romantic love, came from Plato of Greek mythology, who in the Symposium celebrated "not the non-sexual love of a man for a woman, but the loving interest that Socrates took in young men."

Prima Donna: The main singer in an opera. From the Italian for, 'first lady.'

♀

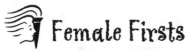 # Female Firsts

1997: Kim Campbell became the first female Prime Minister of Canada.

1997: In April, the International Female Boxing Association was formed to promote women boxing throughout the world as a genuine, professional and athletic competition.

1997: Madeleine K. Albright became the first woman Secretary of State and the highest-ranking woman in the U.S. government.

1997: Catherine Chabaud of France became the first woman to finish a nonstop solo round-the-world voyage in a time of 140 days.

1997: Anita DeFrantz of the U.S. became the first female vice-president of the International Olympic Committee executive committee.

1997: Nawal El Moutawakel became the first Muslim woman ever elected as a member of the International Olympic Committee. She was also the first woman from an Islamic nation to win an Olympic medal that year.

1998: Fashion designer, entrepreneur and author, Vivienne Poy, became the first Canadian of Chinese descent, and the only Asian to be appointed to the Senate.

1998: April Heinrichs became the first woman named to the National Soccer Hall of Fame in the U.S.

1998: At age 26, Christina Sanchez became the first female matador to fight in Madrid's famed Les Ventas ring.

1999: Teenagers Serena and Venus Williams became the first sisters to win singles titles in world tennis matches on the same day, when Venus won the IGA Superthrift Tennis Classic hours after Serena won at the Open Gaz de France. Later that year, the two squared off against each other at Wimbledon and Venus beat Serena two games to one to win the match.

♀

The Cottage Hospital

By Loretta Sherren, Fredericton, New Brunswick

It was several years after Confederation before Canadian rules and regulations played a significant role in Newfoundland's cottage hospital system. Primitive equipment and treatment remained well into the fifties. Nurse's aides were still hired right off the street, so to speak, and given only on-the-job training before performing tasks that would today be considered both illegal and criminal. A severe shortage of nurses in the province left the smaller hospitals strapped for help, and then as now, someone had to take care of the sick.

The cottage hospitals were managed mostly by matrons, many of whom where British, as was the case at the hospital where I was employed as a nurse's aide. Our matron came to Newfoundland with a load of emotional baggage. The man she was to marry had been killed in the London Blitz, and it was this tragedy that brought her to Newfoundland. She was an excellent nurse with a kind and caring attitude and totally dedicated to her profession, but she had a drinking problem that she tried without success to hide. In fact, most of our superiors had something to hide.

With the exception of the doctor and cook, room and board was provided in the hospital for the staff. Pay for aides was $48 per month for working six, 12-hour shifts per week, and even though we were all over the age of 18, there was a strictly enforced curfew of 10 p.m. sharp. We had no control over wages and working conditions, a steady diet of corn beef hash or the long hours, but the curfew was another matter! We were young and full of life and having to be back from a dance on a Saturday night by 10 p.m., just wouldn't do! The first escape door was at the end of the corridor in our upstairs quarters, and we began using the fire escape. On dance nights we simply went back to the hospital and signed in at 10 p.m, then went upstairs and climbed the fire escape and went back to the dance until midnight.

Because the cottage hospital was not equipped to treat the more seriously ill patients, they were transferred to the larger hospitals. The patients were always escorted by a nurse's aide and this gave the matron the opportunity to replenish her supply of booze. We all participated in her ritual, and understanding her need for privacy and our own need for a paycheque, we kept our mouths shut. Besides, she was a good boss and none of us wanted to see her get in trouble. Though already gray, she was a young and attractive lady whose life the war had changed forever. Apart from those evenings when she invited both nurses and aides to play cards with her, she lived a solitary life, and her loneliness showed.

With the exception of maternity cases, the night shift was usually less demanding than day shift. Once the lights went out at 10 p.m., there was quiet to do the things that could only be done in the quiet of night. Sterilization of the maternity and surgical trays, rolling bandages, that arrived loose in large cartons, and writing up patient charts, were just part of the nightly routine. We were also required to cook our own midnight meal. Most nights a couple of the local R.C.M.P. officers came by around midnight for a coffee break. There being no television and all of us too poor to own a radio, they also brought a daily news report.

On one particular night, the police officers brought more than just a news report. They brought a drunk who was totally out of his cups and ready to fight dragons. Using foul and abusive language, and knocking over everything in his path, he was pinned down and given enough of a tranquilizer to knock out a horse, but not him! The police stayed until he appeared to be sleeping, then left. Ten minutes later, I checked on him and he was gone! Panic ruled. While the police were quickly called back, the matron was alerted to search the staff quarters. Some time later he was found sitting in a bucket in the scrub room drinking sassafras, a solution used to delouse patients. The following day he was taken by police to cool his heels in the city jail, but the old

Waterford might have been a better place for him.

The night shift was staffed by three people: two aides and a nurse. My partner was also my best friend. Prior to working as a nurse's aide, she had been a second year nursing student and was much better trained than me. Having been caught drinking, she was suspended from completing her studies for one year. One night she suggested we test ourselves for TB. I told her I didn't have TB and neither did she. She reminded me that I had escorted patients with TB and had certainly been exposed to the germ. This sort of thing was forbidden, and I didn't want to be caught, but she had a point. She applied the patches and to avoid detection, we kept our arms covered until it was time for the patch to come off. To my surprise mine was positive! There was more than just my life at stake, we had to confess! I was immediately sent to see a chest specialist, removed from working on the wards and transferred to the out-patient clinic for three months. The inactive germ, fortunately never became active, and our goofing off ceased.

The doctor was a witty Irishman. He and his Swedish born wife were a childless couple, but he had a special fondness for children and was rarely seen making his rounds without a child in his arms. Many of the children were from isolated areas where the only transportation was by train, and families rarely got to visit, if at all. The doctor, too, was not without his little secret. His wife, a strikingly beautiful blond, was a thief! Once a month this wonderful man had to visit the few store owners and pay off bills for the items his wife had stolen. He had an arrangement with the store owners to keep the matter secret. His wife was sent away for treatment, and before her feet left the ground, everybody knew the secret.

The night nurse usually on my shift was a soft spoken, redhead and a very nice person to work with. She was secretly married to one of the officers who came for coffee breaks. R.C.M.P. officers were required to give five year's service before getting married, and this one had six months to go. Somehow the marriage was prematurely revealed and his career was destroyed. Feeling betrayed and with her own career hanging in the balance, our fun-loving, practical joker became both worried and sad. The song, "Once I had a secret love, that lives within the heart of me," was very popular at the time and seemed to have been written just for her. Gradually things sorted themselves out and she returned to her old self. The power of love it is thought, is an all redeeming power.

One night a tiny baby suffering from a severe case of gastroenteritis, died just after midnight. The small body was dressed, wrapped in a blanket and placed on a steel tray to be taken to the morgue. It being February, and a very stormy night, I intended leaving the baby in the hospital until daylight. Besides, it was pitch dark, and the very thought of going to the morgue at this time of night turned my insides to jelly! Two hours later the nurse ordered me to make the trip to the morgue. She's either joking or out of her cotton pickin' mind I thought. "You're joking." I said. But the look on her face told me it was no joke.

The morgue was at the far end of a large field and near the woods. It was cold and the snow was very deep. I pleaded the storm and the fact that I was not properly dressed to go out in such bad weather. She grabbed her cape from the hook and threw it at me, tossed the doctor's hip rubber boots at my feet, stuck a flashlight in my hand and said, "Any more excuses?" She was being a real witch and so out of character that I should have been suspicious then, but I wasn't. My partner was sitting with a maternity patient. I tried to bribe her into switching places with me but she said, "Are you nuts?" Something here was strangely out of place and I couldn't put my finger on it.

Cursing under my breath and sweating bullets from fright, I picked up the tray and went out the door. I put the tray on top of the snow and pushed it in front of me with one hand, while holding the flashlight with the other, and ploughed a path to the morgue. The blowing snow was blinding, but I managed to find the door and get it open. As I picked up the tray with both hands I dropped the flashlight in the snow and couldn't reach it. I could see the light underneath the snow and decided to get it on my way out. The next step I took sent me sprawling on my face. I had tripped over a stretcher that shouldn't have been there. I was thinking the caretaker would get a piece of my mind for this, when I put my hands down to push myself up and felt hair!

With the tray secured on a shelf, I stepped over the corpse on the floor and ran like hell. I was back at the hospital in a heartbeat, and I heard the laughter before I reached the door. I took a minute to catch my breath and get a hold of myself, then I went in. My partner had disappeared like a scalded cat when she heard the door, but the nurse was doubled over with laughter. She gained control long enough to blurt, "Oh, I forgot to tell you about the man who hung himself this morning at Pine Tree. That's his body in the morgue!" "I know," I snapped, "he told me, but the living are more dangerous than the dead, now go to hell!" It was a week before we mentioned it again, but twice in the middle of a meal she had to leave the table to avoid laughing in my face. It wasn't funny, but in the end I laughed too.

In 1955 Canadian rules and regulations were implemented and many young ladies who had seen the handwriting on the wall and had the means, already had their R.N.A's and all but a handful of N.A's were given their pink slips and it was time to move on. Wages doubled overnight and everything else changed accordingly. Forty years later, few, if any, of the old cottage hospitals are still standing, but the memories will last forever?

♀

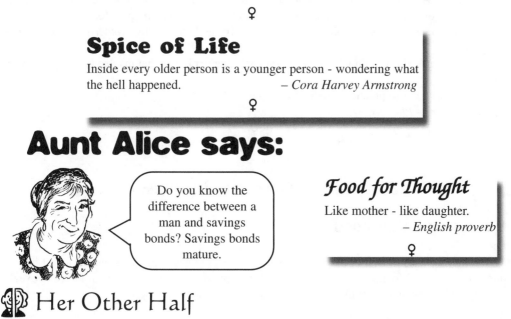

Spice of Life

Inside every older person is a younger person - wondering what the hell happened.
– Cora Harvey Armstrong

♀

Aunt Alice says:

Do you know the difference between a man and savings bonds? Savings bonds mature.

Food for Thought

Like mother - like daughter.
– English proverb

♀

Her Other Half

Just To Be Sure

A doctor and his wife are having a fight at the breakfast table. He got up in a rage and said, "And you are no good in bed either," and storms out of the house. After sometime he realized he was nasty and decided to make amends so he rang her up. She came to the phone after many rings and the irritated husband said, "What took you so long to answer the phone?"

"I was in bed," she said.

"In bed this early, doing what?"

"Getting a second opinion."

♀

🐃 Adam's Ribbing
The Life of a Cabby

"Turn your meter on said the housewife to the waiting taxi driver in her driveway as she placed her three young children in the back seat, and ran back into the house, "I'll be back in a minute."

When the brawling, bawling and crawling over seats had gone on for nearly 15 minutes, the mother came out and and said, "How much do I owe you?"

"We haven't gone anywhere yet," said the cab driver.

"Oh, I don't want to go anywhere. I just wanted to make a long-distance call and I wanted some peace and quiet. Here's the fare, and thanks for waiting."

♀

Life's Funny Experiences
At Attention

We recently visited Newfoundland to attend a friend's wedding. My brother-in-law was the best man. We, of course, refer to the job of the best man as that of "standing up" for the groom. We spent the day in St. John's shopping and we were hurrying home so my brother-in-law could get to rehearsal.

My nephew asked his mom what rehearsal meant. She explained that his dad had to practise for the wedding.

"What, Daddy has to practice standing up?!" he exclaimed.

Bud Sizemore – Phoenix, Arizona

♀

🐾 Animal Mating - Fact and Fantasy – *Ron Young*

Confusing Fatherhood

Fact:

Although she only does it once a year, when the female Prairie Dog gives birth, each of her litter may have a different father. This is a result of her extreme four to five hour bout of sexual activity with as many as five different males during conception.

Fantasy:

In big families, special days
For most dads, mostly a maze
And forgetting them, a fair, forgone conclusion
Just imagine, how bewilderin'
For Poppa Prairie's many children
Who, on father's day, are faced with mass confusion

♀

Life, Love & Laughter

Tickle and Bight *By Lucy Fitzpatrick–McFarlane*

Change of Life

The whole thing started slowly six months ago. I'd wake up in the middle of the night shivering, feeling hot one minute and cold the next. I couldn't go back to sleep and I felt worried and anxious for reasons I couldn't explain. I tried everything to relax, even counting sheep, but after an hour or so, they seemed to be going in slow motion. I felt so sorry for the poor things that I started helping them get over the fence and come morning, I'd be exhausted. I was unable to concentrate on anything for longer than a minute and I'd burst into tears if anyone looked at me scow ways. I felt older than God's cow and when I'd get home from work, I'd lay on the couch like a rag doll. If the phone happened to ring beside me, I'd say, "It's 8:30 at night, who could be phoning at this late hour?"

Then, the hot flashes hit me with a vengeance, sending electrical currents scorching through my body and zapping every ounce of energy I had left. I felt grouchy all the time and literally turned into a witch overnight. I never swept the kitchen floor for almost a week because I was afraid I'd fly off on the broom handle. I started throwing temper-tantrums like a spoiled child, going on a rampage at the drop of a hat one minute, and the next I'd be smiling and jolly again. My family thought I was going stark, raving mad, because I'd get sudden bursts of energy in the middle of the night and start cleaning the house, often ousting them out of their beds. And talk about being forgetful! Sometimes I couldn't even remember buddy's name. You know, the fella I married 25 years ago...wassisname. I got so absent-minded that even if I heard a good bit of gossip, I couldn't pass it on to anybody because I couldn't remember it seconds later. I started doing the oddest things, like washing my pantyhose in the birdbath outside, going to work wearing odd shoes and getting simple messages and directions mixed up. At one point, I actually set a bowl of Meow Mix on the table for lunch and gave the cats the ham sandwiches. I kid you not. It was the most scary thing I've ever experienced, so I decided it was time I saw a doctor.

The doctor quietly listened to my story, making notes and occasionally nodding his head. "How old are you now, Lucy? 48?" I nodded my agreement and took a deep breath. "Well, what's wrong with me? Is it Alzheimer's?"

"I think you've hit mid-life crisis, Lucy," he said.

"You're telling me," I said. "I almost burned the house down yesterday because I put the pot holders in the hot oven and left the roast on top of the stove."

"I mean, you've started the change of life. You know, menopause," he said calmly.

It hit me like a ton of bricks. Menopause. I listened intently as he recounted the symptoms associated with the loss of female hormones and everything seemed to fall in place. I was experiencing every darned thing: Severe hot flashes, night sweats, insomnia, fatigue, mood swings, irritability, confusion, memory loss, depression, aches and pains, dry eyes, vaginal atrophy and loss of sexual drive. By the time he'd finished telling me all this good news, I wondered how I managed to get to this office with all those things screwed up on my pitiful body. I brightened up when he told me about the Hormone Replacement Therapy or HRT, as it is commonly called, but when he told me the downside, my hot flashes overwhelmed me. Not to worry, he said, I had a choice. I could put up with the way I was feeling, but if I decided on the hormones, there was an increased risk of developing breast or uterine cancer, gall bladder problems, thrombosis and possibly ovarian cancer. If I didn't take the increased estrogen in the HRT, then I was not going to be protected from coronary heart disease, osteoporosis, colon cancer, memory loss and maybe Alzheimer's disease. Wow, that's some price to pay for the

Life, Love & Laughter

Life, Love & Laughter

privilege of having reproductive glands. I was smack in the middle of menopause, so I knew it was too late to ask for a sex change. "Why don't you just put me out of my misery, take me out back and shoot me," I moaned.

After a long talk, I opted for the hormone replacement therapy. At that moment, the letters H R T spelled out three words that explained how I felt: Haggard, Revengeful and Testy. I'm beginning to think that woman was created before man, that perhaps Eve was a rough draft and Adam the up-dated version, with all the glitches ironed out. Now, I realize that you men think this is a woman's subject, but that's not true, so put down the remote control and listen up. After all, this difficult time in a woman's life was aptly named by a male, for the very word MEN-O-Pause implicates you, now doesn't it? Besides, who else but a man can change a woman's life, make her feel irritable, give her mood swings, cause hot flashes and make her feel depressed? I don't want to frighten you, but statistics show that by the year 2000, four million Canadian women (the baby boomers) will be starting their transition into menopause, so you'd better gear up. Just imagine, four million hormone-deprived, tempermental women to deal with! You men will be right in the middle of them every day, because you'll meet them on the highway, at the office, department stores, in places of business and in every public place. And then you'll have to go home to your wife. Need I say more? Hormone Replacement Therapy may very well be the most important words you'll ever hear. H R T: Husbands, Run, Take cover for your own safety. Trust me, I know what I speak of because when my change of life started, my husband had no idea anything was amiss until I threatened to hit him over the head with the frying pan when he offered to do the dishes. Normally, I would've jumped at the chance, but I had no idea that my hormones had given up and my tank was running on empty, so neither of us was prepared for my reaction. Fact is, I thought I was too young to hit that plateau in my life, so I never once read up on the problems of menopause.

Allow me to offer a few tips to all you unsuspecting, unprepared husbands as you enter the transition into menopause with your spouses. If your wife tells you she's having a hot flash, don't take it as an invitation to get frisky. Just lie absolutely still in bed and take deep breaths until her face and neck loses the red colour. If she appears irritable and is banging dishes around in the kitchen, don't even think of asking her to iron a shirt for you. Should you be awakened at 3 a.m. to find her pulling the bed sheets out from under you to wash them, let her have them, because she may not get this sudden spurt of energy to clean house for another three months. If she seems distracted or forgetful, never ask what's for dinner or you may find yourself wearing the spaghetti sauce. If she prepares to leave the house for work with the tail of her dress tucked into her pantyhose, don't say a word about it. Let her scream at somebody else instead of you, and if she kisses the cat and pats you on the head, don't take it personally. Think carefully before you say a word if you awake at night and find her anxiously pacing the floor. Never, under any circumstances, ask this question, "Honey, now that you're up, can you bring me a glass of water?" No matter how lovely she looks, don't compliment her unless you know for a fact that she's not in the middle of a mood swing, for she'll undoubtedly think you're criticizing her and you'll find yourself locked out of the house. Pretend you don't notice all of the odd things you see her do, agree with everything she says and for heaven sakes, don't even attempt to open your gob if she's anywhere near a sharp object when she gets a hot flash. And above all, be patient, understanding and loving at all times, if you can get a word in edgewise without upsetting her. Remember, the change of life will pass. It may take 5 to 10 years, but it'll pass. But take heart, there's light beyond the tunnel, for some women claim that the hormone replacement therapy makes them feel rejuvenated, almost like a teenager again. And when that times comes, I hope you men can handle it.

Reprinted from Downhomer *magazine.*

♀

🐝 Her Other Half

Up When He's Down

A husband and wife had a bitter quarrel on the day of their 40th wedding anniversary. The husband yells, "When you die, I'm getting you a headstone that reads, 'Here Lies My Wife - Cold As Ever.'"

"Yeah?" she replies. "When you die, I'm getting you a headstone that reads, "Here Lies My Husband. Stiff at last."

♀

📝 Female Firsts

1999: In June, Carolina Morace became the first female coach of a men's professional soccer team in Italy.

1999: Chamique Holdsclaw became the first woman basketball player to win the Sullivan Award, America's top amateur athlete award.

1999: In August, the first national Ironman event ever held inside the continental U.S. was held in Lake Placid, New York. It was won by Canadian Heather Fuhr.

2000: The first Award of Excellence of the National Soccer Coaches Association of America's Women's Committee winner was April Heinrichs, the women's soccer coach at the University of Virginia.

2000: Germany's Hanka Kupfernagel won the first women's winter cyclocross title in 50 years of world championships in the Netherlands.

2000: In February, the first great-grandmother to walk across the U.S., Doris Haddock, finished the 14-month walk which took her from California to Washington, DC. The 90-year-old Dublin, New Hampshire woman, walked an average of 10 miles per day on her trek, which was to advocate for campaign finance reform.

2000: The first joint-nominees in the Sullivan Award's 70-year history to win the athletic award, were identical twins Kelly and Coco Miller.

2000: At age 36, jockey Julie Krone became the first woman elected to thoroughbred racing's hall of fame. She was also the only woman to have won the Triple Crown of horse racing.

2000: Kristine Lilly became the first player in the history of international soccer to play in 200 games for her country when she played for the U.S. team against Canada in Portland, Oregon. The US team beat the Canadian team with a score of 4-0.

2000: Gianna Angelopoulos-Daskalaki, a 44-year-old lawyer from Greece, became the first woman to head an Olympics organizing committee.

2000: Seilala Sua won the women's discus at the NCAA Outdoor Track-and-Field Championships to become the first woman to win the same field event four times.

♀

Life, Love & Laughter

PRETTY FANNY GOFF

Tryphena Goff—or as she was generally known, Pretty Fanny Goff—was born at Portugal Cove about the commencement of the 19th century. I think that the original pet name must have been pretty Pheenie, her christian name being Tryphena, and not Frances, but Fanny she was generally called. She was the daughter of Mr. George Goff, innkeeper and chopman at Portugal Cove. Goff's Inn was a celebrated hostel in its day; the elite of the land visited it and stayed there when enroute from St. John's to the large ports in Conception Bay. Pretty Fanny's mother was the daughter of a Mr. and Mrs. Pottle of Bonavista. At the commencement of the reign of King George III, Mr. Pottle was a Captain in the Guards and Mrs. Pottle (nee Miss Jennings, a great-niece of the celebrated Sarah, first Duchess of Marlborough), was a lady-in-waiting to Queen Charlotte.

In the summer of 1761, the couple eloped, came to this country and settled at Bonavista. While pursuit was being made after them in the direction of Gretna Green, this loving couple got quietly down to Poole in Dorset and embarked on a ship bound for Newfoundland. Had they been caught it would have gone hard with them both, but especially the man, for he had deserted the King's colours. On the return voyage, the ship in which the Pottles left England was lost with all hands, and the place of their residence and hiding remained so long unknown to the authorities that they escaped punishment for their elopement.

On August 24, 1787, their eldest daughter, Mary, a tall aristocratic-looking woman, who possessed a fair share of her mother's good looks, was married at Bonavista to George Goff, an Englishman. He was said to have been the illegitimate son of a member of the Royal family of England. George Goff and Mary Pottle were married by a Mr. Akerman, who was an S.P.G. lay-reader at Bonavista, and had a license to marry from the Bishop of Nova Scotia of whose Diocese Newfoundland then formed a part.

After his wife's death, Captain Pottle came to reside with his daughter Mary Goff at Portugal Cove. Here he died about 1826 and was buried beside his granddaughter Tryphena. He has been described as being a tall and handsome man, clean shaven and ruddy of countenance, and though advanced in years, very upright in stature. He wore a three-cornered hat, his hair in a queue, a coat with gilt buttons, scarlet silk vest, blue cloth pants, silk stockings fastened with silver clocks at the knee, and shoes with silver buckles.

He was not popular at the Cove. Once I asked an old woman who knew him why this was. "It was because he lived to spoil trade", she said. How was that I asked. "In this way", she said. "One day mother sent me to the Inn to sell a basket of eggs to Mrs. Goff. While Mrs. Goff was counting the eggs and placing them in a dish on the counter, her father, who was sitting by the fire in the bar-room smoking a long church-warden pipe, said "Don't buy those eggs, Mary, they aren't fit to eat, for all the Portugal Cove hens are fed on fish maggots." Mrs. Goff laughed and said, "Oh father, these are all right, for Mrs. Nealy feeds them only on potatoes and milk with a little Indian meal."

(How is it that some non-natives appear to take pleasure in writing and speaking disparagingly of Newfoundland and its people? To my mind such conduct is a decided indication, to say the least, of defective education, and possibly of low origin on the part of those who are guilty of it.)

Miss Jennings was an heiress, and it is certain that her relations strongly objected to her union with Captain Pottle, which they considered a decided misalliance on her part, hence the elopement. (I have known not a few men who were by birth of lowly origin, but were nevertheless wholly and altogether gentlemen in mind and action. Captain Pottle's jest, if it was a jest, was decidedly unrefined and what you might expect from a costermonger who sold strawberries by the pottle.)

But to return to the subject of this narrative, Pheenie Goff was remarkable for great beauty of face and figure. She had a sweet voice. What is best of all, she was as good as she was beautiful. In a land that always has been noted for the beauty of its women, she was considered to be of her time the most beautiful woman in Newfoundland. All who knew her loved her and she was quite as much liked by the women as by the men.

An old lady at Portugal Cove who knew Phennie Goff well, said that she had such an expressive countenance that having once looked thereupon you could not withdraw your gaze. She had a host of admirers among the naval and military men, of who there were many in Newfoundland at that time. At that time she had more than one excellent offer of marriage, but she refused all except one. That favoured one was a Newfoundlander named Barter who carried on a profitable business at Brigus, Conception Bay.

Mr. Barter has been described by one who knew him, as being tall, rather powerfully built, and a very handsome man. The couple were well matched. The wedding was to take place in March, 1823. Preparation was made for it on a large scale at Goff's Inn, but the wedding was not to be. Less than a fortnight before it was to take place, the intended bride was smitten by typhoid fever. More than one doctor from St. John's hurried to the bedside to render assistance, but all human help was in vain.

From the first, poor Pheenie felt that it would be so, and was said to have been resigned to the Divine will. She was even cheerful, saying with the simplicity of an innocent child that the Divine Master wanted her for his bride and that she was quite content to go to him and to be "safe in the arms of Jesus" for evermore. So she fell asleep.

She left a loving message for her intended earthly bridegroom, telling him not to grieve for her, but to get ready to meet his God, for it would not be long ere he too passed "behind the veil". From what will appear presently it is doubtful if Mr. Barter ever received this message.

As the time drew near for his wedding he loaded a sleigh with presents for the bride and bridesmaids, and tackling his horse thereto left Brigus to drive around the Bay on the ice to Portugal Cove. There was then no telegraphic communication in Newfoundland, and he was quite ignorant of the terrible news that awaited his arrival at Portugal Cove.

Mr. Barter whiled away the tedium of his journey with a happy song. On the morning of the very day on which he was to have been married, and on the afternoon of which his intended bride was to be buried, he reached the house of Mr. William Squires of St. Phillip's. He entered Mr. Squires' home joyfully, asking for breakfast, and saying that this was to be the happiest day of his life. Mr. Squires and family were exceedingly troubled, and at first could say nothing, for they knew of Miss Goff's death and were getting ready to attend her funeral. But in a little while, Mr. Squires, recovering in a measure his composure, took poor Barter into a private room, and there as gently as he could broke to him the sad tidings of Miss Goff's death. After hearing this dreadful news, which fell upon him like a bolt from heaven, Mr. Barter spoke not a word but harnessed his horse and drove back to Brigus. There he speedily settled his affairs and taking to his bed, died within three days of a broken heart. His intended wife's death-bed prophecy had a speedy fulfillment. They were lovely and beautiful in their lives and in death they were not divided.

In 1823 there was no regular graveyard at Portugal Cove in connection with the Church of England. Pretty Pheenie Goff's remains were interred under an apple tree in her father's garden, a place where she had often sat on summer evenings. A head-stone was erected to her memory, though from time and neglect the inscription thereon is almost illegible. Miss Goff was buried by a lay-reader named Curtis who preached, it is said, an impressive sermon upon the occasion.

It is only the Light and the Peace that comes from the Manger at Bethlehem that can make bearable such trying incidents in life's journey.

Author Unknown

♀

Life, Love & Laughter

Life, Love & Laughter

Quillings

Erosion *E. J. Pratt*

It took the sea a thousand years,
A thousand years to trace
The granite features of this cliff
In crag and scarp and base.

It took the sea an hour one night
An hour of storm to place
The sculpture of these granite seams
Upon a woman's face

♀

Ennellene

Absence makes
The heart grow fonder
But abstinence makes it
Fonder of wander

♀

Spice of Life

Old age ain't no place for sissies.

– Bette Davis

♀

Animal Mating – Fact and Fantasy *– Ron Young*

The Codfish (and the Chicken)

Fact:

The Codfish population is dwindling at an alarming rate, especially around the coasts of Newfoundland and Labrador where they once were so plentiful they could be "drawn up in baskets." Many reasons are attributed to this catastrophe, but there is no way the female codfish is to blame. After mating, a large female cod can lay as many as ten million eggs, which constitutes about one-third of her body weight. In human terms, this is like a 120 pound woman giving birth to one or more babies that in total weigh 40 pounds.

Unlike the domestic hen, which is growing in numbers and now outnumber humans, and who usually lays only one egg, and complains and cackles about that, the codfish gives birth without a whimper.

Fantasy:

The codfish lays ten million eggs
The cherished chicken, one
The codfish never cackles
To tell us what she's done
This rhyme is for Ms. Codfish
In effort to explain
Why folks in species everywhere
Who always win and gain
Are those who oftener cry "foul"
And loudlier complain

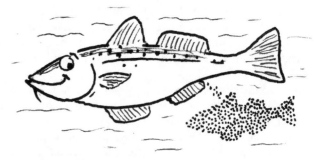

♀

Tickle and Bight *By Lucy Fitzpatrick–McFarlane*

Life is Full of Irony

I have a confession to make. It's not something that I am proud of, but perhaps if I admit it publicly, I'll feel better about myself. Truth is, I am guilty of laughing at the wrong things at the wrong time. There. I've said it. I came to the realization a while ago when I actually saw humour in a tragic story that I heard on the evening news. I won't blame you if you judge me harshly, because it was downright heartless of me considering the circumstances. It was a story about a pregnant woman who was charged with the attempted murder of her unborn child after she shot herself in the vagina. I was very relieved that the child survived and I felt sorry for the woman, because I knew that only a disturbed person would do such a thing. Now if

she had just left well enough alone, I would've had no problem with it, but no, the story took another twist. The woman claimed she had no idea she was pregnant, but rather she was depressed and was trying to kill herself. Now that's when I felt this pressure well up inside me and before I could control it, a giggle escaped and built to a crescendo until I dissolved in laughter. Call me macabre if you will, but if I wanted to commit suicide, I think I'd be hard pressed to even entertain the idea of getting a gun and shooting myself in the crotch.

I'm not at all happy about discovering the dark side of my personality, but I can't help the way I am. I've never considered myself insensitive, but there are times when I read the newspaper or listen to the news and my imagination shifts into overdrive. Perhaps it is the way the story is presented, but my reaction is never the same as anyone else's. I always seem to find irony in every situation, especially in stories that are true. And sometimes truth can be stranger than fiction. Let me give you a few examples. Awhile ago I saw a headline in a U.S. newspaper that read, "Thief leaves calling card." A robber entered a home by breaking a window and although he had no qualms about stealing all the jewelry and valuables, he suddenly developed a guilty conscience, a mistake which led police straight to his door. Believe it or not, he felt so bad about breaking the window that he left a note of apology for the homeowners, and his credit card number to pay for the broken window. Then there was another man who tried to rob a bank. He broke through the wall of the bank with a blow torch, only to find that his efforts were useless because the torch had set fire to all the paper money. Now this one may sound awful, but again, this really did happen. A man who was always trying to get rid of a pesky cat finally caught it one day and after he doused the poor animal with gasoline, he set the cat on fire. Call it justice if you will, but the man's cruel act got him exactly what I think he deserved, for the cat ran under the house and you guessed it, the house burned down.

Oh, yes, strange things happen to people and while something may seem traumatic at the time, when you look at it in retrospect, it is only then that you can see the humour in it. Let's face it. We're only human and we all do and say things in the heat of the moment. Mothers do it all the time, particularly when they're faced with a situation when she fears for her child's safety. Often the words that come out of her mouth doesn't reveal the anxiety she's feeling. "If you fall out of that tree and break your leg, don't come crying to me!" Personally, I'm not responsible for any of my actions when I'm under stress or if there's an emergency. My reaction is totally unpredictable, ranging from anger to tears to hysteria. My son still reminds me about the time he

Life, Love & Laughter

swallowed a nickel when he was six and I rushed him to the hospital. I have no recollection of even driving there myself, but Tim says I ran every red light. It seems that when the doctor said he was out of danger and that the nickel would eventually re-surface, that I expressed my relief in a violent way. Tim maintains that I hugged him first then shook the living daylights out of him in front of the doctor. "If you ever do something dangerous like that again, I'll kill you!"

Stress does some strange things to me and sometimes when I get nervous, I giggle. Not a very endearing quality, ask my sister and brother. Why, I almost ruined the most important day in their lives when I was only 15 years old. Helena and Harve got married in a double wedding ceremony and I was a bridesmaid for the first time. I was very shy then and felt uncomfortable standing at the altar in front of a church full of people. I got so nervous that I began to quiver all over and my knees were knocking. I might have been fine had it not been for mom, because she was late and when she got into the pew beside me, I noticed she had her new hat on backwards. I could feel the laughter building up inside me, for mom got all flustered when daddy reached over and yanked her hat the right way around. And then I heard her gasp as she grabbed me by the arm, "Oh, the dear Lord! I think I forgot to put on me drawers, Lucy!" she whispered in my ear. "I can't kneel down in front of the priest to take communion with no pants on, what if someone can see under my dress?" That did it. I took to giggling and I couldn't stop. Even in front of the priest when the couples were exchanging solemn vows, I tittered and laughed so hard that the little pillbox hat that was perched on my head, fell down over my eyes. My sister nearly broke my rib cage with her elbow, but in my heightened nervous condition, I laughed even more. I just couldn't stop no matter how hard I tried. Needless to say, my reaction put a dent in the ceremony and the priest was appalled at my lack of respect in a house of worship. It was just one of those things that you wished had never happened.

It's funny how life has a way of twisting things around when you least expect it, isn't it? Mary Dwyer, a Newfoundlander who is now deceased, once told me how her good intentions backfired when she first started teaching school in 1921. Ambitious and full of ideas, the young school teacher was determined to make a good impression in the small outport, and she did, but not in the way she expected. She wanted to get acquainted with the parents of every child in her class and the perfect opportunity came when one of her 3rd graders told her his grandfather had died. Mary decided to go visit the boy's grandmother. It was customary back then to wake the deceased in the home and everybody brought food so that the family didn't have to prepare meals, so Mary baked a cherry cake to take with her. She introduced herself to the woman as Johnny's teacher and extended her sympathy. "Your grandson told me about your dear husband's death," she said, "And I've come to extend my deepest sympathy.."

The woman seemed taken aback at first when Mary offered the cake, she was immediately ushered into the kitchen. For an hour the widow talked about how much her dead husband suffered before he died and as she talked, she ate slice after slice of cake. It occurred to Mary that the woman didn't seem overly distraught and that there were no mourners in the house, but not wanting to appear insensitive, she politely listened. Finally, Mary stood up and asked if she could go pay her respects to her dearly departed and say a few prayers. The woman's face lit up and stuffing the last of the cake into her mouth, she opened the porch door. "God love ya, maid. Indeed you can see poor Pete!" she said. "The graveyard's just up yonder beyond that hill. Come on, then. I'll show you the way!"

It seemed that the child left out one small detail about his grandfather's death. The poor man had been dead for three years.

Oh, no, the subject of death is not one to be scoffed at, but there is yet another story on the same vein that is sad, but in retrospect, amusing. Shirley Laslo, a friend here in Niagra Falls, told me about a funeral that never took place. Back 70 years ago, her grandfather apparently fell off a rooftop and when her distraught grandmother found his lifeless body on the ground, she presumed he was dead. As we did in Newfoundland, the deceased was prepared for burial in his good suit and waked in the parlor. A few hours later while mourners were gathered in the kitchen crying over the tragic accident, from the doorway, a shadow appeared and there stood the dead man rubbing his head. "What's all the commotion here? You're making enough noise to wake the dead!" he bellowed.

Thinking he had risen from the dead, everybody started screaming and running in different directions. The screams startled Shirley's grandfather so much, that he ran too and the others thought he was chasing them. When things settled down, the family realized that the man had only been knocked unconscious and had no recollection of what happened or even that he had been prepared for burial. He was totally bewildered.

"Why am I wearing my good suit?" he asked his wife. "We're not having company again, are we?"

When Shirley finished her story, I just couldn't help it. I burst into unabashed laughter. Life is just full of irony, isn't it?

♀

Food for Thought

Millions long for immortality who do not know what to do with themselves on a rainy Sunday afternoon. – *Susan Ertz*

♀

Spice of Life

A good many men still like to think of their wives as they do of their religion, neglected but always there. – *Freya Stark*

♀

Animal Mating - Fact and Fantasy – *Ron Young*

Put That Ugly Thing Away

Fact:

If sex is a turnoff because of your significant other's apparatus, thank God you are not a female Bushbaby, who is related to both monkeys and apes. The penis of the male bushbaby is not only twisted into weird and different shapes, but has spikes, bristles, and bumps.

Fantasy:

If at the altar you feel antsy
About your preordained pregnancy
Knowing that the only way is with a two-some
Just think that if your choice had, maybe
Left you with an adult male bushbaby
Then your present prospect's not all that gruesome

♀

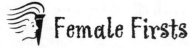 Female Firsts

2000: The first national sports education program designed exclusively for mothers, was launched on Mother's Day in the U.S. Called 'C'mon Mom,' the event's purpose was to help mothers to get involved as volunteer coaches and as sideline spectators.

2001: At age 59, Jody Conradt, a veteran coach for 32 years with the Texas Longhorns, became the first women's basketball coach to work 1,000 games.

2001: Jutta Kleinschmidt of Germany, became the first woman to win the Paris-Dakar road rally at age 38.

2001: Ann Bancroft, 45, of the US, and Liv Arnesen, 47, of Norway, became the first women to cross the Antarctic land mass on skis. Each woman pulled 240-pound sleds during the expedition.

2002: Janica Kostelic, a 20-year-old Croatian woman, became the first Alpine skier to win four medals at a Winter Olympics with her gold medal performance in the giant slalom, giving her 3 golds and one silver for the Salt Lake Games.

2003: Hayley Wickenheiser, a 24-year-old Canadian woman, became the first woman to score a goal in a men's pro hockey game when she assisted on a goal for her Finnish League team, the Kirkkonummi Salamat.

2003: Regina Jacobs became the first woman to break the four-minute mile in the indoor 1,500 meters at the Boston Indoor Games.

2003: Oprah Winfrey became the first African-American woman ever to make *Forbes* magazine's list of global billionaires. *See also page 103.*

2003: On October 10, Shirin Ebadi became the first Iranian and the first Muslim to win the Nobel Peace Prize for her efforts in promoting peaceful and democratic solutions in the struggle for human rights.

2003: On October 21, Newfoundland and Labrador elected 10 females in the Provincial election, the highest number of females ever elected in the province.

♀

Quillings

Revelations – By Ron Young

Since time began, wars have raged
The victors were the strong
Yet all the times man fought for peace
Man never got along
And for every coup, war, conflict, fight
Man never learned to do it right
Man never found a way to be
Better than his insecurity

Behind man always, through his strife
Were lover, mother, girlfriend, wife
Is it time to take another stance?
And give the womenfolk a chance
And if they can't give it a go
We can always say, "I told you so"
Or maybe when they have succeeded
Will negatives, no more be needed?

♀

Life, Love & Laughter

Appetizers
&
Enhancers

Seal Flipper Pastry (for ship's crew)

Geraldine Prim, St. John's, Newfoundland (nee O'Brien, Cape Broyle, Newfoundland)

Ingredients:
4 lbs flour
4 ozs baking powder
1 tsp salt
3/4 lb margarine
1 1/2 litres milk

Directions:
Mix dry ingredients together, add margarine. Mix until crumbly - add milk, mix to form a soft dough. Do not overmix! Place dough on a lightly floured board and knead lightly. Then roll out until pastry is 3/4" thick before placing over the previously cooked seal flippers in the pan. Covers up to 24 flippers.

Lentil Barley Soup

G. Bussey, Roseneath, Ontario

Ingredients:
1/2 cup lentils
1 medium onion, chopped
1/4 cup barley
2 cups cabbage, chopped
4 cups water
2 stalks celery, chopped
1 can tomatoes (19 oz)
Salt and savory to taste
3 medium carrots, sliced

Directions:
Boil all ingredients slowly until carrots are tender (about one hour), then serve.

Hot Crabmeat – Avocado Salad

Louise Sweetapple, Downsview, Ontario

Ingredients:
1 can (12 ozs) crabmeat drained and cartilage removed
1/3 cup celery, chopped
3 hard cooked eggs, chopped
2 tbsps pimento, chopped
1 tbsp onion, chopped
1/2 tsp salt
1/2 cup mayonnaise or salad dressing
3 large or 4 small ripe avocados
Lemon juice

Appetizers & Enhancers

Appetizers & Enhancers

3 tbsps dry bread crumbs
1 tsp melted butter
2 tbsps slivered almonds

Directions:

Heat oven to 400°F mix crabmeat, celery, eggs, pimento, onion, salt and the mayonnaise together. Cut ripe peeled avocados length-wise in half and remove pits. Brush halves with lemon juice, sprinkle lightly with salt. Fill avocado halves with crabmeat mixture. Toss bread crumbs in butter, spoon over crabmeat. Place in an ungreased shallow baking dish; bake uncovered for 10 minutes. Sprinkle almonds over crumb topping, bake 5 minutes longer or until bubbly. 6 to 8 servings.

Luau Bites

Karen Kennedy

Ingredients:

1 can (284 ml) drained water chestnuts whole
1/2 lb side bacon cut into strips
1/4 cup soya sauce
2 tsps brown sugar

Directions:

Cut bacon in half. Wrap bacon around a water chestnut. Fasten with a wooden toothpick. Chill in mixture of soya sauce and brown sugar for about 1/2 hour. Spoon marinade over occasionally. Drain. Broil in oven until bacon is crispy - turning once. Serve hot.

Homemade Condensed Milk

Alice Vezina, Renfrew, Ontario

Ingredients:

1 cup skim milk powder
2/3 cup icing sugar
1/3 cup boiling water
2 tbsps melted butter

Directions:

Blend until smooth. Keep in refrigerator. Yield 1 1/4 cups = 1 can condensed milk.

Cream Cheese Frosting

Geraldine Prim, St. John's, Newfoundland (nee O'Brien, Cape Broyle, Newfoundland)

Ingredients:

1 pkg (3 oz) cream cheese (softened)
1/4 cup butter (softened)
2 cups icing sugar
1/2 tsp vanilla
2 tsps milk (if necessary to spread evenly)

Directions:

Beat cream cheese into softened butter in a medium size bowl with a mixer, then beat in icing sugar with vanilla. (add milk if necessary to make spreading easier).

Spaghetti Dressing

Geraldine Prim, St. John's, Newfoundland (nee O'Brien, Cape Broyle, Newfoundland)

Ingredients:
2 lbs hamburger meat
1 stick celery
1 can tomato paste (small)
2 onions, chopped finely
1/2 tsp red pepper
1/4 lb salt pork, chopped finely
1/2 green pepper
1 can tomatoes (large)
1/2 garlic clove

Female Facts

Advised From The Beginning of Democracy
In 1776, John Adams, one of America's founding fathers, received a letter from his wife, Abigal, that read: "If particular care and attention is not paid to the ladies, we are determined to foment a rebellion, and will not hold ourselves bound by any laws in which we have no voice or representation.

Directions:

Fry out salt pork, then add hamburger meat, followed by other ingredients. Cook 3 hours, stir often, add a little water.

The Famous Scottish Dumpling

Margaret Crocker, Kitchener, Ontario (nee MacMillan, Scotland)

Ingredients:
350 g (12 oz) plain flour
100 g (4 oz) fresh white breadcrumbs
225 g (8 oz) shredded suet
225 g (8 oz) dark soft brown sugar
1 tsp baking powder
1 tsp mixed spice
1 tsp ground ginger
1/2 tsp cinnamon
1 tbsp golden syrup
1 tbsp marmalade
3 tbsps black trecle
1 tbsp milk
2 large carrots (grated)
575 g (20 oz) dried mixed fruit
Two large eggs, beaten

Female Facts

A Duck By Any Other Name
"Hello my Ducky," is a common greeting up to this day in Newfoundland and Labrador, and is always said with the kindest and friendliest of intents. Its origins however, come from the amorous intents of men in 16th century London, England. Any British prostitute who worked the docks was called a 'docky.' That later evolved into 'ducky,' but before it made its way to respectability and to this side of the ocean, it found yet another use. The term 'lame duck,' which indicates a person who defaults on debts, alluded to prostitutes who had lost their looks and could no longer be counted upon to bring in any money.

Directions:

Mix all ingredients together to make quite a firm mixture, then put a large tea-towel into a pan of boiling water and boil for one minute. Drain until cool enough to handle, then squeeze dry. Spread on work surface and generously sprinkle with flour. This forms the seal or crust around the dumpling while it is boiling. Spoon the mixture into the middle of the cloth, shaping it into a neat round. Gather up the cloth and tie securely, leaving room for the dumpling to expand slightly. Bring a large pan of water to a boil. Place the dumpling on a trivet or an upturned saucer. Cover and boil for three hours, topping up the water with boiling water as necessary. Remove from pan and leave to stand for five minutes before removing cloth. Cut into slices, and serve hot with cream, custard or brandy butter. (Serves 8)

Biscuits

G. Bussey, Roseneath, Ontario

Ingredients:
2 cups flour
4 tbsps margarine
3 tsp baking powder
3/4 cup milk
1/2 tsp salt
1/4 cup melted margarine

Spice of Life

The only reason I would take up jogging is so that I could hear heavy breathing again.
– Erma Bombeck

Directions:
Sift flour, baking powder and salt together. Cut in margarine until mixture resembles coarse cornmeal. Stir in milk. Knead 1/2 minute. Roll 1/4 inch thick and spread margarine on dough. Roll up like a jelly roll. Cut off 1 inch thick slices and place around edges of casserole. Bake at 425°F for 25 minutes or until biscuits are lightly browned.

Marshberry Jelly

Helen Crocker, Kitchener, Ontario (formerly of Heart's Delight, Newfoundland)

Ingredients:
4 cups of marshberries
2 cups water
Granulated sugar

Female Facts

In 1997, over two-thirds of women in prison in the U.S. had at least one child under the age of 18 years.

Directions:
Pick over and wash marshberries. Boil water in a saucepan and add berries. Boil for 20 minutes, then force through a sieve, pressing all juice from the boiled berries. Cook juice for 3 minutes, then add 3/4 cup granulated sugar for each cup of juice and cook for another 2 minutes. Pour into a sterilized jar and seal. This is a very old recipe and was handed down to the family for 5 generations. We use it in place of cranberry sauce. It is better than cranberry sauce.

Bread Pudding

Janice Hunter, Kitchener, Ontario, (formerly of Heart's Delight, Newfoundland)

Ingredients:
8 ozs stale bread
4 ozs raisins

Spice of Life
Don't look back - they may be gaining on you.

2 ozs brown sugar
2 ozs finely chopped suet (fat)
1/2 tsp mixed spice
1/4 tsp cinnamon
1/4 tsp ginger
1 egg
Milk

Food for Thought

The difference between courtship and marriage is like the difference between the pictures in a seed catalogue and what comes up. – *James Wharton*

Directions:

Break bread into small pieces and soak in cold water for 15 minutes. Then squeeze as dry as possible. Put into a bowl and beat out lumps with a fork. Add raisins, sugar, suet, spices, and mix well. Add beaten egg and enough milk to enable the mixture to drop easily from a spoon. Pour into a well-greased bread pan and bake at 300°F for 50 minutes. When done, turn out onto a hot dish and dredge with sugar. Serve hot with custard.

Smokey Salmon Spread

Louise Sweetapple, Downsview, Ontario

Ingredients:

2 cans salmon (200g or 7 3/4 oz)
1 250 g (8 oz) package cream cheese
2 tsps grated onion
2 tsps fresh lemon juice
1 tsp grated horseradish
1/4 tsp salt
1/4 tsp liquid smoke
1/4 cup chopped toasted almonds
Fresh parsley

Female Facts

More Seniors Are Women
Women make up a relatively large share of the senior population, especially in the very oldest age range. In 1995, Canadian women constituted 58 per cent of the population aged 65 and over and 70 per cent of the population aged 85 and over.

Directions:

In a bowl blend flaked salmon, cheese, onion, lemon juice, horseradish, salt and liquid smoke. Refrigerate covered over night. Shape mixture into a ball. Roll in almonds. Garnish with parsley sprigs. Serve with small biscuits, thinly sliced bread or raw vegetable sticks. Makes about 20 servings.

Dipping Sauce

Louise Sweetapple, Downsview, Ontario

Ingredients:

2 tsps curry powder
1 1/2 cups Hellmann's mayonnaise
1/2 tsp dry mustard
1/2 tsp salt (or less) salt
Dash pepper
1 tsp or more grated onion

Spice of Life
September is the month when children will return to school, and many a mother will return to bed.

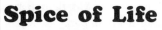

Appetizers & Enhancers

Directions:
Stir all ingredients well together in a bowl to make a dipping sauce for carrots sticks, celery sticks, cauliflower flowerettes, etc.

Egg Rolls
Donna Chafe

Ingredients:
2 lbs medium minced meat
3 or 4 tsps salt
8 cups cabbage (shredded)
1 tsp pepper
8 cups bean sprouts
6 tbsps Worchestershire Sauce
2 cups diced onions
6 tbsps soya sauce
1 cup diced celery
6 tbsps MSG
2 cans sliced mushrooms
6-8 pkgs egg roll covers (thawed enough to separate)
1 jar of Mazola oil or any polyunsaturated oil
Egg whites

Female Facts

Mohammed's Child Bride
Ishah Bint Ab Bakr, whose father supported the prophet Mohammed, became the child bride of the prophet after the battle of Bakr in AD624. Mohammed died when Ishah was 18, leaving no male heir. Ishah maintained her position of power through tremendous courage, intelligence and learning, and became an authority on Muslim tradition. She was very important for her active role in the civil war, but was defeated and captured in a battle near Basra in 656, called the 'Battle of the Camel.' She was only released after promising to abandon political life. Ishah is still an established name in the tradition of Islam.

Directions:
Sauté meat on low heat to remove grease (drain and add to bean sprouts, cabbage, diced onions, celery and mushrooms in a very large bowl, then mix together with salt, pepper, Worchestershire Sauce, soya sauce and MSG. Brush edges of egg roll covers with the egg whites and place 1 tbsp of mixture in the centre and fold. Fry in hot fat and cool. Sample one and then freeze. To serve: reheat in 400°F oven approx. 10 minutes.

Plain Toutons
Gladys Meaney

Ingredients:
4 cups flour
4 tsps baking powder
1 tsp salt
1/2 lb salt pork (diced)

Female Facts

Employed Women Healthier
Employed, married women have the best health profile whether or not they have children. Employed, unmarried women rank next, but those with children (single moms) have worse health than those without children. Unemployed Canadian women, married or unmarried, with and without children have poorer health.

Directions:
Fry pork slightly - cool. Mix flour, baking powder and salt together. Add enough cold water to make dough firm. Fry in pork scruncheons and fat. Pat out and cut. Deep fry in hot fat or in frying pan.

Cheddar Chutney Nibblers

Stephanie Woodford

Ingredients:
20 Ritz Crackers (any flavour)
1 pkg (227g) Cracker Barrel old cheddar cheese
1/2 cup (125 ml) chutney (or prepared cranberry sauce)
Chopped pecans

Directions:
Cut cheese into 20 slices. Place 1 slice of cheese on each cracker and top with 1 tsp (5 ml) chutney. Top with pecans. Bake at 350°F (180°C) for 5 minutes or until cheese starts to melt. Serve immediately. Makes 20 appetizers. Preparation time: 5 minutes. Cooking time: 5 minutes.

Hot Crab and Swiss Bites

Susan Lewis

Ingredients:
20 Ritz Crackers (any flavour)
1 can (42 oz/120 g) crab meat, drained
1/4 cup (50 ml) mayonnaise
2 green onions, chopped
1/2 cup (125 g) grated Kraft swiss cheese

Directions:
Mix together crab, mayonnaise, green onions and cheese. Place 2 tsps (10 ml) crab mixture on each cracker. Bake at 350°F (180°C) for 5 minutes. Serve immediately. Makes 20 appetizers. Preparation time: 5 minutes. Cooking time: 5 minutes.

Brie–Berry Bites

Megan Doyle

Ingredients:
16 Ritz Crackers (any flavour)
1 pkg (125 g) Kraft brie cheese
8 strawberries, cut in half

Directions:
Cut brie cheese into 16 wedges. Place one wedge on each cracker and top with strawberry half. Makes 16 appetizers. Preparation time: 5 minutes.

Salmon Ball

Wanda Sullivan

Ingredients:
8 oz pkg cream cheese
2 cans (7 oz) red salmon

Appetizers & Enhancers

Appetizers & Enhancers

1 tbsp lemon juice
2 tsps finely chopped onion
1 tsp horseradish
1/4 tsp salt
1/2 cup chopped pecans
3 tbsps parsley

Directions:

Mix together first six ingredients, then form into a ball and refrigerate several hours. Remove from refrigerator and roll ball in pecans and parsley mixture until well coated. Keep chilled. May be frozen. Thaw 4 hours before serving. Serve with crackers and grapes.

Heavenly Jam

Judy Rimmer

Ingredients:

2 pkgs strawberry jello
1 can (20 oz) crushed pineapple
5 cups rhubarb
5 cups sugar

Directions:

Cut rhubarb into small pieces. Add sugar and pineapple. Let sit at room temperature for 12 hours. Boil. Reduce heat for 20 minutes. Stir in jello until dissolved. Cool and bottle.

Pickled Eggs

Judy Rimmer

Ingredients:

Eggs
3 tsps peppercorns (optional)
9 cups white vinegar
6 tsps mixed pickling spices - tied in a cheesecloth bag
4 1/2 tsps salt

Directions:

Hard boil as many eggs as desired, then cover immediately with cold water. Combine remaining ingredients, bring to a boil and then simmer for 10 minutes. Cool. Remove egg shells. Put eggs into a large glass jar. Pour cooled vinegar mixture over them, and seal for at least 3 weeks. Enjoy!

Spinach Dip

Emily Price

Ingredients:
1 small bottle Hellmann's Mayonaise or 1 cup
1 cup sour cream
1 pkg Knorr Swiss vegetable soup mix
1 small can water chestnuts cut up
2 green onions (chopped)
1 pk frozen spinach rinsed and drained well (Fresh spinach may be used, just cook and drain)
Round pumpernickle bread

Directions:
Mix all ingredients except bread together to stand overnight. Cut top off bread, cut out centre of bread into cubes. Arrange on platter around scooped out crust and fill crust with dip about 1 hour before serving.

Coconut Icing

Betty Healey

Ingredients:
1 cup sugar
1 cup coconut
1 tsp vanilla
1/2 cup butter
1 can (14 1/2 oz) of milk, dilute with 1 can water

Directions:
Bring to a boil. Punch fork holes in cake. Pour hot frosting as soon as cake is taken from oven.

Cheese Sauce

Donna Phillips

Ingredients:
2 tbsps butter
2 tbsps flour
1/4 tsp salt
1/8 tsp pepper
1 cup milk
1/2 cup shredded cheddar cheese
Mustard (optional)

Directions:
Melt butter in a saucepan and stir in flour, salt and pepper. Add milk a little at a time, stirring continuously. Then add shredded cheddar cheese into the white sauce, and a little mustard if desired. Continue cooking over medium heat for 15 minutes. Serve over cooked broccoli, cauliflower or other vegetables. (May be reheated; to do so add a little more milk while heating.)

Female Facts

Breast Cancer Most Diagnosed
Breast cancer is the most frequently diagnosed cancer in Canadian women, accounting for 30 per cent of all cancer cases.

Spice of Life

Could the charming brides be described as "lovely women, very well-groomed"?

Food for Thought

Always be smarter than the people who hire you.
– Lena Horne

Appetizers & Enhancers

Appetizers & Enhancers

Partridgeberry Salad

Robyn Mason

Ingredients:
1 cup water
1 pkg Jell-O - any red flavour
2 cups frozen partridgeberries
1 cup diced apples

Directions:
Dissolve Jello into boiling water, then add berries and diced apples. Stir and set. Delicious served with turkey or cold cuts. Also may be served with sour cream as an appetizer.

Female Facts

Female Eating Disorders
Of all people with eating disorders, 95 per cent are female. Of those between the ages of 14 and 25, one to two per cent have anorexia, and 3 to 5 per cent have bulimia. As many as 10 to 20 per cent show eating behaviours associated with anorexia and bulimia.

Bacon Roll–Ups

Darlene Lane

Ingredients:
1 lb bacon, cut in half
1 can mushroom soup (10 oz)
1/2 pkg onion soup mix
1 loaf bread (no crust)

Directions:
Cut bread into fingers and flatten. Combine soups and spread over bread, and roll up, then wrap a piece of bacon around roll and hold with a toothpick. Broil until brown on top, then turn and broil bottom.

Female Facts

First Canadian Girls' School
Margaret Bourgeoys opened a girls school on Montreal Island in 1658, and later, using recruited French and Canadian girls, organized a boarding school for girls in Montreal, a school for Indian girls, and a domestic arts school. She is best known as being the founder of the Congregation de Notre Dame de Montreal.

Turkey and Mushroom Croustades

Betty Anne Meaney

Croustade Ingredients:
20 slices of sandwich bread (crust removed)
Melted butter

Croustade Directions
Brush both sides of each bread slice with melted butter: press gently into large muffin pans. Bake at 350°F for 15 to 20 minutes or until golden. (Croustades may be made ahead and frozen).

Filling Ingredients:
1/4 cup butter
3 tbsps flour
1 small onion chopped (optional)
1 cup milk

Food for Thought

If you think you can, you can. And if you think you can't, you're right.
– *Mary Kay Ash*

Spice of Life

A diet is for women who are thick and tired of it.

1 cup finely chopped mushrooms
1/4 tsp salt
1 can flakes of turkey (drain and flake with a fork)
Few grains cayenne pepper
Freshly ground black pepper
1 tsp lemon juice
Parsley flakes

Food for Thought

If you tried to do something but failed, you are still much better off than if you tried to do nothing and succeeded.

Filling Directions:

In a medium saucepan, melt butter. Sauté onion and mushrooms until onion is transparent. Stir in flakes of turkey, sprinkle mixture with flour and mix well. Add milk gradually, continue heating and stirring until mixture thickens and comes to a boil. Remove from heat, stir in salt, pepper, cayenne pepper and lemon juice. Fill each croustade with filling. Place on a cookie sheet and heat in a 350°F oven for 10 minutes or until bubbly. Sprinkle with chopped parsley and serve hot. Makes 20 croustades.

Old-Fashioned Potato Bread

Gail Van Wort, Stoney Creek, Ontario

Ingredients:
2 cups warm water (115°F)
2 pkgs active dry yeast
1/2 cup sugar
1 tbsp salt
1 cup warm mashed potatoes, unseasoned
1/2 cup butter or margarine, softened
2 eggs
7 1/2 cups unsifted all-purpose flour
3 tbsps butter or margarine

Spice of Life

A Newfoundland lighthouse keeper was asked how he met his wife and he said that he had advertised for a woman to do some light house work. Apparently their marriage is headed for the rocks!
– *Cracks from Clyde*

Directions:

Put warm water in a large bowl. Sprinkle with the yeast; stir until dissolved. Add sugar and salt; stir until dissolved. Add unseasoned mashed potatoes, soft butter, eggs, and 3 1/2 cups of flour. With an electric mixer at medium speed, beat until smooth (about 2 minutes). Gradually add remaining flour; mixing with a wooden spoon or by hand, until dough is smooth and stiff enough to leave sides of bowl. Melt 1 tbsp of butter and brush over dough. Cover with double thickness of tin foil or plastic wrap. Let rise in fridge for about 2 hours or until double in bulk. Punch down dough. Refrigerate overnight. Next day turn out dough onto a lightly floured board, knead dough until smooth and elastic and blisters appear on surface (about 10 minutes). Divide dough in half and shape each half into a smooth ball about 6 inches in diameter. Place each in a 9-inch cake pan, or you can use muffin pans or square bread pans. Melt remaining 2 tbsp of butter and spread over dough. Cover with towel. Let rise in a warm place free of drafts until the dough doubles in bulk. (1 1/2 hours to 2 hours). Preheat oven to 400°F. Bake until dough sounds hollow. When bread is done, brush melted butter over cooked bread. Remove from pans.

Appetizers & Enhancers

Appetizers & Enhancers

Herb Rice

Connie Fowlow, Goulds, Newfoundland (nee Mason, formerly of St. John's, Newfoundland)

Ingredients:
1 cup instant, long grain rice
2 large onions, chopped
3 tbsps margarine
1/2 tsp marjoram
1/2 tsp savoury
1/2 tsp rosemary
1/2 tsp salt
3 chicken bouillon cubes
2 cups hot water

Female Facts

Always In Fashion
The most-lasting of all woman's fashion has been the sar (sari), of India, which has been popular for over 5,000 years.

Directions:
Put rice, onion and margarine in frying pan. Cook until rice is golden brown; stirring constantly. Add water, chicken cubes, salt and seasonings; bring to a boil. Reduce heat and cook for about 40 minutes, covered. Serves 3-4.

Veggie Pizza

Norma Clarke, Peterborough, Ontario, (nee Atkinson, Herring Neck, Newfoundland)

Ingredients:
2 pkgs refrigerator crescent rolls
1 (8 oz) pkg cream cheese
3/4 cup mayonnaise
1 tsp dillweed
1/4 cup milk

Spice of Life

Beauty in women is that potent personal alchemy which usually transforms the best of men into fools.

Directions:
Spread crescent rolls out on a baking sheet. Bake crust for 10 minutes at 350°F. Blend together cream cheese, mayonnaise, dillweed and milk; spread on baked crust. Top with raw vegetables of your choice and shredded cheese, if desired.

Devilled Eggs

Edna Million, St. John's, Newfoundland

Ingredients:
Hard-boiled eggs (1 per guest/person)
Mayonnaise, or a similar salad dressing
Relish
Pickled onions (diced)
Pickles (diced)
Paprika

Food for Thought

Because his wife is of such a delicate nature, a man will avoid using certain questionable descriptive words all through his married life. And then one day he picks up a novel she is reading and is nonplussed to find five of the words in the first chapter.

Directions:

To hard-boil an egg, boil for 10-15 minutes. Cut the cooled eggs in half, scoop out all the yolks. In a bowl, mash together the yolks and any, or all, of the relish, onions or pickles. Add mayonnaise, a tablespoon-full at a time, and add only enough to make the mixture creamy. There should be 3 parts yolk for every 1 part other ingredients. When all is thoroughly blended, use a spoon to refill the now empty egg whites with the mixture. Sprinkle each with paprika. Arrange on a serving tray, preferably one that isn't green.

Devilled Squidlets

Sue Bonderski, Ottawa, Ontario

Ingredients:
2 large squid hoods
1/4 cup fresh parsley, chopped
1/4 cup lemon juice
1 tbsp oil
2 tsps brown sugar
1/2 tsp dry mustard
1/4 tsp tabasco sauce

Female Facts

President of Malta
In 1947, Agatha Barbara became Malta's first woman Member of Parliament. She remained an MP for the next 35 years, holding down two ministerial positions during that time. In 1982 she became President of the Republic of Malta.

Directions:

Cut squid lengthways into 1cm. strips, thread onto toothpicks. Combine remaining ingredients, except parsley, in a bowl. Add squid to the liquid and put in the refrigerator to marinate for a few hours. Barbecue squid, brushing with marinade, until tender. Sprinkle with parsley before serving. Yields 24.

Mushroom Caps Stuffed with Herb Cheese

Maria Young, St. Philip's, Newfoundland (nee Hardy, Port aux Basques, Newfoundland)

Ingredients:
16 medium mushrooms
3 tbsps whipped cream cheese
1 tbsp fresh parsley, or basil
2 tsps parmesan cheese, grated
1 small garlic clove, minced
2 tsps plain, dried bread crumbs

Spice of Life

Perfume counters in department stores are scentsational places.

Directions:

Preheat oven to 450°F. Remove stems from mushrooms and chop (save caps). Using a fork, combine chopped mushrooms, cream cheese, parsley (or basil), parmesan cheese and garlic; mix well. Fill each cap with equal amounts of mixture and arrange in an 8 x 8 non-stick baking pan. Sprinkle bread crumbs on top. Pour 1/4 cup water into bottom of pan and bake approximately 8 - 10 minutes, until mushrooms are fork tender and lightly brown.

Appetizers & Enhancers

Mushrooms with Herb Cheese Filling

Sue Bonderski, Ottawa, Ontario

Ingredients:
30 small mushrooms
100 g ham, chopped
1 tbsp fresh chives, chopped
1/3 cup cheese, grated
1/4 cup stale bread crumbs
1/4 tsp dried tarragon leaves
Pinch cayenne pepper

Directions:
Remove stems from mushrooms, chop stems finely. Combine stems with remaining ingredients in a large bowl, mixing well. Spoon mixture into mushroom caps. Barbecue on foil or pan until tender.

Christmas Salad

Claudine Barnes (nee Pye, Cape Charles, Labrador)

Ingredients:
1 can mandarin oranges, with juice
1 cup crushed pineapple, drained
1 cup miniature marshmallows
1 small container sour cream
1/2 cup coconut

Directions:
Mix all ingredients together and let set for 24 hours.

Christmas Salad

Viola Mauger, Port aux Basques, Newfoundland

Ingredients:
1 pkg lime Jello
1 cup boiling water
1 (8 oz) pkg cream cheese
1 small can crushed pineapple
1 cup nuts
1 cup celery, chopped
1 cup miniature marshmellows
1 pt whipping cream

Directions:
Prepare Jello with water. Set until ready to gell, then add cream cheese, pineapple, nuts, celery and marshmallows. Mix well and chill until almost set. Fold in whipped cream.

Food for Thought

Sleeping alone, except under doctor's orders, does much harm. Children will tell you how lonely it is sleeping alone. If possible, you should always sleep with someone you love. You both recharge your mutual batteries free of charge. – *Marlene Dietrich*

Female Facts

Dressed To Drink
During the reign of Catherine I of Russia, women were forbidden to get drunk at parties, and men were forbidden to get drunk before nine o'clock. During that time, ladies of the court, including Catherine's own daughter, Princess Elizabeth, went to transvestite parties in order to get around the rule.

Appetizers & Enhancers

Sweet Hungarian Pancakes

Madge Witzing, London, Ontario (nee Bailey, Baie Verte, Newfoundland)

Ingredients:

2 large eggs, separated
1 cup milk
1/2 cup flour
1 tbsp sugar
1 tbsp rum (optional)
1/8 tsp salt
2 tbsps butter, melted
3/4 cup jam (strawberry, raspberry, etc.)
1/2 cup ground hazelnuts
2 tbsps icing sugar

Female Facts

On May 12, 1969, 39-year-old Sharon Sites Adams, set sail in her 31 foot sailboat to sail alone, 5,618 miles eastward across the Pacific Ocean. On July 26, she arrived in San Diego harbour to become the first woman to sail the Pacific solo.

Directions:

Beat egg yolks in a medium size mixing bowl until thoroughly blended. Add milk, flour, sugar, rum and salt; beat with a wire whisk until smooth. Blend in melted butter. Refrigerate for 1 hour. Beat egg whites until stiff, but not dry; fold into batter; combine well. Lightly grease an 8-inch heavy skillet or omelet pan with butter. Place over moderate heat until a few drops of water sprinkled in skillet dance. Stir batter. Remove pan from heat and pour 3 tbsps of batter into the pan; quickly tilt pan in all directions to coat the bottom with batter. Return to heat; cook until lightly browned. Turn; cook for a few seconds on other side. Transfer to a warm plate. Continue in the same manner; stirring batter before making next pancake. Stack pancakes with waxed paper between each one. Keep warm until all pancakes are cooked. Place 1 1/2 tbsps jam in center of each pancake; roll. Place side by side on a platter. Combine hazelnuts and sugar; sprinkle over pancakes. Heat in a 325°F oven for 10 minutes. Makes about 6 servings. These pancakes are great with ice cream and rolled in the same manner and topped with chocolate or butterscotch sauce.

American French Toast

June Gates, Woodstock, Ontario

Ingredients:

3/4 cup butter or margarine, melted
1 1/2 cups brown sugar
1 1/4 tsps cinnamon
12 slices of bread
5 eggs, well beaten
1/2 tsp salt
1 1/2 - 1 3/4 cups milk

Female Facts

America's Canadian Sweetheart
In the days of silent films, "America's Sweetheart" Mary Pickford, who was really Canadian-born Gladys Smith, was one of the first real movie stars. She made the amazing sum of $350,000 a film in 1917.

Directions:

Mix butter, sugar and cinnamon together. Sprinkle about 1/3 of the mixture in the bottom of a 9" x 13" pan. Cover with 6 slices of bread and sprinkle with another 1/3 brown sugar mixture. Cover with remaining 6 slices of bread and sugar mixture. Mix the well-beaten eggs, salt and milk together. Pour carefully over the bread. Place in the fridge overnight. Bake in the morning at 350°F for about 45 minutes. Serve with maple syrup.

Appetizers & Enhancers

Egg in the Hole

Norma Clarke, Peterborough, Ontario, (nee, Atkinson, Herring Neck, Newfoundland)

Ingredients:
1 slice of bread
Butter
1 egg

Spice of Life
After paying for the big wedding, the only thing a father has left to give away is the bride.

Directions:
Butter bread on both sides. Cut a hole in the middle of the bread. Grease a frying pan and put heat on medium. Place a slice of bread in the pan; drop egg in the hole and fry on both sides. Serve with syrup.

Aunt Madeline's Cabbage Rolls

Rosemarie Reynar, North York, Ontario (nee Stratton of Lewisporte, Newfoundland)

Ingredients:
1 egg
1 tsp salt
Dash pepper
1/4 cup onion, finely chopped
2/3 cup milk
1 lb ground beef
3/4 cup rice, cooked
Cabbage leaves
1 can tomato soup
1 tbsp brown sugar
1 tbsp lemon juice

Female Facts

Black and Blue
Women have been checking men's collars for signs of lipstick for over 8,000 years. Back then, in ancient Egypt, which is as far back as there are traces of lipstick, the popular colour wasn't red or even hot pink, it was blue-black.

Directions:
Combine egg, salt, pepper, onion and milk. Mix well. Add beef and cooked rice, mixing with a fork. Immerse cabbage leaves in boiling water for 3 minutes or until limp, drain. Place 1/2 cup meat mixture on each leaf. Fold in sides and roll ends over meat. Place rolls in a long baking dish. Blend together soup, sugar and lemon juice. Pour over rolls. Bake at 350°F for 1 1/4 hours. Baste once or twice with sauce.

Penne with Herbed Tomato-Tuna Sauce

Rosalind Fraser, Garson, Ontario

Ingredients:
1 tbsp olive oil
1 small onion, chopped
1 clove garlic, minced
1 can tomatoes, chopped
1/2 cup chicken stock
1 tsp dried basil

Food for Thought
A house is no home unless it contains food and fire for the mind as well as for the body. – *Margaret Fuller*

1 can tuna, drained
1/3 cup fresh parsley
3 cups penne
Salt and pepper, to taste

Directions:

Heat oil in a saucepan; add onion and garlic. Cook for 5 minutes, stirring occasionally. Add tomatoes; stir in chicken broth and basil. Simmer uncovered for 10 minutes. Stir in tuna and simmer for 5 minutes. Add salt, pepper and parsley. Cook penne; drain off excess water. Toss with tomato mixture and serve.

Stuffed Pumpkin

Agnes Gaultois, Kindersley, Saskatchewan

Ingredients:
1 medium pumpkin
1 onion, chopped
1 lb ground meat
2 cups rice
1 medium green pepper, chopped
1/2 stalk celery, finely chopped
1 can cream of chicken soup
1 can mushroom pieces, drained
3 tbsps brown sugar
1 tbsp soya sauce
Salt, to taste

Directions:

Cut off the top of the pumpkin. Scoop out all pulp and seeds. Brown meat in a saucepan with a little butter; add onion and green pepper. When partly cooked, add the rest of the ingredients. Rub inside of the pumpkin with a little salt and fill with cooked mixture. Put lid back on pumpkin and place on a cookie sheet. Bake at 350°F for 1 hour or more. Serve as is, or on bread pieces or nacho chips.

Pasta Salad with Dressing

Ada Gillis (nee Mercer), Dartmouth, Nova Scotia

Salad Ingredients:
3 cups three-colour fusilli pasta
2 ripe tomatoes (diced)
1/2 cup cucumber (diced)
1/2 green pepper (chopped)

Salad Directions:

Cook pasta (according to package directions), drain, cool and combine with other ingredients.

Appetizers & Enhancers

Appetizers & Enhancers

Dressing Ingredients:
2/3 cup sugar
1/2 cup olive oil (extra virgin preferably)
1/3 cup ketchup
1/4 cup white vinegar
1 tsp salt
1/4 tsp black pepper
1 tsp paprika

Dressing Directions:
Combine ingredients in a bowl and beat with egg beater until smooth. Pour over pasta salad and refrigerate for two hours.

Creamy French Icing

Doreen Sooley, Perth-Andover, New Brunswick

Ingredients:
2 tbsps water
4 1/2 tbsps white sugar
2 1/3 cups sifted icing sugar
1 egg
2/3 cup Fluffo shortening
1 tsp vanilla

Directions:
Boil water and sugar together for a few minutes. Mix icing sugar and egg together; blend with sugar and water mixture. Add shortening and vanilla. Beat with electric mixer until creamy.

Banana Icing

Winnie Marshall, Stephenville, Newfoundland

Ingredients:
1/2 cup butter
1/2 cup mashed bananas
3 1/2 cups sifted icing sugar
1 tsp vanilla
1 tbsp lemon juice

Directions:
Cream together butter and mashed bananas. Gradually blend in icing sugar, vanilla and lemon juice. Chill to proper spreading consistency. Makes enough to fill and frost two 8-inch layers.

Female Facts

Working Women Abuse
In Canada, 25 per cent of working women report that they were subject to physical, verbal or sexual abuse at work.

Female Facts

From Orphanage to Legislature
Although Dorothy Lavinia Brown was only five months old when her unmarried mother placed her in an orphanage, she later became the first African American female surgeon in the Southern U.S. Later, in 1966, she became the first African American woman to be elected to the Tennessee State Legislature for a two-year term.

Food for Thought

The day will come when men will recognize woman as his peer, not only at the fireside, but in councils of the nation. Then, and not until then, will there be the perfect comradeship, the ideal union between the sexes that shall result in the highest development of the race. – *Susan B. Anthony*

Fresh Whipping Cream for all Seasons

Marjorie Baetzel (nee Noseworthy), St. John's, Newfoundland

Ingredients:
1 (250 ml) carton whipping cream
1/2 tsp icing sugar

Spice of Life

I have a friend who says her idea of roughing it is staying at motels without room service.

Directions:
Open the carton of whipping cream and taste test to assure its freshness, then place in freezer until it is needed. Remove from the freezer a day before needed and place in regular fridge to thaw. When ready to whip, put icing sugar in a bowl. Add thawed cream and whip on high speed. When cream is stored in a bottle, it will stay fresh for about a week.

Vanilla Extract

Alice Vezina, Renfrew, Ontario

Ingredients:
1 vanilla bean
1 cup vodka or brandy

Spice of Life

Better to have loved and lost a short person than never to have loved a tall.
– *David Chambless*

Directions:
Place vanilla bean and vodka or brandy in an airtight, opaque container; seal bottle tightly and store in a dark cupboard for 4 weeks. To get the full flavour of the bean, break into pieces and make sure each piece is covered with liquid. The longer the bean is left in the bottle, the stronger the mixture's vanilla flavour. This homemade mixture can be used in a recipe that calls for vanilla.

Sweetened Condensed Milk Substitute

Alice Vezina, Renfrew, Ontario

Ingredients:
2/3 cup butter or margarine
2/3 cup hot water
1 1/2 cups granulated sugar
2 cups dry skim milk powder (do not reconstitute)

Food for Thought

It is always incomprehensible to a man that a woman should refuse an offer of marriage.   – *Jane Austen*

Directions:
Put butter in a large microwave-proof bowl. Microwave on high for 1 minute or until melted. Gently stir in hot water. Stir milk powder and sugar together. Add to butter mixture. Microwave on high for 3 1/2 - 5 minutes or until mixture boils, whisking every minute. For best results, let cool and refrigerate overnight before using. Makes 2 cups.

Appetizers & Enhancers

Appetizers & Enhancers

Parsnip and Apple Puree

Violetta Hollett, Toronto, Ontario

Ingredients:
4 large cooking apples, peeled and chopped
2 lbs parsnips, peeled and chopped
1/2 cup chicken stock or canned broth
2 tbsps brown sugar
1 tsp ground coriander
Pinch cinnamon

Food for Thought
You will find that friendships based solely upon gratitude are similar to photographs; both fade with time.

Directions:
Place apples and parsnips in a saucepan, add stock and sprinkle with sugar and spices. Cover and let simmer for 20 minutes or until parsnips are tender. Add more stock if required. Drain, reserving liquid. Transfer to food processor. Puree, adding liquid as needed. Makes 6 servings.

Molasses Coady

Bertha Smith, Clarenville, Newfoundland

Ingredients:
1 cup molasses
1/4 cup water
1/4 cup butter
1 tbsp vinegar

Spice of Life
Don't accept rides from strange men, and remember that all men are strange.
– Robin Morgan

Directions:
In a saucepan, combine all ingredients together. Heat to boiling, then simmer for 10 minutes, stirring occasionally. Serve over pudding.

Hot Seafood Dip

Dianne Tilley, Dartmouth, Nova Scotia

Ingredients:
1 pkg cream cheese
1 can (5 1/2 ozs) crab meat
2 tbsps green onion, chopped
1/2 tsp horseradish
Dash tabasco sauce
1 tbsp milk
1/4 tsp salt
1 tbsp lemon juice
Green pepper, chopped (to taste)
1 dash pepper
1/3 cup slivered almonds (for garnish)

Female Facts
Canadian Breast Cancer Stats
Over 99 per cent of breast cancer is found in women. One in nine Canadian women will develop breast cancer at some point during their lifetime. One in 27 will die from it. Twenty-two per cent of breast cancer cases occur in women under age 50; 48 per cent of cases occur in women ages 50 to 69; 30 per cent of cases occur in women age 70 and over. Since 1986, mortality rates for women with breast cancer have declined by 20 per cent, and are currently at their lowest since 1950. The average five-year survival rate for women with breast cancer is 82 per cent.

Directions:
Combine all ingredients (except almonds) together. Mix well, then garnish with slivered almonds. Warm in oven for 20 minutes at 350°F and serve. A great dip for crackers or chips.

Salt Substitute
Lila Young, St. John's, Newfoundland

Ingredients:
1 tbsp dry mustard
1 tbsp garlic powder
1 tbsp onion powder
1 tbsp paprika
1 1/2 tsps black pepper
1 tsp basil
1 tsp thyme

Directions:
Combine ingredients well and place in a shaker jar. This can be used to replace salt any time a recipe calls for it. This recipe is worth a lot more than its salt.

Partridgeberry Fowl Stuffing
Ron Young, St. John's, Newfoundland

Ingredients:
4 cups bread crumbs
1 medium onion (chopped)
4 celery sticks (chopped very fine)
1 tsp salt
1 tsp Mount Scio savoury
1/8 tsp pepper
1 cup partridgeberries (fresh or frozen and thawed)
2 cups apples (peeled, diced and sprinkled with lemon juice)
Butter or margarine

Directions:
Melt butter in a frying pan. Add onions and celery and sauté. Combine bread crumbs, salt, savoury and pepper, and add to onion and celery mixture. Stir in partridgeberries and apples and stuff your turkey, chicken, duck, goose or turr before cooking.

Zippy Cranberry Sauce
Maria Young, St. Philip's, Newfoundland

Ingredients:
3 cups fresh or frozen cranberries
1 orange (cut in quarters)
1 cup sugar
1/4 cup Grand Marnier

Female Facts

Woman's Fault?
Research indicates that a significant percentage of young men and women believe it is okay to coerce a woman to have sex. In a 1992 Toronto study, 31 per cent of males and 22 per cent of females agreed when asked, "If a girl engages in necking or petting and she lets things get out of hand, is it her own fault if her partner forces sex on her?"

Food for Thought
You can tell who handles the money in families nowadays - they're making women's handbags bigger and men's wallets smaller.

Spice of Life
A newspaper article that started, "A local couple gave birth to triplets today....." had a headline that read, "Three of a kind gives pair full house!"

Directions:
Place cranberries, orange and sugar in a blender and chop. Add Grand Marnier and serve with turkey or whatever.

Newfoundland Dumplings

Daphne Parr, St. Lunaire, Newfoundland

Ingredients:
1 cup flour
2 tsps baking powder
1/2 tsp salt
1/2 cup milk

Food for Thought

If you obey all the rules,
you miss all the fun.
– *Katharine Hepburn*

Directions:
Blend together the flour, baking powder and salt. Stir in milk. Drop by spoonfuls over hot stew or soup. Cover and simmer 15 minutes without lifting lid. Serve immediately.

Food for Thought

Before you begin a thing, remind yourself that difficulties and delays quite impossible to foresee are ahead. If you could see them clearly, naturally you could do a great deal to get rid of them but you can't. You can only see one thing clearly and that is your goal. Form a mental vision of that and cling to it through thick and thin.

– *Kathleen Norris*

Female Facts

No one knows why, but 90 percent of women who walk into a department store immediately turn to the right.

Spice of Life

The best way to keep children home is to make the home atmosphere pleasant--and let the air out of the tires.

– *Dorothy Parker*

Appetizers & Enhancers

Main Course Meals

Glazed Chicken

Cindy Ings, Fort McMurray, Alberta (nee Gidge, Cobb's Arm, Newfoundland)

Ingredients:
3 lbs chicken parts, skin removed
2/3 cup salad dressing
2 tbsps chili sauce
1 tbsp sweet relish
1 tbsp lemon juice
1 tsp Worcestershire Sauce
1 pkg dry onion soup mix
1/2 cup apricot jam
1 tbsp brown sugar

Female Facts

Dumb Blondes
The legend that all blonde women are dumb started in 1760 when the blonde Countess of Coventry, England, died of lead poisoning because her vanity caused her to use too much make-up.

Directions:
Arrange chicken in a greased casserole dish or small roaster. Mix salad dressing, chili sauce, relish, lemon juice and Worcestershire Sauce in a small bowl. Stir in soup mix, jam and brown sugar. Spoon over chicken being sure to get some on every piece. Bake, uncovered at 350°F for about 1 hour until tender. Baste chicken at half-time. Serves 4 to 6.

Ham Cauliflower Bake

Cindy Ings, Fort McMurray, Alberta (nee Gidge, Cobb's Arm, Newfoundland)

Ingredients:
5 cups cauliflower pieces
Water, to cover
1 can cream of chicken soup
1/3 cup light sour cream
1 can whole mushrooms, drained
1/4 cup chopped green onion
1/2 cup grated medium cheddar cheese
2 cups cubed cooked ham (3/4 inch)
3/4 cup grated medium cheddar cheese

Female Facts

Conquering Woman
Aethelflaed, the Saxon Queen, known as Lady of the Mercians, led her army to the conquest of Derby and Leicester in AD917. At the time of her death in AD918, she had won authority over parts of Wales and Northumbria, had won the allegiance of York and was planning campaigns further north.

Directions:
Cook cauliflower in water in a large saucepan until tender, then drain. Mix next 6 ingredients in a medium bowl. Stir in cauliflower. Turn into ungreased 2-quart (2L) casserole dish. Sprinkle with second amount of cheese. Bake, uncovered, in 350°F oven for 30-40 minutes. Makes 4 generous servings.

Texas Hash

Cindy Ings, Fort McMurray, Alberta (nee Gidge, Cobb's Arm, Newfoundland)

Ingredients:
1 lb ground beef
3 large onions, sliced

Food for Thought
A smile is a curve that can set a lot of things straight.

Main Course Meals

Main Course Meals

1 large green pepper, chopped
1/2 cup uncooked rice
2 tsps salt
1 to 2 tsps chili powder
1/8 tsp pepper
1 (16 oz) can whole tomatoes

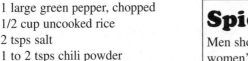

Spice of Life

Men should think twice before making widowhood women's only path to power.   *– Gloria Steinem*

Directions:

Cook and stir ground beef, onions and green pepper in a 10-inch skillet until beef is brown. Drain. Stir in tomatoes with liquid and remaining ingredients. Pour into an ungreased 2-quart (2L) casserole dish. Cover and cook in 350° F oven until rice is tender and liquid is absorbed (About 1 hour).

Doris's Cod Sound Hash

Doris Senior, St. John's, Newfoundland

Ingredients:
1 lb pkg salted cod sounds
1 dozen potatoes (medium, peeled)
1 medium onion, chopped
1 small piece salt pork
1/4 tsp pepper
1/4 tsp salt

Food for Thought

When we love, we always have something so say.
   – Mary Wortly Montagu

Directions:

Soak sounds in cold water for about 4 hours, then clean sounds removing any black spots on them. Cook potatoes and sounds together in a boiler. When potatoes are cooked, sounds will be cooked also. Mash potatoes in large bowl. Cut sounds into small pieces then add to mashed potatoes. Cut salt pork into small pieces and fry them with chopped onions. When cooked, stir salt pork fat and onion into the mashed potatoes and saute sounds. Add salt and pepper, then stir all together. Spoon the ingredients into a casserole dish or roaster and bake for 30 minutes at 350°F.

Meat Roll

Margaret Crocker, Kitchener, Ontario (nee MacMillan, Scotland)

Ingredients:
400 g (1 lb) best steak
340 g (12 oz) lean bacon
1 large onion, chopped finely
1 pkg small butter biscuits, crushed finely
2 eggs beaten
Sprinkling nutmeg
Pinch of salt

Food for Thought

The average man is more interested in a woman who is interested in him than he is in a woman with beautiful legs.   *– Marlene Dietrich*

Directions:

Mince the steak and bacon together (Your butcher will do this. Ask him nicely.) Add the onion, biscuit crumbs and beaten eggs, mixing well. Add the seasonings, again mixing well. Fill two 1 lb mason jars or a steamer. Place in a pan of boiling water on a trivet or a tin foil plate and boil for three hours, topping up the water with boiling water as necessary.

Potato Casserole

G. Bussey, Roseneath, Ontario

Ingredients:
8 cups cooked potatoes, cut up
1 can cream of mushroom soup (undiluted)
1/2 cup margarine, melted
1 pint sour cream
1 tsp salt
1/2 cup onion, chopped
2 cups cheese, grated
2 cups Corn Flakes, crushed
1/4 cup margarine, melted

Directions:
Combine first 8 ingredients. Pour into a greased casserole dish. Mix crushed Corn Flakes and margarine together. Cover casserole with the buttered Corn Flakes. Bake at 350°F for 40 minutes.

Female Facts

Tin Lizzie
In Henry Ford's time the most common name for female domestics was Lizzie. Maids worked hard all week, then often took the family children to church on Sundays, which Henry's new Model T Ford automobile did for many, earning it the name, "Tin Lizzie."

Ham and Potato Balls

Helen Crocker, Kitchener, Ontario, (formerly of Heart's Delight, Newfoundland)

Ingredients:
6 boiled potatoes
1 tbsp melted butter
1 cup evaporated milk
2 well beaten eggs
1 cup finely chopped cooked ham
Salt (to taste)

Food for Thought

The way I see it, if you want the rainbow, you gotta put up with the rain.   *– Dolly Parton*

Directions:
Mash potatoes and add a few grains of salt, melted butter and evaporated milk. Mix well and add beaten eggs and ham. Mould into egg-shaped balls and roll in flour. Fry in hot fat, until nicely browned, then serve with your favourite sauce.

Minced Chicken

Janice Hunter, Kitchener, Ontario (formerly of Heart's Delight, Newfoundland)

Ingredients:
1 lb cooked chicken
Salt and pepper (to taste)
4 poached eggs
1 pt white sauce (1/4 cup milk, 3/4 cup chicken stock)

Directions:
Boil chicken complete with bones and trimmings for 90 minutes, then use stock to make sauce. When sauce is cooked, add minced chicken. Serve hot in shallow dish with poached eggs on top. Serves four.

Ham Rissoles

Janice Hunter, Kitchener, Ontario, (formerly of Heart's Delight, Newfoundland)

Ingredients:
1/2 lb cooked ham
4 ozs fresh grated bread crumbs
2 tbsps mashed potatoes
4 tbsps white sauce (1/4 cup milk 3/4 cup chicken stock)
2 beaten eggs
Salt and pepper
Parsley
Deep-frying fat

Spice of Life

It's hard to be funny when you have to be clean. – *Mae West*

Directions:
Mince ham and mix with the bread crumbs and potatoes. Place in a small pan and, heating gently, add half of the beaten egg and white sauce. Season well and spread on plate. Divide into 6-8 equal portions and leave to cool. Shape into rissoles, coat with remaining egg and bread crumbs and fry until golden brown in deep frier. You can substitute ham with pork, veal, lamb or beef.

Veal Loaf

Janice Hunter, Kitchener, Ontario (formerly of Heart's Delight, Newfoundland)

Ingredients:
1 lb cooked veal
1/2 lb sausage meat
1 oz bread crumbs
Salt and pepper (to taste)
1 egg
Flour (or egg and bread crumbs)
Fat for basting
Gravy or salad

Female Facts

Charity Jean Fowlow of Bishop's Cove, Conception Bay was one of Chatelaine Magazines' *Women of the Year* in 1974. Apart from her civic activities with the Epilepsy Association and the Canadian Red Cross, Jean was Mayor of Stephenville from 1969 to 1974.

Directions:
Finely chop veal and mix with sausage meat and bread crumbs. Season to taste and add beaten egg, mix thoroughly adding gravy or stock until mixture is well moistened, but not very wet. Form into a short thick roll and coat lightly with flour or egg and bread crumbs. Heat some fat in a saucepan and baste the veal load. Bake at 375°F for 60 minutes, basting occasionally. Serve hot with gravy, or cold with salad.

Mashed Potato Casserole

Sue Reeder

Ingredients:

1 pkg 3 oz cream cheese (softened)
1 tsp garlic salt
1/4 tsp pepper
1/2 cup sour cream
2 1/2 to 3 lbs potatoes (cooked and mashed well)
2 tbsp butter or margarine
Paprika or parsley sprigs for garnish (optional)

Directions:

In a bowl, stir together cream cheese, garlic salt, pepper and sour cream until smooth. Cook and mash potatoes until lumps are all gone. Then add cheese mixture and spoon potatoes into dish. Dot with butter and bake at 400°F for 25 minutes. These potatoes are really good served with ham or any meat dish. Garnish with paprika or parsley sprigs.

Food for Thought

My divorce came as a complete surprise to me. That will happen when you haven't been home in eighteen years. *– Pro golfer, Lee Trevino*

Devilled Halibut

Colleen Norman

Ingredients:

1/4 cup minced onion
3 tbsps butter
2 tbsps flour
1 cup milk
1 1/2 tsps prepared mustard
2 tsps Worcestershire Sauce
2 tsps lemon juice
1 egg beaten
2 cups flaked cooked halibut
1/2 cup bread crumbs
Salt to taste

Female Facts

At the End of Her Rope
In the past, men have been known to put a rope around their wives' necks and lead them down to the marketplace, where livestock were auctioned. There, she would be sold to the highest bidder, the same as if she were his prize pig.
The first known case of an Englishman selling his wife to another man was in 1533. Researchers found documentation for nearly 400 of these such transactions, up until it was discontinued late into the 1800s.

Directions:

Sauté onion in butter for 5 minutes. Sprinkle with flour and gradually add milk, stirring constantly until mixture reaches boiling point. Add salt, mustard, Worcestershire Sauce, lemon juice, egg and halibut. Mix lightly and divide among 6 buttered baking dishes. Sprinkle with bread crumbs. Bake at 350°F for 20 minutes. Serves 6.

Fresh Cod Casserole

Geraldine Cole

Ingredients:
2 lbs fresh cod
Onion

Spice of Life

Women can do any job men can and give birth while doing it. *– Allan Heavey*

Celery
Green pepper
1 cup milk
Sliced, old-fashioned cheese
Salt and pepper (to taste)

Directions:

Grease oven-proof dish and place a layer of cod in a cooking pan, then add a layer of onion, celery and green pepper. Put another layer of cod on top, then add a layer of onion and salt and pepper to taste. Spread 1 cup of milk over above layers. Top with slices of old fashioned cheese. Bake at 375°F for 30-45 minutes.

Chicken Hurry

Stephanie Hawco

Ingredients:
3 lbs chicken parts
1/2 cup ketchup
1/4 cup water
1/2 cup packed brown sugar
1 pkg dry onion soup

Directions:

Arrange chicken parts in a small roaster or casserole dish. In a small bowl, combine ketchup, water, sugar and soup mix. Mix together well. Spoon over chicken making sure some is on every piece. Bake covered at 350°F for 1 hour or until tender. Serves 4-6.

Codfish Soufflé

April Doyle

Ingredients:
1 cup salt cod fish
2 cups diced potatoes
1 tbsp butter
2 eggs separated
2 tbsps ketchup

Directions:

Shred the codfish and soak for 30 minutes in cold water. Drain. Boil fish with potatoes in water until potatoes are tender. Drain and mash the fish and potatoe mixture together; add butter and beat until light. Sir in beaten egg yolks and ketchup. Fold in stiffly beaten egg whites and turn into a greased 1 1/2 quart casserole dish. Place in a pan of hot water and bake at 375°F for 20 minutes. Serves 4 to 6.

Main Course Meals

Old Fashioned Baked Beans

J. Andrews, Yellowknife, North West Territories

Ingredients:
2 lbs dried beans
1 medium onion - sliced
1/4 cup tomato ketchup
1/4 cup brown sugar
3/4 lb salt pork - sliced
1/2 cup molasses
1 tbsp mustard
Pepper to taste

Female Facts

An Anatomical Analogy
Albert Einstein, who discovered the theory of relativity, described his discovery in the following manner: "Sit with a pretty girl for an hour, and it seems like a minute; sit on a hot stove for a minute and it seems like an hour - that's relativity."

Directions:
Wash beans and add enough water to cover two inches above beans. Boil until tender. Place in a deep casserole dish mixed with other ingredients and bake until crisp and brown. Serve piping hot.

Baked Spareribs in Honey Sauce with Potato Balls

Dorothy Wade

Ingredients:
2 lbs spareribs, cut in serving pieces
1 onion
1/4 cup soya sauce
1/4 tsp pepper
1/2 tsp salt

Spice of Life

I was in a beauty contest once. I not only came in last, I was hit in the mouth by Miss Congeniality.   – *Phyllis Diller*

Directions:
Combine ingredients together in a saucepan, boil for 1 1/2 hours or until spareribs are tender. Drain, arrange spareribs in a baking pan. Set aside while you make sauce.

Sauce Ingredients:
1 tbsp ginger powder
1/2 cup honey
2 tbsps brown sugar
1 tsp salt
2 tbsps soya sauce
1 onion minced
1 tbsp Worcestershire Sauce

Female Facts

Canadian Women's Life Expectancy
The average life expectancy for a Canadian woman is 80.6 years, about 7 years longer than the average man.

Sauce Directions:
Blend ingredients together. Pour over spareribs, bake at 400°F for 10-15 mins.

Serve with Potato Bacon Balls (next page).

Main Course Meals

Main Course Meals

Potato Bacon Balls Ingredients:
1 lb potatoes, boiled and mashed
1 egg beaten
1/4 tsp salt
1/4 tsp pepper
1 cup cooked bacon (chopped)
1/2 cup pineapple juice
1/4 cup brown sugar

<table>
<tr><td>

Spice of Life
Marriage is like a game of poker. You start out by holding hands, and often end up with an unaffordable loss.

</td></tr>
</table>

Directions:
Combine first 4 ingredients together. Shape into balls and roll in the chopped bacon. Arrange in a small greased pan. Bake at 350°F for 15-20 minutes. Boil pineapple juice and brown sugar together for 5 minutes. Use to baste potato balls.

Swiss Potato Casserole

Theresa Earles

Ingredients:
5 medium potatoes, peeled and thinly sliced
2 medium onions (coarsely grated)
2 1/2 cups grated Swiss or Gruyere cheese
1 tsp ground pepper
1/4 tsp nutmeg
1/2 stick butter
Chopped parsley
Salt to taste

<table>
<tr><td>

Food for Thought
You can buy cookies, but you can't buy love.   *– Raquel Welch*

</td></tr>
</table>

Directions:
Mix potatoes, onions, cheese, salt, pepper and nutmeg thoroughly. Grease 8" spring form pan with butter. Pour mixture into pan. Bake for 1 hour at 450°F or until golden brown. Turn out on a platter and garnish with parsley. Serves 6.

Jellied Salmon Loaf

Laurie Laracey

Ingredients:
1 canned salmon (16 ozs)
1 tbsp unflavoured gelatin
2 tbsp cold water
1 hard cooked egg, sliced
Stuffed olives
Salad dressing to taste

<table>
<tr><td>

Female Facts
Hail the Woman Chief
As head of a society of Six Nations matrons, Mary Brant, a Mohawk woman, was consulted by all of the Indians on any matters of importance and, using her influence, encouraged the Indians to remain loyal to England.

</td></tr>
</table>

Directions:
Drain and flake salmon. Soften gelatin in cold water. Dissolve over hot water and add to salad dressing. Add flaked salmon. Line loaf pan with wax paper. Cover bottom with slices of egg and olives. Pack mixture into mold and chill till firm. Serve on crisp lettuce and salad dressing. Serves 4 to 6 with tossed salad, crisp rolls and butter.

Quick Casserole
Christa Hawco

Ingredients:
2 tbsps cooking oil
2 lbs round steak
1 can cream of mushroom soup (10 oz)
1/4 cup water

Directions:
Cut meat into serving size pieces, brown in heated oil in frying pan. Transfer to casserole dish or small roaster. In a small bowl, combine soup with water. Pour over the top of meat. Cover, bake at 350°F for 1 to 1 1/2 hours or until tender. Serves 5-6.

Spice of Life

The secret of a happy marriage is to tell your spouse everything but the essentials.   – *Cynthia Nelms*

Chicken Casserole
Pauline Bennett

Ingredients:
1 average size broccoli
2 or 3 chicken breasts
1 can of cream of chicken soup
1 can of Carnation milk
2 tbsps salad dressing
Pepper
Salad dressing
1/4 cup grated cheese
Bread crumbs

Dressing Ingredients:
4 slices bread
1 onion
Savoury
Butter to moisten
Pinch of salt and pepper to taste

Female Facts

Along The Amazon
When explorer Francisco de Orellana found a race of strong and virile women living in South America, he called them Amazons. Francisco's knowledge of Amazons was from the race of women warriors who, according to Greek mythology, did battle with such great male warriors as Hercules. The word Amazon comes from the Greek *a* meaning, "without" and *mazon* meaning, "breasts." (The "Amazons" were said to have cut off their right breasts so they would have greater freedom of movement while maneuvering their swords and other weapons.) The world's mightiest river, the Amazon, was given its name by Francisco and was so named because of the mighty "Amazon" women he discovered living on its banks.
NOTE: The Amazon is not only the widest river on Earth, at times it is six miles wide, but brings a full 20 per cent of all the fresh water out of the planet's rivers into all the world's oceans. The force of its current can be felt more than a 100 miles out to sea.

Directions:
Cook broccoli for 10 to 15 minutes in salted water. Drain, then layer broccoli, dressing (see Dressing Ingredients or use Stove Top Stuffing) and chicken in a greased casserole dish with broccoli on bottom. Mix soup, canned milk and salad dressing to make a creamy sauce. Pour over layer along with grated cheese and bread crumbs to top. Repeat layers several times and bake for 1 hour at 325°F. Delicious served with crisp salad and rolls.

Main Course Meals

Grandma's Lopscoush (Salt Beef Stew)

Kyla Kofey

Ingredients:
Salt beef - cut up into bite size pieces
Carrots - sliced into stew size pieces
Turnip - sliced into stew size pieces
Potatoes - sliced into stew size pieces
Cabbage - shredded (or in small pieces)
Onion - chopped

> ## Spice of Life
> We are all born charming, fresh, and spontaneous and must be civilized before we are fit to participate in society. – *Miss Manners (Judith Martin)*

Directions:
Judge the quantities by the size of the crowd you're feeding, then boil salt meat about an hour in water. Add carrot, turnip and potatoes. Just before these vegetables are fully cooked, add chopped onions and cabbage. Finish cooking. This is so simple, but so delicious. It's just like Jiggs dinner in a stew form.

Fish Cakes

Mona Bursey, Charleston, Newfoundland

Ingredients:
2 chopped onions
6 cooked potatoes
2 cups salt fish (cooked and boned)
1/2 cup bread crumbs
1/4 tsp pepper
1/4 tsp savoury
1 egg, well beaten

> ## Food for Thought
> A woman should have enough education so she doesn't have to look up to anyone. She should also have enough to be wise enough not to look down on anyone.

Directions:
Cook onions in a small amount of water. Mash potatoes and fish together. Add onions and seasoning. Add egg and combine well. Form into cakes, and roll in bread crumbs. Fry in rendered pork fat until brown.

Homemade Chow

Judy Rimmer

Ingredients:
6 cups cabbage
3 tsps salt
6 cups onions
1 tsp curry powder
1 1/2 cups sugar
1 tsp tumeric
3/4 cup flour
1 tbsp dry mustard

> ## Female Facts
>
> **Buttering Herself Up**
> If your husband complains about the paints, powders, oils, etc, which you use, remind him that Empress Anne who ruled Russia during the 18th century, never cared for bathing in water. She instead wiped herself down daily with melted butter.

Main Course Meals

4 cups white vinegar
1/2 cup water

Directions:
Finely chop cabbage and onion; add vinegar and boil for 5 minutes. Add sugar and salt. Make a paste from the remaining ingredients and stir into hot pickle. Boil for 10-15 minutes. Let cool a little before bottling.

Spareribs are Peachy
Judy Rimmer

Ingredients:
2-3 lbs spareribs
1 cup brown sugar
4 jars of baby food peaches
2 tsps ginger
1 cup ketchup
2 tsps salt
Pinch of pepper
2/3 cup vinegar

Spice of Life

The average man is forty-two around the chest, forty-four around the waist, ninety six around the golf course, and a nuisance around the house.

Directions:
Cook spareribs in oven for 1/2 hour. Pour off excess fat. Add mixture and continue cooking for 1 hour. Excellent served over white rice.

Maritime Madness
Judy Flynn

Ingredients:
1 lb ground beef (lean)
1 can (10 ozs) cream of mushroom soup
1/2 cup chopped onion
1 tbsp parsley flakes
1 tsp salt
1/4 tsp pepper
1/2 tsp sage
3 tbsps ketchup
1 tbsp barbecue sauce
1/2 tsp garlic powder
1/2 cup rolled oats

Female Facts

Bringing in the Sheep
During The First World War, the wife of President Woodrow Wilson bought a flock of sheep to keep the White House lawn cropped. The sheep not only cropped the lawn, but the sale of their wool by Mrs. Wilson raised $100,000 for the Red Cross.

Directions:
Combine all ingredients in a large bowl. Mix together well. Pat down in a 1 1/2-quart casserole dish. Bake covered 50 minutes at 350°F. Remove cover and bake about 15 minutes to brown. Serves 4.

Main Course Meals

Main Course Meals

Seven Layer Dinner

Lillian Phillips

Ingredients:
3 thinly sliced raw potatoes
2 thinly sliced raw onions
3 medium sliced carrots
1/2 cup regular uncooked rice
14 oz can green peas
1 lb pork sausage
10 oz can tomato soup
1 can water
Salt and pepper (to taste)

Female Facts

Beautiful Need Not Apply
Nineteenth-century educator and first superintendent of US Army nurses, Dorothea Dix, looked for only, "strong women who were not good-looking," as nurses for her staff.

Directions:
Grease a deep casserole dish. Arrange a layer of potatoes in bottom, cover with a layer of onion slices, add layer of carrots, then sprinkle with rice and pour in peas with their liquid. Top with sausages arranged in a wheel-spoke pattern. Add soup mixed with water and salt and pepper to taste, and a pinch or two of your favourite herb. Cover and bake at 325°F for 1 hour. Turn sausages over and bake uncovered for 1 more hour.

Meat Casserole

Janet Edwards

Ingredients:
1 small cabbage
1 lb ground beef
1 onion
1/2 cup rice uncooked
1 can tomato soup
1 cup water

Female Facts

Among single young women who had sexual intercourse during a six month period, only 60% of 15-17 year-olds and 69% of 18-24 year-olds always used a method of contraception (1998 Canadian Contraception Study)

Directions:
Chop cabbage, place in casserole dish. Brown meat and onion and stir in rice. Pour over cabbage. Mix soup and water together and pour over mixture. Bake 1 hour at 325°F.

Sweet and Sour Chicken Legs (Wings or Spareribs may also be used)

Minnie Wheeler

Ingredients:
4-6 chicken legs seasoned and rolled in flour
2 tbsps cooking oil
1 small onion chopped
2/3 cup orange juice
1/3 cup ketchup

Spice of Life

The only man who can fool all the women all the time is a fashion designer.　　　*– Unknown*

1 tbsp brown sugar
1 tsp soya sauce
1/4 tsp ginger
1/4 tsp garlic

Food for Thought

A woman past forty should make up her mind to be young - not her face.   – Billie Burke

Directions:

Cover chicken in flour and brown on both sides in pre-heated oil in frying pan. Place chicken into a covered baking dish, then put remaining ingredients in a pot. Bring to a boil and pour over chicken. Cover and bake for 25 minutes at 350°F. Turn chicken over in sauce and continue to bake for 30 minutes at 325°F. Delicious with steamed rice.

Meat Loaf

Ida Purchase, Laurenceton, Newfoundland

Ingredients:
1 lb lean ground beef
1/2 cup onion, chopped
1 cup tomato juice or tomato sauce
1 cup rolled oats
1 tbsp prepared mustard
1 egg
Salt and pepper

Spice of Life

A woman who takes things from a man is called a girlfriend. A man who takes things from a woman is called a gigolo.   – Ruthie Stein

Directions:

Combine all ingredients thoroughly. Bake at 325°F for just over an hour.

Mexican Casserole

Denise Hibbs (nee Jenkins), Springdale, Newfoundland

Ingredients:
1 lb ground beef
1 (12 oz) jar salsa
1 cup sweet corn
3/4 cup mayonnaise
1 tbsp chili powder
2 cups crushed tortilla chips
2 cups cheese, shredded
Lettuce and tomato (optional)

Food for Thought

An archaeologist is the best husband a woman can have: the older she gets, the more interested he is in her.
          – Agatha Christie

Directions:

Brown meat and drain. Stir in salsa, corn, mayo and chili powder. Layer 1/2 meat mixture, chips and cheese in a casserole dish. Repeat layers. Bake at 350°F for 20 minutes. Top with shredded lettuce and tomatoes, if desired.

Main Course Meals

Chicken and Broccoli Casserole

Denise Hibbs (nee Jenkins), Springdale, Newfoundland

Ingredients:
2 pkgs frozen broccoli
2 cups cooked chicken, diced
2 cans cream of mushroom soup
1 cup mayonnaise
1 tsp lemon juice
1/2 tsp curry powder
Cheddar cheese, shredded
Buttered bread crumbs

> ## Food for Thought
> Whenever you want to marry someone, go have lunch with his ex-wife.   *– Shelley Winters*

Directions:
Layer chicken, broccoli and cheese into a casserole dish. Mix remaining ingredients and pour over layered ingredients. Top with buttered bread crumbs. Bake at 350°F for 1 hour.

Chicken and Rice Casserole

Danessa Quinlan, Birchy Bay, Newfoundland

Ingredients:
1 cup of rice
1 chicken, cut in pieces
1 can cream of mushroom soup
1 can cream of chicken soup
1 pkg onion soup mix
1 tbsp Worchestershire Sauce
2 cans warm water
1-2 cups cheddar cheese, grated

> ## Female Facts
> **Colour-Blindness Genes**
> When a colour blind mother and a father with normal vision reproduce, the daughters will have normal vision, while the sons will be colour blind.

Directions:
Spread rice in casserole dish. Arrange chicken on top. Mix remaining ingredients and pour over chicken. Bake, covered, at 375°F for 2 hours.

Broccoli and Rice Casserole

Danessa Quinlan, Birchy Bay, Newfoundland

> ## Spice of Life
> For a single woman, preparing for company means wiping the lipstick off the milk carton.
> *– Elayne Boosler*

Ingredients:
1 pkg broccoli
1 cup uncooked rice
2 tbsps butter
1/4 cup chopped onion
1 can cream of chicken soup (or cream of mushroom)
1/2 cup grated cheddar cheese

Directions:

Cook broccoli and drain. Fry onion in butter; add rice and soup mixture. Place broccoli in casserole dish; pour mixture over broccoli. Place cheese on top. Bake at 350°F for 30 minutes.

Potato and Cheese Casserole

Danessa Quinlan, Birchy Bay, Newfoundland

Ingredients:

2-3 lbs potatoes
1 small tub sour cream
1 can cream of chicken soup (or cream of mushroom)
1 1/2 cups cheddar cheese, grated
3-4 tbsps onion, finely chopped

> ### *Food for Thought*
> It is possible that blondes also prefer gentlemen.
> – *Mamie Van Doren*

Directions:

Boil potatoes. When cooled, chop into 3/4-inch pieces. In a small bowl, mix remaining ingredients. Combine potatoes with cheese mixture; place in a greased casserole dish. Bake at 350°F for 30 minutes.

Beef and Vegetable Casserole

Leone Smith, St. Catharines, Ontario (nee Chafe, Petty Harbour, Newfoundland)

Ingredients:

1 1/2- 2 lbs stewing beef
1 small turnip, diced
4-5 carrots, sliced
6-8 medium potatoes, diced
1 medium onion, chopped
1/2 tsp thyme
1 tsp basil
1 large can tomatoes
1 cup bread crumbs
Salt and pepper, to taste

> ### Female Facts
> **Better Odds Than Lottery Tickets**
> The odds against a mother giving birth to quadruplets are more than half-million to one.

Directions:

Brown beef in frying pan. Combine all ingredients, except bread crumbs, in a medium-sized roasting pan. Top with bread crumbs. Bake at 350°F for 1 1/2 - 2 hours or until vegetables are cooked and meat is tender. Makes 4-5 servings.

Oven Fried Rice

Mrs. Margaret Pettipas, Dartmouth, Nova Scotia

Ingredients:

2 cups long-grain rice
1 pkg Lipton onion soup mix
1/4 cup soya sauce

> ### Spice of Life
> Alimony is always having to say you're sorry.
> – *Philip J. Simborg*

1/3 cup oil
3 cups water
1 can mushrooms (save 1/3 cup of juice and add to mixture)

Directions:
Combine all ingredients and place in covered casserole dish. Bake at 350°F for 1 1/4 hours.
Note: Any left over meat, chicken or pork can be added to this. Freezes well.

Hash Brown Casserole

Selina Statnyk, Leduc, Alberta

Ingredients:
2 lbs frozen hash browns
2 cups sour cream
1 large can mushroom soup
1/2 cup melted butter
1 medium onion, finely chopped
Salt (to taste)
2 cups cheddar cheese, grated

Directions:
Mix all ingredients, except cheese, together. Spread in a 9" x 13" pan. Sprinkle with cheddar
cheese (parmesan cheese is optional). Bake at 350°F for 1 - 1 1/2 hours.

Broccoli Casserole

Shirley Tibert, Lewis Lake, Nova Scotia

Ingredients:
6 broccoli stalks
2 cups hot water
1 envelope onion soup mix
2 tbsps lemon juice
1 tsp oregano
1 1/2 cups Minute Rice

Directions:
Peel and slice broccoli stalks. Place in a saucepan with water and soup mix. Cook for 15
minutes. Add lemon juice, oregano and rice; bring to a boil. Cover and let stand for 10 minutes.
Can be served by itself or with pork chops, chicken, sausage or steak.

Potato Casserole

Edna Fudge, Gimli, Manitoba

Ingredients:
1 (16 oz) pkg frozen hash browns
1 medium onion, chopped

Female Facts

Divorce BC
Divorce was around before the Roman Catholic, or any
Christian church was founded. In ancient Rome, divorce
was quite prevalent among the
upper classes, according to
Roman author, Lucius Seneca,
who wrote, "...Distinguished
ladies count their years...by
the number of their
husbands."

Spice of Life

When I'm good, I'm very, very good,
but when I'm bad, I'm better!
– *Mae West*

Food for Thought

Age doesn't always bring wisdom. Sometimes
age comes alone.

Main Course Meals

1 green pepper, chopped
2 cans cream of mushroom soup, undiluted
1 cup sour cream
8 oz cheddar cheese, shredded
1 cup Corn Flakes, crushed

Spice of Life

The best way for a woman to forget her troubles is to wear a pair of tight shoes.

Directions:

In a bowl, mix frozen hash browns, onion, green pepper, soup, sour cream and cheddar cheese. Place in casserole dish and top with Corn Flakes. Bake at 350°F for 50 minutes. Can be prepared a day ahead and reheated. Delicious.

Turkey Casserole

R. Maxwell Winters, Saint John, New Brunswick

Ingredients:
1 cup celery, chopped
1/2 cup onion, chopped
1 can mushrooms (save juice)
2 cups cooked turkey, chopped
2 cans cream of mushroom soup
1 large can chow mein noodles

Female Facts

Cheating Italian Women
Fifty-one per cent of Italian women between the ages of 20 and 60 believe that cheating on spouses is healthy for a relationship.

Directions:

Cook celery and onions slightly in butter or margarine; add mushrooms. In a large bowl, mix soup and turkey together, diluting soup with 1/4 or 1/2 cup of juice from mushrooms. Add 1/2 can of noodles. Add previously-cooked celery, onions and mushrooms. Place in a casserole dish and top with remaining noodles. Bake at 350°F for 25-30 minutes.

Tortellini with Mushroom and Garlic Sauce

Frances Ivany, Cranbrook, British Columbia (formerly of Port Rexton, Trinity Bay, Newfoundland)

Ingredients:
1 (450 g) pkg tortellini, frozen or fresh
1 tbsp butter
1 small green pepper, cut in strips
1 small red pepper, cut in strips
1 small onion, cut in strips
1 can cream of mushroom and garlic soup
1/2 cup milk
Parmesan cheese

Food for Thought
Sex is such a personal thing. Why do we think of sharing it with another person?   – Lily Tomlin

Directions:

Cook tortellini as per package directions. Melt butter in a frying pan, saute peppers and onion for 3 minutes. In a bowl, combine soup and milk, blending well. Add to vegetables in frying pan; bring to a boil for 5 minutes. Add tortellini and cook for another 5 minutes. Sprinkle with parmesan cheese. Makes 4 servings.

Main Course Meals

Main Course Meals

Cabbage Casserole

Ashlynn McLoughlin, Millbrook, Ontario

Ingredients:
1 lb ground beef
1 cup onion, diced
1 tsp salt
1/8 tsp pepper
1/4 cup rice
1 (10 oz) can tomato soup
1 can water
1 tbsp brown sugar
1 tbsp lemon juice
3 cups shredded cabbage

Directions:
Brown ground beef and onion. Drain excess fat. Add salt, pepper, rice, soup, water, sugar and lemon juice. Place cabbage in casserole dish. Cover with rest of ingredients. Do not stir. Bake at 350°F for 1 hour.

> *Food for Thought*
> Happiness is good health and a bad memory. – *Ingrid Bergman*

Swedish Potatoes

Netta Polak, Ajax, Ontario

Ingredients:
6 large potatoes, cooked
3/4 cup sour cream
4 oz cream cheese
1 1/4 tsp onion salt
1/4 tsp white pepper
2 tbsps butter

Topping Ingredients:
3/4 cup bread crumbs
1 1/2 tbsps butter, melted

> **Female Facts**
>
>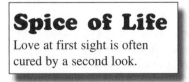
>
> **Couldn't Say No**
> Any bachelor living in Scotland in 1288 (and for some years after) could face a fine of up to one pound, a large sum at the time, for refusing to marry any woman who proposed to him during leap year.

Directions:
Beat all ingredients, except topping, until smooth; turn into a greased casserole dish. Sprinkle with topping ingredients. Bake at 350°F for 30 minutes. Remove and let stand for 10 minutes before serving.

Scalloped Turkey au Gratin

G. Kennedy, Ottawa, Ontario

Ingredients:
2 1/2 cups roasted turkey, diced
1 (10 1/2 oz) can condensed cream of chicken soup
1/2 cup water
1/2 cup aged cheddar cheese, cubed
1/4 tsp thyme

> **Spice of Life**
> Love at first sight is often cured by a second look.

1/8 tsp basil
1/4 cup crushed cracker crumbs
2 tbsps leftover turkey dressing (optional)
Chinese noodles or plain rice

> ## *Food for Thought*
> Wise is the woman who fortifies her life with friendships.

Directions:

Preheat oven to 400°F. Combine turkey, soup, water, cheese and seasonings in a buttered 1 1/2-quart casserole dish. Top with cracker crumbs. Bake for 20-25 minutes or until bubbly. Serve with Chinese noodles or plain rice. Note: Leftover turkey dressing adds flavour.

Cod Casserole

Norma Clarke, Peterborough, Ontario (nee Atkinson, Herring Neck, Newfoundland)

Ingredients:
1 lb cod fillets
1 onion
Salt and pepper, to taste
Prepared mustard
Green pickle relish
1 can tomato soup

> ## *Food for Thought*
> A lot of people have gone through life's revolving door on another person's push.

Directions:

Place cod in casserole dish and add onion, salt and pepper. Spread mustard and relish over cod. Add tomato soup and bake at 350°F until done.

Tuna Casserole

Marion Scheers, Edmonton, Alberta

Ingredients:
2 cups cooked macaroni
1 can flaked tuna
1 can cream of celery soup
1 can peas and carrots
1/4 cup milk

> ## Female Facts
> **Domineering President**
> U.S. President Calvin Coolidge was a very domineering husband, who would not allow his wife to supervise even the domestic part of White House life. All housekeeping plans, including meals, had to be approved by him. The President's approval was also needed before she was allowed to buy her own clothes.

Directions:
Combine all ingredients in a casserole dish and heat in oven for 1/2 hour at 325°F.

Quiche

Peter O'Brien, Happy Valley, Labrador

Ingredients:
1 lb lean ground beef
1 onion, chopped
1/2 cup green pepper, chopped
Salt and pepper, to taste

> ## Spice of Life
> "A nymphomaniac is a women as obsessed with sex as the average man."
> – *Mignon McLaughlin*

Robin Hood Flaky Pie Crust
1/2 cup mayonnaise
3/4 cup milk
3 eggs
1 tbsp cornstarch
1/2 lb mozzarella cheese, cubed

Directions:

Brown meat with onion, green pepper, salt and pepper. Place in a prepared pie shell. Beat mayonnaise, milk, eggs and cornstarch with whisk or spoon. Pour over meat; spread cubed mozzarella over top of meat sauce. Bake at 400°F for 35-40 minutes. When cooked, let stand for 5 minutes.

Olive Pasta

Tena Feaver, Thedford, Ontario

Ingredients:
1 lb spaghetti or linguini
2 tbsps olive oil
1 medium red onion, chopped
2 cloves of garlic, crushed
2 dozen oil-cured black olives (not canned), chopped and pitted
2 tbsps orange rind, grated

Directions:

Cook spaghetti (or linguini) in boiling salt water until just tender. Meanwhile, in a non-stick skillet, heat oil over medium heat. Add onions and garlic and fry for 5-7 minutes (do not brown). Reduce heat to low, add olives and orange rind. Heat thoroughly. Drain cooked spaghetti, and serve topped with mixture.

Margaret's Casserole

Margaret McNiven, Brantford, Ontario

Ingredients:
1 lb ground beef
1 can chicken with rice soup
1 cup soda cracker crumbs
1 egg
1 tsp sea salt
1 tsp pepper
1 tsp sage (or poultry seasoning)
1 tsp prepared mustard
1 onion, chopped
1 tbsp ketchup (heaping)
1 pkg onion soup mix

Main Course Meals

Food for Thought

Speaking of Eleanor Roosevelt: No woman has so comforted the distressed or so distressed the comfortable.
– Clare Boothe Luce

Spice of Life

I don't have a bank account, because I don't know my mother's maiden name.
– Paula Poundstone

Female Facts

Rapes Not Reported
Less than 10 per cent of Canadian university and college women who are abused by their dating partners report their experiences to someone in authority at their school. There are many reasons for women's failure to report including: failure to recognize "date rape" as sexual assault; feeling responsible in some way for the assault; fear of not being believed and shame at having been violated. The majority of date and acquaintance rape victims are young women age 16 to 24. According to the Canadian Panel on Violence Against Women, 31 per cent of sexual assaults occur in dating and acquaintance relationships.

Directions:
Mix all ingredients and bake at 350°F for 1 hour.

Gertrude's Macaroni and Cheese Casserole

Gertrude Cahill, St. John's, Newfoundland

Ingredients:
Juice from 1 can of tomatoes
1 1/2 cups macaroni, cooked
2 slices of cheese
1 tbsp butter
Dash of salt

> ## Food for Thought
> Women never have young minds. They are born 3,000 years old.
> *– Shelagh Delaney: A Taste of Honey*

Directions:
Prepare all ingredients in a baking dish and bake for 20 minutes at 300°F.

Fish and Vegetable Stew

Norma Clarke, Peterborough, Ontario (nee Atkinson, Herring Neck, Newfoundland)

Ingredients:
1 1/2 cups fresh cod
1 cup potatoes
1/2 cup celery, chopped
1/2 cup green pepper, chopped
1 large onion
1 1/2 cups carrot, grated

> ## Spice of Life
> When I meet a man I ask myself: "Is this the man I want my children to spend their weekends with?"
> *– Rita Rudner*

Directions:
In a casserole dish, add layers of fish, potato, celery, green pepper and onion. Finally, add grated carrot. Bake at 350°F for 45 minutes or until cooked.

Boiled Beans

Krista Miller, Mount Pearl, Newfoundland

Ingredients:
2 1/2 cups navy beans
3/4 cup salt beef, cut in cubes
1 large onion, chopped
2 tbsps brown sugar
2 tbsps ketchup

> ## Spice of Life
> Whenever I'm caught between two evils, I take the one I've never tried.
> *– Mae West*

Directions:
Place beans in a saucepan and add cold water to cover 1 inch above the beans. Boil for 1/2 hour; drain off water. Add fresh, boiling water, salt beef, onion, brown sugar and ketchup. Continue to boil for 1 1/2 - 2 hours or until beans are tender.

Main Course Meals

Chili Relleno Casserole

Denise (Wadden) Maher, St. John's, Newfoundland

Ingredients:
12 ozs ground pork
1 small onion, chopped (optional)
2/3 cup chunky salsa
3/4 cup milk
4 eggs
1/4 cup flour
1/2 tsp pepper
1/4 tsp garlic powder
2 cups Monterey Jack cheese, grated
1/2 bottle chili peppers (or Jalepeno peppers)

Directions:
Brown pork until crumbly and well done. Add onions; drain fat. Add salsa and cook until thick (few minutes). In a separate bowl, beat together milk, eggs, flour, pepper and garlic. Stir in cheese. Lightly grease an 8" x 8" dish or large quiche dish. Spread peppers on bottom; layer pork mixture, then egg mixture. Bake, uncovered, at 350°F for 35 minutes. Let stand 10 minutes before serving.

Low-Fat Scalloped Potatoes

Peter Marsh, Grand Falls-Windsor, Newfoundland

Ingredients:
1/4 cup flour
1/2 tsp dill weed
3/4 tsp salt
1/8 tsp pepper
2 cups skim milk
6 medium potatoes, sliced (1/4-inch thick)
1 large onion, thinly sliced

Directions:
Stir flour, dill weed, salt and pepper together in a saucepan. Mix in milk gradually until no lumps remain. Heat and stir until it boils and thickens. Remove from heat. Place 1/2 potatoes and 1/2 onion in 2-quart casserole dish. Pour 1/2 sauce over top. Repeat layers. Cover and bake at 350°F for 1 1/2 hours or until potatoes are tender. Remove cover for a few minutes to brown.

Female Facts

Dying To Find Out
Sarah Bernhardt, the famous French actress had such a fascination with death that she sometimes slept in the rosewood coffin she had begged her mother to buy for her. As a teenager, she would often visit Paris morgues to look at the dead bodies of people who were dragged from the Seine River. She was 79 when she finally gave her coffin its intended use.

Spice of Life

The Rose Bowl is the only bowl I've ever seen that I didn't have to clean.
– Erma Bombeck

Female Facts

Newfoundland Filmmaker
Best known for her work as a documentary filmmaker, Barbara Doran's projects have been broadcast worldwide, although the mini-series *Random Passage* was her first venture producing feature-length TV drama. Barbara recently returned to her native Newfoundland after 18 years in Montreal, where she directed and produced more than 20 documentaries.

Main Course Meals

Betty Lou's Hamburg Stew

Betty Lou (formerly of Appleton, Ontario) and Syd George (formerly of Howley, Newfoundland), Gloucester, Ontario

Ingredients:
1 onion, chopped
2 cloves garlic, chopped
1 lb hamburger meat, extra lean
1 cup ginger ale
1/2 cup ketchup
1 green pepper
Dash of pepper
Dash of Worcestershire Sauce
3 or 4 potatoes
Frozen corn
Baby peas
1/2 cup maple syrup

> ## Female Facts
> **The Evil That Women Do**
> The Brothers Grimm, who produced 200 fairy tales, had a 'grim' outlook on women. Their stories contained 16 wicked mothers or stepmothers, 23 evil female witches, and 13 young women who harmed or killed the men who loved them. The bad guys numbered only three wicked fathers or stepfathers, only two evil male witches, and only one man who harmed a woman, his bride.

Directions:
Cook onion until limp. Add garlic cloves, according to one's taste. Add meat, ginger ale, ketchup, green pepper, pepper and Worcestershire Sauce; cook until meat is well browned. Arrange potatoes on top. Cook until potatoes are nearly done. Stir in corn, peas and maple syrup. Simmer until potatoes are done.

Turkey Casserole

Lillian Davis, Okanagan Falls, British Columbia

Ingredients:
1 3/4 cups sour cream
1 (28 oz) can cream of chicken soup
2 cups broccoli
4 cups turkey
Stove Top stuffing
Melted butter

> ## Food for Thought
> Life is either an adventure or nothing. *– Helen Keller*

Directions:
Put sour cream, soup, broccoli and turkey in a buttered casserole dish. Top with Stove Top stuffing. Drizzle with melted butter or margarine. Bake at 325°F for 1 hour.

Lasagna Roll-Ups

Selina Statnyk, Leduc, Alberta

Ingredients:
8 lasagna noodles
1 (10 oz) pkg frozen, chopped spinach
1 container Ricotta cheese
1 1/4 cups parmesan cheese

> ## Spice of Life
> Life! Can't live with it, can't live without it.
> *– Cynthia Nelms*

Main Course Meals

1/2 tsp salt
1/4 tsp nutmeg

Sauce Ingredients:
2 tbsps oil
1 large, chopped onion
2 cloves garlic, minced
1/2 tsp salt
1 tsp sugar
1/2 tsp basil
1/2 tsp oregano
1 (5 oz) can Hunts tomato sauce with bits

Female Facts

Evil Queen
Believing that stepmothers already had it rough enough and didn't "need that kind of image," when Walt Disney created the movie *Snow White,* the villain became an evil queen instead of an evil stepmother. I guess he figured queens could handle it more than stepmothers

Directions:
Cook lasagna noodles; rinse, drain and set aside on paper towels. Thaw spinach and drain well. Combine Ricotta cheese and 1 cup parmesan cheese, spinach, salt and nutmeg; spread over length of each noodle. Roll up as for jelly roll; set on side in baking dish. For sauce, sauté onion and garlic in oil. Add remaining ingredients; simmer for 10 minutes. Spoon over noodles in a baking dish. Cover and bake at 325°F for 1 hour. Remove and sprinkle with 1/4 cup parmesan cheese. (Freezes well).

Aunt Doris's Meatloaf

Maria Young, St. Philip's, Newfoundland (nee Hardy, Port aux Basques, Newfoundland)

Ingredients:
1 1/2 lbs ground beef
1 large onion
1 cup cracker crumbs
1/4 tsp salt
1/2 can tomato sauce
1 egg
1/2 can tomato soup
1/2 can water
2 tbsps vinegar
2 tbsps prepared mustard
2 tbsps brown sugar

Food for Thought

I have everything now I had 20 years ago - except it's all lower.
– *Gypsy Rose Lee*

Directions:
Mix together beef, onion, cracker crumbs, salt, tomato sauce and egg. Place in a loaf pan. Mix together tomato soup, water, vinegar, mustard and brown sugar; pour over meat loaf. Bake at 350°F for 1 - 1 1/2 hours.

Hearty Roast and Vegetables

Sharon L. Begin, Dundas, Ontario

Ingredients:
2 1/2 - 3 lbs beef chuck pot roast

Spice of Life
I base my fashion taste on what doesn't itch.
– *Gilda Radner*

Main Course Meals

1 tsp seasoned salt
1/2 tsp dried marjoram leaves
1/4 tsp celery seed
1/4 tsp pepper
1 clove garlic, finely chopped
1/2 cup water
1 (10 oz) pkg frozen brussel sprouts
4 medium carrots, cut in strips
2 medium potatoes, cut in strips
2 medium turnips, cut in eighths
1 medium onion, cut in rings, separated
1/2 tsp salt
Parsley

Female Facts

Eastern Education
During the reign of the Yuan emperors in China, between 1260 and 1368, women were educated and even allowed to attend medical school. It took more than 600 years for that to happen in the western world.

Directions:

Trim excess fat from beef, rub Dutch Oven with fat and brown beef. Sprinkle with seasoned salt, marjoram, celery seed, pepper and garlic; add water and heat to boiling. Reduce heat; cover and simmer for 1 1/2 hours. Rinse brussel sprouts under running cold water to separate. Add vegetables to Dutch Oven, placing sprouts on top; sprinkle with salt. Add 1/4 cup of water if necessary and heat to boiling. Reduce heat; cover and simmer until beef and vegetables are tender, 30-40 minutes. Sprinkle with parsley. Makes 5-6 servings.

African Beef

Daphne Edison, Dryden, Ontario (nee Norman, Roddickton, Newfoundland)

Ingredients:
2-3 lbs cubed beef
2 medium onions, chopped
1 can tomato soup
1 can mushrooms
2 celery stalks, diced
1/4 cup brown sugar
1/4 cup vinegar
1 tbsp Worchestershire Sauce
1/2 tsp garlic powder
Salt and pepper, to taste

Spice of Life

The poor wish to be rich, the rich wish to be happy, the single wish to be married, and the married wish to be dead.   *– Ann Landers*

Directions:

Brown beef in a hot frying pan, adding a little oil. Spice as desired; add to medium roasting pan. In medium bowl, combine remaining ingredients. Stir well; add to meat mixture. Bake at 300°F for 3 hours. Serve over rice.

Beef and Sausage Sloppy Joes

Daniel Greenland, St. John's, Newfoundland

Food for Thought

It is not fair to ask of others what you are unwilling to do yourself.
– Eleanor Roosevelt

Ingredients:
2 tsps vegetable oil

1 cup onions, chopped
2 tsps garlic, minced
8 ozs lean ground beef
8 ozs mild Italian sausage, chopped, casings removed
4 cups fresh tomatoes, chopped (or 28 oz can tomatoes, drained)
1 1/2 tsps dried basil
1 tsp chili powder
1/2 tsp dried oregano
2 tbsps parmesan cheese, grated (optional)

> ## Food for Thought
> Happiness is not a station you arrive at, but a manner of travelling. – *Margaret Lee Runbeck*

Directions:
In a large non-stick skillet, heat oil over medium heat; add onions and garlic and cook for 4 minutes or until softened. Add ground beef and sausage, breaking up meat with a spoon, and cook for 5 minutes, or until no longer pink. Drain off excess fat. Add tomatoes, basil, chili powder and oregano; bring to a boil, reduce heat to low and simmer uncovered for 30 minutes, stirring occasionally. Serve over toasted hamburger buns. Sprinkle with parmesan cheese, if desired.

Pepper Steak

Norma Clarke, Peterborough, Ontario, (nee Atkinson, Herring Neck, Newfoundland)

Ingredients:
Fresh meat
Salt and pepper (to taste)
1 onion
1/2 green pepper
1/4 cup soya sauce
1 Oxo cube
1/2 cup hot water
1 can tomatoes

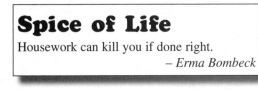

> ## Spice of Life
> Housework can kill you if done right.
> – *Erma Bombeck*

Directions:
Cut meat into squares and sprinkle with salt and pepper. When partially cooked, add onion and green pepper. Continue cooking until meat is tender. Add soya sauce. Dissolve Oxo cube in hot water. Add tomatoes. Let simmer for 1/2 hour. Serve with mashed potatoes or rice.

Sweet and Sour Sauce and Meat Balls

Judy McLoughlin, Millbrook, Ontario

Ingredients:
1/2 cup water
1/2 cup brown sugar
1/4 cup vinegar
1/4 cup ketchup
1 tsp soya sauce
1 tbsp flour
1 lb ground beef

> ## Female Facts
> Bev Crummell was the first woman elected president of the St. John's Metro Softball Umpires Association and was the first woman to officiate in the St. John's Softball League on June 18, 1986.

Wet sliced bread or crumbs
1 egg
1 tsp salt
1 tsp pepper
1 onion
2 tbsp parmesan cheese
1 tsp garlic, minced

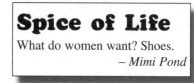

Spice of Life
What do women want? Shoes.
                              – *Mimi Pond*

Directions:

Combine water, brown sugar, vinegar, ketchup, soya sauce and flour to form sauce. Combine remaining ingredients and form into small balls. Fry meatballs until brown. Drain grease and add sauce to meatballs. Place in oven and bake at 350°F until cooked.

Hawaiian Spareribs

Maisie Moyles, Carmanville South, Newfoundland

Ingredients:
1 14-16 oz can pineapple chunks
1/4 cup honey
1/4 cup white vinegar
1 tsp salt
1 tsp Worcestershire Sauce
1/4 tsp ground ginger
5 lbs pork back ribs, cut into single rib portions

Food for Thought
Love is like quicksilver in the hand. Leave the fingers open and it stays. Clutch it, and it darts away.   – *Dorothy Parker*

Directions:

Drain pineapple juice into shallow roasting pan. Stir in honey, vinegar, salt, Worcestershire Sauce and ginger (reserve pineapple). Add ribs, stirring to coat ribs. Cover pan tightly with foil. Bake in 325°F oven for 2 hours or until tender. During last 10 minutes, add reserved pineapple chunks. Arrange ribs and pineapple on warm platter and serve.

Sweet and Sour Pork Chops

Donna Cheeseman, St. John's, Newfoundland

Ingredients:
Pork chops
1 onion, chopped
1/2 cup orange juice
2 tbsps orange marmalade
2 tbsps brown sugar
1 tbsp vinegar

Female Facts
International Women's Day began in 1910 but the roots went back to March 8, 1857 when women textile workers in New York demonstrated against the 12-hour work day, low wages and awful working conditions.

Directions:

Brown pork chops and drain off fat. Place pork chops and onion in pan. Mix together remaining ingredients and pour over pork chops and simmer for 45 minutes, covered. Add slices of oranges as a garnish.

Mrs. Picnic Ham Shoulder

Marilyn Pumphrey, St. John's, Newfoundland

Ingredients:
1 3-5 lb ham (shoulder)
5 whole cloves
1 can pineapple slices
1/2 cup whole cherries (red or green)
1 cup brown sugar
Dash of dry mustard
1 tsp cinnamon

Spice of Life

Outside every thin woman is a fat man trying to get in.   – *Katherine Whitehorn*

Directions:
Parboil ham for 1-2 hours. Remove from water and cool; score ham and insert whole cloves. Apply pineapple slices and cherries to scored ham. Combine brown sugar, mustard and cinnamon. Sprinkle over ham. Bake at 350°F for 1 hour, basting occasionally.

Roast Pork with Clementines

Ron Pumphrey, St. John's, Newfoundland

Ingredients:
4 lbs pork loin roast
1 cup clementine juice
1 bay leaf, finely crumbled
1 clove garlic, finely minced
1/2 tsp thyme
1 tbsp cornstarch
3 clementines, peeled and sectioned
2 Granny Smith apples, cored and cut into wedges
Salt (to taste)

Food for Thought

A timid man said to his wife, "We're not going out tonight and that's semi-final."

Directions:
The day before, place pork in a dish just large enough to hold it, fat side up. Stir the clementine juice with bay leaf, garlic and thyme and pour evenly over the pork roast. Cover and refrigerate overnight, or at least 12 hours. Turn meat at least once during this time and baste with marinade. About 3 hours before serving, preheat oven to 325°F. Lift the roast from the marinade, reserving the mixture. Place the meat, fat side up, in a roasting pan and roast, covered, for 2 1/2 hours; baste several times with the pan juices. Then, uncover and generously baste the entire roast with the marinade mixture. Continue roasting, uncovered, for an additional 1/2 hour or until the roast has turned a golden colour and a meat thermometer inserted into the centre registers 170°F. Baste every ten minutes with marinade. As soon as the pork is finished cooking, remove to a large platter and cover to keep warm. (Let the meat sit for at least 15 minutes before slicing). Pour pan juices into a saucepan and add any remaining marinade. Blend cornstarch with a tbsp. of cold water. Whisk into the pan juice mixture and boil over medium heat, stirring constantly, until thickened, about 5 minutes (add a little more cornstarch if it's not thick enough). Add salt to taste. As a beautiful garnish for the roast, peel and section the clementines and slice the unpeeled apples into thin wedges. Alternate apple and clementine sections around the roast. Serve several slices of fruit with each slice of roast. Serve pan juices in a gravy boat. Serves 8.

Main Course Meals

Coated Roast Pork

Pearl White, Trenton, Ontario (nee Flight, Small Point, Newfoundland)

Ingredients:
2-3 lbs shoulder pork
4 tbsps soy sauce
1 tbsp sherry
1 tbsp cornstarch
1/4 tsp pepper
1/4 tsp MSG
2 garlic cloves, crushed

> ### Spice of Life
> A man can sleep around, no questions asked, but if a woman makes 19 or 20 mistakes she's a tramp. *– Joan Rivers*

Directions:
Preheat oven to 275°F. Place roast on a rack in a dripping pan. Blend remaining ingredients and spread over entire surface of meat. Roast 45-50 minutes per pound. Meat will be crisp on the outside, but tender and juicy on the inside. Serve either hot or cold.

Bublem Squeak

C. Milley Johnson, Port Union, Newfoundland (formerly of Little Catalina, Newfoundland)

Ingredients:
Salt pork, diced
1 medium onion, sliced
Leftover turnip
Leftover carrots
Leftover potatoes
Leftover cabbage

> ### Female Facts
> **First Women's Votes**
> The earliest nation to give women the right to vote was New Zealand in 1893, followed by Australia in 1902 and Finland in 1906.

Directions:
Fry salt pork in an iron frying pan (do not brown). Add onion and cook a little. Add leftover turnip and carrot, which have been sliced or cubed. Add enough water to simmer. Add potatoes and cabbage. Salt to taste.

Pork Chops and Rice

Marie Schultz, Sherwood Park, Alberta

Ingredients:
1 tbsp vegetable oil
6 pork chops
1 medium onion, chopped
1/4 cup green pepper, chopped
1 cup uncooked rice
1/2 tsp salt
1/4 tsp pepper
2 cups beef broth
1 tbsp Worchestershire Sauce
2 tomatoes, sliced

> ### Female Facts
> **From the Horse's Mouth**
> Not only do race-winning camels generally cost more than race-winning horses, all racing camels are female.
>
>

Main Course Meals

Directions:

Heat oil in skillet; brown pork chops. Place 3 pork chops in bottom of a 2-quart, oven-proof casserole dish. Sauté onion and green pepper in pork chop drippings. Place rice on top of pork chops in casserole. Place onion and green pepper on top of rice. Sprinkle with salt and pepper. Cover with remaining 3 pork chops. Combine beef broth with Worchestershire Sauce. Pour over pork chops and rice. Place tomatoes on top. Bake covered at 350°F for 1 hour.

Oven-Baked Bar-B-Q Ribs

Pat Jackman, Holland Landing, Ontario

Ingredients:
2 lbs pork side ribs
1 small bottle ketchup
1 large onion, chopped fine
1/2 cup water
1/4 cup celery, chopped
3 tsps vinegar
3 tsps brown sugar
3 tsps Worchestershire Sauce
1/4 tsp prepared mustard

Food for Thought
Any smart woman will tell you that the best way to a man's heart is through his ego.

Directions:

Cut ribs into individual pieces, fry or boil to remove fat. Place in a roasting pan and prepare remaining ingredients in a bowl; pour over ribs. Bake at 350°F for 35-40 minutes. Stir occasionally. Do not cover. Serve with baked or mashed potatoes, buttered carrots and salad or any other favourite vegetable.

Jodi's Pork Chops

Ethel Nixon, Fredericton, New Brunswick (nee Jones, St. Philip's, Newfoundland)

Ingredients:
1/2 cup ketchup
1/2 cup sugar
1/4 cup Worchestershire Sauce
1 cup coffee
2 tbsps vinegar
1 small onion, sliced
1/2 tsp salt
1/8 tsp pepper
Pork chops

Female Facts

First in Farming, First in Culture
The first 'gods' of fertility and culture were actually goddesses. That's because women were the first to plant crops and the first to decorate their habitations.

Directions:

Combine all ingredients (except pork chops) in a saucepan and simmer for 10 minutes. Pour sauce over uncooked pork chops. Bake covered at 350°F for 1-1 1/2 hours, depending on thickness of pork chops.

Barbecued Pork Chops

Peter Marsh, Grand Falls-Windsor, Newfoundland

Ingredients:

8 boneless loin pork chops (fat removed)
1/2 cup tomato paste
2/3 cup white vinegar
1/2 tsp salt
1/8 tsp ground cloves
1/2 tbsp liquid sweetener
1 tbsp prepared mustard
2 cups fresh mushrooms, sliced
2 cups onion, chopped

Spice of Life

Before we make love my husband takes a painkiller.   *– Joan Rivers*

Directions:

Spray frying pan with non-stick cooking spray. Brown pork chops on both sides. Stir next 6 ingredients in medium saucepan; heat until boiling. Add mushrooms and onion. Arrange pork chops in a small roasting pan and spoon sauce over top. Cover and bake at 350°F for 1 1/2 hours.

Beef Stroganoff

Mary (Peggy) Bourgeois (nee Mercer), Mount Pearl, Newfoundland

Ingredients:

2 tbsps butter or margarine
2 tbsps shortening
1 1/2 pounds sirloin steak (cut in cubes)
1 tsp salt
1/2 tsp pepper (or to taste)
2 sliced onions
1/2 pound sliced mushrooms
4 tbsps flour
1 (10 oz) can beef broth bouillon
1 (10 oz) can water
2 tbsps Worcestershire Sauce
2 tbsps ketchup
1 bay leaf
1 tsp thyme
1 cup sour cream

Female Facts

And the Gin Wasn't Even Aged
In the 1700s an English coachman exchanged his wife for a bottle of gin.

Directions:

Melt butter and shortening in a large frying pan and add steak. Cook steak until brown, adding salt and pepper. Just before meat is brown, add onions and mushrooms. Cook a little longer. Sprinkle with 4 tbsp flour and stir. Slowly add bouillon and then water, stirring constantly. Then add Worcestershire Sauce, ketchup, bay leaf and thyme. Cover and cook on low heat for 3/4 hour, stirring occasionally. Add sour cream before serving. Serve over hot rice, noodles or boiled potatoes.

Main Course Meals

Bacon 'N' Baked Beans

Marg Mitchell, Halifax, Nova Scotia

Ingredients:
1/2 lb bacon
1 (14oz) can beans with molasses
1 (14oz) can lima beans (drained)
1 (14oz) can kidney beans (drained)
1 (14oz) can tomatoes (skinless)
1/2 cup brown sugar
1/4 cup molasses
2 medium onions (diced)
1 tsp mustard

Directions:
Fry bacon until it is crisp then cut into 1-inch pieces. Mix bacon with other ingredients and bake at 350°F for 1 1/2 hours. If too juicy, remove cover and bake at 400°F until juice is absorbed. Makes 8 to 10 servings.

> ## Food for Thought
> Life has got to be lived - that's all there is to it. At seventy, I would say the advantage is that you take life more calmly. You know that "this too shall pass!"
> – Eleanor Roosevelt

Taco Platter

Ina Belcher, Tonawanda, New York (nee MacPherson, St. John's, Newfoundland)

Ingredients:
1 1/2 lbs lean hamburger meat
1/2 cup water
1 pkg taco seasoning mix
16 ozs softened cream cheese
1/4 cup milk
2 medium size tomatoes, chopped
1 cup green onion, chopped
1 1/2 cups shredded lettuce
3/4 cup honey barbeque sauce
1 1/2 cups shredded cheddar cheese
1 bag of tortilla chips

> ## Female Facts
> **A Frenchman Wouldn't Do It**
> Long before the Anglo-Saxon population of England was conquered by the French-speaking people of Normandy, they were the only society known to humankind where a man could divorce a woman because she was too passionate. Vive la France!

Directions:
Brown meat (until no longer pink), then add water and seasoning mix and simmer for 5 or 6 minutes. Put aside when cooked. Then combine cream cheese and milk and mix well. Spread cream cheese on serving platter. Top with meat mixture. Then add tomatoes, onions and lettuce. Drizzle on barbecue sauce. Top with shredded cheese. Serve with the chips.

> ## Spice of Life
> The easiest way to find something lost around the house is to buy a replacement.

Large Family Seven Layer Dinner

Bonnie Butler, Hamilton, Ontario (nee Fudge, Seal Cove, White Bay, Newfoundland)

Ingredients:
5 large potatoes (sliced)
3 carrots (cubed)
1 large onion (sliced thinly)
1 cup of minute rice
1 pkg pork chops
2 cans tomato soup
Salt and pepper (to taste)

Spice of Life

When we talk to God, we're praying. When God talks to us, we're schizophrenic.
– Lily Tomlin

Directions:

In a roaster, place a layer of sliced potatoes on bottom, then place onion, carrot cubes and uncooked rice on top. Mix 1 can soup with 1 can of water and pour over ingredients in roaster. Salt and pepper pork chops to taste and place on top of ingredients in roaster. Mix the second can of soup with water and pour over pork chops. Cover and bake at 350°F for 2 hours.

Fish Stew

Bernadette Kennedy, Foxtrap, Newfoundland

Ingredients:
1 1/2 lbs fresh fish fillets
1 large onion sliced
4 tbsps butter
1 cup ketchup
2 tbsps lime juice
2 tbsps bottled steak sauce
Dash of Worcestershire Sauce
Salt and pepper (to taste)

Female Facts

First Ladies Live Longer
Not counting assassinations, since 1860, American Presidents have had a 40 per cent higher mortality rate than their wives.

Directions:

Sauté onion in butter in heavy skillet until soft. Add ketchup, lime juice, steak sauce, Worcestershire Sauce, salt and pepper. Bring sauce to a boil. Cut fish into chunks and arrange in sauce. Cover and simmer 20 minutes or until fish flakes easily. Serves 4.

Pinwheel Vegetarian Casserole

G. Bussey, Roseneath, Ontario

Ingredients:
3 large onions, chopped
3 1/2 cups frozen mixed vegetables
4 tbsps margarine
2 1/2 cups milk
4 tbsps flour

Food for Thought
Getting divorced just because you don't love a man is almost as silly as getting married just because you do. – *Zsa Zsa Gabor*

1/2 lb Colby cheese
Salt to taste

Directions:
Sauté onions. Pour hot water over the frozen vegetables. Drain and place in casserole. Make a cream sauce with margarine, flour and milk. Add colby cheese and stir until it melts. Add salt.

Vegetarian Meat Balls

G. Bussey, Roseneath, Ontario

Ingredients:
1/2 cup walnuts, chopped
1 tsp salt
1 cup dry bread crumbs
1 tsp poultry seasoning
1/2 cup cracker crumbs
5 eggs
1/2 cup grated cheese
1 clove garlic, chopped

Directions:
Mix and form into balls. Fry in deep fat. Place in dish and cover with sauce.

Sauce Ingredients:
1 onion, chopped
1 can pineapple tidbits and juice
1/2 cup water
2 tsp lemon juice
1/2 cup brown sugar
1 cup tomato ketchup
2 tbsps cornstarch

Sauce Directions:
Sauté onion, add pineapple and juice, then water, lemon juice, brown sugar and ketchup. Bring to a boil. Add cornstarch diluted with cold water. Stir quickly into sauce, cook until clear. Add to meat balls. Bake 30 minutes.

Spice of Life

Never lend your car to anyone to whom you have given birth. – *Erma Bombeck*

Food for Thought

It is far more impressive when others discover your good qualities without your help.
                    – *Miss Manners (Judith Martin)*

Female Facts

Formidable Foes
For two centuries an army of about 2,500 fighting women were feared in the neighbouring kingdoms of their native Dahomey in West Africa. The women carried bows and arrows, guns and huge knives to protect and further the advantage of the king, who was husband to all of them. The great female army was finally crushed by French forces in 1892.

Main Course Meals

Sweets
&
Treats

Pink Angels

Eileen Durnford,
Doyles, Newfoundland

Main ingredients:
2 cups graham wafers
2 tbsps brown sugar
1/2 cup melted butter
1/8 tsp salt

Topping Ingredients:
1 can condensed milk
1 tsp vanilla
2 cups coconut
Pink icing

Filling Ingredients:
2/3 cups water
1/2 cup sugar
1/2 lb dates
1 tsp lemon juice

Female Facts

Fought Like Men
When two women, Mary Read of England, and Anne Bonny of Ireland, who had led separate but notorious lives, met on the same ship in 1719, both disguised as men, they joined forces with a male privateer captain named Rackham, and seized the ship. After many acts of piracy, their ship was attacked and eventually captured. Only one male pirate joined them in the hand-to-hand combat on deck to avoid capture. Before Captain Rackham was hanged, Anne is said to have told him, "If you had fought like a man you need not have been hanged like a dog." Anne's fate is unknown, but Mary died of a fever in prison while waiting to be hanged herself.

Filling Directions:
Add water, sugar and dates. Cook together until thick, stir well, add lemon juice before using.

Directions:
Blend main ingredients together and press in 9" x 9" pan. Bake for 5 minutes at 350°, then add filling. Mix all topping ingredients except icing together, topping the product. Bake another 25 minutes and allow to cool before adding icing.

Snicker Doodles

Floss LeDrew, Pasadena, Newfoundland

Ingredients:
1 cup margarine or butter
1 1/3 cup light brown sugar
2 eggs
1 tsp vanilla
3 cups flour
1 tsp soda
1 tsp cream of tarter
1/4 tsp salt
2 tsps cinnamon
3 tbsps sugar

Spice of Life

Some people ask the secret of our long marriage. We take time to go to a restaurant two times a week. A little candlelight, dinner, soft music and dancing. She goes Tuesdays, I go Fridays. - *Henny Youngman*

Directions:
Beat butter and sugar until creamy. Beat in eggs and vanilla until smooth. In a small bowl, stir together flour, soda, cream of tarter and salt. Gradually add flour mixture to butter mixture.

Sweets and Treats

Blend thoroughly. Combine in a small bowl, cinnamon and sugar. Form dough into balls then roll in cinnamon. Bake at 325°F for 12-15 minutes until the bottom edges are "lightly brown."

Carrot Cake

Geraldine Prim, St. John's, Newfoundland, (nee O'Brien, Cape Broyle, Newfoundland)

Ingredients:
2 cups sifted flour
2 tsps baking soda
1 tsp baking powder
1 tsp salt
2 tsps ground cinnamon
1 3/4 cups sugar
1 cup vegetable oil
3 eggs
1 tsp vanilla
2 cups shredded carrots
1 cup flaked coconut
1 cup coarsly chopped walnuts
1 can (8 1/4 ozs) crushed pineapple (partially drained)

> ## Food for Thought
> In a great romance, each person basically plays a part that the other really likes.
> – *Elizabeth Ashley*

Directions:
Grease baking pan and dust lightly with flour and tap out excess. Mix flour, baking soda, baking powder, salt and cinnamon in a large bowl. Mix well and add in order the sugar, oil, eggs and vanilla. Beat together with wooden spoon until smooth. Then stir in the rest and beat until well beaten (a good whipping). Then pour into 9" x 12" pan and bake for 45 minutes at 355°F.

Brown Sugar Cake

Helen Crocker, Kitchener, Ontario (formerly of Heart's Delight, Newfoundland)

Ingredients:
1 cup butter
2 cups brown sugar
3 eggs beaten
3 cups sifted flour
3 tsps baking powder
1 tsp salt
Juice and rind from one large orange
6 cups raisins
3 cups currants
2 cups peel
1 1/2 cups of red cherries
1 1/2 cups green cherries

> ## Female Facts
> **First Female Over the Pole**
> In 1955, when, at the age of 68, Louise Arner Boyd, an American explorer of the Arctic Ocean, became the first woman to fly over the North Pole. The Norwegian government had earlier awarded Boyd the Chevalier Cross of the Order of Saint Olav for her efforts in 1928, when Boyd led an expedition to find Norwegian Arctic explorer Roald Amundsen, who had disappeared while flying a rescue mission.

Directions:
Cream butter and sugar together. Add beaten eggs, continue beating until mixture is very light. Sift flour, baking powder and salt together, and reserve a little of the flour for flouring the fruit. Add sifted dry ingredients to the egg mixture then add orange juice and rind. Finally fold in

Sweets and Treats

floured fruit. Use a large 10" pan which has been greased and well lined with wax paper. Bake at 275°F for 3 hours.

Peanut Marshmallow Squares

Louise Sweetapple, Downsview, Ontario

Ingredients:
1/2 cup butter
1/2 cup crunchy peanut butter
1 pkg butterscotch chipits
1 1/2 cups coloured marshmallows

> ### *Food for Thought*
> Many people have a wrong idea of what constitutes true happiness. It is not attained through self-gratification, but through fidelity to a worthy purpose.   *– Helen Keller*

Directions:
Melt butter and peanut butter on stove, turn off heat after melted, and stir. Then add butterscotch chipits and stir until dissolved. Cool for 5-10 minutes. Add coloured marshmallows. Put in a square 8" pan and keep refrigerated.

Ritz-Pecan Tortes

Louise Sweetapple, Downsview, Ontario

Ingredients:
3 egg whites
1/4 tsp cream of tartar
1 cup sugar
1/2 tsp vanilla
3/4 cups chopped pecans
20 Ritz Crackers, finely crushed
1/2 pint whipping cream

> ### Female Facts
> **Freedom For All**
> Mercy Otis Warren, who argued that women's alleged weaknesses were due simply to inferior education, became an admired ally of most of the rebel leaders in Massachusetts. She was a confidante of John Adams, a big promoter of the revolutionary cause.

Directions:
Preheat oven to 325°F. Beat egg whites and cream of tartar until stiff. Fold in sugar, vanilla, pecans and Ritz Cracker crumbs. Grease well, two 9" round cake pans, fill with egg white mixture. Bake for 30 minutes at 325°F. Cool for 15 minutes. Remove from pans.
Whip cream until stiff. Spread between two layers and refrigerate for 24 hours. Top with additional whipped cream.

Drizzled Chocolate Mint Bars

Louise Sweetapple, Downsview, Ontario

Ingredients:
1 cup chipits - chocolate mint chips
1/2 cup margarine or butter
1/4 cup icing sugar
1 egg
1 1/2 cups Honey Maid graham wafer crumbs

Spice of Life

There is so little difference between husbands you might as well keep the first.
– Adela Rogers St. John's

Sweets and Treats

1/2 cup chopped walnuts
2 cups icing sugar
2 tbsps milk
Green food colouring (optional)

Directions:
Melt chipits and 1/4 cup margarine over hot water. Reserve 1/4 cup for top drizzle. Add icing sugar and egg to remaining melted chipits and beat well. Stir in wafer crumbs and nuts. Press evenly on bottom of an 8" square pan. Chill. Cream 1/4 cup softened margarine, icing sugar and milk until fluffy. Add green colouring, if desired. Spread evenly over base in pan. Drizzle reserved melted chipits over top. Chill until firm. Cut into bars. Makes about 3 dozen bars.

Boiled Cake

Alicia Windsor

Ingredients:
2 cups boiling water
1/2 lb butter
1 cup white sugar
1 tsp clove
2 tsps cinnamon
1 pkg raisins
3 cups flour
2 tsps baking soda
1 tsp vanilla

Directions:
Boil first 6 ingredients, cool, then add flour, vanilla and baking soda. Bake at 350°F for 1 hour.

Christmas Bread

Rita Yetman

Ingredients:
2/3 cup lukewarm water
2 tsps sugar
2 envelopes yeast
2/3 cup scalded milk
1/2 cup sugar
1 1/4 tsps salt
6 tbsps shortening
3 well beaten eggs
6 cups sifted flour
3 cups mixed fruit

Directions:

Measure into a large bowl 2/3 cup lukewarm water and 2 tsps sugar. Stir until sugar dissolves. Sprinkle with 2 envelopes of yeast. Let stand for 10 minutes, then stir well. Scald 2/3 cup milk and stir in 1/2 cup sugar, 1 1/4 tsp salt and 6 tbsps of shortening. Cool to lukewarm and add to yeast mixture. Stir in 3 well beaten eggs and 3 cups of flour, beat until smooth. Stir in 3 cups of fruit and work in 3 more cups of flour. Knead dough until smooth and elastic. Place in a greased bowl. Cover, let rise in a warm place until double in bulk. Knead down and divide into 3 equal portions. Make 3 small buns or 1 large bun out of each portion. Put in pans and let rise to double in bulk again. Bake at 250°F for 45 minutes.

Lassie Pork Toutons

Anne Marie McGrath

Ingredients:
1 cup finely diced salt pork
1/2 tsp baking soda
4 cups all purpose flour
4 tsps baking powder
1/2 tsp salt
1/4 cup butter or margarine
1/2 cup molasses
1 cup water

> ## Female Facts
> **Wringer Invented by Woman**
> Ellen Eglui invented the clothes wringer for washing machines and sold the patent for just $18, because of her colour. "You know I am black and if it was known that a Negro woman patented the invention, white ladies would not buy the wringer. I was afraid to be known because of my colour, in having it introduced into the market, that is the only reason," she said.

Directions:

Fry out salt pork until crisp (drain well). Sift dry ingredients into a bowl. Cut in butter or margarine. Add scruncheons (fried fat pork cubes) and mix well with a fork. Combine molasses and water. Add to flour mixture, stirring lightly. Roll out on a floured board or pastry sheet. Cut into rounds and place on a greased and floured baking sheet. Bake at 400°F for 15 minutes.

Perfect Cream Puffs

Barbara Healey

Ingredients:
1/4 cup butter
1/4 tsp salt
1/2 cup boiling water
1/2 cup flour
2 eggs

Spice of Life

A liberated woman is one who has sex before marriage and a job after.
– *Gloria Steinem*

Directions:

Add butter and salt to boiling water in saucepan. Add flour all at once, stir vigorously with a wooden spoon until mixture forms stiff ball in centre. Remove from heat, add eggs one at a time, beating well after each addition, until mixture is smooth. Mixture will be very stiff, drop from tablespoon on a lightly greased cookie sheet or muffin pan. Bake in a hot oven at 425°F for 15 minutes. Reduce heat to 375°F and bake for 25 minutes longer. Smaller puffs, 15 to 20 minutes. Fill with your favourite filling.

Sweets and Treats

Filling Ingredients:

1 can crushed pineapple
1/2 cup sugar
1 pkg custard powder or 3 tbsps with 1/2 cup milk (a tsp of sugar will prevent lumps)
1 can Nestles Cream

Filling Directions:

Cook on medium heat or until thick. Remove from heat, cool for 5 minutes, add 1 can Nestles Cream. When cool, fill cream puffs.

Newfoundland Squares

Crystal Wall

Ingredients:

1 cup flour
1/3 cup brown sugar
1/2 cup margarine
1 cup coconut
1 cup walnuts
2 eggs
1 1/2 cups brown sugar

Female Facts

Going in Style
The Dutch-Javanese dancer known as Mata Hari was a German spy, the most famous spy of WWI. When she was arrested, convicted and ordered to be executed by a French firing squad, she ordered a tailor-made suit and white gloves which she was wearing when she was shot.

Directions:

Mix together the flour, 1/3 cup of brown sugar and margarine and press into greased 9" x 9" pan. Bake at 300°F for about 10 minutes, or until delicate brown. Chop the coconut and walnuts. Beat the eggs until they are light. Gradually beat in 1 1/2 cups brown sugar, add coconut and nuts. Spread this mixture over the baked crust. Bake at 325°F for 40 minutes.

Rice and Apple Pudding

Sandy Ivany

Ingredients:

6 apples, sliced (other fruits may be substituted)
2/3 cup water
4 tbsps butter
1/3 cup sugar
1/4 tsp salt
1 1/2 cups cooked rice
1/2 cup marmalade

Spice of Life

For two people in a marriage to live together day after day is unquestionably the one miracle the Vatican has overlooked. – *Bill Cosby*

Directions:

Slice apples. Add water, butter, sugar and salt, simmer until tender. Line bottom and sides of a greased 8" x 8" baking dish with part of the rice. Fill with cooked apples and spread marmalade over top. Cover with remaining rice. Bake at 350°F for 15 to 20 minutes. Let stand until cold. Unmold and turn onto a serving plate. Serve with desired pudding sauce. Serves 6.

Sweets and Treats

Never Fail Banana Bread

Lorraine Ezekiel

Ingredients:
3 mashed bananas
1/4 cup melted butter
1 cup sugar
2 eggs
1 1/2 cups flour
1/4 tsp salt
1 tsp baking powder

Directions:
Add mashed bananas to melted butter. Add sugar and eggs. Mix well. Add flour, salt and baking powder, mixing well. Bake at 350°F for 1 hour. For variety, you can add baking gumdrops, raisins or nuts.

Two Layer Cocoa Squares

Elaine Gill

Top Ingredients:
1 cup coconut
3 tsps flour
1/2 tsp baking powder
3/4 cup milk
1/2 tsp vanilla
1 cup brown sugar

Bottom Ingredients:
5 tbsps cocoa
1/4 cup brown sugar
1 1/2 cups flour
1/2 cup butter (melted)

Directions:
Mix together ingredients for bottom layer and press into a 9" x 9" pan. Mix together ingredients for top layer and pour over bottom layer. Bake at 350°F for 30 minutes. Cool and cut into squares.

Figged Pudding

Mona Bursey, Charleston, Newfoundland

Ingredients:
3 cups bread crumbs
1 cup raisins
1/4 tsp salt

Food for Thought

Never doubt that a small group of thoughtful committed citizens can change the world. Indeed, it is the only thing that ever has. – *Margaret Mead*

Female Facts

Doing Her Part For Procreation
In a 16 month period beginning in 1880 and ending in 1881, a Prussian woman gave birth to 11 children during two pregnancies. She had sextuplets and quintuplets, in that order.

Spice of Life

Everything you see I owe to spaghetti. – *Sophia Loren*

Sweets and Treats

Sweets and Treats

1/2 cup brown sugar
1 tsp ginger
1 tsp allspice
1 tsp cinnamon
3 tsps molasses
1/4 cup melted butter
1 tsp baking soda
1/2 cup flour
1 tsp hot water

Spice of Life

Marriage is a word which always means commitment - but so does insanity.   – *Daniel Quinn*

Directions:

Soak bread for a few minutes, then squeeze out water. Measure without pressing down. Combine bread crumbs, raisins, salt, sugar and spices. Mix with a fork. Add molasses, melted butter and baking soda, which has been dissolved in hot water. Add flour and mix well. Pour into pudding bag and tie tightly. Boil for 1 hour.

Lassy Buns

Judy Rimmer

Ingredients:

3/4 cup butter
1 1/2 cups molasses
1/2 cup hot water
1 tsp cinnamon
1 tsp allspice
1 tsp cloves
1 tbsp baking soda
4 1/2 cups flour
Pinch of salt
2 tbsps baking powder

Female Facts

Golf, as a Woman's Sport
Although golf wasn't invented in Scotland, it was perfected there, and it is with that country that the game is mostly associated. Its popularity was demonstrated there by no less than Mary Queen of Scots, who, when she was informed that her husband, Lord Darnley, had been murdered, finished the round of golf she was playing before leaving to make funeral arrangements. *See also page 196.*

Directions:

Cream butter and molasses. Then add hot water. Sift all dry ingredients together and stir into mixture. Roll out into 1/2 inch thickness and cut. Bake at 375°F for 12-15 minutes.

Raisin Buns

Judy Rimmer

Ingredients:

1 1/2 cups flour
Pinch of salt
1/4 cup coconut
1/4 cup sugar
1/2 cup butter or margarine
1 egg
1/4-1/2 cup milk
1 cup raisins
4 tsps baking powder

Food for Thought

It is the duty of the host to make guests feel at home - it is the duty of the guest to remember they are not.   – *Groenfeldt*

Directions:
Mix together and roll into 1/2 inch thickness. Cut into circles and bake at 400°F for 10-12 minutes.

Grandma's One Bowl Applesauce Cake

Genevieve Dalton

Ingredients:
2 1/4 cups flour
1 tsp salt
1 tsp baking soda
1 tsp cinnamon
1/2 cup soft butter
1 cup molasses
1 egg
3/4 cup raisins
1 cup apple sauce

> ## Spice of Life
> A dressmaker sews what she gathers, and a farmer gathers what she sows.

Directions:
Combine dry ingredients in a mixing bowl. Cut in butter, add molasses, egg and applesauce. Beat in and stir in raisins. Bake at 350°F 40-50 minutes.

Boiled Raisin Cake

Josephine Tubin, Lasalle, Quebec

Ingredients:
1 cup butter or margarine
1 cup white sugar
1 cup dark raisins
2 tsps cinnamon
1 1/2 tsps ground cloves
1/2 tsp salt
2 cups boiling water
1 cup brown sugar
3 1/2 cups flour
2 tsps baking soda

> ## Female Facts
> **Hounding the First Lady**
> Thinking that her divorce was final, Rachel Robards married Andrew Jackson, who was a young lawyer in Nashville at the time. The couple, when they found out about it, had the divorce finalized and married a second time. This time legally. When Andrew later ran for president, his campaign was hounded by vulgar retellings of the story. On the eve of his election Rachel died, leaving Jackson permanently embittered.

Directions:
Boil ingredients (except flour and baking soda) until butter is melted. Let liquid cool, then add flour and baking soda. Bake in greased tube or bundt pan at 325F for 1 hour.

Impossible Pie

Mary Lewis

Ingredients:
4 eggs
2 cups milk
2/3 cups sugar

> ## Spice of Life
> The sole purpose of children's middle names is so they know when they're really in trouble.

1/2 cup flour
1/2 cup margarine
1 tsp vanilla
1/2 tsp salt
1 cup coconut

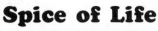

Spice of Life

No matter which cart I choose at the store, mine will be the one with the wobbly wheel.

Directions:

Mix together all ingredients and blend for 15 seconds. Pour into a well buttered 9" plate. Bake for 40 minutes at 350°F.

Coconut Bars

Robyn Phillips

Food for Thought

A mother is that dear person who listens to your problems until you're bored with them.

Ingredients:
1 cup melted margarine
2 cups graham wafer crumbs
2 cups coconut
1 can sweetened condensed milk
6 ozs chocolate chips

Directions:

Mix all together. Place in a 8" x 8" inch pan. Bake at 350°F for half an hour. Sprinkle with 6 ounces of chocolate chips. Place in refrigerator until cool. Cut into bars.

Salt Pork Buns

Kathleen Earles

Female Facts

A Female Freud

Anna Freud, daughter of Sigmund Freud, and a psychoanalyst herself, founded the Hampstead Child Therapy Course and Clinic in London in 1947, and served as its director after 1952. The author of numerous scientific books and papers, she also helped found the annual periodical, *Psychoanalytic Study of the Child*, in 1945.

Ingredients:
1 cup fine chopped salt pork
1/4 cup butter
4 cups flour
1/2 cup molasses
8 tsps baking powder
1 1/2 cups water
1/2 tsp salt

Directions:

Fry pork in butter and drain well. Add to dry ingredients in a bowl. Combine molasses and water, then add to flour mixture and stir. Roll and cut into buns. Bake at 400°F for 15 minutes.

Newfoundland Dumplings

Daphne Parr, St. Lunaire, Newfoundland

Food for Thought

Most of us go to our graves with our dreams still inside us.

Ingredients:
1 cup flour
2 tsps baking powder

Sweets and Treats

1/2 tsp salt
1/2 cup milk

Directions:

Blend together the flour, baking powder and salt. Stir in milk. Drop by spoonfuls over hot stew or soup. Cover and simmer for 15 minutes without lifting lid. Serve immediately.

Mock Apple Fritters

Maria Hiscock, Grand Bank, Newfoundland

Ingredients:

24 graham wafers
1 cup butter
1 cup brown sugar
1 cup chopped pecans

Spice of Life

Even if man could understand women he still wouldn't believe it. – A. W. Brown

Directions:

Arrange wafers on a greased cookie sheet with sides. Melt butter, stir in brown sugar and boil for exactly 2 minutes. Stir in pecans, spread evenly over wafers. Bake at 350°F for 8 - 10 minutes. Watch them carefully. Do not over cook. Cut in half and remove from pan while still warm. Cool on rack, store in air-tight container.

Molasses Muffins

Claudine Barnes, Corner Brook, Newfoundland (nee Pye, Cape Charles, Labrador)

Ingredients:

3 cups flour
1 tsp baking powder
2 tsps baking soda
1/2 tsp salt
1 tsp mixed spice
1 tsp cloves
1/2 cup margarine
3/4 cup sugar
2 eggs
1/2 cup molasses
1 cup milk
1 cup raisins, optional

Female Facts

The Hand That Rocks The Cradle

New York socialite Jenny Jerome, who invented the Manhattan Cocktail, accredited her abundant energy to the fact that she was one-eighth Iroquois Indian. After she married an Englishman named Lord Randolph Churchill and moved to England, she continued to be a socialite, and her energy didn't abate, even while she was pregnant. She was at a party at the ancestral castle of Blenheim when the labour pains started, and before she could be taken to a hospital she gave birth to her since-famous son, Winston Churchill, in a ladies cloakroom.

Directions:

Sift dry ingredients together. Cream margarine and sugar together, beat in eggs one at a time; beat in molasses. Stir in dry ingredients with milk, stirring just enough to blend. Add more milk if too dry. Add raisins. Fill muffin pans 2/3 full. Bake at 350°F for 15-20 minutes. May be iced if desired.

Sweets and Treats

By The Bay Blueberry Muffins

Herb Greening, Botwood, Newfoundland

Ingredients:
2 cups flour
3 tsps baking powder
1/4 cup sugar
1 tsp orange rind
Pinch allspice
Pinch nutmeg
Pinch cinnamon
1/4 cup butter or margarine
1 egg
1 cup milk
1 1/2 cups blueberries

Female Facts

The Idea Was Good Enough
Although the idea of *Life*
magazine was conceived by
Clare Luce Booth, her husband,
Henry Luce, founder of *Time*, Incorporated would not
let her take part in the development and running of *Life*.

Directions:
Combine dry ingredients. Cut in butter with a pastry blender. Mix egg and milk together and add to dry ingredients. Add blueberries and rind. Batter will be thin. Pour into muffin pans and bake for 20 minutes in pre-heated 400°F oven.

Blueberry Hill Muffins

Frances Butt, Winterbrook, Newfoundland

Ingredients:
1/2 cup margarine
1 cup sugar
2 eggs
1 cup sour cream
1 tsp vanilla
2 cups flour
1 tsp baking powder
1 tsp baking soda
1/2 tsp salt
1 1/2 cups blueberries

Spice of Life

Love thy neighbour as yourself, but
choose your neighbourhood.
– Louise Beal

Directions:
Cream margarine and sugar, add eggs; mixing well. Mix sour cream and vanilla together; add to dry ingredients alternately with egg mixture. Stir in blueberries. Bake at 400°F for 25-30 minutes. Makes 24 muffins.
Note: You can substitute sour cream with 1 cup milk mixed with 1 tbsp lemon juice. If berries are frozen do not thaw.

Sweets and Treats

Maple Syrup Muffins

Shirley MacDonald, Fredericton, New Brunswick

Ingredients:
1/2 cup margarine
1/2 cup white sugar
1 tsp salt
1 1/4 cups flour
2 tsps baking powder
3/4 cup rolled oats
1/2 cup milk
1/2 cup maple syrup

Glaze Ingredients:
1 tsp butter
1/2 cup icing sugar
1 tbsp maple syrup

Female Facts

The Hand That Rocks The Big Cradle

A woman known as Mrs. Loring probably changed the course of American history. The years 1776 and 1777 were very successful for the British forces, which had severely damaged Washington's revolutionary forces at White Plains, Fort Washington, Brandywine and Germantown. The British could easily have defeated the Americans during the ferocious winter of 1777-78 at Valley Forge, but they never attacked. General Sir William Howe, commander-in-chief of the British forces, chose to stay in the warm comfort of nearby Philadelphia in the company of Mrs. Loring. By spring, the Colonial army was in a more favourable position and were able to survive and continue the fight.

Directions:

Soften margarine; blend in sugar and salt. Add dry ingredients, except oats. Blend with pastry cutter until crumbly. Mix in oats. Blend milk and syrup together; pour over dry mixture. Stir only to moisten. Bake at 350°F for 20 minutes. While still warm, combine glaze ingredients and spread over muffins.

Orange and Date Muffins

Marion Scheers, Edmonton, Alberta

Ingredients:
1 medium orange
1/2 cup orange juice
1/2 cup dates, chopped
1 egg
1/2 cup margarine, room temperature
1 cup flour
1/2 cup whole wheat flour
1 tsp baking powder
1 tsp baking soda
1/4 tsp salt
1/2 cup sugar
1/4 cup wheat germ

Food for Thought

No one can make you feel inferior without your consent.
– *Eleanor Roosevelt*

Directions:

Cut orange into eight sections removing seeds; put in blender. Add orange juice and dates and blend thoroughly. Add egg and margarine and blend again. Mix both types of flour, baking powder, baking soda, salt, sugar and wheat germ in a bowl. Mix in the blender. Bake at 350°F for 20 minutes. Makes 1 1/2 dozen.

Sweets and Treats

Bean Muffins

Maria Hiscock,
Grand Bank, Newfoundland

Ingredients:
1 cup boiling water
1 cup raisins
3 eggs
1 cup cooking oil
2 cups white sugar (or less)
1 tsp vanilla
1 (14 oz) can beans in tomato sauce
3 cups flour
1/2 tsp salt (or less)
1 tsp baking soda
1 tsp cinnamon
1 tsp baking powder
1 cup nuts (optional)

Directions:
Stir boiling water and raisins together and set aside. Beat eggs, oil, sugar, vanilla, and well-mashed beans together. Add other ingredients, including the raisins and water. Mix well; fill greased or paper-lined muffin pans. Bake at 325°F for 30 minutes.

Female Facts

Indecent Exposure
Although Australian swimming star Annette Kellerman's bathing suit consisted of a full, short-sleeved top and trousers that extended almost to her knees, she was still arrested for indecent exposure when she wore it at a Boston beach in 1909.

Grandma's Tea Buns

Beulah Cooper, Gander, Newfoundland

Ingredients:
3 cups flour
4 tsps baking powder
1/2 cup sugar
Pinch of salt
1/2 lb butter
1 egg, beaten
1/2 cup milk
1 cup raisins

Spice of Life

If you haven't got anything nice to say about anybody, come sit next to me.
– *Alice Roosevelt Longworth*

Directions:
Combine flour, baking powder, sugar, salt and butter. Mix together egg, milk and raisins; add to flour mixture in small amounts, stirring with a fork. Roll out on a floured board and cut out buns. Bake at 400°F for 15-20 minutes on a greased baking sheet. Rub a little butter on top of buns before removing from sheet.

Raisin Buns

Wendy Warren, North West Brook, Newfoundland

Ingredients:
2 1/2 cups flour
5 tsps baking powder
1/2 cup sugar
1/2 cup margarine
1 cup raisins
3/4 cup cold milk

Food for Thought
You will stay forever young and vibrant by growing old gracefully.

Directions:
Sift dry ingredients in a bowl. Cut in margarine; add raisins. Add enough liquid to make a soft dough. Roll into bun shapes; place in pans and bake at 425°F for 15-20 minutes.

Etta's Buns

Etta Wareham, Fort Amherst, Newfoundland (nee Vallis, Ramea, Newfoundland)

Ingredients:
1 pkg yeast
1 egg
1 cup milk
3 1/2 cups flour
1 tsp salt
1/3 cup sugar
1/3 cup margarine

Spice of Life
We're all in this alone. – *Lily Tomlin*

Directions:
Soak yeast in warm water. Mix egg in milk and let warm to room temperature. Mix flour, salt and sugar together and mix in with the margarine. Add liquids and knead as you would for bread. Let rise. Roll out and cut into triangles. Let rise again (about 20 minutes). Bake at 350°F for 15-20 minutes.

Hot Cross Buns

Debbie Marnell, St. John's, Newfoundland

Ingredients:
2 1/2 cups flour
1/2 tsp salt
4 tsps baking powder
3/4 tsp cinnamon
2 tbsps brown sugar
1/4 tsp nutmeg
2 tbsps peel, finely chopped
1/2 cup currants
1 egg, beaten

Female Facts
Imposing Poets
The famous 19th century English poet and novelist George Eliot was actually a woman named Mary Ann Evans, while 20th century Canadian poet and soldier (who was killed during WWI) Joyce Kilmer was actually a man named Alfred Joyce Kilmer.

Sweets and Treats

2 tbsps shortening, melted
1/2-1/3 cup milk

Directions:

Sift together dry ingredients; add sugar and fruit. Make well in centre; add egg, shortening and part of the milk. Work all together, adding more milk as required to make a nice dough. Turn out on a floured board; divide into small pieces with floured hands. Shape into small buns and place close together in a greased shallow pan. With a sharp knife make deep cross cuts in top; let stand for 10 minutes. Brush with butter and sprinkle with sugar. Bake at 400°F for 25-30 minutes.

Miller Rolls

Joyce Miller, Mount Pearl, Newfoundland (formerly of Horwood, Newfoundland)

Ingredients:
1/2 cup lukewarm water
1 tsp sugar
1 pkg quick-rising yeast
4 tsps sugar
1 tsp salt
1 cup milk
4 cups flour
4 tbsps butter, melted

Spice of Life

I married beneath me. All women do.
– *Nancy, Lady Astor*

Directions:

Place water, 1 tsp sugar and yeast in a small bowl; stir and let stand for 10 minutes. Stir again and add 4 tsps sugar, salt and milk; beat lightly. Add flour and butter; beat lightly. Knead to a soft pliant dough, using more flour if needed. Put in a greased bowl and cover. Set in a warm place and let rise to double in size. Knead again and rise a second time. Roll and cut into small buns. Let rise 20 minutes and bake at 350-375°F for 20 minutes. While still warm, brush with melted butter.

Cinnamon Rolls

Daphne Rideout, Springdale, Newfoundland

Ingredients:
2 cups flour
4 tsps baking powder
1/2 tsp salt
4 tbsps shortening
3/4 cup milk
4 tbsps sugar
1/2 tsp cinnamon

Female Facts

Giving Birth a Killer
Each year, 515,000 women (one every minute) die from pregnancy-related causes. The vast majority of these deaths occur in developing countries. An African woman's lifetime risk of dying from pregnancy-related causes is one in 16; in Asia, it's one in 65. In Europe, it's one in 1,400.

Directions:

Sift flour, baking powder and salt together. Rub shortening in with fingertips. Slowly add milk and mix to a soft dough. Roll out on a slightly floured board to 1/2-inch thickness. Spread with cinnamon and sugar mixture. Roll like a jelly roll. Cut slices 3/4-inch thick. Bake in an oven at 450°F for 10-15 minutes. Makes 12 rolls.

Sweets and Treats

Health Food Scones

Marion Scheers, Edmonton, Alberta

Ingredients:
1 3/4 cups whole wheat flour
4 tsps baking powder
1 tsp baking soda
1/2 tsp salt
1/3 cup brown sugar
1 1/2 cups rolled oats
2/3 cup margarine
2/3 cup raisins
1 cup buttermilk or sour milk
2 eggs

Directions:
Mix flour, baking powder, baking soda, salt, brown sugar and oats into a bowl. Cut in margarine. Add remaining ingredients. Drop by spoonfuls and bake at 350°F for 10 minutes. Do not overbake.

Female Facts

Helping the Cause
Apart from being the first woman to direct an officially sanctioned archeological excavation, Hetty Goldman, worked for the Red Cross in New York City during WWI. After the war, she went back to Greece to give help to the Jewish communities there. She was later active in bringing refugees escaping Nazism into the United States.

Baking Powder Biscuits

Daphne Rideout, Springdale, Newfoundland

Ingredients:
2 cups flour
4 tsps baking powder
1/2 tsp salt
4 tbsps shortening
3/4 cup milk

Food for Thought
She has a contagious smile; if you are not very careful, you might catch it.

Directions:
Sift flour, baking powder and salt together. Rub shortening in with fingertips. Add milk slowly and mix to a soft dough. Roll out on a slightly floured board to 1/2 inch thickness. Cut with a biscuit cutter. Bake in an oven at 450°F for 10-15 minutes. Makes 12 biscuits.

Nanny's Doughnuts

Deborah Lonergan-Freake, Timmins, Ontario

Ingredients:
3 tbsps butter or margarine
1 cup white sugar
1 tsp vanilla flavouring
2 eggs
3 cups flour
1/2 tsp salt
4 tsps baking powder
1/4 tsp nutmeg
2/3 cup milk

Spice of Life

When I go to the beauty parlour, I always use the emergency entrance. Sometimes I just go for an estimate.
– *Phyllis Diller*

Directions:
Cream together butter, sugar and vanilla; beat in eggs. Measure flour, salt, baking powder and nutmeg in another bowl. Add dry ingredients to butter mixture and gradually add milk. Mix thoroughly into a soft dough. Pat dough to 1/3-inch thickness on cutting board. Cut out doughnuts and deep fry in melted shortening or vegetable oil at 380°F for approximately 2 minutes per side, or until golden brown.

Salt Pork Toutons

Frances Butt, Winterbrook, Newfoundland

Ingredients:
1 cup salt pork, finely chopped (to make scrunchions)
4 cups flour, sifted
8 tsps baking powder
1/2 tsp salt
1/4 cup margarine
1/2 cup molasses
1 1/2 cups water

> *Food for Thought*
> Life becomes beautiful and ceases to be stale when we dare to come up with a new recipe.

Directions:
Fry out salt pork and drain well. Sift dry ingredients into a bowl. Cut in margarine. Add scrunchions and mix well with a fork until pork is well scattered. Combine molasses and water; add to the flour mixture and stir lightly. Roll out on a floured board to 1/2-inch thickness. Cut into desired shapes. Place on lightly floured baking sheet. Bake at 400°F for 15 minutes.

Old-Fashioned Christmas Sweet Bread

C. Milley Johnson, Port Union, Newfoundland (formerly of Little Catalina, Newfoundland)

Ingredients:
2 pkgs dry yeast
4 cups lukewarm water
2 tsps granulated sugar
1 cup molasses
3 tbsps butter, melted
12 cups flour
6 tbsps granulated sugar
4 tsps salt
3 cups raisins
2-3 tsps caraway seed (optional)

Female Facts

In Your Dreams
Queen Rnavalona of Madagascar made it illegal to dream about her. It is not known if anyone ever confessed to this crime.

Directions:
Dissolve yeast in 1 cup of lukewarm water and 2 tsps sugar. Combine 3 cups lukewarm water, molasses and butter. Sift remaining dry ingredients; add raisins and caraway seed. Stir dissolved yeast into molasses mixture. Stir in flour mixture. Knead for about 10 minutes. Place in a greased bowl and turn dough over 2 or 3 times to grease the top to prevent a crust from forming. Cover; let rise until doubled (about 2 hours). Divide dough into 4 or 5 pieces and form into loaves. Place in greased pans and let rise until doubled in bulk (about 1 hour). Bake at 375°F until loaves give

Sweets and Treats

a hollow sound when tapped (about 1 hour). Brush tops with melted butter while hot, if a soft crust is desired.

Christmas Bread

Doreen Wells, St. John's, Newfoundland (formerly of Seal Cove, Fortune Bay, Newfoundland)

Ingredients:
2/3 cup lukewarm water
2 tsps sugar
2 pkgs yeast
2/3 cup scalded milk
1 1/2 cups white sugar
2 1/4 tsps salt
6 tbsps shortening
3 eggs, well beaten
6 cups sifted flour
1 1/2 cups cherries
1 1/2 cups raisins

> # Spice of Life
> Learn to laugh at life and at yourself. Most of what you worry about will still be here long after you are gone.

Directions:
In bowl, add water and 2 tsps sugar; stir until dissolved. Sprinkle in yeast; let stand for 10 minutes, then stir well. Scald milk; remove from heat and stir in 1 1/2 cups sugar, salt and shortening. Cool to lukewarm, then add yeast mixture. Stir in eggs and 3 cups of flour; beat until smooth. Stir in fruit and work in 3 more cups of flour. Knead dough until smooth and elastic. Place in a greased bowl; cover and let rise in a warm place until doubled. Knead dough and divide into equal portions. Place in pans and let rise until doubled. Bake at 375-400°F for 3/4 hour.

Christmas Plum Pudding

Patti Stanley, Sharon, Ontario (nee O'Neal, St. John's, Newfoundland)

Ingredients:
4 cups flour
1 tbsp cinnamon
1/2 tsp salt
2 cups stale bread crumbs
2/3 cup brown sugar
1 lb suet, finely chopped
4 cups currants, cleaned and dried
2 cups seeded raisins
1 cup mixed peel, finely chopped
1/2 cup blanched almonds
1/2 cup maraschino cherries, halved
5 eggs
2 cups orange juice

> # Female Facts
> **He Just Gave It Its Name**
> Although the Fallopian tube was named for Gabriel Fallopius, a 16-century Italian anatomist, it took another three centuries to learn what its function was.

Sweets and Treats

Sweets and Treats

Directions:
Sift flour, cinnamon and salt together. Add bread crumbs, sugar and suet. Add currants, raisins, mixed peel, almonds and cherries. Beat eggs; mix with fruit juice. Add to first mixture and mix thoroughly. Place greased cloth in a glass bowl and fill with mix; do not press down. Pull four corners together and tie with a string. Place bowl in a pot of water, cover with greased brown paper which extends over side of bowl, place on lid and steam for 2 hours. Steam again approximately 2 hours before serving. Serve with thick sauce or plain custard. To keep, hang up in cool, dry and dark place. Best if over a year old.

Christmas Bangbelly

Jennifer Earle,
Mount Pearl, Newfoundland

Ingredients:
3 cups rice, cooked
1 1/4 cups salt pork, cubed
1 cup molasses
1 cup flour
1 tsp baking powder
1 1/2 tsps baking soda
1 tsp cinnamon
1/2 tsp allspice
1/4 tsp cloves
1/4 tsp mixed spice
2 cups raisins

> # Female Facts
>
> **Kennedy Matriarch Given Award**
> Rose Fitzgerald Kennedy gave her life to her children. As a mother she nurtured, stimulated and challenged nine children, among them the 35th President of the U.S., John F. Kennedy, and two U.S. Senators, Robert F. Kennedy and Edward M. Kennedy. She was equally caring to the rest of her children and worked to keep her family's unity and faith in God strong. The Tribute to Motherhood Award was presented to Mrs. Kennedy through her son, Senator Edward Kennedy in April, 1990, at her 100th birthday party. She died in 1995 at the age of 105.

Directions:
Cook rice and allow to cool; add salt pork and molasses. Sift together flour, baking soda, baking powder and spices. Add raisins, mixing all ingredients together. Pour into a 9" x 9" greased pan. Bake at 350°F for 1 1/4 hours.

Newfoundland Tea Buns

Diane Whyte, Dartmouth, Nova Scotia

Ingredients:
1 egg
1/2 cup milk
1 cup raisins
1/2 cup sugar
3 cups flour
1/2 tsp salt
5 level tsps baking powder
1 cup margarine

> # Food for Thought
> In the days of antiquity, brides carried bushels of wheat, not bouquets of colourful flowers.

Directions:
Stir egg, milk and raisins with a fork in a bowl and set aside. Rub together the sugar, flour, salt, baking powder and margarine and add the raisin mixture from the bowl. Pat or roll out lightly on a floured board or waxed paper, about 1 to 1 1/2 inches thick. Cut out with a small floured glass. Bake at 400°F for 15-20 minutes on a greased cookie sheet.

Zucchini-Carrot Bread

Elizabeth Cleary,
St. John's, Newfoundland

Ingredients:
3 eggs
1 cup vegetable oil
1 1/2 cups packed brown sugar
1 cup grated and drained zucchini
1 cup grated carrot
2 tsps vanilla
2 1/2 cups flour
1 tsp baking soda
1 tsp baking powder
1 tsp salt
3 tsps cinnamon
1/2 cup bran cereal
1 cup chopped nuts

Female Facts

He Got The Last Word
Here's an unconfirmed story of a woman who really got mad at her significant other. Monsieur Regnier, her husband, was the equivalent of todays Crown (or District) Attorney. She was trying to make a point to him at home one day when he rebuked her by saying, "Be silent woman, you talk nonsense." With that she stormed out of the room and refused to speak to him, even after he went to her room (after several days) and apologized profusely. Not only that, she wouldn't speak to anyone else either, not for the rest of her life. When her daughter asked for permission to marry, she was said to merely nod in assent.

Directions:
In a large mixing bowl, beat eggs with oil. Stir in sugar, zucchini, carrot and vanilla. Sift in flour, baking soda, baking powder, salt and cinnamon and add bran cereal. Fold in nuts. Bake in two, well-greased 8 1/2" x 4 1/2" loaf pans at 350°F, for 1 to 1 1/2 hours.

Mocha Layer Cake

Doreen Halfrey, Framingham, Massachusetts (nee Young, Black Duck Brook, Newfoundland)

Ingredients:
1 Sarah Lee reduced-fat pound cake
1 (8oz) container of fat-free frozen Cool Whip
1/4 cup water
1 tbsp instant coffee
2 squares semi-sweet baking chocolate

Spice of Life
I don't care what is written about me so long as it isn't true.
– Dorothy Parker

Directions:
Thaw pound cake and Cool Whip the day before in the refrigerator. In a small saucepan, heat water and coffee. Add chocolate, stirring until melted and well blended. Cool to room temperature. In the meantime, slice thawed pound cake into 4 slices lengthwise. Carefully mix Cool Whip into chocolate mixture with spatula until well blended. Spread between layers of pound cake and over the outside.

Nana's Apple Cake

Betty and Joanne Bulgin, Sag Harbor, New York

Ingredients:
1 cup sugar
1 egg
1/4 lb butter, melted

Food for Thought
Wise sayings often fall on barren ground, but gentle words will never be thrown away.

Sweets and Treats

Sweets and Treats

1 1/2 cups flour, sifted
1/2 cup raisins
1 tsp baking soda
1/4 tsp salt
1/4 tsp cinnamon
1/4 tsp allspice
1/4 tsp nutmeg
1/2 cup walnuts
5 medium apples

Directions:

Preheat oven to 350°F. Grease and flour 8" x 8" pan. Beat sugar, eggs and butter until creamy. Mix dry ingredients together and mix with sugar mixture. Pare and core apples; cut in small pieces. Coat apples in batter. Spread in pan and bake until toothpick inserted in centre comes out clean.

Annabelle's Crumb Cake

Joanne and Betty Bulgin, Sag Harbor, New York

Ingredients:
2 cups flour
2 tsps baking powder
Pinch of salt
1 1/2 cups sugar
3/4 cup butter
1 tsp lemon extract
3/4 cup milk
2 eggs, separated
1/2 cup walnuts, chopped

Directions:

Sift together flour, baking powder and salt. In another bowl add sugar, butter and lemon extract; mixing together to consistency of crumbs. Set 3/4 cup of crumbs aside. Beat together milk and egg yolks; add to flour mixture. Fold in 2 well beaten egg whites. Pour half of mixture in a well-greased pan, sprinkle on 1/4 cup of crumbs. Pour rest of batter in pan and sprinkle with crumbs and walnuts on top. Bake at 325°F for 30-40 minutes, or until done.

Mystery Zucchini Cake

Frances Pelley, Edmonton, Alberta (formerly of Deer Lake, Newfoundland)

Ingredients:
3 eggs
1 1/3 cups sugar
1/3 cup oil
1/2 cup margarine
1 tsp vanilla

1 tsp cinnamon
1/2 tsp salt
1 tsp baking soda
3/4 tsp baking powder
1 (8 oz) pkg cream cheese
2 cups zucchini, grated (squeeze out juice)
3 cups flour
1/2 cup nuts (optional)

Directions:

Beat eggs, sugar, oil, margarine, vanilla, cinnamon, salt, baking soda, baking powder and cream cheese until foamy. Add zucchini, mixing well. Add flour and beat for 2 minutes. Fold in nuts. Pour in a large cake pan and bake at 350°F for 55-60 minutes.

Sauerkraut Chocolate Cake

Patti Stanley, Sharon, Ontario (nee O'Neal, St. John's, Newfoundland)

Ingredients:

2/3 cup sauerkraut
2/3 cup butter
2 1/4 cups sifted all-purpose flour
1/2 cup unsweetened cocoa
1/4 tsp salt
1 tsp baking powder
1 tsp baking soda
1 1/2 cups sugar
3 large eggs
1 tsp vanilla
1 cup water or strong coffee

Directions:

Rinse and drain sauerkraut; chop coarsely. Bring butter to room temperature. Using a fork, combine flour, cocoa, salt, baking powder, and baking soda in large bowl. Cream butter at medium speed with an electric mixer. Gradually add sugar; add eggs one at a time, then vanilla. Alternately, add flour mixture and water or coffee, beginning and ending with flour. Stir in sauerkraut and pour into two greased and floured 8-inch round or square pans. Bake at 350°F for 25-30 minutes. Fill and frost with a chocolate fudge frosting, or mocha whipped cream.

Rhubarb Cake

Joyce Marshall, Whitby, Ontario

Ingredients:

2 cups flour
1 1/2 cups white sugar

Food for Thought

Those who do not complain are never pitied. – *Jane Austen*

Female Facts

It's the Name That Counts

Saudi Arabia has many princes and princesses today, including at least 10,000 descendants of King Abdul Aziz Ibn Saud, who ruled the land from 1932 until his death in 1953. This might seem a very large number of offshoots for one man, except for the fact that the king had 300 wives, whose descendants are given royal titles.

Spice of Life

I'll try anything once.
– *Alice Roosevelt Longworth, on giving birth at age 41.*

Sweets and Treats

1/2 cup shortening or margarine
2 cups rhubarb, chopped
1 tsp baking soda
1 tsp vanilla
1 tsp cinnamon
1 cup sour milk (use vinegar to sour milk)
1 egg

Topping Ingredients:
1/4 cup white sugar
1 tsp cinnamon

Directions:
Mix all ingredients together, adding rhubarb last. Pour into buttered 9" x 13" pan. Combine cinnamon and sugar; sprinkle over cake mixture. Bake at 350°F for 30-40 minutes.

Allister's Famous Cherry Cake
Allister James L. Freake, Timmins, Ontario

Ingredients:
1 cup butter
2 cups white sugar
1/2 cup boiling water
1/2 cup milk
3 cups flour
3 eggs
1 tsp baking powder
1/2 tsp salt
1 tsp lemon flavouring
1 tsp almond flavouring
1 1/2 cups cherries

Directions:
Cream together butter and sugar. Mix boiling water and milk. Add to sugar and butter; gradually add 1 cup of flour and 1 unbeaten egg. Beat mixture until creamy. Gradually add second cup of flour and second egg. Mix baking powder and salt with 1/3 cup of flour. Add to mixture with last egg and lemon and almond flavouring. Beat mixture until creamy. Fold in flour-dredged cherries. Bake at 325°F for one hour, then cover loosely with foil and continue baking for another 1/2 hour. Check to ensure centre is fully baked.

Bishop's Cake
William Fowlow, St. John's, Newfoundland

Ingredients:
2 cups raisins
1 cup currants
1/2 lb dates
2 cups water

> ## *Food for Thought*
> Fashion wears out clothes faster than we do.

> # Spice of Life
> Good taste is the worst vice ever invented.
> *– Edith Sitwell*

> # Female Facts
> **Director of Operations for NASA**
> Apart from her flying time on helicopters, often from ships, and her being the veteran of three space flights, logging more than 894 hours in space, and many other achievements, Wendy B. Lawrence also served as Director of Operations for NASA at the Gagarin Cosmonaut Training Center in Star City, Russia. There her responsibility was for the coordination and implementation of mission operations activities in the Moscow region for the joint U.S./Russian Shuttle/Mir program.

> # Female Facts
> **Anorexia and Bulimia**
> In Canada, 200,000-300,000 females between the ages of 13 and 40 have anorexia, two times this amount have bulimia.

Juice of 1 orange
1 1/2 tsps cinnamon
1 tsp nutmeg
1/2 tsp allspice
1/2 cup butter
1/4 cup oil
2 tsps vanilla
2 tsps baking soda
1 cup cherries
1 cup mixed fruit
2 cups whole wheat flour

Directions:

Combine raisins, currants, dates, water, orange juice, cinnamon, nutmeg and allspice in a large saucepan; boil for 10 minutes. Let cool. Add remaining ingredients. Bake in tube pan at 325°F for 1 1/4 hours.

Sponge Cake

Norma Clarke, Peterborough, Ontario (nee, Atkinson, Herring Neck, Newfoundland)

Ingredients:
3/4 cup sugar
3 eggs
1 cup flour
2 tsps baking powder
1/4 tsp salt
1 tsp vanilla
1/4 cup water

Directions:

Beat eggs and sugar together until stiff. Sift flour and baking powder three times. Combine salt, vanilla, and 1/4 cup water; mix a little. Combine all ingredients and put mixture in pan; place in oven at 400°F for 10-15 minutes. Custard frosting is good for sponge cake.

Mincemeat Cake

Marion Scheers, Edmonton, Alberta

Ingredients:
1/4 cup butter
3/4 cup sugar
2 eggs, slightly beaten
1 tsp vanilla
1 cup mincemeat
3/4 cup flour
1/2 tsp baking powder
1/2 tsp salt
1/2 cup nuts
Chocolate chips

Spice of Life

I arrived in Hollywood without having my nose fixed, my teeth capped, or my name changed. That is very gratifying to me.
— *Barbra Streisand*

Food for Thought

A passionate interest in what you do is the secret of enjoying life. — *Julia Child*

Female Facts

The Medieval Best Man
A medieval tradition known throughout Europe as *jus primae noctis*, gave the right to the lord of any manor to be the first to sleep with any bride within his domain, on her wedding night.

Sweets and Treats

Directions:

Cream butter, sugar, eggs, vanilla and mincemeat until fluffy. Add flour, baking powder, salt and nuts. Pour into a 9" x 9" greased pan; bake at 350°F for 35 minutes. Sprinkle chocolate chips on top and put back in oven until chips are melted. Spread with a spoon.

Applesauce Cake

Marion Scheers, Edmonton, Alberta

Ingredients:

1/2 cup margarine
1 cup sugar
1 egg
1 tsp baking soda
1/2 tsp salt
1/4 tsp cloves
1/4 tsp nutmeg
1 tsp cinnamon
1 cup applesauce
2 cups flour
2/3 cup raisins

Spice of Life

The important thing in acting is to be able to laugh and cry. If I have to cry, I think of my sex life. If I have to laugh, I think of my sex life.
– *Glenda Jackson*

Directions:

Cream margarine and sugar together. Add egg, beat well. Add baking soda, salt, cloves, nutmeg and cinnamon. Add applesauce and flour alternately. Add raisins last. Bake at 350°F for 45 minutes.

Drumstick Cake

Daphne Edison, Dryden, Ontario (nee Norman, Roddickton, Newfoundland)

Base Ingredients:

2 cups crushed vanilla wafers
1/2 cup chopped nuts
1/4 cup butter, melted
3 tbsps peanut butter

Filling Ingredients:

1 (8 oz) pkg cream cheese
1/2 cup sugar
1/2 cup peanut butter
2 tsps vanilla
4 eggs
1 large Cool Whip (thawed)
1/2 cup hot fudge sundae sauce

Food for Thought

I feel we are all islands in a common sea.
– *Anne Morrow Lindberg*

Directions:

Mix all base ingredients together. Use approximately 1 cup of the mixture for the base. Press in bottom of a 9" x 13" baking dish. Keep remainder for topping. With electric mixer, cream the sugar, cream cheese and peanut butter in a large bowl, then add vanilla and blend in eggs, one at a time, at high speed. Fold in Cool Whip with a spatula, then spread over the base. Drizzle hot fudge sauce over top. Put knife through diagonally. Sprinkle remaining crumbs on top. Freeze cake. Remove from freezer 1/2 hour before serving. May be refrozen. Serve covered in 1/2 cup hot fudge sundae sauce.

One-Minute Cake

Alice Bye, Oliver, British Columbia

Ingredients:
1/2 cup brown sugar
2 tbsps cocoa
1/2 cup margarine
1 egg
Vanilla
1 2/3 cups graham wafer crumbs
1/2 cup chopped nuts

Female Facts

Liked Her Cross Eyes
The cross-eyed wife of General Ulysses S. Grant wanted to have the problem corrected, but Grant refused to let her because he liked her that way.

Directions:
Mix brown sugar and cocoa together. Cream margarine, then add to sugar mixture and stir well. Add beaten egg, then cook for 1 minute. Add vanilla, then the crumbs and nuts. Mix well and put in an 8" x 8" pan. Ice when cool.

Baked Pot Cake

Jackey Locke, Topsail, Newfoundland

Ingredients:
1 1/2 cups butter
1 1/2 cups sugar
3 eggs
2 tsps vanilla
3 1/2 cups flour
3 tsps baking powder
1 tsp salt
1 (15 oz) can evaporated milk
1 1/2 cups coconut
3 cups raisins, floured
1 1/2 cups candied cherries

Female Facts

Like a Greek Goddess
To copy the smoothness and beauty of statues of ancient Greece, beauty-conscious women of the time would sometimes pluck all their facial hair, including their eyebrows.

Directions:
Cream butter and sugar together; add eggs and vanilla flavouring, beating well. Sift dry ingredients together; add to creamed mixture alternately with milk. Add coconut, floured raisins and cherries. Pour into a well-lined round pan (9" diameter x 3" deep). Bake at 300°F for 2 1/2 hours. Allow to cool for 30 minutes before removing from pan.

Sweets and Treats

Jelly Cake

Mel Hynes, St. John's, Newfoundland

Ingredients:
2 cups flour
2 tsps baking powder
1/4 tsp salt
1/2 cup butter
3/4 cup sugar
2 eggs, beaten
1 tsp vanilla
3/4 cup milk
Partridgeberry jam

Directions:
Sift flour, baking powder and salt together. Cream butter until soft and gradually blend in sugar, creaming until fluffy. Add eggs and beat vigorously until light and fluffy. Add vanilla; stirring thoroughly. Add flour mixture and milk alternately in 3 or 4 portions, beginning and ending with flour and beating until smooth. Pour into two round 8" greased layer pans lined with waxed paper. Bake at 350°F for 25-30 minutes. Cool; spread partridgeberry jam between layers.

Reliable Chocolate Cake

Pauline Seward, St. John's, Newfoundland

Ingredients:
2 cups unsifted all-purpose flour
3/4 tsp baking soda
1 tsp salt
1/2 cup vegetable shortening
1 1/3 cups sugar
2 eggs
3 squares unsweetened chocolate, melted
1 1/4 cups milk
1 tsp vanilla

Directions:
Combine flour, baking soda and salt together; stirring to mix well. Cream vegetable shortening; add sugar gradually and cream together until light and fluffy. Add eggs, one at a time, beating well after each. Add melted chocolate and blend. Add flour mixture alternately with milk, beating well after each addition. Add vanilla. Turn batter into two deep round 8" or 9" layer pans which have been lined with wax paper. Bake at 350°F for 30-40 minutes.

Spice of Life
Did you know that a woman puts make-up on her so a man will put the make upon her?

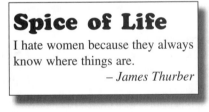

Spice of Life
I hate women because they always know where things are.
— *James Thurber*

Blueberry Spice Cake

Grant Young,
St. Philip's, Newfoundland

Ingredients:
1/2 cup butter
1 1/4 cups brown sugar
2 eggs, beaten
2/3 cup milk
3/4 cup fresh blueberries
2 1/2 cups flour
1 tsp baking powder
1 tsp salt
1 tsp cinnamon
1 tsp nutmeg
1/2 cup raisins

Female Facts

Light Up My Life
After Benjamin Franklin's *Poor Richard's Almanac* published instructions on making personal lightning rods in 1753, women of Europe starting wearing lightning rods in their hats with a wire trailing to the ground.

Directions:

Cream butter and sugar together; add eggs one at a time, beating after each addition. Add sifted flour, baking powder, salt, cinnamon and nutmeg to butter mixture alternately with milk. Fold in floured blueberries and raisins. Turn into a buttered and flour-coated 9" x 9" pan. Bake at 350°F for 50 minutes.

Barcardi Rum Cake

Ruby Marsh, Grand Falls-Windsor, Newfoundland (nee Rowsell, Leading Tickles, Newfoundland)

Cake Ingredients:
1 cup pecans or walnuts, chopped
1 yellow cake mix (520 g)
1 pkg (92 g) vanilla instant pudding
4 eggs
1/2 cup cold water
1/2 cup vegetable oil
1/2 cup Barcardi rum

Food for Thought

Mother to daughter in local department store: "If it has anybody's name on it, it's too expensive."

Glaze Ingredients:
1/2 cup butter
1/4 cup water
1 cup sugar
1/2 cup Barcardi rum

Directions:

Preheat oven to 325°F. Grease and flour a 10-inch tube pan or 12-cup fluted pan; sprinkle nuts over bottom of pan. Combine all cake ingredients; blend well. With electric mixer at medium speed, beat for 4 minutes. Pour batter over nuts, bake 1 hour. Cool; invert on serving plate. Prepare glaze by melting butter over medium heat. Stir in water and sugar and boil for 5 minutes, stirring constantly. Remove from heat and stir in rum. To glaze, prick top of cake with fork. Spoon and brush glaze evenly over top and sides, allowing cake to absorb glaze. Repeat until all

Sweets and Treats

glaze is used. Serves 12. Note: If using a cake mix that has pudding added, omit vanilla pudding and use only 3 eggs and 1/3 cup oil.

Blueberry Cheesecake

Bernadette Bishop, St. John's, Newfoundland

Ingredients:
2 cups graham wafer crumbs
1/2 cup butter, melted
7 oz sugar or icing sugar
16 oz cream cheese
1 tsp lemon juice
16 oz carton cream
2-3 cups blueberries

Female Facts

Love Me, Love My Cats
Because her relatives had been unkind to her pet cats before she died in 1917, an Austrian woman burned all her money rather than leave it to them.

Directions:
Combine graham wafer crumbs and butter in a bowl. Mix until moist. Spread crumb mixture into pan and press firmly. Bake graham wafer mixture at 350°F for 10 minutes; let cool. Combine sugar, cream cheese and lemon juice in a large bowl. Fold in cream and blueberries. Spread mixture over cooled graham wafer crumbs.

Lite Cheesecake

Charlotte Goodwin, Lynn Lake, Manitoba (nee Gallant, Stephenville Crossing, Newfoundland)

Ingredients:
1 3/4 cups graham wafer crumbs
1/2 cup margarine, melted
3 tbsps sugar
1 pkg Dream Whip
1 (250 g) pkg cream cheese
1 cup icing sugar
1 can pie filling (your choice)

Food for Thought
A perfect wife could also be a partner who doesn't expect a perfect husband.

Directions:
Mix graham wafer crumbs, margarine and sugar together. Spread into 8" x 12" pan; set aside. In a medium mixing bowl blend Dream Whip, cream cheese and icing sugar; whip until smooth. Pour over base. Use can of pie filling or make up filling using a little sugar and cornstarch to thicken slightly. Refrigerate.

Rich Wedding Cake

Mrs. Cyril Martin, St. Vincent's, St. Mary's Bay, Newfoundland

Ingredients:
6 cups Sultana raisins
6 cups seedless raisins
3 cups currants

Food for Thought
I finally figured out the only reason to be alive is to enjoy it.
                                              – *Rita Mae Brown*

1/2 lb cherries
3 cups mixed peel
8 oz dates
2 cups walnuts
3 tsps baking powder
1/2 tsp salt
4 tsps cinnamon
1 tsp nutmeg
2 tsps allspice
1/2 tsp cloves
3 1/2 cups flour
1 lb butter
2 cups sugar
12 eggs yolks
12 egg whites
1 tsp vanilla
1/2 cup grapefruit juice
1 tsp almond extract
1/2 cup molasses
1/2 cup strong coffee

Female Facts

Good Night, Sir Knight
Chivalry, which means "honourable behaviour, especially toward women," was the forte of the shining knight of medieval times, but was not necessarily as honourable as fairy tales tell us. A knight was only required to be chivalrous to women of his own class. Knowing the history of mankind, how he treated the peasant women of his era is not hard to imagine. Interestingly, we learned about the king of all knights, King Arthur, and his famous knights of the round table, from a poem. Yet, the poem which showed nothing but piety, valour, loyalty, courtesy and gentleness toward women, was written by a convict. When he wrote the famous story of the king in his, *Morte d'Arthur*, Sir Thomas Malory was serving time in jail. Apart from having been convicted of extortion and looting a monastery, he had also been convicted of two counts of rape. So much for good knights.

Directions:
Grease 3 wedding cake pans (4", 6" and 8" in diameter) lined with greased, heavy brown paper. Combine fruits and nuts; dust with a little flour and let stand overnight. Stir baking powder, salt, all spices and flour together. Cream butter; add sugar gradually, beating between additions. Add egg whites and yolks and other liquids, and blend in dry ingredients. Fold in floured fruits and nuts. Fill prepared pans 2/3 full. Bake at 275°F for 4-6 hours until done.

Chocolate Pecan Fruit Cake

Charlene Jenkins, Springdale, Newfoundland

Ingredients:
4 1/2 cups mixed candied pineapple and cherries
2 cups roasted pecans, coarsely chopped
3 ozs semi-sweet chocolate, finely chopped
4 ozs unsweetened chocolate, finely chopped
1 cup golden raisins
2 cups all-purpose flour
2 tsps baking powder
1/2 tsp salt
3/4 cup unsalted butter
1 cup granulated sugar
6 eggs
3/4 cup brandy
1 tsp vanilla

Female Facts

Lucky Owl
You may not give a hoot, but Florence Nightingale used to carry a pet owl in her pocket wherever she went, whether it was in England or the far-off Crimea, where she became famous.

Directions:

To roast pecans, spread nuts on baking sheet and roast at 350°F for 10 minutes or until lightly browned. Or microwave, uncovered, on high for 8-10 minutes or until lightly browned and fragrant, stirring every 2 minutes. In a large bowl, toss together pineapple, cherries, pecans, chocolate and raisins; toss with half of the flour. Stir together remaining flour, baking powder and salt; set aside. In a large bowl, beat butter and sugar until light and fluffy; add eggs one at a time, beating thoroughly. Beat in 1/4 cup brandy and vanilla. Gradually stir in dry ingredients until well blended. Stir in fruit mixture. Scrape into a greased 9" x 13" cake pan, tapping pan on counter to eliminate air pockets; smooth top. Bake at 300°F for 1 1/2 hours or until cake tester inserted into centre comes out clean. Let cool in pan on rack. Cut cake crosswise into 6 bars. Heat remaining brandy, but do not boil. With skewer, make several holes through cake; pour in brandy. Moisten pieces of cheesecloth with brandy; wrap around individual bars. Wrap in waxed paper, then foil; store in airtight container in cool, dry place for at least 1 week or up to 2 months, checking occasionally and adding more brandy if cake begins to dry.

Boiled Fruit Cake

Daphne Rideout, Springdale, Newfoundland

Ingredients:
2 cups water
1 pkg raisins
1 pkg dates
3/4 tsp salt
1 tsp cinnamon
1 tsp cloves
1/2 cup Mazola oil
2 tsps vanilla
2 cups whole wheat flour
1 tsp baking powder
2 tsps baking soda
1/2 cup chopped nuts

Directions:

Combine water, raisins, dates, salt, cinnamon, cloves and oil together in a medium sauce pan, and bring to a boil for 20 minutes. Let cool. Once cooled, add vanilla, flour, baking powder, baking soda and chopped nuts. Bake at 325°F for 1 hour. This cake is great for diabetics as it contains no added sugar.

White Fruit Cake

Beulah Cooper, Gander, Newfoundland

Ingredients:
1 cup butter
2 cups sugar
4 eggs, beaten
1 cup crushed pineapple

1 lb raisins
1 cup red cherries
1 cup green cherries
2 cups coconut
3 1/2 cups flour
3 tsps baking powder
1 cup milk
2 tsps vanilla

Directions:
Cream butter and sugar together. Add eggs and pineapple. Dredge fruit with flour and coconut; add to mixture. Add flour and baking powder alternately with milk. Add vanilla and bake in greased tube pan for 1 1/2 hours at 300°F.

Jelly Fruit Cake

Josephine Jenkins,
Springdale, Newfoundland

Ingredients:
2 cups boiling water
2 pkgs cherry jelly
1 1/2 cups brown sugar
1/2 lb butter
1 tsp allspice
1 tsp cloves
1 tsp cinnamon
1/2 tub cherries
1 pkg currants
1 pkg raisins
4 cups flour
3 tsps baking soda

Directions:
Put 2 cups of boiling water into a bowl. Add jelly, then butter and brown sugar. Stir together. Add remaining ingredients and mix together. Bake at 275°F for 2 1/2 hours.

Boiled Fruit Cake

Violet Shiner, South Brook, Newfoundland

Ingredients:
1 pkg cherries
1 pkg raisins
1 pkg dates
1 pkg peel or mixed fruit
1 tsp cloves
2 tsps cinnamon
1 tsp nutmeg
1 tsp allspice

Sweets and Treats

1/2 lb butter
3 eggs
3 1/2 cups flour
1 pkg chopped nuts
2 1/2 cups brown sugar
3 tsps baking powder
2 tsps baking soda
2 1/2 cups water

Directions:

Boil fruit and spices in water in a large saucepan for 1/2 hour. Allow to cool completely. Add butter and eggs. Mix in flour, nuts, brown sugar, baking powder and baking soda. Bake at 350°F for 2 hours.

Diet Dark Fruit Cake

Jessie Chaulk, St. John's, Newfoundland

Ingredients:
2 cups raisins
2 cups water
1/2 lb dates
1 cup unsweetened orange juice
1 tsp nutmeg
1 tsp cinnamon
1/2 cup Mazola oil
2 tsps vanilla
2 tsps baking soda
1 cup cherries
2 1/2 cups whole wheat flour

Directions:

In a medium saucepan combine raisins, water, dates, orange juice, nutmeg and cinnamon; boil for 15 minutes. Add remaining ingredients and bake at 350°F for 1 3/4 hours in a tube pan.

Mashed Potato Fruit Cake

Rex Pippy, Mount Pearl, Newfoundland (formerly of Small Point, Newfoundland)

Ingredients:
1 cup mashed potatoes
1 cup sugar
1/2 cup shortening
1/2 cup molasses
1 tsp cinnamon
2 tsps ginger
1/2 tsp cloves
1 pkg raisins
1 pkg currants
1/2 cup hot water

Food for Thought

There is no possible way to be a perfect mother, and a thousand ways to be a good one.

Female Facts

A Lot of Young Americans
The average woman in 17th-century America gave birth to 13 children.

Spice of Life

I have received much of my looks from my parents, and even more from over-the-counter makeup.

1 1/2 tsps baking soda
1/2 tsp salt
2 1/2 cups flour
1 egg (optional)

Spice of Life

No matter how old she is, every mother watches her middle-aged children for signs of improvement.

Directions:
Mash potatoes while hot. Add sugar and shortening; mix well. Add molasses, spices and floured fruit. Add hot water with salt and soda added. Stir in flour; beat well. Batter should be stiff. One egg may be added if desired. Bake for 3 hours in medium (300°F) oven. This cake keeps well.

Apple Dessert

Bertha Smith, Clarenville, Newfoundland

Ingredients:
1 1/2 cups graham wafer crumbs
1/2 cup melted margarine
1 can condensed milk
1 tub sour cream
1/2 cup lemon juice
1 can apple pie filling
Cinnamon (optional)
Chopped nuts (optional)

Food for Thought

Women wish to be loved without a why or wherefore; not because they are pretty or good or well-bred or graceful or intelligent, but because they are themselves.

Directions:
Combine graham wafer crumbs and margarine. Spread on bottom of a greased pie dish. Mix together condensed milk, sour cream and lemon juice. Pour into graham shell. Carefully spread pie filling on top. Sprinkle with cinnamon and nuts, if desired. Bake at 300°F for 20 minutes. Cool at least 3 hours or overnight.

Fool-Proof Apple Pie

Linda Nicholas, Fort McMurray, Alberta (originally from Brown's Arm, Newfoundland)

Crust Ingredients:
2 cups flour
2 tbsps sugar
1/2 cup margarine
1/4 cup shortening
1/4 tsp baking powder
5 tbsps cold water

Filling Ingredients:
8 apples, peeled and sliced
1/2 cup sugar
2 tbsps cornstarch
1/4 tsp cinnamon

Female Facts

Maternal Hoops
For those who can remember the hoop skirts, they were invented to conceal the pregnancy of the French Empress Eugenie.

Sweets and Treats

Directions:
Crumb together first 5 crust ingredients with pastry blender or fork. Then add water, enough to form a ball without crumbling. Roll out half of the dough for the bottom crust and half for the top. Stir together the filling ingredients and pour into uncooked pie crust (be sure to puncture holes in top crust). Bake at 350°F for approximately 1 hour or until golden brown.

Raspberry Tarts

Maisie Moyles, Carmanville South, Newfoundland

Ingredients:
2/3 cup butter
1/2 cup brown sugar
1 egg
1 tsp vanilla
1 1/2 cups flour
Raspberry jam

Filling Ingredients:
1/3 cup butter
1/4 cup brown sugar
1 egg
2 tsps lemon juice
1/2 cup flour
1/2 tsp baking powder

Female Facts

The Mother Tongue
The country of England would not be English-speaking today if it weren't for the women who lived there the last time it was conquered by a non-English-speaking country. The invading country was Normandy, now a province of France; the invading King became known as William, The Conqueror. The year was 1066, and the deciding battle is what is now known as the Battle of Hastings. The French-speaking invaders married English women, who, back then as now, were mothers above all. The English-speaking mothers had the biggest influence on their children, and they taught them to speak English. If it weren't for that, what would North Americans be speaking today?

Directions:
Cream butter and brown sugar in a bowl. Beat in egg and vanilla. Blend in flour. Divide evenly and press into 12 ungreased tart pans, or muffin cups. Place 1 tsp raspberry jam in each tart shell. For filling, cream butter and brown sugar. Beat in egg and lemon juice. Stir in flour and baking powder. Spoon mixture into tart shells covering jam. Bake in 350°F oven for about 20 minutes, or until golden brown.

My Peach Pie

Maisie Moyles, Carmanville South, Newfoundland

Ingredients:
1 graham wafer pie crust
2 cans thick cream
1 pkg vanilla mousse
1 can sliced peaches
1/2 cup milk

Spice of Life

In the spring a young man's fancy, but a young woman's fancier.

Directions:
In the bottom of the pie crust, put 1 can of cream and most of the peaches, saving a few for the top. Blend the vanilla mousse with the milk, spread over the peaches. Spread the other can of cream over the mousse and place remaining peaches on top. I usually make this in the night and serve it the next day. Wonderful!!

Sweets and Treats

Bakeapple Custard Meringue Pie

Betty Lou (formerly of Appleton, Ontario) and Syd George (formerly of Howley, Newfoundland),
Gloucester, Ontario

Ingredients:
1 10-inch deep pie shell, baked
4 egg yolks
1/3 cup sugar
3 tbsps cornstarch
1 1/2 cups 2% milk
1 tsp butter
3/4 tsp vanilla extract
1 tsp orange peel, grated
19 ozs frozen or fresh bakeapples

Meringue Ingredients:
4 egg whites
1/4 tsp cream of tartar (optional)
1/4 cup cold water
1/4 cup sugar

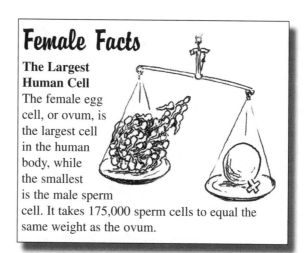

Female Facts

The Largest Human Cell
The female egg cell, or ovum, is the largest cell in the human body, while the smallest is the male sperm cell. It takes 175,000 sperm cells to equal the same weight as the ovum.

Directions:
Preheat oven to 325°F. To make custard, whisk together egg yolks, sugar and cornstarch in the top of a double boiler. Add milk and continue to whisk until custard becomes very thick. Whisk in butter. Remove from heat and add vanilla and peel, blending well. Let cool slightly and spread evenly over the bottom of the pie shell. Let stand until set, about 10 minutes. In a small saucepan, heat bakeapples; bring to a boil. Reduce heat and simmer, stirring for 5 minutes. Remove from heat. Carefully spoon bakeapples over custard layer, covering completely. To make a meringue, beat egg whites with (or without) cream of tartar until foamy. Add water and continue beating at low speed. Add sugar, 1 tbsp at a time, beating for about 2 minutes after each addition. Continue beating until the meringue is glossy and forms stiff peaks. Pile meringue on the pie, gently spreading to cover the pie. Bake for 15-18 minutes or until golden brown.

Apple Pie

Emma Martin, Catalina, Newfoundland

Ingredients:
1 (9-inch) pie shell
1 1/2 lbs apples
1/4 cup butter or margarine
2 tbsps lemon juice
2 tbsps sugar
1 (8 oz) pkg cream cheese
1 1/2 cups milk
1 (3 1/2 oz) pkg vanilla pudding
1 pkg Jell-O

Food for Thought
You can choose your friends, but you only have one mother. – *Max Shulman*

Sweets and Treats

Directions:

Prick edges and bottom of pie shell; bake for 10 minutes until lightly browned; let cool. Core and cut apples into 1/4-inch slices. Melt butter in a large skillet over medium heat; add apples and lemon juice. Saute for 2 minutes until apples are tender; add sugar. Cook for 1 minute. Remove from heat; let cool. In a bowl, mix cream cheese at high speed until smooth; add 1 cup milk and pudding, blending together. Add remaining milk; beat for an additional minute. Spoon into pie shell; arrange apples overlapping each other. Brush with melted jelly or dissolve jelly with 1 cup boiling water and 1/2 cup cool water. When it begins to jell pour over apples. Refrigerate 1-2 hours. Makes 8 servings.

Female Facts

Female Pope?

That Pope John VIII was really a woman named Agnes dressed like a man has never been proven, or disproven. She "was accepted without question in Catholic circles for centuries," writes historian J.N.D. Kelly in his Oxford Dictionary of Popes. Sources say that Agnes's face was one of the papal busts in the cathedral at Siena in Tuscany for about 200 years. It had been carved around 1400. The story was first recorded in history by Martin of Troppau, a Polish Dominican Friar. According to him, Agnes was born in Germany of English missionary parents. She was very intelligent and, knowing that she would never better herself as a woman in a man's world, disguised herself as a man at age 12. She then travelled to Athens in company with a "learned man' who was also a monk, as well as her teacher and lover. Dressed in the sexless clothing of the clergymen of the day, no one suspected she was a woman, and according to Martin she "made such progress in various sciences that there was nobody equal to her." Because of her abilities and her vast knowledge of the scriptures, she became a cardinal in Rome, where she was later elected as Pope John Anglicus in AD855. The story is that her guise might have gone undetected except for an affair she had with a chamberlain who was much younger than her. The affair and her true sex were discovered. The version of the story of the discovery varies, but the most popular version is that the Pope was attempting to mount her horse when she went into labour and gave birth to a son. One version of the story from that point on was that she was then banished to a convent where she lived in penance while her son grew up to be a bishop. Another version says that immediately after she gave birth the crowd tied her feet to the horse's tail, then stoned her to death as she was dragged along a street in AD858, after serving for more than two years as Pope.

Diet
&
Diabetic
Recipes

Diabetic Shortbread

Shirley MacDonald, Fredericton, New Brunswick (formerly of St. John's, Newfoundland)

Ingredients:
1/2 lb Becel margarine
1/2 cup rice flour
1/2 cup sugar
1 3/4 cups flour

Directions:
Mix ingredients and drop on an ungreased cookie sheet. Bake at 325°F for 22-25 minutes.

Nutritional Information:
(3 - 1 1/2 rounds)
Starch: 1
Calories: 158
Fat and oil: 2
Carbohydrates: 15 g
Protein: 2 g
Fat: 10 g

> ## Spice of Life
> I only know that people call me a feminist whenever I express sentiments that differentiate me from a doormat or a prostitute.   *- Rebecca West*

> ## *Food for Thought*
> We've chosen the path to equality, don't let them turn us around.
> *- Geraldine Ferraro (The first woman to be nominated as Vice President of the United States)*

Diabetic Cake

Shirley MacDonald, Fredericton, New Brunswick (formerly of St. John's, Newfoundland)

Ingredients:
2 cups hot water
3 cups raisins
1 cup dates
1/2 tsp low sodium
1 tsp cinnamon
1 tsp nutmeg
1/4 cup liquid sweetener
2 cups sifted whole wheat flour
1 cup sifted white flour
1 tsp baking powder
2 tsps vanilla
2 tsps baking soda
1 1/3 cups mixed fruit

> ## Female Facts
> **The Game of Give and Take**
> In 1899, one of the world's wonders, Stonehenge of England, was owned by Sir Edmund Antrobus, who charged admission to visitors. Sir Edmund offered it to the government for £125,000 (about $300,000 American), but they didn't buy it. So in 1915, Cecil Chubb, as a gift for his wife, bought it at auction for £6,600. Whether Mrs. Chubb appreciated the gift or not is not known, but three years later, Cecil gave Stonehenge to the nation with a Deed of Gift, specifying that free access to the historical sight be maintained.

Directions:

Boil water, raisins, dates, sodium, cinnamon, nutmeg and sweetener for 30 minutes, and let cool. Add flour, baking soda, baking powder, mixed fruit and vanilla, then bake for 30 minutes at 350°F. Reduce heat to 325°F and bake another 45 minutes. Makes two, 2 lb loaves.

Nutritional Information:
(1/2 inch slice)
Calories: 119

Diet & Diabetic Recipes

Starch: 1
Fruit: 1
Oil: 1

Finger Jell-O

Shirley MacDonald, Fredericton, New Brunswick (formerly of St. John's, Newfoundland)

Ingredients:
4 pkgs plain gelatin
3 small sugar free Jell-O
4 cups hot water

Directions:
Mix until dissolved. Chill until set and slice. Keeps well at room temperature.

Clam Chowder

Shirley MacDonald, Fredericton, New Brunswick (formerly of St. John's, Newfoundland)

Ingredients:
1 can whole baby clams (5 oz)
Water
1 medium size potato, peeled and chopped
1/4 onion, chopped
2/3 cup evaporated skimmed milk
1/4 tsp each pepper and thyme leaves
1 tbsp lite margarine

Directions:
Drain clams. Save juice. Add water to juice to measure 2/3 cup. Combine liquid, potato and onion in medium saucepan. Bring to a boil, reduce heat and simmer until potato is tender.
Add milk, pepper and thyme leaves. Increase heat to medium high. Cook and stir 2 minutes. Add margarine. Cook 5 minutes or until chowder thickens, stirring occasionally.
Add clams - cook and stir 5 minutes.

Dietary Exchange:
1 starch/bread, 1 milk, 1 lean meat

Spicy, Smothered Shrimp

Shirley MacDonald, Fredericton, New Brunswick (formerly of St. John's, Newfoundland)

Ingredients:
3 tbsps canola oil
1/4 cup flour
1 cup chopped onion
1 cup chopped pepper
4 cloves garlic, minced

Diet & Diabetic Recipes

1 14 oz can vegetable broth
1/2 tsp salt
1/4 cup chopped celery
2 medium diced carrots
2 1/2 lbs large shrimp, peeled and deveined
1 tsp crushed red pepper
1 tsp hot pepper sauce
4 cups hot cooked rice
Parsley

Food for Thought

The most important thing in a relationship between a man and a woman is that one of them be good at taking orders. – *Linda Festa*

Directions:

Heat oil in a Dutch oven over medium heat. Add flour, cook and stir until flour mixture is a deep golden brown (10-15 minutes). Add onion, pepper, carrots, celery and garlic, cook and stir 5 mins. Stir in vegetable broth and salt, bring to a boil. Simmer until veggies are tender (10 minutes). Stir in shrimp, red pepper and pepper sauce; simmer until shrimp are opaque (6-8 minutes). Pour into 8 shallow bowls. Top each with 1/2 cup rice. Sprinkle with parsley.

Exchange: 1 1/2 starch/bread, 3 lean meat, 1 veggie

Corn and Cheddar Chowder

Shirley MacDonald, Fredericton, New Brunswick (formerly of St. John's, Newfoundland)

Ingredients:

1 cup chopped onion
1 tbsp margarine
2 tbsps flour
2 1/2 cups fat free, reduced sodium chicken broth
1 cup frozen whole corn kernel
1 can cream corn (16 oz)
1/2 cup diced red pepper
1/2 tsp hot pepper sauce
3 oz shredded sharp cheddar cheese
Freshly ground pepper (optional)

Female Facts

From Peace Prize to Prime Minister
Helen Clark was awarded the annual Peace Prize of the Danish Peace Foundation for her work in promoting peace and disarmament in 1986, and was elected Prime Minister of New Zealand in 1999.

Directions:

Cook onion in margarine in a large saucepan over medium heat. Sprinkle with flour, stir and cook 1 minute. Add broth; bring to boil stirring frequently. Add whole and creamed corn, pepper and pepper sauce. Cover, simmer for 15 minutes. Remove from heat. Stir in cheese gradually until melted. Ladle into soup bowls. Sprinkle with black pepper (optional). Makes 6 servings.

Nutritional Information:

Calories: 180
Starch/bread: 1 1/2
Fat: 1
Lean meat: 1/2

Spice of Life

What would men be without women?
Scarce, sir, mighty scarce. – *Mark Twain*

Crab Salad

Shirley MacDonald, Fredericton, New Brunswick (formerly of St. John's, Newfoundland)

Ingredients:
12 cups washed and torn romaine lettuce
2 cups diced ripe tomatoes or halved cherry tomatoes
12 ozs fresh or canned crabmeat (drained)
1/4 cup crumbled blue or gorgonzola cheese
1/4 cup cholesterol-free bacon bits
Pinch ground pepper
3/4 cup fat-free Italian or Caesar dressing

Spice of Life
Show me a woman who doesn't feel guilt and I'll show you a man.   *– Erica Jong*

Directions:
Cover large platter with lettuce. Arrange tomatoes, crabmeat, cheese, bacon bits and pepper over lettuce. Add dressing just before serving. Toss well. (Can be made, covered and kept in refrigerator up to 5 hours. Be sure to add dressing just before serving.) Makes 8 servings.

Mocha Crinkle

Shirley MacDonald, Fredericton, New Brunswick (formerly of St. John's, Newfoundland)

Ingredients:
1 3/4 cups flour
3/4 cup cocoa
2 tsps instant espresso or coffee granules
1 tsp baking soda
1/4 tsp salt
1/8 tsp pepper
1 1/3 cups light brown sugar
1/2 cup vegetable oil
1/4 cup low-fat sour cream
1 egg
1 tsp vanilla
1/2 cup powdered sugar

Female Facts
Several Firsts
May Edward Chinn was the first African-American woman to graduate from Bellevue Hospital Medical College, one of the first female African-American physicians in New York City, and the first African-American woman to intern at Harlem Hospital. Her work in cancer research helped in the development of the Pap smear, a test for early detection of cervical cancer. She did not retire from private practice until she was 81 years old.

Directions:
Mix flour, cocoa, espresso, baking soda, salt and pepper in a bowl and set aside. Beat sugar and oil in a medium bowl at medium speed until well blended. Beat in sour cream, egg and vanilla. Beat in flour mixture until soft dough forms. Form into ball. Refrigerate 3-4 hours, or until firm. Put powdered sugar in a shallow bowl. Cut into 1-inch pieces and roll into a ball, then roll in powdered sugar. Use ungreased cookie sheets. Bake 10-12 minutes at 350°F until cookies are firm to touch. Don't overbake. Cool on wire racks.

Nutritional Information:
1 cookie per serving - 1/2 bread/starch

Diet & Diabetic Recipes

Walnut Cocoa Macaroons

Shirley MacDonald, Fredericton, New Brunswick (formerly of St. John's, Newfoundland)

Ingredients:
1/3 cup crushed walnuts
3/4 cup quick oats
1/3 cup packed brown sugar
6 tbsps cocoa (unsweetened)
2 tbsps flour
4 egg whites
1 tsp vanilla
1/2 tsp salt
1/3 cup sugar

Food for Thought

When a girl marries she exchanges the attentions of many men for the inattention of one.
– Helen Rowland

Directions:
Stir walnuts, oats, brown sugar, cocoa and flour in a medium bowl, mix well and set aside. Preheat oven to 375°F, then reduce to 325°F. Combine egg whites, vanilla and salt in a dry mixing bowl. Beat with electric mixer on high until soft peaks form. Gradually add sugar and continue beating on high until stiff peaks form. Gradually fold in dry mixture with rubber spatula. Drop level tbsps of dough onto cookie sheet, then bake 15 to 17 minutes, or until tops of cookies no longer look wet. Store in loosely covered container. Makes 3 dozen cookies.

Nutritional Information:
3 cookies - 1/2 fat, 1 starch/bread

Texas Style Chili

Shirley MacDonald, Fredericton, New Brunswick (formerly of St. John's, Newfoundland)

Ingredients:
1 lb lean hamburger
2 cups onions, chopped
5 garlic cloves, minced
2 tbsps chili powder
1 tbsp ground cumin
1 tsp ground oregano
2 1/2 cups fat-free sodium-reduced beef broth
1 cup prepared salsa
2 cans (16 ozs each) pinto or red beans (drain and rinse)
1 cup chopped ripe tomatoes
1/2 cup nonfat sour cream

Female Facts

Canadian Women in Labour Force
In Canada, 58 per cent of females over the age of 15 are in the labour force.

Directions:
Heat large saucepan and spray with Pam. Add hamburger meat, onions and garlic; cook for about 5 minutes, or until pinkness is gone. Sprinkle mixture with spices and mix well. Add broth and salsa, bring to a boil. Cover and simmer approximately 45 minutes. Stir in beans and simmer another 30 minutes, stir occasionally. Put into bowls and top with tomatoes and sour cream. (Tastes even better if made the day before and refrigerated.) Makes 8 servings.

Diet & Diabetic Recipes

Diet & Diabetic Recipes

Nutritional Information:
Calories: 268
Starch/bread: 1 1/2
Lean meat: 2 1/2
Vegetable: 1

Spice of Life
How many husbands have I had?
You mean apart from my own?
– *Zsa Zsa Gabor*

Pumpkin Pie

Shirley MacDonald, Fredericton, New Brunswick (formerly of St. John's, Newfoundland)

Ingredients:
1 frozen, 9" pie shell (Bake according to directions on box)
1 can of pumpkin (15 oz)
2 egg whites
1 cup evaporated skim milk
1/3 cup maple syrup
1 tsp cinnamon
1/2 tsp ginger
1/3 cup sugar
1/2 tsp salt

Female Facts
Belief in Marriage
In Canada, five per cent of women believe that
they benefit more from marriage than men do.

Directions:
Combine all ingredients in a large bowl. Mix well. Pour into pie shell. Bake 15 minutes at 425°F, reduce to 350°F and bake an additional 45-50 minutes until centre is set.

Nutritional Information:
Fat: 1
Starch/bread: 2

Food for Thought
The first problem for all of us, men and women, is not to learn, but to unlearn. – *Gloria Steinem*

Christmas Squares

Shirley MacDonald, Fredericton, New Brunswick (formerly of St. John's, Newfoundland)

Ingredients:
30 marshmallows
2 cups graham wafer crumbs
30 cherries (bottled) red, green or mixed
1/2 cup nuts (chopped)
1 can condensed milk
Coconut

Female Facts
Sex in a Public Place
In Canada, 33 per cent of women 40 to 49
years old have had sex in a public place.

Directions:
Cut marshmallows and cherries into small pieces. Add finely chopped nuts, mix together, add condensed milk and mix again. Cover bottom of 8" x 11" pan with coconut and wafer crumbs. Put mixture in and pack down. Sprinkle with more coconut. Cover and place in fridge.

Hamburger Casserole

Shirley MacDonald, Fredericton, New Brunswick (formerly of St. John's, Newfoundland)

Ingredients:
2 lbs ground beef
2 onions, chopped
Salt and pepper to taste
1 can tomato soup
2 tbsps ketchup
1 tsp Worcestershire Sauce
Stove Top Stuffing or homemade stuffing

Spice of Life

Women have a much better time than men in this world. There are far more things forbidden to them. – *Oscar Wilde*

Directions:
Fry hamburger and onions together. Add salt and pepper and place in a casserole dish; add soup, ketchup and Worcestershire Sauce. Place stuffing on top. Bake for 1/2 hour. Serve with mashed potatoes and your favourite vegetable.

Cheese Cookies

Shirley MacDonald, Fredericton, New Brunswick (formerly of St. John's, Newfoundland)

Ingredients:
1 cup butter
1 cup grated cheese
1 1/2 cups flour
Marmalade or jam

Food for Thought

People think at the end of the day that a man is the only answer. Actually a job is better for me. – *Princess Diana*

Directions:
Cream cheese and butter together. Add flour to make dough soft enough to roll. Cut with a cookie cutter. Bake at 350°F until light brown. When cool, spread marmalade on one and place another on top. (Your favourite jam may also be used).

Bean Pot Casserole

Shirley MacDonald, Fredericton, New Brunswick (formerly of St. John's, Newfoundland)

Ingredients:
1 pkg onion soup mix
1 tbsp prepared mustard
1 can beans (28 oz)
2 tbsps brown sugar
1/2 cup tomato ketchup
8-10 wieners, sliced
1/4 cup water

Female Facts

A Girdle-maker's Paradise
A decree of Queen Catherine de Medici, who died in 1589, was that the waist size of ladies of the French court be no bigger than 13 inches.

Directions:
Combine all ingredients together in a 2-quart dish. Bake uncovered at 350°F for 1 hour. Stir occasionally. Makes 4-6 servings.

Diet & Diabetic Recipes

Rhubarb Relish

Shirley MacDonald, Fredericton, New Brunswick (formerly of St. John's, Newfoundland)

Ingredients:
5 lbs rhubarb (cut up)
1 tsp cinnamon
5 lbs brown sugar
1 tsp allspice
3 cups vinegar
1/4 tsp cayene pepper
1 tsp cloves

> ## *Food for Thought*
> If we are to achieve a richer culture, rich in contrasting values, we must recognize the whole gamut of human potentialities, and so weave a less arbitrary social fabric, one in which each diverse gift will find a fitting place.   – *Margaret Mead*

Directions:
Combine ingredients in a large pot. Simmer down to 2/3rds of quantity. Seal in hot, sterilized jars. Excellent with roast beef.

Southern Pecan Pie

Shirley MacDonald, Fredericton, New Brunswick (formerly of St. John's, Newfoundland)

Ingredients:
3 eggs
2/3 cup sugar
Dash of salt
1 cup dark corn syrup
1/3 cup melted butter
1 cup pecan halves

> ## **Spice of Life**
> Marriage is the continuous process of getting used to things you never expected.
> – *Daniel Quinn*

Directions:
Beat 3 eggs thoroughly with sugar, salt, corn syrup and melted butter. Add pecan halves and pour into a 9" unbaked pastry shell. Bake in moderate 350°F oven for 50 minutes, or until knife inserted halfway between centre and edge comes out clean. Then cool.

Carrot Raisin Cake

Bernadette Kennedy,
Foxtrap, Newfoundland

Ingredients:
1/2 cup oil
1/4 cup brown sugar
4 eggs
3 cups grated carrot
2 cups whole wheat flour
1 tsp baking powder
2 tsps cinnamon
1 tsp baking soda
1/2 cup raisins

> ## **Female Facts**
> **Education Up, Birth Rates Down**
> A survey of 106 developing countries shows that as the literacy level of women increases, the fertility rates decline. This is because literate women tend to marry later and are more likely to use family planning. It also showed that infant mortality rates decline because mothers with even one year of schooling tend to take better care of their babies. Immunization rates are also on the rise because literate mothers are more likely to seek medical care for their children.

Directions:
Put oil and brown sugar in a bowl and beat together. Add eggs one at a time. Then add carrot. Mix together flour, baking powder, cinnamon and soda and add to mixture. Add raisins. Bake in tube pan at 350°F for one hour.

Diet Pineapple Muffins

Bernadette Kennedy,
Foxtrap, Newfoundland

Ingredients:
1/2 cup oil
2 eggs, well beaten
1 tsp vanilla
1 cup crushed pineapple (unsweetened)
1 cup grated carrot
1 1/2 cups whole wheat flour
1 tsp baking soda
1 tsp baking powder
1/2 tsp salt
3/4 cup dates
3/4 cup raisins

Directions:
Mix well. Bake in greased muffin pans for 20 minutes at 325°F.

Basic Health Drink

Bernadette Kennedy, Foxtrap, Newfoundland

Ingredients:
1 cup orange juice
3/4 cup yogurt
1 banana, cut into 1-inch-long pieces
2 tbsps powdered milk

Directions:
Toss ingredients into your blender in order, then whip at medium speed until smooth. So good.

Diet Cheesecake

Faith Snow, North River, Newfoundland

Ingredients:
1 1/2 cups graham wafer crumbs
1/4 cup Becel margarine
3 pkgs Equal
1 pkg Lucky Whip, prepared
1 pkg light Philadelphia cream cheese
1 can light cherry pie filling (or other fruit)

Female Facts

First Woman on Record
Anna En Hedu is the first female name recorded in technical history. The daughter of Sargon of Akkad, who established the Sargonian Dynasty in Babylon some 4000 or so years ago, was appointed chief priestess of the moon goddess of the city. This was a position of great power and prestige. It was only with the sponsorship of the high priestess that a leader could achieve a legitimate claim to rule. The priests and priestesses in Sumeria and Babylon established a network of observatories to monitor the movements of the stars. The calendar they created is still used today for certain religious events, like Easter and Passover.

Spice of Life

Trust your husband, adore your husband, and get as much as you can in your own name.
– *Joan Rivers (advice from her mother)*

Food for Thought

In my heart, I think a woman has two choices: either she's a feminist or a masochist.   – *Gloria Steinem*

Directions:
Press mixture of wafer crumbs, margarine and 1 pkg Equal into a 9" x 12" pan. Reserve 1 1/2 tbsp of mixture to sprinkle on top. Cream together Lucky Whip, cream cheese and 2 pkgs Equal, fold into cheese mixture and spread over crumbs. Spread pie filling over cheese mixture and sprinkle remaining crumbs on top. Chill for 12 hours, or overnight.

Boiled Diet Cake

Faith Snow, North River, Newfoundland

Ingredients:
2 cups water
1 cup orange juice (or) 1 orange (grated peel included)
1 pkg raisins = 2 cups
1/2 lb chopped dates = 2 pkgs
1 tsp nutmeg
2 tsps cinnamon
2 tsps vanilla
1/2 cup oil
1 cup cherries
1 cup mixed fruit
2 cups whole wheat flour
2 tsps baking soda
1 cup walnuts (optional)

Directions:
Boil water, orange juice, raisins, chopped dates, nutmeg, cinnamon and vanilla in saucepan until orange juice nearly boils away. Let cool, add 1/2 cup oil and mix thouroughly. While still mixing, add remaining ingredients and bake at 300°F for 1 hour and 15 minutes.

Diet Dessert

Faith Snow, North River, Newfoundland

Ingredients:
1 pkg diet orange Jell-O
1 tub light Cool Whip
1 tub low-fat cottage cheese
1 can drained pineapple (14 oz)
1 can orange sections

Directions:
Mix together and let cool.

Diet & Diabetic Recipes

Diabetic Mushrooms and Cabbage

Faith Snow, North River, Newfoundland

Ingredients:
1 tbsp minced onion
2 tbsps Becel margarine
2 cups shredded cabbage
1 cup canned sliced mushrooms
1 tbsp vinegar
1 tsp salt
1/8 tsp pepper

Female Facts

Minimum Wage Workers Mostly Women
A full-time, year-round minimum-wage worker in the United States does not earn enough to bring a two-person family above the poverty line. Nearly two-thirds of the minimum-wage workforce is female, the vast majority of whom are adults, not teenagers.

Directions:
Sauté onion in margarine in a large frying pan for 1 minute. Add cabbage and mushrooms including liquid, vinegar, salt and pepper. Stir cabbage mixture well. Cover and cook for 15 minutes.

Sugar Free Fudge

Anne Brown, Coley's Point, Newfoundland

Spice of Life

If you want to sacrifice the admiration of many men for the criticism of one, go ahead, get married.
– *Katharine Hepburn*

Ingredients:
480 g Paneer Cream Cheese, softened
2 blocks unsweetened chocolate squares (30 gms each), melted and cooled
1/2 cup crushed sugar-free tablets
1 tsp vanilla extract
1/2 cup chopped peanuts

Directions:
In a small mixing bowl, beat the cream cheese, chocolate, sugar-free tablets and vanilla until smooth. Stir in peanuts. Pour into an 8" square baking pan lined with foil. Cover and refrigerate overnight. Cut into 16 squares. Serve chilled.

Anna-Banana Milk Shake

Anne Brown, Coley's Point, Newfoundland

Food for Thought

Men are not the enemy, but the fellow victims. The real enemy is women's denigration of themselves. – *Betty Friedan*

Ingredients:
1 banana, frozen
3/4 cup skimmed milk
Freshly ground nutmeg to taste
Sugar-free tablets as required

Directions:
Fully freeze the banana. Thoroughly purée in a blender or food processor all ingredients. Serve immediately. Makes one portion.

Diet & Diabetic Recipes

Diet & Diabetic Recipes

Carrot and Raisin Cake

Anne Brown,
Coley's Point, Newfoundland

Ingredients:
6 egg whites
1 cup apple juice concentrate
2/3 cup canola oil
1/4 cup water
3 cups unbleached white flour
1 tbsp baking powder
1 tsp baking soda
1 tsp salt
2 tsps cinnamon
1/4 tsp nutmeg
2 cups raisins
2 cups carrots (4-6 medium)

> ## Female Facts
> **Famous Five: Persons Case**
> The Persons Case is a legal history milestone in Canada. Five women from Alberta (Henrietta Muir Edwards, Nellie McClung, Louise McKinney, Emily Murphy and Irene Parlby), known as the Famous Five, asked the Supreme Court of Canada to declare that women were persons under the law. When the Supreme Court turned them down, they appealed to the British Privy Council. The Privy Council found for the women on October 18, 1929, declaring that women were persons under the law, a giant leap for womankind.

Directions:
Preheat oven to 350°F. Stir together egg whites, apple juice concentrate, oil and water. Set aside. Sift together dry ingredients: flour, baking powder, baking soda, salt, cinnamon, and nutmeg. Put raisins in warm water to plump. Meanwhile, grate carrots and spray two round 9" cake pans with non-stick pan spray. Gently stir wet ingredients into dry ingredients just until moistened. Drain raisins, and fold in carrots and raisins. Pour into cake pans, and bake at 350°F for 25 to 30 minutes. Then reduce heat to 325°F for 8 to 12 more minutes.

Sassy Sandwich Pizza

Anne Brown, Coley's Point, Newfoundland

Ingredients:
1 loaf French bread (1lb)
1 cup pizza sauce
1-2 cups shredded mozzarella cheese
1 can sliced mushrooms (4 oz), drained
1 can artichoke hearts (16 oz), drained
1/2 large green pepper, sliced
1/2 large red or yellow pepper, sliced
1/2 red onion, chopped
1 can sliced black olives (2 oz), drained
Coarsely cracked black pepper

Spice of Life

When men reach their 60s and retire, they go to pieces. Women go right on cooking.
– *Gail Sheehy*

Directions:
Slice loaf in half lengthwise and spread each half with equal amounts of ingredients. Sprinkle lightly with black pepper. Bake at 350°F for 7 to 10 minutes, or until cheese melts. Slice each half into fourths. Serves 6-8.

Nutritional Information:
Calories: 253
Protein: 11 g
Carbohydrates: 41 g
Fiber: 5 g

Tomato-Rosemary Chicken

Rosemary (Dolly) Krauss
(nee Stamp, St. John's, Newfoundland)

Ingredients:
12 boneless, skinless chicken breast halves (4 pounds total)
1/2 tsp salt
1/4 tsp black pepper
1/4 cup all-purpose flour
2 tbsps vegetable oil (or olive oil)
2 tbsps butter (or margarine)
5 cloves garlic, chopped
1/4 lb proscuitto, chopped
1/3 cup dry white wine
1 tbsp chopped fresh rosemary or 1 tsp dried, crumbled
12 plum tomatoes, diced
1/2 cup chicken broth

Food for Thought

We stand now where two roads diverge. But unlike the roads in Robert Frost's familiar poem, they are not equally fair. The road we have long been travelling is deceptively easy, a smooth superhighway on which we progress with great speed, but at its end lies disaster. The other fork of the road—the one "less travelled by"—offers our last, our only chance to reach a destination that assures the preservation of the Earth. – *Rachel Carson*

Directions:
Season both sides of chicken breast halves with salt and pepper. Place flour on a sheet of waxed paper. Turn chicken in flour to coat both sides; shake off any excess and place chicken on another piece of waxed paper. Heat oven to 375°F. Heat 1 tbsp oil and 1 tbsp butter in a large non-stick skillet over medium-high heat. Add 6 chicken breast halves and sauté until lightly browned, about 3 minutes per side. Place chicken in a 15" x 10" x 1" jelly-roll pan in a single layer, filling half of the pan. Repeat with remaining oil, butter and chicken. Bake chicken in a heated 375°F oven for 20 minutes or until internal temperature registers 170°F on an instant-read thermometer. Meanwhile, add garlic and proscuitto to skillet; cook over medium heat, stirring constantly, 3 minutes. Add wine and rosemary; cook 2 minutes, stirring up any browned bits from bottom of skillet. Add tomatoes and broth. Bring to a boil. Reduce heat; simmer 10 minutes. Place chicken on a serving platter; pour sauce over top. Serve immediately.

Nutritional Information:
Calories: 257
Protein: 34 g
Sodium: 377 mg
Cholesterol: 89 mg
Fat: 11 g
Carbohydrates: 5 g

Exchanges: 4 Low-Fat Meat; 1 Vegetable

Female Facts

Hillary, Arkansas Woman of the Year
Before becoming First Lady of the U.S., Hillary Rodham Clinton developed her special concern for protecting the best interests of children and their families. She was named Arkansas Woman of the Year in 1983 and Arkansas Mother of the Year in 1984.

Diet & Diabetic Recipes

Dolly's Chocolate Almond Meringues

Rosemary (Dolly) Krauss (nee Stamp, St. John's, Newfoundland)

Ingredients:
1/2 cup sugar, divided
1/4 cup ground almonds
1 tbsp unsweetened cocoa
1 tsp cornstarch
2 egg whites
1/8 tsp cream of tartar
1/2 tsp vanilla (or 1/4 tsp almond extract)

Spice of Life

Men are creatures with two legs and eight hands.
– *Jayne Mansfield*

Directions:
Preheat oven to 250°F. Spray a foil-lined baking sheet with non-stick spray. In a small bowl, mix 2 tbsps of sugar with almonds, cocoa and cornstarch. In a stainless steel or glass bowl, beat egg whites with an electric mixer until frothy. Add cream of tartar and beat on high speed until soft peaks form. Gradually add flavouring and remaining sugar. Beat until stiff and shiny. Gently fold cocoa mixture into meringue. Drop cookie mixture from a teaspoon onto the baking sheet to form small mounds. Leave about 2 inches between each mound. (Mixture could also be piped through a large pastry bag fitted with a large star tube.) Bake at 250°F for 40 minutes. Cookies should be dry and slightly browned. Cool completely. Store in a tightly covered container.

Nutritional Information:
Calories: 18
Protein: trace g
Sodium: 7 mg
Cholesterol: 0 mg
Fat: 0.3 g
Carbohydrates: 4 g
Exchanges: 1/4 Bread/Starch

Female Facts

Nadia Comaneci
Romanian gymnast Nadia Comaneci became a favourite of fans and the media at the 1976 Summer Olympics in Montréal, Canada, where she won three gold medals and a bronze in individual competition, and a silver team medal.

Krauss's Chocolate Kahlua Cake

Rosemary (Dolly) Krauss (nee Stamp, St. John's, Newfoundland)

Ingredients:
1 devil's food cake mix (18.25 oz)
1 small (1 oz) box sugar-free, instant chocolate pudding mix
1 cup non-fat vanilla yogurt
1/4 cup canola oil
1/3 cup skim milk
1 large egg
3 large egg whites
1/3 cup Kahlua liqueur
1/3 cup semisweet chocolate chips
Cocoa

Food for Thought

If it's a woman, it's caustic; if it's a man, it's authoritative.
– *Barbara Walters*

Directions:
Preheat oven to 350°F, then coat a 13" x 9" baking pan with non-stick cooking spray and dust with cocoa. Place all ingredients except chocolate chips in a large bowl. Beat with mixer for 2 minutes or until well blended. Stir in chocolate chips. Pour batter into prepared pan and bake for 50 minutes, or until toothpick inserted in middle comes out clean. Cool before cutting.

Nutritional Information:
Calories: 205
Protein: 3 g
Sodium: 209 mg
Cholesterol: 13 mg
Fat: 8 g
Carbohydrates: 31 g
Exchanges: 2 Bread/Starch; 1-1/2 Fat

Food for Thought

I've learned from experience that the greater part of our happiness or misery depends on our dispositions and not on our circumstances. – *Martha Washington*

Poppy's Lemon Poppy Seed Cake

Rosemary (Dolly) Krauss (nee Stamp, St. John's, Newfoundland)

Ingredients:
1 cup all-purpose flour
1/2 cup sugar
1/3 cup poppy seeds
1-1/2 tsps baking powder
1/2 tsp baking soda
1/8 tsp salt
1/4 cup margarine, melted
2 large egg whites, or 1/4 cup egg substitute
1/2 cup fat-free milk
3 tbsps fresh lemon juice
1 tsp finely grated lemon zest
1 tsp pure vanilla extract
2 tbsps powdered sugar

Female Facts

Skating to Fame
American figure skater Peggy Gale Fleming won the national title at the 1964 United States Figure Skating Championships and went on to win the world title in 1966, 1967 and 1968. After Fleming's victory at the 1968 world championships, she retired from competitive skating and subsequently performed in ice shows and television specials. She also became a television commentator.

Directions:
Preheat the oven to 350°F. Prepare a 9" x 9" baking pan with non-stick pan spray. Combine the flour, sugar, poppy seeds, baking powder, baking soda and salt in a large bowl. Add the margarine, egg whites, milk, lemon juice, zest and vanilla. Mix just until the dry ingredients are moistened. Pour into the prepared pan. Bake 30 minutes, or until the cake springs back when the center is lightly pressed. Cool on a wire rack. Sift powdered sugar over the cake. Cut into 3-inch squares to serve.

Nutritional Information:
Calories: 183
Protein: 4 g
Sodium: 242 mg
Cholesterol: 0 mg
Fat: 7 g

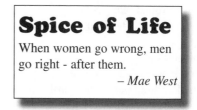

Spice of Life

When women go wrong, men go right - after them.
– *Mae West*

Carbohydrates: 26 g
Exchanges: Other Carbohydrate: 1 - 1/2, Fat: 1 - 1/2

Corn Muffins

Rosemary (Dolly) Krauss (nee Stamp, St. John's, Newfoundland)

Ingredients:
1/2 cup corn meal
1 cup flour
1 tbsp baking powder
3/4 cup skim milk
1 tbsp butter or margarine, melted
1 egg

> ## Food for Thought
>
> A woman's head is always influenced by her heart; but a man's heart by his head.
> — *Lady Marguerite Blessington*

Directions:
Mix dry ingredients together. Add lightly beaten egg, milk and butter. Mix just until moist. Bake in muffin pans lined with cupcake papers for 20 minutes at 400°F.

Nutritional Information:
Calories: 95
Protein: 5 g
Fat: 2.5 g
Carbohydrates: 15 g

Curry Chicken

Anne Brown, Coley's Point, Newfoundland

Ingredients:
6 single chicken breasts, skinned, boned, washed
3 tsps oil
1/2 onion, chopped
2 cloves garlic, crushed
1/2 cup low sodium chicken broth
1 1/2 cups water
1/2 tsp cumin
1/2 tsp coriander
1/2 tsp tumeric
1/8 tsp allspice
1/8 tsp ginger
Dash dried fennel
Dash ground black pepper
1 tsp coconut flavouring

> # Female Facts
>
> **All That Jazz**
> Maria Fisher had a long and illustrious career as a film actress, appearing in over 60 films in the 1930s and '40s. She was also a leading soprano with the London Opera Company, as well as with the Columbia Opera Company in Washington, D.C., where she hosted and performed on a classical radio program. She founded the American Opera School and the Beethoven Society of America. Believing that "Jazz is America's classical music," she founded the Thelonious Monk Institute of Jazz.

Directions:
In a large skillet, sauté chicken breasts in 2 tsps of oil until golden on both sides. Remove chicken from pan. Saute garlic and onion in remaining oil 5-7 minutes. Add broth, water and all of the spices to garlic/onion mixture. When well blended, return chicken pieces to skillet. Cover

and simmer over medium heat for 30 minutes. Stir in coconut flavouring. Serve over rice or rice/grain mixture.

Nutritional Information:
Calories: 145
Protein: 19 g
Sodium: 43 mg
Cholesterol: 52 mg
Fat: 6 g
Carbohydrates: 2 g
Exchanges: 3 low-fat meat

Chicken and Spinach Salad

Anne Brown, Coley's Point, Newfoundland

Ingredients:
6 oz fresh spinach
2 oranges, peeled and cut into chunks
2 cups cooked and cubed chicken
2 cups fresh strawberries

Dressing Ingredients:
2 tbsps red wine vinegar
3 tbsps orange juice
1 - 1/2 tbsps canola oil
1/4 tsp dry mustard
1/3 tsp poppy seeds

Directions:
Mix dressing ingredients and refrigerate. Wash spinach and tear into bite size pieces. Add oranges, chicken and strawberries. Serve with dressing.

Nutritional Information:
Calories: 135
Sodium: 46 mg
Cholesterol: 31 mg
Fat: 4 g
Carbohydrates: 10 g
Exchanges: 1 fruit, 1 1/2 lean meat

Scottish Scones

Anne Brown, Coley's Point, Newfoundland

Ingredients:
1 cup unbleached all-purpose flour
1 cup whole wheat flour
1 tsp baking powder

Female Facts

Entrepreneurial Woman of the Year
In 1980 Liz Claiborne was named the fashion industry's first Entrepreneurial Woman of the Year. A year later her firm made a public stock offering, after which it began to diversify, adding petite, dress and shoe divisions. In 1986, Liz Claiborne, Inc. was listed among the Fortune 500 for the first time.

Spice of Life

Marriage is when two people are under the influence of the most violent, most insane, most delusive and most transient of passions. They are required to swear that they will remain in that excited, abnormal and exhausting condition continuously until death do them part.   *– George Bernard Shaw*

Female Facts

Higher Doorways For Women
One time women's headgear was so tall in France, that the queen had the doorways of the royal palace at Vincennes raised so the ladies of the court could pass through without ducking.

Diet & Diabetic Recipes

Diet & Diabetic Recipes

1/2 tsp salt
4 tbsps whipped butter
1 cup buttermilk
1/2 cup golden raisins

Food for Thought

If you must hold yourself up to your children as an object lesson, hold yourself up as a warning and not as an example.

Directions:
Preheat your oven to 400°F. Coat a baking sheet with non-stick cooking spray. In a large bowl, sift the dry ingredients together. Add the butter and mix it into the flour with your fingers. Add buttermilk and knead into a soft dough. Knead in the raisins. On a floured board, roll out the dough until 1/2" thick. Cut dough into 16 rounds. Place on a baking sheet and bake for 15 to 20 minutes, or until golden in colour. Serve warm or let cool and store in an airtight container.

Nutritional Information:
Calories: 97
Protein: 3 g
Sodium: 115 mg
Cholesterol: 7 mg
Fat: 3 g
Carbohydrates: 16 g
Exchanges: 1 Starch/Bread

Female Facts

One-Third Illiterate
One out of three women in the world today cannot read or write.

Cinnamon Apple Pork Tenderloin

Anne Brown, Coley's Point, Newfoundland

Ingredients:
1 lb pork tenderloin
2 apples, peeled, cored, sliced
2 tbsps cornstarch
2 tbsps raisins
1 tsp ground cinnamon

Food for Thought

We still live in a world in which a significant fraction of people, including women, believe that a woman belongs, and wants to belong, exclusively in the home. – *Rosalyn Sussman (Nobel Prize-winning medical physicist)*

Directions:
Preheat the oven to 400°F. Place the pork tenderloin in a roasting pan or casserole dish with a lid. Combine the remaining ingredients in a bowl and stir. Spoon the apple mixture around the pork tenderloin. Cover and bake for 40 minutes. Remove the lid and spoon the apple mixture over the tenderloin. Return to the oven and bake 15-20 minutes longer until tenderloin is browned and cooked through.

Nutritional Information:
Calories: 270
Protein: 20 g
Sodium: 148 mg
Fat: 10 g
Carbohydrates: 13 g
Exchanges: 3 Medium Fat Meat; 1 Fruit

Spice of Life
Honesty has ruined more marriages than infidelity.
– *Charles McCabe*

Ginger Sweets

Anne Brown, Coley's Point, Newfoundland

Ingredients:
1/4 cup frozen apple juice concentrate
1/4 cup granulated fructose
1/2 cup margarine
1 egg
1/2 tsp vanilla
1 cup flour
1/2 tsp baking soda
1/4 tsp salt
2 tsps ginger
1/2 cup chopped walnuts (optional)

Directions:
Mix juice concentrate and fructose together, then in a large bowl, cream this together with the margarine, egg and vanilla. Beat for 3 minutes. Combine dry ingredients separately and add slowly to beaten mixture, continuing to beat. Stir in nuts. On a baking sheet, which has been coated with non-stick spray, drop cookies by spoonfuls about 2 inches apart. Bake at 350°F for 8 minutes. Remove from sheet with metal spatula. Makes 24 cookies.

Nutritional Information:
Calories: 85
Protein: 2 g
Sodium: 85 mg
Cholesterol: 11 mg
Fat: 6 g
Carbohydrates: 7 g
Exchanges: 1/2 Bread; 1 Fat

Cinnamon Pumpkin Torte

Anne Brown, Coley's Point, Newfoundland

Ingredients:
Non-stick cooking spray
1 pkg (18.25 oz) low-fat yellow cake mix
1/4 cup low-fat margarine, melted
1 egg, slightly beaten (or 1/4 cup egg substitute)
1 can (30 oz) pre-spiced pumpkin pie mix
2 eggs, beaten (or 1 cup egg substitute)
2/3 cup canned, evaporated skim milk
2 tbsps sugar
1 tsp cinnamon

Food for Thought

Put duties aside at least an hour before bed and perform soothing, quiet activities that will help you relax.

– Dianne Hales

Female Facts

National Ballet of Canada
Dancer, choreographer, director and teacher Celia Franka, whose stage name is Celia Franks, has played a central role in ballet in this country, including being the founder of The National Ballet of Canada.

Spice of Life

Good humour is one of the best articles of dress one can wear in society.

Diet & Diabetic Recipes

Diet & Diabetic Recipes

Directions:
Preheat oven to 350°F. Coat a 9" x 13" cake pan with cooking spray. Set aside 1 cup of yellow cake mix. Mix margarine and one egg and add to remaining cake mix. Slightly press dry mixture into bottom of pan to form a crust. Combine pumpkin pie mix, two remaining eggs, and evaporated skim milk. Pour over prepared bottom crust. Mix the 1/8 cup reserved cake mix, sugar and cinnamon and sprinkle over pumpkin filling. Bake 45 to 55 minutes, or until filling is set. Makes 24 servings.

Nutritional Information:
Calories: 163
Sodium: 256 mg
Cholesterol: 27 mg
Fat: 3 g
Carbohydrates: 31 g
Exchanges: 1-1/2 Bread/Starch; 1 Vegetable

Texas Red Chili

Anne Brown, Coley's Point, Newfoundland

Ingredients:
2 tbsps vegetable oil
1 beef brisket (about 2 lbs), cut into 1/4-inch cubes
1 cup chopped onion
3 jalapeno chilies, halved, seeded and finely chopped
2 cloves garlic, finely chopped
1/4 cup chili powder
1 tbsp ground cumin
1/2 tsp salt
1/2 tsp ground red pepper (cayenne)
1 can (13-3/4 ozs) beef broth
2 cans (14-1/2 ozs each) stewed tomatoes
1 bottle (12 ozs) beer
1 bay leaf
Lime wedges for garnish

> ### Female Facts
> **Nobel Prize in Physics**
> In 1963, Maria Goeppert-Mayer was awarded the Nobel Prize in Physics for her ground-breaking work in models of the nucleus of atoms.

> ### Food for Thought
> All women are misfits. We do not fit into this world without amputations. *– Marge Piercy*

Directions:
Heat oil in a Dutch Oven over medium-high heat. Working in batches, saute brisket until browned, about 10 minutes. Transfer to a plate. Add onion, jalapenos and garlic to drippings in pot; cook over medium-low heat until onion is very tender, about 8 minutes. Stir in chili powder, cumin, salt and red pepper; cook 1 minute. Return meat to pot. Stir in broth, tomatoes, beer and bay leaf. Heat to boiling. Lower heat; then simmer, with cover slightly ajar, until meat is tender (about 1 1/2 hours). For the last 20 minutes, uncover to thicken chili. To serve, ladle chili into bowls. Garnish each bowl with lime wedge. Makes 8 servings.

Nutritional Information:
Calories: 334
Protein: 30 g

Sodium: 712 mg
Cholesterol: 84 mg
Fat: 17 g
Carbohydrates: 15 g
Exchanges: 1 Bread/Starch; 4 Medium-Fat Meat

Cognac-Laced Truffles

Anne Brown, Coley's Point, Newfoundland

Ingredients:
1/4 cup cognac
1/2 cup heavy cream
11 squares (1 oz each) semisweet chocolate, chopped
3 squares (1 oz each) white baking chocolate, chopped
1 square (1 oz) unsweetened chocolate, chopped
3/4 cup confectioners' sugar

Coating Ingredients:
2 tbsps unsweetened cocoa powder
2 tbsps confectioners' sugar

Directions:
Line two baking sheets with waxed paper. Heat cognac in a small saucepan just to simmering. Remove from heat. Add cream. Bring to simmering. Place all the chocolate and 3/4 cup confectioners' sugar in a food processor and whirl 1 to 2 minutes or until finely chopped. With machine running, add cream mixture in a steady stream. Process until smooth. Scrape into a medium-size bowl. Refrigerate just until thick enough to hold shape (about 1 hour). Drop rounded teaspoonfuls onto prepared baking sheets. With your hands, quickly shape into balls. (Refrigerate to firm while working if necessary.) Place in a freezer for 30 minutes. Prepare coating: Sift cocoa powder and confectioners' sugar into a small bowl. Add truffles, 3 at a time; toss to coat. Refrigerate in airtight containers up to 1 month. Serve at room temperature.

Nutritional Information:
Calories: 76
Protein: 1 g
Fat: 5 g
Carbohydrates: 8 g
Exchanges: 1/2 Starch/Bread, 1 Fat

Shrimp Scampi

Anne Brown, Coley's Point, Newfoundland

Ingredients:
1 tbsp butter
2 tbsps olive oil
4 cloves garlic, finely chopped
1 lb large or medium shrimp, peeled and deveined

Female Facts

Good Night Mom
After she was crowned Queen Victoria at the age of 18, the monarch's first act was to remove her bed from her mother's room.

Spice of Life

Prince to kidnapped damsel in ugly pink gown, "Nobody in his right mind would rescue a damsel in dis dress."

Diet & Diabetic Recipes

Diet & Diabetic Recipes

1/4 cup dry white wine
1 tbsp fresh lemon juice
1/2 tsp salt
1/8 tsp black pepper
1 tbsp dry seasoned bread crumbs
2 tbsps chopped fresh parsley

Directions:

Heat butter and oil in a large non-stick skillet over high heat. When butter starts to brown, add garlic. Lower heat; cook 1 minute, stirring to prevent garlic from overbrowning. Add shrimp; cook 2 minutes, stirring occasionally. Add wine, lemon juice, salt and pepper; cook 2 minutes or until shrimp are cooked through. Stir in bread crumbs and parsley. Serve immediately. Serves 4.

Nutritional Information:

Calories: 172
Protein: 15 g
Sodium: 473 mg
Cholesterol: 142 mg
Fat: 11 g
Carbohydrates: 3 g
Exchanges: 2 Medium-Fat Meat

Pork Cutlets Mexicano

Anne Brown, Coley's Point, Newfoundland

Ingredients:

2 tbsps butter
1/3 cup finely chopped red onion
1 1/2 tsps finely chopped garlic
2 tbsps all-purpose flour
4 boneless pork cutlets (1-1/4 lbs total), slightly flattened
1/4 tsp ground cumin
1/2 cup chicken broth
1/2 tsp red-wine vinegar
1 cup salsa

Directions:

Melt butter in a large non-stick skillet over medium-high heat. Add onion and garlic; sauté, stirring occasionally, 2 minutes or until softened. Meanwhile, place flour on waxed paper. Lightly coat cutlets in flour, shaking off excess. Add cutlets to skillet; sauté 2 minutes per side or until golden brown. Add cumin, broth, vinegar and salsa; cook about 4 minutes or until the meat is cooked through.

Nutritional Information:

Calories: 258
Protein: 27 g
Sodium: 872 mg
Cholesterol: 94 mg

Fat: 12 g
Carbohydrates: 8 g
Exchanges: 3 - 1/2 Medium-Fat Meat; 1 Vegetable

Ratatouille

Anne Brown, Coley's Point, Newfoundland

Ingredients:
1 small eggplant, cut into 1/2-inch cubes
Salt and freshly ground black pepper
2 tbsps extra virgin olive oil
2 large red bell peppers, seeded and cut into 3/4-inch pieces
4 small zucchini, sliced
1 onion, coarsely chopped
4 cloves garlic, minced
1 lb fresh tomatoes, chopped, or 1 can (28 oz) whole tomatoes, drained and chopped
1/3 cup chopped fresh basil

Directions:
Sprinkle eggplant lightly with salt and let drain in a colander for 30 minutes. Pat dry, then in a non-stick skillet heat 1 tbsp oil over medium-high heat. Add eggplant. Stir and cook until soft and browned, about 6 to 7 minutes. Transfer eggplant to bowl. Add remaining oil to pan and heat until hot. Add red peppers, zucchini, onion and garlic. Cook vegetables, stirring until tender, about 3 to 5 minutes. Mix in tomatoes, basil and eggplant. Stirring occasionally, cook on low heat 15 to 20 minutes or until all vegetables are very tender. Add salt and pepper to taste. Ratatouille, a specialty of the Provence region of France, is a popular and versatile dish that uses large amounts of produce. The tomatoes and eggplant create a juicy, stew-like sauce that accentuates the flavours of basil and garlic. Serve it hot as a side dish or over grain for an entree. This version also tastes great when served cold.

Nutritional Information:
Calories: 123
Protein: 4 g
Sodium: 200 mg
Fat: 5 g
Carbohydrates: 19 g
Exchanges: 3 - 1/2 Vegetable, 1 Fat

Meatloaf

Anne Brown, Coley's Point, Newfoundland

Ingredients:
5-6 slices bacon, cooked and crumbled
1/2 cup diced onion
1/2 cup diced celery
1 1/2 lbs ground beef
1/2 lb ground pork

Diet & Diabetic Recipes

2 eggs
1/4 cup Worcestershire Sauce
1/2 tsp parsley
Honey barbecue sauce
3 slices Italian bread
Salt and pepper, to taste

Female Facts

Big on Business
In Canada, 30 per cent of businesses are owned or operated by women.

Directions:
Preheat oven to 350°F. Cook bacon, then remove from pan, reserving some of the grease. Sauté onion and celery briefly in a small amount of bacon grease until soft. Mix all ingredients together, except for crumbled bacon and bread. Spray loaf pan with cooking spray. Place bread on bottom of pan. Spread meatloaf mixture evenly in pan. Cover with foil and bake at 350°F for 1 hour and 20 minutes. Remove from oven and drain carefully. Spread with honey barbecue sauce and crumbled bacon. Place in oven for about 10-15 minutes, just enough to glaze. Remove from oven, let stand for 5 minutes, then enjoy!

Smoked Ham with Cranberry Chutney

Anne Brown, Coley's Point, Newfoundland

Ingredients:
1 boneless, fully-cooked smoked ham, 4-6 lbs

Spice of Life

My perfume is so expensive, I have to pay for it through the nose!

Chutney Ingredients:
1 can(16 oz) whole-berry cranberry sauce
1 can (8.25 oz) crushed pineapple, unsweetened, drained
1 bottle (5 oz) prepared horseradish

Ham Directions:
Preheat oven to 325° F. Place ham in a shallow baking pan. Bake, uncovered, in a 325° F oven for 1 to 1 1/2 hours, or until meat thermometer registers 140°F. Remove from oven; slice thinly to serve.

Chutney Directions:
Meanwhile, combine remaining ingredients in a medium bowl. Transfer to a serving bowl, serve immediately, or cover and chill until serving time. Serve chutney alongside ham.
Yield: approximately 2-1/2 cups.

Nutritional Information:
(Per 2 tbsp serving of chutney, without ham):
Calories: 53
Fat: 1 g
Carbohydrates: 11 g
Cholesterol: 3 mg
Sodium: 23 mg
Exchanges: 3/4 fruit

Food for Thought

I think the key is for women not to set any limits.   – *Martina Navratilova*

Pot Roast with Root Vegetables

Anne Brown, Coley's Point, Newfoundland

Ingredients:

1 boneless beef chuck roast (6 pounds), trimmed and tied; or 2 chuck steaks (3 pounds each)
1 1/2 tsps salt
1 tsp coarsely ground black pepper
3/4 tsp ground cinnamon
3/4 tsp ground ginger
1/4 tsp ground cloves
1/4 tsp ground nutmeg
1 tbsp vegetable oil
1 lb small onions, cut into quarters
2 cans (14 1/2 oz each) beef broth or 3 1/2 cups beef stock
1/2 cup dry red wine
1 tbsp Worcestershire Sauce
1 bay leaf
10 small red potatoes, each cut into quarters
2 large turnips (8 oz each), peeled and cut into 1 1/2 inch pieces
3 carrots, peeled and cut into 1 1/2 inch pieces
2 small parsnips (4 oz each), peeled and cut into 1 1/2-inch pieces

> ## Food for Thought
> Don't compromise yourself. You are all you've got. – *Janis Joplin*

Directions:

Preheat oven to 350°F. In a cup, combine salt, pepper, cinnamon, ginger, cloves and nutmeg. Use to rub on roast. In an 8-quart Dutch oven, heat oil over medium-high heat until very hot. Add roast and cook until well browned. Transfer roast to plate. Add onions to Dutch oven and cook, stirring occasionally, until golden. Stir in broth, wine, Worcestershire Sauce, and bay leaf; heat to boiling. Return roast to pot; cover and place in oven. Bake 2 1/2 hours, then stir potatoes, turnips, carrots and parsnips. Bake until meat and vegetables are very tender, about 1 1/2 hours longer. Transfer roast to a warm platter. With slotted spoon, remove vegetables from pot. Place two cups of vegetables in food processor fitted with knife blade and puree. Skim and discard fat from pot liquid. With food processor running, pour liquid into pureed vegetables. Spoon remaining vegetables around roast and serve with sauce. Bake 4 hours.
Makes 12 main-dish servings.

Nutritional Information:

Each serving:
Calories: About 421
Protein: 38 g
Carbohydrates: 33 g
15 g total fat (5 g saturated)
Cholesterol: 114 mg
Sodium: 799 mg

> ## Female Facts
> ### Audrey Hepburn Worked for UNICEF
> Although Belgian-born, Audrey Hepburn became one of Hollywood's best-known stars with her leading roles in films, she later (in 1988) became a special ambassador to the United Nations Children's Fund (UNICEF) and spent the last years of her life working for needy children, especially in Africa and Latin America.

Diet & Diabetic Recipes

Tuna Casserole

Anne Brown, Coley's Point, Newfoundland

Ingredients:
1 box white cheddar macaroni and cheese
Water (for cooking macaroni)
1 can albacore tuna, drained
1/2 tbsp unsalted butter
1/8 cup unsalted butter
1/2 onion, chopped
1 cup skim milk
1 cup saltine cracker crumbs
3/4 cup cheddar cheese, low-fat, shredded

Spice of Life

I didn't want to be rich, I just wanted enough to get the couch reupholstered.
– Kate (Mrs. Zero) Mostel

Directions:
Preheat oven to 350° F. Boil water to make macaroni and cheese. Cook pasta and drain. In the meantime, chop your onion, open and drain your tuna and get ready to launch into tuna casserole land. In a medium-sized skillet, melt your measly 1/2 tablespoon of butter. (I'm trying to be good about the butter, but sometimes I slip a little extra in.) Now sauté your onion and as it turns clear, add the drained tuna. Then add the milk, butter and sauce packet from the box of macaroni and cheese and cook till it thickens. Mix everything together except the saltines and cheddar, and place it in a lightly greased casserole dish. Top with saltines and then cheese. Bake for about 15 minutes, give or take. Serves 4.

Nutritional Information:
(Per serving)
Calories: 216 (kcal)
Total fat: 11 g (46% calories from fat)
Protein: 9 g
Carbohydrates: 19 g
Cholesterol: 25 mg
Sodium: 430 mg
Exchanges: 1 Grain (Starch); 1/2 Lean Meat; 0 Vegetable; 0 Fruit; 2 Fat; 0 Other Carbohydrates

Female Facts

Body Image
In Canada, 90% of females experience dissatisfaction with body image.

Tangy Apricot Chicken

Anne Brown, Coley's Point, Newfoundland

Ingredients:
8 chicken thighs, skin removed
1 cup fruit-sweetened apricot jam
1/4 cup fat-free Thousand Island dressing
Fresh ground pepper, to taste

Food for Thought
Instead of getting hard ourselves and trying to compete, women should try to give their best qualities to men - bring them softness, teach them how to cry.   – Joan Baez

Directions:
Preheat the oven to 350° F. Spray a small baking dish with nonstick cooking spray. Wash the chicken and blot dry with paper towels. Stir the jam into the dressing. Coat the chicken with the apricot mixture and place in the baking dish. Season with pepper to taste. Bake for 30-35 minutes or until the meat juices run clear and the meat is cooked through. Serves 4.

Nutritional Information:
Per serving (without syrup or preserves):
Calories: 333
Total fat: 11 g (3 g saturated fat)
Carbohydrates: 29 g
Cholesterol: 99 mg
Sodium: 366 mg
Sugars: 18 g
Protein: 29 g
Dietary fiber: 3 g
Exchanges: 2 Fruit; 4 Lean Meat

Apple Sausage Rolls

Anne Brown, Coley's Point, Newfoundland

Ingredients:
1 lb turkey or beef sausage
2 cups diced apples
2 cups bread crumbs
1 small onion, diced

Directions:
Preheat oven to 350°F. On waxed paper, roll out turkey or sausage into a rectangle 1/2-inch thick. Combine apples, bread crumbs, and onions; spread over meat. Start from the long end and roll as for jelly roll. Place in a 9" x 13" baking dish. Bake for 45 minutes. Serves 8.

Nutritional Information:
(Per serving)
Calories: 263
Fat: 10 g
Protein: 16 g
Carbohydrates: 31 g
Cholesterol: 50 mg
Sodium: 673 mg
Exchanges: 2 meat, 1-1/2 bread, 1/2 vegetable, 1/2 fruit, 1 fat

Broiled Vegetable Sandwich

Anne Brown, Coley's Point, Newfoundland

Ingredients:
1 small zucchini, julienned
1/2 cup cider vinegar
1 tsp chopped, pickled jalapenno peppers
1/2 medium red bell pepper, julienned
1 slice tomato

Female Facts

Women and Violent Crime
Every 9 seconds a woman is beaten in the United States, and every 3 minutes a woman is raped. A Canadian woman is nine times more likely to be killed by her spouse than by a stranger. More women are injured or killed by abuse than by automobile crashes and muggings. One in 10 Canadian woman is beaten regularly, and on average, every 17 minutes a woman is raped in this country. Domestic violence is the leading cause of injury to women between the ages of 15 and 44 in the United States.

Food for Thought

I can honestly say that I was never affected by the question of the success of an undertaking. If I felt it was the right thing to do, I was for it regardless of the possible outcome. – *Golda Meir*

Spice of Life

Many a girl who elopes wishes later that she had just let her imagination run away with her.

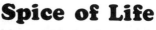

Diet & Diabetic Recipes

1 slice sweet, red onion
2 tsps extra-virgin olive oil
3 dashes black pepper
1 deli-style rye roll (3-1/2 oz)
1 slice low-fat Swiss cheese

Food for Thought

If you want something said, ask a man;
if you want something done, ask a
woman.   – *Margaret Thatcher*

Directions:
Place the zucchini strips in a small lidded container and add the cider vinegar and jalapenno
peppers. Cover and refrigerate for at least 2 hours. Set the oven to broil and spray the broiler pan
with nonstick cooking spray. Drain the marinade from the zucchini mixture and place the strips
on the broiler pan. Add the bell pepper, tomato and onion to the broiler pan. Drizzle with olive
oil and sprinkle with black pepper. Broil until the vegetables are brown and soft, about 15
minutes. Using a pair of tongs, carefully layer the vegetables on a roll and top with cheese. For
more flavour, marinate all the vegetables for 8 hours before broiling.

Note: This recipe is moderately high in sodium.
Exchanges: 4 Starch; 1 Lean Meat

Peanut Butter and Jelly Heart Sandwiches

Anne Brown, Coley's Point, Newfoundland

Ingredients:
2 tbsps peanut butter (creamy or crunchy)
2 tbsps preserves or jelly (strawberry or raspberry)
1 stick red licorice (about 6 inches long)
2 slices bread

Spice of Life

You can't get spoiled if you
do your own ironing.
               – *Meryl Streep*

Directions:
Cut bread slices into heart shapes using a large cookie cutter, or make a template out of
cardboard. Carefully cut around the template with a sharp knife. Cut licorice in shape of an
arrow, if desired. Spread peanut butter on one slice of bread; spread preserves on the other slice.
Place the licorice stick diagonally on the peanut buttered slice of bread. Put both slices of bread
together to make a sandwich, gently press together.

Nutritional information:
(Per sandwich)
Calories: 369
Fat: 18 g
Cholesterol: 0 mg
Sodium: 429 mg
Protein: 13 g
Carbohydrates: 66 g

Female Facts

Treating Polio
Elizabeth Kenny, as a bush country nurse in Australia,
devised methods for treating poliomyelitis by stimulating
and re-educating the affected muscles, rather than
immobilizing patients with splints and casts. The Elizabeth
Kenny Institute in Minneapolis, Minnesota, was set up in
1943 to train nurses and physiotherapists in her methods.

Diet & Diabetic Recipes

Baked Orange French Toast

Anne Brown, Coley's Point, Newfoundland

Ingredients:
1/4 cup fresh orange juice
2 large egg whites
1/2 tsp pure vanilla extract
6 slices day-old French bread, cut 1-inch thick
1 tbsp powdered sugar
1 medium orange, peeled and cut into 6 wedges

Preheat oven to 350°F. Prepare a cookie sheet with nonstick pan spray. Beat the orange juice, egg whites and vanilla together in a large bowl. Dip the bread slices on both sides and place them on the prepared cookie sheet. Spoon any remaining juice mixture over the slices. Bake for 15 to 17 minutes, or until golden brown, turning once after 8 minutes. Serve hot, sprinkled with powdered sugar and garnished with orange wedges. Makes 6 slices (3 servings).

Nutritional Information
(Per Serving - 2 slices)
Calories: 185
Total Fat: 2 g
Carbohydrates: 35 g
Protein: 7 g
Sodium: 306 mg
Cholesterol: 1mg
Fiber: 2 g
Exchanges: 2 starch, 1/2 fruit

Fiber Rich French Toast

Anne Brown, Coley's Point, Newfoundland

Ingredients:
1/4 cup liquid egg substitute
1/4 cup nonfat milk
1/8 tsp vanilla extract (or to taste)
1/4 tsp ground cinnamon
1/2 tsp brown sugar
2 slices whole-grain bread
1 tsp chopped pecans

Directions:
Preheat a medium nonstick skillet over medium heat. Mix together the egg substitute, milk, vanilla, cinnamon and brown sugar in a small, wide-mouth bowl (a soup plate works best). Dip the bread in the egg mixture, coating both sides. Place the bread in the skillet and cook until both sides are brown, turning with a spatula. Place the toast on a serving plate and sprinkle with chopped pecans. Top with sugar-free syrup or all-fruit preserves and serve immediately. Makes 1 serving.

Food for Thought

Women who seek to be equal with men lack ambition.   – *Timothy Leary*

Female Facts

Life After Death
A dying woman will still be able to give life if scientists are correct in their belief that it is possible to save the eggs of a dying woman's ovaries. That will make it possible for her to have children, even after she is dead, and no longer capable of conception.

Diet & Diabetic Recipes

Nutritional Information:
Per Serving (without syrup or preserves)
Calories: 214
Total fat: 4 g (1 g saturated fat)
Carbohydrates: 33 g
Cholesterol: 1 m
Sodium: 437 mg
Fiber: 4 g
Protein: 14 g
Sugars: 8 g
Exchanges: 2 bread/starch, 1 very lean meat

Food for Thought

The vote means nothing to women. We should be armed.   *– Edna O'Brien*

Diabetic Friendly Strawberry Rhubarb Compote

Anne Brown, Coley's Point, Newfoundland

Ingredients:
3 cups strawberries
1 1/2 cups finely chopped rhubarb
3/4 cup honey or sugar
1 tsp vanilla extract
1 tsp lemon juice

Food for Thought

Too many of us worry about what people think of us when they don't.

Directions:
Clean and cut strawberries into quarters. Place chopped rhubarb in saucepan with honey or sugar. Cook over medium heat until tender. Add strawberries; cook 7 minutes more. Remove from heat; stir in vanilla and lemon juice. Serve warm or cold, over waffles, pancakes or with yogurt. Makes 4 servings.

Nutritional Information:
(Per serving - 1/4 recipe)
Calories: 192
Fat: 1/2 g
Carbohydrates: 48 g
Cholesterol: 0 mg
Sodium: 3 mg
Dietary fiber: 3 g
Calcium: 56 mg
Protein: 1 g
Exchanges: 2 starch/bread, 1 fruit

Female Facts

The Best Legs in The War
In 1943, as WWII raged, Betty Grable was Hollywood's top draw and was reported to be the highest paid woman in the United States. Although she acted in 42 movies, she became famous for her world-renowned swimsuit poster, owned by one out of every five U.S. servicemen in World War II. Grable had the legs shown on that poster insured for one-quarter million dollars, a large amount of money in 1943.

Waffle Sandwiches

Anne Brown, Coley's Point, Newfoundland

Ingredients:
1 tbsp chunky peanut butter
2 tbsps mashed banana

1 tbsp honey
2 light frozen waffles, toasted (such as Aunt Jemima Light)

Directions:
Combine peanut butter, banana and honey in a small bowl. Spread on toasted waffles. Makes 1 serving.

Nutritional Information:
(Per Serving)
Calories: 249
Total fat: 9 g
Saturated fat: 3 g
Carbohydrates: 45 g
Protein: 7 g
Fiber: 8 g
Cholesterol: 0 mg
Sodium: 558 mg
Exchanges: 1 fruit, 2 bread, 1 fat

Blueberry Pineapple Delight Cake

Anne Brown, Coley's Point, Newfoundland

Ingredients:
1 can (20 oz) crushed pineapple in juice, undrained
2 cups fresh or frozen blueberries
1 box (18.25 oz) lemon cake mix
2/3 cup light brown sugar
1/2 cup margarine or butter, melted

Directions:
Preheat oven to 350°F. In a 13" x 9" x 2" baking pan coated with nonstick cooking spray, spread the pineapple and blueberries over the bottom of the pan. Sprinkle evenly with the cake mix and brown sugar. Drizzle margarine evenly over the top. Bake 45 to 50 minutes, or until bubbly. Makes 16 Servings.

Nutritional Information
(Per Serving)
Calories: 251
Total fat: 10 g (2 g saturated fat)
Carbohydrates: 39 g
Cholesterol: 8 mg
Sodium: 315 mg
Protein: 2 g
Fiber: 1 g
Exchanges: 2 other carbohydrates, 1/2 fruit, 2 fat

Female Facts

The Living Legacy Awards
The Women's International Center, which presents The Living Legacy Awards given each year, was founded in 1982 by Gloria Lane as a non-profit organization dedicated to women and their great contributions to humanity. More than 100 people have received the awards (not all are women) and the list reads like a who's who of the most distinguished people in the world, including many within these pages.

Food for Thought

To be loved,
be lovable.
      – *Ovid*

Diet & Diabetic Recipes

Golden Lemon Cake

Anne Brown, Coley's Point, Newfoundland

Ingredients:
Non-stick vegetable cooking spray
1 pkg (18 oz) lemon cake mix
1/3 cup vegetable oil
2 eggs
2 cups unpeeled yellow squash, grated
3/4 cup unsweetened, crushed pineapple, well drained
1/2 cup sliced almonds

Directions:
Preheat oven to 325°F. Spray a 9" x 13" pan with cooking spray and set aside. In a large mixing bowl, beat together the cake mix, oil and eggs at low speed until moistened. Continue beating at medium speed for 2 minutes. Fold in squash, pineapple and almonds, thoroughly blending all ingredients. Pour batter into a 9" x 13" prepared pan and bake for 45 to 55 (or 60 to 70 minutes in a Bundt pan). Cake is done when a cake tester comes out clean. You can also use a 12 cup Bundt or tube pan. Makes 16 Servings.

Nutritional Information:
(Per Serving)
Calories: 215
Total fat: 10 g
Carbohydrates: 31 g
Dietary fiber: 2 g
Protein: 3 g
Cholesterol: 34 mg
Sodium: 220 mg
Exchanges: 2 bread/starch, 2 fats

Diabetic Friendly Blueberry Cobbler

Anne Brown, Coley's Point, Newfoundland

Ingredients:
1/2 cup (1 stick) 30% fat-reduced margarine
1 cup self-rising flour
1/2 cup sugar, divided
3/4 cup nonfat milk
1 tsp vanilla extract
2 cups fresh blueberries
1/2 cups water
1 tsp cinnamon
1/4 tsp nutmeg

Diet & Diabetic Recipes

Directions:
Preheat oven to 350°F. Melt butter in a shallow 1 1/2 quart baking dish. Combine flour, 1/4 cup sugar, milk and vanilla in a mixing bowl; pour evenly over butter. Combine berries, remaining 1/4 cup sugar (combined with cinnamon and nutmeg) and water. Spoon evenly over flour mixture. Do not stir. Bake 40 to 45 minutes. Makes 6 servings.

Nutritional Information:
(Per Serving)
Calories: 247
Total fat: 8 g
Carbohydrates: 41 g
Trace cholesterol
Protein: 3 g
Dietary fiber: 4 g
Sodium: 464 mg
Exchanges: 2 bread, 1/2 fruit, 1-1/2 fat

Food for Thought

God gave women intuition and femininity. Used properly, the combination easily jumbles the brain of any man I've ever met. – *Farrah Fawcett*

Diabetic Friendly Strawberry Rhubarb Cobbler

Anne Brown, Coley's Point, Newfoundland

Filling Ingredients:
3/4 cup sugar
2 tbsps all-purpose flour
1 tsp cinnamon
1 tsp finely grated orange zest
4 cups coarsely chopped (3/4-inch pieces) rhubarb
2 cups sliced strawberries

Topping Ingredients:
1 cup all-purpose flour
2 tbsps sugar
1 tsp baking powder
1/4 tsp baking soda
1/4 tsp salt
2 tbsps margarine, chilled and cut in bits
2/3 cup low fat buttermilk

Female Facts

Bird in a Gilded Cage
Lawyer, politician, broadcaster, Julia Verlyn "Judy" LaMarsh, as Minister of National Health and Welfare in the Pearson cabinet, saw the implementation of several important pieces of legislation, including the Canada Pension Plan. Among her books was *Bird in a Gilded Cage*, about her life in politics.

Filling Directions:
Preheat oven to 400°F. In a bowl, combine sugar, flour, cinnamon and orange rind. Add rhubarb and strawberries; toss to mix. Spread mixture in an 8-cup shallow glass or ceramic baking dish (do not use metal); bake for 10 minutes.

Topping Directions:
In a large bowl, mix flour, sugar, baking powder, baking soda and salt. Using two knives or pastry blender, cut in margarine until mixture is size of small peas. With fork, stir in buttermilk until mixture is moistened and soft dough forms. Drop by spoonfuls in 6 evenly spaced mounds on hot fruit. Bake for 25 minutes, or until top is golden. Serves 6.

Diet & Diabetic Recipes

Company Apple Tart

Anne Brown, Coley's Point, Newfoundland

Ingredients:

3 apples, peeled, cored and cut into wedges
1/4 cup light olive oil or canola oil
1 cup egg substitute
1 cup skim milk
1/4 cup plain nonfat yogurt
1/4 cup sugar
1/4 tsp nutmeg
1/2 tsp cinnamon
1 tsp lemon juice
1 tsp vanilla extract
2 tsps almond extract
3/4 cup all-purpose flour
1/2 cup whole wheat flour
2 tbsps sliced almonds

Directions:

Preheat oven to 350°F. Spray a 10-inch quiche pan or pie pan with cooking spray. With a food processor, use slicing disk to thinly slice apple wedges. Layer apple slices (about 3-1/2 cups) into prepared pan. Put oil, egg substitute, milk, yogurt, sugar, spices, lemon juice and extracts into food processor. Process until smooth, scraping sides once or twice. Add flours and pulse 3 or 4 times until flours are incorporated, occasionally scraping sides. Do not overmix. Pour mixture over apples. Sprinkle with almonds. If mixture does not all fit into prepared pan, spray custard cups with cooking spray and fill with remaining mixture. Bake 40 to 45 minutes, or until puffed and browned and cake tester comes out clean when inserted in center. Cool about 15 minutes before serving. Cover and store in a refrigerator. Bring to room temperature before serving. Makes 10 servings.

Nutritional Information:

(Per serving)
Calories: 78
Fat: 7 g
Carbohydrates: 24 g
Protein: 6 g
Cholesterol: 1 mg
Sodium: 60 mg
Fiber: 2 g
Exchanges: 1 bread/starch, 1/2 fruit, 1 fat (2 carbohydrate choices)

Female Facts

Intelligence Service
At one time the highest ranking woman in the U.S. Intelligence Service and later California State Senator, Lucy Killea is an outspoken environmentalist, especially against nuclear waste. And although she abhors abortion, she still fights for the right of women to make a choice.

Food for Thought

Because I am a woman, I must make unusual efforts to succeed. If I fail, no one will say, "She doesn't have what it takes." They will say, "Women don't have what it takes."   – *Clare Boothe Luce*

Spice of Life

One of the reasons I don't see eye to eye with Women's Lib is that women could have it all on a plate if only they knew it. They don't have to be pretty either.   – *Charlotte Rampling*

NOTE: For the benefit of those who already own Volumes 1 and 2 of *Downhomer Household Almanac & Cookbook*, this index covers recipes for all three volumes.

NOTE: For the benefit of those who already own Volumes 1 and 2 of *Downhomer Household Almanac & Cookbook*, this index covers recipes for all three volumes.

NOTE: For the benefit of those who already own Volumes 1 and 2 of *Downhomer Household Almanac & Cookbook*, this index covers recipes for all three volumes.

NOTE: For the benefit of those who already own Volumes 1 and 2 of *Downhomer Household Almanac & Cookbook*, this index covers recipes for all three volumes.

NOTE: For the benefit of those who already own Volumes 1 and 2 of *Downhomer Household Almanac & Cookbook*, this index covers recipes for all three volumes.

NOTE: For the benefit of those who already own Volumes 1 and 2 of *Downhomer Household Almanac & Cookbook*, this index covers recipes for all three volumes.

NOTE: For the benefit of those who already own Volumes 1 and 2 of *Downhomer Household Almanac & Cookbook*, this index covers recipes for all three volumes.

NOTE: For the benefit of those who already own Volumes 1 and 2 of *Downhomer Household Almanac & Cookbook*, this index covers recipes for all three volumes.

NOTE: For the benefit of those who already own Volumes 1 and 2 of *Downhomer Household Almanac & Cookbook*, this index covers recipes for all three volumes.

NOTE: For the benefit of those who already own Volumes 1 and 2 of *Downhomer Household Almanac & Cookbook*, this index covers recipes for all three volumes.

NOTE: For the benefit of those who already own Volumes 1 and 2 of *Downhomer Household Almanac & Cookbook*, this index covers recipes for all three volumes.

NOTE: For the benefit of those who already own Volumes 1 and 2 of *Downhomer Household Almanac & Cookbook*, this index covers recipes for all three volumes.

NOTE: For the benefit of those who already own Volumes 1 and 2 of *Downhomer Household Almanac & Cookbook*, this index covers recipes for all three volumes.

NOTE: For the benefit of those who already own Volumes 1 and 2 of *Downhomer Household Almanac & Cookbook*, this index covers recipes for all three volumes.

NOTE: For the benefit of those who already own Volumes 1 and 2 of *Downhomer Household Almanac & Cookbook*, this index covers recipes for all three volumes.

NOTE: For the benefit of those who already own Volumes 1 and 2 of *Downhomer Household Almanac & Cookbook*, this index covers recipes for all three volumes.

NOTE: For the benefit of those who already own Volumes 1 and 2 of *Downhomer Household Almanac & Cookbook*, this index covers recipes for all three volumes.

NOTE: For the benefit of those who already own Volumes 1 and 2 of *Downhomer Household Almanac & Cookbook*, this index covers recipes for all three volumes.

NOTE: For the benefit of those who already own Volumes 1 and 2 of *Downhomer Household Almanac & Cookbook*, this index covers recipes for all three volumes.

NOTE: For the benefit of those who already own Volumes 1 and 2 of *Downhomer Household Almanac & Cookbook*, this index covers recipes for all three volumes.

NOTE: For the benefit of those who already own Volumes 1 and 2 of *Downhomer Household Almanac & Cookbook*, this index covers recipes for all three volumes.